World Cultural Leaders of the Twentieth Century

Volume I

World Cultural Leaders of the Twentieth Century

Volume I
A–K

Jennifer L. Durham

Peter Stansky, consulting editor

ABC-CLIO

Santa Barbara, California
Denver, Colorado
Oxford, England

146942

Library of Congress Cataloging-in-Publication Data
Durham, Jennifer L.
World cultural leaders of the twentieth century / Jennifer L. Durham
    p.   cm.
Includes bibliographical references and index.
   ISBN 1-57607-038-7 (alk. paper)
   1. Arts, Modern—20th century.   2. Artists—Biography—Dictionaries.
I. Title.
NX456.D885   2000
700'.92'2—dc21   00-009209
                                                            CIP

06 05 04 03 02 01 00   10 9 8 7 6 5 4 3 2 1

ABC-CLIO, Inc.
130 Cremona Drive, P.O. Box 1911
Santa Barbara, California 93116-1911

This book is printed on acid-free paper ∞.
Manufactured in the United States of America.

In memory of Loretta Tipping Maloney
(June 20, 1918–May 21, 1994)
and Mildred Lillian Hollard Hansley
(November 4, 1910–March 8, 2000)

Contents

List of World Cultural Leaders of the Twentieth Century

Preface

World Cultural Leaders of the Twentieth Century highlights the lives and accomplishments of more than 400 men and women whose contributions to literature, art, film, dance, music, and theater helped shape international twentieth-century culture. American figures, with the exception of those whose work had significant international dimensions, have been omitted from the present volume and are treated extensively in ABC-CLIO's American Cultural Leaders (1993).

A major strand in the development of twentieth-century music was the departure from traditional tonality. Arnold Schoenberg led this departure with his atonal twelve-tone system, in which compositions are formed from a row of twelve tones in the chromatic scale. The twelve-tone system was further explored by his pupils Alban Berg and Anton von Webern as well as countless other composers. Russia's Igor Stravinsky explored Neoclassical idioms before turning to twelve-tone music in his later career and was also one of the major forces in twentieth-century music.

Notable too are the composers who sought to preserve their respective native folk traditions in their work. The folk songs Béla Bartók collected during his extensive travels around his native Hungary figured prominently in his music, as did Andalusian folk tradition in the work of Spain's most prominent composer of the twentieth century, Manuel de Falla.

Britain produced a series of influential composers that began with Sir Edward Elgar, a composer in the late Romantic style, in the early part of the century. Benjamin Britten, Sir William Walton, and Ralph Vaughan Williams continued the British tradition later in the century. Russia produced such noted composers as Sergei Prokofiev and Dmitry Shostakovich.

France and Germany contributed a number of experimental figures in music. The work of Claude Debussy and Maurice Ravel has been described as "musical impressionism." Darius Milhaud composed a large body of polytonal music, while both Pierre Boulez and Karlheinz Stockhausen conducted extensive experiments with serialism (in which musical elements are arranged without regard for tonality) and electronic music. Bruno Maderna was another major contributor to electronic music. The work of France's Olivier Messiaen was equally experimental but more eccentric, employing such diverse sounds as Gregorian chant and birdsong. Erik Satie, famous for his use of bizarre sounds like typewriters and sirens and for such instructions as to play "light as an egg," was another central figure in experimental composition. Before he turned to writing Broadway musicals, Germany's Kurt Weill composed music that went hand in hand with the "epic theater" embraced by the playwright Bertolt Brecht.

Not to be forgotten either is the advent of rock and roll in the 1960s. This volume treats three of the major forces in rock and roll, all from Britain—The Beatles, The Rolling Stones, and Led Zeppelin. Also from Britain, Lord Andrew Lloyd Webber incorporated popular music into opera, producing such international sensations as Cats, The Phantom of the

Opera, *Les Miserables*, and *Jesus Christ Superstar.*

Although the twentieth century was essentially a time of experimentation in music, some musicians and composers aimed their work at preserving older traditions or preferred to compose tonal music. With his operas and symphonic poems, drawing from the tradition of Richard Wagner, Richard Strauss continued the late Romantic style of the nineteenth century into the twentieth and was one of the century's most influential figures in opera. Arnold Dolmetsch devoted his career to revitalizing old English music through reconstruction of old instruments and performances of traditional song. In Germany Paul Hindemith rejected Schoenberg's atonality.

Compositions require performers to be heard. The operas of Strauss, Giacomo Puccini, and others showcased the talents of a number of talented sopranos, including Dame Joan Sutherland, Dame Maggie Teyte, Renata Tebaldi, Dame Elisabeth Schwarzkopf, Montserrat Caballé, and Dame Kiri Te Kanawa. The famous Three Tenors—José Carreras, Luciano Pavarotti, and Enrico Caruso—appeared on operatic stages around the world and in the 1990s embarked on a series of highly popular concerts. Other notable voices include those of the contralto Kathleen Ferrier and the bass Feodor Chaliapin, who gained fame in the early part of the century for his interpretation of the title character in *Boris Godunov*. The impresario Sir Rudolf Bing, general manager of the Metropolitan Opera of New York from 1950 to 1972, furthered the careers of many of the century's leading voices and conductors.

Mstislav Rostropovich and Pablo Casals were the twentieth century's most renowned cellists. The Russian Sergei Rachmaninoff and the Ukrainian Sviatoslav Richter rank among the century's finest pianists, and France's Jean-Pierre Rampal earned worldwide fame as a flutist.

Finally, a number of conductors were highly influential in popularizing both composers and performers. Britain's witty and colorful Sir Thomas Beecham championed the music of Frederick Delius and helped popularize that composer's work in England. Many performers appeared under the precise baton of Arturo Toscanini and in the ebullient interpretations of Wilhelm Fürtwangler. The Russian-American Serge Koussevitzky was instrumental in popularizing the works of American, French, and Russian composers during his tenure at the Boston Symphony Orchestra. Other noted conductors of the twentieth century include Herbert von Karajan, Sir Georg Solti, and Bruno Walter, who was best known for his interpretations of the works of Gustav Mahler.

The field of literature is perhaps the widest and most diverse. A succession of works now accepted as literary classics came from Europe, including James Joyce's *Ulysses* and Franz Kafka's *The Trial* and *The Castle*. In the early part of the century the Bloomsbury Group, an informal group of progressive artists and writers, produced such authors as Virginia Woolf and E. M. Forster. Britain also produced many prolific writers whose bodies of work sometimes exceeded 100 volumes. A number of widely read works emerged from their pens— Aldous Huxley's *Brave New World*, George Orwell's *Animal Farm* and *1984*, Anthony Burgess's *A Clockwork Orange*, H. G. Wells's *The War of the Worlds* and

The Time Machine, Joseph Conrad's *Heart of Darkness*, and others. In their fiction and nonfiction writings, the outspoken G. K. Chesterton and Hilaire Belloc, both prolific writers influenced by staunch Catholic persuasions, championed a philosophy they called "distributivism" that rejects large concentrations of power in both governmental and corporate settings in favor of small, localized power centers.

Hispanic literature produced a number of distinguished figures. Miguel de Unamuno in the early part of the century and later Camilo José Cela were among Spain's most influential novelists. Cela, a member of the Generation of 1927, employed violent imagery in a literary style called *tremendismo*. In his short stories and poetry the Argentinian Jorge Luis Borges embraced *ultraísmo*, a literary style that also used striking imagery. "Magical realism," which combines realism with fantastic elements, was the trademark style of the popular Colombian novelist Gabriel García Márquez.

Three major writers to emerge from Russia and the Soviet Union in the twentieth century were Maxim Gorky, Boris Pasternak, and Aleksandr Solzhenitsyn. While Gorky formulated the Socialist Realism style that was to dominate Russian literature for most of the twentieth century, Solzhenitsyn devoted his efforts to exposing atrocities perpetrated by the Soviet state, many of which he experienced firsthand. Pasternak produced a body of poetry but is best known for his tragic Revolution-era novel, *Dr. Zhivago*.

The century's best-known mysteries, thrillers, and detectives came from Britain. Sir Arthur Conan Doyle introduced the infamous sleuth Sherlock Holmes in *A Study of Scarlet* (1887). The detectives Hercule Poirot and Miss Jane Marple were the creations of the prolific mystery writer Dame Agatha Christie. Ian Fleming created James Bond, secret agent 007, while John Le Carré and Len Deighton authored series of successful spy novels.

Twentieth-century literature also reached into the erotic, the bizarre, and the mythological. Writers such as Anaïs Nin, D. H. Lawrence, and Colette treated erotic themes extensively in their work. Mystery and the occult were the driving forces behind the bizarre tales of Algernon Blackwood. J. R. R. Tolkien formulated an entire mythology that was the basis of his popular *The Hobbit* and *The Lord of the Rings* trilogy.

From Italy Umberto Eco fashioned complex novels from his extensive knowledge of signs and symbols. That country also produced such controversial and outspoken writers as Gabrielle D'Annunzio and F. T. Marinetti, the latter of whom was a chief proponent of Italian Futurism—a movement that praised the motion, speed, and velocity of the twentieth century. Hermann Hesse, Thomas Mann, and Günter Grass rank among Germany's chief novelists of the twentieth century.

As in all aspects of culture, the work of twentieth-century French writers was essentially marked by a rejection of tradition in favor of experimentation. With his *La Nouvelle Revue Française*, André Gide helped launch the careers of many French writers. Albert Camus and Jean-Paul Sartre led the French existentialists in the World War II era and addressed what they saw as the hopelessness and absurdity of life.

Writers such as Nigeria's Chinua Achebe explored the clash between native African culture and Western influence. Oe Kenzaburo emerged as Japan's leading novelist in the post–World War II generation, while India's prolific Rabindranath Tagore was his country's leading writer.

Britain had a strong tradition of poetry during the past century that began with a group of antiwar poets during the World War I era. Of the three of these treated in this volume—Sigfried Sassoon, Wilfred Owen, and Rupert Brooke—only Sassoon survived the war. Another generation of politically oriented poets arose in the 1930s to which four figures were central. The four—Louis MacNeice, Stephen Spender, W. H. Auden, and C. Day-Lewis—were dubbed "MacSpauday" by their critics. Most influential, however, was the American-born T. S. Eliot, a pioneer in modern verse and experimentation in style.

With lyrical verse rich in mysticism and Irish tradition, W. B. Yeats was the undisputed leader in Irish poetry of the twentieth century. Seamus Heaney, winner of the Nobel Prize for Literature in 1995, was another central figure in Irish poetry. The Welsh poet Dylan Thomas contributed some of the best-known English-language lyric poetry of the century. Surrealism was a major force in French poetry and was advanced by poets such as Paul Éluard.

A major early figure in Russian poetry was Alexander Blok, who embraced Symbolism in the early 1900s. Reacting against the Symbolists, poets such as Anna Akhmatova and Osip Mandelstam advocated a plainspoken, simplistic style of verse known as Acmeism. Joseph Brodsky followed later in the century and was expelled from the Soviet Union for writing introspective verse that did not conform to the dictates of Socialist Realism.

A number of poets distinguished themselves in the Spanish-speaking world. The Andalusian Federico García Lorca was a member of the Generation of 1927 in Spain and was that country's leading poet before he lost his life in the Spanish Civil War in 1936. Two Hispanic poets, Mexico's Octavio Paz and Chile's poet-diplomat Pablo Neruda, earned Nobel Prizes for Literature.

The Russian director Konstantin Stanislavsky, formulator of the widely used Stanislavsky Method, was a central and highly influential dramatic theorist in the early 1900s and advocated a form of acting that required actors to become intimately acquainted with their characters. A more experimental vein emerged in the "epic theater" of Bertolt Brecht, who purposely sought to establish distance between actor and audience. The Theater of the Absurd playwrights, such as Eugène Ionesco, Jean-Paul Sartre, and Samuel Beckett, created plays with illogical plots and sparse dialog to mirror what they saw as the absurdity of life.

During the Irish Literary Renaissance Dublin's Abbey Theatre hosted the nationalistic dramas of Yeats, Sean O'Casey, J. M. Synge, and others. The Italian Dario Fo, winner of the Nobel Prize for Literature in 1997, brought a highly controversial blend of satire, comedy, and mime to world stages after World War II.

The central figure in early-twentieth-century British theater was George Bernard Shaw, who authored dozens of plays tinged with social satire and worked extensively with the director-playwright Harley Granville-Barker. Shaw and Granville-Barker stripped what they considered elements of entertainment from their plays in an effort to emphasize the intellectual and social messages of their productions. Over the years Shaw's plays showcased some of England's most famous actors, such as Sybil Thorndike. Later playwrights to find success in Britain included Tom Stoppard and Harold Pinter.

Sir Nöel Coward was a central figure in the British comedy of manners and was noted for his satiric portrayals of the British upper classes. Another trend in modern British theater was the revival of the Shakespearean tradition at the Old Vic, led in particular by the director Sir Tyrone Guthrie and the actor-director Sir John Gielgud, who was well known for his portrayals of Shakespearean characters. Sir Laurence Olivier, Peter O'Toole, Sir Alec Guinness, and other international film personalities started their acting careers on the British stage.

In South Africa Athol Fugard devoted his efforts to exploring the apartheid system, and later postapartheid society, through his plays. Wole Soyinka, Nigeria's leading playwright, combined elements of his native Yoruba tradition with Western literary styles. The Caribbean poet and playwright Derek Walcott explored the clash between Western culture and native Caribbean culture in his work.

The film era began in the early 1900s with the advent of silent film. France's Abel Gance was a pioneer from this time period. The Soviet director and theorist Sergei Eisenstein flourished during the Stalinist years and was responsible for introducing "the montage of film attractions" as well as many other technical innovations that heavily influenced the development of filmmaking throughout the world. Italian film had a strong tradition in the work of the Neorealists, a post–World War II movement led by Roberto Rossellini and Luchino Visconti that employed improvisation and an informal approach to filming. The work of Federico Fellini, creator of such films as *8 1/2* and *La Dolce Vita*, had its roots in the Neorealist tradition, as did the films of French New Wave directors such as Jean-Luc Godard and François Truffaut in the 1950s. Louis Malle, although not associated with the French New Wave, emerged as a director in France during the same period and made the career of the famed French actress Jeanne Moreau. In Sweden Ingmar Bergman directed a series of philosophical films that included *The Seventh Seal*, and his films were responsible for launching the career of actor Max von Sydow.

After contributing to the development of film in his native Hungary and working in Europe and the United States, Sir Alexander Korda settled in England and founded London Film Productions in 1931. Two years later Korda's *The Private Life of Henry VIII* marked the beginning of a long series of lavish films that employed international acting talents. British film was strong in the second part of the century as well. Sir Carol Reed and Sir David Lean were two of its most prominent directors, the latter directing such successful epic films as *Doctor Zhivago* and *Lawrence of Arabia*. More recently, Mike Leigh satirized British middle-class life in his films and recently gained acclaim for such films as *Naked* and *Secrets and Lies*.

With the release of *Drunken Angel* in 1948, Akira Kurosawa brought Japanese film to international audiences. In the post–World War II era, Rainer Werner Fassbinder probed postwar middle-class

German society. Spain's Luis Buñuel introduced Surrealism into a number of highly controversial films during the World War I era. In the 1930s director Josef von Sternberg began a series of films that propelled actress Marlene Dietrich to international stardom.

Finally, two figures in particular did significant work in the realm of documentary filmmaking. Britain's John Grierson coined the term *documentary* in the 1920s and was involved in many documentary projects during his lifetime. The Dutch director Joris Ivens worked in the Netherlands, the United States, Eastern Europe, and elsewhere, creating leftist-tinged documentaries that address social conditions.

One figure emerged as the central personality of dance—that of the Russian-born impresario Sergei Diaghilev. His Ballet Russes (1909–1929) catapulted some of the twentieth century's leading dancers to international fame, including the athletic and enigmatic Vaslav Nijinsky, the dainty Anna Pavlova, and Tamara Karsavina, who danced with the Ballet Russes from 1909 to 1922.

The twentieth century's best-known choreographers showcased their work through Diaghilev's Ballet Russes as well. Michel Fokine was Diaghilev's chief choreographer from 1909 to 1914, during which time he created such standards as *Petrushka* and *Le Carnaval*. Leonide Massine and George Balanchine, the latter of whom worked with Diaghilev during the company's final years, also got their starts as choreographers for the Ballet Russes. In addition to dancers and choreographers, Diaghilev enlisted the talents of avant-garde painters and composers. Léon Bakst contributed lavish set and costume designs to many of his productions. Pablo Picasso, Maurice Ravel, and Claude Debussy are among many others who contributed ballet scores, costume designs, and scenery to Ballet Russes productions.

After the demise of the original Ballet Russes following Diaghilev's death in the late 1920s, Britain produced a number of noteworthy figures in dance. Central among them was Sir Frederick Ashton, chief choreographer for the Royal Ballet from 1933 to 1970. The delicate Alicia Markova (who started her career with Diaghilev's Ballet Russes), and later Dame Margot Fonteyn—the celebrated partner of the Russian dancer Rudolf Nureyev for a decade and a half—were two figures who emerged from the British ballet tradition and gained international acclaim. As a dancer and choreographer, Sir Robert Helpmann brought dramatic creations to British and Australian ballet.

The popular and athletic Mikhail Baryshnikov continued the Russian tradition for world audiences in the latter half of the century, dancing with the Kirov Ballet from 1966 to 1974, when he defected to the West. Roland Petit was a central figure in French ballet in the second half of the century, bringing a blend of classical ballet, fantasy, and modern dance to international audiences. Two figures were central to the development of modern, expressionistic dance—the choreographer-dancers Mary Wigman and Kurt Jooss.

Twentieth-century painting was dominated by "isms" marking countless abstract or semiabstract experimental styles that flourished most forcefully in Germany, France, and Spain. Henri Matisse led a group of painters disparagingly dubbed the "Fauves" (wild beasts) by a critic who objected to their use of bold, striking color. Analytical and Synthetic Cubism developed through the experimentation of Pablo Picasso and Georges Braque beginning in 1908 and was a major influence on the subsequent development of abstract painting.

Influenced by the Norwegian painter Edvard Munch, the German Expressionists flourished during the same period in that country. Circles of Expressionist painters such as The Bridge and The Blue Rider included Wassily Kandinsky, Ludwig Kirchner, Emil Nolde, Egon Schiele, Oskar Kokoschka, and others. Although a diverse group whose paths would soon diverge, the Expressionists shared a dislike for academic painting and a preference for bold color and distorted, sometimes abstract forms.

Spain's Salvador Dalí led the Surrealist movement in painting, crafting bizarre, dreamlike juxtapositions of objects. Also to emerge from Germany were those such as Käthe Kollwitz and George Grosz who used their art to further strong political and social beliefs. In England Francis Bacon painted distorted, grotesque figures in violent color. The brother and sister Augustus and Gwen John carried on the tradition of portraiture in that country, the former producing many portraits of well-known figures of his day and the latter known for her depictions of women.

Sculptors such as Emile-Antoine Bourdelle and Aristide Maillol evolved their monumental works from the nineteenth-century French master Auguste Rodin. The dominant trend in sculpture, however, was a move toward abstraction, seen particularly in the creations of Britain's Barbara Hepworth, Henry Moore, and the painter-sculptor Ben Nicholson as well as those of the Romanian-born Constantin Brancusi. The trademark of the Swiss-born Alberto Giacometti was his preference for tall, thin figures. Switzerland's Jean Tinguely was a pioneer in kinetic sculpture, fashioning his works to emit strange noises and sounds and even to self-destruct. In his "readymades," the French sculptor Marcel Duchamp used everyday objects. Other sculptors of note include Italy's Marino Marini, who produced a series of works on equestrian themes, female figures, and portraits, and Umberto Boccioni, who applied the Futurist principles in Marinetti's writing to sculpture.

Working in the early twentieth century, the architects Josef Hoffman, Baron Victor Horta, Henry van de Velde, Adolf Loos, and others anticipated the development of the International Style by combining functionality with decorative elements influenced by the Art Nouveau movement. Walter Gropius, the chief theorist behind the purely functional International Style that rejected all decorative elements in architecture, founded the Bauhaus in 1919. The Bauhaus served as a training ground for such figures as Ludwig Mies van der Rohe, creator of the modern skyscraper. Peter Behrens applied the International Style to industrial design, and Le Corbusier was best known for his application of the International Style to city planning and public buildings.

Not all architects of the past century, however, accepted the International Style. While it influenced the work of Finland's Alvar Aalto, he retained an expressive functionality in his designs. The Glasgow architect Charles Rennie Mackintosh favored simplicity in his designs for private homes but rejected the severity of the International Style. In England Sir Edwin Lutyens rejected the International Style altogether, seeking to retain a traditional look in his gabled dwellings.

The figures chosen for this volume represent a broad slice of world cultural developments of the twentieth century. They are meant as representatives of the dominant influences in music, theater, dance, painting, sculpture, literature, and architecture. It is hoped that the reader will take advantage of the extensive cross-referencing and suggestions for additional reading at the end of each entry to gain a more complete understanding of the individual's contribution to twentieth-century world culture.

This book was a massive undertaking that could not have been realized without the generous assistance and patience of many individuals. I would like to thank the following for their assistance, support, and advice, in many forms, during this project: Mom, Dad, Michael, Grandma, John and Sylvia, John and Phyllis, Jasper, Alex, Cyrus, and Missy. Many thanks are also due to Dr. Peter Stansky and Todd Hallman for their work in choosing the people to be included in this book and much more; Silvine Marbury Farnell, who went above and beyond the call of a copy editor's duty and made particularly valuable contributions to the entries on literary figures; Connie Oehring for her hard work and patience during production; and Liz Kincaid for coordinating the artwork.

World Cultural Leaders of the Twentieth Century

Volume I

Aalto, Alvar

(February 3, 1898–May 11, 1976)
Architect, Furniture Designer, City Planner, Teacher

One of the most internationally influential architects of the twentieth century, Finland's Alvar Aalto (born Hugo Alvar Henrik Aalto) combined the functionality of other modern architects with his own organic, expressive style and the use of indigenous materials. During his long and successful career Aalto designed more than 200 buildings or groups of buildings in Europe, the United States, and the Middle East.

Aalto was born in Kuortane, Finland, then part of the Russian Empire. His family moved to Alajäri and then to Jyväskylä. His mother died in 1903; his father, a surveyor, then married her sister. As a child Aalto displayed a mild interest in architecture and began to take notice of the buildings around him. He graduated from the Jyväskylä Normal School in 1916. Before he moved on to the Polytechnic Institute in Helsinki, he designed his first architectural piece, a wooden portico for his parents' home.

Aalto fought in the Finnish War for Independence (1918–1919) and graduated from the institute in 1921. Over the next several years he traveled around and began to enter his architectural designs in competitions. Eventually, he returned to Finland, setting up a practice in Jyväskylä. Aalto soon began to win competitions for building designs and gained opportunities to execute them. His earliest buildings reflect the classical-traditional style then dominant in Finland. Aalto used stucco and masonry as well as wood, a traditional building material in Finland. His major early works include railroad employees' housing (1923) and a Workers' Club (1924), both in Jyväskylä.

In 1925 Aalto married Aino Marsio, also an architect. Although there is debate over how much she contributed to his designs, she worked closely with him until she died in 1949. Aalto moved his office to Turku in 1927. There he worked in partnership with Erik Bryggman until 1933. His move to Turku marked a new direction in his style and the beginning of his success as an architect. He received a major commission to design the Turun Sanomat Building, a newspaper office in Turku. The resulting building signaled a break from traditional architecture and is particularly noteworthy for its functionality and the tapered columns supporting the roof of the pressroom. Aalto's next major success was the tuberculosis sanatorium at Paimio. Like many of his designs from this period, the building was finished with a smooth white surface. Sunlit balconies opened out into scenic views for the patients.

The Municipal Library at Viipuri (now Vyborg) attracted international attention as an example of the International Style and an innovative library design. Begun in 1927 and completed in 1935, it demonstrates Aalto's concern with interiors as well as exteriors. He designed the auditorium furniture in laminated wood and covered the undulating ceiling with wood. Circular skylights illuminated the reading room. A large glass window-wall and two-level lending room are among the building's other notable features. With the library building, he began to move away from the strict functionality of the modernist architects. The building was destroyed in the Russo-Finnish war, after which it fell under the control of the Soviet Union and remained in a state of disrepair. An international campaign to restore the building began in the early 1990s.

In 1933 Aalto moved his practice to Helsinki. Around this time he began to find success as a furniture designer as well as an architect. He constructed many chairs and other pieces with laminated wood, aiming to create furniture that was both visually appealing and functional. A show of his work in London (1933) contributed significantly to his international reputation as a furniture designer. With his wife and Mairea Gullichsen, he founded the Artek Company (1935) to manufacture and sell his furniture.

Aalto's notable architectural designs of the 1930s include the Finnish pavilions for the world fairs in Paris (1937) and New York (1939–1940). He increasingly used organic materials such as wood and glass. Aalto also designed the interior of the Savoy Restaurant in Helsinki (1937) and a country home near Noormarkku, Villa Mairea, for the Gullichsens. The Sunila cellulose factory (1936–1939, expanded 1951–1954) included an employee village and marked his first major success designing multiple-building sites.

From 1940 to 1947 Aalto lived in the United States and taught at the Massachusetts Institute of Technology (MIT). While at MIT he designed the Baker House, a student dormitory that overlooks the Charles River. Aalto returned to Finland in 1948 and immersed himself in designing buildings for war-ravaged Helsinki. Following the death of his wife in 1949 he married Elissa Mäkiniemi, an architect who also came to collaborate with him.

Over the next two decades Aalto designed many buildings for Helsinki, including the National Pension Bank and Finlandia Hall, Helsinki (1971, enlarged 1974), the city's lakeside cultural center and home of the Helsinki Philharmonic Orchestra. Pollution caused deterioration in the building's original white Carrara marble surface, and the damage sparked a controversy in the 1980s over how to restore it. Proponents of the more durable granite lost to the supporters of marble (among whom was Aalto's widow), who sought to maintain the building's intended appearance. Renovations began in 1997.

Aside from his work in Helsinki, Aalto completed numerous international commissions as well as buildings elsewhere in Finland. Abroad he designed an apartment building in Bremen (1958), a post and telegraph office in Baghdad (1958), a church in Bologna (1966), Mount Angel Abbey Library, near Salem, Oregon (1967–1970), and an art museum in Iran (1970). His other works in Finland include a sawmill at Varkaus (1945); college buildings at Otaniemi (1949–1964) and Jyväskylä (1952–1957); a church at Vuoksenniska, Imatra (1956–1958); the Community Center in Seinäjoki (1962; expanded 1967); and the Taidemuseo in Jyväskylä (1973), later renamed the Alvar Aalto Museum.

Aalto's later work is marked by his use of organic forms and his reliance on indigenous materials for effect, as in the Säynätsalo town hall group (1950–1952), in which he combined metal (copper), brick, and wood. While his designs never abandoned the functionality of his early work, he imbued his buildings with more expressive styles than did other modern architects.

He was a member of numerous academies and international societies, including the Academy of Finland (as its president from 1963 to 1968) and the Congrès Internationaux d'Architecture Moderne (1928–1956). Aalto received numerous awards for his work, including the Royal Gold Medal for Architecture from the Royal Institute of British Architects (1957) and the Gold Medal from the American Institute of Architects (1963).

BIBLIOGRAPHY

Pearson, Paul David, *Alvar Aalto and the International Style*, 1978; Quantrill, Malcolm, *Alvar Aalto: A Critical Study*, 1983; Schildt, Gorän, *Alvar Aalto: The Decisive Years*, 1986; Schildt, Gorän, *Alvar Aalto: The Mature Years*, 1989.

Achebe, Chinua

(November 16, 1930–)
Novelist, Poet

Chinua Achebe, Nigeria's chief novelist of the twentieth century, depicts in his novels the conflict between European and West African cultures during the years of colonial rule in Africa as well as the political troubles arising from military dictatorships in the postcolonial period. Although he writes in English, he avoids traditional European literary styles to create a subtly ironic medium rich in the folklore and speech of his own people. He was one of the first African writers to gain a wide readership in the English-speaking world and has been honored with nearly two dozen honorary degrees to date.

Achebe was born Albert Chinualumogu Achebe into a Christian family in Ogidi, a town in eastern Nigeria. His father was an Igbo evangelist heavily involved in the church, and Achebe studied at church schools as a youth. Many of his classes were taught in English.

He attended Government College, a secondary school, in Umuahia. There he met the poet CHRISTOPHER OKIGBO, with whom he would found a publishing company in 1967. He later attended the University College in Ibadan and studied medicine, literature, history, and religion. Some of his first published writings appeared in the *University Herald*, which he edited for a year.

After years of education in English, Achebe began to investigate the culture and traditions of West Africa. He resented the British rule of Nigeria that had been established in 1906 as well as the British perspective on African culture that dominated his education and characterized such novels as JOSEPH CONRAD's *Heart of Darkness*. Following his graduation in 1953 Achebe took a job working for the Nigerian Broadcasting Corporation in Lagos. In 1956 he traveled to London and studied with the British Broadcasting Corporation (BBC).

Achebe's first two novels, *Things Fall Apart* (1958) and *No Longer at Ease* (1960), began in part as an answer to

JOYCE CARY's *Mister Johnson,* the title character of which is a Nigerian civil servant who accepts the values of the British colonial administration, even as it destroys his life. The tragic story of the first begins at the arrival of British missionaries in Nigeria in the late 1800s. Okonkwo, a prominent member of an Igbo village in Nigeria, is successful within his traditional culture but steadfastly resists the introduction of the European order. Okonkwo's resentment manifests itself in destructive ways and ends in his own suicide. *No Longer at Ease* portrays the tragic fall from grace of a young Nigerian (Okonkwo's grandson) who embraces British culture.

In 1961 Achebe married Christie Chinwe Okoli. His next novel, *Arrow of God,* followed in 1964. The story is set in Nigeria in the 1920s and again explores the conflict between European colonialism and traditional Nigerian culture. The conflict takes place in the character of Ezeulu, a priest of the god Ulu who loses the support of his village. He rejects the offer of an office from British authorities, yet at the same time he suffers alienation from his own people; he is trapped helplessly between the two cultures. In 1969 Achebe made his first trip to the United States, where he lectured with Gabriel Okara and Cyprian Ekwensi. When he returned to Nigeria he became a research fellow and later a professor at the University of Nigeria. Beginning in 1970, he served as director of two publishing companies.

A Man of the People (1966), Achebe's first novel set in the postcolonial era, criticizes corrupt African dictatorships. After a gap of twenty years in publishing novels, Achebe finished *Anthills of the Savannah* (1987), a disturbing portrayal of West African life under military dictatorships that follows in the vein of *A Man of the People.* He was paralyzed from the waist down in an accident in 1990.

Among his other works are the short stories collected in *Girls at War* (1972); a children's book co-written with John Iroaganachi, *How the Leopard Got His Claws* (1973); books of poetry, *Beware, Soul-Brother* (1971) and *Christmas in Biafra* (1973); and the essays of *Morning Yet on Creation Day* (1975), later revised as *Hopes and Impediments: Selected Essays 1965–1987* (1988); and *The Trouble With Nigeria* (1983). In 1971 Achebe helped found the literary magazine *Okike: An African Journal of New Writing,* and in 1984 he began publishing *Uwa ndi Igbo: A Journal of Igbo Life and Culture.*

BIBLIOGRAPHY

Carroll, David, *Chinua Achebe,* 1980; Currey, James, *Chinua Achebe: A Biography,* 1997; Innes, C. L., *Chinua Achebe,* 1990.

Akhmatova, Anna

(June 23, 1889–March 5, 1966)
Poet, Translator

The life of the Russian poet Anna Akhmatova was marked by a long series of personal tragedies, in addition to the suffering she endured as an accused enemy of the Soviet regime. Akhmatova's confessional, plainspoken poetry is highly personal, dealing largely with love, religion, and the suffering of the Russian people under the Soviet regime. She was instrumental in introducing Acmeism into Russian poetry and is widely considered one of Russia's leading poets of the last century.

Akhmatova was born Anna Andreyevna Gorenko in Bolshoy Fontan, near Odessa, Ukraine. Her father was a naval engineer who disliked her poetic ambitions. From her mother she heard poetry, but her parents kept few books. Akhmatova went to school in Tsarskoe Selo when she was 10. After suffering from a strange illness when she was 11, she began to write poetry and was soon devouring the works of other poets. Her father, who did not want his family name associated with poetry, told her to use a pseudonym, and she chose the Tatar name of her maternal grandmother.

In 1903, she met the poet Nikolay Gumilyov, who for years was obsessively in love with her. Her rejections of him led to his three failed suicide attempts before they married in 1910. More importantly for Akhmatova's career, Gumilyov and she were associated with a group of poets known as Acmeists, who formed as a reaction to the Symbolists. The Acmeists, who also included OSIP MANDELSTAM, embraced a straightforward and simple style, with an emphasis on precise form.

Akhmatova studied law at the Kiev College for Women beginning in 1907. The Acmeist periodical, *Apollon*, published from 1910 to 1917, included her poetry. The first collection of her verse, *Vecher (Evening)*, was published in 1912, followed by *Chyotki (Rosary)* in 1914. Tragic difficulties of love, a reflection of her unhappy relationship with Gumilyov, form the primary theme of both volumes. *Rosary* was so popular that it even became the basis for a game, in which one person recited a portion of a poem and another finished it.

The social, military, and political events of Russia always affected Akhmatova deeply. The collection *The White Flock* (1917) included some poetry inspired by the war, such as "In Memoriam, July 19, 1914." Other themes include her continuing preoccupation with love and poetic inspiration. After divorcing Gumilyov in 1918, she married Vladimir Shileyko, and their relationship proved to be even more disastrous. The poems of her next small volume, *Plantain* (1921), appeared again in the larger *Anno Domini MCMXXI* (1922).

Anno Domini MCMXXI expresses a thoroughly pessimistic outlook, a product of the war, the Bolshevik Revolution, and the blood spilled in Russia. Among those who lost their lives during this tumultuous period was Gumilyov, who was executed in 1921 on false charges of participating in counterrevolutionary activity. Soviet authorities began to denounce Akhmatova's poetry in the mid-1920s, and from then until 1940 none of her verse was published in the Soviet Union.

Akhmatova turned to earning her living translating the works of other poets, including Victor Hugo and RABINDRANATH TAGORE. During this time she also wrote a number of essays on Aleksandr Pushkin as well as a cycle of poems memorializing those who perished under Stalin, *Requiem* (1963). Unlike many of her contemporaries, she refused to emigrate following the Revolution, and for many years she remained critical of those who chose to go abroad. Akhmatova lost many of her friends and family to arrests, executions, and suicides, including Gumilyov, Mandelstam, and the poet Marina Tsvetaeva.

With the outbreak of World War II, Soviet critics temporarily lifted their unofficial ban on Akhmatova's work. In 1940, several poems appeared in *The Star*, and in 1941 she delivered a radio address to the women of Leningrad. She was evacuated to Tashkent and spent part of her time reading poetry to wounded soldiers. This experience served as the source for some of her later poetry. The year 1946 brought a fresh clash with Soviet censors. Andrey Zhdanov, speaking for the Central Committee of the Communist Party, declared Akhmatova's poetry "completely individualistic" and denounced her as "half nun, half harlot." Soviet authorities destroyed copies of a planned volume of her poetry.

Akhmatova's son, Lev Gumilyov, was arrested on numerous occasions and in 1949 was sent to Siberia. In a vain effort to obtain his release, Akhmatova wrote poems praising Stalin that appeared in *The Little Light;* he was not released until after Stalin's death. After the dictator's death Akhmatova herself was rehabilitated and permitted to publish her poetry. Her longest and most complex work, *Poema bez geroya (Poem without a Hero)*, was written over a twenty-two-year period between 1940 and 1962.

Akhmatova also wrote memoirs about ALEXANDER BLOK, AMEDEO MODIGLIANI, and Mandelstam. She counted among her close friends BORIS PASTERNAK; in her later years she became a significant source of inspiration for a younger generation of poets, most notably JOSEPH BRODSKY. In 1964, she received Italy's Etna-Taormina prize, and the following year, Oxford University awarded her an honorary doctorate.

BIBLIOGRAPHY

Haight, Amanda, *Anna Akhmatova: A Poetic Pilgrimage*, 1976; Ketchian, Sonia, *The Poetry of Anna Akhmatova: A Conquest of Time and Space*, 1986; Reeder, Roberta, *Anna Akhmatova: Poet and Prophet*, 1994.

Alain-Fournier

(October 3, 1886–September 22, 1914)
Novelist, Short-Story Writer

The literary reputation of Alain-Fournier, whose life was cut short by World War I in 1914, rests almost entirely on his only finished novel, *The Wanderer*. His celebrated correspondence with the critic Jacques Rivière, his closest friend and his brother-in-law, was published after his death.

Alain-Fournier was born Henri-Alban Fournier in La Chapelle-d'Angillon, France. His parents, both teachers, moved the family to the small village of Epineuil-le-Fleuriel, where Fournier spent most of his childhood. The village's rural setting provided the idyllic background of *The Wanderer*, and Fournier cherished the area for the rest of his life. In 1898 his parents sent him to the Lycée Voltaire in Paris against his will. He excelled academically, earning more than a dozen prizes during his years there. In 1901–1902 Fournier went to the Naval Academy at Brest, and in 1902 he enrolled in the Lycée Bourges.

At the Lycée Lakanal, where he studied in 1903, Fournier met his lifelong friend Rivière. Both took an interest in Symbolist poetry, and Fournier began to write his own verse the same year. A chance meeting in 1905 shaped much of Fournier's literary output. Outside a Paris art exhibit, he spotted the blond and blue-eyed Yvonne de Quiévrecourt, whose beauty captured his imagination. She did not reciprocate Fournier's romantic interests but came to embody an ideal of youth and beauty in his mind. The poem "From across the Summers" (1905) recounts his meeting with her, and she was the inspiration for Yvonne de Galais in *The Wanderer*.

In 1905, Alain-Fournier went to London and there began his long correspondence with Rivière. His first published work, the prose poem "The Body of Woman," appeared in the *Nouvelle revue française* in 1907. He was drafted the following year and entered the officer's training school. The prose poem "Madeleine" belongs to 1909 and captures one of Fournier's central themes, the conflict between reality and the ideal. Madeleine and Tristan have suffered through failed loves and unsuccessfully strive after an ideal one.

The year 1909 was eventful for Fournier in many other ways. Rivière married his sister, Isabelle. He underwent a religious crisis that led him to Lourdes, sent him searching in the Bible, and briefly led him to consider becoming a monk. He finished his military service the following year and, having now failed the national teacher's examination twice, became a reviewer for the *Journal* and lived with Jacques and Isabelle Rivière.

Fournier wrote the short story "The Miracle of Three Village Women" in 1910; it begins with three women who romanticize their pasts to compensate for the unpleasantness of their present lives. When they return to their husbands, they find that the men have passively participated in the beating of Madame Henry's sister, the beautiful Marie, by her fiancée, who had grown angry about her relationship with a previous lover. "The Miracle of the Farm Wife," also written in 1910, appeared in *La grande revue*.

In 1912, Alain-Fournier went to work for the son of a former French president. *The Wanderer* (1928), later published as *The Lost Domain*, was first published serially as *Le Grand Meaulnes* in the *Nouvelle revue française* in 1913. François Seurel narrates the novel, and its hero is the idealistic Augustin Meaulnes. Alain-Fournier describes Meaulnes's meeting with a beautiful girl and his subsequent search for her, but what distinguishes the book is the power with which it evokes an almost mythic rural setting based on the author's youthful idyll in Epineuil-le-Fleuriel.

In 1913, Alain-Fournier began writing a second novel, *Colombe Blanchet*, which he never finished. The war cut his life and work short; in 1914, he was reported missing during the Battle of the Marne. Much of his work appeared after his death, and *The Wanderer*, which had enjoyed only a modest success during his lifetime, gained classic status in France and is the cornerstone of his literary reputation. *Miracles*, a collection of his poetry and prose, was published in 1924, and his correspondence with Rivière also appeared posthumously.

BIBLIOGRAPHY

Arkell, David, *Alain-Fournier: A Brief Life*, 1986; Gibson, Robert, *The Land without a Name: Alain-Fournier and His World*, 1975; Gurney, Stephen, *Alain-Fournier*, 1988.

Amis, Kingsley

(April 16, 1922–October 22, 1995)
Novelist, Poet, Critic, Teacher

In the eyes of contemporary critics, the publication of *Lucky Jim* in 1954 established Kingsley William Amis as one of the "Angry Young Men," British writers of the 1950s whose work protested against social rigidity and injustice. Amis wrote nineteen additional novels during his lifetime, none of which matched *Lucky Jim*'s success. All were marked by a critical and even cynical outlook, and by extensive use of parody and satire. He also wrote poetry and essays.

Amis was born in London and grew up in the city's suburb of Norbury. His father was not wealthy but did everything he could to further his son's education. Amis studied at the primary school of St. Hilda's and subsequently at Norbury College. At the latter, he published his first short story, "The Sacred Rhino of Uganda." With a scholarship, he entered the City of London School, where he wrote for the school magazine.

By this time, Amis had already acquired a reputation as a talented mimic, a tendency that would emerge in the parody and satire of his later work. In 1941, he entered St. John's College, Oxford, where he formed a friendship with the poet and novelist PHILIP LARKIN. World War II put a temporary halt on his studies, and from 1942 to 1945 he served in the Royal Corps of Signals. After returning to Oxford, he met JOHN WAIN; he earned his degree in English in 1949.

Although most famous as a novelist, Amis published poetry before he became successful in fiction. His first volume, *Bright November*, appeared in 1947. Many of these poems were written during his war service. Uncertainty after the war forms a major theme in *Bright November*, as does love. The object of his affections at this time was the subject of "Poem for Hilary," Hilary Ann Bardwell, whom he married in 1948; he later married the novelist Elizabeth Jane Howard. Critics included Amis in a group of poets they dubbed "The Movement," in which they also included ELIZABETH JENNINGS, Larkin, and Wain.

The Movement was not a formal group, but their poetry was popularized in the 1950s anthology *New Lines*. Their verse was straightforward and plain-spoken with tight form and little use of metaphor. Amis's later collections of verse include *A Frame of Mind* (1953), *A Case of Samples* (1956), and *A Look round the Estate* (1963). The latter especially reflects the cynicism of his later years. His cynicism was both political ("On Goliath") and religious. In poems such as "New Approach Needed," Amis argued that Jesus was an inadequate savior for mankind. His *Collected Poems 1944–1979* was published in 1979.

In 1949, Amis began his academic career, which lasted until 1963, with a teaching position at the University College of Swansea in Wales. He scored a major success with the publication of his first novel, the humorous *Lucky Jim* (1954), which won the Somerset Maugham Award in 1955. Jim Dixon is a young and disgruntled assistant lecturer at a British college. Although he is not always a sympathetic character in Amis's portrayal, Dixon's grievances are real. He detests having to publish and speak on hollow, boring subjects in order to keep his job in the History Department. He has an affair with a colleague, Margaret Peel. In the end, Dixon makes his final exit from the academic scene in triumph, free at last of its social pretentiousness. The novels *The Uncertain Feeling* and *I Like It Here* followed in 1955 and 1958.

Take a Girl Like You (1960) explores the sexual tension between Patrick Standish and Jenny Bunn, two opposites. The protagonist of *One Fat Englishman* (1963) is the greedy and miserable publisher Roger H. St. John W. Micheldene. With *The Green Man* (1969), Amis toyed with the realm of the supernatural. Maurice Allington, landlord of an old inn, The Green Man, narrates the story of his confrontation with the ghost of Dr. Thomas Underhill, a seventeenth-century man suspected of murdering his wife.

Amis experimented with fiction in several genres. *The Anti-Death League* (1966) is a spy thriller with a more serious tone than his previous novels. Using the pseudonym Robert Markham, he contributed *Colonel Sun* (1968) to the James Bond series. *The Riverside Villas Murder* (1973) is a detective story that unfolds around the murder of Christopher Inman. His murderer and former mistress, Mrs. Trevelyan, has an affair with the young and unwitting Peter Furneaux, who is helping Colonel Manton solve the mystery of Inman's murder.

In *We Are All Guilty* (1992), Amis examines the notion that society is responsible for an individual's behavior. The delinquent Clive seriously hurts a night watchman when he breaks into a warehouse. Clive has a host of supporters all insisting that he cannot be held responsible for the crime, the only exception being a police sergeant. Amis's other novels include *The Egyptologists*, co-written with Robert Conquest; *I Want It Now* (1968); *Girl, 20* (1971), set in London during the 1960s; *Ending Up* (1974); *Jake's Thing* (1978); *Stanley and the Women* (1984), which earned widespread condemnation from feminists and other critics; *The Old Devils* (1986), winner of the Booker Prize; *The Folks That Live on the Hill* (1990); and *The Russian Girl* (1994).

Among Amis's other works are the short-story collection *My Enemy's Enemy* (1962) and his *Memoirs* (1991). Amis's son, Martin Amis, has also become a well-known novelist. Amis was knighted in 1990. Amis was a founder figure in both poetry and literature in the 1950s. The unpretentious style and use of traditional poetic devices in Amis's verse helped form the foundation of the Movement poetry, and *Lucky Jim* was a central work among the Angry Young Men.

BIBLIOGRAPHY

Bradford, Richard, *Kingsley Amis*, 1989; Fussell, Paul, *The Anti-Egotist: Kingsley Amis, Man of Letters, 1994*; Gardner, Philip, *Kingsley Amis*, 1981; Jacobs, Eric, *Kingsley Amis: A Biography*, 1995; McDermott, John, *Kingsley Amis: An English Moralist*, 1989; Moseley, Merritt, *Understanding Kingsley Amis*, 1993; Salwak, Dale, *Kingsley Amis, Modern Novelist*, 1992.

Andrić, Ivo

(October 9, 1892–March 13, 1975)
Novelist, Short-Story Writer, Poet

The Serbo-Croat language author Ivo Andrić, best known for three novels published after World War II, explored the religious, ethnic, and historical elements of his native Bosnia in his short stories, novels, and poetry. He received the Nobel Prize for Literature in 1961.

Andrić was born into a Catholic family in Dolac, in what is now Bosnia, near Travnik. His father died of tuberculosis when Andrić, an only child, was two, and Andrić then went to live with an aunt in Višegrad. The Višegrad landscape was the center of centuries-old ethnic and religious conflicts and would furnish the material for much of his writing. He attended school beginning at age 6, then moved to Sarajevo for high school and lived there with his mother. Although he disliked his later schooling, it was during his days as a student that he developed his interest in writing.

In 1912 Andrić enrolled at the University of Zagreb and then studied in a succession of universities in Vienna, Cracow, and later Graz, where he earned a doctorate. Along with many other students who opposed Austro-Hungarian rule, Andrić was a member of the National Revolutionary Youth Organization and as a result spent part of World War I in prison. After his release in 1915 he spent the next two years interned in Bosnia. In 1918 Andrić returned to Zagreb, where he helped found the journal *The Literary South*. Two early collections of poetry, *Ex Ponto* (1918) and *Anxieties* (1920), belong to this period.

Although his literary reputation began to grow, the royalties from his work proved insufficient for a living. After the war he joined the Yugoslavian diplomatic service, a position that took him all over Europe between the two world wars. Andrić wrote short stories during these years. His first, "The Journey of Alija Derzelez," was published in 1920. The majority of these stories, like his novels, are set in the Yugoslavian landscape.

In 1941 Andrić, then in Berlin, left the diplomatic service and returned to Belgrade after the German invasion of Yugoslavia. He wrote the three novels for which he is most famous during World War II. *Bosnian Story* (1945) is set in the period from 1807 to 1814, during the brief existence of a French consulate in Travnik that was established during the Napoleonic wars. In the story Andrić explored the effect of the Western consulate on the Eastern cultures in Bosnia. *The Bridge on the Drina* (1945) is an epic chronicle spanning a period from the sixteenth century to the beginning of World War I. The stone bridge in the novel forms a symbolic center for the variety of religious and ethnic elements that inhabit the region. First built by the Ottoman Vezir in the sixteenth century, it serves as the focal point of all of the novel's action and represents an established way of life until its destruction in World War I. *The Woman from Sarajevo* (1945) focuses on the character of Rajka Radaković, a neurotic Yugoslavian miser.

In 1966 Andrić married Milica Babić, a costume designer. His other works include the unfinished novel *Omer Pasha Latas*, published posthumously; *Signs by the Roadside*, a series of philosophical essays and sketches; and *Devil's Yard* (trans. 1962), a novella set inside a Turkish prison.

Bibliography

Hawkesworth, Celia, *Ivo Andrić: Bridge Between East and West*, 1984; Popovic, Radovan, *Ivo Andrić: A Writer's Life*, 1989.

Anouilh, Jean

(June 23, 1910–October 3, 1987)
Playwright, Director

A major figure in French theater, Jean-Marie-Lucien-Pierre Anouilh wrote more than fifty plays in numerous styles. Noted for his penchant for experimentation and carefully crafted productions of social issues, he used his plays as vehicles for commentary and investigation but stopped short of philosophical presentation. Even when he incorporated historical and mythological episodes in his plays, they retained a modern spirit.

Anouilh was born in Bordeaux, France, and moved to Paris with his family as an adolescent. He studied law and worked for a time in advertising before he entered the world of theater—as secretary to the actor and director Louis Jouvet. Influenced by Jouvet and by the experimental director Jacques Coupeau, Anouilh began to write his own plays.

His early plays, which Anouilh dubbed "Pièces noires" (black plays), are presented in a naturalistic style and have negative resolutions. The protagonist of *L'Hermine (1932; The Ermine)*, the first black play, is the impoverished orphan Frantz. Frantz's love for Monime leads him to try several businesses to enable him to earn enough money to marry her. When these fail, he begins to consider murdering Monime's benefactor, the duchesse de Granat, the first of many older aristocratic women to appear in Anouilh's plays. When Frantz actually does commit the murder, his deed has the unexpected effect of alienating Monime, so he confesses. *Jézabel*, another dark play, followed the same year.

Le voyageur sans bagage (1937; Traveler without Luggage) marked Anouilh's first popular success and offered a sharply critical look at post–World War I bourgeoisie. The protagonist, Gaston, has been suffering from amnesia since World War I. When his benefactor, the duchesse Dupont-Dufort, tries to find a home for him among the many who lay claim to him, she by chance chooses his real family. Gaston soon discovers, however, that his past is full of unpleasantness—theft, wronging his friends, and other misdeeds. He tries to reject his past and grabs at a fictional one when the opportunity presents itself.

Like Gaston, many of Anouilh's characters are restless, in search of something more than they have, on the verge of major decisions, or living in illusions—like Georges in *Le rendez-vous de Senlis*.

An unhappily married man, he falls in love with Isabelle and tries to create an ideal atmosphere by hiring actors to impersonate his parents. Isabelle uncovers the ruse but still loves him in the end. The heroine of *La sauvage (Restless Heart;* 1938), Thérèse Tarde, struggles to come to terms with the differences in background between herself and her lover, Florent, a rich piano player.

During World War II, Anouilh served briefly in the military. He lived in Paris during the Nazi Occupation and, having a largely apolitical outlook, did not join the Resistance. The war years marked the period in his work during which he wrote several plays derived from Greek myth, all of which in fact addressed the problems of his own time. These include *Medea*, first performed in 1937, *Eurydice* (1942), and the tragedy *Antigone* (1942). Many consider *Antigone*, his story of the rebellious niece of Créon who defies her uncle's orders and buries her brother, Polynice, among the finest of his works. The plot is based on the ancient tragedy by Sophocles, but Anouilh's version clearly celebrates the Resistance.

L'invitation au château (1947; *Ring 'Round the Moon*), a fairy tale rife with comedy, switches gears entirely. The story concerns the identical twins Horace and Frédéric, the latter of whom pursues the rich Diana. Horace, in love with Diana, concocts a scheme to pair his brother with Isabelle, a scheme that, after a few complications, finally works. *The Waltz of the Toreadors* (1952) is one of many farces by Anouilh to include the character of General Saintpé. The life of the retired general, stuck in an unhappy marriage, is disturbed by the appearance of his longtime mistress Ghislane de Sainte-Euverte. The general has carried on his relationship with her by correspondence. Ghislane seeks to prove that the general's wife is having an affair, and after a series of tragicomic turns, she ends up with the general's son, Gaston.

Flashback, one of Anouilh's favorite devices, forms an integral part of two historical plays in which the heroes choose death rather than compromise their beliefs. *The Lark* (1953) presents the trial of Joan of Arc interspersed with flashbacks of her past. *Becket, or, The Honor of God* (1959) depicts the life Thomas à Becket, Archbishop of Canterbury and twelfth-century martyr.

Anouilh's versatile technique and presentation style included comedies, tragedies, farces, and the *comédie-ballet*. His vivid characterizations, critical eye, and ability to weave tight, dramatic plots were a major force in French theater.

The Trousers (1978) takes place in France when the Women's Liberation Movement has come to power. The protagonist, Léon, finds himself accused before the Committee of Liberated Women, and among his alleged crimes is fathering the child of his maid. When the baby is born black, proving he is not its father, the Committee drops the charge, but he is found guilty of other offenses against women and flees to Switzerland. Anouilh's other plays include *Thieves' Carnival* (1938); *Ring 'Round the Moon* (1947); *Poor Bitos* (1956); *The Baker, The Baker's Wife, and The Baker's Boy* (1968); *Dear Antoine; or, The Love That Failed* (1969); *The Goldfish; or, My Father, This Hero* (1970); *Do Not Awaken the Lady* (1970); and *The Arrest* (1975). He also wrote many film scenarios and translated other plays.

BIBLIOGRAPHY

McIntyre, H. G., *The Theatre of Jean Anouilh*, 1981; Smith, Christopher Norman, *Jean Anouilh: Life, Work, and Criticism*, 1985.

Antonioni, Michelangelo

(September 29, 1912–)
Director, Producer

Michelangelo Antonioni began making his abstract and metaphorical films at roughly the same time FEDERICO FELLINI and ROBERTO ROSSELLINI embarked on their own film careers. Antonioni was influenced by the Neorealists, and he is best known for his films of the 1950s and 1960s. His cinematic style is characterized by the use of symbolic imagery and landscapes as well as sparse plot and his films convey some of the century's most compelling images of desolation and isolation.

Antonioni was born in Ferrara, in northern Italy, and grew up in relative comfort and prosperity, a factor he has cited as a prime influence on his film career. As a child he designed puppets and the structures to go with them, and as an adolescent he began to paint. Antonioni attended local schools and later commuted to the University of Bologna,

Michelangelo Antonioni (AKG)

where he studied the Greek and Roman classics and economics. He began to go to the cinema and write harsh, outspoken film criticism, which was heavily edited by Fascist censors.

By 1939, Antonioni had decided to try to make it in the cinema and moved to Rome. Success eluded him at first, and he worked in a series of odd jobs. After working for a while as an editor for the magazine *Cinema*, Antonioni was fired for political reasons. The magazine was run by the Fascist Entertainment Guild, of whom Vittorio Mussolini, son of the dictator, was director. Antonioni then studied briefly at the Centro Sperimentale di Cinematografia.

Antonioni got his start in film in the Neorealist movement. Among the early scripts he worked on was Rossellini's *A Pilot Returns* (1942), and he later traveled to France to work with the French director Marcel Carné on his *Les visiteurs du soir*. In 1943, Antonioni began his first film, the short *Gente del Po* (1947; *People of the Po*), a documentary about fishermen who lived along the Po River. During this time Antonioni also worked as a translator to earn money and wrote film criticism for the underground paper *Italia libera*. He was unable to finish *Gente del Po* until after the war; then, until 1950, he worked on a series of other short documentaries.

Cronaca di un amore (1950; *Story of Love*), Antonioni's first feature film, brought some success. The story concerns Fontana, a Milanese industrialist; his wife, Paola; and her lover, Guido. When he looks into Paola's past, Fontana discovers that Paola and Guido may be at fault in the death of Guido's former fiancée. Paola and Guido renew their affair, and she wants to kill Fontana. Fontana perishes in a car accident that may or may not have been set up, and his death separates Paola and Guido forever.

Antonioni's films are marked by their character studies and ambiguous plots, plots that are secondary to symbolic presentation. Obtrusive, metaphorical objects, long tracking shots, barren landscapes, and industrial scenes are all typical components of the bleak outlook he conveys. He has either written or co-written the majority of his screenplays, which depict alienation, isolation, corruption, and decadence in modern society.

Le amiche (1955) concerns a circle of corrupt women in Turin. When Clelia arrives to help establish a branch of a fashion house, she becomes involved with the manipulative Momina and the suicidal Rosetta. When Rosetta's lover, Lorenzo, breaks with her, she kills herself. Clelia blames Momina for her death and finally leaves Turin for Rome, abandoning her own lover as well.

L'avventura (1959; *The Adventure*), Antonioni's first international success, is the first in a trilogy of films. Anna, a passenger on a yacht, disappears on a cruise in the Lipari Islands. Among those who search for her are her lover Sandro and her friend Claudia, who fall in love and live in relative happiness until Claudia finds him with a call girl. *L'avventura* was the first of many Antonioni films to star Monica Vitti. *La notte* (1961; *Night*) and *L'eclisse* (1962; *The Eclipse*) completed the trilogy.

Deserto rosso (1964; *Red Desert*) was Antonioni's first color film, and he was so meticulous in his color choices that he had a field painted gray to achieve the effect he wanted. Vitti plays Giuliana, a despairing married woman in search of meaning and love. Antonioni places her against a bleak industrial landscape, ravaged by technological advance.

In *Blow-Up* (1966), Antonioni's first major English film, David Hemmings plays Thomas, an arrogant fashion photographer. One day in the park he takes photographs of a happy couple, one of whom is Jane (Vanessa Redgrave). Jane will do anything to get the pictures back, and when Thomas develops them, he makes a startling discovery. In the background he has photographed a murder. Thomas makes blow-ups of his prints and goes to the park, where his discovery of the dead body proves his suspicions. He wonders about the details, but they are never brought to light, and he continues to live his corrupt existence. *Zabriskie Point* (1970), set in the turbulent atmosphere of 1960s counterculture, was Antonioni's first American film.

Antonioni's other films include *I vinti* (1952); *La signora senza camelie* (1952–1953); *Chung Kuo China* (1972); *The Passenger* (1974), starring Jack Nicholson and Maria Schneider; *Identification of a Woman* (1982); and *Beyond the Clouds* (1995). *The Mystery of Oberwald* (1980), adapted from JEAN COCTEAU's play *The Eagle Has Two Heads*, was shot on videotape and employs experimental coloring and editing.

BIBLIOGRAPHY

Arrowsmith, William, *Antonioni: The Poet of Images*, 1995; Leprohon, Pierre, *Michelangelo Antonioni: An Introduction*, 1963; Rifkin, Ned, *Antonioni's Visual Language*, 1982.

Arp, Jean

(September 16, 1887–June 7, 1966)
Painter, Sculptor, Poet, Short-Story Writer, Essayist

Jean Arp assimilated the influences of German Expressionism, Dadaism, and Surrealism, forging his own abstract style marked by his treatment of curvilinear forms. Arp's work in numerous styles—including stone sculpture, painted wood reliefs, torn paper creations, collages, and lithographs—contributed to the development of abstract art in the second half of the century.

Arp was born in Strassburg, Germany, now Strasbourg, France. He began to draw at a young age. While studying at the Strasbourg School of Fine Art, Arp tired of "everlasting copying of stuffed birds and withered flowers." During a 1904 visit to Paris he discovered modern art, and the following year he entered the Weimar Art School in Germany. After studying there from 1905 to 1907, he enrolled in the Académie Julien in Paris in 1908.

By 1911 Arp had associated himself with a number of modern artists, including WASSILY KANDINSKY. The same year, he helped organize an exhibition at Lucerne entitled *Moderne Bund*, featuring his own works as well as those of PABLO PICASSO, HENRI MATISSE, and others. While in Munich in 1912, Arp briefly involved himself in the activities of the Expressionist group Der Blaue Reiter (The Blue Rider).

Arp moved to Paris in 1914, enabling him to meet avant-garde artists such as Picasso and ROBERT DELAUNAY as well as the writer Max Jacob. With the outbreak of World War I, he moved to Zurich, where with Tristan Tzara, Hugo Ball, and others he helped found the Dadaist movement. The Dadaists rejected traditional, representational forms of art and saw all aspects of existence as art.

Inspired by the elementary forms embodied in his children's blocks, Arp created what he termed his first "essential" picture in Zurich. Rebelling against traditional oil-on-canvas creations, Arp created and exhibited collages, tapestries, and fabrics. By 1917 the angular forms of his early works had given way to the curvilinear and biomorphic forms that characterized the remainder of his work.

While in Switzerland, Arp also created his first painted wood reliefs. Works such as *Plant Hammer* (1917) and *Birds in an Aquarium* (1920) combine separate, sometimes painted, pieces of wood cut into abstract shapes. He returned to the medium throughout his career, and among his major works is a large wood relief for Harvard University's Graduate Center (1950).

Arp collaborated with other artists, such as KURT SCHWITTERS and MAX ERNST, and moved to Germany after the war. In 1921 he married the artist Sophie Tauber, and three years later they settled in Meudon, near Paris. In the mid-1920s, he fell under the influence of the Surrealists in Paris, taking part in the first exhibition of Surrealist paintings at the Galerie Pierre in 1925. His Surrealist works, which Arp described as "interpretive," bear titles such as *Moon Frog* and *Navel Bottle*. Arp worked in many media. His *Mountain, Table, Anchors, Navel* (1925) is an oil on cardboard with shapes cut from the picture. Many of his collages use string and other materials.

Following his Surrealist period, Arp began to concentrate on the perfection of forms. He and his wife joined the Cercle et Carré (Circle and Square) group and in 1931 helped found the Association Abstraction-Création. During the 1930s he began to sculpt, primarily working in metal and stone. His smooth, abstract, and organic forms bear some resemblance to the work of the English sculptors BARBARA HEPWORTH and HENRY MOORE. Among the works that reflect these qualities are *Human Concretion* (1935) and *Stone Formed by the Human Hand*, in Jura limestone.

During World War II, Arp returned to Zurich, where Sophie died in 1943. He returned to Meudon after the war and continued to create his abstract works in various media. Among his later works is a large metal-on-cement piece for the Ciudad Universitaria in Caracas, Venezuela.

Aside from art, Arp also created poetry, sketches, and essays in both French and German—he used the name Hans Arp when he wrote in German. Marcel Jean edited two collections of his writings: *Arp on Arp: Poems, Essays, Memories by Jean Arp* (1972) and *Collected French Writings* (1974).

BIBLIOGRAPHY

Read, Herbert Edward, *Arp*, 1968; Read, Herbert Edward, *The Art of Jean Arp*, 1968; Soby, James Thrall, ed., *Arp*, 1958.

Ashton, Frederick

(September 17, 1904–August 18, 1988)
Choreographer, Dancer, Director

Frederick William Mallandaine Ashton distinguished himself as the primary choreographer for England's Royal Ballet from 1933 to 1970, producing original ballets such as *Façade* and *A Month in the Country* and choreographing other classics. Though not noted for his originality, he established himself as a respected veteran in the ballet world. Ashton danced minor roles himself and worked with leading dancers of his era, such as Dame MARGOT FONTEYN and RUDOLF NUREYEV.

Ashton was the youngest son of a British diplomat; he was born in Guayaquil, Ecuador, and attended a Dominican school in Lima, Peru, where the family moved in his youth. When he was 13, he saw ANNA PAVLOVA dance in Lima, sparking his interest in the ballet. His family's disapproval, however, prevented him from pursuing his interest until later. Beginning in 1919, Ashton spent several unhappy years as a student at Dover College in England.

After his father's suicide, Ashton's mother moved to England. While Ashton worked in a merchant's office and lived with her, he secretly took lessons from LÉONIDE MASSINE. His mother's disapproval when she found out threatened to end his dancing career, but she relented when he fell ill from disappointment. Ashton continued to study with Massine until his departure from England and then studied under Marie Lambert. At the same time, he attended all the performances he could, among which were some of the final productions of SERGEY DIAGHILEV's Ballets Russes.

Ashton's debut as a dancer took place in 1925 at the Palace Pier in Brighton. He danced the role of Monsieur du Chic in Ashley Dukes's *The Tragedy of Fashion* (1926) as well as choreographing the piece—one of his early choreographic efforts. The ballet portrays the story of a fashion designer (Monsieur du Chic), who commits suicide when his masterpiece fails to win approval. Ashton's other early works as a choreographer include *The Fairy Queen* (1927), based on Henry Purcell's opera; Dukes's *Jew Süss* (1929), based on writings by LION FEUCHT-WANGER; *Capriol Suite* (1930); and Ashton's own *Regatta* (1932).

In 1933, Ashton joined the Vic Wells Ballet (eventually the Sadler's Wells Ballet and then the Royal Ballet), where he would remain as primary choreographer until 1970. He continued to dance in secondary roles but distinguished himself primarily as a choreographer. In Ashton's own *Mephisto Valse* (1934), with music by Franz Liszt, he danced the part of Mephisto. Other early Ashton ballets include *Façade* (1931), loosely based on poetry by Edith Sitwell with music by WILLIAM TURNER WALTON; *Mercury* (1931); *Pas de deux* (1933); *Les rendezvous* (1933); *Les patineurs* (1937); *Symphonic Variations* (1946); and *Scènes de ballet* (1948) with Igor Stravinsky's music.

In 1950, Ashton created the one-act *Illuminations* for the New York City Ballet. He tailored the 1963 ballet *Mar-guerite and Armand* to Fonteyn and Nureyev, the former of whom he worked with extensively. Over the years he also choreographed classics such as *Cinderella* (1948); MAURICE RAVEL's *Daphnis and Chloë* (1951), originally created for the Ballets Russes; *Sylvia* (1952); and *Orpheus* (1953).

Ashton was an essentially optimistic individual, and he designed his ballets to bring out the beauty of the dance rather than to make strong statements. Many of his ballets have become part of standard repertoire.

Ashton's ventures into film were largely unsuccessful. He contributed choreography to *Tales of Hoffmann* (1951) and in 1970 choreographed and danced the part of Mrs. Tiggy-Winkle in *Tales of Beatrix Potter*. Among his later ballets are *Ondine* (1958); *La fille mal gardée* (1960); *The Dream* (1964), a one-act ballet; *Monotones* (1965–1966), with music by ERIK SATIE; *Jazz Calendar* (1968); *Enigma Variations* (1968); *Siesta* (1972); *A Month in the Country* (1976), adapted from the Russian author Ivan Turgenev's play; and *Rhapsody* (1981), with music by SERGEY RACHMANINOFF. His *Five Brahms Waltzes in the Manner of Isadora Duncan* (1975–1976) was written for the dancer Lynn Seymour.

Ashton served as the Royal Ballet's associate director from 1952 to 1963 and its director from 1963 to 1970. He was knighted in 1962.

BIBLIOGRAPHY

Kavanagh, Julie, *Secret Muses: The Life of Frederick Ashton*, 1996; Vaughan, David, *Frederick Ashton and His Ballets*, 1977.

Asturias, Miguel Ángel

(October 19, 1899–June 9, 1974)
Novelist, Playwright, Poet, Diplomat, Short-Story Writer, Translator

The Guatemalan writer Miguel Ángel Asturias reached the height of his popularity in Latin American literature in the 1960s. His best-known works are his novels, beginning with the publication of *The President* in 1946. Asturias won the Nobel Prize for Literature in 1967.

Asturias was born in Guatemala City, Guatemala. His father was a magistrate, and his mother taught school. The family moved to the country for political reasons until 1908, when they returned to the city atmosphere. In 1922 Asturias helped found the Popular University, which offered free classes to those who could not afford an education. He took a degree in law from the University of San Carlos of Guatemala and moved to Europe in 1923.

In Paris Asturias studied anthropology at the Sorbonne. He had already developed an interest in Indian culture—his dissertation for his law degree, "The Social Problem of the Indian," earned a Gálvez Prize in Guatemala. While in Paris he helped translate French versions of the Maya *Popol Vuh* and *Annals of the Cakchiquels* into Spanish. His first major work was a book of Maya-inspired tales titled *Legends of Guatemala* (1930). Also important to his literary development was the influence of the Paris Surrealists, in particular the movement's founder, ANDRÉ ROBERT BRETON. The Surrealists' emphasis on the subconscious and the psyche formed one of the major elements in Asturias's fiction, as did the Guatemalan political atmosphere.

Asturias returned to Guatemala in 1933 and was rarely far from politics. In 1942 he was elected to the Guatemalan Congress, and in 1946 he began nine years of service as a diplomat, working mostly in Central and South America. When a new dictatorship arose in Guatemala in 1954, Asturias fled abroad. From 1966 to 1970 he served as Guatemala's ambassador to France in Paris.

His first novel, *The President* (1946), is about a Latin American dictator whose administration is rife with intricate intrigues and corruption. The title character was inspired by Manuel Estrada Cabrera, dictator of Guatemala from 1898 to 1920. *Men of Maize* (1949) incorporates many Maya legends into its three major subplots, whose characters are very loosely connected. In the first, local Indians refuse to cooperate with the forced commercialization of corn, their sacred crop. A guerrilla war erupts between government forces and Indian rebels, and the murder of the rebel leader brings a traditional Indian curse on the conspirators.

In the second part, María Tecún has fled with her children from her husband, a blind man who raised her and later married her. He regains his sight after an operation and embarks on a years-long search for María. Eventually he is wrongly jailed and finds María when she comes to visit her son, who has also been unjustly imprisoned. In the third section, the Indian mail carrier Nicho Aquino arrives home to find his wife missing. After a complicated search for her, he learns that she slipped into a well and died. Nicho is contacted by a descendant of mountain spirits with whom he undergoes a psychic and spiritual journey.

A trilogy of novels beginning with *The Strong Wind* (1950) explores the exploitation of Indian workers on banana plantations. *The Strong Wind* begins as a foreign fruit company (the U.S.-based United Fruit Company) is clearing hostile terrain in Guatemala. It was followed by *The Green Pope* (1954) and *The Eyes of the Buried* (1960). Asturias's later novels include *The Little Bejeweled One* (1961), *Mulata de tal* (1963), *Bad Thief* (1969), and *The Talking Machine* (1971).

Also among Asturias's writings are a number of plays. The first two, *Culculcán* and *Soluna*, draw heavily from Maya legends. *La audencia de las confines* (1957) is based on Bartolomé de Las Casas, the Spanish missionary known as the "Apostle of the Indians." His other plays include *Blackmail* and the comedy *Dry Dock.*

In addition to novels and plays, Asturias also wrote short stories and poetry. Among his volumes of short stories are *Lida Sal's Looking Glass* (1967) and *Weekend in Guatemala* (1956), a collection of short stories about Castillo Armas's invasion of Guatemala in 1954. His poetry anthology *Sien de Alondra* was published in 1949. Asturias contributed regularly to Latin American journals during his lifetime and was awarded the Lenin Peace Prize in 1966.

BIBLIOGRAPHY

Callan, Richard J., *Miguel Ángel Asturias*, 1970.

Auden, W. H.

(February 21, 1907–September 29, 1973)
Poet, Playwright, Essayist, Critic, Librettist

Influenced by the poets T. S. ELIOT and WILLIAM BUTLER YEATS, Wystan Hugh Auden began to write poetry in the early 1920s and became one of the twentieth century's major poets. His early verse belongs with the work of a generation of Oxford-educated poets who rose to prominence in the 1930s and shared strong opposition to Fascism and a commitment to radical left-wing political ideals. Auden stands out among those poets for his ability to address the problems of England, then deep in the Depression, in verse that is irreverent, witty, and beautifully crafted. In the 1940s and onward, Auden cultivated a more personal and reflective style of poetry that is both simple and lyrical.

Auden was born in York, Yorkshire, England and moved to Birmingham with his family when he was 2. There his father worked as a medical officer for the city schools and a professor of public health at the University of Birmingham. His mother, too, was in the medical profession and worked as a nurse. At the age of 8 he entered St. Edmund's Preparatory School in Surrey, where he met his lifelong friend Christopher Isherwood. Five years later, he went to Gresham's, a private school at Holt, Norfolk. Following his family's interests, he studied science and biology and thought of becoming a mining engineer. However, Auden had other interests as well, such as acting in school plays and writing poetry. Throughout his life he was to retain a wide spectrum of interests.

Auden's first published poem appeared in a school periodical in 1922. Three years later he entered Christ Church College, Oxford, where he continued to study sciences but took many other classes as well. He enjoyed his English literature classes and attended some of J. R. R. TOLKIEN's lectures on Old English—an important influence on his early poetry.

At Oxford, Auden absorbed poetry of all sorts, including the modern verse of T. S. Eliot, and became a well-known poet at the university himself. For the time being, he rejected the Anglican tradition of his upbringing. His associates included fellow poets STEPHEN SPENDER, LOUIS MACNEICE, and C. DAY-LEWIS, all of whom shared during the 1930s a left-wing political outlook that manifested itself in their verse. Auden was the most active and self-confident poet and the acknowledged leader of the group. Spender handprinted a limited edition of Auden's first collection of poetry in 1928, but soon Auden found a wider audience with *Poems* (1930).

Along with the verse in *The Orators* (1932), the early poems are sometimes marred by obscurity, but the energy and force with which they expressed in poetic form the psychological and economic ills of England created a strong impression, winning Auden an audience immediately. In them Auden assimilated an extensive range of influences, from Sigmund Freud to Anglo-Saxon verse, which influenced poems such as "The Wanderer," whose opening line illustrates how Auden could capture both the music and the tone of Anglo-Saxon poetry: "Doom is dark and deeper than any sea-dingle." "Miss Gee, a Ballad," show Auden's mastery of both popular ballad rhythms and Freud, with its picture of a repressed woman who dies of cancer. Wherever he traveled, Auden absorbed the landscape, and his poetry is filled with imagery from both cities and countryside.

After graduating from Oxford, Auden traveled to Germany with Isherwood and fell in love with the German language. He returned to England in 1929 and taught that year in London. In 1930 he took a teaching position at the Larchfield Academy in Scotland, replacing the departing Day-Lewis. In 1932 he taught at Down's School, Colwall.

In the mid-1930s, Auden's poetry grew increasingly political and social in nature as he embraced Marxism. Works such as the volume *On This Island* (1937) reflect not only a more political tone, but also a clearer, less obscure style. A 1937 journey to Spain (which inspired the poem *Spain* of the same year) signaled the beginning of his disillusionment with Communism and his return to his Anglican roots. Intending to drive an ambulance for the Loyalists during the civil war, he was shocked when he arrived in Spain to find all the churches closed.

In spite of the political overtones of much of his verse from these years, Auden remained wary of politics. He treated other themes in his poetry as well, such as the role of the artist, in poems such as "The Novelist" and "Musée des Beaux Arts" (1938). In spite of his homosexuality, he married Erika Mann, daughter of the German novelist

THOMAS MANN, for the sole purpose of obtaining for her a British passport to escape Nazi Germany in 1935.

For the experimental Group Theatre in London, Auden wrote several plays, on most of which he collaborated with Isherwood. *The Dance of Death*, which he wrote alone, is a musical verse play and was first performed in 1934. Three joint efforts with Isherwood followed: *The Dog Beneath the Skin* (1935), *The Ascent of F6* (1936), and *On the Frontier* (1938). Beginning in 1935, he wrote commentaries for documentary films for the General Post Office Film Unit in London, such as *Coal Face* (1935) and *Night Mail* (1936), both of which featured music scores by BENJAMIN BRITTEN.

Two travel books date from the end of the decade as well. The first of these, *Letters from Iceland* (1937), followed a trip to that country with MacNeice. Auden remained fascinated with Iceland throughout his life, as he believed it the home of his paternal ancestors. The publication of *Journey to a War* (1939) followed a trip to China with Isherwood.

In 1939 he and Isherwood moved to the United States, where he settled in New York and became a U.S. citizen in 1946. His poetry became increasingly nonpolitical and more reflective, shaped by his renewed interest in Christianity and by his avid reading of the works of the Danish philosopher Søren Kierkegaard. It appeared in periodicals such as the *New Yorker*. His published volumes of verse from this time include *Another Time* (1940), which contains his well-known "September 1, 1939," and *The Double Man* (1941), containing the poem "New Year Letter." During the 1940s he wrote three major long poems, the Christmas oratorio *For the Time Being* (1944), *Sea and the Mirror*, and *The Age of Anxiety* (1947). For the last of these, which treats four figures in a Manhattan bar, Auden won the Pulitzer Prize in 1948.

During his last years, Auden spent much of his time in Europe, passing summers first on the Italian island of Ischia and later at a farmhouse in Austria. With his then companion, Chester Kallman, an American poet, he wrote a number of opera librettos in collaboration with composers such as IGOR STRAVINSKY and HANS WERNER HENZE. With the former they created *The Rake's Progress* in 1951; and with Henze they finished *Elegy for Young Lovers* (1961) and *The Bassarids* (1966).

Auden's later volumes of verse include *The Shield of Achilles* (1955), *Homage to Clio* (1960), *About the House* (1965), *City without Walls* (1969), and the posthumously published *Thank You, Fog* (1974). The title poem from the first of those volumes is one of Auden's best. The sea-nymph Thetis comes to the smith of the gods for a shield for her son, Achilles, just as Homer tells the story in his *Iliad*. But in Auden's poem, when Thetis looks over the smith's shoulder for all the beauty Homer describes,

> There on the shining metal
> His hands had put instead
> An artificial wilderness
> And a sky like lead,

and all the horrors of modern warfare.

In general, however, the last poems carry a lighter, more personal tone than his earlier verse. In the 1960s he revised and arranged many of his poems and published them as *Collected Shorter Poems 1927–57* (1967) and *Collected Longer Poems* (1969).

Auden also edited works by others, such as *An Elizabethan Song Book* (1956) and *The Collected Poems of St. John Perse* (1972); wrote essays and reviews; and taught at many American universities and colleges. A volume of criticism, *The Dyer's Hand*, was published in 1962. Auden returned to England to teach at Oxford in 1972. He received numerous awards during his lifetime, including the National Book Award for *The Shield of Achilles*.

Auden's body of poetry covers a wide variety of themes—treatments of landscape, psychological explorations, dedications to individuals (such as "Friday's Child," written in honor of the German Lutheran theologian Dietrich Bonhoeffer, who was hanged at the concentration camp in Flossenbürg by the Nazis in 1945), the political and social poems of the thirties, love, and religion. He has been considered the most versatile and intellectually vigorous of poets writing in English in this century, but perhaps too ready to alternate seriousness with flip-pancy to deserve to be called great. He himself seems to have seen himself not as a "great poet," but in the tradition of the Roman poet Horace, and in one of his light later poems, "The Horatians," it seems likely he imagines himself saying, with others in that tradition, that poets "can only/ . . . look at/ this world with a happy eye/ but from a sober perspective."

Auden did more than that, but even if he had only done that supremely well, surely he should be granted a kind of greatness.

BIBLIOGRAPHY

Callan, Edward, *Auden: A Carnival of Intellect*, 1983; Carpenter, Humphrey, *W. H. Auden: A Biography*, 1981; Davenport-Hines, R. P. T., *Auden*, 1995; Fuller, John, *W. H. Auden: A Commentary*, 1998; Hecht, Anthony, *The Hidden Law: The Poetry of W. H. Auden*, 1993; Johnson, Wendell Stacy, *W. H. Auden*, 1990; Osborne, Charles, *W. H. Auden: The Life of a Poet*, 1979; Rodway, Allan Edwin, *A Preface to Auden*, 1984; Smith, Stan, *W. H. Auden*, 1985; Wright, George Thaddeus, *W. H. Auden*, 1969.

Awoonor, Kofi Nyidevu

(March 13, 1935–)
Poet, Novelist, Diplomat

The Ghanaian writer Kofi Awoonor is best known for his novel *This Earth, My Brother* and poetry that contrasts traditional African culture with European influences in West Africa. He has also held a number of prominent political posts as a representative of the government of Ghana.

Awoonor was born in Wheta, Gold Coast (now Ghana), during the last years of the British colonial period. His family was of the Ewe people, and Ewe culture and customs are heavily incorporated into his work. His grandmother's renditions of traditional Ewe oral poetry (dirge) helped shape the rhythms of his own verse. Awoonor earned his undergraduate degree at the University of Ghana at Legon in 1960. After graduating, he worked with the Ghana Film Corporation.

His first book of poetry, *Rediscovery and Other Poems*, appeared in 1964 under the name George Awoonor-Williams. Poems such as "The Weaverbird" sharply criticize European colonialization in Africa. Awoonor likened European colonizers to the destructive weaverbird, which invades a host tree and takes it over. The conflict between indigenous African culture and European culture is a primary theme in Awoonor's poetry. He presents the latter as a destructive force on African traditional customs and criticizes Africans who fall under European influence. Elements of Ewe culture and folklore are woven into his poetry and combined with Western literary influences.

For political reasons, Awoonor left Ghana in 1966. He subsequently earned a master's degree in London and a doctorate in comparative literature from the State University of New York at Stonybrook in 1972. His volume of poetry *Night of My Blood* was published in 1971, and the collection *Ride Me, Memory* (1973) deals with his time in America.

After lecturing in the United States, Awoonor returned to Ghana in 1975. Authorities arrested him for alleged involvement in an antigovernment conspiracy. He spent several months in prison and after his release taught at the University College of Cape Coast. His prison experience inspired the volume of poetry *The House by the Sea* (1978).

Awoonor has also written two novels, the better known of which is *This Earth, My Brother* (1971). Its protagonist, Amamu, is a lawyer in postcolonial Ghana. *Comes the Voyager at Last* (1991) concerns an African American who travels to Ghana. Awoonor's other works include the poetry collection *The Latin American and Caribbean Notebook, Volume I* (1992) and *The Breast of the Earth: A Survey of the History, Culture, and Literature of Africa South of the Sahara* (1975). He has edited or coedited the literary journals *Okyeame* and *Transition* as well as the volume *Messages: Poems from Ghana* (1970). In the 1980s and 1990s Awoonor served in a number of political and diplomatic posts for Ghana's government, including that of ambassador to the United Nations.

BIBLIOGRAPHY

Egudu, Romanus, *Four Modern West African Poets*, 1977.

Bacon, Francis

(October 28, 1909–April 28, 1992)
Painter, Decorator

Francis Bacon's pessimistic paintings stand out for their depictions of grotesque and savage figures in psychological and emotional torment. He set his human subjects in landscapes of loneliness, violence, and despair, all conveyed in eye-catching color. Bacon's mature expressionistic style shows the influence of the German Expressionists of the early twentieth century, and his paintings are unique in the intensity of their violence.

Bacon was born in Dublin to a father who trained racehorses. A local clergyman tutored him privately at home, and he briefly attended the Dean Close School in Cheltenham. His family moved frequently back and forth between England and Ireland. As a child Bacon suffered from asthma, an ailment that was to excuse him from military service during World War II. When he was 16, he left his parents for a life of drifting in Western Europe.

In 1925 Bacon went to London, then on to Munich and Berlin in 1926. He supported himself by working at odd jobs and taking interior decorating commissions. Bacon went to Paris later that year and finally settled in London in 1929. Having been inspired by a Picasso exhibition he saw in Paris, he began to paint in watercolor. Bacon gradually moved away from interior design and devoted more of his time to painting.

Bacon began to paint in oils, the medium for which he is best known. Single paintings appeared in exhibitions in 1933, and he held his first one-man show in London the following year. Few of his early paintings survive—he destroyed many of them in 1943. His works remained essentially unknown until 1945, when he attained recognition for his *Three Studies for Figures at the Base of a Crucifixion* (1944) and *Figure in a Landscape* (1945).

From 1947 to 1950 Bacon spent much of his time in Monte Carlo, dividing his time between there and London. He began his series of heads in 1948. The first two works in the series depict distorted, skull-like heads against ominous backgrounds of black and gray. Above the open mouth of the sixth *Head*, the forehead disappears into the background. The grotesque forms of the *Heads* characterize most of the tormented, terrorized, or lonely figures in his body of work.

Although the human figure appears in most of his work, his first portrait of a named individual came in 1951 with his depiction of the artist Lucian Freud. In 1956 he began a series of paintings on the Dutch artist Vincent van Gogh (1853–1890). Muriel Belcher, a friend and manager of the Colony Club in the Soho district of London, was the subject of a 1959 portrait and of *Sphinx—Portrait of Muriel Belcher* (1959). In 1964 he began a series of portraits of his friend Isabel Rawsthorne. His friend George Dyer was the subject of numerous portraits, including a triptych Bacon painted after his death (1972–1974). Bacon's portraits were not portraits in any conventional sense—as in his *Heads*, the faces are contorted and evince great psychological and emotional pain.

A portrait of Pope Innocent X by the Spanish painter Diego Velázquez (1599–1660) formed the basis for Bacon's nightmarish *Screaming Popes* series, begun in 1949. His graphic red-and-orange triptych *Three Studies for a Crucifixion* (1962) also depicts violence within a religious framework. Most of Bacon's paintings depict human figures, but he sometimes used animal subjects, as in his *Study of a Baboon* (1953).

Bacon's works gained increasing popularity in the 1950s. The Institute of Contemporary Arts in London held a major exhibition of his work in 1955. Three years later his work was exhibited in Turin, Italy. By the 1970s his work was well known in the United States and Europe. Among Bacon's other paintings are a depiction of the screaming nanny from SERGEY EISENSTEIN's *Battleship Potemkin*, numerous studies based on photographs by the American motion-picture pioneer Eadweard Muybridge (1830–1904), several self portraits, and his *Orestia* triptych (1981).

BIBLIOGRAPHY

Davies, Hugh Marlais, *Francis Bacon*, 1986; Gowing, Lawrence, and Hunter, Sam, *Francis Bacon*, 1989; Peppiatt, Michael, *Francis Bacon: Anatomy of an Enigma*, 1997.

Bakst, Léon

(February 8, 1866–December 28, 1924)
Painter, Costume Designer, Illustrator, Clothing Designer

Best known for his vivid, elaborate scenery and costume designs for impresario SERGEY DIAGHILEV's Ballets Russes, Léon Bakst designed costumes for some of the most notable dancers of his era—VASLAV NIJINSKY, TAMARA KARSAVINA, and Ida Rubenstein. He contributed his provocative and sometimes erotic scenery to *Schéhérazade, Daphnis and Chloe, The Sleeping Beauty*, and many other ballets presented to international audiences in the early twentieth century.

Bakst was born Lev Samoylovich Rosenberg in Russia. The details of his birth and family name are somewhat confused. His year of birth has been given as 1866, 1867, and 1868, and it is unclear whether he was born in Grodno or St. Petersburg. His father's original name had been Bakst, but he had changed it to Rosenberg. Bakst remained dedicated to his family's Jewish faith throughout his life. Growing up, he was fascinated with the theater and began making toy theater models for his younger siblings, for whom he became responsible when his parents divorced.

Concentrating on drawing and sculpture, Bakst studied art at the Imperial Academy of Arts in St. Petersburg, where he met the future portraitist Valentin Serov. Bakst was expelled from the Academy after he painted a *Pietà* that depicted biblical figures—the Virgin and the disciples—as Jewish peasants. In 1893

Costume for Scheherezade (1910) by Léon Bakst
(Ann Ronan/Image Select)

Bakst went to Paris, where he studied under the Finnish master Albert Edelfelt (1854–1905).

Bakst's early works mainly consist of portraits. Through his acquaintance with Dima Filosofov, he met Diaghilev, with whom he founded the journal *Mir Iskusstva* (*World of Art*) in 1899. During this time Bakst also gained the friendship of MARC CHAGALL and married (in 1903) Lubov Pavlovna Gritzenko, the daughter of millionaire Pavel Treiakov. Their marriage, however, was short-lived on account of his numerous affairs and his personal torment over having outwardly converted to Christianity in order to marry her.

By 1903, Bakst was designing sets for Russian theaters, but he also worked as an illustrator and portraitist and would not devote his energies entirely to set design until after a successful Paris exhibition of his works in 1906. In 1908 he designed sets for the choreographer MICHEL FOKINE. For one of his early flamboyant and vivid Ballet Russes designs—*Cléopâtre* (1909)—he created a large, elaborate chamber with columns and statues. Also among the *Cléopâtre* creations was the costume for the young ballerina Ida Rubenstein's lead role.

The same year he contributed some costumes to *Une nuit d'Egypte*, but a greater success came the following year with *Schéhérazade* (1910). Bakst's scenery for the highly successful ballet employed curtains and carpets as well as erotic, shocking designs and vibrant color. For *Le carnaval* (1910) he designed lower-profile costumes. His work for *Les Orientales* (1910)—for which he designed costumes for Nijinsky and Karsavina—and *Le Dieu Bleu* (1912) carry an oriental flavor.

In spite of his stormy relationship with Diaghilev, Bakst designed sets and/or costumes for numerous Ballets Russes productions, including *The Firebird* (1910), *Le spectre de la rose* (1911), *Narcisse* (1911), *Thamar* (1912), *L'après-midi d'un faune* (1912), *Daphnis et Chloé* (1912), and *La légende de Joseph* (1914). Diaghilev, however, began to turn to the Paris avant-garde—PABLO PICASSO, HENRI MATISSE, and many others—for costumes and scenery.

During his career as a stage designer, Bakst designed numerous costumes for Rubenstein's appearances in ballets such as *The Martyrdom of Saint Sebastian* (1911), *Salomé* (1912), and *Artémis troublée* (1922). He contributed designs to numerous other ballets, including *Aladdin* (1919), *Moskwa* (1922), *Phaedre* (1923), and *Istar* (1924). In spite of the work's commercial failure, his extensive designs for a London production of Peter Ilyich Tchaikovsky's *The Sleeping Beauty* (1921; again with the Ballets Russes) are often considered his best work. It includes elaborate curtains, many costumes, and designs for numerous scene changes.

Aside from his work in the theater, Bakst also designed women's fashions, a number of which appeared in *Harper's Bazaar*. He visited the United States in 1922 and helped convert a Baltimore bowling alley into the Evergreen Theatre. His fascination with the female form manifested itself in his stage designs as well as in the many nude female figures he sketched and painted. Among his patrons was James de Rothschild, for whose townhouse he painted murals.

BIBLIOGRAPHY

Levinson, André, *Bakst: The Story of the Artist's Life*, 1971; Schouvaloff, Alexander, *Bakst: The Theatre Art*, 1991; Spencer, Charles, *Léon Bakst*, 1973.

Balanchine, George

(January 22, 1904–April 30, 1983)
Choreographer, Dancer, Composer

Trained in the tradition of the St. Petersburg ballet, George Balanchine extended the classical principles of his background and was the most influential and active choreographic force in twentieth-century neoclassical ballet. After choreographing for SERGEY DIAGHILEV's Ballets Russes during the company's final years (1925–1929), Balanchine settled in the United States and ultimately became the driving force behind the New York City Ballet for almost thirty-five years. Balanchine also choreographed for Broadway musicals and Hollywood films.

Balanchine was born Georgy Melitonovich Balanchivadze to Georgian parents in St. Petersburg, Russia. His father was a composer. In 1914 Balanchine entered the Imperial School of Ballet at the Mariinsky Theatre, and after his first unhappy year there he made his stage debut as a cupid in *The Sleeping Beauty* in 1915. When the Soviets gained control of the government in 1917, the school closed and reopened the following year as the Soviet State School of Ballet.

Balanchine remained at the school and in 1920 choreographed his first piece, danced to Anton Rubenstein's *Nuit* (*Night*). The same year he choreographed the experimental ballet *Le boeuf sur le toit* (1920), by JEAN COCTEAU and DARIUS MILHAUD.

He joined the Mariinsky Company following his graduation in 1921, but he began to move increasingly away from performing and toward choreography. At the same time he pursued musical interests, studying at the Petrograd Conservatory from 1921 to 1924. Around 1923 he began to choreograph for the experimental Young Ballet.

In 1924, while on tour in Europe with the Soviet State Dancers, Balanchine decided not to return to the Soviet Union. The following year he joined Sergey Diaghilev's Ballets Russes in Paris, replacing as ballet master Bronislava Nijinska. *Barabau* (1925) was his first work for the Ballets Russes, but his mature, distinctly neoclassical style did not emerge until *Apollon Musagéte* (1928).

Le fils prodigue (*The Prodigal Son*, 1929) was also among the ten works Balanchine choreographed for the Ballets Russes before Diaghilev's death in 1929. Notable, too, among these was *Le chant du rossignol* (*The Song of the Nightingale*, 1925), Balanchine's first of many collaborative efforts with the composer IGOR STRAVINSKY, whom he deeply admired for many years.

After the disbanding of the Ballets Russes, Balanchine worked in London, Paris, and elsewhere and choreographed, both in 1932, *La concurrence* and *Cotillion*. In 1933 he helped found and served as chief choreographer for Les Ballets, and while on tour with them he met the American Lincoln Kirstein.

On Kirstein's invitation, Balanchine moved to the United States the same year and helped organize the School of American Ballet and the American Ballet Company, which for many years was closely associated with the Metropolitan Opera in New York.

Among the many works he produced there were *Serenade* (1934), choreographed to music by Peter Ilyich Tchaikovsky, and *Le baiser de la fée* (*The Fairy's Kiss*, 1937).

On Your Toes (1936) was the first of more than two dozen Broadway musicals Balanchine choreographed. He also ventured into the world of Hollywood filmmaking, contributing choreography to films such as *The Goldwyn Follies* (1938) and *Star Spangled Rhythm* (1942).

The American Ballet remained loosely together after severing its ties with the Met in 1938, and three years later it went on a major Latin American tour with Kirstein's Ballet Caravan (founded 1936). After working with the Ballet Russe de Monte Carlo for two years (1944–1946), Balanchine rejoined Kirstein, who founded the Ballet Society in 1946. Two years later it became the New York City Ballet. Balanchine was to remain artistic director and chief choreographer of this group until 1982, and to it he contributed more than 150 works. In 1963 the Ford Foundation awarded eight million dollars to the ballet and its affiliates.

Balanchine's prolific output spans a wide variety of styles and music. He worked often with Stravinsky's music, presenting three Stravinsky Festivals between 1937 and 1982 and collaborating with him in 1962 on the television ballet *Noah and the Flood*. The famous Christmas ballet *The Nutcracker* (1954), for the New York City Ballet, is one of his best-known works. Among his other major productions were *Liebeslieder Walzer* (1960), *A Midsummer Night's Dream* (1962), *Harlequinade* (1965), *Don Quixote* (1965), *Jewels* (1967), *Coppélia* (1974), *Vienna Waltzes* (1977), and *Dance in America* (1968).

In his approach to choreography, Balanchine was cool-headed, methodical, and intellectual. He was known for his keen sense of characterization, and his formal training in both music and dance enabled him to assimilate those different aspects of the production into his dance movements.

BIBLIOGRAPHY

Buckle, Richard, *George Balanchine, Ballet Master*, 1988; Garris, Robert, *Following Balanchine*, 1995; Haggin, B. H., *Discovering Balanchine*, 1981; McDonagh, Don, *George Balanchine*, 1983; Scholl, Tim, *From Petipa to Balanchine: Classical Revival and the Modernization of Ballet*, 1994; Taper, Bernard, *Balanchine: A Biography*, 1984.

Balthus

(February 29, 1908–)
Painter, Costume Designer

A close friend of the Surrealist poet PAUL ÉLUARD and the painter ALBERTO GIACOMETTI, Balthus (Count Balthasar Klossowski de Rola) began his painting career in the avant-garde atmosphere of Paris. His reclusive personality and desire for independence kept him from associating with particular schools of painting, and, though often mysterious, his landscapes, portraits, still lifes, and other subjects are unique examples of modern figurative painting.

Balthus was born Balthasar Klossowski to Polish parents in Paris. His father was a stage designer, art historian, and painter, and both parents introduced him to the arts at a young age. At the beginning of World War I, Balthus's parents took him to Berlin. They separated three years later, after which he lived in both Germany and Switzerland. When he was young, the poet RAINER MARIA RILKE urged him to publish a book of sketches about a lost cat, Mitsou, and contributed a preface to the work. Balthus also began to create stage designs around the age of fourteen.

Rilke would support Balthus for the rest of his life. With his assistance and that of ANDRÉ GIDE, he settled in Paris in 1924 and studied painting. He began to paint in earnest, and his subjects are most often city scenes, landscapes, portraits (most of which are women), female nudes, interiors, and occasional still lifes.

Balthus's early portraits of women are often erotic. In 1933–1934 he provoked a controversy in Paris when he exhibited three such paintings—*Cathy Dressing* (1933), *Alice* (1933), and *The Guitar Lesson* (1934). During the same two years he completed a series of illustrations for Emily Brontë's *Wuthering Heights*. He painted many nudes over his career, including *Nude with Pink Jacket* (1927), *Large Reclining Nude* (1965), *Nude at Rest* (1977), and *Nude with a Guitar* (1983–1986). Like the subjects of his portraits, they appear in a variety of positions—provocative, relaxed, or sleeping.

Balthus's great love of cats was not confined to his childhood *Mitsou* creations. They appear everywhere in his paintings, staring into mirrors, sitting passively by his female figures, or, as in his famous *Thérèse* (1938), drinking from a saucer of milk. The first painting in his *Cat with Mirror* series was begun in 1977, and Balthus painted himself as *The King of Cats* in 1935.

The subjects of his portraits often look washed-out or somber. In much of his painting, Balthus uses muted, earthy browns, golds, and greens that convey a subdued atmosphere. Such is the tone of his portrait of *Princess Maria Volkonka Aged Twelve* (1945). Balthus also painted portraits of the Baroness Alain de Rothschild (1958) and the painters ANDRÉ DERAIN (1936) and JOAN MIRÓ with his daughter (1937–1938).

Balthus's landscapes show a variety of influences, including Chinese landscape painting. His *Cherry Tree* (1940) portrays a woman on a ladder picking cherries in an orchard. Some landscapes, such as the dark *The Mountain* (1943), convey a mysterious, brooding atmosphere. Others with the same kind of atmosphere include *The Farm* (1958) and *Landscape With Cows* (1958).

In the 1930s Balthus did a series of paintings on Moroccan subjects, including *Garrison in Morocco* (1933). Inspired by his future wife Setsuko, he painted a series of Japanese women in the 1960s and 1970s. He also painted numerous city scenes, among which is *Le passage du commerce Saint-André* (1954). Balthus also painted still lifes and contributed designs for the theater, including sets and/or costumes for productions of Shakespeare's *As You Like It* (1934), Antonin Artaud's 1934 production of *The Cenci*, a production of ALBERT CAMUS's *State of Siege* (1948), and a production of Ugo Betti's *The Isle of Goats* (1957).

Balthus's work began to gain international recognition in the 1950s. In 1956 the Museum of Modern Art in New York held a major exhibition of his work, and retrospectives of his work were held in the United States and France in the 1980s. From 1961 to 1977 Balthus served as director of the French Academy in Rome. An obscure and secretive figure, he has continued to live and work in France.

BIBLIOGRAPHY

Leymarie, Jean, *Balthus*, 1982; Roy, Claude, *Balthus*, 1996.

Bardot, Brigitte

(September 28, 1934–)
Actress

Cast as a sensuous, open, and amoral blonde, the French screen actress Brigitte Bardot skyrocketed to fame as an international sex symbol in the 1950s and 1960s. With Catherine Deneuve and JEANNE MOREAU, she was one of the leading French actresses of her day and broke contemporary sex taboos on screen before she retired in 1973.

Bardot was born into a well-off family in Paris. Her father was an industrialist involved in liquid oxygen manufacturing as well as an amateur photographer who had his own cine camera and liked to film the family. Like most middle-class mothers, Bardot's was intent upon molding her daughter into a respectable young woman. To this end she dressed Bardot well, made her up, and enrolled her in

Brigitte Bardot (AKG)

ballet lessons at the Conservatoire Nationale de Danse. During her school years she attended Hattemer, a private school, but academic study never interested her.

Wearing a plaid dress and a ponytail, Bardot appeared on the cover of *Elle* (May 8, 1950), then the leading women's magazine in France. A very attractive young woman, she went looking for notice and soon attracted the attention of Roger Vadim (assistant to the director Marc Allégret), who fashioned her into a blonde sex symbol. She appeared in the gossip magazine *Paris-Match* and in 1952, in spite of her lack of any formal training in acting, made her film debut in Jean Boyer's low-budget comedy *Le trou normand* (1952; *Crazy for Love*), set in a village inn in Normandy.

Her outraged father took legal action to have portions of his bikini-clad daughter censored from her next film, *Manina, la fille sans voile* (1952), in which she played the leading role.

The same year she married Vadim—the first of several husbands, who included Jacques Charrier and the millionaire Gunther Sachs. In 1954 she traveled to Italy and made two films, *Tradita* and *Helen of Troy*, the latter a film in Technicolor directed by the American Robert Wise. In the early 1950s she made her only stage appearance in JEAN ANOUILH's *L'invitation au château*.

The sensuous and expressive Bardot appeared in film after film, including RENÉ CLAIR's first color film, *Les Grandes Manoeuvres* (1955). Before their marriage ended, she starred in two pictures directed by Vadim, *Et Dieu créa la femme* (1956; *And God Created Woman*) and *Les bijoutiers du claire de lune* (1958; English title *The Night Heaven Fell*). Cast as Juliette Hardy in the former, she plays an attractive, blossoming orphan who marries and ultimately gives in to the strong sexual desires that lead her away from her husband. Breaking contemporary standards against nudity in film, *And God Created Woman* was a sensation in the United States and established Bardot as an international sex symbol.

In the 1960s Bardot appeared in several more serious roles, starring in Henri-Georges Clouzout's *La verité* (1960; *The Truth*) and LOUIS MALLE's *Vie privée* (1961; *A Very Private Affair*). In JEAN-LUC GODARD's *Le Mépris* (1963; *Contempt*), she acted the part of Camille Javal, wife in a failing marriage to a writer under contract to rewrite a screenplay of a Fritz Lang film.

Bardot's other notable films include Malle's musical comedy *Viva Maria!* (1965; with Moreau), Henry Koster's *Dear Brigitte* (1965), and Godard's *Masculin-Féminin* (1966; *Masculine Feminine*). In spite of her divorce from Vadim, she continued to work with him throughout her film career in such productions as *Si Don Juan était une femme* (1973; *If Don Juan Were a Woman*).

After making her final film, *L'histoire très bonne et très joyeuse de Colinot Trousse-Chemise* (1973; *The Good and Happy Tale of Colinot Lifter-of-Skirts*), she retired from acting and devoted herself to the cause of animal rights. She established the animal-welfare organization Foundation Brigitte Bardot in 1976. Her autobiography, *Initials B.B.*, was published in 1996.

BIBLIOGRAPHY

Frischauer, Willi, *Bardot: An Intimate Biography*, 1978; Haining, Peter, *The Legend of Brigitte Bardot*, 1983; Roberts, Glenys, *Bardot*, 1984.

Barlach, Ernst

(January 2, 1870–October 24, 1938)
Sculptor, Playwright, Illustrator

Although he dissociated himself from formal art movements, Ernst Barlach began to sculpt in the climate of the German Expressionists in the early 1900s. He is best known for his monumental human figures, often carved from wood, and was one of only a few sculptors to produce large works in that medium. Barlach also sketched, painted, and wrote plays.

Barlach was born in Wedel, Holstein, Germany. His father was a doctor and came from a family full of amateur painters, so Barlach was exposed to the visual arts at a young age. He studied at the School of Applied Art in Hamburg and from 1891 to 1895 attended the Academy of Art in Dresden. The following year he lived in Paris, where he studied briefly at the Académie Julien and executed a number of sketches.

The earliest influence on Barlach's style was the Art Nouveau movement, which emphasized sinuous, flowing lines and work in the decorative arts. Living in Wedel and Berlin, he worked in ceramics, and he taught at the Trade School of Ceramics in Hoehr in 1904–1905. However, Barlach distanced himself from formal association with any particular school, and in his later life chose to live in provincial towns away from the cities where artistic movements thrived.

The catalyst for the development of his mature style as a sculptor was a trip to Russia in 1906, during which he was deeply moved by the Russian peasantry and developed an admiration for Russian wood carvings. Scenes from the peasant culture dominate his sketches from that period and provided subject matter for sculptures such as *Russian Beggar Woman* (1906), a ceramic depiction of a seated female figure leaning over with her head to her knees.

Barlach's mature sculptures are characterized by their massive size and their rough, chiseled surfaces. He often worked in wood but also cast bronze and ceramic sculptures. Barlach's figures are heavily clothed male and female depictions, often in motion (as in *The Avenger*, 1914), with strong expressions on their faces (*Horror*, 1923), or playing instruments (*The Flute Player*, 1936).

He reached the height of his popularity as a sculptor in the 1920s and 1930s; during the same period he completed World War I memorials and religious figures. Barlach's work was not immune to the Nazi censorship that followed their rise to power in 1933. His *Das Wiedersehen* (1926; *The Reunion*) was included in the famous Degenerate Art exhibit in 1937, and his work was removed from German museums during the Nazi era.

Aside from sculpting, Barlach wrote seven plays, poetic dramas he sometimes illustrated himself. *Der tote Tag* (1912; *The Dead Day*) relates the story of a mother who stifles her son and tries to prevent him from maturing. She also hampers his efforts to find his father, who, as it later turns out, is a God-figure. Other plays include *Der Findling* (1922; *The Foundling*) and *Die Suendflut* (1924; *The Deluge*), winner of the Kleist Prize.

Barlach's studio in Güstrow, Germany, was later converted into a museum. Many of his works are held at the Ernst Barlach House in Hamburg.

BIBLIOGRAPHY

Chick, Edson M., *Ernst Barlach*, 1967; Werner, Alfred, *Ernst Barlach*, 1966.

Baroja y Nessi, Pío

(December 28, 1872–October 30, 1956)
Novelist, Short-Story Writer

Pío Baroja was the leading novelist of the Generation of '98 in Spain. When he died in 1956, his body of work included more than 100 novels and volumes of short stories, including his monumental 22-volume series *Memoirs of a Man of Action* (1913–1928).

Baroja was of Basque ancestry, born in San Sebastián, Spain. His father was a mining engineer who kept a large library and encouraged his sons to read and write. The family was relatively prosperous and in 1879 moved to Madrid, where Baroja attended the Instituto de San Isidro. From 1887 to 1890 Baroja studied medicine at the University of Madrid. After graduating he briefly worked as a municipal doctor in Cestona. In 1896 he returned to Madrid to manage his aunt's bakery, a position in which he remained until 1902.

Baroja's first writings were published in Spanish periodicals. He was a member of the Generation of '98, a term that applies loosely to a group of Spanish writers whose work is often characterized by advocacy of liberalization and reform, a negative outlook, and deep roots in regional Spanish culture. Other members of the Generation of '98 include MIGUEL DE UNAMUNO, ANTONIO MACHADO, and Baroja's friend Azorín.

Baroja's first book, a collection of short stories titled *Somber Lives*, was published in 1900. *The House of the Aizgorri* (1900) was inspired by the author's visit to a distillery. In the novel Baroja depicted the downfall and final destruction of a distillery in the town of Arbea. The distillery symbolizes the town's decadence, embodied in the corrupt members of the Aizgorri family. His other early novels include *The Lord of Labraz* (1903) and *Zalacaín the Adventurer* (1909), one of Baroja's own favorites.

Eleven trilogies belong to Baroja's body of work. The most famous, *The Struggle for Life*, was published in 1904 and is set in the slums of Madrid. Baroja described the squalid conditions in which prostitutes, criminals, beggars, and other down-and-outs lived in Spain's capital city. The character of Manuel Alcázar, who eventually abandons his life and odd jobs among the city's social outcasts to marry into the bourgeoisie, appears in all three novels.

The trilogy *Agonies of Our Time* (1926–1927) reflects Baroja's own travels to Germany, Holland, and Denmark and is partially set in those countries. The author painted a dim picture of post–World War I Europe, including its political and philosophical trends. Its main character is Jose Larrañaga, a well-traveled, forlorn, and pessimistic intellectual. In the trilogy, Baroja was critical of theologians, political leaders, and philosophers, all of whom offer no hope of improvement. Another theme present in the trilogy is Larrañaga's failed relationships with women—a German girl, Nelly, and his cousin Pepita. A man's inability to form a lasting relationship with a woman is a prominent theme in Baroja's body of work, stemming from his own romantic troubles (he never married or found lasting love).

The experiences Baroja gained through his travels around the world and his conversations with other people often worked their way into his stories. Baroja wrote in an abrupt style and drew from the tradition of the Spanish picaresque novel. His protagonists are usually weak-willed or flawed in some way, and the author's outlook is decidedly pessimistic and cynical. Baroja also targeted established religion, evident in portrayals of faithless priests in novels such as *Friar Beltrán's Nocturne* (1929). The American novelist Ernest Hemingway was heavily influenced by Baroja and visited him just before Baroja's death in 1956.

The massive series *Memoirs of a Man of Action* (1913–1928) consists of more than twenty volumes. The central character is a nineteenth-century rebel, Eugenio Aviraneta Ibargoyen Echegaray y Alzate, a nephew of Baroja's great-great-grandfather. Baroja's ancestor in many ways resembles himself—he opposes religion and looks much older than his age. Through the series Aviraneta matures from something of an idealist who lacks the will to act toward his aims to a full-fledged man of action.

The outbreak of the Spanish Civil War in 1936 spurred Baroja to flee to Paris, where he would live for the next four years. During his residence in France, he completed the novels *Susana* (1937) and *Laura* (1937). His brief attempts to involve himself in politics were unsuccessful; he failed in his runs for councilman in 1909 and Congress in 1918. In 1934 he was elected to the Royal Spanish Academy. His other works include the essays collected in *Yesterday and Today* (1939) and *Strolls of a Solitary Man* (1955).

BIBLIOGRAPHY

Patt, Beatrice P., *Pío Baroja*, 1971.

Barrault, Jean-Louis

(September 8, 1910–January 22, 1994)
Director, Actor, Producer

Jean-Louis Barrault and his wife, Madeleine Renaud, established an internationally famous repertory company, Compagnie M. Renaud–J.L. Barrault. Barrault acted in, directed, and produced many of the company's productions, bringing a unique blend of classic theater and the work of modern and avant-garde playwrights to the public. He is also noted for his contributions to the art of pantomime.

Barrault was born in Le Vésinet, France. His father, a chemist who worked in a mental asylum, loved politics and espoused a socialist ideology. Typhus took his life during World War I, when Barrault was eight. His mother remarried, and Barrault attended a local school. As a student, he liked to learn but often found himself in trouble with the teachers for his disruptive behavior.

After considering several professions, Barrault entered the world of theater. He studied under Charles Dullin and learned pantomime under the actor and mime Étienne Decroux. Early on Barrault was introduced to the works of Paul Claudel and other playwrights of all schools, a variety that was to mark his career. The influences on him were both classical and contemporary, from William Shakespeare and Miguel de Cervantes to modern playwrights such as Claudel, JEAN-PAUL SARTRE, and EUGÈNE IONESCO. The work of the Russian actor-director KONSTANTIN STANISLAVSKY also had a significant influence on Barrault, as did the Surrealists.

At the Théâtre de l'Atelier, Barrault acted in productions such as *Volpone* and *Richard III*. His first independent project

came with his adaptation of William Faulkner's *As I Lay Dying* (1935), and it was followed with works by Cervantes and others. He had soon founded his own company.

With the encouragement of Jacques Coupeau, Barrault joined the Comédie-Française in 1940. His first production with the group, *Le Cid*, was followed by one of his many *Hamlet*s. Among his many acting and directing roles with the group are Claudel's *The Satin Slipper* and his final role, Moron in Molière's *La Princesse d'Elide*. The Comédie-Française provided Barrault with the chance to make his most important acquaintance, that of his future wife, Madeleine Renaud.

Renaud and Barrault founded their own repertory company at the ThéâtreMarigny, the Compagnie M. Renaud–J.L. Barrault. The company's first production, ANDRÉ GIDE's translation of *Hamlet*, was followed by Pierre Marivaux's *False Confessions*. In 1947, Barrault adapted FRANZ KAFKA's *The Trial* with Gide, and he would later produce Kafka's *The Castle*. Barrault aimed to draw half of his material from classics and the other half from modern plays. The company performed the works of avant-garde playwrights such as Sartre, Ionesco (*Rhinoceros*, 1960), JEAN ANOUILH, JEAN COCTEAU (*Bacchus*), and ALBERT CAMUS as well as Shakespeare and the nineteenth-century Russian playwright Anton Chekhov (*The Cherry Orchard*).

The company's diverse material ranged from melodramas to operettas, a variety that helped propel the group to international fame. Barrault was involved in production, direction, and acting. In 1950, the group embarked on its first tour of South America. Two years later it first performed in North America, in New York and in Canada. In 1960, the company embarked on a tour of major cities around the world.

In 1959, Barrault moved his company to the Odéon, later renamed the Théâtre de France, where he served as director until 1968. Among his productions there were works by Samuel Beckett, Jean Genet's *The Screens* in 1966, and his final production there, Claudel's *Tête d'Or* in 1968. Barrault also served as director of the Théâtre des Nations (1965–1967, 1972–1974) and the Théâtre D'Orsay (1974).

Barrault's acting career was not limited to the stage. His first role in film, which he secured with the help of Gide's nephew, came in 1936 with *Les beaux jours*. His other films include *Drôle de drame* (1937), *Farinet ou l'or dans la montagne* (1937), and *La ronde* (1950). In his best-known film role, he played the mime Deburau in Marcel Carné's *Les enfants du paradis* (1945). Barrault's other works include the books *The Theatre of Jean-Louis Barrault* (1959), and *Memories for Tomorrow: The Memoirs of Jean-Louis Barrault* (1974).

BIBLIOGRAPHY

Barrault, Jean-Louis, *Memories for Tomorrow: The Memoirs of Jean-Louis Barrault,*1974.

Barrie, J. M.

(May 9, 1860–June 19, 1937)
Playwright, Novelist

The Scottish playwright James Matthew Barrie created Peter Pan, the boy who refused to grow up, one of the most popular childhood characters of all time. In his novels and plays, Barrie portrayed both the idyllic happiness of the child's world and the erosion of that happiness in adulthood. His many plays were produced in London alongside the works of George Bernard Shaw, John Galsworthy, and other playwrights of his day.

The son of a weaver, Barrie was born in Kirriemuir, Forfarshire, Scotland. The happiness of his early childhood ended at the age of 6, when his older brother, David, died in a skating accident. His death traumatized Barrie as well as his mother, to whom he maintained a strong attachment for the rest of her life. His biography of her, *Margaret Ogilvy*, was published in 1896. In 1868, Barrie moved to Glasgow to live with an older brother and studied at the Glasgow Academy, the first in a series of schools he would attend. He studied at the University of Edinburgh and in 1883 began to contribute to the *Nottingham Journal*.

Two years later, Barrie moved to London and worked as a freelance writer, contributing to, among other publications, the *St. James Gazette*. His first

J. M. Barrie (Ann Ronan/Image Select)

was published in 1900, the last of Barrie's novels.

By this time Barrie had already begun to write plays and had some early successes with productions of *Ibsen's Ghost* (1891) and *Walker, London* (1892). His unhappy marriage to the actress Mary Ansell began in 1894, and in 1897 he met Sylvia Llewellyn Davies. Davies's five sons were the first to hear Barrie's now famous Peter Pan stories. *The Little White Bird* (1902) contained some of the tales, but more successful was the play *Peter Pan, the Boy Who Wouldn't Grow Up.* In this classic fantasy, Peter Pan persuades three ordinary children, Wendy, John, and Michael, to learn to fly and to come away with him to the Never Land, where he is the captain of the Lost Boys (lost by careless nursemaids and brought to the Never Land by the fairies) and leads them in battles with the Indians and pirates who also inhabit the island. The world of a child's imagination becomes a place one can fly to, leaving the burden of having to grow up into a boring adult behind, and Barrie's feeling for this world allowed him to make this his best work. The play, first produced at the Duke of York's Theatre on December 27, 1904, was later published as a book, and much later made into an animated film by Walt Disney (1953).

Barrie's marriage ended when his wife left him in 1900, and his life was further complicated by the death of Sylvia Davies. Barrie practically adopted her sons, two of whom were killed, one in World War I and one in a drowning. After his divorce, he lived near two of the major figures in theater of his day, Shaw and HARLEY GRANVILLE-BARKER.

Peter Pan embodies the spirit of childhood wonder, love of adventure, and in-

major book, *Auld Licht Idylls*, was published in 1888, followed by *A Window in Thrums* (1889). The stories are set in Thrums, a Scottish town based on Barrie's native Kirriemuir. In the novel *The Little Minister* (1891), a Scottish minister falls in love with a gypsy and must deal with his congregation's reaction. The story was dramatized in 1897.

Other novels followed before Barrie turned his efforts primarily to the theater. In *Sentimental Tommy* (1896), a 5-year-old boy, Tommy Sandys, lives with his impoverished mother in London. His mother dies when he is 11, and Aaron Latta, her former lover, raises Tommy and his sister, Elspeth. At the age of 15, the budding writer Tommy leaves Thrums. *Tommy and Grizel*, its sequel, nocence, but, unsurprisingly, the themes of Barrie's adult plays are less positive; he tends to portray the adult world as corrupt and disordered. *The Admirable Crichton* (1902), a four-act play, demonstrates the absurdity of the class structure in England. Lord Loam, owner of a house in Mayfair where the typical elements of class hierarchy are in place, plays a game with his household in which class distinctions are removed. The butler, Bill Crichton, emerges as the leader of the group during the game, played out on a desert island. Crichton not only possesses the practical knowledge needed for survival, he is successful when his entrepreneurial spirit is allowed to flourish. His return to the role of servant when the game is over has an almost tragic impact.

The role of women is the theme of two other Barrie plays, *What Every Woman Knows* (1908) and *The Twelve-Pound Look* (1910). In the latter, Kate, working for her ex-husband, Harry, discloses the reason she left him. It was not, as Harry had presumed, that she had found another man. Kate believed Harry took away her freedom and, when she could type well enough, she felt confident enough to leave him.

In his plays, Barrie employed elaborate stage effects, which posed complications in more than one instance. The difficulty of the scene changes from Lord Loam's house to the desert island nearly resulted in its failure to open, and the flying children in *Peter Pan* also posed problems. His final play, *The Boy David* (1936), is an adaptation of the story of the early years of the biblical David before he became king. AUGUSTUS JOHN designed an elaborate set for the original production, but it failed to win much acclaim. Barrie's work came to be seen as embarrassingly sentimental and whimsical, and he is for the most part only remembered as the author of *Peter Pan*.

Barrie's other plays include *Quality Street* (1901); *Alice Sit-By-The-Fire* (1905); *Pantaloon* (1905); *Rosalind* (1912); *The Will* (1913); *A Kiss for Cinderella* (1916); *Dear Brutus* (1917); *Mary Rose* (1920); and *Shall We Join the Ladies?* (1921). He was made baronet in 1913 and awarded the Order of Merit in 1922. Barrie became chancellor of the University of Edinburgh in 1930.

BIBLIOGRAPHY

Birkin, Andrew, *J. M. Barrie and the Lost Boys*, 1979; Jack, Ronald D. S., *The Road to the Never Land: A Reassessment of J. M. Barrie's Dramatic Art*, 1991; Ormond, Leonee, *J. M. Barrie*, 1987.

Bartók, Béla

(March 25, 1881–September 26, 1945)
Composer, Pianist, Teacher

Béla Bartók was Hungary's most accomplished composer of the twentieth century. After starting out primarily as a pianist, he embarked on a prolific career as a composer, forging his own style, which combined traditional tonality with elements of Hungarian folk music. His lifelong study of regional music resulted in the publication of thousands of East European and North African folk songs previously known only in local oral traditions.

Bartók was born in Nagyszentmiklós, Hungary (now Sînnicolau Mare, Romania). Both parents were musically talented and exposed him to music as a boy. His father died when he was 7, and his mother taught him to play the piano. Bartók was composing when he was not yet 10, and his first recital at age 11 featured his own composition, *The Course of the Danube*. While he finished his primary education, he studied music under László Erkel and Anton Hyrtl.

At age 18, Bartók enrolled in the Budapest Academy of Music. Although he had been accepted at the renowned Vienna Conservatory, he broke with tradition and chose to study in Budapest. Bartók's decision was influenced by one of his role models, the composer Ernö Dohnányi, who also studied in Budapest, and his choice corresponded with a resurgence of Hungarian nationalism in the late nineteenth century.

Bartók's course of study in Budapest was primarily based on the work of German composers, and he showed the most promise as a pianist. Early in his composing career he was influenced by the German composers Richard Wagner (1813–1883) and RICHARD STRAUSS as well as the Hungarian composer Franz Liszt. However, Bartók was swept up in the nationalistic fervor then emerging in Hungary, and even his first major compositions have a distinct Hungarian flavor. The music of his symphonic poem *Kossuth* (1904) draws from Strauss, but its subject is the nineteenth century Hungarian nationalist Lajos Kossuth, who failed in his 1849 attempt to establish an independent Hungarian republic. *Kossuth* proved popular with the Hungarian public and brought Bartók his first taste of fame abroad.

With his lifelong friend and fellow composer Zoltán Kodály, Bartók conducted extensive research on Hungarian folk songs beginning in 1905. The two composers recorded them, transcribed them for piano, and incorporated their rhythms, melodies, and other peculiarities into their own work. The investigation of Magyar, Romanian, North African, and Turkish folk music was a lifelong interest for both composers, and by Bartók's death in 1945, they had produced numerous volumes containing thousands of folk songs. Bártok frequently spent summers traveling to remote regions of Eastern Europe and Morocco to collect folk songs.

In 1907 Bartók began teaching piano at the Academy, replacing his old piano teacher István Thomán. Around this time he also developed an interest in the work of the French impressionistic composer CLAUDE DEBUSSY. In 1908, he completed *Violin Concerto No. 1.* for the woman he was then involved with, the violinist Stefi Geyer. The following year he married Márta Ziegler, and they had one son, Béla. Bartók taught piano at the Academy until 1934 and composed six volumes of teaching pieces entitled *Mikrokosmos* (1926–1939).

Bartók's six string quartets are often considered his best works. He composed the First String Quartet in 1908. The Second String Quartet (1915–1917) followed his 1913 trip to North Africa and incorporates elements of the region's folk music. The musically diverse, one-movement Third String Quartet (1927) and the five-movement Fourth String Quartet (1928) are marked by their dissonant harmonies. His Fifth String Quartet appeared in 1934 and his Sixth String Quartet in 1939.

After Bartók and his first wife divorced in 1923, he married the pianist Ditta Pásztory. Their son, Péter, was born in 1924. In addition to his activities as a composer, teacher, and collector of folk music, Bartók toured Europe and the United States extensively as a pianist. Fleeing the German occupation of Hungary, he and his wife moved to the United States in 1940. Columbia University hired him as a research assistant, and he was able to continue his study of folk music.

Among Bartók's stage works are the one-act opera *Duke Bluebeard's Castle* (1911), the one-act ballet *The Wooden Prince* (1914–1916), and the one-act pantomime *The Miraculous Mandarin* (1918–1919). His piano works include *Allegro Barbaro* (1911), *Romanian Dances from Hungary* (1915), and *Out of Doors* (1926).

Aside from his research on folk music, Bartók's chief contributions to music were his variations of traditional tonality. His music is often characterized by driving, asymmetrical rhythms, modality, and the innovative use of chromatic scales as well as counterpoint and polyphony. Although Bartók was influenced by the work of Debussy and Arnold Schoenberg, he did not use the atonality characteristic of their compositions.

Bartók's other works include Symphony in E-Flat (1902); Piano Concerto No. 1 (1926), Piano Concerto No. 2 (1930–1931), and Piano Concerto No. 3 (1945), finished by Tibor Serly; Piano Quintet (1903–1904); Violin Concerto No. 2 (1938); Sonata No. 1 (1921) and Sonata No. 2 (1922), both for violin and piano; the choral work *Cantata Profana* (1930); Concerto for Orchestra (1943), originally performed by the Boston Symphony Orchestra; the orchestral works *Transylvanian Dances* (1931) and *Music for Strings, Percussion, and Celesta* (1936); Sonata for Two Pianos and Percussion (1937); Sonata for Solo Violin (1944); and *Village Scenes* (1924), consisting of five songs. He died of leukemia in 1945.

BIBLIOGRAPHY

Gillies, Malcolm, ed., *The Bartók Companion*, 1993; Griffiths, Paul, *Bartók*, 1984; Stevens, Halsey, *The Life and Music of Béla Bartók*, 3d ed., 1993.

Baryshnikov, Mikhail

(January 28, 1948–)
Dancer, Director, Choreographer, Actor

The Latvian-born dancer Mikhail Baryshnikov was the world's most famous male dancer in the 1970s and 1980s and is frequently praised for his graceful leaps and the naturalness with which he executes difficult roles. His vitality, strength, and grace have carried him through hundreds of leading roles for ballet companies in the Soviet Union and the United States.

Baryshnikov was born in Riga, Latvia, to Nikolai Baryshnikov and Alexandra Kiseleva. His mother abandoned the family when he was 12, soon after he had enrolled in a ballet school in Riga. From the start, Baryshnikov loved the ballet and excelled as a student. In 1963 he entered the Vaganova School, which was a stepping-stone to the Kirov Ballet in Leningrad. For the next three years he studied dance under Alexander Ivanovich Puskhin, who taught in the classical Russian tradition.

Baryshnikov joined the Kirov ballet in 1966; his first role was as a peasant in a production of *Giselle*. He quickly became the ballet company's star. In addition to solo performances, in which he was allowed a measure of creativity, he played leading roles in *Gorianka* (1968) and *Vestris* (1969), choreographed for him by Leonid Yakobson. Baryshnikov's other performances with the Kirov ballet included Adam, opposite Irina Kolpakova's Eve, in a 1971 production of *The Creation of the World*, Albrecht in *Giselle* (1972), and roles in *Don Quixote* and *The Sleeping Beauty*.

Although Baryshnikov was popular in the Soviet Union, the rigid demands of the guardians of politically acceptable theater stifled his creativity. After a series of performances in Canada in 1974 he defected to the West and eventually settled in the United States. He joined the American Ballet Theatre (ABT) the same year. With his first major role at the ABT, again as Albrecht in a production of *Giselle*, Baryshnikov became a sensation among ballet-goers in the United States. In a period of four years, he danced more than forty roles for the company and choreographed versions of *The Nutcracker* (1976) and *Don Quixote* (1978). Other productions in which he starred at the ABT are *Petrouchka*, Alexander S. Pushkin's *The Queen of Spades; Le spectre de la rose*, and Twyla Tharp's *Push Comes to Shove.*

In 1978 Baryshnikov joined the New York City Ballet Company and worked extensively with the Russian-born choreographer GEORGE BALANCHINE. His more than twenty roles for the company include the poet in *La sonnambula* and the harlequin in *Harlequinade*. From 1980 to 1989 he served as the artistic director for the ABT. Aside from ballet, Baryshnikov received an Oscar nomination for his role in the movie *The Turning Point* (1977), costarring Shirley MacLaine and Anne Bancroft. He has appeared in other movies, *White Nights* (1985), *That's Dancing!* (1985), and *Dancers* (1987), and starred in a Broadway production of FRANZ KAFKA's *The Metamorphosis* (1989). In 1990, with the choreographer Mark Morris, Baryshnikov founded the White Oak Dance Project, a modern dance company with which he continues to perform.

BIBLIOGRAPHY

Smakov, Gennady, *Baryshnikov: From Russia to the West*, 1981.

Bax, Arnold

(November 8, 1883–October 3, 1953)
Composer

Arnold Edward Trevor Bax, to give him his full name, was a member of a generation of composers in England who attained popularity between World War I and World War II. After establishing himself with several symphonic poems, Bax went on to compose seven symphonies and many piano and chamber works. Bax composed in the neoromantic style characteristic of English music from that time period and is especially noted for his lush chromatic harmonies. Influenced by the Irish Renaissance in the early 1900s, he also wrote poetry and short stories.

Bax was the eldest of four children and was born in London. He was particularly close to his brother, Clifford Bax, who became a writer. His father was a barrister and an active member of the Royal Society of Antiquaries, and he extensively researched the Bax family history. Bax's mother was organized, active, and very attentive to social status. As a boy he attended the preparatory school of Argyll House, and later, when his family moved, Heath Mount in Hampstead. At home the young Bax was exposed to much literature and loved to read. Among his other hobbies were painting, drawing, and doing crossword puzzles.

His great passion, however, was music, to which he was introduced in part by his paternal grandfather. Bax learned to play the piano at a young age. By the time he was 13, he was accompanying a choral society. In 1900 he entered the Royal Academy of Music, where he studied the piano and began to compose seriously. At that time, the academy was under the direction of Sir Alexander Campbell Mackenzie, who disliked modern trends in music. Bax composed a number of works performed at the school, including a *Celtic Song Cycle* (1904). He won the Gold Medal for piano in 1905.

Upon the completion of his studies the same year, Bax, enamored with the Romantic works of Richard Wagner (1813–1883) and RICHARD STRAUSS, went to Dresden for a short period of time. He next went to Ireland, where he fell in love with the country, its legends, and the literature of the Irish Renaissance. Bax absorbed the poetry of WILLIAM BUTLER YEATS and, with his brother Clifford, frequented the circles of Æ, JAMES STEPHENS, and other figures of the literary revival then going on in Ireland.

Under the pseudonym Dermot O'Byrne, Bax published verse and short stories

Arnold Bax (Ann Ronan/Image Select)

while in Ireland. Some of the latter appeared in the *Irish Review* and were later collected as *Children of the Hills*. Although not as interested in the occult and esoteric doctrines as Yeats, Bax absorbed from the Irish myths and legends a certain sense of spirituality that manifests itself in his music. Irish folk songs also exerted an influence on his subsequent compositions. In 1909 he wrote the symphonic poem *In the Faëry Hills* (1909), based on a section of *The Wanderings of Oisin*.

In 1910 Bax went to Russia with a Ukrainian woman and there immersed himself in the social life of St. Petersburg. When his affair with her ended, he returned to England and in 1911 married Elsa Sobrino, the daughter of a Spanish concert pianist. Having seen SERGEY DIAGHILEV's Ballets Russes in London, he composed the ballet score *Tamara* (1911) and dedicated it to the dancer TAMARA KARSAVINA. Bax would later compose *The Truth about the Russian Dancers*, based on a scenario by J. M. BARRIE, for the Ballets Russes (1920).

The years 1916–1917 saw major triumphs in his career, with three symphonic poems, *The Garden of Fand*, *Tintagel*, and *November Woods*. In 1917 he also completed his *Symphonic Variations* for piano and orchestra, which was given its premiere by pianist Harriet Cohen. Cohen, with whom Bax developed a close relationship, performed many of his subsequent works and premiered four of his piano sonatas.

Between the two world wars, Bax completed seven symphonies. A talented pianist, he wrote many works for the piano as well as more than thirty chamber works. Among the latter are his *Nonet* for winds, strings, and harp (1931) and several string quartets. Bax did not write for the opera but composed many songs. Among these are *Five Irish Songs* (1922), settings of poems by JOHN MILLINGTON SYNGE.

Bax's music is often described as Romantic and impressionistic. He did not care for the atonal music of modern composers such as ARNOLD SCHOENBERG and relied on the chromatic harmony characteristic of nineteenth-century music. His work has a spiritual quality and effectively evokes scenes from nature, particularly his much beloved sea. Bax received the Gold Medal from the Royal Philharmonic Society in 1931. He was knighted in 1937 and became Master of the King's Musick in 1941. The universities of Oxford and Durham awarded him honorary degrees.

BIBLIOGRAPHY

Foreman, Lewis, *Bax: A Composer and His Times*, 1983; Scott-Sutherland, Colin, *Arnold Bax*, 1973.

Beatles, The

Harrison, George
(February 25, 1943–)

Lennon, John Winston
(October 9, 1940–December 8, 1980)

McCartney, James Paul
(June 18, 1942–)

Starr, Ringo
(July 7, 1940–)

Four men from working-class backgrounds in Liverpool, England—John Lennon, Paul McCartney, George Harrison, and Ringo Starr—elevated rock music from pop entertainment to art with innovative albums such as *Sgt. Pepper's Lonely Hearts Club Band* (1967). The musical experimentation and philosophical lyrics of their later work had a profound impact on much of the rock music that followed it in Britain and the United States.

The group that became known as The Beatles began when Lennon and McCartney started working together in 1957; Harrison also joined their band later that year. Along with drummer Tommy Moore and bassist Stu Sutcliffe, they formed The Beatles in 1959. Pete Best replaced Moore in 1960. The group that became famous ended up with Lennon on rhythm guitar, Harrison on lead guitar, and McCartney playing bass. Ringo Starr (real name Richard Starkey) replaced Best on drums in 1962.

The Beatles began performing covers of American rock-and-roll songs by singers who had influenced them—Carl Perkins, Buddy Holly, and others—in Liverpool and Hamburg. EMI's Parlophone released their first single, "Love Me Do," in 1962. It and every subsequent Beatles record was produced by George Martin. Their next two singles, "Please Please Me" and "From Me to You," both released in 1963, reached top positions on the charts. These and other early Beatles hits such as "She Loves You" (1963), "I Want to Hold Your Hand" (1963), and "Can't Buy Me Love" (1964), were written by Lennon and McCartney, as were most of the Beatles' later songs. Their early albums include *Please Please Me* (1963), *With the Beatles* (1963), *Meet the Beatles* (1964), and *Help!* (1965).

"Beatlemania" soon swept the United States, and in 1964 the Beatles landed in New York to perform on the *Ed Sullivan Show*. Along with their "rival" band THE ROLLING STONES, who also caused a sensation on both sides of the Atlantic in the early 1960s, the Beatles were part of the British Invasion. Unlike the Rolling Stones, the Beatles disliked the raucous mobs of screaming fans that attended their concerts and followed them around. They increasingly preferred studio art to stage entertainment. Beginning with *Rubber Soul* (1965) and *Revolver* (1965), their music began to evolve from simple pop songs toward more complex musical and lyrical arrangements, evident in such songs as "Nowhere Man" (1965) and "Eleanor Rigby" (1965).

The years 1966 and 1967 marked a turning point for the Beatles. In 1966, the band gave its last performance in San Francisco and ceased touring, devoting more time to composing albums in the studio. Lennon remarked to a reporter that the Beatles were "more popular than Jesus Christ," provoking an uproar in the United States. Brian Epstein, who originally discovered the Beatles and had managed them since 1961, died of an accidental overdose of sleeping pills in 1967. Around this time Lennon also began his high-profile relationship with Yoko Ono, which caused a significant amount of tension among the Beatles.

Sgt. Pepper's Lonely Hearts Club Band (1967) was the Beatles' most experimental album to date. It is considered one of the first concept albums, an album in which all the songs combine to form a whole work of art. Psychedelic songs such as "Lucy in the Sky with Diamonds" incorporated electronic sounds and landmark studio production techniques. The music also reflects their experiences with the hallucinogenic drug LSD. Harrison in particular developed an interest in Indian mysticism, and the sitar also began to figure in the Beatles' music, as did orchestral arrangements. The famous *Sgt. Pepper's* album cover features the faces of figures as diverse as Bob Dylan and Karl Marx.

The songs of *Magical Mystery Tour* (1967), such as the psychedelic "Strawberry Fields Forever" and "I Am the Walrus," evidence the Beatles' continuing musical experimentation. *The Beatles* (1968), better known as the White Album,

was a double record and featured songs such as "Ob-La-Di Ob-La-Da" and the hard-driving "While My Guitar Gently Weeps," one of Harrison's most powerful contributions to the band's body of work. The White Album was the first to be released on the Beatles' newly formed record label, Apple Records, and it reflected a growing divergence of interests among the individual band members. Their popular single "Hey Jude" also reached the top of the charts in 1968.

The albums *Yellow Submarine* and *Abbey Road*, both released in 1969, are less cohesive than *Sgt. Pepper's* and the White Album. More and more the Beatles drifted apart. Although Lennon and McCartney continued to write most of the band's songs, they worked less closely than they had before. The release of *Abbey Road* sparked a "Paul is dead" rumor, and people combed the album for evidence to support it. *Let It Be* (1970) was the Beatles' final album.

The Beatles disbanded in 1970 amidst a series of personal and financial quarrels. Each of them subsequently pursued his own work. Lennon recorded a series of solo albums, the most famous of which is *Imagine* (1971), before his 1980 death at the hand of an assassin in New York. McCartney formed the band Wings and later recorded his own albums; his most recent effort is the Celtic-flavored orchestral work *Standing Stone* (1997). Harrison has recorded solo albums as well as two records as a member of the Traveling Wilburys, who also include musicians Bob Dylan, Tom Petty, Jeff Lynne, and the now-deceased Roy Orbison. Starr has played drums for many other artists. A popular three-volume Beatles *Anthology* was released in 1995–1996, featuring a new song written by Lennon and recorded by McCartney, Harrison, and Starr, "Free as a Bird."

The Beatles' influence on rock music was monumental. In an era when most bands covered material written by other artists, they wrote their own songs and helped pave the way for other musicians to do so. Their unprecedented experiments with electronic music and studio production in albums such as *Sgt. Pepper's* opened new musical paths for other artists to explore. *Sgt. Pepper's* also popularized the concept album, used by other bands such as The Kinks, The Moody Blues, and Pink Floyd. For the first time, people began to consider rock music not just mere pop entertainment, but serious art.

Among the many honors the Beatles have received are the Grammy Trustees Award in 1972 and induction into the Rock and Roll Hall of Fame in 1988. Queen Elizabeth II named all of them Members of the Order of the British Empire in 1965, but Lennon relinquished his award in 1969. The Queen knighted McCartney in 1997.

Along with albums, the Beatles made several films: *A Hard Day's Night* (1964), *Help!* (1965), and *Magical Mystery Tour* (1967). The German artist Heinz Edelmann created the animated movie *Yellow Submarine* in 1968.

BIBLIOGRAPHY

Davies, Hunter, *The Beatles*, 1968; Kozinn, Allan, *The Beatles*, 1995; McKeen, William, *The Beatles: A Bio-Bibliography*, 1989; Tobler, John, *The Beatles*, 1984; Turner, Steve, *A Hard Day's Write: the Stories Behind Every Beatles Song*, 1994.

Beauvoir, Simone de

(January 9, 1908–April 14, 1986)
Novelist, Short-Story Writer, Essayist, Philosopher, Playwright, Journalist

With JEAN-PAUL SARTRE and ALBERT CAMUS, Simone Lucie-Ernestine-Marie-Bertrand de Beauvoir (as she was christened) was a leading proponent of existentialist thought in the World War II era. Having gained international acclaim as a philosopher, novelist, and advocate of feminism, she was at the forefront of the feminist movement in the 1960s and 1970s. Her treatise on the role of modern women, *The Second Sex*, has become a staple of feminist literature.

Beauvoir was born in Paris. Though the family had been well-off, its fortunes declined soon after her birth. Her mother, a devout Catholic, was overbearing and favored her over her younger sister. Beauvoir shared her father's religious skepticism and by the age of 14 had become an atheist. As a child she liked to read and write, producing her first written works at the age of 7. Beginning in 1913 she attended the Cours Adeline Désir, a Catholic school. Beauvoir earned a degree in literature and philosophy at the Sorbonne in 1927. After studying at the École Normale Supérieure and the Sorbonne, she earned her degree in philosophy in 1929.

Simone de Beauvoir (AKG)

During her studies Beauvoir met the existentialist philosopher Sartre. They maintained a lifelong, open love affair but lived together only briefly. Beauvoir began to teach in 1931, took a position at the Lycée Molière in Paris in 1936, and continued to teach until 1943. That year saw the publication of her first novel, *L'invitée* (1943; *She Came To Stay*), a fictional account of the triangular relationship she and Sartre had with a young woman, Olga Kosakiewicz. Through the character of Françoise, she explored her own feelings of jealousy toward the second woman, even though Beauvoir did not violate her philosophical acceptance of her open relationship with Sartre.

Beauvoir and Sartre spent World War II in Paris. In 1945 they began to edit the review *Le Temps Modernes*. Both actively participated in the French Resistance, which forms the backdrop of her next novel, *Le Sang des autres* (1945; *The Blood of Others*). In *Tous les hommes sont mortels* (1946; *All Men Are Mortal*), Beauvoir explored the existentialist question of immortality in a tale set during the Italian Renaissance and afterward. The protagonists are the actress Régine and Fosca, who claims he is immortal. Having rejected her own belief in God, Régine erroneously comes to believe her love for Fosca will replace God and render her immortal.

Beauvoir published many nonfiction works as well. Her philosophical work *Pour une morale de l'ambiguité* (*The Ethics of Ambiguity*) appeared in 1927. She is perhaps best known for her feminist treatise *Le deuxième sexe* (1949; *The Second Sex*). Using various disciplines such as history, biology, and economics, she attempted to define the role of modern women. In her view, the earliest Western philosophers established women as "the other," paving the way for patriarchal societies.

The novel *Les mandarins* (1954; *The Mandarins*) derives from the experience with the Resistance she and Sartre shared during World War II. Although Beauvoir has denied the allegations, many critics believe she based several of the main characters on herself, Camus, and Sartre. *The Mandarins* is a portrait of postwar intellectuals as they try to redefine their roles as philosophers and political activists after participating in the Resistance.

Beauvoir involved herself in numerous political activities after the war, embracing the causes of Algerian liberation in the 1950s and abortion rights in the 1970s. With Sartre she visited Cuban leader Fidel Castro in 1960. In 1974 she became president of the French League of Women's Rights.

In her later life Beauvoir began to explore the dilemmas of middle and old age. *La femme rompue* (1968; *The Woman Destroyed*) consists of three stories about women struggling in middle age. The nonfiction works *Une mort très douce* (1964; *A Very Easy Death*) and *La vieillesse* (1970; *Old Age*) recount her mother's death from cancer and explore the treatment of the elderly.

Beauvoir wrote many autobiographical works, including *Mémoires d'une jeune fille rangée* (1958; *Memoirs of a Dutiful Daughter*), *La force de l'âge* (1960; *The Prime of Life*), *La force des choses* (1963; *Force of Circumstance*), and *Tout compte fait* (1972; *All Said and Done*). *La cérémonie des adieux* (1981; *Adieux: A Farewell to Sartre*) recounts Sartre's last years. Among her other works are the play *Les bouches inutiles* (1945; *Who Shall Die?*); the short-story collection *Quand prime le spirituel* (1979; *When Things of the Spirit Come First*); the volume of letters *Lettres au Castor et à quelques autres* (1983); and the travel books *La Longue Marche: Essai sur la Chine* (1957; *The Long March*) and *L'Amérique au jour de jour* (1948; *America Day by Day*). In 1973 she began writing a column in *Le Temps Modernes*. The following year, she became president of the League of Women's Rights, and in 1975 she won the Jerusalem Prize.

BIBLIOGRAPHY

Appignanesi, Lisa, *Simone de Beauvoir*, 1988; Ascher, Carol, *Simone de Beauvoir: A Life of Freedom*, 1981; Bair, Deirdre, *Simone de Beauvoir: A Biography*, 1990; Brosman, Catharine Savage, *Simone de Beauvoir Revisited*, 1991; Evans, Mary, *Simone de Beauvoir*, 1996; Fallaize, Elizabeth, *The Novels of Simone de Beauvoir*, 1988; Francis, Claude, *Simone de Beauvoir: A Life, A Love Story*, 1987; Keefe, Terry, *Simone de Beauvoir*, 1998; Mahon, Joseph, *Existentialism, Feminism, and Simone de Beauvoir*, 1997; Moi, Toril, *Simone de Beauvoir: The Making of an Intellectual Woman*, 1994; Vintges, Karen, *Philosophy as Passion: The Thinking of Simone de Beauvoir*, 1996.

Beckett, Samuel

(April 13, 1906–December 22, 1989)
Playwright, Novelist, Critic

The Irish writer Samuel Barclay Beckett (who wrote in French as well as English) is best known for plays such as *Waiting for Godot*, which present unflinchingly the absurd dilemma of the powerless individual consciousness trying to make sense of the world, exploring, as Beckett himself said, "impotence, ignorance, . . . that whole zone of being that has always been set aside by artists as something . . . incompatible with art." Beckett also wrote several novels that explore the same zone. In 1969, he received the Nobel Prize for Lit-

Samuel Beckett (Fragment Publishing)

erature, "for his writing, which—in new forms for the novel and drama—in the destitution of modern man acquires its elevation." It is in such paradoxical terms that Beckett's work is often praised, for revealing the destitution of humanity in the modern world, yet also for finding in that destitution, as one critic put it, "an ironically sorrowful joy," or, as another put it, "affirming beneath all affirmation."

Beckett was born into a middle-class Protestant family in Foxrock, County Dublin, Ireland. His mother in particular was devout and pious, and his relationship with her was troubled throughout his life. The young Beckett enrolled in school in Dublin and later, when he was 14, in the Portora Royal School in what is now Enniskillen, in Northern Ireland. Beckett later studied at Trinity College in Dublin, where he earned a degree in Romance languages.

After his graduation he taught briefly in Belfast before moving to Paris in 1928. Beckett gained the friendship of fellow Irish writer James Joyce, then in Paris. Joyce became a primary influence on his early work. Two years later Beckett returned to Ireland to teach, and he subsequently traveled around Europe. After his return to Paris in 1937, he suffered a serious stab wound and was visited frequently by Joyce during his recuperation. Beckett, who joined the French Resistance during World War II, fled Nazi-occupied Paris during World War II when the Gestapo arrested other members of his group. For the rest of the occupation he worked in the unoccupied portion of France. After a brief return to Ireland in 1945, he again settled in Paris.

A prominent figure in Beckett's work, particularly as it matured, is the person trapped in an absurd world, confused about the meaning of his existence, and suffering from the belief that all actions amount to no more than exercises in futility. His early work includes the poem *Whoroscope* (1930), about the French philosopher René Descartes, an essay on Marcel Proust entitled *Proust* (1931), and *More Pricks Than Kicks* (1934), a collection of ten stories about an Irish intellectual, Belacqua Shuah. The novel *Murphy* (1938) concerns a Mr. Willoughby-Kelly, who finds himself physically attracted to a prostitute, Celia. Celia's demand that he get a job destroys their plan to marry.

Watt (1953), written during World War II, showed the beginnings of what became Beckett's mature style and was the first of his novels to create a pervasive atmosphere of absurdity. Its protagonist, Watt, fights for his sanity while performing routine work in the home and service of a mysterious Mr. Knott, whom neither he nor the reader ever meets. After the war Beckett began writing in French, most notably his trio of novels *Molloy* (1951), *Malone Dies* (1951), and *The Unnamable* (1953). (Since Beckett did his own translations, only the English version of the title is given here.)

Beckett's most famous work is perhaps the play *Waiting for Godot*. Roger Blin directed its first production at the Théâtre de Babylone in Paris in 1953, and it became the first of Beckett's works to win significant international recognition. The story takes place on a deserted road (represented by a bare stage), where two tramps, Vladimir (called Didi) and Estragon (called Gogo), wait in vain for an ambiguous figure named Godot, encountering only a rich (and cruel) man and his slave. Most of the play shows them finding ways to kill time—"We always find something, eh Didi, to give us the impression we exist?" The play gained instant recognition as a portrayal of the human condition in the twentieth century, where God seems absent and materialism dominant, but part of its appeal also lies in its humor, and in the obscure sense it creates that somewhere more meaning exists.

Along with EUGÈNE IONESCO and other French playwrights, Beckett is often associated with the Theater of the Absurd, although he thoroughly disliked this label and did not consider his work a part of the movement. Absurdist plays are characterized by minimal dialogue, undeveloped characters, illogical situations and plots, and other elements aimed at depicting the irrationality of existence.

Among Beckett's other plays from the 1950s and the 1960s is the one-act *Endgame* (1957), in which the characters try in vain to fill time with repetitions of the meaningless routines that seem to offer them some identity, but in the end give in, remaining unmoving and silent. The main character in *Krapp's Last Tape* (1958) is a bitter old writer who makes annual recordings about the previous year on his birthday. In the story he listens to the tape he made on his thirty-ninth birthday and records a new one, again trying in vain to convince himself that his life has some meaning. In *Play* (first performed 1963), three characters find themselves eternally trapped in a love triangle. The story continues on and on with no resolution and, to emphasize its repetitiveness, is performed exactly the same way twice.

Beckett also wrote several plays that feature women as their main characters. In *Happy Days* (1961), an optimistic, complacent middle-aged woman, Winnie, sinks into the ground, her optimism apparently unshaken by this strange occurrence. In *Not I*, the only thing illuminated on stage is a mouth reciting in a female voice. Beckett wrote this play and two others, *That Time* (1976) and *Footfalls* (1976), for the actress Billie Whitelaw. Whitelaw also starred in a London production of *Rockaby* (1981), a monologue.

In 1961 Beckett married Suzanne Deschevaux-Dumesnil, his longtime companion. He accepted the Nobel Prize for Literature in 1969 but, shunning the publicity, sent a representative to Stockholm to receive it for him. In the early 1980s he completed a trio of novels, collected as *Nohow On* in 1996. The first of these, *Company* (1980), incorporated many childhood memories and was followed by *Ill Seen Ill Said* (1981) and *Worstward*

Ho (1983). His other works include *Echo's Bones* (1935), the radio play *All That Fall* (1957), *How It Is* (1961), *Stories and Texts for Nothing* (1967), *The Lost Ones* (1972), *Stirrings Still* (1986), the unfinished novel *Dream of Fair to Middling Women* (written in the early 1930s and published in 1992), and the three-act play *Eleutheria* (written just after World War II and published in 1995).

The plays from the 1950s and 1960s, especially *Waiting for Godot, Krapp's Last Tape, Endgame,* and *Happy Days,* are the ones that are generally considered classics. His later work, though still evocative, is so stripped down or obscure that it has had less impact. The last work, *Stirrings Still,* a brief and sometimes inaccessible yet beautiful and haunting play, has been seen as a fitting epitaph for Beckett, especially its first sentences: "One night as he sat at his table head on hands he saw himself rise and go. One night or day. For when his own light went out he was not left in the dark."

BIBLIOGRAPHY

Bair, Deirdre, *Samuel Beckett: A Biography,* 1978; Cronin, Anthony, *Samuel Beckett: The Last Modernist,* 1996; Knowlson, James, *Damned to Fame: The Life of Samuel Beckett,* 1996.

Beckmann, Max

(February 12, 1884–December 27, 1950)
Painter, Graphic Artist, Teacher

Deeply affected by the bloodshed he witnessed during World War I, the German Expressionist painter Max Beckmann rose to prominence with his tormented, grotesque depictions of the horrors he witnessed. As was the fate of many artists and intellectuals of his time in Germany, the Nazis confiscated hundreds of his works and forced him into exile when they rose to power in 1932. Beckmann's best-known works are his massive allegorical triptychs and his numerous self-portraits, and all are infused with a disturbing and profound sense of disquiet and uneasiness.

Beckmann was born in Leipzig, Germany. His father was a prosperous flour merchant. As a youth he studied at the Braunschwig gymnasium, but he was more interested in pursuing the artistic ambitions that emerged early in his life, and he particularly admired the Dutch painter Rembrandt (1606–1669). Beckmann studied at the Weimar Academy from 1900 to 1903. There he absorbed the conservative classical influence of the Academy, studying under Hans von Marées. In 1904 Beckmann moved to Berlin and began to paint under the influence of German Impressionists such as Lovis Corinth. Two years later he joined the Berlin Secession, an avant-garde movement opposed to the dominant traditional representational art.

After Beckmann met the Norwegian expressionist painter Edvard Munch, he too began to develop the expressionistic style for which he is best known. During World War I he served in the medical corps, an experience that led to a mental breakdown and to a pronounced change in the tone of his work. Beckmann's depictions now grew violent and grotesque as he investigated relationships between volume and space.

Heavy brush strokes, contorted lines, and bold, vibrant color recur in his paintings from this era, as in *The Descent from the Cross* (1917) and *The Night* (1918–1919). The emaciated Christ figure being lowered from the cross in the former is as shocking a scene as the violent, brutal depiction of murder in the latter. Unlike contemporaries such as GEORGE GROSZ, Beckmann never aimed at direct political and social statement but kept his commentary to an individual level. *The Dream* (1921) depicts a veteran and amputee, cradling a large fist under one of his half cut-off arms, on a ladder blowing a trumpet while an indifferent blond girl looks on. All of these canvases are crowded with disturbing figures interacting in atmospheres pervaded with an overwhelming spirit of chaos.

At this time Beckmann was also experimenting with graphic art, completing an early series of lithographs entitled *Hell*. He did most of his work in graphic arts during his years in Germany, with the notable exception of his later series *Day and Dream* (1946). For much of his graphic art he worked in drypoint, a technique that involves scratching a metal plate.

Beckmann's work grew in popularity in Germany during the 1920s, leading to his appointment as a professor at the Städel School of Art in Frankfurt, many exhibitions in Germany, and a gold medal for artistic achievement from the city of Düsseldorf. His fortunes changed, however, with the rise of the National Socialists. The Nazis declared Beckmann's art "degenerate" in 1932 and over the next several years confiscated some six hundred of his works.

Around this time Beckmann had begun the first of his nine allegorical triptychs. The vividly colored *Departure* (1932–1933) is filled with the violence and death of his earlier work, with such depictions as a man with amputated hands—seated, with the bloody stubs of his arms tied above his head—and a woman facing execution. Other paintings from this period include *View of Genoa* (1927), in which a dark shadow hanging over the city contrasts with the vibrant green of the water; *Girls with Playful Dogs* (1933), a depiction of two young women and five dogs in the park that offers a high-contrast interplay of color; and *Journey on the Fish (Man and Woman)* (1934).

Having been forced from his professorship and increasingly in fear of his life, Beckmann fled with his wife to Amsterdam in 1937. He worked there for ten years, completing his noted triptychs *The Actors* (1942) and *Blindman's Bluff* (1945). The colorful, busy scenes in the latter begin in the left panel with a crowd of figures who seem lost in uneasy thought. The frenzied figures in the center panel are wildly playing harps, horns, and other instruments, while a blindfolded man dominates the right panel. The triptych *Beginning* (1946–1949), completed after he settled in the United States, depicts his childhood and schooling.

Beckmann taught for three years at Washington University in St. Louis and then moved to New York. By this time he had developed his own expressionistic style and symbolic vocabulary, and the violence and tension of his earlier canvases toned down in his later work. The moral, self-searching bent in his work is nowhere more evident than in the approximately eighty self-portraits he is known to have produced. Beckmann often depicted himself in costume, wearing tuxedos, sailor's caps (*Self-portrait in Sailor Hat*, 1926), or clown's uniforms. *Self-portrait with Cigarette* (1923) depicts the artist sitting pensively and holding a cigarette in his raised right hand, with a dark shadow cast over the right side of his face. Other self portraits include *Self-portrait with Red Curtain* (1923) and *Self-portrait with Green Curtain* (1940)."

Beckmann put the finishing touches on his final triptych *Argonauts* (1949–1950) the day he died.

BIBLIOGRAPHY

Haftmann, Werner, A. Hentzen, and W. S. Lieberman, *German Art of the Twentieth Century*, 1957; Lackner, Stephan, *Max Beckmann*, 1977.

Beecham, Thomas

(April 29, 1879–March 8, 1961)
Conductor

A colorful personality, popular with the English public, Sir Thomas Beecham conducted the major international orchestras of his day and was responsible for founding several of them. He was an outspoken critic of the state of English music in his day, and introduced international musical figures such as Feodor Chaliapin to the British public. Beecham enthusiastically promoted the work of composer FREDERICK DELIUS, about whom he later wrote a biography.

Beecham was born into a wealthy family in St. Helens, Lancashire, England. His father, one-time mayor of St. Helens, was fond of music. Beecham studied at the University of Oxford and was largely self-taught in the music field he later entered. In 1899 he made his first public appearance as a conductor with the Hallé Orchestra, with which he was to work until the end of World War II. Six years later, Beecham debuted in London conducting the Queen's Hall Orchestra. In 1906 he conducted with his New Symphony Orchestra.

Beecham conducted both orchestras and operas. In 1910 he embarked on a sequence of operas, and following World War I he founded the British National Opera Company. In 1911 he introduced impresario SERGEY DIAGHILEV's Ballets Russes to London audiences. Beecham was responsible for popularizing the talents of a number of noted figures in his day, including Delius and the Russian singer FEODOR CHALIAPIN.

Known for his strong opinions about the deficiencies of British music and his sharp wit, Beecham would go to great lengths to emphasize a point. In 1935, to prove the weight an Italian name carried with England's opera-going public, he announced with fanfare the arrival of a newly discovered Italian operatic soprano, Lisa Perli, who was to sing Mimi

Portrait of Thomas Beecham superimposed over the Royal Opera House (Ann Ronan/Image Select)

earned rave reviews she had not previously received from critics.

In 1928 Beecham conducted the New York Philharmonic, substituting for ARTURO TOSCANINI. The following year he conducted Delius's major compositions at Queen's Hall. In 1932 he founded the London Philharmonic Orchestra, and in 1933 he became artistic director at Covent Garden. Beecham spent much of World War II conducting in Australia, Canada, and the United States, where he conducted the Seattle Symphony from 1941 to 1943 and the orchestra of the Metropolitan Opera in New York (1942–1944). After the war ended, he returned to England and founded the Royal Philharmonic Orchestra in London.

A great champion of Delius and JEAN SIBELIUS, Beecham also included in his repertoire many eighteenth-century composers. He conducted from memory and gave interpretive and instinctual, rather than strict, renditions of music. He was knighted in 1916 and made a Companion of Honor in 1957. In 1917 he succeeded to his father's baronetcy. Beginning in 1910, Beecham recorded many works. He published two books, the autobiography *A Mingled Chime* (1943) and the biography *Frederick Delius* in 1959.

BIBLIOGRAPHY

Blackwood, Alan, *Sir Thomas Beecham: The Man and the Music*, 1994; Cardus, Neville, *Sir Thomas Beecham: A Memoir*, 1961.

in an upcoming production of *La Bohème*. Perli was in fact the experienced singer Dora Labette, who as an Italian

Behrens, Peter

(April 14, 1868–February 27, 1940)
Architect, Painter, Graphic Artist, Designer, Typographic Designer

Trained as an artist, Peter Behrens was an influential force in the development of modern architecture in Germany, particularly in the application of his functional geometric style to industrial design. He employed and was a direct influence on a generation of younger modern architects that included LUDWIG MIES VAN DER ROHE, Bauhaus founder WALTER GROPIUS, and LE CORBUSIER. Behrens also designed furniture, appliances, cutlery, decorative objects, and typefaces.

Behrens was born in St. Georg, Hamburg. His father was a prosperous landowner from Holstein, and both parents died before he was 15. As an adolescent, having inherited a sizable sum of money from his parents, he went to live with a guardian. Behrens attended school in Altona before entering the Gewerbeschule in Hamburg. In 1886 he enrolled at the Kunstschule (Art School) in Karlsruhe (1886), and he subsequently studied privately under Ferdinand Brütt in Hamburg and Hugo Kotschenreifurt in Munich. In 1889 he married Lilli Krämer.

Behrens started out as a painter and graphic artist influenced by the tradition of Realism and by the Impressionists. In 1892 he exhibited his *Zecher bei gelbem Lampenlicht* (1893; *Toper by the Yellow Lamplight*) in the Munich Secession, and in 1894–1895 he painted numerous landscapes. Behrens also began to design woodcuts influenced by the Japanese printmakers and the Art Nouveau movement then blossoming in Germany. *Sturm* (1896), one such large woodcut, depicts a massive bird flying in front of trees blowing in a turbulent wind.

Toward the end of the decade, Behrens began to devote himself increasingly to the applied arts, designing ceramics, porcelain, fabrics, glass, and carpets. Many of his designs were manufactured commercially, including tea sets, dishes, and vases. In 1900 the grand duke of Hessen invited Behrens to Künstlerkolonie, a new art colony in Darmstadt. There Behrens designed his own home the following year.

Around the same time, Behrens designed his first interiors. In 1900 he created a dining room for his friend Otto Erich Hartleben. Three of his interiors formed part of the German section at the First International Exhibition of Modern Decorative Arts in Turin in 1902. The following year he designed another dining room for the poet Richard Dehmel. These and other early designs were heavily influenced by the curvilinear forms, undulating lines, and decorative focus of the Art Nouveau movement.

Behrens took a post as director of the arts-and-crafts school in Düsseldorf in 1903. Commissions for larger projects soon followed—a private home for the industrialist Gustav Obenauer in 1905, a concert hall in Cologne (1906), and a crematorium at Delstern (1906–1907). During this time he had also begun to develop the first of several typefaces he created, which include Behrens-Schrift (1902), Kursiv (1906–1907), and Behrens Mediäval (1914).

In 1907 Emil Rathenau, general director of the large manufacturing company Allgemeine Elektricitäts Gesellschaft (AEG), put Behrens to work designing for all aspects of the company's operation. The years 1907–1914 marked his most intense involvement with the AEG, and during that time he designed everything from factory complexes and workers' housing to clocks, kettles, fans, and a particularly successful arc lamp. Behrens also designed the company's logo, a special typeface for AEG, and its stationery.

As his career progressed, Behrens moved increasingly away from the Art Nouveau influence toward the International Style advanced by Mies van der Rohe, Gropius, and Le Corbusier. His New Ways (1923–1925), a privately commissioned house in England, was one of the earliest examples of the use of modern architecture for private dwellings in that country.

Among his later works are the Catholic Community House at Neuss (1907); the head office for the Mannesmannröhren-Werke in Düsseldorf (1911–1912); the administrative building for the Continental Rubber Company in Hannover-Vahrenwald (1911–1920), which was destroyed during World War II; the German embassy at St. Petersburg (1911–1912), which shows influences of classical architecture; The Gasgesellschaft (1911–1912), or Gasworks—a large industrial complex marked by its series of cylindrical towers; the offices for the Dyeworks Höchst (1920–1924); the Frankfurter factory for the Austrian Tobacco Administration at Linz (1930); and the Ring der Frauen pavilion (1931), a white, flat-roofed building composed of circular elements.

BIBLIOGRAPHY

Windsor, Alan, *Peter Behrens: Architect and Designer*, 1981.

Belloc, Hilaire

(July 27, 1870–July 16, 1953)
Poet, Novelist, Critic, Journalist, Essayist

The massive output of the French-born British writer Joseph-Pierre Hilaire Belloc includes more than 150 novels, volumes of poetry, biographies, and histories as well as countless articles and essays that appeared in journals over his lifetime. Belloc's broad knowledge extended to history, politics, religion, and literature. His writing was heavily colored by his devout Catholic belief, and his confrontational manner made him one of the most controversial figures in England in the first half of the twentieth century.

Belloc was born in La Celle-Saint-Cloud, France. His mother, Elizabeth Parkes, was English and a supporter of women's suffrage. She knew many prominent literary figures and was the great-granddaughter of Dr. Joseph Priestley, the Englishman-turned-American who discovered oxygen. Belloc's father, a lawyer, died when he was two, a blow from which his mother never really recovered. She eventually moved the family to England, and Belloc studied at the Oratory School in Birmingham.

Hilaire Belloc (Ann Ronan/Image Select)

After considering several professions, Belloc determined to pursue journalism and began to submit reviews to the *Pall Mall Gazette*. He was drafted into the French Army and served for a year. Upon his release, he entered Balliol College, Oxford. He was successful academically there, receiving first class honors in history and serving as the president of the debating society. However, Belloc's intentions of pursuing an academic career were frustrated when he was denied a fellowship on repeated occasions.

Unable to gain a teaching position, he decided to write. In 1896, he married Elodie Hogan, an American for whom he had twice journeyed across the United States before she agreed to become his wife. Elodie's death in 1914 was a devastating blow for Belloc. His first book of verse, *Verses and Sonnets*, was published in 1895 and largely ignored. His other volumes of serious poetry include *Verses* (1910) and two volumes entitled *Sonnets and Verse* (1923 and 1938). Belloc's serious poetry is classical in form, incorporates his historical knowledge, and treats themes of love, religion, the poor, landscape, and death.

Belloc's light verse, much of it for children, was more successful in terms of popularity. *The Bad Child's Book of Beasts* (1896), a collection he intended as moral verse written with an appealingly lighthearted ferociousness and illustrated by Belloc's friend Basil T. Blackwood, proved to be very popular upon its publication. It was followed by other volumes such as *The Modern Traveller* (1898), *The Moral Alphabet* (1899), *Cautionary Tales for Children* (1907), *More Peers* (1911; for adults), and *New Cautionary Tales* (1930).

Around the turn of the century, Belloc moved to London, where he became fast friends with G. K. CHESTERTON and his brother, Cecil. Belloc and Chesterton, dubbed "Chesterbelloc," held a then-unpopular stance in opposing England's role in the Boer War and imperialism in general. The two also embraced an economic vision they called "distributivism," which aimed to limit concentrations of power and wealth to small, localized areas. They objected to both socialism and capitalism, the former of which concentrates power in a central government and the latter of which leaves control in the hands of a few wealthy capitalists.

Belloc's career in politics lasted only a few years. He became a British subject in 1902 and in 1906 began four years of service as a representative for Salford in Parliament. Belloc ran as a Liberal but soon found himself at odds with the party. Disgusted by the corruption he saw in politics and under too much stress from the demands his office placed on him, he retired. During World War I, he contributed popular military essays to the journal *Land and Water*.

Several of Belloc's satirical novels dating from this period reflect his view of the political corruption he saw. These include *Mr. Clutterbuck's Election* (1908), about a man who buys a seat in Parliament; *A Change in the Cabinet* (1909); and *Pongo and the Bull* (1910). Along with *The Postmaster-General* (1932), these novels reflect Belloc's belief that money and power ruled Britain's democracy. He saw the party system as a sham, with leaders from supposedly opposing parties in collusion with one another in the interests of money and power.

Outside the political realm, Belloc satirized academics, journalists, and capitalists in his novels. *Lambkin's Remains* (1900), an indictment of the academic world inspired by his troubles at Oxford, was followed by a satire on journalists, *Caliban's Guide to Letters* (1903). The main character of *The Mercy of Allah* (1922) is a wealthy and unscrupulous capitalist, Mahmoud.

In *Emmanuel Burden* (1904), Burden, the owner of a hardware store, finds himself the victim of the wiles of the financier I. Z. Barnett. Barnett desires to control the store to enable him to exploit a colony in Africa. Barnett's powers of manipulation at first succeed on Burden but do not work on his smarter friend Abbott, whose business Barnett is also after. Belloc wrote novels in other styles, including the historical novel *The Gir-*

ondin (1911), set during the French Revolution; *The Haunted House* (1927); the love story *Belinda* (1928); *The Man Who Made Gold* (1930); and *The Hedge and the Horse* (1936). Chesterton illustrated many of his novels.

Belloc was never a stranger to public controversy, but he carried on his most heated war of words with H.G. WELLS. In particular he objected to the progressive, evolutionary vision of humanity Wells laid out in his *Outline of History*. The quarrel produced several volumes of argumentation and rebuttal from both sides, culminating in Belloc's *A Companion to Mr. Wells's "Outline of History"* (1926).

Belloc wrote many historical and biographical works in an engaging, nonacademic style. He was a lifelong, devout Catholic, and his Catholic worldview influenced both his historical perspective and his contemporary observations. In spite of frequent criticism from the academic world, he refused to use footnotes or write in a scholarly manner. His works on the French Revolution include *Danton* (1899), *Robespierre* (1901), *Marie Antoinette* (1909), and *The French Revolution* (1911). Among his other historical works are his four-volume *History of England* (1925–1931) and biographies of many French and English monarchs.

Belloc's political writings include *The Party System* (1911), co-authored with Cecil Chesterton, which attacked the party system in England. In *The Servile State* (1912), he argued that Britain's subjects were handing over their freedoms to the welfare state. His later political writings include *The House of Commons and Monarchy* (1920) and *An Essay on the Restoration of Property* (1936). Belloc's pilgrimage on foot from Toul, in the northeast of France, to Rome provided the subject matter for *The Path to Rome* (1902), his best-known travel book. His other works include the essay collections *Hills and the Sea* (1906), *On Nothing* (1908), and *On Something* (1910) as well as books of literary criticism. He re-ceived an honorary doctorate of laws from Glasgow University in 1920.

BIBLIOGRAPHY

Markel, Michael H., *Hilaire Belloc*, 1982; Wilson, A. N., *Hilaire Belloc*, 1984.

Bennett, Arnold

(May 27, 1867–March 27, 1931)
Novelist, Playwright, Screenwriter, Critic

Enoch Arnold Bennett wrote more than thirty novels, and is particularly noted for his straightforward portrayals of lower-class people in the Five Towns, the region formerly known as the Potteries in England. Bennett's narratives carry a realistic and subdued tone and generally treat the lives of unremarkable individuals. He also wrote plays, essays, articles, and books of practical advice.

Bennett was the eldest of nine children born in Burslem, Staffordshire, England, in the Five Towns, a region with a centuries-old tradition of pottery making. His childhood was marked by the abnormally high expectations his parents, and particularly his father, held for him. He studied at the Infants' Wesleyan School and when he was 10 entered the Endowed School. Bennett was an exceptional student at these and at the last school he was to attend, the Newcastle Middle School in Newcastle-under-Lyme. At the age of 16, under pressure from his father, he quit school to work as a clerk in his father's office.

In 1889, Bennett moved to London, where he continued to work as a clerk

Arnold Bennett (Ann Ronan/Image Select)

before he became an assistant editor of the magazine *Woman*, to which he contributed advice to women under the pseudonym "Gwendolyn." His first published story, a parody, appeared in *Tit-Bits* and won a small award. After the publication of his first novel, *A Man from the North* (1898), Bennett conclusively decided to devote himself to writing.

Other novels followed and were published serially, including *The Ghost about Carl Foster*, about a medical student who goes to London and gets wrapped up with the musical comedy stars Rosa and Alresca. Carl, in love with Rosa, is haunted by the ghost of Rosa's dead lover. *The Grand Babylon Hotel* appeared in 1902, and *The Gates of Wrath* was published the following year.

Bennett, who loved everything French, was influenced by French Realists such as Gustave Flaubert. With a few exceptions, he used the omniscient narrator to tell his stories. Death is an ever-present force in his narratives, propelling characters into new situations or providing final ends to their tragic histories. His characters are average people in average situations—there is little of the bizarre, abnormal, or fantastic in his stories. Bennett's commentary is subtle.

Anna of the Five Towns (1902), one of Bennett's most acclaimed novels, is the first to unfold completely in his favorite setting. In the story, the heiress Anna Tellwright's life is anything but remarkable, except perhaps for the brief period of time covered in the book. She becomes engaged to Henry Mynors, who promises to give her a routine and uneventful life as a husband, and submits to her fate as his wife at the end of the novel.

Bennett moved to France in 1903 and married the actress Marguerite Soulie in 1907. Their marriage proved to be relatively unhappy and ended in 1921. Even before he arrived in Paris, he had begun to devour the works of literature he had missed when he quit school to work for his father. The varied cultural atmosphere of Paris suited his taste, but he returned to England in 1912. He purchased a yacht, the *Velsa*, the same year and memorialized it in *From the Log of the Velsa* (1914).

Love and sexual themes form the center of many of Bennett's novels. In *Lenora* (1903), the return of Arthur Twemlow causes upheaval in the lives of Lenora Stanway, her Victorian husband John, and their daughters. The end result is John's suicide and Lenora's liberation, as she is now free to be with Arthur, with whom she has fallen in love. *Sacred and Profane Love* (1905), one of Bennett's most controversial novels, is narrated in the first person by Carlotta, a young woman in her twenties. In the story Bennett covers her sexual awakening and maturity, beginning with her first sexual encounter at age 21.

The Old Wives' Tale (1908), another of the works many critics consider among Bennett's best, depicts the tragic lives of Constance and Sophia Baines. Both girls fall in love and get married, Sophia to the salesman Gerald Scales and Constance to Samuel Povey. Povey dies and Scales deserts Sophia. Circumstance brings the two aged women back together, until the news of the demise of Sophia's husband kills her as well. Constance outlives her for a few years.

In *Buried Alive* (1908), Bennett showed a penchant for humor. The protagonist, a middle-aged artist, Priam Farll, suffers greatly from the death of his valet, Henry Leek. Leek served as his link to a world from which Farll hid, in spite of the success of his paintings. Farll takes advantage of Leek's death by pretending he is the one who has died. He marries Alice Challice, who had formerly pursued Leek as a potential husband. Farll begins to paint again to support his family, and the public uncovers his real identity. Bennett later adapted *Buried Alive* as the play *The Great Adventure* (1913).

Clayhanger (1910), a serious work, is the first volume in Bennett's trilogy *The Clayhanger Family* (1905). The protagonist Edwin Clayhanger leaves school as an innocent and naive young man and goes to work in his overbearing father's print shop. He wins the friendship of the wealthy Orgreaves and at their home falls in love with Hilda Lessways. His intentions of marrying her are frustrated by his father's reaction when he asks for a raise and by Hilda's marriage to another man. After many years, when Edwin's father has died, he meets Hilda again and plans to marry her. The trilogy's succeeding volumes, *Hilda Lessways* (1911) and *These Twain* (1916), deal with Hilda's life and their marriage, respectively.

Bennett's later novels are diverse. For the setting of *Riceyman Steps* (1923), he chose Clerkenwell, a lower-middle-class area in London. *Lord Raingo* (1926) offers a portrait of a prosperous, middle-aged man seeking a new direction in his life. *Imperial Palace* (1930) is a lengthy novel set in a luxury hotel and marked by its incorporation of many characters and episodes.

Among Bennett's plays are *What the Public Wants* (1909), staged on the West End; *The Honeymoon* (1910), about a couple arguing about their honeymoon; *The Love Match* (1922); and *Body and Soul* (1922). Many of his novels were also adapted as plays. Bennett's greatest success in the theater came with *Milestones*, co-written with Edward Knoblock. The play ran for a year at the Royalty Theater beginning in 1912.

The story of *Milestones* carries on for three generations before reaching a positive resolution. John Rhead breaks with his longtime partner Samuel Sibley over the question of building iron ships. Gertrude, John's sister, also ends her engagement to Samuel. A quarter of a century passes and finds John pushing his daughter, Emily, into an unhappy marriage in spite of her love for another man. In another twenty-five years, Emily adopts the same attitude toward her own daughter, Muriel, who becomes the first in the family to follow her own heart.

Bennett's other works include the novel *Helen with the High Hand* (1910); *Piccadilly*, a film script that Alfred Hitchcock directed as *Punch and Judy* in 1929; the three-volume *The Journals of Arnold Bennett, 1896–1928* (1932–1933); and many books of essays, criticism, and practical advice.

BIBLIOGRAPHY

Broomfield, Olga R. R., *Arnold Bennett*, 1984; Drabble, Margaret, *Arnold Bennett: A Biography*, 1974; Squillace, Robert, *Modernism, Modernity, and Arnold Bennett*, 1997.

Berg, Alban

(February 9, 1885–December 24, 1935)
Composer

ARNOLD SCHOENBERG and two of his students, Alban Maria Johannes Berg and ANTON VON WEBERN, comprise the Second Viennese School in twentieth century music and were the major early composers in Schoenberg's twelve-tone method. In his mature years, Berg, who along with Schoenberg was first influenced by the late Romantics, imbued the system Schoenberg formulated to bring structure to atonal music with a greater sense of expression and flexibility than did either Schoenberg or Webern.

Berg was born into an upper-middle-class Catholic family in Vienna, Austria. His father was a merchant and died when Berg was 15. Living in Vienna, Berg gained exposure to a variety of cultural

Alban Berg (Ann Ronan/Image Select)

influences in his youth. At home, too, he was exposed to his mother's music and painting and his siblings' musical interests. He at first aspired to be a poet and was to maintain a lifelong interest in literature. However, in his teens he began to compose music. After failing his matriculation in 1903, Berg unsuccessfully attempted suicide.

Berg's eldest brother, Charley, took some of his work to Schoenberg in 1904. Schoenberg, impressed by Berg's work, initially took him on as a student free of charge, giving him his first formal instruction. Through Schoenberg he met another important influence on his work, his lifelong close friend and fellow composer Anton von Webern. At the time Berg studied with him, Schoenberg was experimenting with atonality, in which a work lacks a definite key, and working toward the development of his twelve-tone composition style. Berg faithfully defended Schoenberg's controversial work when it brought heated criticism. His own early work, such as the *Seven Early Songs* (1905–1908) was also influenced by late Romantic composers such as Gustav Mahler (1860–1911), RICHARD STRAUSS, and Richard Wagner (1813–1883). Mahler's widow, Alma, supported Berg's career throughout his life.

The single-movement Piano Sonata (1907–1908), influenced by the late Romantics, was Berg's first major work to see public performance. With his String Quartet (1910), Berg moved permanently into atonal composition. His early work *Five Orchestral Songs* (1912), a setting for verse by the Viennese poet Peter Altenberg, formed part of a 1913 concert that included works by Schoenberg, Webern, and Mahler. A riot instigated by musical opponents broke out during the performance.

In 1911 Berg married Helene Nahowski. Fragile health and asthma plagued him for most of his life, often hampering his ability to work. World War I also interrupted Berg's composing career, and his work in the war ministry from 1915 to 1918 further compromised his health. Before the war he had begun his operatic masterpiece *Wozzeck*, with libretto based on the German dramatist Georg Büchner's *Woyzeck*, and he completed it in 1921.

Berg wrote *Wozzeck*'s score in "atonal style," although the work is not atonal in a strict sense, and dedicated it to Alma Mahler. It premiered at the Berlin State Opera in 1925, conducted by Erich Kleiber. The expressionistic opera's unique combinations of vocal and instrumental elements, along with the use of "speech song" (in which the line between speech and song is blurred), helped make the opera an international success. The plight of the protagonist, a soldier who suffers at the hands of the leaders of society, was close to Berg's heart. It was one of the few atonal operas to gain widespread acceptance, and the work's popularity stabilized Berg's fragile financial situation.

The Chamber Concerto for violin, piano, and thirteen wind instruments (1925) was written for Schoenberg's fiftieth birthday and was Berg's first major work to use serialism. *Lyric Suite for String Quartet* (1926) was partly inspired by Berg's affair with Hanna Fuchs-Robettin and was the first of his major works to depart from less structured atonality to Schoenberg's more systematic approach, the twelve-tone method. In this system, a composer forms a row of twelve tones from the notes of the chromatic scale, and the composition is written from each tone in sequence. Berg's later works combine the twelve-tone system with other styles.

The rise of Nazism in Germany in 1933 was costly to Berg's career. Authorities labeled his music "degenerate" and forbade its performance. Equally distressing to Berg was the expulsion of Schoenberg, who was Jewish and was then teaching in Berlin, from Germany. Schoenberg moved to the United States in 1933, and Berg never saw him again.

Berg's last major works were his unfinished opera, *Lulu* (1937), drawn from two plays by Frank Wedekind, *Earth Spirit* and *Pandora's Box*, and his Violin Concerto. The composer Friedrich Cerha finished *Lulu* after Berg's death, and it was not performed until 1979. The violinist Louis Krasner commissioned the Violin Concerto, which Berg shaped into a requiem for Manon Gropius. Gropius was the daughter of Alma Mahler and her second husband, the architect Walter Gropius, and died in her teens. Berg dedicated the concerto "to the memory of an angel."

Berg was elected to the Prussian Academy of Arts in 1930. His work became better known after his death than it had been during his lifetime, and his mastery of Schoenberg's twelve-tone style after 1925 influenced many later twentieth-century composers. He died of septicemia in 1935. Among his other works are *Four Songs* (1909), *Four Pieces for Clarinet* and Piano (1913), *Three Orchestral Pieces* (1915), and *Der Wein* (1929), a concert aria written for the Viennese soprano Ružena Herlinger and orchestra using poetry by Charles Baudelaire.

BIBLIOGRAPHY

Carner, Mosco, *Alban Berg: The Man and the Work*, 2d ed., 1983; Monson, Karen, *Alban Berg*, 1979; Redlich, H. F., *Alban Berg: The Man and His Music*, 1957.

Bergman, Ingmar

(July 14, 1918–)
Director, Screenwriter

The Swedish filmmaker Ernst Ingmar Bergman is the most successful Scandinavian director in world cinema. In his extensive body of films, most written and directed by himself, he weaved unique symbolic dreamscapes that explore themes of life, death, loss of faith, religion, sexuality, hopelessness, and childhood. Although he is primarily known for his work in the cinema, he has also enjoyed a long and successful career as a theater director in Sweden and Germany.

Bergman was born in Uppsala, Sweden, and moved to Stockholm with his parents. His mother and father (a Lutheran pastor) were strict disciplinarians and subjected Bergman and his siblings to sometimes cruel punishments. The emotionally painful events of his childhood were to resurface in many of his films. Bergman attended Palmgren's School as a youth. After a brief period serving in the military that resulted in partial deafness, he enrolled in Stockholm University, where he studied literature, history, and art.

Bergman's career in the arts began in the theater. At the university he devoted much of his time to writing, directing, and acting for the student theater. He staged plays by MAURICE MAETERLINCK, Shakespeare, August Strindberg, and many others as well as his own, such as *The Death of Punch* (1942). Bergman later became a trainee director at the Mäster Olofsgården Theatre and at the Sagas Theatre.

A meeting with Carl-Anders Dymling, head of the Svensk Filmindustri, began Bergman's film career. He joined the Filmindustri as a scriptwriter, and the first of his scripts to see production was *Frenzy* (1944; American title *Torment*), directed by Alf Sjoeberg. Following its success, Bergman soon began writing and directing his own films. His first, *Crisis*, appeared in 1945, followed by *Prison* (1949; American title *The Devil's Wanton*). From 1952 to 1959 Bergman served as director of the Malmö municipal theater and continued to stage plays.

In the film *Sawdust and Tinsel* (1953; American title *The Naked Night*), Harriet Andersson plays the mistress of a circus owner. This film made considerable use of one of Bergman's trademark cinematic techniques, facial close-up shots. Dream sequences and visions also play a significant role in his body of films. *A Lesson in*

Ingmar Bergman (AKG)

nius, who comes face to face with Death as a living character. *Wild Strawberries* (1957), a circular story based in part on Bergman's childhood, is an examination of the passage of time and human failures. An elderly professor faced with death recalls events from his childhood that he believes led to his failures later in life.

A few years later, Bergman filmed a trilogy that examined questions of religion, love, and doubt. The first, *Through a Glass Darkly* (1961), centers on four family members who grapple with belief in God. Its successor, *Winter Light* (1963), paints a picture of hopelessness and disbelief. A minister loses his faith and can offer little consolation to a suicidal parishioner who comes to him for help. In the third film, *The Silence* (1963; originally entitled *God's Silence*), two very different sisters and a son of one of them find themselves stranded in a city that speaks a language they cannot understand. Outside there is a war in progress; inside the sex-obsessed Anna and intellectual Ester compete for the affections of Anna's son, Johan. The chaotic world outside is framed in words they cannot understand and appears devoid of meaning. The sexual scenes in the movie provoked bitter attacks that almost resulted in its being banned in several countries.

Bergman bought a country home on the island of Fårö and filmed a series of projects there, including *Persona* (1966), *Hour of the Wolf* (1968), *The Shame/Shame* (1968), and *A Passion/The Passion of Anna* (1969). *The Rite/The Ritual* (1969) is a psychological portrait of two actors and an actress subjected to a torturous inquisition when authorities accuse them of staging an obscene show.

Love (1954), *Journey into Autumn* (1955; American title *Dreams*), and *Smiles of a Summer Night* (1955) followed; the latter, which examines the love, troubles, and sexuality of four couples during a summer night, became his first international success.

Set in medieval Europe, *The Seventh Seal* (1957) is considered one of Bergman's masterpieces. Like many of his films beginning around this time, it examined conflicts between good and evil, faith and disbelief, and life and death. It began as a play Bergman wrote entitled *Wood Paintings* and was partially inspired by church murals he frequently gazed upon as a youth. The actor Max von Sydow played a knight, Anto-

The Touch (1971) was his first film both in English and in color. The color red dominates the story of a woman dying of cancer in Cries and Whispers (1972), which earned an Oscar for cinematography.

Bergman filmed a television version of Mozart's The Magic Flute in 1974. Face to Face (1976), blurring the distinction between reality and dreams, portrays the shattering of a psychiatrist's sanity after an attempted rape. Autumn Sonata (1978), filmed in Oslo, Norway, stars INGRID BERGMAN as a concert pianist and treats the strained relationship with her daughter. His final film for the cinema, Fanny and Alexander (1983), won four Academy Awards. Bergman retired from the cinema and subsequently directed two films for television, After the Rehearsal (1983) and The Blessed Ones (1985). He continued to direct plays in Stockholm after his retirement.

Bergman's films earned numerous awards, including several Academy Awards and prizes from the Cannes Film Festival. The Magic Lantern, his autobiography, was published in 1988. His other films include Waiting Women (1952), Summer with Monika/Monika (1952), The Magician (1958), So Close to Life/Brink of Life (1958), The Virgin Spring (1960), The Devil's Eye (1960), Now About All These Women/All These Women (1964), Hour of the Wolf (1966), Scenes from a Marriage (1974), Paradise Place (1977), The Serpent's Egg (1977), and From the Life of the Marionettes (1980).

BIBLIOGRAPHY

Bergman, Ingmar, The Magic Lantern: An Autobiography, 1988; Cowie, Peter, Ingmar Bergman: A Critical Biography, 1982.

Bergman, Ingrid

(August 29, 1915–August 29, 1982)
Actress

Known for her aura of intelligence, charm, beauty, and sensitivity to her characters, the Swedish actress Ingrid Bergman appeared in more than sixty films, plays, and television dramas in the United States, Sweden, Germany, France, Italy, and Britain. Her most famous films include Casablanca, Gaslight, and Anastasia. A high-profile affair with and subsequent marriage to the Italian film director ROBERTO ROSSELLINI in the early 1950s led to a series of unsuccessful films before she returned to Hollywood in 1956.

Bergman was an only child born in Stockholm. Her father was an unsuccessful painter who also owned a camera shop. After the successive deaths of her mother when she was 2 and her father and aunt when she was 12, Bergman went to live with an uncle. She studied at the Lyceum School for Girls and, with the reluctant agreement of her uncle, was able to win a scholarship to the Royal Dramatic Theatre in Stockholm, where she enrolled in 1933. Soon afterward she met her first husband, the dentist Peter Lindstrom.

Ingrid Bergman (Ann Ronan/Image Select)

With Lindstrom's encouragement she decided to pursue a career in film. Her first break came when she visited a film studio and attracted the attention of a director. Bergman debuted on screen as the maid Elsa in *Munkbrogreven* (*The Count of the Monk's Bridge*, 1935). *Branningar* (*Ocean Breakers*) featured her as a fisherman's daughter who becomes pregnant during an affair with a guilt-ridden minister. Over the next five years she made ten films in Sweden, among which are *En kvinnas ansikte* (*A Woman's Face*, 1938) and *Intermezzo* (1939). In 1938 she also made a film for Universum Film AG in Germany.

Impressed by her performance in *Intermezzo*, David O. Selznick brought her to the United States for a Hollywood remake of the film in 1939. The new film, *Intermezzo (A Love Story)*, which also starred Leslie Howard, featured Bergman as a piano teacher who has an adulterous affair with Swedish violinist Holger Brandt (Howard). Her performance earned her international stardom. The following year Bergman appeared as Julie in a Broadway production of *Liliom*.

Over the next several years Bergman starred in a series of highly successful films that elevated her to superstardom. After appearing in *Dr. Jekyll and Mr. Hyde* (1941), she starred opposite Humphrey Bogart in the World War II–era classic *Casablanca* (1942). The following year she played Maria in a film version of Ernest Hemingway's *For Whom the Bell Tolls* (1943).

Her performance in *Gaslight* (1944) won her first Academy Award for best actress, and *Saratoga Trunk* and *The Bells of St. Mary's* followed in 1945. In 1945 and 1946 she made two films with Alfred Hitchcock, *Spellbound* and *Notorious*, the latter costarring Cary Grant. Bergman also made *Under Capricorn* with Hitchcock in England in 1948. Her leading role in *Joan of Arc*, a part she had long wanted to play, was less successful.

In a famous letter to Rossellini, Bergman offered to act in one of his films if he was interested. The unsuccessful *Stromboli* (1950) was the immediate result of the letter. Her subsequent affair with Rossellini resulted in the birth of a son, a divorce from Lindstrom, and the temporary alienation of her American audience. Selznick's initial public portrayal of Bergman as a wholesome and respectable figure contributed to the scandal that ensued.

Bergman and Rossellini married in 1950, and two years later she gave birth to twin daughters, Isabella (now a well-known actress herself) and Isotta. The two made a series of films together that were, in general, unsuccessful. These include *Europa '51* (1952; *The Greatest Love*, 1954), made in France; *Un viaggio in Italia* (1954; *Journey to Italy*, 1955), filmed in Italy; and *Fear* (1955), filmed in Germany. In 1955 she also appeared in JEAN RENOIR's *Paris Does Strange Things*.

Bergman returned triumphantly to Hollywood after her divorce from Rossellini, starring in the title role of *Anastasia* (1956), for which she won another Academy Award. She married her third and final husband, the Swedish theater impresario Lars Schmidt, two years later. Bergman continued to make films in the United States, including *The Inn of Sixth Happiness* (1958), *The Yellow Rolls-Royce* (1964), and *Cactus Flower* (1969). Her portrayal of a Swedish missionary in a film version of AGATHA CHRISTIE's *Murder on the Orient Express*

(1974) won her an Academy Award for best supporting actress.

Among her notable later roles were her portrayal of a concert pianist in INGMAR BERGMAN's *Autumn Sonata* (1978) and her final role, that of Israeli prime minister Golda Meir in the television play *A Woman Called Golda* (1981). For the latter she was posthumously awarded an Emmy for outstanding actress in a miniseries.

In addition to her high-profile screen career, Bergman occasionally acted on stage. Her plays include *Hedda Gabler* (Paris, 1962); *A Month in the Country* (England, 1965); GEORGE BERNARD SHAW's *Captain Brassbound's Conversion* (Lon-

don, 1971); and *The Constant Wife* (New York, 1975). Bergman also appeared in the television plays *The Turn of the Screw* (1959), *Hedda Gabler* (1963), and *The Human Voice* (1967). She died of cancer on her sixty-seventh birthday. Her autobiography, *My Story*, was published in 1980.

BIBLIOGRAPHY

Bergman, Ingrid, *My Story*, 1980; Leamer, Laurence, *As Time Goes By: The Life of Ingrid Bergman*, 1986; Quirk, Lawrence J., *The Complete Films of Ingrid Bergman*, 1970; Spoto, Donald, *Notorious: The Life of Ingrid Bergman*, 1997; Taylor, John Russell, *Ingrid Bergman*, 1983.

Betjeman, John

(August 28, 1906–May 19, 1984)
Poet, Journalist

In his poetry, Sir John Betjeman combined traditional forms with modern subject matter, creating poems that are at times sentimental and nostalgic and at times mildly satirical. He is chiefly remembered for verse rich with the images he admired—the landscape and topography of England's towns and countrysides as well as the ritual and customs of the Anglican Church—and the musical quality he created with his manipulation of meter and rhyme, which, combined with his enormous popularity during his lifetime, led to his appointment as poet laureate in 1972.

Betjeman was the only child of a successful businessman and his wife, a dedicated Christian Scientist. His father's

family boasted a long line of inventors, and his grandfather's invention of the Tantalus proved particularly profitable. This tendency did not manifest itself in Betjeman, who disappointed his father when he refused to involve himself in the family business. His childhood was relatively tranquil until his parents hired a cruel nurse to care for him, who, according to Betjeman, inflicted permanent damage to his psyche with her stories and threats of hell.

At the Highgate Junior School, Betjeman found himself a pupil of the American poet T. S. ELIOT, to whom he gave a volume of his early poetry. Eliot apparently never commented on the verses. From Highgate Betjeman moved on to the Dragon School in Oxford and later Marlborough College, where he gained the friendship of Louis MacNeice. After finishing his studies at Marlborough, he attended Magdalen College, Oxford, and studied under C S. Lewis. Betjeman's lackadaisical work habits and indulgence in sensual pleasure conflicted with the academic discipline Lewis demanded, and the two mutually disliked one another.

Betjeman began to write poetry in his youth. He worked to mold words to bring out sound, rhythm, and musicality using traditional form and meter. Frequent excursions around England, during which he carefully observed topography and architecture, provided him with the many images of railways, towns, and countrysides that recur throughout his poetry. Although he was never an outstanding student, he devoured books of poetry and literature and involved himself in Oxford's literary scene.

Another important influence on Betjeman's verse was his reception into the Anglican Church, to which he grew increasingly devoted with age. Betjeman counted among his friends the staunchly Catholic Evelyn Waugh, who tried his best to convert him. Waugh did not shake Betjeman's devotion, but he was more successful with Betjeman's wife, the independent and multitalented Penelope Hester Chetwode. Betjeman's stormy marriage to her eventually broke up.

After working briefly as a cricket master, Betjeman took a job writing for the *Architectural Review* in 1931. Throughout the decade, he continued to work as a journalist. Betjeman's first books of poetry, *Mount Zion* (1933) and *Continual Dew* (1937) are his least serious works. Some of the poems amount to mild satires of middle-class attitudes and behaviors, while others evoke his fascination with the customs of the church.

Old Lights for New Chancels (1940) and *New Bats in Old Belfries* (1945) are notable for their evocations of the English landscape—towns, railways, chapels, and rural settings. Some of the poems are religious in nature and reflect Betjeman's continual preoccupation with death, but they lack any strong philosophical attitude.

In his poems, Betjeman is sentimental about the old, dying order giving way to modern society. "Middlesex," part of *A Few Late Chrysanthemums* (1954), which many critics consider his finest volume of verse, mourns the proliferation of suburbs that destroy the countryside. Death is again a repeated theme in the collection, and in particular Betjeman's own sense of guilt stemming from his father's death. His later volumes of poetry include *Collected Poems* (1958), *High and Low* (1966), *A Nip in the Air* (1974), *Church Poems* (1981), and *Uncollected Poems* (1982). *Summoned by Bells* (1960), his autobiography in blank verse, treats his life from his childhood to his days at Oxford.

In addition to poetry, Betjeman wrote extensively on architecture, travel, and topography. His first book on architecture, *Ghastly Good Taste*, was published in 1933, and among his others is *A Pictorial History of English Architecture* (1972). *Vintage London* (1942), *English Cities and Small Towns* (1943), the *Collins Guide to English Parish Churches*, *First and Last Loves* (1952), *London's Historic Railway Stations* (1972), and a number of travel guides are among his other works.

Critical assessment of his works has generally held the collections of the 1940s and 1950s in highest regard. If he did not capture the universal admiration of critics in his later life, he found immense popularity with the English public and became a popular television personality in England. His charming personality off the air was marked by a number of odd quirks, among which was his lifelong attachment to his childhood teddy bear, Archibald. He was knighted in 1969 and in 1972 succeeded CECIL DAY-LEWIS as poet laureate.

BIBLIOGRAPHY

Taylor-Martin, Patrick, *John Betjeman: His Life and Work*, 1983.

Bing, Rudolf

(January 9, 1902–September 2, 1997)
Impresario

Often described as "autocratic" and "imperious," Sir Rudolf Franz Josef Bing was the general manager of New York's Metropolitan Opera from 1950 to 1972. Under Bing's management, the Met grew into one of the most internationally prestigious opera houses and attracted top stars from all over the world.

Bing was born in Vienna, and his father was a successful Austrian industrialist. At home he was exposed to musical influences, and as an adolescent he nursed ambitions to sing. Bing took voice lessons and later attended the University of Vienna. He found his calling, however, when he went to work for a bookstore. When the store expanded its sphere of operation to include concert and opera management, Bing became involved in the business that was to become his career.

In 1927 Bing moved to Berlin and began working for various agencies casting singers for operas. With Carl Ebert, he managed the Charlottenberg Opera in Berlin (1931). When the rise of National Socialism forced him from Germany, Bing settled in England and in 1935 was given the post of general manager at the Glyndebourne Opera Company. During World War II he worked in a department store.

Following the war (1947), Bing helped found the Edinburgh Festival, which afterward grew into a successful and popular annual music event. In 1950 he became general manager at the Met, where his controversial reign lasted more than two decades. As a manager Bing was uncompromising and involved himself in every aspect of the theater's operation—securing performers and conductors, choosing the shows, and overseeing with meticulous care the costumes and scenery.

Bing was notorious for his high-profile feuds with soprano Maria Callas (whom he fired in 1968) as well as with many other figures, including the conductor George Szell and the Danish tenor Lauritz Melchior. On the other hand, it was Bing who broke the long-standing racial barrier, when he secured the African-

American contralto Marian Anderson for the role of Ulrica in *Un ballo in maschera* in 1955. While under Bing's management, the theater moved from Thirty-ninth Street to the Lincoln Center in 1966.

Under Bing's leadership, the Met attracted the world's most renowned opera stars and conductors,— including singers ELISABETH SCHWARZKOPF, Callas, RENATA TEBALDI, JOAN SUTHERLAND and conductors HERBERT VON KARAJAN, GEORG SOLTI, and Leonard Bernstein. He was sometimes criticized for staging too many Italian romantic operas and too few modern works, but he knew what the audience liked. Prior to his departure from the Met, he appointed James Levine, who had debuted as a conductor at the Met in 1971, principal conductor. Bing was knighted in 1971 and published two memoirs, *5,000 Nights at* *the Opera* (1972) and *A Knight at the Opera* (1981).

Although Bing lived to the age of 95, the last fifteen years of his life were tragic ones. Following his wife's death in 1983, his mental health deteriorated. Suffering from Alzheimer's disease, he married a younger widow with a history of mental illness and began giving her large sums of money. In 1987 his guardian Paul Guth succeeded in having him declared incompetent and freezing his assets, and his marriage was annulled because he could not remember having wed his bride. He died of respiratory failure in 1997.

BIBLIOGRAPHY

Bing, Sir Rudolf, *5,000 Nights at the Opera*, 1972; Bing, Sir Rudolf, *A Knight at the Opera*, 1981.

Blackburn, Thomas

(February 10, 1916–August 13, 1977)
Poet, Novelist, Playwright, Teacher, Critic

Thomas Blackburn's early volumes of poetry, published during the 1950s, coincided with the emergence of poets such as KINGSLEY AMIS and JOHN WAIN, who were seen by critics as belonging to a group dubbed "The Movement," but Blackburn did not follow them in their plainspoken style and avoidance of metaphor. Influenced by the Irish poet WILLIAM BUTLER YEATS, Blackburn used strong imagery derived from legends and myths in his early works. His later poetry was intensely personal and addressed his own experiences and dilemmas.

Blackburn was born in Hensingham, Cumbria, England. His father, a rigid and excessively strict clergyman, had a profound impact on Blackburn's psychology. After studying at a public school, he began to study law at the University of Cambridge. Law was his father's choice, but it did not suit Blackburn. He turned to alcohol, an addiction that would trouble him for the rest of his life, and suffered a nervous breakdown.

As part of his recovery, Blackburn underwent psychoanalysis. In addition to pursuing an interest in Freud and Jung, he devoured the writings of poets and philosophers from Friedrich Nietzsche to William Blake. Upon his recovery, he studied English at the University of Durham, from which he graduated in 1940. His first marriage to Joan Arnold did not last, and in 1945 he married the painter Rosalie de Méric. During World War II, Blackburn, a pacifist, worked for the London Stretcher Party and elsewhere.

Blackburn's first major volume of poetry, *The Holy Stone*, was published in 1954, along with several others during that decade. As mentioned above, his early poetry shows the heavy influence of Yeats, and much of it employs mythological imagery and traditional form. Blackburn's 1960 poem "The Sediment" won a Guinness Award. Later collections include *A Smell of Burning* (1961), *A Breathing Space* (1964), and *Selected Poems* (1976).

For much of his adult life, Blackburn taught at various schools around England—Marylebone Grammar School in London, the University of Leeds, the College of St. Mark and St. John, Chelsea,

and Whitelands College, Putney—and was noted for his enthusiastic teaching style. In his later life, Blackburn maintained he had experienced a series of visions and dreams. A significant experience occurred in a Welsh cottage, and after the vision he believed he had died. *Post Mortem* (1977) was written after this occasion. The posthumous *Bread for the Winter Birds* followed in 1980.

Among Blackburn's other works are the radio play *A Place of Meeting*, produced by the British Broadcasting Corporation in 1956; *Robert Browning* (1967); *The Price of an Eye* (1961), a collection of criticism; the musical drama *The Judas Tree* (1967), with music by Peter Dickinson; his autobiography, *A Clip of Steel* (1969); and the novel *Feast for the Wolf* (1971).

BIBLIOGRAPHY

Blackburn, Thomas, *A Clip of Steel: A Picaresque Autobiography*, 1969; MacVean, Jean, ed., *The Adjacent Kingdom: Collected Last Poems*, 1988.

Blackwood, Algernon

(March 14, 1869–December 10, 1951)
Novelist, Short-Story Writer, Writer of Children's Books

Algernon Henry Blackwood's mysterious tales of the supernatural and occult have made him something of a cult figure among readers of fantasy and horror fiction. His high-impact, suspenseful, and emotional tales influenced other writers in the genre, such as the American H. P. Lovecraft. In the later years of his life, he became a popular storyteller in British Broadcasting Corporation (BBC) radio and television.

Blackwood was born into an upper-class family in Shooters Hill, Kent, England. When he was a child, the family moved to Crayford, which provided settings for some of his stories.

The family moved again to a house near Beckenham, also in Kent. Blackwood's father, Sir Arthur Blackwood, was the dominant influence on his young life. The elder Blackwood was Permanent Secretary of the Post Office and had experienced a profound religious conversion after fighting in the Crimean War. A devout Christian and lay preacher, he first stimulated his son's interest in spirituality, though his son's spirituality did not take a direction of which he approved. The younger Blackwood's imagination was further fired by his father's love of the outdoors, travel, and telling ghost stories.

Education was less pleasant for Blackwood. He attended a series of rigid private schools, one of which was the School of the Moravian Brotherhood at Köningsfeld in the Black Forest region of Germany, another locale that later provided settings for his fiction. In 1888 he entered the University of Edinburgh to study agriculture in hopes of establishing himself as a farmer. However, agriculture failed to capture his interest, and he preferred to spend his time investigating spiritualism. When he was twenty, he went to Canada, where he wrote for the *Canadian Methodist Magazine*.

Blackwood's interest in spiritualism began with the discovery of Patanjali's *Yoga Aphorisms* among his father's books. For the elder Blackwood, the book was evidence of a disturbing trend, but his son was impressed when he read it. Blackwood read the writings of Madame Blavatsky and became a theosophist. He also met the psychic researcher Frank Podmore and with him investigated his first haunted house. It was an interest for the rest of his life, and his stories, such as "The Empty House," include many haunted-house tales.

By 1890 Blackwood had abandoned his formal studies and moved to Canada, where he wrote for the theosophist magazine *Lucifer* and helped found the Theosophical Society's branch in Toronto. When a farm venture failed, he moved to New York and worked as a reporter. A number of experiences there, including interviews with criminals and experimentation with morphine, contributed to his future work. After a brief interlude searching for gold in Minnesota, Blackwood returned to New York and worked for the *New York Times*.

Blackwood's North American days, recounted in his *Episodes Before Thirty* (1923), came to an end when he returned to England in 1899 and helped establish a dried milk company. His first book of short stories, *The Empty House* (1906), received widespread critical acclaim. The second volume, *The Listener* (1907), contains one of his most famous stories, "The Willows." *John Silence* (1908) introduced his most popular character, the psychic detective of the title, and was his most successful volume up to that date.

Later collections include *The Lost Valley* (1910); *Pan's Garden: A Volume of Nature Stories* (1912); *Incredible Adventures* (1914), containing the novellas "A Descent Into Egypt," "The Regeneration of Lord Ernie," and "The Damned," as well as two other stories; *The Wolves of God, And Other Fey Stories* (1921); *Tongues of Fire and Other Sketches* (1924); and *Shocks* (1935).

For a time Blackwood was a member of the Hermetic Order of the Golden Dawn, stimulus for his novel *The Human Chord* (1910). In it, Robert Spinrobin is working for the retired minister Philip Skale. Skale has a group of people who, with training, hope to be able to speak the name of Jehovah and gain power over Him. Blackwood also developed a firm belief in past lives, and he later came to believe that he was a reincarnated American Indian. Reincarnation and past lives form the primary focus of two novels published in 1916, *Julius Le Vallon: An Episode* (1916) and *The Wave: An Egyptian Aftermath* (1916) as well as *Karma: A Reincarnation Play* (1918).

During World War I, Blackwood wrote war propaganda stories and worked as a British spy in Switzerland. He traveled widely around Europe and continued his inquiries into mystical matters, visiting the mystic George Ivanovitch Gurdjieff (1872–1949) in France in the 1920s. Among Blackwood's novels, *The Centaur* (1911), about the spiritual quest of the reporter O'Malley, is one of his most popular and was his own favorite. This novel was heavily influenced by the theories of the German psychologist and physicist Gustav Fechner (1801–1887). Others include *Jimbo: A Fantasy* (1909); *The Education of Uncle Paul* (1909); *A Prisoner in Fairyland* (1913); *The Extra Day* (1915); *The Garden of Survival* (1917); *The Promise of Air* (1918); *The Bright Messenger* (1921), sequel to *Julius Le Vallon;* and *Dudley and Gilderoy: A Nonsense* (1929).

Blackwood wrote less frequently in his later years but gained popularity for the stories he read on BBC radio and television productions. His other works include children's books, such as *Sambo and Snitch* (1927), *Mr. Cupboard* (1928), and *The Fruit Stoners* (1934), as well as plays.

BIBLIOGRAPHY

Ashley, Mike, *Algernon Blackwood: A Bio-Bibliography*, 1987.

Blais, Marie-Claire

(October 5, 1939–)
Novelist, Poet, Playwright

The Quebec-born novelist Marie-Claire Blais conveys in her work a pessimistic view of contemporary violence and social oppression, the forces that shape her characters and determine their destinies. She often sets her novels in rural and urban Quebec but has also used American and French backdrops for her work. She is the first novelist to write so intensely of the "dark side" of modern life in Quebec.

Blais was born in Quebec City, Quebec, Canada, and was the eldest of five children. Her father was an engineer, but the large family strained his income. As a young child Blais nursed an ambition to write, beginning her first novel at the age of nine. She was sent to secondary school at the Convent of St. Roch but quit to go to work. For several years Blais worked in a series of secretarial jobs.

Her break as a writer came as a result of taking night classes at Laval University, where she met two figures who would prove important to the development of her career. The first of these was literature professor Jeanne Lapointe, who took a special interest in promoting and encouraging female authors. Father Georges-Henri-Lévesque, who founded the School of Social Sciences at Laval, was directly responsible for selling Blais's first novel to a publisher. The resulting work, *La belle bête* (*Mad Shadows*), appeared in 1959 and attracted the attention of several prominent critics.

Mad Shadows tells of contemporary violence and social oppression, the principal concern in nearly all the rest of her writing. This particular story is a sordid tale of jealousy, murder, and violence that unfolds on a farm in rural Quebec. There live the widowed Louise and her two children, the intelligent but unattractive Isabelle-Marie and her handsome but dull brother Patrice. Isabelle-Marie, driven by the rejection she encounters because of her looks and jealous of their mother's preference for Patrice, is determined to destroy him, first by starving him and then by plunging his attractive face into boiling water. She falls in love with a blind neighbor, who also rejects her when he recovers his sight. Eventually she destroys the sources of her oppression—murdering her mother, burning the farm, driving her brother to suicide, and killing herself.

Having moved to Montreal the same year she finished *Mad Shadows*, Blais followed with the stories *Tête blanche* (1960) and *Le jour est noir* (1962; *The Day Is Dark*). She received a grant to study in France (1961) and, with the encouragement of critic Edmund Wilson, a Guggenheim Fellowship that enabled her to study in the United States. For the rest of the decade she lived on Cape Cod, where she formed friendships with the antiwar activist Barbara Deming and the artist Mary Meigs. Under Deming's influence, Blais grew increasingly concerned with the United States's involvement in the Vietnam War.

Une saison dans la vie d'Emmanuel (1965; *A Season in the Life of Emmanuel*), perhaps Blais's best-known work, depicts the deaths of the children in a large Quebec farming family. Central to the story is the tragic and symbolic fate of the aspiring poet Jean Le Maigre, one of the children, who is sent to a monastery, contracts tuberculosis, and dies. *David Sterne* (1967), her next novel, unfolds amidst the climate of the Vietnam War and reflects Blais's antiwar sentiment more strongly than any of her other work.

Blais left Cape Cod in 1969 and moved to France with Meigs. A year earlier she had begun her semiautobiographical trilogy—*Manuscrits de Pauline Archange* (1968; *Manuscripts of Pauline Archange*), *Vivre! Vivre!* (1969; *To Live! To Live!*), and *Les Apparences* (1970; *The Appearances*), published collectively in English as *The Manuscripts of Pauline Archange* (1970). Like Blais, the protagonist is a girl who overcomes her social circumstances in Quebec and becomes a successful writer.

Several other novels followed before she returned to Quebec in 1975, including *Le Loup* (1972; *The Wolf*), *Un Joualonais sa Joualonie* (1973; *St. Lawrence Blues*), and *Fièvre et autres textes dramatiques* (1974; *Fever and Other Dramatic Texts*). In *Une liason parisienne* (1976) Blais took aim at Paris literary culture. *Le sourd dans la ville* (1979; *Deaf to the City*), among her more successful novels, was later adapted for film by Mireille Dansereau.

With *Pierre, ou la guerre du printemps 81* (1984; *Pierre, or the War of the Spring of 1981*), Blais attempted to reconstruct her vision of the twentieth-century climate of violence in the mind of protagonist Pierre, who is a clear product of his surroundings. As an adolescent Pierre joins a motorcycle gang. Blais reveals his consciousness through interior monologue largely constructed from news snippets she spent months gathering. In two novels, *L'Nuits de l'Underground* (1978; *Underground Nights*) and *L'ange de la solitude* (1989; *The Angel of Solitude*), Blais has explored lesbian themes.

L'exécution (1968; *The Execution*), staged at the Montreal at the Théâtre du Rideau Vert, was the first major production of Blais's plays. A two-act study of violence and the corrupting influence of power, the story concerns three boys who murder a schoolmate. Her other dramatic works include *L'océan* (1977; *The Ocean*); *Sommeil d'hiver* (1984; *Sleep of Winter*); and *L'ile* (1988; *The Island*).

Blais's other novels include *L'insoumise* (1966; *The Fugitive*) and *Visions d'Anna* (1980). Her autobiographical *Parcours d'un écrivain: Notes américaines*, appeared in 1993.

BIBLIOGRAPHY

Green, Mary Jean, *Marie-Claire Blais*, 1995.

Blasco Ibáñez, Vicente

(January 29, 1867–January 28, 1928)
Novelist, Essayist, Playwright, Politician, Short-Story Writer

The Spanish author and member of the Generation of '98 Vicente Blasco Ibáñez is most famous for his novel *The Four Horsemen of the Apocalypse*. In addition to his prolific literary output, Blasco Ibáñez was a politician, editor, agitator, and influential orator in his lifetime.

Blasco Ibáñez was born in Valencia, Spain, to Aragonese parents who owned a small grocery store. He studied at the Colegio Levantino and later at the University of Valencia, where he earned a law degree. In his youth he loved to tell stories and write, and he completed his first novel at the age of 14. At age 16 he moved to Madrid, and until 1892 he wrote numerous romance novels.

Blasco Ibáñez involved himself heavily in politics from the time he was a teenager. He was a born leader, often speaking before political groups in Madrid and Valencia and stirring protests on the university campus. For the duration of his life he remained staunchly antimonarchist, and his vocal advocacy of a Spanish republic repeatedly landed him in jail and sent him into exile. He suffered injuries in several duels over political issues.

In 1890 Blasco Ibáñez was exiled to Paris, where he wrote his *History of the Spanish Revolution* (1870–1874). Having returned to Spain the following year, he married his cousin María Blasco del Cacho and founded the Republican political paper *El Pueblo*. In 1898 he was elected to the first of six terms in the Spanish Parliament as a representative of the Republican Party.

Blasco Ibáñez's novels fall into several categories. The early novels are set in his native Valencia, depict the lives of the middle and lower classes, and employ elements of Naturalism and Symbolism. His first major work in this style is *Rice and a Carriage* (1894). In *Among the Orange Trees* (1900), the weak-willed Rafael replaces his father in the legislature after the latter's death. While engaged to another woman, he falls in love with the experienced and world-weary Leonora, generating a scandal that forces them to flee the area. They are pursued by Don Andrés, who convinces Brull to return to his respectable life and marry a woman he does not love.

Reeds and Mud (1902), another major "Valencia" novel, is set around an inhospitable lake. The story revolves around the family of the veteran fisherman Tío Paloma. Paloma, a hardworking and proud man, tries to train his grandson, Tonet, to fish. Tonet, however, is lazy and prefers to indulge in sensual pleasure. He has an ongoing affair with Neleta, who marries a tavern owner in his absence. Upon her husband's death, Neleta inherits his money on the condition that she remain single, but she is pregnant with Tonet's baby. After giving birth to the child in secret, Tonet plans to abandon the baby on a doorstep but instead throws the child into the lake. Tonet's dog retrieves the corpse, and Tonet commits suicide. Other Valencia novels include *The Mayflower* (1895), *The Cabin* (1898), and *Sónnica the Courtesan* (1901).

Beginning with *The Cathedral* (1903), Blasco Ibáñez incorporated strong elements of social and religious protest and set his novels outside of Valencia. He used characters to relate his own philos-ophy in a didactic manner, as in *The Cathedral*'s Gabriel Luna. Luna, an atheist and antimonarchist, returns to Toledo after a life of turmoil. When he tries to convert others to his political and religious ideas, they misinterpret his intentions and plan to steal jewelry from the cathedral. One of them kills Gabriel when he tries to stop them. *The Intruder* (1904), *The Wine Cellar* (1905), and *The Horde* (1905) also belong to this group of novels.

The Naked Maja (1906) begins Blasco Ibáñez's series of psychological novels. One of his most noteworthy works of this period is *Blood and Sand* (1908). The subject of the psychological study is Juan Gallardo, a champion bullfighter whose bravado has elevated him from poverty to stardom. Gallardo, married to another woman, has an affair with Doña Sol, who proves to be the ruin of his career. When she leaves him the weakened Gallardo suffers a series of mishaps in the ring before a bull mortally wounds him.

Blasco Ibáñez lived in Paris during World War I. There he wrote a series of war novels, including his most famous work, *The Four Horsemen of the Apocalypse* (1916). The story takes place in France, and it and his other war novels reflect his strong support for the Allies in the war. The story served as the basis of a successful Hollywood film starring Rudolph Valentino. *The Argonots* (1914) and *Mare Nostrum* (1918) are also among his war novels.

Blasco Ibáñez's later novels include a number of works about Spain and Spanish figures, such as *The Pope of the Sea* (1925) and *At the Feet of Venus* (1926). His other works include *The Judge* (1894), his only play; the travel books *In the Land of Art* (1896), *Orient* (1907),

Argentina and Its Grandeurs (1910), and *A Novelist's Tour of the World* (1924–1925); the essay collection *Mexican Militarism* (1921); the short-story collections *Valencian Stories* (1896) and *The Condemned Woman* (1908); *The Dead Command* (1909); *The Enemies of Women* (1919); *Alfonso XIII Unmasked* (1924); *In Search of the Great Khan* (1929); *The Knight of the Virgin* (1929); and *The Phantom with Wings of Gold* (1930). He became a member of the French Legion of Honor in 1906 and was awarded an honorary doctorate from George Washington University in 1919.

BIBLIOGRAPHY

Day, A. Grove, and Knowlton, Edgar C., *V. Blasco Ibáñez*, 1972.

Bliss, Arthur

(August 2, 1891–March 27, 1975)
Composer

A leading English composer, Sir Arthur Edward Drummond Bliss, to give him his title and his full name, absorbed the influences of the avant-garde French composers in his early works but was also influenced by the British composer EDWARD ELGAR. Bliss, noted for his experimental combination of music and voice, produced a varied output including choral symphonies, operas, cantatas, ballet music, and film scores.

Bliss was born in London and inherited the love his mother—who died when he was four—had of music and the piano. His father, an American with many relations in New England, sent him to school as a young boy and enrolled him in dancing lessons with a Mrs. Wordsworth. Bliss studied at the preparatory school of Bilton Grange, followed by the Rugby School. At the latter he developed a love for the music of Elgar, then England's leading composer, and visited him on several occasions.

Following his graduation from Rugby in 1909, Bliss continued to study the piano and began to play the viola. From 1910 to 1913 he studied music at Cam-

Arthur Bliss (Ann Ronan/Image Select)

bridge, and in 1913–1914 he attended the Royal College of Music, where he studied under Charles Villiers Stanford. Service in World War I interrupted Bliss's music career, and his brother was killed in combat. Following the war Bliss joined the Catholic Church, and he married Trudy Hoffmann in the United States in the 1920s.

Bliss began to compose in earnest after the war, pursuing an experimental style in works such as *Rhapsody* (1919), for solo voices and chamber ensemble, *Madam Noy* (1920), which he dubbed "a Witchery Song," and *Rout* (1920), for chamber orchestra and voice. Other early works include his *Mêlée Fantasque* (1921), *Introduction and Allegro* (1926), and *Hymn to Apollo* (1926). In *A Colour Symphony* (1922; revised 1932), Bliss devised the four movements to suggest the colors purple, red, blue, and green.

In 1930 Bliss completed a major choral symphony, *Morning Heroes* (1930), based on the theme of war in general and World War I specifically. In the first movement, a soldier prepares to leave his home to go to war. The second movement describes the arming of a city as war approaches. In the third movement, Bliss addresses the thoughts and emotions of a soldier and the wife he has left. The final two parts of *Morning Heroes* depict battle scenes and World War I, incorporating texts by the poet WILFRED OWEN.

In 1935 Bliss finished the first of three film scores, *Things to Come* (1935; a film based on H. G. WELLS's novel). *Men of Two Worlds* and *Welcome the Queen* followed in 1945 and 1954. Bliss also composed music for theatrical productions such as *As You Like It* and *The Tempest*. Bliss's full-length opera *The Olympians* (1945), a collaborative effort with J. B. PRIESTLEY, was produced by PETER BROOK in 1949 at Covent Garden. He wrote numerous cantatas, including *The Beatitudes* (1962), for the opening of the cathedral at Coventry; *Mary of Magdala* (1963); *The Golden Cantata*, written for the Cambridge Quincentenary in 1963; *The World is Charged with the Grandeur of God* (1969); and *Shield of Faith* (1974).

Ninette de Valois, the choreographer, dancer, and founder of the Royal Ballet, choreographed the first of Bliss's ballets, *Checkmate* (1937), an allegorical game of chess. The production featured an all-star cast, with FREDERICK ASHTON as Death, ROBERT MURRAY HELPMANN as the Red King, and MARGOT FONTEYN as the leader of the Black Pawns. Helpmann choreographed two additional ballets by Bliss, *Miracle in the Gorbals* (1944) and *Adam Zero* (1946). The latter Bliss designed as an allegory of the stages of life.

In his later work, Bliss was less daring with his musical experimentation. Among his more conservative compositions are *Conversations* for chamber orchestra (1920); quintets for oboe (1927) and for clarinet and strings (1932); the pastoral *Lie Strewn the White Flocks* (1929); *Music for Strings* (1935); a Piano Concerto (1938); *Meditations on a Theme by John Blow* (1955); *The Lady of Shallot* (1958); *Tobias and the Angel* (1960), a television opera adapted from the apocryphal book of Tobit; and the song cycle *Angels of the Mind* (1968), one of numerous works that incorporated the poetry of Kathleen Raine.

Bliss was knighted in 1950 and three years later became Master of the Queen's Music, a position in which he wrote ceremonial music. In 1963 he received the Gold Medal from the Royal Philharmonic Society.

BIBLIOGRAPHY

Bliss, Arthur, *As I Remember*, 1989; Craggs, Stewart R., *Arthur Bliss: A Sourcebook*, 1996.

Blok, Alexander

(November 28, 1880–August 7, 1921)
Poet, Dramatist

A principal exponent of Symbolism in Russia before the 1917 revolution, Aleksander Aleksandrovich Blok (to give him his full Russian name) established himself as his country's leading Symbolist poet. He was a contemporary of the Acmeist poets ANNA AKHMATOVA and OSIP MANDELSTAM, who rejected the lyrical, metaphorical qualities of Symbolists like Blok in favor of plainspoken verse. Blok later supported the Bolshevik uprising and devoted his efforts to writing politically and socially oriented poetry.

Blok was born into a wealthy, cultivated family in St. Petersburg, Russia. His father was a law professor of German (Holstein) ancestry at the University of Warsaw and separated from his mother before he was born. Blok went to live with his mother's family, which was full of distinguished scientists and intellectuals. At the age of five he began to write his own verse. Blok attended gymnasium (high school) before entering the University of St. Petersburg to study law. He later abandoned law and earned a degree in philology in 1906.

The primary influences on Blok's early poetry were the image of the "Eternal Feminine" or "Sophia" principle propounded by the poet Vladimir Solovyov (1853–1900) and the poetry of the French Symbolists, such as Paul Verlaine. The heavenly Sophia, whom Solovyov viewed as the embodiment of eternal divine wisdom and spiritual beauty, is the central figure in his first volume *Stikhi o prekrasnoy dame* (1904; *Songs to the Beautiful Lady*).

In 1903 Blok married Liubov Mendeleyeva, an actress and the daughter of the chemist D. I. Mendeleyev. Initially a happy union, the marriage inspired much of his verse from the period, verse in which Liubov came to embody the Lady Beautiful. Blok's other principal concerns were the musicality and rhythm he worked feverishly to perfect.

The focus of Blok's poetry, however, soon turned to social ills, political upheaval, human suffering, and Russia's role in the future of the world. *Neznakomka* (1906; *The Unknown Woman*) retained the mystical quality of *Verses About the Lady Beautiful*, but *Gorod* (1904–1908; *The City*) and *Snezhnaya Maska* (1907; *Mask of Snow*) addressed his new concerns. Blok wrote many poems full of religious imagery during a visit to Italy in 1909.

Although not a political activist, Blok embraced the cause of the Bolsheviks and supported the 1917 uprising. His support for the Bolsheviks amounted to a rejection of his own upper-class background, but nevertheless the peasants on the family estate burned and destroyed his property. Blok went to work for the new Bolshevik government as an editor and writer. Much to his dismay, the authorities instructed him to write propagandistic pieces and began to attack his poetry. True, he was given the congenial task of editing the works of Mikhail Lermontov (1814–1841), but then the authorities rejected his introduction to them, and he was further discouraged.

Although rife with despair, his later poetry retains flickers of hope. *Rodina* (1907–1916; *Homeland*) and *Skify* (1918; *Scythians*) are political works, the latter depicting Russia's experiment in Communism as a beacon of hope for the rest of the world. Blok seemed to view the violence of the revolution as a necessary means to a good end in the ballad *Dvenadtsat* (1918; *The Twelve*, 1920). The poem depicts the mission of twelve Red Army men: "To get the bourgeoisie / We'll start a fire, a worldwide fire, and drench it in blood. / The good Lord bless us!"

Blok's disillusionment with the Bolshevik system and the vision of disintegration that accompanied it manifest themselves in his latest works, among which is the narrative poem *Vozmezdiye* (1910–1921; *Retribution*). Blok also wrote plays. Destitute and nearly starving, he fell ill and died in 1921.

BIBLIOGRAPHY

Chukovskii, Kornei, *Alexander Blok as Man and Poet*, 1982; Forsyth, James, *Listening to the Wind: An Introduction to Alexander Blok*, 1977; Vogel, Lucy E., *Alexander Blok: The Journey to Italy*, 1973.

Boccioni, Umberto

(October 19, 1882–August 16, 1916)
Painter, Sculptor, Graphic Artist

While F. T. MARINETTI led Italy's Futurist movement in the written word, Umberto Boccioni was Futurism's foremost visual artist. Boccioni and the Futurists were primarily concerned with conveying the motion, velocity, and dynamism of the modern age. In accordance with these ideals, Boccioni's Futurist paintings and sculptures depict violent, dynamic, and abstract forms in vivid color.

Boccioni was born in Reggio di Calabria, Italy. His father worked for the government and frequently moved the family around, resulting in an erratic early education for Boccioni. During his youth Boccioni developed a love for literature. Sometime around 1898 he moved to Rome, where he studied under the portraitist Giacomo Balla (1871–1958). Balla worked in the style of the Divisionists, who, like the Pointillists of France, applied small strokes of pure pigment to the canvas that when viewed from a distance seem to combine.

From Balla Boccioni acquired his predilection for using complementary colors. At this time he painted mostly

Untitled Futurist painting by Umberto Boccioni (Ann Ronan/Image Select)

semirealistic landscapes and portraits, such as his *Campagna romana* (1903; *Roman Landscape*), *Self Portrait* (1905), and numerous portraits of women. From 1903 to 1906 he exhibited with the Società degli Amatori e Cultori. His paintings also appeared in exhibitions with a group calling themselves the "Salon des Refusés," made up of artists whose paintings had been rejected for the Società's exhibitions.

Not fully satisfied with Balla's style, Boccioni sought new directions in his art. By 1907 he was using bolder color and had moved to Venice, where he fell under the influence of the more theoretical Divisionism embraced by Gaetano Previati

(1852–1920). The avant-garde artistic trends in Europe—Expressionism, Symbolism, and Cubism—also interested Boccioni, and under their influence he began to experiment with his style. Works such as *Mourning* (1910) belong to this experimental period, during which he began to use distorted forms and more violent colors. The same year, Boccioni exhibited more than forty of his creations in Venice.

In 1910 Boccioni met Marinetti, and with others such as Luigi Russolo and Carlo Carrà he continued to formulate the ideals of the Futurist movement that Marinetti had already begun. After Marinetti's *Futurist Manifesto* (1909), which appealed to literary concerns, Boccioni signed his name to the provocative *Manifesto of the Futurist Painters* (1910), which called for a destruction of the art of the past. Its more theoretical sequel, *Technical Manifesto of the Futurist Painters* (1910), insisted that "motion and light destroy the material nature and look of solid bodies." The Futurist artists called for depictions of technology, machinery, and other representations of modern society, in dynamic and violent forms.

Riot in the Gallery (1909), a depiction of chaos and mayhem, had already demonstrated Boccioni's new move toward dynamic motion and light. *The City Rises* (1910–1911) is a violent picture with the barely recognizable forms of humans and horses in frenzied motion. The composer and pianist Feruccio Busoni, whose portrait Boccioni painted in 1916, later purchased *The City Rises* in London.

A disgruntled observer vandalized Boccioni's violently colored *The Laugh* (1911) at a Milan exhibition. His was not the only criticism of the new Futurist aesthetic. Ardengo Soffici vehemently attacked the Futurists in the Florence review *La Voce*, after which Boccioni provoked a physical fight with him.

Undaunted by criticism, Marinetti and the Futurists sought to extend Futurism to the rest of Europe. Boccioni and others visited France in 1911 and held an unsuccessful exhibition in Paris the same year. He took from Paris a deeper appreciation of Picasso's Cubism, which influenced his later paintings to a certain extent. The Futurists subsequently exhibited in most of Europe's major cities.

Boccioni's other works include his *States of Mind* (1911–1912), which depicts dynamic swirls and planes of deep blue-greens and other vibrant colors; *Elasticity* (1912); *Abstract Dimensions* (1912); *Dynamism of a Cyclist* (1913); and his most famous work, *Unique Forms of Continuity in Space* (1913). All of these works demonstrate his concern with complementary colors, intersection of force lines and planes, and portrayal of velocity and motion.

Boccioni extended his painting theories to sculpture. In 1912 he published the *Manifesto of Futurist Sculpture*, in which he advocated the combination of glass, wood, electric lights, cement, and other unconventional materials. He also sought to combine multiple subjects into single sculptures, as in his *Head + House + Light* (1912). *Development of a Bottle in Space* (1913), a bronze sculpture, attempts to shows the emergence of a bottle. A number of his sculptures were exhibited in Paris in 1913.

Futurist theorists eventually extended their ideas to all aspects of the culture, including politics. Like Marinetti, Boccioni embraced an extreme nationalism that glorified war and violence. He volunteered to fight in World War I and lost his life after falling off a horse in 1916. His other works include etchings and the book *Pittura, scultura futuriste* (1914; *Futurist Painting and Sculpture*).

BIBLIOGRAPHY

Coen, Ester, *Umberto Boccioni*, 1988; Golding, John, *Boccioni's Unique Forms of Continuity in Space*, 1972; Taylor, Joshua Charles, *The Graphic Work of Umberto Boccioni*, 1961.

Bonnard, Pierre

(October 3, 1867–January 23, 1947)
Painter, Graphic Artist, Illustrator

Pierre Eugène Frédéric Bonnard, known for his brilliantly colored, luminous paintings, got his start as an artist with a group of painters known as the Nabis (see MAURICE DENIS), who placed heavy emphasis on decorative elements and used flat areas of color and curvilinear forms. In the early 1900s he was associated with *Intimisme*, a style so named because its adherents painted intimate domestic scenes.

Bonnard was born in Fontenay-aux-Roses, France. He entered school in 1877 and studied at two different lycées. According to the wishes of his practically-minded father, he studied law and went to work in a government office in 1888. While working there, he attended the École des Beaux-Arts, and in 1889 he achieved his first success in the realm of art when he sold a poster for La France Champagne.

Bonnard soon devoted himself to art, trying unsuccessfully for the Prix de Rome and then entering the Académie Julien. There he met Maurice Denis, ÉDOUARD VUILLARD, and others who would form the core of the Nabis during the 1890s. Denis, a devout Catholic and the leader of the group, saw his art from a religious perspective, but Bonnard's outlook was secular.

With the Nabis, nevertheless, Bonnard shared a devotion to the decorative arts and a style influenced by the sinuous lines of the Art Nouveau movement in Germany, and by the work of the French Postimpressionist Paul Gauguin. In 1890 Bonnard shared a studio with Denis, Vuillard, and later the artist Aurélien Lugné-Poë in Montmartre. Another influence on his work at this time was his interest in Japanese prints, evident in such works as *Partie de Croquet* (*Croquet Party*, 1892). He exhibited at the Salon des Indépendants in 1891; he was to show his work there often in the future. In addition to painting scenes from Montmartre and from everyday life, Bonnard created posters, stained glass, screens, and scenery for the theater.

Following their work with the Nabis, both Bonnard and Vuillard were associated with the Intimists, who focused on interpreting domestic interiors. Throughout his life, Bonnard's subject matter was confined to a handful of subjects—landscapes, still lifes, lighted domestic scenes (*The Dining Room*, 1913), and everyday scenes indoors and out. Oil lamps recur frequently, as in *La lampe*, 1895–1896, as do nudes on lavish beds (*Siesta—The Artist's Studio*, 1908–1910).

He contributed illustrations to many books and periodicals, including his brother-in-law Claude Terrasse's *Petites scènes familières* and *Petit solfège illustré* (1893), the avant-garde review *La revue blanche*, the Symbolist poet Paul Verlaine's *Parallèlement* (1900), and an edition of Octave Mirbeau's *La628-E-8* (1908). The Paris art dealer Ambroise Vollard published his lithograph series *Quelques aspects de la vie de Paris* (*Aspects of Paris Life*, 1899).

The exploration of color and mood was Bonnard's principal focus as a painter. Many of his works are difficult to date due to his habit of returning to them over long periods of time to add color to the surface. In 1910 Bonnard, as many other painters had done, discovered the south of France and began to paint scenes from that sunlit area, such as his seascapes at Cannes and Saint-Tropez on the Riviera. From 1915 until the end of the 1920s he painted many nudes, including a long series of nudes in baths, among which is *La sortie de la baignoire* (*Getting Out of the Bath*, 1930). Self-portraits appeared from time to time as well, showing the artist with somber, serious expressions on his face. In 1925 he married his longtime model and companion Maria Boursin.

BIBLIOGRAPHY

Hyman, Timothy, *Bonnard*, 1998; Royal Academy of Arts, *Pierre Bonnard*, 1966; Watkins, Nicholas, *Bonnard*, 1994.

Borges, Jorge Luis

(August 24, 1899–June 14, 1986)
Poet, Short-Story Writer, Essayist, Teacher

The Argentinean short-story writer and poet Jorge Luis Borges introduced the Spanish literary style known as Ultraísmo to Latin American literature; he is best known, however, for the popular fantastic short stories he wrote in his later career, which made him one of Latin America's most beloved and widely read authors of the twentieth century.

Borges was born in Buenos Aires, Argentina, into a middle-class Argentinian family. His father's family had some British ancestry, and he had a long line of ancestors on his mother's side who had made names for themselves in Argentinian history. Borges learned both English and Spanish as a child. His father was a teacher with intellectual interests and an extensive library of English literature, which became the primary influence on Borges's career. Borges was tutored at home until he was nine and then attended a public school. Although he was a gifted student, his classmates ridiculed him and rendered his days as a student intolerable. In 1914 Borges went to Geneva to study at the Collège de Genève, where learned French, German, and Latin.

When Borges graduated in 1919 he moved with his family to Majorca, and then to Spain in 1920. In Spain he met ultraist writers, a group who used forceful, unconventional imagery and complex metrical schemes in their poetry. Borges returned to Buenos Aires in 1921 and, with other writers, founded the ultraist literary magazine *Prisma*. Although he would later reject the ultraists, his early poetry employed ultraist imagery. His first book of poetry, *Fervor of Buenos Aires* (1923), celebrated his native Buenos Aires. Other volumes soon followed, such as *The Moon Opposite* (1925) and *San Martin Notebook* (1929). Borges also wrote a number of essays, helped found several literary journals, and completed a biography of the poet Evaristo Carriego (1930).

A Universal History of Infamy (1935) collected his early short stories. Among them is "Streetcorner Man," one of his most popular early stories. A gang member, Juárez, is challenged to a duel and flees from his challenger, Francisco Real. Francisco dies from wounds in another duel, probably with the narrator, who is a friend of the dishonored Juárez's. At this point in his literary career, Borges followed fairly conventional narrative style and did not yet employ the complex symbolic language he used in his later stories.

In 1937, Borges, not yet successful enough to support himself with the earnings from his writing, took a position at the Miguel Cané Library, a job that he found thoroughly monotonous. His experiences at the library served as the basis of his short story "The Library of Babel" (1941) a nightmarish depiction of a sort of overwhelming universal library that appeared in his *Fictions* (1945).

In 1938, shortly after the death of his father, Borges scraped his head against a newly painted window. He suffered blood poisoning from the accident and nearly died. The hallucinations he experienced during his shaky recovery as well as his mother's reading aloud of C. S. LEWIS's *Out of the Silent Planet*, had a profound effect on his future stories, which began to take on a more fantastic atmosphere. A fictional account of the accident appears in Borges's short story "The South," also published in *Fictions*. In addition to the aftereffects of his accident, Borges continued to suffer from another physical ailment, a worsening hereditary blindness that had plagued his father. Nevertheless, during this time he cowrote a series of detective stories using the pseudonym H. Bustos Domecq. The stories appeared as *Six Problems for Don Isidro Parodi* (1942).

Borges became director of the National Library in 1955 and the following year became a professor of English and American literature at the University of Buenos Aires. Around the same time he lost nearly all of his sight and had to dictate his writings, which began again to include poetry, to others. Still a relatively unknown writer, he won the Formentor Prize in 1961 (along with the Irish dramatist SAMUEL BECKETT), giving him his first international fame.

Among Borges's later stories, "The God's Script," published in *The Aleph* (1949), is a fine example of the fantastic nature of his stories. In the story, a Mayan priest is jailed by a Spanish conquistador. With a jaguar in the cell beside him, the priest tries to figure out why his god (the Wheel, or the universe) has been defeated. As he languishes in his cell, he has a vision and is united with the god. He finally gains the ability to read a secret inscription on the jaguar's skin, but he determines to go to his grave without uttering the secret of universal understanding he has attained.

At the age of 67 Borges married his first wife, Elsa Astete Millán, but their marriage lasted only three years. His other works include the essays in *Other Inquisitions, 1937–1952* (1952); *Extraordinary Tales* (1955); *Dreamtigers* (1960), a collection of poetry and prose; *Personal Anthology* (1961); *Labyrinths* (1962); *The Book of Imaginary Beings* (1967); *Dr. Brodie's Report* (1970); and *The Book of Sand* (1975). Borges died from liver cancer in Geneva.

BIBLIOGRAPHY

Barnstone, Willis, *With Borges on an Ordinary Evening in Buenos Aires: A Memoir*, 1993; Rodríguez Monegal, Emir, *Jorge Luis Borges: A Literary Biography*, 1970; Thomas di Givanni, Norman, ed., *The Borges Tradition*, 1995.

Boulez, Pierre

(March 26, 1925–)
Composer, Conductor

As a composer Pierre Boulez contributed to the development of serialism, an outgrowth of ARNOLD SCHOENBERG's twelve-tone system by extending it to tonal color, rhythm, and other musical elements when it had been previously applied primarily to harmony and melody. Like Germany's KARLHEINZ STOCKHAUSEN, he experimented with the use of electronic instruments and sounds in musical composition. Boulez has also enjoyed a successful career as a conductor of the modern repertoire and has recorded extensively.

Boulez was born into a Catholic family in an apartment above a pharmacy in Montbrison, France. His father, more devoted to the Church than was his mother, was an engineer and a technical director in a steel manufacturing plant. At the age of seven Boulez entered the Institut Victor de la Prade, a Catholic seminary and high school. He received a classical education and excelled as a student, particularly in the areas of science and mathematics. At the age of six he began taking piano lessons, and his talent as a musician soon became apparent. Boulez first heard orchestral music on a radio his father brought back from the United States. As a teenager he rejected Catholicism and came into increasing conflict with his father, who wanted him to go into engineering.

Boulez next studied mathematics and music at the Collège de Saint-Étienne, and then at the University of Lyon. At the latter he heard his first live orchestra and attended his first opera—a production of *Boris Godunov*. With the support of his sister, he finally summoned the courage to defy his father and chose music as a career. In 1944–1945 he studied harmony under OLIVIER MESSIAEN at the Paris Conservatoire. Messiaen's varied musical interests—which included Gregorian chants and birdsong—and his teaching style, which fostered an atmosphere of freedom and experimentation, suited Boulez's temperament better than did the narrowness and discipline of the strict academic teachers. In the meantime, he earned money playing the ondes martenot, an electronic keyboard instrument.

Much as he enjoyed Messiaen, however, Boulez felt the need of something more; he studied Schoenberg's twelve-tone technique under one of the composer's students, René Leibowitz, in 1945–1946. After breaking unhappily with Leibowitz, Boulez in 1948 became director of JEAN-LOUIS BARRAULT's Renaud-Barrault Company at the Théâtre Marigny. There he inaugurated in 1954 a series of chamber concerts, Les Concerts du Petit-Marigny, later called the Domaine Musicale. For the most part, the concerts presented the works of modern composers such as Schoenberg, ANTON VON WEBERN, ALBAN BERG, and IGOR STRAVINSKY.

Boulez's compositions at this time, such as his *Le Visage Nuptial*, a setting of verse by the French poet René Char that Boulez composed after a stormy love affair, have a violent and disturbing tone. Schoenberg's twelve-tone system applied to pitch, but Boulez and other composers like Karlheinz Stockhausen extended his work to rhythm and tonal

Pierre Boulez (Gamma)

color. His Sonatine for flute and piano (1946) employs the twelve-tone system. His popular and aggressive Second Piano Sonata (1948) was a significant piece in the development of serialism.

In the 1950s Boulez began to devote himself more to conducting. Treating mostly the works of modern composers, he has conducted CLAUDE DEBUSSY, Stravinsky, and many of his own compositions. In 1958 he went to work for the Southwest Radio Symphony Orchestra in Baden-Baden, West Germany. From 1967 to 1972 he served as principal guest conductor at the Cleveland Orchestra in Ohio. Boulez also worked with the BBC Symphony Orchestra and the New York

Philharmonic, where he became music director in 1971. After resigning this position in 1977, he returned to Paris to direct the Institut de Recherche et de Coordination Acoustique/Musique. In 1995 he became principal guest conductor at the Chicago Symphony Orchestra. Boulez has recorded numerous works, particularly of modern composers, with the Cleveland Orchestra, the Chicago Symphony Orchestra, the London Symphony Orchestra, and the New York Philharmonic.

Boulez, who has always expressed what he thinks of the work of others, maintained a tense but respectful relationship with Stockhausen as they introduced new elements into music.

Boulez's most significant serialist works include *Polyphonie X* (1951); *Le marteau sans maître* (*The Hammer without a Master*, 1954) for voice and six instruments, another setting of Char's verse; *Pli selon pli* (*Fold According to Fold;* first performed 1960), incorporating the poetry of the French Symbolist poet Stéphane Mallarmé; and the Third Piano Sonata, which uses elements of chance, and is thus an example of what is called aleatory music. In *Structures, Book I* (1952), for two pianos, a partial collaboration with Messiaen, Boulez used a twelve-tone series from Messiaen's work.

Boulez scored some of his work for electronic instruments as well. Additional works include *Structures, Book II* (completed 1961), for two pianos; *Éclat* (1965) for chamber orchestra of fifteen instruments; *Domaines* (1968) for solo clarinet and twenty-one instruments; *Rituel* (1975), for orchestra; and *Répons* (first performed 1981), for chamber orchestra, six solo instruments, and computer. His writings include *Penser la musique aujourd'hui* (1964; *Thinking of Music Today*), *Relevés d'apprenti* (1966; *Raised from Apprenticeship*), and *Par volonté et par hasard* (1975; *By Choice and by Chance*).

BIBLIOGRAPHY

Peyser, Joan, *Boulez*, 1976; Stacey, Peter F., *Boulez and the Modern Concept*, 1987.

Bourdelle, Émile-Antoine

(October 30, 1861–October 1, 1929)
Sculptor

For thirteen years an assistant to the French sculptor Auguste Rodin (1840–1917), Émile-Antoine Bourdelle created large, monumental sculptures that combine influences of Rodin's Romantic works with those of ancient Greek and Romanesque art. Giving his sculptures fragmented, rough surface textures, he imbued his subjects with expressiveness and sensitivity.

Bourdelle was born into a working-class family in Montauban, France. At the age of fifteen he won a scholarship to the École des Beaux-Arts in Toulouse, where he studied sculpture. In 1884 he went to the École des Beaux-Arts in Paris, also working in the studio of John-Alexandre-Joseph Falguière (1831–1917). More important than his academic training in shaping his sculpting style, however, were the Romanesque art he saw in Toulouse and his years (1893–1906) working as Rodin's assistant.

His early figures, such as the smooth-faced, wide-eyed boy of *Head of a Montauban Boy* (1886), lack the rough-hewn surfaces of his mature work. In 1889 he executed several Adam figures cast in bronze, depicting the guilt-ridden biblical figure conscious of his sin. From Bourdelle's earliest years, the composer Ludwig von Beethoven was a recurring subject in Bourdelle's work. *Beethoven* (1903) depicts the head of the composer, and five years later he executed a *Hand of Beethoven*. The full-length *Draped Figure of Beethoven* (1910) and a *Mask of Beethoven* (1925) were only two of the more than twenty likenesses of the composer Bourdelle executed over his career.

In spite of his work for Rodin, Bourdelle turned away from the naturalistic style of the great sculptor and forged a style that draws from classical Greek and Romanesque sources. His mature work is marked by its rough, uneven surfaces and human figures in dramatic, expressive poses. In 1900 he completed his major work *Head of Apollo*, which recalls ancient Greek sculpture and marked a turning point in his style. A decade later, Bourdelle achieved his first major success with a bronze *Hercules the Archer*, the subject of numerous other sculptures by him.

Male and female nudes form another core in Bourdelle's subject matter. *Small Boy* (1905) depicts the nude subject of its title standing upright with his back arched. The nude in *The Cloud* (1905–1907) is a plump female figure lying on her back. Other nudes include the *Crouching Bather* (1906–1907) and the walking *Young Bacchante* (1907).

Among Bourdelle's many portraits is *Sculptress Resting* (1905–1908), which depicts his wife leaning on her right arm to support herself and staring into the air. In 1914 he completed a life-sized bust of the Alsatian surgeon Dr. Koeberlé. A life-sized portrait of Isadora Duncan (1927–1928) depicts the famed American dancer in flowing costume, her arms raised expressively in the air.

In spite of the success of Bourdelle's monumental sculptures, he found it difficult to escape the shadow of his better-known teacher Rodin. His other works include *Noble Burdens* (1911), an eight-foot-high sculpture of a mother holding a baby; reliefs for the Théâtre des Champs-Élysées; *Apollo and His Thought* (1912); the *Dying Centaur* (1914), a piece that depicts the death of paganism; the *Monument to the Fighters of Montauban* (1893–1902); and the massive *Monument to General Alvear* at Buenos Aires. He also taught, converting his studio into the Académie de la Grande-Chaumière.

BIBLIOGRAPHY

Cannon-Brookes, P., *Émile-Antoine Bourdelle: An Illustrated Commentary*, 1983; National Gallery of Canada, *Antoine Bourdelle, 1861–1929*, 1961.

Bowen, Elizabeth

(June 7, 1899–February 22, 1973)
Novelist, Short-Story Writer

Elizabeth Dorothea Cole Bowen is best known for her poignant treatment of the lives of young, British upperclass women in novels of manners.

She created a series of young female protagonists, who, through the experiences narrated, begin their transformations from innocent youth to mature adulthood. Bowen also wrote short stories and essays.

Bowen, of the Anglo-Irish gentry, was an only child born in Dublin. As a young girl she divided her time between the family estate, Bowen's Court, near Kildorrey, County Cork, and Dublin. Her father, a barrister in Dublin, suffered a nervous breakdown when she was 7, and her mother took her to southern England to live. Bowen attended Downe House School in Kent and later the London County Council School of Art. When she was 13, her mother died of cancer, the disease that took her own life many years later.

The short story "Breakfast," written when Bowen was 20, marked the beginning of her literary endeavors. Her first collection of stories, *Encounters*, was published in 1923, the same year she married Alan Charles Cameron, secretary for education of the Oxford School System.

The Hotel (1927), Bowen's first novel, written after a winter stay at a hotel in Bordighera, introduces the first of her many young female protagonists who find themselves in conflict with their surroundings when they are on the verge of adulthood. The 22-year-old, inexperienced Sydney Warren goes to the hotel of the title to visit a cousin but does not fit in with the other guests. The exception is the self-interested Mrs. Kerr, who seems more sophisticated than the others Sydney meets. Sydney rejects, accepts, and then rejects again a marriage proposal from James Milton, an older Anglican minister. She begins to understand Mrs. Kerr's selfish motivations, a realization that forms part of her new maturity.

Bowen's next novel, *Joining Charles*, was published in 1929. Like Sydney Warren, the central character of *The Last September* (1929) is an inexperienced young woman. During her last months at an Irish country house in Danielstown, the 19-year-old orphan Lois Farquar begins to move into adulthood with the self-knowledge she gains from her ill-fated relationship with the English officer Gerald Lesworth. Lois's story unfolds against the backdrop of the troubles that plagued Ireland in the early part of the century.

The Death of the Heart (1938), one of Bowen's most acclaimed novels, is divided into three sections based on a phrase from the baptismal ceremony of the Anglican Book of Common Prayer— "The World," "The Flesh," and "The Devil"—the three things the godparents must renounce on behalf of the infant who is being baptized. The story unfolds around the emotional quest of Portia Quayne, a 15-year-old orphan who goes to live with her half-brother Thomas and his wife, Anna.

Bowen worked for the Ministry of Information during World War II and served as an air-raid warden. The war forms the backdrop of *The Heat of the Day* (1949), set during the bombing of London. Stella Rodney is older and more experienced than Bowen's previous protagonists. Harrison, who is attracted to her, comes to her with the news that her lover, Robert Kelway, has been giving secrets to the Germans. Robert initially denies the charge, but, as it turns out, his spying stems from enmity toward England and his almost inhuman mother.

Bowen's husband, Cameron, died in 1952, after which Bowen moved to Bowen's Court, the family home she had inherited in 1930. She sold the home in 1960 and returned to England. Her other novels include *To the North* (1932); *The*

House in Paris (1935); *A World of Love* (1955); *The Little Girls* (1964); and *Eva Trout, or The Changing Seasons* (1969). The title story of her collection *The Demon Lover, and Other Stories* (1945; published in the United States as *Ivy Gripped the Steps*) is one of her best-known, and among her other short-story collections is *A Day in the Dark, and Other Stories* (1965). Bowen's other works include the autobiographical *Bowen's Court* (1942); *Collected Impressions* (1950); *A Time in Rome* (1960); *Afterthought: Pieces About Writing* (1962); and *Pictures and Conversations* (1975). She was made Commander of the British Empire in 1948 and Companion of Literature in 1965. Both Trinity College, Dublin, and Oxford awarded her honorary doctorates of letters. Bowen also lectured widely in the United States and England.

BIBLIOGRAPHY

Austin, Allan E., *Elizabeth Bowen*, rev. ed., 1989; Craig, Patricia, *Elizabeth Bowen*, 1986; Lassner, Phyllis, *Elizabeth Bowen*, 1990.

Brancusi, Constantin

(February 21, 1876–March 16, 1957)
Sculptor

A major contributor to the development of modern abstract sculpture, Constantin Brancusi raised himself from illiteracy and a peasant background to become one of the most influential artists in Paris. His works employ ovoid (egglike) and other organic shapes and include lengthy series on particular themes, among which are birds in flight, female faces, and tall columns.

Brancusi was born Constantin Brîncusi into a peasant family in Hobita, Romania. He did not attend school and only later taught himself to read and write. In his childhood he was occupied with tending his family's flocks, during which time he learned to carve tools and designs in wood. Romanian peasant carvings, with which he had intimate familiarity, influenced his later sculpture. Brancusi was a restless child and at the age of 9 ran away to Tirgu-Jiu, in the Oltenia region. There he worked for a dyer until his mother came to retrieve him.

Two years later Brancusi ran away permanently, taking a job at an inn in Slatina. He subsequently worked in a restaurant in Craiova, where he remained for several years. Brancusi never abandoned his love for wood carving and during this time is said to have constructed a violin from an orange crate. At some point his woodwork impressed an industrialist, who sent him to the Craiova School of Arts and Crafts in 1894.

At the School of Arts and Crafts, Brancusi primarily studied woodworking. From 1896 to 1898 he traveled, went to Vienna, and earned a living as a woodworker. In 1898 he won a sculpture contest that enabled him to study at the Bucharest School of Fine Arts. The same year, he sculpted a clay bust of Gheorghe Chiu, a revolutionary hero and well-known political figure who helped found the School of Arts and Crafts as well as a bust of the emperor Vitellius. While Brancusi studied there, the curriculum at Bucharest was modeled on the École des Beaux-Arts in Paris.

In spite of his increasing disillusion with formal academic strictures, the school purchased some of his sculptures, such as the *Écorché* (1902), and bestowed upon him a number of awards. Brancusi sympathized with a group of students who rebelled against the academic strain in art.

In 1903 a Bucharest military hospital gave him his first commission—to sculpt a bust of General Carol Davila. After completing military service, he developed an interest in the work of the French sculptor Auguste Rodin (1840–1917). He lived in Munich until 1904 and then journeyed (largely on foot) to Paris. There he studied at the École des Beaux-Arts under Antonin Mercié and washed dishes at a restaurant to support himself. Brancusi's early sculptures, such as *Pride* (1905), the bronze head of a girl, are representational pieces and show the influence of Rodin.

Brancusi had his first exhibitions in Paris in 1906. The following year, he was commissioned to sculpt a funeral monument for a Romanian landowner. Brancusi exhibited two well-received works at the Tinerimea Artistica exhibition, an annual show that featured the works of emerging talents.

Around 1908, however, Brancusi began to move away from strictly representational sculpture. He abandoned modeling (in which a sculpture is rendered by building up materials) and began to carve directly. His first version of *The Kiss* (1908) is a symmetrical, abstract stone interpretation of two lovers kissing in an embrace. *Sleeping Muse* (1908), an abstract depiction of a woman's face, is another recurring theme in his work. In 1909 he formed a friendship with AMEDEO MODIGLIANI, who under his influence began a series of sculptures.

Brancusi was soon using ovoid shapes as the basis of his sculpture. He devoted almost as much attention to the bases of his works as he did to the actual figures. With *Maiastra* (1912), he began his long series of abstract depictions of birds in flight, a theme to which he would return for nearly thirty years. One of his bird sculptures generated a legal battle with U.S. customs officials, who believed the abstract piece was a secret industrial part. The case was resolved in his favor. In 1912 he won the first prize for sculpture at the Bucharest Salon, and the following year he exhibited five works in several American cities. Among these was his popular bust *Mademoiselle Pogany*.

Brancusi finished the first of his famous *Columns*, which consist of repeated rhomboid or pyramidal shapes, in 1918. Two decades later one of his columns, a one-hundred-foot-tall sculpture in cast iron, was placed in a public garden in Tirgu Jiu with two other works, *Gate of the Kiss*, and *Table of Silence*. The sculpture *Princess X* (1920) generated a public scandal. A polished bronze piece, it depicts a human in a phallic form. His other sculptures include *The New-Born* (1915); *The Beginning of the World*, also known as his sculpture for a blind man; and *The Fish* (first version 1922). In the 1930s the Maharajah of Indore commissioned him to create a temple, but the Maharajah's death prevented the realization of the project.

Although he rendered many of his sculptures in bronze or stone, Brancusi often returned to wood carving, sometimes creating wood versions of future sculptures. He completed his first major wood sculpture, *The Prodigal Son*, in 1914. From 1917 to 1930 he made *The Cups*, a series of wood carvings. Brancusi also made furniture, utensils, and other objects from wood.

Brancusi earned world fame for his abstract sculptures during his lifetime and influenced a generation of younger abstract sculptors that included HENRY MOORE and BARBARA HEPWORTH. His first one-man show came in 1926, when the Brummer Gallery in New York held a major exhibition of his work. He lived and worked in Paris, where he formed friendships with many of the city's avant-garde artists, literary figures, and musicians. Among them was the composer ERIK SATIE, who inspired him to design a costume for a ballerina in his ballet *Gymnopédies*. The Solomon R. Guggenheim Museum in New York held a major exhibit of his work in 1955. Upon his death, Brancusi left his workshop and its contents to the Museum of Modern Art in Paris.

BIBLIOGRAPHY

Balas, Edith, *Brancusi and Rumanian Folk Traditions*, 1987; Geist, Sidney, *Brancusi: A Study of the Sculpture*, 1967; Miller, Sanda, *Constantin Brancusi: A Survey of His Work*, 1995.

Braque, Georges

(May 13, 1882–August 31, 1963)
Painter, Sculptor, Graphic Artist

With PABLO PICASSO, Georges Braque pioneered the development of Analytical and Synthetic Cubism in the early twentieth century and was an influential force in the development of modern abstract art. After brief periods of impressionistic and Fauvist landscape painting, he turned to Cubism, still lifes, and more abstract forms. His period of energetic experimentation lasted until the early 1920s and included new developments in form, style, and texture.

Braque was born in Argenteuil, France, and moved with his family to Le Havre in 1890. His father and grandfather owned a successful house-painting business, and both were amateur painters. Braque often accompanied his father when he painted, and his father sought to train him in the family business. He attended a local school, where he excelled in athletics and learned to play the flute. When he was 15, he enrolled in a night class at an art academy in Le Havre. In 1899 Braque was apprenticed to a painter and decorator, and he eventually moved to Paris.

From his apprenticeship Braque acquired decorative skills that manifest themselves in his later paintings, such as his ability to imitate wood grains and marble surfaces. After serving in the military for a year, he determined to paint for a living—an ambition his family supported. From 1902 to 1904 he studied in Paris at the Académie Humbert, and he also studied briefly at the École des Beaux-Arts. At the Louvre in Paris, he developed an admiration for Egyptian and Greek art. The French Impressionists, however, were the dominant influence on Braque's early painting style.Then in 1905 he saw the exhibition of the Fauves (or "wild beasts," so named for their bold use of color) at the Salon d'Automne in Paris. Under the influence of HENRI MATISSE, ANDRÉ DERAIN, and other Fauves, Braque intensified the colors in his own paintings. *La Ciotat* (1907) is a lyrical landscape with deep blue sky, hills, and trees. At this point in his career, Braque concentrated on Fauvist landscape, as in *Landscape at L'Estaque* (1906) and *Le Mas* (1906).

Around 1907 Braque discovered the works of Paul Cézanne (1839–1906), from whom he adopted a focus on geometric forms. The loose, free forms of his Fauvist paintings evolved into more strict geometric shapes, as in *View from the Hôtel Mistral, L'Estaque* (1907). *Houses at L'Estaque* (1908) is a composition of geometric shapes and angular planes in pale greens and yellows, and it and other paintings directly anticipated the development of Analytical Cubism.

Braque slowly gained a reputation as a painter and in 1907 sold a number of his works after an exhibition at the Salon des Indépendants. The same year he began his association with art dealer Daniel-Henry Kahnweiler, who had his own gallery and ardently promoted the Cubist works of both Braque and Picasso. Kahnweiler exhibited a number of Braque's works in his gallery in 1908,

after which Paris critic Louis Vauxcelles commented disparagingly on the "cubes" Braque used as the basis of his forms.

The poet Guillaume Apollinaire introduced Braque to Picasso at the latter's studio in Montmartre. Braque's initial reaction to Picasso's famous proto-Cubist painting *Les Demoiselles d'Avignon* (1907) was a negative one, but the two painters soon developed a strong friendship and began working closely together. Critics still debate exactly what each artist contributed to Cubism, but one of Braque's most certain contributions came in the development of geometric forms.

By 1909 Braque and Picasso were well into the development of the first phase of Cubism, which the painter JUAN GRIS called Analytical Cubism. In *Guitar and Fruit-dish* (1909), *The Mandolin* (1910), and other paintings of the period, Braque used low-key browns, oranges, blues, greens, and grays. Lighting from different sources highlights the sharply fragmented surfaces of Analytical Cubism.

During the early phase of Cubism, the subjects of Braque's paintings moved increasingly away from landscapes toward still lifes. *Still Life with Musical Instruments* (1910–1911) is one of many Cubist still lifes from this period. Fruit, musical instruments, and bottles recur throughout his work for the rest of his career. *Mandolin, Glass, Pot and Fruit* (1927) depicts such objects in earthy browns, blues, and greens. He painted numerous works, such as *Violin and Glass* (1910–1911), in oval shape. In a further effort to move away from traditional representation, Braque used stenciled letters in *The Portuguese.*

Around 1910 or 1911, Braque created his first engravings, among which is *Fox*

(1911). In what was to become the first papier collé, Braque in 1912 affixed pieces of wallpaper to the drawing *Fruit Dish and Glass*. Both he and Picasso began to combine other nontraditional elements with painting in their collages. *Glass, Bottle, and Newspaper* (1913) combines newspaper clippings, simulated wood grain, and other items.

In 1912 Braque married Marcelle Lapré and settled in a house at Sorgues, near Avignon. He contributed to the early development of Synthetic Cubism, abandoning severe geometric shapes for looser forms, as in *Still Life with Playing Cards* (1913). He served in World War I as an infantry sergeant and received both the Légion d'Honneur and the Croix de Guerre. In 1917 Braque suffered a serious head injury from shrapnel at Carency, from which it took him months to recover. During his recuperation he published (1917), with the assistance of Pierre Reverdy, a collection of aphorisms as *Thoughts and Reflections on Painting* in the review *Nord-Sud*.

As Spanish nationals, both Picasso and Gris were exempt from military service during the war. Braque was incapacitated for a time while they continued to develop Synthetic Cubism, but upon his recovery he immersed himself in the new developments. Synthetic Cubist paintings, such as his *The Musician* (1917–1918), substitute broader planes and brighter colors for the fragmented surfaces and muted tones of Analytic Cubism. During this time Braque also experimented with texture, mixing foreign elements such as ash, metal filings, and sawdust into his paints and incorporating his skill imitating wood and marble surfaces.

In the 1920s, after moving away from Cubism, Braque continued to paint still lifes, some with tall, vertical shapes. In 1923 and 1925, he accepted commissions from ballet impresario SERGEY DIAGHILEV for Ballets Russes productions of *Les Fâcheux* and *Zéphyre et Flore*, both based on works by Molière. He would return to set design in 1949, when he created for the French actor and director Louis Jouvet the scenery for a production of Molière's *Tartuffe*.

The rest of Braque's output is marked by his series of paintings on single subjects. These include series of canephores (1922–1926); guéridons, or small tables (1928–1929); sixteen etchings to illustrate Hesiod's *Theogony* (1932); billiard tables (1944–1952); and studio interiors (1949–1956).

As World War II approached, Braque worked on a death-infused *Vanitas* series in which the dominant objects are skulls, crosses, and rosary beads. His relatively limited output of sculpture also dates from the World War II era. During the last years of his life, Braque was too ill to work on large-scale paintings and created jewelry designs, some of which were exhibited in Paris in 1963.

Braque achieved international fame during his Cubist years and in 1937 won the Carnegie Prize. Major retrospectives of his work have been held around the world. In 1961 he became the first living artist to have his work exhibited at the Louvre.

BIBLIOGRAPHY

Cafritz, Robert, *Georges Braque*, 1982; Mullins, Edwin, *The Art of Georges Braque*, 1968; Rubin, William, *Picasso and Braque: Pioneering Cubism*, 1989; Zurcher, Bernard, *Georges Braque, Life and Work*, 1988.

Brecht, Bertolt

(February 10, 1898–August 14, 1956)
Playwright, Theorist, Director, Poet

Bertolt Brecht worked out the theory of "epic theater," a mode of presentation that establishes distance between the audience and the characters in a play, and became one of the most influential theater directors in the twentieth century. Brecht's plays carried a strong anti-capitalist bent and established him as a prominent anti-Nazi voice after his exile from Germany in 1933.

Brecht was born Eugen Berthold Friedrich Brecht in Augsburg, Germany, the first child of middle-class parents. His mother came from a Protestant background, and his father's family was Catholic; the couple raised their children as Protestants. Although rebellion came naturally to Brecht in school, he excelled in his studies. At age 15, he helped establish a literary magazine, *The Harvest*, which printed some of his own stories. He frequently wrote poetry; both his stories and his poetry tended toward morbid themes. In 1917, in order to avoid being drafted, he moved to Munich to study medicine.

German Expressionism influenced Brecht's earliest plays, as did the works he was fond of reading by RUDYARD KIPLING, the French Symbolist poet Arthur Rimbaud (1854–1891), the fifteenth-century French lyric poet François Villon (c. 1431–1463), the French Symbolist poet Paul Verlaine (1844–1896), and the German playwright Frank Wedekind (1864–1918). His first play, *Baal* (1918), is a provocative and anarchistic drama written in poetic style. Its hero, Baal, is a bisexual murderer who callously uses both men and women. *A Manual of Piety* (1927) collected Brecht's often sexually explicit poetry and songs.

In 1924, Brecht moved to Berlin, where he remained until 1933. Working with the German composer KURT WEILL, he wrote the musical *The Threepenny Opera* in 1928, based on *The Beggar's Opera* (1728) by John Gay. Like his "Epic opera," *Rise and Fall of the City of Mahogany* (1930), also with Weill's music, it painted a dark picture of capitalism and the bourgeois mentality. Brecht also began to write "exemplary plays," which broke with all traditional theatrical form and attempted to teach audiences.

Brecht's opposition to Hitler forced him into exile in 1933. He lived in Scandi-

Bertolt Brecht (Fragment Publishing)

navia until 1941, when he moved to the United States. Brecht wrote prolifically in his exile. In *Mutter Courage und ihre Kinder* (1941; *Mother Courage and Her Children*), a mute daughter of a brutal businesswoman, Anna Fierling, sacrifices her life to warn her village of impending attack. *Leben des Galilei* (1943; *Galileo*) portrayed the famous inventor of the telescope as a thief who stole the idea for his instrument from one of his students. When he discovers on his own that the earth is round instead of flat, the Catholic hierarchy forces to him to publicly renounce his discovery, which it considers heretical. *Der gute Mensch von Sezuan* (1943; *The Good Woman of Setzuan*) portrays a Chinese woman, Shen Te, who remains determined to act morally in the midst of corruption and evil influences. Throughout the play, she is vexed by her evil male cousin, Shui Ta, who, as it turns out, is only herself in disguise. In writing his plays, Brecht frequently had uncredited help from others. Nevertheless, the plays remain essentially Brecht's, and they represent the first great examples of epic theater as he was later to define it.

Among Brecht's later plays are *Der authealtsame Autsteig des Arturo Ui* (1947; *The Resistable Rise of Arturo Ui*), a metaphorical look at Hitler's rise to power that suggests people could have prevented it. Written in the postwar period when East and West were vying for control of Germany, *Der Kaukasische Kreidekreis* (1948; *The Caucasian Chalk Circle*) depicts the struggle for a child, Michel, between a wealthy mother and Michel's maid, Grusha. Grusha saves the child when the mother deserts it, but later the mother goes to court to regain her child, claiming to be motivated by mother love. It is obvious, however, that

the mother's only interest in her son is the inheritance she can claim if she gains custody of him. Presiding over the dispute is a judge, who despite his drunkenness, cowardice, and corruption, can see the obvious truth. He orders Michel placed in the middle of a chalk circle and has the two women pull on his arms. The mother pulls hard, while Grusha tugs gently to spare the child from pain. Grusha, having proved her love, is awarded custody. The final song draws the Marxist moral—land should go to those who will make it productive, whether they have legal title to it or not, as the child should go to the woman who loves him.

As his career and ideology progressed, Brecht developed elaborate ideas about theater and the presentation of drama. He viewed the theater as a platform for interpreting history and teaching audiences from a Marxist perspective. From his viewpoint, drama needed a style of delivery compatible with the perspective of social/historical evolution fundamental to Marxist thought. He sought to divide the audience from the characters, and thus from the illusion that the actors portrayed reality. Instead of identifying with the characters, audiences were encouraged to look at them critically and to think about the ideas the author is expressing, creating what Brecht called the "alienation effect." Certain devices helped achieve the separation between audience and performer—actors delivered their lines in monotonous voices, wore masks, were interrupted by authorial commentary in some form, or spoke in asides. Lights illuminated the entire stage rather than just the action.

In 1948 Brecht moved to Zürich, and in 1949 he traveled to East Berlin and sub-

Breton, André Robert

(February 19, 1896–September 28, 1966)
Poet, Novelist, Critic, Essayist

The French writer André Breton founded the Surrealist movement in Paris in 1924 with his *Surrealist Manifesto*. He devoted his adult life to defining the movement's principles, creating Surrealist literary works, and promoting the work of other Surrealist writers and painters.

Breton was born in Tinchebray, France, the only child of a seamstress and a police official. Throughout his childhood and adulthood he found himself at odds with his domineering mother, and he generally retained unhappy memories of his childhood. After his family moved to Pantin, an industrial suburb of Paris, Breton attended both Catholic and public schools and usually excelled in his studies.

Several influences in Breton's early life would affect his literary career. He grew up in a mixed religious atmosphere—his father was an avowed atheist and his mother was a devout Catholic. In 1907 he enrolled in what is now the Lycée Chaptal, where, in spite of his waning interest in school, he developed his fondness for poetry, particularly French Symbolist poets such as Stephane Mallarmé and Arthur Rimbaud. A 1910 trip to Germany inspired his interest in German Romantic literature. He was encouraged by PAUL VALÉRY, who read and critiqued his writings.

After his graduation Breton enrolled in medical school. During World War I he served in several military medical positions, including a post at a psychiatric hospital. His interest in mental illness, coupled with his interest in Sigmund Freud's theories on the subconscious, played a direct role in his literary work. With Philippe Soupault and Louis Aragon, Breton founded the literary review *Littérature* in 1919, around the same time that he joined the Dadaists. The Dadaists, who originated in Zürich, were a nihilistic group of antiartists who disliked Western culture and rejected traditional art forms.

Breton became interested in automatic writing, in which one writes down thoughts as they come to mind. With Soupault he wrote *Magnetic Fields* (1920), one of the major pieces of automatic writing of the time. Automatic writing would become one of the characteristics of the Surrealist movement, which Breton initiated in 1924 with his *Surrealist Manifesto*. Breton and other Surrealists sought to merge the conscious and unconscious worlds. They considered the subconscious of prime importance in creative activity and believed rational thought inhibits creativity. Other prominent Surrealists included MARCEL DUCHAMP, JOAN MIRÓ, JEAN ARP, MAX ERNST, and, until his expulsion from the movement, the Spanish painter SALVADOR DALÍ.

Breton's novel *Nadja*, a surrealistic account of his encounters with a young woman, appeared in 1928. With the poet PAUL ÉLUARD he cowrote *The Immaculate Conception* (1930). The same year he published a second Surrealist manifesto. In *The Communicating Vessels* (1932), Breton likened the relationship between dreams and consciousness to the balance achieved between a liquid connected with a gas in an experiment.

Along with other Surrealists, Breton joined the Communist Party in the early 1930s, but he became disillusioned with the leadership of Joseph Stalin. With his wife, Jacqueline, he traveled to Mexico in 1938, where the exiled Bolshevik Leon Trotsky was staying. Breton stayed with the painter DIEGO RIVERA and his wife, the painter FRIDA KAHLO, and spent time talking and traveling with both Rivera and Trotsky.

Breton spent part of World War II in the United States, where he successfully promoted Surrealism. He returned to France in 1946. His other prose works include *The Lost Steps* (1924), *Legitimate Defense* (1926), *Surrealism and Painting* (1926), *Mad Love* (1937), *Arcanum 17* (1944), and *The Key to the Fields* (1953). His poetry includes the love poems collected in *The Air of Water* (1934); *Poems* (1948); and *Constellations* (1959), written to accompany works by Miró.

BIBLIOGRAPHY

Browder, Clifford, *André Breton, Arbiter of Surrealism*, 1967; Caws, Mary Ann, *André Breton*, 1971; Polizzotti, Mark, *Revolution of the Mind: The Life of André Breton*, 1995.

Britten, Benjamin

(November 22, 1913–December 4, 1976)
Composer, Conductor, Pianist

With his thoroughly British-flavored music, Edward Benjamin Britten was one of England's foremost composers after the death of Sir EDWARD ELGAR. His massive and varied body of music includes the opera *Peter Grimes*, the choral work *War Requiem*, *The Young Person's Guide to the Orchestra*, and many other vocal and instrumental compositions. Britten also enjoyed a successful career as a pianist and conductor.

Britten was born on St. Cecilia's Day (worth noting because St. Cecilia is the patron saint of music), in Lowestoft, Suffolk, England; he was the youngest of four children and inherited his interest in music from his mother. With the full encouragement of his father, a dentist, she was an amateur singer and a member of the Lowestoft Choral Society. Britten took his first piano lessons from her when he was 5, the same age at which he composed his first work. From 1928 to 1930 he attended Gresham's School in Holt, Norfolk. Throughout his childhood, he actively composed plays, symphonies, tone poems, and other works, parts of which would later reappear in compositions such as his *Simple Symphony* (1934).

Britten excelled in the schools he attended, but they afforded him little opportunity to pursue his interest in music, so he took private lessons. The most significant of his teachers was the viola player and composer Frank Bridge. Bridge's perfectionistic style and strict attention to technique were lasting influences on Britten, as were his efforts

Benjamin Britten (Decca)

to expose his young pupil to contemporary music. In 1930, Britten won a scholarship to the Royal College of Music in London, where he studied piano with Arthur Benjamin and composition under John Ireland, and won the Ernest Farrar Prize for composition.

The year 1935, when Britten met the poet W. H. AUDEN, marked the beginning of several years of collaboration between the two men. Auden worked with Britten or contributed text to several of his works, including the song cycle *Our Hunting Fathers* (1936), *On This Island* (1937), and the opera *Paul Bunyan* (1941). Britten's *Hymn to St. Cecilia* (1942) used Auden's text and honored his martyred patron saint. Both men worked

at the General Post Office's film division, collaborating on the short films *Coal Face* and *Night Mail.*

Britten was homosexual; he originally met his lifelong companion, the tenor Peter Pears, in 1934 and established a permanent relationship with him in 1937. From then on, they traveled and performed together, and Britten composed many works specifically for Pears. From 1939 to 1942 they lived in the United States. Upon their return to England, they were exempted from military service as conscientious objectors. Britten's lifelong pacifism is evident in his choral work *War Requiem* (1962), which incorporates the Latin Mass for the Dead and poetry by WILFRED OWEN.

Paul Bunyan (1941), Britten's first opera, was completed in the United States and has largely been forgotten. Much more successful was *Peter Grimes* (1945), with libretto by Montagu Slater based on George Crabbe's poem "The Borough." The main character of Britten's psychological study is an introverted fisherman driven to suicide, and Britten tailored the role for Pears. The *Sea Interludes* from *Peter Grimes* are often performed separately. The richly colored *The Rape of Lucretia* (1946) was the first of Britten's "chamber operas," or smaller scale operas, written for the English Opera Group that he and Pears helped found. A comedy, *Albert Herring* (1947) followed. Britten and Pears also helped found the Aldeburgh Festival, where there is now a center that hosts classes and performances, in 1947.

Gloriana (1953), which Britten wrote for Queen Elizabeth II's coronation, was first performed at Covent Garden. The opera was based on the relationship between Elizabeth I and Lord Essex and featured choreography by JOHN CRANKO. Britten's other operas include *Billy Budd* (1951), with libretto by Eric Crozier and E. M. FORSTER based on Herman Melville's tragic novella; *The Turn of the Screw* (1954), based on Henry James's classic ghost story; *A Midsummer Night's Dream* (1960), a version of William Shakespeare's fantastic comedy; *Death in Venice* (1973), based on THOMAS MANN's story of love and corruption.

Although Britten familiarized himself with and admired the work of contemporary composers, his varied music is largely traditional and English. In both music and subject matter, he most often drew from British poets, playwrights, novelists, and composers (particularly the seventeenth-century English composer Henry Purcell [1659–1695]). Outside of England, Britten admired the composers ALBAN BERG, Gustav Mahler (1860–1911), and DMITRY SHOSTAKOVICH as well as European literary figures such as Mann and the nineteenth-century French Symbolist poet Arthur Rimbaud.

Noye's Fludde (1958) was based on a fifteenth century miracle play about Noah and the ark. (Medieval miracle plays retold biblical stories for a popular audience, often bringing in touches of humor.) Between 1964 and 1968, Britten composed three "church parables," *Curlew River* (1964), *The Burning Fiery Furnace* (1966), and *The Prodigal Son* (1968), all three with libretto by William Plomer. English influences did not dominate completely: Britten's interest in Japanese Noh theater is particularly evident in *Curlew River*.

Among Britten's many vocal works and song cycles are *Les Illuminations* (1939), for high voice and strings, a setting of poems by Rimbaud; *Seven Sonnets of Michelangelo* (1940), for solo voice and piano; *Ceremony of Carols* (1942), for harp and treble voices; *The Holy Sonnets of John Donne* (1945); *Winter Words* (1953), a setting of Thomas Hardy's verse; and *Songs and Proverbs of William Blake* (1965).

Britten's most famous instrumental works are the *Simple Symphony* (1925), for strings; *Sinfonietta* (1932), for chamber orchestra; the *Spring Symphony* (1949), for chorus, boys' choir, and orchestra; three string quartets, several concerti, and *The Young Person's Guide to the Orchestra* (1945). The latter uses Purcell's music to introduce the listener to each of the instruments of the orchestra. Symphony in D Major for Cello and

Orchestra (1963) and several cello suites were written for the Russian cellist MSTISLAV ROSTROPOVICH, whom Britten met in 1960.

Britten was made a Companion of Honor in 1953, was awarded the Order of Merit in 1965, was made a life peer in 1976, and won several international awards. His other works include *Variations on a Theme of Frank Bridge* (1937); five canticles (1947–1974); the score for Cranko's ballet *The Prince of the Pagodas* (1956); and arrangements of other composers' music.

BIBLIOGRAPHY

Evans, Peter, *The Music of Benjamin Britten*, 1979; Holst, Imogen, *Britten*, 3d ed., 1980; Kennedy, Michael, *Britten*, 1981; Oliver, Michael, *Benjamin Britten*, 1996; Palmer, Christopher, ed., *The Britten Companion*, 1984.

Brodsky, Joseph

(May 24, 1940–January 28, 1996)
Poet, Essayist, Playwright

Joseph Brodsky's lyrical and meditative poetry first became known through *samizdat*, the clandestine literature that began to be circulated in the Soviet Union in the 1950s. When the Soviet authorities expelled him from the country in 1972, Brodsky settled in the United States and wrote poetry, essays, and plays in Russian and English. He received the Nobel Prize for Literature in 1987, "for an all-embracing authorship, imbued with clarity of thought and poetic intensity."

Brodsky was born Iosip Aleksandrovich Brodsky in Leningrad, now once again St. Petersburg. His father was a commercial photographer who lost his job more than once because he was Jewish. The family lived in a cramped, communal apartment and often survived from income brought in by his mother. Brodsky quit school when he was 15 and began the first of a long series of odd jobs. Meanwhile, he developed an interest in poetry and began to write.

Brodsky learned Polish and English, enabling him to read and earn money translating the works of poets such as John Donne and Czeslaw Milosz. The then aged poet ANNA AKHMATOVA, though her style differed dramatically from Brodsky's, served as an important source of inspiration to him. Brodsky involved himself with the Leningrad literary scene, and his poetry began to appear in *samizdat* publications such as the journal *Sintaksis*. Among his early poems are "Isaac and Abraham" and "The Great Elegy to John Donne," both written in 1963.

Brodsky's poetry is personal, elegiac, and lyrical, full of metaphor and wordplay.

Though his verse is entirely apolitical and cannot be called dissident literature, its emphasis on the personal and the spiritual conflicted with the aims of Socialist Realism, the style Soviet authorities demanded (see MAXIM GORKY). Brodsky was arrested on several occasions, although he never actually served a sentence.

The most serious incident occurred in 1964, when he was arrested and charged with "social parasitism." Brodsky was found guilty and sentenced to five years of hard labor in Siberia, a region with which he was familiar firsthand. However, a transcript of his trial smuggled to the West demonstrated to the world the absurdity of the proceedings. Under pressure from other writers in the Soviet Union and abroad, Soviet authorities commuted his sentence.

Brodsky's troubles were not over once he was released. He continued to publish poetry and gained increasing popularity, especially in the West. His first collection, *Short Poems and Long Poems*, was published in the United States in 1965. *A Halt in the Wasteland* followed in 1970. Brodsky was denied permission to attend international writers' conferences on multiple occasions. In May 1972, he was given a visa and told to leave the country.

Several of Brodsky's friends who remained in the Soviet Union were subsequently arrested for publishing his work. Abroad, Brodsky found a friend in the English poet W. H. AUDEN, who secured money for him to go to the United States. He immediately obtained a position as poet-in-residence at the University of Michigan in Ann Arbor (1972–1980) and subsequently taught literature at Mount Holyoke in Massachusetts. Brodsky gave poetry readings and lectured widely in the United States until his death in 1996.

In the United States, Brodsky loved the spirit of individualism he believed Americans embodied. Although he sometimes wrote in English, he usually wrote in Russian and translated his works. His later volumes include *A Part of Speech* (1980) and *To Urania* (1988). *So Forth: Poems* (1998), his final collection, contains poems of a deeply personal nature, including meditations on death, life, and nature.

Among Brodsky's other works are the essay collections *Less Than One* (1986), *On Grief and Reason: Essays* (1994), and *Watermark* (1992), the last of which consists of Brodsky's observations on the spirit, scenery, and architecture of Venice; the plays *Democracy!* and *Marbles;* and *Homage to Robert Frost* (1996), a volume to which he contributed with SEAMUS HEANEY and DEREK WALCOTT. Brodsky was poet laureate of the United States from 1991 to 1992.

BIBLIOGRAPHY

Heaney, Seamus, *The Singer of Tales: On Joseph Brodsky*, 1996; Polukhina, Valentina, *Joseph Brodsky: A Poet for Our Time*, 1989.

Brook, Peter

(March 21, 1925–)
Director, Producer

Noted for both his Shakespeare productions in England and his experimental modern productions based in France, Peter Stephen Paul Brook (to give him his full name) has enjoyed a varied and successful career in the theater. His experimental approach to the theater incorporates mysticism, humanism, and the ideas of several modern directors. Brook has also directed films.

Brook was born in London and studied at Gresham's School and at the University of Oxford. He entered the theater as a teenager, directing a production of *Dr. Faustus* at the Torch Theatre when he was 18, and quickly established himself as one of England's foremost directors. After directing at the Birmingham Repertory Theatre he worked as a director at the Royal Opera House from 1947 to 1950. Abandoning opera, he began to direct some of Britain's leading actors in Shakespearean plays. Over the next several years he directed both Shakespearean and modern plays, including *Vicious Circle* (1945), with ALEC GUINNESS; *Venice Preserv'd* (1953) with Paul Scofield and JOHN GIELGUD; *Titus Andronicus; The Winter's Tale; Men Without Shadows;* and *King Lear* (1962).

Brook helped introduce the works of modern French playwrights such as JEAN-PAUL SARTRE, JEAN GENET, and JEAN COCTEAU to England. Under the influence of experimental dramatists such as Antonin Artaud, BERTOLT BRECHT, and Jerzy Grotowski, he explored many possibilities in the presentation of plays. In 1964 he embraced Artaud's concept of the Theater of Cruelty, reworking traditional spatial arrangements and downplaying dialog, with which he was able to experiment at the LAMDA Theatre.

Many of Brook's productions from the 1960s carry strong political elements, including his international success, Peter Weiss's *Marat/Sade* (1962). *US* sharply criticized American involvement in the Vietnam war. A more lasting influence on

Brook's outlook, however, was an interest in Eastern spiritual traditions that took him to India, Africa, and Afghanistan. Assisted by two instructors—Jane Heap and then Madame Jeanne de Salzmann—he delved into the writings of the Russian-born mystic George Gurdjieff (1866–1949).

Brook began to develop his own ideas on the theater, which he has elaborated in volumes such as *The Empty Space* (1968), *The Shifting Point, 1946–1987* (1987), and *The Open Door: Thoughts on Acting and Theater* (1995). In contrast to theorists like GORDON CRAIG he does not grant equal status to all elements of production. The individual actor, he asserts, is the most powerful force on the stage. Music, scenery, and costumes are minimized. A director, in Brook's view, is the primary force behind the presentation of a play. Brook has also written extensively on the utilization of space on the stage.

Feeling restricted in his ability to experiment freely in England, Brook moved to France in 1970. In 1968 he had founded the International Centre of Theatre Research, where he spent much of his time working with actors to develop alternative acting techniques and expressive body movements. Brook has consistently sought modes of expression that transcend the language barrier and speak in universal terms to audiences. In 1971, working with the poet TED HUGHES, he created an entirely new language in the play *Orghast*, performed at the Shivaz Festival. In Paris he ran the Bouffes du Nord theater, where he used an international cast of actors to put his ideas on the theater into action.

The Man Who (produced 1993) ranks among his most successful later works. Derived from Oliver Sacks's book *The*

Man Who Mistook His Wife for a Hat, the play concerns a group of patients with mental and neurological disorders. Four actors portray numerous doctors and patients. Among the latter are a man suffering with Tourette's Syndrome, a man who is unable to recognize common objects, and a man trapped in a chair.

Mahabarata (1985) was perhaps Brook's most ambitious production. A nine-and-a-half-hour marathon spectacle, it premiered in a limestone quarry in the south of France. The play recreates the Indian epic poem depicting the familial war between the Pandavas and the Kauravas, written between 300 B.C. and 300 A.D.. Brook conceived the idea for the production in 1973; it required twelve years of research, actor training, and visits to India.

Among Brook's other productions are Shakespeare's *Timon of Athens* (1974) in Paris; *Ubu Roi* (1977) in Paris; Shakespeare's *Antony and Cleopatra* (1979) in England; SAMUEL BECKETT's *Happy Days; La tragédie de Carmen; Je suis un phénomène*, a play that examines the psyche of a man with a photographic memory; Shakespeare's *The Tempest* (1987); Anton Chekhov's *The Cherry Orchard* (1988); *The Ilk*, an examination of an African tribe; *Pélleas and Méllisande* (1992); and *Qui est là?* (1996). He has also directed numerous motion pictures, including *The Beggar's Opera* (1953), *Lord of the Flies* (1963), *Tell Me Lies* (1968), *King Lear* (1971), a film based on Gurdjieff's autobiography, *Meetings with Remarkable Men*, and *La tragédie de Carmen* (1984). His *Memoirs* relate the formative influences on his life and theatrical ideas.

BIBLIOGRAPHY

Hunt, Albert, *Peter Brook*, 1995; Jones, Edward Trostle, *Following Directions: A Study of Peter Brook*, 1985.

Brooke, Rupert

(August 3, 1887–April 23, 1915)
Poet

Rupert Chawner Brooke was the most idealistic and traditional of a generation of English World War I poets that included WILFRED OWEN and SIEGFRIED SASSOON. His most famous compositions are his wartime sonnets, written in 1914 not long before his death.

Brooke was born in Rugby, Warwickshire, England, and attended the Hillbrow preparatory school and Rugby School, where his father was housemaster. He earned praise for his poetry as early as 1904, when his "The Pyramids" was recognized in a school contest. The following year, he won a scholarship to King's College, Cambridge, where he studied classics and English literature over the next several years.

Brooke was handsome, charming, romantic, and, to those who knew him, deeply emotional. The time at King's College was important to the development

Rupert Brooke (Ann Ronan/Image Select)

of many aspects of his character. One of his primary interests was in the dramatic arts, and he shared with a group of other students an interest in Elizabethan drama. In 1907 Brooke and his acquaintances formed the Marlowe Dramatic Society (named for the Elizabethan dramatist Christopher Marlowe), of which he became president. Among the plays in which he acted was a 1907 production of Marlowe's *Dr. Faustus* (as Mephistophilis). He wrote his dissertation, *John Webster and the Elizabethan Drama*, in 1911.

Brooke's years at Cambridge were also marked by the development of his socialist political philosophy. He joined the Cambridge Fabian Society (see GEORGE BERNARD SHAW) in 1907 and became its president in 1909. During this time Brooke met or associated with many literary and intellectual figures, including Shaw, H. G. WELLS, Leonard Woolf (the husband of the writer Virginia Woolf), E. M. FORSTER, and the biographer and critic Lytton Strachey. He would later break with Woolf, Forster, Strachey, and the rest of the Bloomsbury Group (see VIRGINIA WOOLF), objecting to their tendency toward homosexuality and to Strachey for personal reasons.

In 1910, Brooke moved to the Vicarage in Grantchester, the backdrop for one of his most famous poems, "The Old Vicarage, Grantchester" (1912). In 1910 he also temporarily assumed his father's position at Rugby following the latter's death. Brooke's first book of poetry, *Poems*, was published in 1911 and contained "Dining-Room Tea" and "The Fish." Brooke's verse shares the lyrical and romantic character of Georgian poetry, incorporating images from nature and filled with emotion. His strong political beliefs rarely appear as direct statements. In spite of his comparatively small output, he is considered one of the major Georgian poets of the early twentieth century.

In the atmosphere of a failing love affair in 1912, Brooke suffered a nervous breakdown and went to Cannes to recover. His only play, *Lithuania* (1912), was written the same year. Its dark story takes place in Lithuania, where a family plots the murder of a wealthy stranger who has come to them in search of shelter. The murdered stranger, it turns out, is a long lost son who has returned with money. *Lithuania* received little attention, and it was performed initially only in Chicago.

Working for the *Westminster Gazette*, Brooke traveled to the United States, Canada, and the South Seas in 1913. He stayed for a period of time on the island of Tahiti, where he had an affair with a Tahitian woman who appears as Mamua in his poem "Tiare Tahiti." "The Great

Lover," "Heaven," and other poems were also written during this period. With the exhaustion of his funds in 1914, Brooke returned to England and obtained a commission in the Royal Naval Division. He fell ill in Egypt in 1915, died of blood poisoning, and was buried on the island of Skyros.

The five poems that made Brooke famous, the war sonnets, were written in 1914 and were first published in *New Numbers*. The sonnets express a melancholy idealism quite different from the work of other war poets of his generation—perhaps at least partly because Brooke never actually saw combat. In "The Soldier," last and most popular of the sonnets, Brooke wrote: "If I should die, think only this of me: / That there's some corner of a foreign field / That is forever England." Many of Brooke's poems also appeared in Edward Marsh's *Georgian Poetry, 1913–1915*, and several collections of his work were published following his death.

BIBLIOGRAPHY

Laskowski, William E., *Rupert Brooke*, 1994; Lehman, John, *Rupert Brooke: His Life and His Legend*, 1980; Read, Mike, *Forever England: The Life of Rupert Brooke*, 1997.

Bunin, Ivan

(October 22, 1870–November 8, 1953)
Poet, Novelist, Short-Story Writer

Although the poetry and prose of the Russian author Ivan Alekseyevich Bunin belongs primarily to the twentieth century, he rejected modern trends in literature; he has more in common with the classic Russian authors of the nineteenth century. In 1933 Bunin became the first Russian to win the Nobel Prize for Literature, "for the strict artistry with which he has carried on the classical Russian traditions in prose writing."

Bunin was born in Voronezh, Russia, into an old and established but declining Russian noble family. His father was a jovial man fond of drinking and gambling, whereas his mother was pious and melancholy. From the latter Bunin gained his first taste of literature. The family moved to a more rural atmosphere, his father's estate at Yelets, in 1874. After being tutored by Nikolay Romashkov, a constant stimulus to Bunin's imagination in his childhood, he entered the gymnasium in Yelets at age 8. He wrote his first poem there, but he was a poor student and quit after four years. His elder brother, confined to the family estate for radical political activity, tutored him further. During this time Bunin read classic Russian authors and began to teach himself English.

Bunin's first writings were poems and short stories. His first published poem, "At the Grave of S. Ya. Nadson," lamented the death of the poet Semyon Nadson; it was published in the literary journal *Native Land* in 1887. In 1889 he began working as an editor's assistant for the *Oryol Messenger*, a position that enabled him to publish his short stories and other writings.

Much of his early poetry and prose expresses sorrow and loneliness and is steeped in the struggles of Russian provincial life. Bunin's preoccupation with death is evident in all his work. Although he associated himself with Symbolists and members of other modern literary movements early in his career, he never joined them and generally disliked modern trends in literature. In 1892 he moved to St. Petersburg, where he developed acquaintances with some of Russia's leading literary figures, including the writer MAXIM GORKY, a staunch supporter of his work. In style and in subject matter, however, Bunin's work owes more to Realism and its great nineteenth-century Russian exponents, such as Leo Tolstoy, whom he met in Moscow in 1894, and the playwright Anton Chekhov.

The first volume of Bunin's poetry was published in 1891. The structure and imagery in his poetry is simple and traditional. The collection *Under the Open Sky* appeared in 1898, and the most noteworthy volume from his early years is *Falling Leaves* (1901), which was widely praised by his contemporaries. Bunin's first collection of short stories, *To the Edge of the World*, was published in 1897. Like his poems, his early stories are simple. They generally deal with the Russian provincial gentry and peasantry, and plot plays a less important role than emotion and landscape.

Two journeys in the early 1900s made a lasting impact on Bunin's philosophy and work.

After a 1903 trip to Constantinople, he developed an intense interest in the Middle East and its spiritual traditions. A 1911 journey to Singapore, Ceylon, and Egypt kindled his interest in Buddhism and the Buddha. Although he continued to write poetry and prose set in Russia, such as the sketches in *God's Tree* (1931), he also used Middle Eastern, Far Eastern, and other settings. His work also began to acquire a more philosophical bent.

One of his most famous short stories, "The Gentleman of San Francisco," appeared in 1915; it concerns the sudden death of a wealthy, spiritually bankrupt American businessman traveling in Europe. Love, passion, and romance dominate *Dark Avenues* (1949), his final volume of short stories, largely written during World War II.

For the most part, Bunin distanced himself from politics. The violence associated with the 1905 and 1917 revolutions as well as World War I took an emotional toll on him. He and his wife, Vera Muromtseva, whom he met in 1907, moved to Odessa in 1918. Two years later, with the Red Army's capture of Odessa imminent, they fled to Constantinople and eventually settled in France. For the rest of his life, he divided his time between Paris and his villa in southern France.

Bunin's longer works of fiction include *The Village* (1910), centered around the Russian peasantry, and *Mitya's Love* (1925), about a man driven to suicide by his obsession with a woman who ultimately rejects him. The semiautobiographical *The Life of Arsenyev* (1930) consists of five parts and traces the development of a sensitive poet's philosophy, experience, and art. A sequel, *Lika*, followed in 1939.

Aside from writing, Bunin also gained fame as a translator. His translations of Henry Wadsworth Longfellow's *The Song of Hiawatha*, Byron's *Cain*, and other works, along with his own poetry, earned him three Pushkin Prizes from the Russian Academy. He was elected to the Academy in 1909. His other works include *Tolstoy's Liberation* (1937); *On Chekhov* (published posthumously); and his memoirs, *The Accursed Days* (1926) and *Memories and Portraits* (1950).

BIBLIOGRAPHY

Connolly, Julian W., *Ivan Bunin*, 1982.

Buñuel, Luis

(February 22, 1900–July 29, 1983)
Director

Known for surrealistic films that savagely attack bourgeois values and religion and explore his erotic interests, the Spanish-born filmmaker Luis Buñuel was one of the most controversial directors of the twentieth century.

Buñuel was the eldest of seven children, born in Calanda, Spain. His father was a successful businessman and a veteran of the Spanish-American War, and his mother came from an upper-middle-class family. Buñuel, athletic and a top student, attended Jesuit schools in Zaragoza before he entered the University of Madrid at the age of 17. At the university he studied music and entomology and, more importantly for his artistic interests, gained the friendship of the Surrealist painter SALVADOR DALÍ and the poet FEDERICO GARCÍA LORCA.

In 1920 Buñuel founded a film club at the university. He moved to Paris in 1925 and studied at the Academy of Cinema. Buñuel became an assistant director and by 1928 was able, working closely with Dalí, to direct his first movie, *Un chien andalou* (*An Andalusian Dog*), a short, surrealistic film filled with disconnected bizarre sequences, such as donkeys in pianos, and sexual imagery. Working again with Dalí, he directed *L'âge d'or* (1930; *The Golden Age*), a film highly critical of Catholic clergy, high society, and government officials, who appear as skeletons in the movie. Before a long dry spell in his filmmaking career, Buñuel directed one more film, *Las Hurdes* (1932; *Land Without Bread*), a documentary about peasant life in Las Hurdes, an impoverished region of northern Spain. Early on and throughout his career, Buñuel contributed little in the way of technical innovation to film; he was primarily known for his shocking, controversial messages and the surrealistic atmosphere of his movies.

Back in Spain, Buñuel produced several films for his native country's budding film industry. During the Spanish Civil War, he worked for the Republican side and made propaganda films such as *Madrid 1936* (1937). After moving to the United States in 1938 he worked with Hollywood producers as an adviser, and later in New York, but he made no more films of his own until he moved to Mexico in 1947.

Luis Buñuel directs Delphine Seyrig on the set of the film *The Discreet Charm of the Bourgeoisie* (1972) (Gamma)

His first significant Mexican film, *The Great Madcap* (1949), is a comedy about an alcoholic millionaire whose family convinces him that he has lost all of his money. In it Buñuel returned to one of his favorite themes—mockery of values held by the bourgeois and the wealthy. The more serious *The Forgotten* (1950) is a disturbing psychological portrait of two young boys who grow up in the brutal environment of a Mexico City slum.

In *Él* (1951; *This Strange Passion*), filmed in Mexico, Buñuel explores the neuroses of a middle-class man. Francisco is successful in his career but unmarried and still a virgin at 40. He lures a beautiful woman, Gloria, away from her

lover and marries her, but his neuroses begin to consume him as soon as they marry. Gloria lives in terror of his fits of jealousy and paranoia, which culminate in his attempt to strangle a priest. Francisco eventually enters a monastery. The protagonist of *Ensayo de un crimen* (1955; *The Criminal Life of Archibaldo de la Cruz*) is similarly disturbed. A repressed memory buried inside the outwardly respectable Archibaldo de la Cruz reemerges as a criminal obsession. As a child he witnessed the bloody death of his nurse, which gave him acute pleasure. He resolves to re-create that moment of excitement by murdering a woman, but every attempt to kill a victim fails.

The police refuse to arrest him after he confesses his failed desires, and the exasperated Archibaldo loses his obsession.

Buñuel's antireligious sentiment comes through in *Nazarín* (1958), based on a novel by the Spanish writer Benito Pérez Galdós. Father Nazarín lives his life working and proselytizing among sinners after being ejected from the priesthood. His actions parallel those of Jesus as recorded in the Gospels, but Buñuel depicts his attempts to comfort the suffering and disseminate love as futile and sometimes even harmful. The 1961 film *Viridiana* (1961), shot after Buñuel returned from Mexico to Spain, carries a similar antireligious message. It starred the Mexican actress Silvia Pinal and was banned by Spanish censors. Viridiana (the name of a Catholic saint) is a girl who plans to enter a convent. Her uncle's untruthful claim that he raped her ruins her aspirations for sainthood. She loses her innocence and eventually renounces her vows. The Franco government originally financed the film but later suppressed it. *Viridiana* won the golden palm at the Cannes Film Festival.

Back in Mexico in 1962, Buñuel filmed *The Exterminating Angel* (1962), a black comedy in which a group of dinner-party guests find themselves strangely unable to leave. The force that keeps them there is nothing concrete, but some intangible psychological pull. *Le Journal d'une femme de chambre* (1964; *The Diary of a Chambermaid*) is an anti-Fascist film. A young girl, Célestine (JEANNE MOREAU), finds herself trapped in a bizarre, perverted world when she quits her city job to become a chambermaid for a family in provincial France. *Belle de Jour* (1967), based on a novel by Joseph Kessel, is an erotic drama about a middle-class housewife, Severine (Catherine Deneuve), who pursues her sexual fantasies in a brothel during the day. Her escapades destroy her husband, Pierre (Jean Sorel), who is a hardworking, kind, and loving surgeon.

Buñuel's other films include an adaptation of Daniel Defoe's *Robinson Crusoe* (1952); *Simón del desierto* (1965; *Simon of the Desert*); *Tristana* (1970); *The voie lactée* (1970; *The Milky Way*); the comedy *Le charme discret de la bourgeoisie* (1972; *The Discreet Charm of the Bourgeoisie*), about three wealthy couples who fail at every attempt to eat dinner together, which won the Academy Award for best foreign-language film of the year; *The Phantom of Liberty* (1974); and his final film, *That Obscure Object of Desire* (1977). Buñuel's autobiography, *My Last Sigh*, was published in 1983.

BIBLIOGRAPHY

Aranda, J. Francisco, *Luis Buñuel: A Critical Biography*, 1976; Buache, Freddy, *The Cinema of Luis Buñuel*, 1973; Durgnat, Raymond, *Luis Buñuel*, 1968.

Burgess, Anthony

(February 25, 1917–November 22, 1993)
Novelist, Critic, Composer, Translator

The English novelist and critic Anthony Burgess produced a large volume of literature and criticism marked by his skillful use of language and pointed satire. He is best known, however, for one of his own least favorite works, *A Clockwork Orange*, popularized by American director Stanley Kubrick's film version. The novel reached classic status in English literature and depicts, in a slang Burgess invented, the exploits of a young, violent criminal and society's attempts to rehabilitate him.

Burgess was born John Burgess Wilson in Harpurhey, Manchester, England. His father, a bookkeeper and pianist, raised him as a Catholic. His mother, a dancer, died of the Spanish flu when Burgess was a child. He studied languages and English literature at Bishop Bilsborrow Primary School, Xavarian College, and Manchester University.

After serving in World War II, Burgess held several posts in the field of education. He taught at Birmingham University from 1946 to 1950 and worked for the Ministry of Education for two of those years. From 1950 to 1954 he taught at the Banbury Grammar School. His subsequent post as a civil servant in Malaya (now Malaysia) and Borneo provided the experience and material for *The Long Day Wanes: A Malayan Trilogy* (1964).

Wishing to leave his wife some money, Burgess began writing in earnest when a doctor misdiagnosed him with a terminal brain tumor. Burgess's adeptness with multiple languages enhances the sharp, witty writing that characterizes his satiric commentaries on twentieth-century society. In the futuristic *The Wanting Seed* (1962), world leaders desperately try to bring overpopulation under control.

The comic character of F. X. Enderby, a poet, appears in several of Burgess's novels, including *Inside Mr. Enderby* (1963), *Enderby Outside* (1968), and *Enderby's Dark Lady* (1984). Like Burgess himself, Enderby is an artist forced to confront the pop culture of the 1960s. Burgess's other early novels include *One Hand Clapping* (1961), *Honey for the Bears* (1963), and *Venus* (1964).

A Clockwork Orange (1963), Burgess's least favorite of his own works, ironically became his most popular novel. Its protagonist and narrator, Alex, is a teenage criminal who speaks in a slang-ridden language Burgess invented, Nadsat. Alex's brutal crimes send him to jail, and he becomes a guinea pig in a scientific rehabilitation experiment. Kubrick produced a highly successful film from Burgess's novel but, to Burgess's disgust, omitted the author's ending, which finds Alex maturing out of his criminal behavior. Some of the story's characters reappear in *The Doctor Is Sick* (1966), about a doctor who is diagnosed with a brain tumor.

Burgess's later novels include *Napoleon Symphony* (1974), *Earthly Powers* (1980), *The End of the World News* (1983), *The Kingdom of the Wicked* (1985), *Any Old Iron* (1989), and *A Dead Man in Deptford* (1993). *Byrne: A Novel* (1995) was Burgess's last work, a satiric "novel in verse." Its main character, Michael Byrne, is an Irish Don Juan and artist who disappears in Nazi Germany.

His nonfiction books include *Here Comes Everybody: An Introduction to James Joyce for the Ordinary Reader* (1965); biographies of David Herbert Lawrence, William Shakespeare, and Ernest Hemingway; and his own two-part autobiography. In addition, Burgess composed music, translated, and wrote television scripts, including a translation and adaptation of Edmond Rostand's classic *Cyrano de Bergerac*.

Bibliography

Burgess, Anthony, *Little Wilson and Big God: Being the First Part of the Autobiography*, 1986; Coale, Samuel, *Anthony Burgess*, 1981.

Burton, Richard

(November 10, 1925–August 5, 1984)
Actor, Director

The Welsh-born actor Richard Burton first made his name in the theater and became an international star with his role as Mark Antony in the 1963 film *Cleopatra*. Burton's turbulent off-screen life was marked by five marriages—two of them to Elizabeth Taylor—numerous affairs, and alcoholism. He is best known for his skillful portrayals of Shakespearean characters, but appeared in many other roles as well.

Burton was born Richard Walter Jenkins in Pontrhydyfen, Wales. He was the twelfth of thirteen children of an alcoholic miner and his wife. After his mother's death when he was 2, he went to live with an older sister. Burton attended the Eastern Infants School and became the first member of his family to win a scholarship to the Port Talbot Secondary School. At school he was an above-average, physically active student with a streak of rebellion. During his student years, two teachers, Meredith Jones and Philip Burton, played a formative role in his life. The latter took Richard into his home, tutored him, and helped him obtain a scholarship to the University of Oxford. Richard eventually adopted Burton's name.

Aside from the school productions in which he appeared, Burton acted his first role as Glan in a 1943 production of *The Druid's Rest*. His first success in the theater came with his role as a clerk in Christopher Fry's comedy *The Lady's Not for Burning* (1949) at the Globe Theater in London. In 1948, Burton obtained his first film role in *The Last Days of Dolwyn*, a story about the flooding of a Welsh town. He appeared in several other films before he acted in his first American cinema part, Philip Ashley in *My Cousin Rachel* (1952).

In *The Robe* (1953), the first film to be shown in CinemaScope, Burton played the Roman officer Marcellus Gallio. He rocketed to international fame with his role as Mark Antony in *Cleopatra* (1963), less for his performance than for his highly publicized off-screen affair with his costar, Elizabeth Taylor. Burton and Taylor married in 1964, divorced a decade later, remarried in 1975, and di-

Richard Burton as Henry VIII in *Anne of a Thousand Days* (Ann Ronan/Image Select)

vorced once and for all in 1976. Among the eleven films they made together are the film versions of Edward Albee's *Who's Afraid of Virginia Woolf?* (1966); *The Comedians* (1967); Christopher Marlowe's *Doctor Faustus* (1968), with Burton codirecting and playing Faustus and Taylor as Helen of Troy; and Shakespeare's *The Taming of the Shrew* (1967).

Burton delivered a number of performances as prominent historical figures, including Alexander in *Alexander the Great* (1956); Thomas à Becket in *Becket* (1964); Henry VIII in *Anne of the Thousand Days* (1970); Leon Trotsky in *The Assassination of Trotsky* (1971); and the German composer Richard Wagner (1813–1883) in *Wagner* (1983). His other noteworthy films include versions of JOHN OSBORNE's play, *Look Back in Anger* (1959); Tennessee Williams's play, *The Night of the Iguana* (1964); *The Spy Who Came in From the Cold* (1965), based on a novel by JOHN LE CARRÉ; and Peter Shaffer's play, *Equus* (1977). Burton's final role in film was O'Brien in an adaptation of GEORGE ORWELL's *Nineteen Eighty-Four* (1984).

Throughout his film career, Burton continued to perform in the theater, appearing in several of Shakespeare's plays in London and on Broadway. His 1964 portrayal of Hamlet in JOHN GIELGUD's Broadway production was one of his most popular roles, as was his King Arthur in *Camelot* (1960 and 1980). He delivered his last stage performance in New York in NOËL COWARD's *Private Lives* (1983), opposite Taylor.

Burton's television roles include Heathcliff in *Wuthering Heights* (1958) and Winston Churchill in *Walk with Destiny* (1974). He also recorded radio plays and poetry readings on record. A brain hemorrhage took his life in 1984.

BIBLIOGRAPHY

Alpert, Hollis, *Burton*, 1986; Bragg, Melvyn, *Richard Burton: A Life*, 1988; Junor, Penny, *Burton: The Man Behind the Myth*, 1985.

Caballé, Montserrat

(April 12, 1933–)
Singer

Monteserrat Caballé contributed her warm and powerful soprano voice to many roles in the world's major opera houses, mastering French, Italian, and German repertoire. She is particularly noted for her skill in interpreting Verdi and Donizetti. She recorded her work extensively and gave recitals of Spanish songs and other music, and, like her contemporaries Luciano Pavarotti, José Carreras, and Enrico Caruso, she has dabbled in popular music.

Caballé was born Maria de Montserrat Viviana Concepción Caballé y Folch into a family of modest means in Barcelona, Spain. The Spanish Civil War raged in the background of her early childhood. Caballé attended a local school but showed little interest in her studies. More fascinating to her was the music she heard on the radio or on her parents' records, and she was prone to burst into singing at home. Among the voices she listened to was that of Conchita Badía, under whom she later studied privately. Her first trip to the opera (for a performance of *Madame Butterfly*) came when she was seven.

Caballé next studied at the Conservatorio del Liceo in Barcelona, where her most important instructor was Eugenia Kemmeny. Kemmeny, who was an accomplished athlete as well as a soprano, stressed the cultivation of emotion, breathing, and muscular development. She called her controversial methods "respiratory gymnastics," and her exercises stuck with Caballé for many years. Nevertheless, during her final exam, for which she sang three arias, Caballé fainted. It was not the last time—she was to collapse on several more occasions during her singing career, whether from nerves or from her later diagnosed hypoglycemic condition. Caballé also studied under Badía and Napoleone Annovazzi, for whose orchestra she sang in 1954.

From 1956 to 1959 she sang at the Basel Opera, finding her first success as Mimí in *La Bohème*. At Basel she sang many roles she would repeat throughout her career—Elvira in *Don Giovanni*, Jaroslavna in *Prince Igor*, the title roles in *Aïda* and *Tosca*, and the title role in

Montserrat Caballé (Universal Pictorial and Press Agency)

Richard Strauss's *Salome*, one of her particular successes. In 1959 she joined the Bremen Opera, where she sang, among other roles, Violeta Valéry in Guiseppi Verde's *La Traviata* and the title role of *Madame Butterfly*.

During this time Caballé also began to make guest appearances at major opera houses around the world. In 1964 she debuted in Mexico City in Jules Massenet's *Manon*. She married the tenor Bernabé Martí the same year. The next year saw her American debut and a performance in Gaetano Donizetti's *Lucrezia Borgia* at Carnegie Hall in New York. Her other roles include the Countess in Mozart's *Le nozze di Figaro;* Marschallin in Strauss's *Der Rosenkavalier;* and Marguerite in Gounoud's *Faust*, which she sang for her debut at the Metropolitan Opera House in New York.

Aside from her opera roles, Caballé also gave recitals of Spanish songs and other music. Sometimes overshadowed by her older and more high-profile contemporaries Maria Callas and RENATA TEBALDI, she remained more open to modern music than did they. Freddie Mercury, lead singer of the British rock band Queen and a fan, collaborated with her on "Barcelona," later adopted as a theme song of the Barcelona Olympics.

Caballé recorded an operatic recital for Vergara in 1964 and made many other recordings. Among these are *Salomé; *EMI's first recording of Arrigo Boito's *Mefistofele; La Bohème* for RCA with PLÁCIDO DOMINGO; several works by GIACOMO PUCCINI; the first recording of Verdi's *I vesperi siciliani* as well as numerous other Verdi works; and many Spanish songs.

BIBLIOGRAPHY

Pullen, Robert, and Taylor, Stephen, *Montserrat Caballé*, 1994.

Calvino, Italo

(October 15, 1923–September 19, 1985)
Novelist, Short-Story Writer, Writer of Children's Books

Italo Calvino emerged as a writer in the vein of the Italian Neorealists and later evolved his own blend of fantasy and realism. He achieved fame as a writer with three allegorical fantasies written in the 1950s, and his fiction is sometimes compared to the work of the Argentinean writer JORGE LUIS BORGES.

Calvino was born to Italian parents in Santiago de las Vegas, Cuba. His parents, both botanists, were in Cuba doing research and returned the family to Italy shortly after his birth. Calvino spent his youth on the family farm in the Mediterranean town of San Remo, where he studied at local schools. When he reached university age, he enrolled in the Faculty of Agriculture at the University of Turin, where his father taught. With the Nazi occupation of Italy, Calvino left school and joined a group of partisans in resistance to the Germans. His wartime experience provided the material for his first novel and a number of early short stories.

When the war ended Calvino joined the Communist Party. Nevertheless, he returned to the University of Turin and decided to study literature. He finished his degree with a dissertation on JOSEPH CONRAD and began contributing stories to periodicals. Around this time he met Giulio Einaudi, who later published the majority of his writing. The immediate postwar years marked the period of his most intense political activity, as he involved himself with the Communist Party and contributed to the Communist periodical *L'Unità*.

Il sentiero dei nidi di ragno (1947; *The Path to the Nest of Spiders*), Calvino's first novel, belongs to the Italian Neorealist style, which expressed itself most forcefully in the cinema (see ROBERTO ROSSELLINI). Narrated by an adolescent boy named Pin, the story is based on Calvino's experiences with the partisans during the war. Pin, like many of Calvino's characters, is an innocent, politically unaware youth who essentially joins the partisans by accident, and he knows little of the cause for which he fights. Calvino's short-story collection *Ultimo viene il corvo* (1949; *Adam, One Afternoon, and Other Stories*) follows in the same vein.

During the 1950s Calvino turned to writing fantastic allegories and established himself as a writer of international stature. *Il visconte dimezzato* (1951; *The Cloven Viscount*) was the first in a trilogy of fantasies that brought him international fame. The protagonist of the story is Medardo, a seventeenth-century nobleman. A cannon shot divides Medardo into two halves during a war with the Turks. Medardo's evil half returns home to the horror of everyone, eventually engaging his good half in a duel over a woman. The two halves of Medardo reconcile after the confrontation.

The second fantasy, *Il barone rampante* (1957; *The Baron in the Trees*), depicts a nobleman, Cosimo Piovasco di Rondò, who as a boy climbs into the trees and never comes down.

As penance, a Sister Theodora narrates the third fantasy, *Il cavaliere inesistente* (1959; *The Nonexistent Knight*), about a knight who does not really exist beneath his armor. *I racconti* (*The Tales*), a collection of Calvino's stories, appeared in 1958.

During this time Calvino continued to write political commentary, although he left the Communist Party in 1957. He traveled to the Soviet Union in the 1950s and contributed a number of articles to the Soviet magazine *ABC*. From 1959 to 1966 he coedited a leftist journal with Elio Vittorini. After the 1950s, Calvino's political writings declined, and he devoted his energies more and more to literature.

Calvino returned to a realistic mode to some extent in later works such as *La giornata d'uno scrutatore* (1963; *The Watcher*), a novel that reflects his own disillusionment with the Communist Party. Set during the Italian election of June 1953, the story revisits the political climate of the Resistance era through the Communist poll-watcher Amerigo Ormea. *The Watcher*, like many of Calvino's later works, is more experimental in structure than his earlier works, which follow traditional narrative styles.

A collection of children's stories, *Marcovaldo*, appeared in 1963, and Calvino married the Argentine translator Chichita Singer the following year. He spent much of his adult life in Rome and in Paris, where he lived for sixteen years. His later works of fantasy include *Le cosmi-*

comiche (1965; *Cosmicomics*) and the tales in *Ti con zero* (1967; *T Zero*). Narrated by a mysterious figure known as Qfwfq whose thoughts are presented using stream-of-consciousness technique, *Cosmicomics* relates Calvino's vision of the evolution of the universe.

Other works include *La speculazione edilizia* (1957; *Building Speculation*); *Il castello dei destini incrociate* (1969; *The Castle of Crossed Destinies*); *Le città invisibili* (1972; *Invisible Cities*), built around Marco Polo's voyage to Kublai Kahn's empire; *Se una notte d'inverno un viaggiatore* (1979; *If on a Winter's Night a Traveler*); and *Mr. Palomar* (1983). His essay collection *Una pietra sopra: Discorsi di letteratura e società* (1980; *The Uses of Literature*) consists of pieces that previously appeared in *Il Menabò*. Calvino died of a stroke at the age of 61.

BIBLIOGRAPHY

Adler, Sara Maria, *Calvino: The Writer as Fablemaker*, 1979; Cannon, JoAnn, *Italo Calvino: Writer and Critic*, 1981; Carter, Albert Howard III, *Italo Calvino: Metamorphoses of Fantasy*, 1987; Weiss, Beno, *Understanding Italo Calvino*, 1993.

Camus, Albert

(November 7, 1913–January 4, 1960)
Novelist, Dramatist, Essayist, Philosopher

The French-Algerian existentialist writer Albert Camus examined what he believed was the absurdity, futility, and meaninglessness of life in his novels, essays, and plays, facing the crumbling of all the old systems of belief, yet searching for the possibility of creating an authentic existence. He received the Nobel Prize for Literature in 1957 "for his important literary production, which with clear-sighted earnestness illuminates the problems of the human conscience in our times."

Camus was born in Mondovi, Algeria, which the French controlled until 1962. His father lost his life in World War I when he was less than a year old, and he was raised primarily by his impoverished mother. His elementary school teacher, Louis Germain, recognized him as an exceptional student and helped him further his education. Camus attended the University of Algiers and studied philosophy. In 1930, he suffered the first of several severe bouts with tuberculosis.

From 1930 to 1940 Camus associated himself with young leftist intellectuals in Algeria. He founded and was involved in all aspects—directing, producing, acting, writing—of the Worker's Theater, the theater with which he hoped to bring quality drama to the working classes. In 1934 he married Simone Hié, whose addiction to drugs contributed to the end of their marriage two years later. The first of Camus's published writings, a collection of essays entitled *L'Envers et l'endroit* (*The Wrong Side and the Right Side*), appeared in 1937. In it Camus explored the contrasts between the beauty and pleasures of

Albert Camus (Hulton Getty)

earthly existence and the horror and inevitability of death, introducing questions that would preoccupy his thoughts for the rest of his life. A second collection of essays, *Noces* (*Nuptials*), was published in 1939 and explores similar themes.

In 1940 Camus married his second wife, Francine Faure, and wrote a controversial essay on the condition of Muslims in French Algeria. He moved to Paris and became friends with JEAN-PAUL SARTRE. After being rejected from military service on account of his health, he became involved in the Resistance to the Nazi occupation of France during World War II (usually referred to simply as "the Resistance") and edited the underground newspaper *Combat*. The French government awarded him the Medal of Liberation for his efforts in 1946.

Camus's first published novel, *L'Etranger* (1942; *The Stranger*), is set in Algeria and involves a murderer who is convicted of shooting an Arab. The murderer, Meursault, receives the death sentence less for his crime than for the fact that he remains indifferent to cares others believe should worry him. In an essay entitled *Le Mythe de Sisyphe* (1942; *The Myth of Sisyphus*), originally titled *L'absurde*, Camus examined the question of whether an absurd life is worth living. In Greek mythology, the god Zeus sentenced Sisyphus to spend eternity pushing a rock up a hill and watching it roll back down. Camus likened the futility of Sisyphus's toil to the struggles of people who go through life only to die. Nevertheless, he concluded, "one must imagine Sisyphus happy." Camus developed similar themes in his novel *La Peste* (1947; *The Plague*), and plays such as *Cross Purpose* (1944) and *Caligula* (1945).

In his early years, the basis of Camus's philosophy was the conviction that death renders life and existence meaningless and absurd. He struggled to extract happiness from this absurd life, and in fact he believed it was possible to do so. As he grew older, he embraced a philosophy of personal rebellion, in which one accepts the absurd and stands up against it in the face of absurdity. In the 1951 essay *L'Homme révolté* (*The Rebel*), Camus rejected Marxism and Stalinism as well as Christianity and proposed individual moral rebellion as a solution to the absurd man's problem. Because Camus rejected political and social rebellion in *The Rebel*, many leftist intellectuals, including Sartre, sharply criticized him.

Camus's other works include the novels *La Chute* (1956; *The Fall*) and *Happy Death*, his first novel, not published until after his death; the play *L'Etat de siège* (1948; *State of Siege*); *L'Exil et le royaume* (1957; *Exile and the Kingdom*), a collection of short stories; and the essay collection *L'Eté* (1954; *Summer*), which recalled some of the exuberance of *Noces* and other early essays. He died in a car accident on the way to Paris in 1960.

BIBLIOGRAPHY

Brée, Germaine, *Camus*, 1959; King, Adele, *Albert Camus*, 1964; Lottman, Herbert R., *Albert Camus: A Biography*, 1997.

Caro, Anthony

(March 8, 1924–)
Sculptor

The abstract sculptures for which Sir Anthony Alfred Caro is best known are creations of welded steel, composed of an interplay of beams, rods, and other shapes. As an assistant to the abstract sculptor HENRY MOORE, he was influenced early in his career by Moore's style. Caro's meeting with the American abstract and welded-steel sculptor David Smith in 1959 set him on the path to the mature abstract, constructivist forms of style.

Caro was born in New Maiden, Surrey, England. From 1942 to 1944 he studied engineering at Christ's College, Cambridge. During World War II he served in the Fleet Air Army of the Royal Navy, and in 1946 he began to study sculpture at the Regent Street Polytechnic in London. From 1947 to 1952 he studied at the Royal Academy Schools, and during that time he moved to Much Hadham and worked as Moore's assistant. He married Sheila Girling in 1949. In 1953 he took a teaching position at the School of Art in London, where he remained until 1979.

Moore was the biggest influence on Caro's early sculpture, which consists mainly of figurative works in clay. His sculptures were first exhibited in 1955, and the following year he held his first one-man show at the Galleria del Naviglio in Milan. His style changed radically, however, following a trip to the United States and his meeting with David Smith.

Under Smith's influence, Caro moved into pure abstraction and adopted steel as his primary material. *Midday* (1960), composed of painted yellow steel and one of his best-known works, reflects the shift in his work. An expert welder, he began creating sculptures from beams, thin rods, and sheets of metal, with no bases. Sometimes he painted the metal in striking, solid colors, as in the purple-painted steel sculpture *Shaftsbury* (1965) and the bright-green mix of cylindrical and rectangular shapes entitled *Dumbfound* (1976). In other works, he simply allowed the metal to rust. Other sculptures were interplays of thin, metal bars, such as *Emma Dipper* (1977) and *Emma Dance* (1977–1978).

In 1974 Caro worked at the York Steel Company in Toronto, where he began a series of large steel sculptures that required the use of cranes. Caro created some paper sculptures in the early 1980s as well as stoneware and sculptures in wood and lead. In the 1990s he began to create "sculpitectures," such as the twenty-two-foot-high *Tower of Discovery* (1991), in which the observer can walk around. He was made an honorary member of the American Academy of Arts and Letters in 1979 and knighted in 1987.

BIBLIOGRAPHY

Rubin, William Stanley, *Anthony Caro*, 1975; Waldman, Diane, *Anthony Caro*, 1982.

Carreras, José

(December 5, 1946–)
Singer

With a voice acclaimed for its lyrical qualities and tonal purity, José Carreras attained international fame as an operatic tenor in the 1970s, performing in the standard Italian operatic roles. With PLÁCIDO DOMINGO and LUCIANO PAVAROTTI, he formed the Three Tenors, who gave a number of high-profile concerts around the world in the 1990s.

Carreras was born Josep Maria Carreras-Coll into a Catalan family in Barcelona. Although his parents were not musically inclined, they were supportive of the singing talent and ambition that emerged in their son at a young age. His father was a teacher by profession, and his mother was a hairdresser. For economic and political reasons (his father was a veteran of the Spanish Civil War and had fought against the Franco forces), the family moved briefly to Argentina before returning to Spain. At the age of six Carreras experienced his first inspiration to sing when he saw the film *The Great Caruso* (see ENRICO CARUSO), with Mario Lanza.

From that point on Carreras began to sing around the house, dressing up as a character on occasion. At the age of 8 he saw his first opera—a performance of *Aïda* with RENATA TEBALDI. Soon afterward he gave his first public performance, in a benefit for the National Radio. At the age of 11 he played a small role in a production at the Gran Teatro del Liceo. His family's purchase of a record player augmented his ambition to sing. His interest in his schoolwork was marginal, and his other hobby in his youth was sports.

When he was 17, Carreras began to take singing lessons from Jaime Francisco Puig, a local singer and teacher. He next studied under Juan Ruax, who remained a lifelong friend and whom Carreras warmly described as "the complete opposite of those unbending, overbearing singing teachers who from time immemorial have forced a certain method on their students." Still unsure about pursuing opera as a career, Carreras entered the University of Barcelona, but by 1968 he had decided finally to become an opera singer.

Carreras earned critical acclaim for his Flavio in Vincenzo Bellini's *Norma* in 1970. His performance in that show impressed the soprano MONTSERRAT CABALLÉ, who from then on remained his loyal friend and supporter. Carreras had his first leading role as Gennaro in Donizetti's *Lucrezia Borgia*. Over the next several years Carreras debuted at the major opera cities around the world—New York, London, and finally in Milan at La Scala in 1975. The first of many collaborative efforts with conductor Herbert von Karajan came in Salzburg in 1976, when he sang in Giuseppe Verdi's *Requiem*.

Over the years Carreras continued to appear in the standard Italian operas, and he is particularly known for the lyrical beauty of his Don José in Georges Bizet's *Carmen*. In the mid-1980s he branched out into other forms of music, recording Leonard Bernstein's *West Side Story* with soprano KIRI TE KANAWA. Carreras made his first recordings in 1972 and since then has recorded dozens of operas, songs, and other material. Following his recovery from leukemia in the late 1980s, he participated with Pavarotti and Domingo in the highly successful Three Tenors concerts in 1990 and 1994, an effort that also produced several recordings.

BIBLIOGRAPHY

Carreras, José, *Singing From the Soul: An Autobiography*, 1989.

Caruso, Enrico

(February 27, 1873–August 21, 1921)
Singer

Enrico Caruso charmed world audiences with his warm, lyrical voice in the first two decades of the twentieth century and was the world's most renowned operatic tenor in his day. Caruso was also one of the first artists to offer his music to the public in the form of gramophone recordings.

Caruso was born Errico Caruso into a large, impoverished family in Naples, Italy. A woman from the church nursed and tutored him, helping him endure the conditions of a home life with poor sanitation, frequent illness, and cramped quarters. Caruso sang regularly in his youth—first in the church choir and later at other engagements and with café troupes. A talent for drawing and sketching also emerged, and he earned extra money copying music. His finances prohibited him from taking the singing lessons he desired, but he finally got a break when a persistent friend persuaded Guglielmo Vergine, one of the city's leading teachers, to take him on in exchange for 25 percent of his earnings for five years. (The contract eventually resulted in a legal battle.)

When he was 18, Caruso served two months of a three-year term in the military before he was excused to return to his music lessons. Vergine was sometimes less than helpful to Caruso and regarded him as a minor talent. Caruso debuted on stage at age 21 in Mario Morelli's *L'Amico Francesco* at the Teatro Nuovo in Naples. He began to build his reputation with a successful performance as Loris in the premiere of Umberto Giordano's *Fedora* in Milan in 1898.

Caruso's tenor impressed the composer GIACOMO PUCCINI, and in 1900, thanks to Puccini, Caruso starred as Rodolfo in Puccini's *La Bohème*. The performance, opposite Caruso's longtime mistress, Ada Giachetti, playing the soprano, was a rousing success. Caruso debuted at La Scala, the Milan opera house built by the Austrian archduchess Maria Theresa, in Ruggero Leoncavallo's *La Bohème* (1901), conducted by Arturo Toscanini. Later that season he sang in the premiere of Pietro Mascagni's *Le Maschere* (1901; *The Masks*) and appeared, to great popu-

A cartoon representing Enrico Caruso and Marcella Sembrich in *La Bohème* (Ann Ronan/Image Select)

lar acclaim, as Nemorino in *L'Elisir d'Amore*. He appeared in many subsequent productions at La Scala, including Francesco Cilea's *Adriana Lecouvreur* and Puccini's *La Fanciulla del West* (*The Girl of the Golden West*).

The success of Caruso's performances in Italy led to engagements around the world, including St. Petersburg and Buenos Aires. In a popular production of Puccini's *La Bohème* in Monte Carlo, Caruso first sang opposite the soprano Nellie Melba. He would sing opposite many other top sopranos of his day, including Emmy Destin, Luisa Tetrazzini, and Mary Garden.

Caruso debuted in the United States at the Metropolitan Opera in New York in 1903 in Giuseppe Verdi's *Rigoletto*. He enjoyed a long career singing at both the Metropolitan Opera and Covent Garden in London. Among the many other operas in which he starred during his career are *Mefistofele;* Verdi's *Aïda, Il Trovatore,* and *Un Ballo* (as King Gustavo); Leoncavallo's *I Paglicacci* (as Canio); Puccini's *Manon Lescaut, La Tosca,* and *Madame Butterfly;* and Jacques Halévy's *La Juive* (his final role, as Eléazar).

In the years before World War I, Caruso's life and career began to deteriorate. His relationship with Giachetti ended bitterly, eventually resulting in his successful slander suit against her. His voice began to darken, but on account of his popularity he was not denied engagements. His health also began to worsen. In 1917, he met and later married the American Dorothy Benjamin.

Aside from his success as a live performer, Caruso earned royalties from some of the first gramophone recordings, which he began in 1902 under contract with Fred Gaisberg in London. In the United States, Calvin G. Child of the Victor Company (later purchased by the Radio Corporation of America and known as RCA-Victor) took an interest in recording Caruso's work, and many of his songs were subsequently released on the company's Red Seal series. Like his performances, Caruso's recordings gained enormous popularity. Caruso developed a severe lung infection in 1921 and died later that year.

BIBLIOGRAPHY

Greenfeld, Howard, *Caruso,* 1984; Greenfeld, Howard, *Caruso: An Illustrated Life,* 1991; Jackson, Stanley, *Caruso,* 1972; Scott, Michael, *The Great Caruso,* 1988.

Cary, Joyce

(December 7, 1888–March 29, 1957)
Novelist

The moderate literary output of Arthur Joyce Lunel Cary, always called simply Joyce Cary, falls into three main categories: his fiction set in Africa, which probes the complex political and social situations created by European colonialism so successfully that some of it is still read because of the insight it gives into the inadequacy of all simple and idealistic solutions; his novels on childhood; and his trilogies, in which each volume is narrated by a different character in the story.

Cary was born in Londonderry, Northern Ireland. His father came from a long line of Anglo-Irish landowners, and the family moved to London in his youth. At the age of 10, Cary suffered the first in a lifelong series of tragic losses when his mother died. From his childhood through his adulthood, he was never overly interested in school. Cary studied at the Hurstleigh School in Tunbridge Wells and then at Clifton College, beginning in 1903. In 1906 he went to Paris to study painting, and he returned the following year to study art at the Board of Manufacturers School of Art in Edinburgh. Cary finished his education between 1909 and 1912, studying law at Trinity College, Oxford.

In 1912, Cary joined a Red Cross unit with the Montenegrin army in the Balkans.

The following year, he began seven years of service in Africa that included fighting in the Southwest African Field Force in World War I and working in the Nigerian Civil Service. He returned to Oxford and joined his wife (Gertrude Margaret Ogilvie, whom he had married in 1916) in 1920.

The same year, a number of his short stories appeared in the United States in the *Saturday Evening Post*. His first novel, however, was not published until 1932. As with a number of its successors, *Aissa Saved* takes place in Africa and depicts the multifaceted conflicts in colonial African society. The main character, Aissa, is a Christian convert caught between the demands of her new religion and her old one.

An American Visitor (1933) also unfolds in Africa and examines other conflicts created by the intrusion of colonialism in Nigeria. The American visitor is Marie Hasluck, who marries Brewsher. She and Brewsher believe in minimal intrusion into the Birri province, while another faction seeks to introduce tin mining. Both come into conflict with missionaries. Other novels set in Africa, *The African Witch* and *Mister Johnson*, followed in 1936 and 1939. Cary came to favor independence for African colonies and advocated it in a political work, *The Case for African Freedom* (1941).

In the years surrounding World War II, Cary wrote two novels on the theme of childhood. The protagonist of *Charley Is My Darling* (1940) is a young, rebellious boy who goes to live in the country and leads other kids into trouble. *A House of Children* (1941) is semiautobiographical, with many incidents drawn from Cary's own childhood, and won the James Tait Black Memorial Prize.

The first of Cary's two trilogies begins with *Herself Surprised* (1941). The protagonist is Sara Monday, a country girl who takes a job as a cook for the Monday family. Sara, an emotional woman who perceives the world through feeling rather than thought, marries Matthew Monday and becomes involved with two other men, Tom Wilcher and Gulley Jimson. Wilcher is a staunchly conservative lawyer, whereas Jimson is a volatile visionary artist. Wilcher narrates the second part of the trilogy, *To Be a Pilgrim* (1942), and Jimson narrates the third and most popular of the volumes, *The Horse's Mouth* (1944), acclaimed for its masterfully intense combination of drama and comedy.

Having been rejected for military service in World War II, Cary served in the Civil Defense. In 1942, the Ministry of Information asked him to write a motivational film script for *Men of Two Worlds*. After the war, Cary lost his wife to cancer in 1949 and his son to heart disease four years later.

His second trilogy begins with *A Prisoner of Grace* (1952). Its protagonist, Nina Woodville, is a young orphan who finds herself pregnant by Jim Latter. She marries the politician Chester Nimmo, whom she does not love, and feels trapped in an unhappy marriage for years. When she finally breaks free, she marries Jim, but Chester continues to place demands on her. Jim murders her. An aged Chester Nimmo narrates *Except the Lord* (1953), in which he tells the story of his younger years. *Not Honour More* (1955) is narrated by Jim Latter.

Failing health prevented Cary from completing even the first volume of a third trilogy, *The Captive and the Free*

(1959), a treatment of religious faith and practice. The novel was published posthumously in its unfinished form. He tried his hand at other forms of writing that met with less success. His *Verses* were published in 1909, and his short stories appeared in the posthumously published volume *Spring Song* (1960). His other works include the political pieces *Power In Men* (1939) and *British West Africa* (1946); the play *The King is Dead, Long Live the King* (1939); and a volume of lectures, *Art and Reality* (1958).

BIBLIOGRAPHY

Bishop, Alan, *Gentleman Rider: A Life of Joyce Cary*, 1988; Fisher, Barbara, *Joyce Cary: The Writer and His Theme*, 1980; Roby, Kinley E., *Joyce Cary*, 1984.

Casadesus, Robert

(April 7, 1899–September 19, 1972)
Pianist, Composer

The pianist and composer Robert Marcel Casadesus, one of an extended family of distinguished composers, violinists, cellists, conductors, and actors, was known for his clarity of style and interpretations of the piano works of the French composers and of Wolfgang Amadeus Mozart. Casadesus was also a respected teacher.

Casadesus was born into a large family in Paris. His mother died at his birth, and his father was a traveling actor, so he was raised primarily by grandparents who lived near Paris. He took his first piano lessons from his aunt Rose Casadesus, a concert pianist. At age 11 he entered the Paris Conservatory, where he trained on the piano under Louis Diémer (a former pupil of the composer Franz Liszt) and studied composition under Xavier Leroux. He won several awards for his piano playing there, including the Grand Prix Diémer. In 1917 he made his debut as a professional pianist.

In 1921 Casadesus married the concert pianist Gaby L'Hote, who was also a student of Diémer. He began touring in 1922 and distinguished himself as a piano player around the world. He frequently performed the works of French composers such as Gabriel Fauré (1845–1924), MAURICE RAVEL, CLAUDE DEBUSSY, and Albert Roussel (1869–1937). His American debut came in 1933, as a soloist with the New York Philharmonic Symphony—a performance that impressed the Italian conductor ARTURO TOSCANINI, who was in attendance. Casadesus made many recordings, including all of Ravel's piano music and Eduoard Lalo's *Symphonie Espagnole* with violinist Zino Francescatti, pianist Max Lanner, and the Columbia Symphony Orchestra. He received the Commandeur de la Légion d'honneur and Belgium's Commandeur de l'Ordre de Léopold.

In 1929–1930 Casadesus was professor of musical interpretation at the Conservatory of Genoa, and the following two years he taught at the Conservatory of Lausanne. From 1935 until the eruption of World War II, he taught at the American Conservatory at Fontainebleau. Casadesus was also a composer and in 1917 finished his first work, *Le Voyage Imaginaire*. Among his other compositions are violin sonatas, piano concertos, and two symphonies.

BIBLIOGRAPHY

Casadesus, Gaby, *Mes noces musicales*, 1989.

Casals, Pablo

(December 29, 1876–October 22, 1973)
Cellist, Conductor

Best known for his interpretations of the cello music of Johann Sebastian Bach (1685–1750), the Spanish-born Pablo Casals was one of the foremost cellists of the twentieth century. Exiled from his native country during the Spanish Civil War (1936–1939), he refused to return to Fascist Spain and spent his mature years advocating world peace through music. Casals was also known for his gifts as a teacher.

Casals was of Catalan ancestry, born Pau Carlos Salvador Defillo de Casals in the Tarragonese town of El Vendrell, Spain. The eldest of his mother's surviving children, he was her favorite and the undisputed center of her attention. His father was a piano and organ repairman, singer, organist, and choirmaster, and his interests also extended to science and politics. From him Casals inherited his ardent republicanism and received his first music instruction, starting with piano lessons at the age of 4. Casals attended a local school as a boy and in his spare time enjoyed learning to play obscure instruments.

A major turning point in his life came in 1888, when he heard his first chamber trio perform. Overwhelmed by the music, and particularly the cello, he fell in love with the instrument that would bring him world fame. Over his father's objections, his mother sent him to the Municipal School of Music in Barcelona, where he studied the cello for five years under José García.

García was his most important instructor. Under him Casals felt free enough to develop his own style and dispense with conventional rules of playing. Rather than move the entire left hand, Casals preferred to extend the fingers when possible. He also disliked the generally required rigid pose, in which the cellist plays with stiff arms and elbows to the side of the body. Casals, too, rejected the requirement of using the full length of the bow.

During his time as a student, Casals took part-time jobs playing the cello at cafés, weddings, and other places to earn money. At the age of 14 he discovered Bach's *Six Suites for Unaccompanied Violincello*, which was to become one of his signature pieces as a performer. He

Pablo Casals (Ann Ronan/Image Select)

By 1898 Casals had repaired his relationship with his royal patrons, and the Queen Regent purchased for him a fine cello. His major debut as a cello soloist came the same year at the Concerts Lamoureaux in Paris. Casals soon established himself as one of the finest cellists in Europe, playing for many royal audiences as well as the public.

From 1898 to 1917 he toured extensively in Europe and the Americas. Although he often performed alone, he also appeared with others. His most famous collaboration, with French pianist Alfred Cortot and French violinist Jacques Thibaud, produced more than 150 international performances. As a performer he promoted the works of others he admired, such as the Hungarian composer Emanuel Moór.

In 1919 Casals, with Thibaud and particularly Cortot, helped found the École Normale de Musique in Paris. The following year he established the Orquestra Pau Casals in Barcelona, which he conducted regularly for sixteen years. Each fall and spring, the orchestra gave a series of ten concerts. Casals preferred the works of romantic and classical composers to modern works, but he often included the latter in the repertoire and invited their composers to conduct performances.

When the Spanish Civil War broke out, Casals, an adamant opponent of Fascism, fled his native country and settled in Prades, France. During the civil war and World War II he was active in relief efforts to help Spanish refugees and other war victims. In 1946 he announced his retirement from performing in protest of the Franco government in Spain, but he returned in 1950. The same year he founded, at Prades, an annual Bach Commemorative Festival.

gave his first solo performances in 1889. Four years later, with the financial assistance of the music patron, Queen Regent María Cristina, Casals entered the Madrid Conservatory.

Uncomfortable with the expectations of his royal patrons, who wanted him to compose rather than play the cello, Casals studied briefly in Brussels and finally chose freedom over financial assistance. He moved briefly to Paris and in 1896 moved again to Barcelona, becoming principal cellist of the Gran Teatro del Liceo. In Barcelona he also began his distinguished teaching career, taking over García's duties at the Municipal School of Music.

Casals had recorded some performances prior to 1950 but did so much more actively after his return to public view. In 1956 he settled permanently in Puerto Rico, where he established the annual Casals Festival. He spent his mature years crusading for world peace and calling for an end to the proliferation of nuclear weapons. He performed several times for United Nations Day and widely conducted his own oratorio *El Pessebre* (composed 1944–1946; *The Manger*), a musical call for world peace.

Casals continued to perform into his nineties; he died at the age of 96. In 1989 he was awarded, posthumously, a Lifetime Achievement Award from the National Academy of Recording Arts and Sciences. His recollections, *Joys and Sorrows*, were published in 1970.

BIBLIOGRAPHY

Baldock, Robert, *Pablo Casals*, 1992; Kirk, H. L., *Pablo Casals: A Biography*, 1974.

Cavafy, Constantine

(April 29, 1863–April 29, 1933)
Poet, Essayist

A rigorous critic of himself and his work, Constantine Cavafy never published his poems commercially during his lifetime and printed only a select number of poems privately to circulate among friends. In spite of this fact, the posthumous publication of his small body of work established him as one the major Greek-language poets of the twentieth century. Cavafy was particularly noted for his intimate style and innovative use of both the ancient and modern Greek vernacular in poetic language. He also contributed essays to various periodicals.

Cavafy was born Konstantínos Pétrou Kaváfis into a large Greek family in Alexandria, Egypt, where he spent most of his life. The family business, Cavafy Brothers, took them to Alexandria, but the business eventually failed. His father died when he was 7, and in 1872 his mother moved the family to Liverpool, England.

They remained in England until they returned to Egypt in 1879, and this period of time in Britain was significant in Cavafy's development. Cavafy often spoke English out of preference, and sometimes wrote in English. In 1881, he entered a private school run by A. Papazis.

When hostilities erupted in Egypt, the family spent 1882–1885 in Constantinople. Back in Alexandria after that time, Cavafy worked briefly for the Alexandria paper *Telegraphos* and later at the Egyptian Stock Exchange with one of his brothers. In 1892 he was appointed special clerk at the Irrigation Service (Third Circle) in the Ministry of Public Works, where he worked for three decades. Although his family's fortunes had declined, he remained well connected through them.

Cavafy admired French literature as well as English, and many of his early poems were influenced by the French Symbolists. He translated Charles Baudelaire's (1821–1867) "Correspondances" and was particularly influenced by his work. Cavafy's verse is written in a direct, intimate style and incorporates many colloquialisms. Cavafy wrote in both forms of modern Greek—the first, Katharevousa, still conforms to the usage of ancient Greek, as handed down by the Byzantines, whereas the Demotike is the modern vernacular of Greece.

Cavafy's poetry frequently incorporates Hellenistic and Byzantine imagery ; it reflects his personal despair, which sometimes plunged him into deep depression. His disillusionment with orthodox Christianity and traditional values as well as his frank exploration of his homosexuality, emerge in a number of his poems. Among his better-known poems are "Dünya Güzeli" (1884), "The City" (1894), "Waiting for the Barbarians" (1898), and "Hidden Things" (written 1908; published 1963).

Although never printed in commercial editions, a number of Cavafy's poems were published in periodicals during his lifetime. Early poems appeared in *Hesperos*, a periodical published in Leipzig, Germany, in 1886. Four poems were published in the journal *Grammate* in 1917, and T. S. Eliot published "Ithaka" in his *Criterion* in 1924. He was not well known to the public, but several prominent authors and critics took notice of his work. In 1901 he met the Greek critic Gregory Xenopoulous, who promoted his poetry. In 1915, Cavafy formed a friendship with the British writer E. M. Forster, who wrote an essay on him in *Athenaeum*, a periodical published in London. In his *Alexandria Quartet*, Lawrence Durrell, who lived in Egypt and on the Greek islands, frequently alludes to Cavafy's work.

Cavafy printed "Walls," originally written in Greek and translated into English by his brother, in 1897. In 1904 he printed his *Booklet*, which contained fourteen poems and was expanded as *Booklet, Poems* (1910). Cavafy's verse first appeared in a commercial edition after his death, just before World War II, and the English translation *The Poems of C. P. Cavafy* only appeared in 1951. Among his other works are *Ars Poetica* (1903); the article "The Elgin Marbles" (1891), written in English; and "Genealogy" (1911). He edited the journal *Alexandrian Art* in 1926. Cavafy was awarded Greece's Medal of the Phoenix in 1926 and died seven years later of cancer of the larynx on his seventieth birthday.

BIBLIOGRAPHY

Anton, John P., *The Poetry and Poetics of Constantine P. Cavafy: Aesthetic Visions of Sensual Reality*, 1995; Bien, Peter, *Constantine Cavafy*, 1964; Evans, Robert Charles, *A Critical Introduction to C. P. Cavafy*, 1988; Liddell, Robert, *Cavafy: A Critical Biography*, 1974.

Cela, Camilo José

(May 11, 1916–)
Novelist, Short-Story Writer, Poet, Essayist

Camilo José Cela ranks among the prominent novelists of the post–Civil War generation in Spain. With novels such as *The Family of Pascual Duarte*, he uses a literary style known as *tremendismo*, whose violent, brutal imagery delivers a strong impact. Cela received the Nobel Prize for Literature in 1989 "for a rich and intensive prose, which with restrained compassion forms a challenging vision of man's vulnerability."

Cela was born Camilo José Cela y Trulock in the Galician town of Iria Flavia, Spain. His mother was of English origin, and his father, a customs official, of Galician origin. The family moved around Spain frequently in Cela's youth and eventually settled in Madrid. Cela was a poor student at the numerous Catholic schools he attended. After graduating from the last of them in Madrid, he enrolled at the University of Madrid, where he studied medicine and later law, neither of which appealed to him. Cela began his literary career as a poet; his book of poetry, *Treading the Uncertain Light of Day*, published in 1936, was significantly influenced by the Chilean poet PABLO NERUDA.

Cela achieved the rank of corporal in the forces of the Fascist dictator Francisco Franco during the Spanish Civil War, during which he was seriously wounded. He later rejected the Franco dictatorship, and several of Cela's books were subjected to censorship under Franco's rule. In 1941, suffering from a severe bout with tuberculosis, Cela recuperated in a sanitarium. During his illnesses he read extensively, particularly classic Spanish authors such as Miguel de Cervantes and Lope de Vega.

His first novel, *The Family of Pascual Duarte* (1942), proved to be his most widely read work. He tells the story in the form of fictional memoirs of its protagonist, Pascual Duarte, and supplementary documents from others. Duarte is a violent criminal whose brutal and unpredictable actions torment his family. After he has murdered two victims, his mother and a pimp who has impregnated his wife, he kills a third and is sentenced to die. Pascual's motive for killing his third victim, the wealthy Don Jesús González de la Riva, is left largely as a matter of speculation. The graphic depiction of Pascual's crimes is characteristic of *tremendismo*, a style many critics see as originating with Cela. Although the Spanish authorities confiscated copies of the novel after its second publication, it was translated into many languages and well received internationally.

In 1943 Cela married María del Rosario Conde Picavea. The same year also saw the publication of his novel *The Sanitarium* (*Rest Home*), inspired by his experiences during his bouts with tuberculosis. Cela spent the next several years working tirelessly on *The Hive*, published in 1951. The novel is an experimental literary montage featuring 160 characters and unfolding in a broken sequence over three days in Madrid at the close of 1943. Cela's next novel, *Mrs. Caldwell Speaks to Her Son* (1953), is also fragmentary in nature. He tells the story in the form of the mad ramblings of an overbearing English mother obsessed with her son, Eliacim, who lost his life in a war. During a visit to Venezuela in 1954, Cela was commissioned to write *The Blonde* (1955), a novel set in that country.

His later novels include *San Camilo, 1936* (1969), a work rendered in stream-of-consciousness form and set during the Spanish Civil War; the 1194 episodes that comprise *Requiem of Darkness* (1973); *Mazurka for Two Dead* (1983), set in rural Spain; and *Christ Versus Arizona* (1988). Cela has also written a number of travel books recounting his journeys through Spain and Latin America. They include *Journey to the Alcarria* (1948), *From the Miño to the Bidasoa* (1952), *Jews, Moors, and Christians* (1956), and *The Wheel of*

Idle Moments (1957), relating his journeys through South America. His collections of short stories include *The Passing Clouds* (1945), *The Neat Crime of the Carabiniere and Other Tales* (1947), and *The Windmill and Other Short Fiction* (1956).

After moving to Mallorca in 1954, Cela founded the respected literary review *Papeles de Son Armadans*, published from 1956 to 1979. In addition to receiving the Nobel Prize in 1989, he was admitted to the Royal Spanish Academy in 1957 and has received honorary doctorates from several universities.

BIBLIOGRAPHY

McPheeters, D. W., *Camilo José Cela*, 1969.

Celan, Paul

(November 23, 1920–May 1, 1970)
Poet, Translator

Influenced by the Surrealists and other French poets, Paul Celan contributed ten volumes of verse to post–World War II German poetry. His poetry is largely concerned with the horrors of the Holocaust and the historical plight of the Jewish people. He was one of the most important poets writing in German to give powerful expression to these themes.

Celan was born Paul Antschel into a German-speaking Jewish family in Czernowitz, Romania, now Chernovtsy, Ukraine. Upon his graduation from school in 1938, he went to Tours, France, to study medicine. The following year he returned to Romania to study Romance

languages and literature. The advent of World War II devastated Celan's family. Romania allied itself with the Nazis, and Celan's parents were sent to their deaths in a concentration camp. Celan was interned in a labor camp but escaped death.

After the war ended Celan worked as a translator in Bucharest for several years. In 1948 he moved to Vienna and then to Paris. His first published poems appeared in the Romanian journal *Agora* in 1947. The following year, a major series of poems appeared in Otto Basil's periodical *Plan*. The latter series formed the first cycle of verse in his debut volume of poetry, *Der Sand aus den Urnen* (1948; *The Sand from the Urns*).

Celan's early poetry is lyrical, tinged with romanticism, and among the most personal of his largely impersonal verse. The French poets had the strongest influence on his style, which was marked by rich imagery and precise language. Personal notes arise in poems such as "Nähe der Gräber" ("Nearness of Graves"), which evokes the memory of the mother he lost to the Nazis. Although Celan was not a religious poet, his Jewish heritage and the historical suffering of the Jewish people is the dominant theme in his work.

Mohn und Gedächtnis (1952; *Poppy and Memory*) brought Celan fame in postwar West Germany; it consists of four parts entitled "Der Sand aus den Urnen," "Todesfuge," "Gegenlicht" ("Counterlight"), and "Halme der Nacht" ("Blades of Night"). "Todesfuge" ("Fugue of Death"), an impassioned evocation of a Nazi concentration camp narrated from the perspective of the victims, remains one of his most popular poems.

In 1950 Celan married Gisèle Lestrange, a Frenchwoman to whom he dedicated his next collection of verse, *Von Schwelle zu Schwelle* (1952). With *Von Schwelle zu Schwelle* and its successor, *Sprachgitter* (1959), his poetic language grew more sparse and less lyrical. Perhaps more strongly than any of his collections, *Die Niemandsrose* (1963) expresses his concern with the plight of the Jewish people and his antipathy toward Christianity. He dedicated the volume to OSIP MANDELSTAM, the Russian-Jewish poet and martyr to the Soviet state.

Atemwende (1967) backed away somewhat from Jewish themes, and its first cycle of poems appeared earlier as *Atemkristall* (1965). Celan's later volumes of verse are *Fadensonnen* (1968), *Todtnauberg* (1968), *Lichtzwang* (1970; *Lightforce*), and the posthumous collection *Schneepart* (1971).

Celan's other area of interest was language. He was multilingual and taught languages at the École Normale in Paris. During his lifetime he translated many works from French (including works by JEAN COCTEAU), English, Italian, and Russian. Celan took a keen interest in European literature of both the East and West and often read literary works in the original languages.

Celan received the Georg Büchner Prize in 1960 and co-edited the periodical *L'Ephemère* beginning in 1968. He drowned in 1970 in what appears to have been a suicide. *Speech-Grille and Selected Poems*, an English translation of his poetry, appeared in 1971.

BIBLIOGRAPHY

Colin, Amy D., *Paul Celan: Holograms of Darkness*, 1991; Glenn, Jerry, *Paul Celan*, 1973; Samuels, Clarise, *Holocaust Visions: Surrealism and Existentialism in the Poetry of Paul Celan*, 1993.

Chagall, Marc

(July 7, 1887–March 28, 1985)
Painter, Graphic Artist, Costume Designer

The Russian-born painter Marc Chagall infused the external world with an optimistic sense of the subconscious, and is best known for his use of fantastic elements to create a sense of the joy that lurks in the subconscious, at a time when artists have been more apt to dwell on the darkness. He used a unique style that blended elements of Realism, Impressionism, Fauvism, and Cubism. Chagall is known not only for his paintings but also for the murals and stained-glass windows he executed in his later life.

Chagall was born into a devout Jewish family, in Vitebsk, in what is now Belarus. His father worked in a herring warehouse, while his mother ran a small grocery shop. As a child he attended a Jewish elementary school. Chagall's upbringing and the Vitebsk environment served as material for his work throughout his career. After attending a public school, Chagall began to study painting with Jehuda Pen, a local portraitist who painted in an academic and traditional style he soon grew to dislike. In 1907 he moved to St. Petersburg and studied with the Russian painter and stage designer LÉON BAKST.

Chagall's early paintings often lack the exuberance of his later work. Dark, somber blacks, blues, muted reds, and grays dominate paintings such as *Red Nude* (1908), and *My Fiancée with Black Gloves* (1910), and *Bride With a Fan* (1911). In 1910 Chagall moved to France and eventually settled in an artist's colony known as the Beehive. There, surrounded by the widely varied influences of the Fauvists, Impressionists, Postimpressionists, and Cubists, he began to develop his mature painting style. While some of these influences are evident in his paintings, as for example Cubism in *Cubist Landscape* (1918), Chagall did not ally himself with any school. Instead he began to create his own distinctive style, employing bolder and brighter color schemes, upside-down figures, and floating objects. Typical of this period are the brilliantly colored *I and the Village* (1911), *Self-Portrait with Seven Fingers* (1912), and *The Burning House* (1913).

After two joint exhibitions in Paris, Chagall held his first individual showing in Berlin in 1914. He returned to Vitebsk in 1914 and painted a series of local figures and scenes, including *The Praying Jew* (1914), *Jew in Green* (1914), and *Jew in Red* (1914). The following year he married Bella Rosenfeld, the daughter of a prosperous merchant whom he had long loved before their marriage. Images of Bella appeared in many of his subsequent paintings, including *Bella With a White Collar* (1917), *Bella in Green* (1934) and *The Three Candles* (1938).

As an artist, Chagall found the creative climate in Russia after the 1917 revolution increasingly intolerable. He became commissar of art for the Vitebsk area and, unhappy with the political demands that accompanied his position, moved to Moscow in 1919. Between 1919 and 1922 he dedicated much of his time to the stage. He served as art director of the Moscow Jewish State Theater from 1919 to 1922, designed sets and costumes, and painted a series of murals for the

Kamereny Theater, including *Love on the Stage* and *Dance*.

In 1922 Chagall moved to Berlin, where he developed an interest in printmaking, lithography, and wood engraving. In Berlin he completed a series of autobiographical engravings entitled *Mein Leben* (1922; *My Life*). The following year he moved his family to Paris and began to achieve his first measure of success. He continued to paint in essentially the same vein as he previously had, treating a variety of subjects in such paintings as *The Praying Jew* (1923), *The Falling Angel* (1923–1947), *Lovers in the Lilacs* (1930), *The Circus* (1931), *Solitude* (1933), and *The Bride and the Groom of the Eiffel Tower* (1938–1940). Chagall also traveled widely through Europe and Palestine.

In addition to painting, he began the first of three projects for the Paris art dealer Ambroise Vollard, a series of 107 plates for an edition of the Russian author Nikolay Gogol's *Dead Souls*. Chagall completed another series of prints for an edition of Jean de La Fontaine's *Fables* and had begun work on a series of illustrations for the Bible when Vollard passed away. After World War II, another publisher took over the projects and eventually released completed editions of all three.

The years of World War II were difficult ones for Chagall, and the sadness he felt comes through in many of his paintings of this period. Fleeing the Nazi occupation of France, he moved his family to the United States, where his wife died from an illness in 1944. In a series of paintings using the crucifixion motif, including *White Crucifixion* (1938), *Martyr* (1940), and *Descent from the Cross* (1941), Chagall modified the crucifixion

scene to lament the sacrifice of Jewish lives under the Nazis. Bella is also a recurring image in his paintings of this period, including the gloomy, tragic *Around Her* (1945) and *Wedding Candles*, two halves of what began as a single painting, and the exuberant *The Naked Cloud*.

By this time Chagall's work was widely exhibited in the United States and Europe. Before he returned to France in 1948, his work appeared in two major exhibitions in New York and Chicago. After moving back to France, he married Valentina Brodsky. Many of his paintings in the mid-1950s feature scenes in Paris, including *Bridges Over the Seine* (1954). In 1958, commissioned by the architect Joseph Neufeld and the Women's Zionist Organization, he began designing a number of stained glass windows that appeared in the Cathedral of Metz and later the synagogue of the Hadassah-Hebrew University Medical Center near Jerusalem. The synagogue windows, each of which is dominated by a particular color, depict the biblical blessings given to the twelve patriarchs of the tribes of Israel.

Chagall's hand was employed in decorating several public buildings, including a United Nations window in 1964, the ceiling for the Paris Opera (1964), and the walls for the New York Metropolitan Opera (1966), which featured the murals *The Sources of Music* and *The Triumph of Music*. The National Museum of the Marc Chagall Biblical Message, dedicated to the artist's biblical works, opened in 1973. André Malraux, the writer and French minister of cultural affairs, commissioned three tapestries on the Creation, the Exodus, and the Entry into Jerusalem.

Amidst his other activities Chagall designed scenery and costumes for a number of stage productions in the United States and Europe. These include a 1945 production of Igor Stravinsky's ballet *The Firebird*, a 1958 production of MAURICE RAVEL'S *Daphnis et Chloé* in Paris, and a 1967 production of Wolfgang Amadeus Mozart's *Magic Flute* in New York.

BIBLIOGRAPHY

Alexander, Sidney, *Marc Chagall: A Biography*, 1978; Greenfeld, Howard, *Marc Chagall*, 1990.

Chaliapin, Feodor

(February 13, 1873–April 12, 1938)
Singer, Actor

Feodor Chaliapin rose from poverty to become the most renowned operatic bass of his day. Best known for his defining interpretation of the title part in *Boris Godunov*, Chaliapin appeared around the world as Ivan the Terrible, Don Quixote, and in many other dramatic singing roles. He also performed in baritone roles.

Chaliapin was born Fyodor Ivanovich Shalyapin into an impoverished family near Kazan, Russia. His father was of peasant background and worked as a clerk in the district town council.

Before his brief schooling, Chaliapin was tutored privately at home. When he refused to attend school any further, his father unsuccessfully tried to place him in a number of trades. Showing no interest or skill in working with his hands, Chaliapin dreamed of singing and acting. As an adolescent he sang in a church choir. In Kazan in 1884, he obtained his first role, a minor part in *L'Africaine*.

In search of better work, the family moved to Astrahkhan. His father vehemently objected to his aspirations, and the exasperated Chaliapin left his family at the age of 17. For the next several years he traveled and supported himself with odd jobs. A job singing in a chorus gave him a minor break, and by 1890 he had risen to the rank of soloist. However, Chaliapin continued to endure economic hardship so severe that it led him to the brink of suicide.

His fortunes changed when he met Dimitri Usatov and went to study with him in Tiflis (now Tbilisi, Georgia). Usatov took in the emaciated figure, gave him the only formal musical training he ever had, and secured local singing engagements for him. Chaliapin would remain grateful to his teacher for the rest of his life, and he supported Usatov's widow until she died.

In 1895 Chaliapin sang Mephistopholes in Gounoud's *Faust*, a role he later repeated many times around the world. He found his first success at the Mariinsky Theatre in St. Petersburg in 1896. The same year he joined the Mamontov Private Opera Company, where, in contrast to the Mariinsky, he was granted considerable freedom to experiment. There he also met his first wife, the Italian ballerina Iola Tornaghi.

Once he found himself in comfortable circumstances, Chaliapin began to educate himself in earnest. He immersed himself in literature, drawing, clay modeling, and painting, executing a number of self-portraits. He soon found himself a famous figure, and he took on roles in many languages, including Russian, French, and Italian. His Salieri in Rimsky-Korsakov's *Mozart and Salieri* (1898) was the first of his numerous performances of that role. In 1900 he first worked with the pianist-composer SERGEY RACHMANINOFF, to whom he remained close for the rest of his life.

Among Chaliapin's notable successes were his performances as Ivan Susanin in Mikhail Glinka's *A Life for the Czar* (1901), Philip II in Giuseppe Verdi's *Don Carlos;* Ivan the Terrible in Nikolay Rimsky-Korsakov's *Maid of Pskov* (1914), the title role in Arrigo Boito's *Mefistofele*, the title role in *Don Quixote* (1910, at the Bolshoi Theatre as well as in a film version in 1933), and the Viking Merchant in Rimsky-Korsakov's *Sadko*. He also appeared in Alexander Borodin's *Prince Igor* and in *Judith* and excelled in comic roles, such as Don Basilio in Gioacchino Rossini's *Il barbiere di Siviglia* and Leporello in Wolfgang Amadeus Mozart's *Don Giovanni.*

Chaliapin's most famous interpretation, however, was the title role in Modest Mussorgsky's *Boris Godunov*, an opera about the life of the sixteenth-century tsar. He first performed the role in 1901, repeated it on numerous occasions over the next four decades, and left the stage with Boris Godunov as his final role. A 1921 production at New York's Metropolitan Opera House proved particularly successful.

On stage Chaliapin's tall, broad-shouldered figure and booming voice made him a commanding figure. Known for his dramatic flair as well as his vocal tone, he was both talented and temperamental. His uncompromising demands for perfection made him difficult for others to work with. Immersing himself in his roles, he carefully thought out the facial expressions and psychological states of his characters. Those who saw Chaliapin perform marveled at the complete transformations his face underwent, helped by his skillfully applied makeup, so that he seemed to fit his part perfectly whether he played a peasant or a prince.

Chaliapin performed abroad as early as 1901 (Milan) and appeared in New York in 1907 and in London, at the invitation of SIR THOMAS BEECHAM, in 1913. He left the newly formed Soviet state in 1921 and lived the remainder of his life in Europe. Chaliapin frequently appeared with the Metropolitan Opera Company, the Chicago Civic Opera Company, and his own company. He made hundreds of recordings beginning in 1898 and wrote two autobiographical works, *Pages from My Life* (1926) and *Man and Mask: Forty Years in the Life of a Singer* (1932). In 1984 Chaliapin's remains were moved from Batignolles Cemetery in Paris to the Novodevichy Cemetery in Moscow.

BIBLIOGRAPHY

Borovsky, Victor, *Chaliapin: A Critical Biography*, 1988.

Chesterton, G. K.

(May 29, 1874–June 14, 1936)
Novelist, Poet, Critic, Essayist, Editor

Gilbert Keith Chesterton, known for his jovial temperament, conservative outlook, and clever writing, wrote more than a hundred books in his lifetime. He is perhaps best known for his novels *The Napoleon of Notting Hill* (1904) and *The Man Who Was Thursday* (1908) as well as his series of detective stories featuring Father Brown. His other work includes poetry, biographies, short stories, essays, and theological works.

Chesterton was born at Campden Hill, London, attended St. Paul's School from 1887 to 1892, and later studied art at the Slade School in London. He studied English literature at University College in London. His literary career began there when he met Ernest Hodder Williams, the future governing director of the publishing house Hodder and Stoughton. He began to write reviews for its monthly periodical *Bookman*. In 1901 he married Frances Blogg. Although he began as a political and philosophical liberal, his ideology soon grew more conservative. With HILAIRE BELLOC he edited a conservative weekly journal, and he contributed voluminous essays to his own magazine, *G.K.'s Weekly*, and *The Illustrated London News*. The essays covered a wide range of subject matter, including religion, politics, literary criticism, society, and philosophy.

Chesterton opposed both the large concentrations of power and wealth of corporate capitalism and the forced communalization of socialism. Instead, he believed land, society, and enterprise were best divided into small, privately owned segments, a philosophy dubbed "distributivism." In 1922 he converted to Catholicism, and he remained a devout Roman Catholic for the rest of his life. Both his political and religious beliefs influenced his fiction.

The novel *The Napoleon of Notting Hill* (1904) looks forward to the end of the twentieth century, when the nations of the world have amalgamated into a few large and peaceful empires. When the new king, Auberon Quin, is appointed, he orders the restoration of medieval customs around London as a joke. The matter is no joke to Adam Wayne, who eventually starts a successful civil war and inspires a rebirth of localized patriotism. The story ends on an optimistic note as society begins to redivide itself into smaller segments. *The Man Who Was Thursday* (1908) was an allegorical response to the pessimistic generation prior to World War I. Syme, a poet and secret police agent, infiltrates a circle of anarchists. As it turns out, all six of the others on its inner council are police agents. Each of them is is named for a day of the week (Syme is Thursday). Their leader is the powerful Sunday, who is only revealed to be a fellow agent after the others unite in pursuit of him. The story reflects Chesterton's belief that things are not as bad as they seem and ultimately work toward a good purpose.

In *Manalive* (1912), Chesterton emphasizes the extraordinary nature of life, even in its ordinary things. The main character, Innocent Smith, proves to himself and others the worth of life, his house, and his wife. When he offers to end the lives of some of his negatively disposed friends, he shoots a hole through their hats instead, which he finds quickly restores their appreciation for their own lives. Chesterton's other fiction includes *The Club of Queer Trades* (1905), a collection of short stories, *How I Found Superman* (1909), and above all the Father Brown stories. *The Innocence of Father Brown* (1911) was the first volume in a series of popular detective stories about a priest-sleuth. Chesterton's poetry, including *The Ballad of the White Horse*, reflects the same philosophical themes that appear in his novels and essays. Although his views often spurred controversy, the clever, witty style of delivery that pervades all of his literary output rendered his work more palatable to critics than that of Belloc.

Chesterton wrote works of literary criticism on Robert Browning (1903), Charles Dickens (1906), his friend and contemporary GEORGE BERNARD SHAW (1909), William Blake (1910), and Robert Louis Stevenson (1927). His religious works include *Orthodoxy* (1909), *St. Francis of Assisi* (1923), *The Everlasting Man* (1925), *The Catholic Church and Conversion* (1926), and *St. Thomas Aquinas* (1933).

BIBLIOGRAPHY

Chesterton, G. K., *The Autobiography of G. K. Chesterton*, 1936; Evans, Maurice, *G. K. Chesterton*, 1938; Pearce, Joseph Chilton, *Wisdom and Innocence: A Life of G. K. Chesterton*, 1996.

Chevalier, Maurice

(September 12, 1888–January 1, 1972)
Actor, Singer

Maurice Chevalier charmed millions of moviegoers and theatergoers around the world with his French accent, popular songs, tilted hat, polish in light comedy, and his ability to convey zest for life, even in old age. Chevalier's dozens of films made in France, England, and Hollywood made him an international sensation, and he continued to draw crowds performing on stage throughout his life.

Chevalier was born in a Paris slum. His father, an alcoholic house painter, erupted in violent tirades when he drank and eventually left the family. Chevalier saw him only once afterward. The elder Chevalier's departure left his mother nearly destitute with three sons. Chevalier attended a charity school until he was 10, when he obtained the first in a series of odd jobs to help support his mother. At the age of 12, he started to sing in Paris cafés.

Chevalier's career rose steadily over the next several years. By the age of 16, he had achieved a measure of popularity singing in the music hall scene. Chevalier continued to sing in music halls and operettas in Paris and London over the next several years. Having postponed his mandatory military service, he enlisted in 1913 and eventually fought in World War I.

Maurice Chevalier (Ann Ronan/Image Select)

While recovering from wounds he began to learn English, which served him well in his Hollywood career.

In the meantime, Chevalier had begun making silent films. *Trop Crédule*, his first, appeared in 1908. Before 1924, he appeared in a dozen silent films, with the later ones all directed by Henri Diamant-Berger. Chevalier first sang "Valentine" (written by Albert Willmetz and Henri Christiné), one of his many popular songs, at the Casino de Paris in 1925. Three years later, he starred in his first sound film, *Bonjour New York!*

Chevalier's successful Hollywood career began with the comedy *The Innocents of Paris* (1929), in which he stars as the junk dealer Maurice Marney, who abandons his stage career for a woman. In *The Love Parade* (1930), Chevalier starred as Count Alfred opposite Jeanette MacDonald's Queen Louise. The count marries the queen, resents her ill treatment of him, and succeeds in curing her of her callousness. Both of these films grew into international hits.

The first phase of Chevalier's Hollywood career continued until his return to Europe in 1935. Among the films in which he starred during that phase are *Playboy of Paris* (1930), based on a Tristan Bernard comedy; *The Smiling Lieutenant* (1931); *One Hour With You* (1932); *Love Me Tonight* (1932); *Bedtime Story* (1933), in which he acted the part of the romantic Vicomte de St. Denis, who finds an infant in his car; and *The Merry Widow* (1934).

The Beloved Vagabond (1936), based on a novel by W. J. Locke, was produced in England. RENÉ CLAIR directed *Break the News* (1938), in which Chevalier starred as François Verrier, one of two men in show business who orchestrate a public-ity stunt. Verrier's colleague, Teddy (Jack Buchanan), is allegedly murdered. Political events in the country where he is hiding prevent him from returning before Verrier is convicted of his murder. Clair also directed *Le silence est d'or* (1945; *Silence is Golden*), in which Chevalier plays a film director who is attracted to the same young girl as his actor-protégé.

During World War II, Chevalier's appeal declined. The Germans occupied France, and Chevalier was accused of collaborating with them, charges of which he was later cleared. Following the war, he toured North America with the popular one-man shows he continued performing around the world for two decades.

Chevalier returned to Hollywood in 1957, singing the title song in *The Happy Road* (1957). In *Love in the Afternoon* (1957), he played the father of Ariane Chavasse (Audrey Hepburn). In this and other later films, he played father figures and other roles of older men. These include *Gigi* (1958); *Can-Can* (1960), with Frank Sinatra; *Fanny* (1961); *Jessica* (1962); and *Monkeys, Go Home* (1967), as Father Sylvain in a story about an American who inherits an olive farm in France. Chevalier sang the title song for *The Aristocats* (1970).

In 1958, Chevalier received an Academy Award for his contributions to the field of entertainment. He published several autobiographical volumes: *Man in the Straw Hat* (1946), *With Love* (1960), *I Remember it Well* (1970), and *My Paris* (1972).

BIBLIOGRAPHY

Behr, Edward, *Thank Heaven for Little Girls: The True Story of Maurice Chevalier's Life and Times*, 1993; Harding, James, *Maurice Chevalier: His Life 1888–1972*, 1982.

Chillida, Eduardo

(January 10, 1924–)
Sculptor, Graphic Artist, Illustrator

Known for their massive, abstract forms in granite, iron, steel, and concrete, the sculptures of the Spanish-born Eduardo Chillida Juantegui explore relationships between interior and exterior space. His works stand in public places and buildings around the world. Chillida is also an accomplished graphic artist.

Chillida is of Basque ancestry, born in San Sebastián, Spain. His mother was a soprano. In 1930 he entered a secondary school that emphasized classical studies in the curriculum, and in his youth he was a goalkeeper at the San Sebastián football club. From 1943 to 1946 he studied architecture at the University of Madrid, and the following year he studied drawing at a private school in Madrid.

Chillida experimented with clay and plaster in his earliest sculptures, such as the plaster *Forma* (1949), a headless female figure. In 1950 he married Pili de Belzunce, and the following year he created his first major iron sculpture, *Ilarik*, an abstract work with intersecting geometric forms. About this time he began to work primarily with iron. Chillida's first one-man show came in 1954 at the Clan Gallery in Madrid. The same year he created the first in a long series of sculptures entitled *Yunque de sueños* (1954–1966; *Anvil of Dreams*), many of which consisted of wood bases and iron anvils, and won an award for his work at the Triennale in Milan. The year 1954 also brought an important commission for four iron doors for the Basilica of Aranzazu, and the following year the city of San Sebastian commissioned a stone

sculpture of Sir Alexander Fleming, who discovered penicillin. The iron *Elogio del aire* (*In Praise of Air*, 1956) is one of several small works composed of thin, pointed forms.

An exhibition at the Venice Biennale in 1958 secured Chillida's international reputation as a sculptor. The series of large sculptures entitled *Abesti Gogora*, begun in 1959, marked the beginning of his serious use of wood as a medium. In *Rumor de límites IV* (1959; *Rumor of Limits*), part of a series of seven sculptures rendered in iron and steel, Chillida first began to use steel. *Elogio de la luz* (1965; *In Praise of Light*) is another significant early work.

In the late 1960s and early 1970s Chillida finished several major steel sculptures, including *Comb of the Wind IV* (1969) and *Alrededor del Vacío* (1970; *Around the Void*), the latter of which was placed at the World Bank in Washington, D.C. In 1973 he began to use terra cotta, and he also executed massive abstract sculptures in concrete such as *Lugar de Encuentros III. The House of Johann Sebastian Bach* (1981), *The House of Hokusai* (1981), and *The House of Goethe* (1981) are among his imaginative re-creations of artists' homes. Chillida has often used granite in his later sculptures.

Aside from his work in sculpture, Chillida has also illustrated numerous books. His woodcuts for JORGE GUILLÉN's *Más Allá* won the Diano Marina Prize in Milan 1974. He illustrated Max Hoelzer's book *Meditation in Kastilien* (1968) and the German philosopher Martin Heidegger's *Die Kunst und der Raum* (1969; *Art* and Space). Chillida won an award for his etchings *Euzkadi IV* at the Tenth Biennale of Graphic Arts in Tokyo in 1976.

His other works include his large memorial *Homage to Jorge Guillén* (1982); *Elogio de agua* (1987; *In Praise of Water*), for the Parque de la Creueta del Coll in Barcelona; *Lo profundio es el aire* (1988); *Gravitations* (1988); the massive steel sculpture *De Musica* (1989); and *Elogio del horizonte* (1990).

BIBLIOGRAPHY

Chillida, Eduardo, *Chillida*, 1990; Selz, Peter Howard, *Chillida*, 1986.

Chirico, Giorgio de

(July 10, 1888–November 19, 1978)
Painter, Sculptor

With GIORGIO MORANDI and the Italian Futurist Carlo Carrà, Giorgio de Chirico established the *pittura metafisica* style of painting in Italy. Characterized by their dark, brooding atmospheres, bizarre juxtapositions of places and objects, and faceless human forms, his paintings significantly influenced the development of Surrealism in France. In the 1930s Chirico renounced his earlier work and turned to a more academic style of painting.

Chirico was born into an Italian family living in Vólos, Greece, where his father worked as a railroad engineer. At a young age he began to take drawing lessons, and when his family moved to Athens in 1899 he studied drawing at the Polytechnic and painting with a portraitist. After his father died, the family returned to Italy in 1905. Chirico began painting five years later, producing a series of landscapes, such as his *Enigma* series, that evoke the fantastic, allegorical work of the Swiss painter Arnold Böcklin (1827–1901).

In 1911 Chirico settled in Paris, where he formed friendships with PABLO PICASSO, the French Symbolist poet Guillaume Apollinaire (1880–1918), and other figures of the Paris avant-garde. A *Self Portrait* (1912–1913) from this period shows a left profile of the artist's somber, serious face against a bright green background. In paintings such as *The Soothsayer's Recompense* (1913), *The Uncertainty of the Poet* (1913), *The Mystery and Melancholy of a Street* (1914), and *Metaphysical Composition* (1914), Chirico created bleak cityscapes and placed unusual combinations of objects against backgrounds of darkness and mystery. In his compelling *Metaphysical Composition*, for example, an egg casts a shadow over a long, gray surface, on which sit human feet and other objects. Two red smokestack-like figures rise in the background.

After being conscripted into the army, Chirico found himself in Ferrara in 1915. With Carrà he founded the magazine *Pittura Metafisica* in 1920. The dreamlike paintings of his output from 1915 to the end of the 1920s include *The Seer* (1915),

Giorgio de Chirico (AKG)

Grand Metaphysical Interior (1917), *The Lovers* (1925), and *The Poet and His Muse* (1925). The latter depicts two faceless figures, the gloomy poet dressed in white, slouched in a chair, and receiving consolation from the muse.

Chirico broke with the Surrealists in 1926 but continued to associate with the Paris avant-garde. In 1928 JEAN COCTEAU examined his work in *Le Mystère Laïc*, and the following year he contributed scenery and costume designs to a production by SERGEY DIAGHILEV's Ballets Russes.

His paintings from the late 1920s include *Furniture in a Valley* (1927), which places a roofless interior in an outdoor setting. In 1930 he met his second wife, Isabella Pakszwer, with whom he returned to Italy.

In the 1930s Chirico turned to more classical sources for his inspiration and began to paint in an academic style, becoming an avowed antimodernist. *Horses of the Hellespont* (1936), a fiery picture of two horses under a brilliantly lit sky, conveys an almost apocalyptic tone. Chirico also created a series of nude male warriors, a *Mysterious Baths* series, portraits, and covers and illustrations for *Vogue*. He spent much of 1936–1937 in New York and often used the city as a backdrop for his paintings, for example, *The Mystery of Manhattan* (1973) and *Metaphysical Vision of New York* (1975).

In the 1940s and 1950s, numerous arguments and scandals arose over forgeries of Chirico's work. In his work from the

1960s and 1970s, he sometimes returned to the metaphysical subjects of his early paintings. His other works include the autobiographical *Hebdomeros* (1929), a series of lithographs for an edition of Apollinaire's *Calligrammes* (1930), bronze sculptures, and scenery design.

BIBLIOGRAPHY

Braun, Emily, ed., *Giorgio de Chirico and America*, 1996; Soby, James Thrall, *The Early De Chirico*, 1969; Glenbow Museum, *Four Modern Masters: De Chirico, Ernst, Magritte, and Miró*, 1981.

Christie, Agatha

(September 15, 1890–January 12, 1976)
Novelist, Playwright, Short-Story Writer

The investigative sleuth Hercule Poirot, one of the most famous detectives in modern fiction, was the creation of the British mystery writer Agatha Christie. Christie's bestselling mysteries made her one of the most widely read authors of the twentieth century. Christie also wrote popular plays such as *The Mousetrap* and romance novels.

Christie was born Agatha Mary Clarissa Miller into a well-to-do family in Torquay, Devon, England. She grew up in a house her mother purchased in Ashfield, and her childhood and family life was generally happy. As a young girl she never attended a formal school, but was tutored by her mother, to whom she grew particularly close. She wrote her first stories on her mother's suggestion. Agatha was shy, private, and reserved, traits that characterized her for the rest of her life. Early in her life she considered becoming a professional singer and took music lessons in Paris. In 1914 she married Colonel Archibald Christie, and she served as a nurse in Torquay during World War I while her husband fought.

Christie's wartime medical experience provided her with a thorough knowledge of poisons, often used as the murder weapon in her mysteries. Acting in part on a challenge from her older sister, in 1916 Christie began the first in a long series of engaging mystery novels rife with plot twists and surprises. That first novel, *The Mysterious Affair at Styles* (1920), concerns the murder of a wealthy woman. The eccentric Belgian sleuth Hercule Poirot, who appeared in so many of her subsequent stories, made his first appearance in this book. Christie introduced the second of her two most popular detectives, Miss Jane Marple, in *Murder at the Vicarage* (1930).

The Murder of Roger Ackroyd (1926) was the first of her mysteries to become famous. The same year she generated a real-life mystery of her own. When her husband asked her for a divorce, she disappeared for ten days, the circumstances of which remain a mystery. They officially divorced in 1928, and her second marriage to Sir Max Mallowan two years later proved to be a much happier one.

Christie and Mallowan, an archaeologist, traveled to the Middle East on ar-

Agatha Christie (Universal Pictorial and Press Agency)

Christie also wrote a number of plays. They include her enormously popular *The Mousetrap* (1952), one of the longest running plays in history; *Witness for the Prosecution* (1953), made into a film in 1958; *Murder on the Orient Express* (1934), a film version of which was released in 1978; *Death on the Nile* (1937), produced as a film in 1978; *Ten Little Indians* (1939); and *And Then There Were None* (1940).

Among Christie's other works are six romance novels using the pseudonym Mary Westmacott, including *Absent in the Spring* (1944), *Unfinished Portrait* (1934), and *The Burden* (1956); the short stories collected in *The Thirteen Problems* (1932), *The Hound of Death and Other Stories* (1933), *The Listerdale Mystery and Other Stories* (1934), and *Poirot and the Regatta Mystery* (1943); and finally the posthumously published *Autobiography* (1977). She was created Dame Commander of the British Empire in 1971.

chaeological expeditions. Their excursions to Syria and Iraq provided the material for some of her mysteries, such as *Murder in Mesopotamia* (1930) and *Appointment with Death* (1938). Among her numerous other mysteries are *The Seven Dials Mystery* (1929); *A Murder is Announced* (1950); and *At Bertram's Motel* (1965). Poirot dies in *Curtain* (1975).

BIBLIOGRAPHY

Christie, Agatha, *An Autobiography*, 1977; Gill, Gillian, *Agatha Christie: The Woman and Her Mysteries*, 1990; Morgan, Janet P., *Agatha Christie: A Biography*, 1985; Osborne, Charles, *The Life and Crimes of Agatha Christie*, 1982; Robyns, Gwen, *The Mystery of Agatha Christie*, 1978; Sanders, Dennis, *The Agatha Christie Companion: The Complete Guide to Agatha Christie's Life and Work*

Clair, René

(November 11, 1898–March 15, 1981)
Director, Novelist

René Clair established his directing career among the Parisian avant-garde during the 1920s. After initially opposing the introduction of sound into the cinema, he experimented with the interaction of imagery and sound in several films during the 1930s. Clair spent the World War II years working in Hollywood but was less successful after his return to France.

Clair was born René Chomette in Paris and grew up in the city's market quarter. He served with the French ambulance corps in 1917–1918 and later worked as a journalist for *L'intransigéant*. Clair first entered the cinema as an actor in 1920, appearing in *Le lys de la vie*. Over the next several years he wrote film criticism for *Théâtre et Comoedia Illustrés*, continued to act in films, and began to work as an assistant director in *Carillon de minuit* and other films. Clair first adopted his pseudonym for the screen in 1921.

In 1924 Clair directed his first film, *Paris qui dort* (1923; *The Crazy Ray*; literally, *Paris Who Sleeps*). Set in Paris, the story concerns a night watchman who finds Paris frozen in its tracks. He meets a group of still animate visitors and with them discovers the cause of the sudden paralysis—a scientist with a motion-stopping ray. With the help of his niece, they convince the scientist to undo the paralysis.

Clair's second film, *Entr'acte* (1924), was made to accompany a ballet by ERIK SATIE. Satie and several Dadaist painters appeared in the film. At this time Clair's film technique belonged to the avant-garde and was influenced by the Surrealists and Dadaists. *Entr'acte* is a surrealistic film laced with montage sequences.

Le fantôme du Moulin Rouge (The Phantom of the Red Mill) appeared in 1924, followed the next year by *Le voyage imaginaire (The Imaginary Voyage)*. Protagonist Jean is a weak and timid figure in love with Lucie, who works in his office. *Le voyage imaginaire* is one of Clair's most surrealistic films and contains an intricate dream sequence that reveals Jean's inner world. *La proie du vent* (1926; *The Prey of the Wind*) marked the first of several films for which Lazare Meerson served as art director.

La tour (1928), a brief film about the Eiffel Tower, was followed by *Les deux timides* (1928; *The Two Timid Souls*), the most visually innovative of his silent films. Clair employed flashbacks; jump cuts, split screen, and many other techniques to relate the story of a man in trouble with the law for beating his wife. *Un chapeau de paille d'Italie* (1927; *The Italian Straw Hat*), based on a farce by Eugène Labiche, satirizes middle-class hypocrisies; in it, Clair began to move toward a more conventional approach to filmmaking.

Clair at first disliked the introduction of sound into film, believing sound detracted from "the world of dreams over which the silent cinema reigned." *Sous les toits de Paris* (1930; *Under Paris Rooftops*), his first sound film, concerns a song-seller named Albert who falls in love with Pola. With this film and with *Le million* (1931) and *À nous la liberté!*

(1931; *For Us, Liberty*), he began experimenting with the place of sound in his work.

After the release of *Quatorze juillet* (1933; *July Fourteenth*), Clair traveled to England to film his international success *The Ghost Goes West* (1935). *Break the News*, starring MAURICE CHEVALIER, followed in 1937. Clair was working on *Air pur* when Germany invaded France and never finished the project. He fled France with his family, eventually settling in the United States. During the war he worked in Hollywood.

After the unsuccessful film *The Flame of New Orleans* (1940), Clair finished his most popular Hollywood film, *I Married a Witch* (1942). The story begins during the Salem witch trials of the seventeenth century, with a curse pronounced by a witch burned at the stake. The witch, Jennifer, curses the descendants of her leading accuser, Wooley. And indeed, poor relationships plague Wooley's descendants. In 1940, a lightning strike releases Jennifer's spirit, after which she seduces Wallace Wooley. After a series of twists and turns, they are happily married. *It Happened Tomorrow* (1944) and *And Then There Were None* (1945), adapted from an AGATHA CHRISTIE story, finished his Hollywood films.

Clair returned to Paris in 1946 and completed *Le silence est d'or* (1947; *Man About Town*; literally, *Silence is Golden*), again starring Chevalier. Chevalier plays a film director who takes in a friend's daughter. Both the director and his protégé, Jacques, fall in love with her, but she returns affection only to Jacques. The story ends with the director accepting their love.

Among Clair's later films are *La beauté du diable* (1949; *Beauty and the Devil*),

René Clair (Ann Ronan/Image Select)

adapted from the Faust story; *Les belles-de-nuit* (1952); *Les Grandes Manoeuvres* (1955), his first color film; *Porte de Lilas* (1957; *Gates of Paris*); *Tout l'or du monde* (1961); *Les fêtes galantes* (1965; *Courtly Affairs*). He also wrote several novels: *Adams* (1926; *Star Turn*), *De fil en aiguille* (1941), and *La princesse de Chine* (1951). Clair's other efforts include the radio production *Une larme du diable* (1951; literally, "a tear of the devil"), the stage production *On ne badine pas avec l'amour* (1959; literally, "one does not jest with the devil"), and in 1972 Glück's opera *Orpheus* for the Paris Opera.

Clair received an honorary doctorate from Cambridge University (1956) and was elected to the French Academy in 1960. His *Reflections on the Cinema* was published in 1953. His films often unfold in Paris and are characterized by his unique blend of humor and fantasy, explorations of the dynamics of relationships, and his own scenarios. Although some critics fault his style for superficiality, he infused his films with a distinctive charm that rendered him one of the leading filmmakers of his time. Although he was considered a leader in the avant-garde in the silent film era, Clair's reputation as a filmmaker declined after World War II.

BIBLIOGRAPHY

Dale, R. C., *The Films of René Clair*, 1986; McGerr, Celia, *René Clair*, 1980.

Clark, John Pepper

(April 6, 1935–)
Poet, Playwright, Critic, Translator, Teacher, Editor

The Nigerian poet John Pepper Clark is best known for his lyrical verse and poetic dramas rooted in Nigerian culture and tradition. Clark was one of the first West African poets to be published in English and helped make the traditional Niger Delta *Ozidi Saga* known to the English-speaking world. He has also used the name J. P. Clark-Bekederemo.

Clark was born in Kiagbodo, Nigeria. As a boy he attended several schools and was fond of reading. Upon his completion of secondary school, Clark enrolled at the University of Ibadan, where he edited the journal *Beacon* and helped found the poetry periodical *The Horn*. Many of his earliest poems appeared in these publications. He graduated with an English degree in 1960 and subsequently went to work for the newly formed independent Nigerian government. He wrote editorials and features for the *Daily Express* in Lagos, where he worked from 1961 to 1962.

His first book of poetry, *Poems*, appeared in 1961, as did the play *Song of a Goat*, a one-act verse tragedy about a wealthy man, Zifa, who is sexually impotent and has defied the gods. Zifa's wife's affair with his brother leads to her pregnancy, and an angry Zifa hastily and improperly prepares a ritual goat sacrifice. The incident leads to the suicides of both men. Like most of Clark's work, the play incorporates many Nigerian, and specifically Ijo, customs, beliefs, and traditions.

In 1962 and 1963 Clark went to Princeton University as a Parvin Fellow. His year overseas inspired *America, Their America* (1964), a biting narrative indictment of the United States, its people and culture, and Princeton University. Clark also wrote two plays while he was in the United States. The first, *The Masquerade* (1964), can be seen as a sequel to *Song of a Goat*. In *The Masquerade*, Clark implies that Tufa is the illegitimate son of Zifa's wife. Titi is the daughter of the main character, Diribi, and is engaged to Tufa. When questions about Tufa's background arise, Diribi opposes the marriage, murders his daughter, and later kills Tufa. *The Raft* (1964) is often considered Clark's best play. The simple story is a metaphor for Clark's bleak perception of the human condition: four men drift on a raft on the Niger River, and all eventually meet death in one way or another.

Clark returned to Nigeria in 1963, when he embarked on research into Ijo history and tradition at the Institute of African Studies. The subject of his inquiries was the story of Ozidi (or Azudu), a traditional Niger Delta epic about a heroic son schooled by his grandmother, who has supernatural powers, to avenge his father's murder. Clark collected several versions of the *Ozidi Saga*, translated one of them into English, and used the epic as the basis for subsequent works. Among them are his play *The Ozidi* (1966) and his film *Tides of the Delta* (with Francis Speed), which depicts a performance of the saga.

Clark has published several other collections of poetry. *A Reed in the Tide* (1965) consists of verse published previously as well as new poetry. Many of its poems are shaped by the crises leading up to the civil war in Nigeria in 1966. The verse in *Casualties: Poems 1966–1968* (1970) is largely inspired by the Nigerian civil war. Aside from Nigeria's political scene and native culture, Clark addresses erotic themes in his poetry and laments the adverse effects of European colonialism in poems such as "Ivbie: A Song of Wrong." His other volumes of verse include *A Decade of Tongues* (1981) and *State of the Union* (1981).

Beginning in 1964, Clark taught English at the University of Lagos. He married Ebun Odutola the same year, and with her he founded the PEC Repertory Theater in Lagos in 1982. Clark also served as coeditor of the literary periodical *Black Orpheus*. His other works include the essay collection *The Example of Shakespeare* (1970) and the prose play *The Boat* (1981).

BIBLIOGRAPHY

Egudu, Romanus N., *Four Modern West African Poets*, 1977; Wren, Robert M., *J. P. Clark*, 1984.

Cocteau, Jean

(July 5, 1889–October 11, 1963)
Novelist, Poet, Playwright, Director, Painter

The versatile French avant-garde artist Jean Cocteau began his career as a poet in his teens and became a prolific creator in a wide variety of art forms, including novels, poetry, plays, surrealistic films, and paintings, and in all of these areas he was a major figure in the French avant-garde. Cocteau always insisted that poetry formed the basis for all of his art.

Cocteau was born into a wealthy family of lawyers in Maisons-Laffitte, near Paris, the city in which he spent the majority of his life. His father, a broker and amateur painter, committed suicide when Cocteau was 9. His mother, Eugénie Lecomte, came from a wealthy background, and both parents took an interest in the arts. At the Petit Condorcet and later the Lycée Condorcet, Cocteau

Les Six, a group of French musicians, with Jean Cocteau at the piano and, left to right, Georges Auric, Arthur Honneger, Germaine Tailleferre, Francis Poulenc, and Louis Durey (Ann Ronan/Image Select)

was a poor student and often played the role of class clown. His formal schooling ended when he dropped out at age 16.

In 1908, the actor Édouard de Max sponsored a reading of Cocteau's poetry, thus launching his career in the arts. His first collection of poetry, *La lampe d'Aladin* (*Aladdin's Lamp*), was published when he was 19, and established his reputation as a writer. The following year he met the impresario SERGEY DIAGHILEV, then in Paris with his Ballets Russes. Diaghilev's famous challenge to Cocteau, "Astonish me," resulted in the ballet *The Blue God*, which premiered in 1912 but proved a commercial failure. VASLAV NIJINSKY danced the lead role in a London production the following year. Cocteau supplied the scenario for Diaghilev's ballet *Parade* (1917), accompanied with music by ERIK SATIE and a set designed by Cocteau's friend PABLO PICASSO; it was more successful. In 1920 he created the

scenario for Diaghilev's *Le boueuf sur le toit* (1920; *The Nothing-Doing Bar*), while DARIUS MILHAUD supplied the musical score.

His first book, *Le Potomak* (1912), is a prose fantasy and began as a tale Cocteau invented to entertain a child. Among Cocteau's novels is *Thomas the Imposter* (1923), which reflects his experiences as an ambulance driver for the Red Cross during World War I. The hastily written *Les enfants terribles* (1929; *Children of the Game*) is Cocteau's most widely read novel. The story centers on the brother and sister Paul and Elizabeth, whose father has deserted the family. Cocteau's war experience also contributed to *The Cape of Good Hope* (1919), a collection of poetry inspired by his first experiences flying in airplanes. *Plain-Chant*, a book of lyrical poetry addressed to an angel, appeared in 1923.

In general, Cocteau's work reflects influences of the Symbolists and Surrealists of his era. His acquaintances included the Symbolist writer Guillaume Apollinaire, Picasso, and the writer and painter Max Jacob. Cocteau's intimate relationship with Raymond Radiguet (1903–1923) was also one of the primary influences on his career. Radiguet, introduced to Cocteau by Jacob, was a young poet and novelist who embraced qualities of classicism and simplicity in his writing.

Radiguet's death from typhoid in 1923 plunged Cocteau into a state of despair. He developed an addiction to opium and wrote several works around the time of his recovery. Among them is the lengthy *L'ange Heurtebise*, a tormented poem inspired by his belief that he was in the presence of an angel named Heurtebise. *Opium: journal d'un désintoxication* (1932; *Opium: The Diary of an Addict*) addresses Cocteau's struggle with his addiction. During this period Cocteau also wrote poems in a variety of styles, many of which appear in *Opéra* (1927).

Two of Cocteau's most popular plays derive from Greek myths. *Orphée* (1925; *Orpheus*) is a character study of a poet based on a modernized version of the myth of Orpheus, the son of Apollo, renowned as the first and greatest musician and poet,who rescued his deceased wife (Eurydice) from Hades by the power of his song, then lost her again. The angel Heurtebise again appears in the play, and it premiered at the Théâtre Des Artes in Paris in 1926. *Le machine infernale* (1936; *The Infernal Machine*) is an adaptation of the Oedipus myth, a theme that had also appeared earlier in his collaboration with the Russian composer IGOR STRAVINSKY, *Oedipus Rex*. Cocteau sought to create a "poetry of the theatre," integrating all elements of a production to produce a unified experience.

Cocteau narrated his first film, the autobiographical *Le Sang d'un pòete* (1930; *Blood of a Poet*). He did not make another film until the 1940s. *Le belle et la bête* (1945; *Beauty and the Beast*) is a surrealistic rendering of the children's fairy tale, and he based the film *Orpheus* (1950) on his play of the same title. The actor Jean Marais, to whom Cocteau grew close in the 1930s, starred in many of Cocteau's films and theater productions; his roles include the beast in *Beauty and the Beast* and Galahad in the play *The Knights of the Round Table* (1937).

In the last years of his life and career Cocteau occupied himself with visual arts, an area in which he was significantly influenced by Picasso. In 1950 he decorated the Villa Santo Sospir in Saint-Jean-Cap-Ferrat, and he subsequently painted frescoes for a number of churches. His later volumes of poetry include *Le Chiffre Sept, Clair-Obscur,* and the collection of prose poems *Appogiatures.* Cocteau's other works include the novella *The White Book;* the novel *The Big Split* (1923); and the ballet *The Ox on the Roof* (1920), with music by Darius Milhaud.

BIBLIOGRAPHY

Brown, Frederick, *An Impersonation of Angels: A Biography of Jean Cocteau,* 1969; Crosland, Margaret, *Jean Cocteau,* 1955; Steegmuller, Francis, *Cocteau: A Biography,* 1970.

Colette

(January 28, 1873–August 3, 1954)
Novelist, Short-Story Writer, Critic, Playwright, Librettist

Never having had the idea of becoming a writer, Sidonie-Gabrielle Claudine Colette found her first literary character, Claudine, something of a fictional cult figure in the France of 1900. Although her first husband took the credit for the stories of Claudine, which were published under his name, Colette soon established herself as a leading French writer in her own right. Her dramatic and probing stories explore the difficulties of romantic and sexual relationships, primarily through the eyes of female protagonists; the stories gain depth by being closely intertwined with the cycles of nature.

Colette was born in the Burgundian village of Saint-Sauveur-en-Puisaye, France. Her mother was the dominant influence in her life, instilling in her a love of animals and nature that later emerged as a prominent force in her fiction. Colette's father was a former military man who had lost a leg in battle and become a tax collector. Although she loved to read from her childhood, Colette nursed no ambition to become a writer. In 1890 debt forced the family to move to the neighboring village of Châtillon-Coligny, where her brother worked as a doctor.

Her marriage to Henri Gauthier-Villars (Willy) in 1893 dramatically changed her life. Willy took her from her idyllic country life to the social circles of Paris. Under his influence she began to write while recovering from an illness. The resulting series of novels, known as the "Claudine" books, which bore Willy's name on them, became immediate bestsellers.

The heroine of the semiautobiographical series, Claudine, is a rebellious, and independent character. *Claudine à l'école* (1900) begins as a journal written by the fifteen-year-old Claudine during her final year at school. *Claudine à Paris* (1901) finds her two years older and living in Paris, but as yet unmarried. In *Claudine en ménage* (1902; *Claudine Married*) the heroine has married and, as Colette was when she wrote the novel, is struggling with an unhappy union and confused sexuality. *Claudine s'en va* (1903; translated as *Claudine and Annie*; literally, "Claudine leaves") and *La retraite sentimentale* (1907; *The Sentimental Retreat*) completed the series.

In 1904 Colette published her first novel under her own name, *Dialogues de bêtes*. Unhappy with Willy and unable to endure his infidelities, she separated from him in 1906 and spent the next several years as a music hall performer. Her next major work, *L'ingénue libertine* (1909; *The Gentle Libertine*), consists of two novels about a heroine in a failed search for ideal love.

La vagabonde (1910; *The Vagabond*) marked a major new direction in Colette's writing and is usually considered the first of her mature novels. Written largely backstage during her music hall performances, the story derives from Colette's experiences of these years. The protagonist is the recently divorced music hall performer Renée Néré, who is involved in a new relationship with Maxime. Colette continued the story in the sequel *L'entrave* (1913; *The Shackle*). *L'envers du music-hall* (1913) is a collec-

Colette (AKG)

tion of sketches that recalls her music-hall days.

With her 1912 marriage to Henry de Jouvenel Colette left the music hall circuit and began to write for his paper, *Le Matin*. In 1916 she published *La Paix chez les bêtes* (1916; *Peace Among Animals*), followed by *Mitsou* in 1919. Her marriage to Jouvenel, too, proved unhappy and disastrous. They separated in 1923 and divorced in 1925.

Chéri (1920) and *La Fin de Chéri* (1926) became two of Colette's biggest successes. The protagonist of the title is a young man who has a romantic relationship with Léa de Lonval, an older woman. Their story ends unhappily, with his inability to cope with his life and eventual suicide. Many of her other novels treat what she viewed as a fundamental incompatibility between men and women. *Le blé en herbe* (1923; *Ripening Seed*) explores a romantic relationship between two young protagonists emerging from the innocence of youth. *Duo* (1934) concerns the deterioration of a relationship between Michel and his wife after she has a brief affair. Colette continued the story in the short sequel *Le Toutounier* (1939).

In other novels such as *La maison de Claudine* (1922; *My Mother's House*) and *Sido* (1930) Colette explored themes of childhood innocence and nature. *La chatte* (1933) evinces the deep regard Colette held for animals. In the story, a cat attains such stature in his master's eyes that it breaks up his marriage to a jealous wife who tries to kill it.

In 1935 Colette married Maurice Goudeket, the only one of her marriages that proved to be emotionally fulfilling. There were trials to endure, however: the Gestapo arrested Goudeket in 1942, and after the war Colette suffered from painful and crippling arthritis. Among her later works are *Julie de Carneilhan* (1941) and the short-story collection *Gigi* (1944). The title story of the latter became the basis for a popular musical.

Colette's other works include *La Naissance du jour* (1928; *Break of Day*); *La Seconde* (1929; *The Other One*); *Ces plaisirs* (1932; later titled *Le Pur et l'impur—The Pure and the Impure*); *Mes Apprentissages* (1936; *My Apprenticeship*), a negative account of her first marriage; *Jounral à rebours* (1941; *Looking Backwards*); *De ma Fenêtre* (1942; *From My Window*); and the journals *L'Étoile Vesper* (1946; *The Evening Star*) and *Le Fanal bleu* (1949; *The Blue Lantern*).

Aside from her fiction, journals, and criticism, Colette also wrote plays, ballet scenarios, and libretto. She was elected to the Belgian Royal Academy in 1935 and the French Académie Goncourt in 1945, and in 1953 she was elected a grand officer of the Légion d'Honneur. Her *Oeuvres complètes* ("complete works") were published in 1949–1950.

BIBLIOGRAPHY

Cottrell, Robert D., *Colette*, 1974; Crosland, Margaret, *Colette—The Difficulty of Loving: A Biography*, 1973; Lottman, Herbert R., *Colette: A Life*, 1991; Mitchell, Yvone, *Colette: A Taste for Life*, 1975; Richardson, Joanna, *Colette*, 1983.

Compton-Burnett, Ivy

(June 5, 1884–August 27, 1969)
Novelist

In her twenty novels, the British author Ivy Compton-Burnett is chiefly noted for her ability to dissect family relations in upper-middle-class English families. Her typical family portraits are dominated by one or more controlling individuals who adversely affect the rest of the family.

Compton-Burnett was one of twelve children born into a large upper-middle-class family in London. Her difficult family relations provided material for much of her fiction. Her father was a homeopathic doctor, and her mother was perpetually ill-tempered. None of the children ever had any offspring of their own, and three of them committed suicide. Neither Ivy nor any of her sisters ever married; Ivy lived most of her life in London with her friend, Margaret Jourdain. Her brothers tutored her at home before she went to the Royal Holloway College at the University of London, where she studied classics, graduating in 1906.

Dolores (1911), Compton-Burnett's first novel, was regarded neither by the author nor her critics as a solid work. Fourteen years elapsed before the publication of her next book, *Pastors and Masters* (1925), which showcases the ironic understatement characteristic of her style, set at a boys' school. Manipulation and power struggles—prime elements in all of Compton-Burnett's novels—drive the motley cast of characters. Nicholas Herrick, who with his sister Emily owns the school, steals a manuscript written by Bumpus and claims it as his own writing. Bumpus, who would like to bring out the truth, cannot because his own secrets are too incriminating. The atmosphere Compton-Burnett creates among the characters is one of dishonesty and people feeding off each others' failures. *Brothers and Sisters* (1929), *Men and Wives* (1931), and *More Women than Men* (1933) followed.

Almost without exception, human relationships are the fundamental concern in Compton-Burnett's novels. In particular, she dissects relationships in large families ruined by tyrannical figures, such as a manipulative woman, an authoritarian man, or a lustful man. Her view of these associations is overwhelmingly pessimistic, and children often provide the only sense of freshness or innocence in her claustrophobic family dens. Curt, clipped speech dominates dialogue between characters, emphasizing the ineffective communication that troubles them.

In *Daughters and Sons* (1937), two women, the elderly Sabine Ponsonby and her daughter Hetta, dominate the family. Hetta, whose domain is the day-to-day running of the household, fakes suicide in an attempt to prove that the others need her. Sabine, meanwhile, is concerned with manipulating the relationships in her household. When her granddaughter Frances writes a prize-winning novel using her governess's name as a pseudonym, Sabine wants to marry her son, the novelist John, to the governess. The novel ends in the death of both women.

Manservant and Maidservant (1947) was published as *Bullivant and the Lambs* in the United States and was

Ivy Compton-Burnett (Universal Pictorial and Press Agency)

Compton-Burnett's most successful work in America. The villain of this story, Horace Lamb, differs from other Compton-Burnett autocrats in that he recognizes his own shortcomings when he discovers his wife's intention to leave him. Nevertheless, Horace fails to do anything about them. Intertwined with the family intrigues is a world of manipulation among the servants, chief of whom is the butler, Bullivant.

The shortcoming of Cassius Clare, protagonist of *The Present and the Past* (1953), is his insensitivity. He allows his ex-wife, Catherine, to return to see their children. The visit at first distresses Flavia, his current wife, and the children, who have adapted to their new family situation. Circumstances turn against Cassius when Catherine and Flavia become friends and ignore him, so he fakes a suicide attempt to get attention.

The patriarch Hereward Egerton, married to Ada Merton, manipulates his family through his sexual conquests in *A God and His Gifts* (1963). Hereward's affair with Ada's sister produced the first of his secret illegitimate children, Viola. His legitimate son Merton is engaged to Hetty, Hereward's next conquest. Their union produces a second illegitimate child, Henry. When Hereward's illegitimate and legitimate children grow up, he is forced to reveal his paternity when they become attracted to each other.

Compton-Burnett's other novels include *A House and Its Head* (1935), *Parents and Children* (1941), *Elders and Betters* (1944), *Two Worlds and Their Ways* (1949), *Darkness and Day* (1951), *Mother and Son* (1955), *A Father and His Fate* (1957), *A Heritage and Its History* (1959), *The Mighty and Their Fall* (1961), and *The Last and the First* (1971). She received an honorary doctorate of letters from the University of Leeds in 1960 and was made Dame of the British Empire in 1967.

BIBLIOGRAPHY

Baldanza, Frank, *Ivy Compton-Burnett*, 1964; Nevius, Blake, *Ivy Compton-Burnett*, 1970; Sprigge, Elizabeth, *The Life of Ivy Compton-Burnett*, 1973; Spurling, Hilary, *Ivy: The Life of I. Compton-Burnett*, 1984; Spurling, Hilary, *Secrets of a Woman's Heart: The Later Life of Ivy Compton-Burnett, 1920–1969*, 1984.

Conrad, Joseph

(December 3, 1857–August 3, 1924)
Novelist, Short-Story Writer, Essayist

The Polish-born author Joseph Conrad spent his young adult life at sea and wrote novels that incorporate his varied experiences and explore the deficiencies in human nature. He is widely admired for his masterful use of the English language, which he did not learn until his early twenties.

Conrad was born Józef Teodor Konrad Korzeniowski in Berdychev, Poland, then part of the Russian Empire. His father, a poet, translator, and Polish patriot, was arrested by the Russian authorities and took his family with him into exile in northern Russia in 1861. His mother died from tuberculosis in 1865. After his father's death from the same ailment four years later, Conrad went to live with an uncle, Tadeusz Bobrowski, who was a constant source of support until his death. Conrad read voraciously as a child, particularly translations of English writers, and studied in both Cracow and Switzerland. With assistance from his uncle in 1874, he went to Marseilles, where he began a twenty-year career at sea with the French merchant service.

Conrad's years at sea provided the material for much of his work. The first ship on which he sailed, the *Mont-Blanc*, took him to Martinique. There is speculation about his activities as a steward on the *Saint-Antoine*, which sailed to the West Indies, Colombia, and Venezuela. On this voyage Conrad was purportedly involved in illegal activity, either smuggling or gunrunning for Spanish rebels. Upon his return to France, Conrad shot himself in the chest in a failed suicide attempt.

After his recovery in 1878 he joined the crew of a British steamer, the *Mavis*, and from that point on he lived in England. Two years later he became a second mate. The next voyage that provided significant material for his later work came in 1881 as second mate aboard the *Palestine*, which sailed to the Far East. It was a troubled voyage that ended in the ship's destruction by a devastating fire. Conrad's experiences on this journey appear in his short story "Youth" (1898).

His next important voyage, as second mate aboard the iron ship *Narcissus* (from Bombay) in 1883, contributed to his novel *The Nigger of the "Narcissus"*

Joseph Conrad (Ann Ronan/Image Select)

(1897). In 1886 he earned his master mariner's certificate, and the same year he became a British subject. The following year he was first mate of the *Highland Forest* on a voyage to Java. Its captain, John MacWhirr, became the unremarkable captain MacWhirr in *Typhoon* (1903). Conrad then joined the *Vidar*, which traded in Southeast Asia.

Conrad began to write in 1889 in London. After returning to England from the Belgian Congo in 1891, he sailed as first mate on several ships, retiring from sea life in 1894. The following year he married Jessie George; they had two sons, Borys and John. Conrad's early writings received critical acclaim but were unsuccessful commercially. During his writing career he became a friend of Edward Garnett, who took an early interest in his work as well as gaining the friendship of Stephen Crane, Henry James, H. G. WELLS, and FORD MADOX FORD. Because of the difficulty the English found in pronouncing "Korzeniowski," he used the name Joseph Conrad.

Conrad's works are noteworthy for their skillful use of the English language (his third language, after Polish and French), pessimistic outlook, and investigation of human morality and psychology. The characters in his novels are largely unheroic; at their worst they divorce themselves from reality, and often their own flaws and imperfections inhibit noble ideals they possess. Critics labeled him a writer of sea stories, a reputation he sought to shed throughout his career.

Power and greed motivate the protagonists of Conrad's first novels, *Almayer's Folly* (1895) and *An Outcast of the Islands* (1896), both set in Borneo. The title character of *Lord Jim* (1900) tries to compensate for an unheroic act and redeem himself. *Nostromo* (1904) examines greed in a fictional South American country whose major source of wealth is a silver mine. Dominic Cervoni, first mate of the *Saint-Antoine*, aboard which Conrad sailed as a steward in the 1870s, served as the model for one of *Nostromo*'s characters.

Heart of Darkness (1902), published two years before *Nostromo*, is perhaps Conrad's most famous work. Like its narrator, Marlow (who appears in several of Conrad's works), Conrad traveled into the Congo aboard a river steamboat. He began his difficult voyage in 1890 for the Belgian Company for Commerce, and his journey aboard the *Roi de Belges* closely paralleled the events of *Heart of Darkness*. Marlow sails through the heart of the Congo on the river steamer, anticipating his meeting with the hypnotic Kurtz. Kurtz, whom Conrad based on the trading company's agent at Stanley Falls, Georges Antoine Klein, operates with brutal power in a secluded place where his evil nature is allowed to reign unchecked. At the time of Marlow's arrival, Kurtz suffers from the illness that will later claim his life. Part of Marlow is horrified by what he sees, but he nevertheless finds he is strangely fascinated with the man who seems a pure embodiment of evil. As Kurtz lies dying on Marlow's ship, he utters his famous words, "The horror! The horror!"

Conrad's experience in the Congo was traumatic psychologically, spiritually, and physically. He suffered from dysentery and fever and never fully regained his health. The horrific effects of Belgian exploitation in the area deeply disturbed him, and he was known to say, "Before the Congo I was a mere animal." The

Congo journey also served as the basis for his story "The Outpost of Progress."

With *The Secret Agent* (1907), Conrad turned to European politics. Set in London and steeped in political intrigue, the novel paints a dark picture of radical politics. *Under Western Eyes* (1911), set in tsarist Russia, takes place in the stormy pre-Soviet political climate. Razumov, a philosophy student in St. Petersburg, finds himself in a revolutionary plot against his will.

With the serialization of his novel *Chance* in the *New York Herald* in 1912, Conrad began to enjoy a measure of commercial success. *Victory* (1915) became popular in both the United States and Great Britain. His later works include *The Shadow-Line* (1917), *The Arrow of Gold* (1919), *The Rescue* (1920), and *The Rover*

(1923). Among his other writings are *The Inheritors* (1901) and *Romance* (1903), both written with Ford; the autobiographical *A Personal Record* (1912); *The Congo Diary* (1925); and *Last Essays* (1926). Conrad refused an offer of knighthood in 1924 and died of a heart attack the same year. Conrad's novels, particularly *Heart of Darkness* and *Nostromo*, are still widely read and admired for their mastery of English and probing depictions of corruption and the dark side of human nature against exotic backgrounds.

BIBLIOGRAPHY

Adams, Elbridge L., *Conrad: The Man*, 1976; Bennett, Carl D., *Joseph Conrad*, 1991; Sherry, Norman, *Conrad*, 1988; Tennant, Roger, *Joseph Conrad*, 1981.

Cortázar, Julio

(August 26, 1914–February 12, 1984)
Novelist, Short-Story Writer, Poet, Translator

The Argentinian fiction writer Julio Florencio Cortázar is best known for his experimental novel *Hopscotch* and his many fantastic, surrealistic short stories. He ranks among the most influential Latin American writers of the twentieth century.

Cortázar was born to Argentine parents in Brussels, Belgium, and grew up in Banfield, Argentina. At the age of 12 he enrolled in the Escuela Normal Mariano Acosta and took a degree as a teacher in 1932. In 1935 he began studying at the University of Buenos Aires and later taught high school near the city. His first

book, *Presencia*, a collection of sonnets, appeared in 1938 under the pseudonym Julio Denis. In 1944 he began teaching literature at the University of Cuyo, a position he lost two years later because of his active resistance to Juan Perón, who became Argentina's leader in 1946.

JORGE LUIS BORGES published the first of Cortázar's short stories to see print, "House Taken Over," in 1946. The fantastic nature of the story is typical of Cortázar's early writings as well as much of his later fiction. The story centers around a brother and sister living in financial ease in a house they have inherited. When the mysterious "they" invade part of the house, the apathetic siblings find themselves confined to one portion of the home. The unidentified invading force eventually drives them from the house altogether, and the siblings leave, expressing little shock or reaction.

In 1949 Cortázar published *The Monarchs*, a prose poem based on the myth of the Minotaur. *Bestiary*, his first short-story collection, appeared in 1951. Fleeing the Perón regime, Cortázar moved to Paris permanently the same year. In 1953 he married his first wife, Marries Aurora Bernández. Other short-story collections followed in the 1950s, including *End of the Game* (1956) and *Secret Weapons* (1958). The latter contains "The Devil's Drivel," adapted for MICHELANGELO ANTONIONI's film *Blow-up* (1966).

As he grew older Cortázar became increasingly involved in Latin American politics. During the early 1960s he actively supported the Cuban revolution and traveled frequently to Cuba. He would later support Marxist movements in other Latin American countries, most notably the Sandinistas in Nicaragua. Short stories such as "Meeting" (1964) and "Apocalypse at Solentiname" (1979) were politically oriented, as was his 1973 novel, *A Manual for Manuel*. Nevertheless, he maintained a measure of intellectual distance from pure political revolutionaries, who he felt held too little respect for artists and intellectuals.

In Cortázar's first published novel, *The Winners* (1960), a motley group of contest winners embarks on a river cruise aboard the *Malcolm* only to find themselves trapped in a nightmarish web of intrigue, disease, and tangled relationships. His next novel, *Hopscotch* (1963), is his most internationally famous work on account of its experimental structure. Cortázar suggested an alternative order for reading the novel's chapters but also allowed the reader to finish them in their traditional order. The somewhat disjointed story of *62: A Model Kit* (1968) unfolds as a series of reflections through the eyes of numerous characters and takes its title from chapter 62 of *Hopscotch*.

For much of his adult life Cortázar worked as a professional translator. In 1947 he finished his translating degree, and beginning in 1952 he translated for UNESCO. Among the works of fiction he translated into Spanish are Louisa May Alcott's *Little Women* and Edgar Allan Poe's prose. Cortázar's later short-story collections include *All Fires the Fire* (1966), the humorous *Cronopios and Famas* (1969), *Octahedron* (1974), *Someone Walking Around* (1977), *We Love Glenda So Much* (1980), and *Bad Timing* (1982). Among his other works are the collection of poetry *Peoms and Meops* (1971); his commentary on art, *Territories* (1978); *Rimbaud* (1941); the novel *The Exam*, published posthumously; *Around the Day in Eighty Worlds* (1967); and *A Certain Lucas* (1979). Cortázar died of leukemia in 1984.

BIBLIOGRAPHY

Peavler, Terry J., *Julio Cortázar*, 1990.

Coward, Noël

(December 16, 1899–March 26, 1973)
Playwright, Composer, Actor, Poet, Short-Story Writer, Novelist

Noël Pierce Coward won widespread fame in the English-speaking world with his lightly satiric comedies of the British upper classes in the post–World War I generation. Coward also acted in the theater and in film, wrote musicals, composed music, and wrote short stories and novels. A number of his plays remain part of the standard repertory, and his brand of pointed satire has contributed to the enduring popularity of his plays.

Coward was born in Teddington, Middlesex, England, near London. Having a mother, a navy captain's daughter, who pushed him toward the performing arts, Coward began his career as a professional at an early age. His mother enrolled him in dance classes and his father, a piano tuner, exposed him to music. Coward debuted on stage at the age of 11, when he received a part in a production of the fairy play *The Goldfish*. By 1917 he was playing lead roles, his first in *The Saving Grace*.

After several months, marked by ill health and difficulty, serving in the British Army in 1918, Coward obtained a medical discharge and returned to the theater. He enjoyed some early successes as a playwright with the comedies *I'll Leave It to You* (1920) and *The Young Idea* (1922). But his first major triumph came with the drama *The Vortex* (1923), in which he starred as the drug-addicted Nicky Lancaster. Nicky's mother, Florence, has a habit of chasing younger men. Her latest fling, Tom Veryan, turns out to be the former lover of Nicky's fiancee, Bunty Mainwaring. When Florence and Nicky find Bunty with Tom, both relationships fall apart. Nicky, heartbroken and addicted to drugs, demands that his mother start acting like one.

The three-act *Hay Fever* (1925) was Coward's first success in the style for which he is most famous—the comedy of manners. The action takes place at a weekend party in a British country home, owned by the Bliss family, around a series of romantic mismatches and games.

Other Coward plays from this period include *Fallen Angels* (1925), *Easy Virtue* (1925), *The Queen Was in the Parlour* (1926), *This Was a Man* (1926), *The Marquise* (1927), and *Home Chat* (1927).

The comedy *Private Lives* (1930), written primarily for Gertrude Lawrence, is still widely performed. When the former husband and wife Elyot Chase and Amanda Prynne find themselves in neighboring suites, each on a honeymoon with a new spouse, chaos erupts. Elyot and Amanda each demand to leave the hotel, but neither of their spouses will agree. The resulting arguments end with Elyot and Amanda running off with each other and eventually arguing violently. Victor and Sibyl, their new spouses, find them together and break their relationships. Elyot and Amanda have by now forgiven each other and take off together.

Coward's plays were carefully structured, employed his characteristic clipped speech in the dialogue, and were entertaining and dramatic. He involved himself in all aspects of his projects, often writing, directing, singing, dancing, and acting in a production. Although he is most famous for his comedies, his active association with the impresario C. B. Cochran led to a number of popular reviews for which he composed lyrics, music, and books.

In 1925 Cochran commissioned him to write the book and lyrics for *On with the Dance* (1925), and Coward wrote *This Year of Grace!* in 1927. The operetta *Bitter Sweet* (1929) was one of the most popular products of the Coward-Cochran collaboration. With *Cavalcade* (1931), a play that chronicles the ups and downs of a working-class family and a wealthier one during the Victorian era, production assumed gigantic proportions, requiring an elaborate set, a multitude of characters, and thousands of costumes. *Words and Music* (1932), also proved successful.

Coward composed the music for *London Calling!* (1939), which included his popular parody of the Sitwells, "The Swiss Family Whittlebot." Coward's other popular songs include "Mad Dogs and Englishmen," "Some Day I'll Find You," "Poor Little Rich Girl," "A Room With a View," "Mad About the Boy," and "Marvellous Party." In 1959 he composed the score for the ballet *London Morning* (1959).

Coward enjoyed a long career in film as well as the theater, and many of his plays were adapted into films. In 1935 he appeared in the film *The Scoundrel*. His play *Blithe Spirit* (1941) became the basis for a film. In the story, Ruth Condomime and her husband, Charles, a novelist, throw a dinner party. Among the guests is the medium Madame Arcati, who deeply disturbs Charles by materializing his deceased former wife, Elvira. Elvira wreaks havoc on the household and eventually kills Ruth through a car accident. Calamity ensues when both women materialize in the house. *In Which We Serve* (1942), a war propaganda film, was one of Coward's contributions to Britain's war effort after having been rejected for military service. Coward adapted his play *Still Life* as the film *Brief Encounter* (1946).

Coward continued to write plays in the midst of his other activities. *Relative Values* (1952) unfolds in a house in East Kent around the engagement of Nigel, Earl of Marshwood, to the American film star Miranda Frayle. In *Nude with Violin* (1956), a satire on modern art and its critics, a deceased modernist painter, Paul Sorodin, leaves a letter confessing that he did not paint his widely acclaimed masterpieces. One by one, the valet Sebastien gets rid of the series of ghost painters from various "periods" in Sorodin's career who emerge. Meanwhile, Sorodin's "mourners" plot how to keep the fraud secret and sell his final painting, *Nude with Violin*, from the "Neo-Infantilist" period. Coward made his last West End stage appearance in his *Suite in Three Keys* (1966).

Among Coward's literary endeavors are *Collected Short Stories* (1962); the short stories in *Pretty Polly Barlow* (1964) and *Bon Voyage* (1967); the novel *Pomp and Circumstance* (1960); and the poetry collection *Not Yet the Dodo* (1967). Two volumes of his autobiography appeared during his lifetime and a third was unfinished when he died. His other plays, musicals, and reviews include *A Withered Nosegay* (1922), *Sirocco* (1927), *Design for Living* (1933), *Conversation Piece* (1934), *Tonight at Eight-Thirty* (1936), *Operette* (1938), *Present Laughter* (1939), *This Happy Breed* (1942), *Sigh No More* (1945), *Pacific 1860* (1946), *Peace in Our Time*

(1947), *Home Colonial* (1949), *Quadrille* (1952), *After the Ball* (1954), *Waiting in the Wings* (1960), and *Sail Away* (1961). Coward was knighted in 1970.

BIBLIOGRAPHY

Fisher, Clive, *Noel Coward*, 1992; Hoare, Philip, *Noël Coward: A Biography*, 1995; Kiernan, Robert F., *Noel Coward*, 1986.

Craig, Gordon

(January 16, 1872–July 29, 1966)
Actor, Director, Producer, Essayist, Theorist, Graphic Artist

Although he attained only modest success and recognition during his lifetime, Edward Gordon Craig was an influential force in the development of dramatic presentation in the early twentieth century. Rejecting the realistic tendencies of his age, he took a symbolic and integrated approach to the design of a play's elements. Craig promoted his ideas with his long-running review *The Mask* and in theoretical works on the theater.

Craig was born in Stevenage, Hertfordshire, England. He was the son of the famed actress Ellen Terry (1847–1928) and the architect Edward William Godwin. When his parents separated in 1875 he moved to London with his mother. There he began his theatrical career, studying and acting in Henry Irving's Lyceum Theatre. As early as age 6 he appeared as a super in *Olivia*. From Irving's company Craig received a broad education in the theater, as he appeared in plays ranging from Shakespeare and the classics to modern stage works.

Craig continued touring with acting companies until 1898, when he gave up his stage career. From then on he devoted himself mainly to the development of his ideas on the theater. He founded the periodical *The Page*, to which he contributed expressionistic woodcuts and other items. Hoping to put some of his developing theories into practice, he established the Purcell Operatic Society when he was 28.

His first major production was Purcell's *Dido and Aeneas* (1900), which impressed WILLIAM BUTLER YEATS enough to earn him a commission for designs for the Abbey Theatre. Craig also staged Purcell's *The Masque of Love* (1900) and George Frederick Handel's *Acis and Galatea* (1902). Into these productions he introduced a number of innovative scenic and design elements, among which were the earliest examples of colored overhead lighting. In 1903 he produced Henrik Ibsen's *The Vikings* (1903) for Terry's company at the Imperial Theatre in London.

In 1903 he went to Italy, where he founded the School for the Art of the Theatre at the Arena Goldoni in Florence. In 1904, the same year he began his stormy affair with the American dancer Isadora Duncan, Craig went to Germany at the invitation of Count Harry Kessler. There he wrote *The Art of the Theatre* (1905; later published as *On the Art of the Theatre* in 1911), in which he

Gordon Craig, an actor before turning to design, here shown as Arviragus in Shakespeare's *Cymbeline* (Ann Ronan/Image Select)

called for the creation of an expressive, symbolic theater.

Craig attempted to integrate all elements of a theatrical production—costumes, acting, lighting, and set design—into an artistic whole. He sought a symbolic mode of expression to replace the representational and realistic productions that dominated the era. Objecting to traditional footlighting, he designed a system of suspended overhead lights that enabled directors to control shadow and mood in their productions. Craig also created a mobile stage consisting of movable blocks, allowing the creation of spatial variations.

In an article entitled "The Actor and the Übermarionette" he compared actors to marionettes in a director's hand. Craig wrote of the actor as an element of the production and not as a unique, individual force. These ideas and many others he energetically promoted in his periodical *The Mask*, which he founded in Florence in 1908 and ran until 1929. A skilled graphic artist, Craig presented his scenic designs in *A Portfolio of Etchings* (1908) and other volumes.

In 1907 he began to develop folding screens, which he employed in a production of *Hamlet* at the Moscow Art Theatre (1912). The famed Russian director KONSTANTIN STANISLAVSKY, whose realistic vision of the theater stood diametrically opposed to Craig's symbolic view, was nevertheless intrigued by his theories and invited him to Moscow.

Among Craig's other productions were designs for Eleonora Duse's production of Ibsen's *Rosmersholm* (1906); *The Pretenders* in Copenhagen (1926) for Johann Poulsen; and *Macbeth* in New York (1928). Despite the vigor with which he promoted his ideas, he never became successful enough to operate his own theater company. Nevertheless, his innovative theories of the stage and set designs had a significant impact on the development of dramatic production in the later part of the twentieth century.

Craig wrote numerous theoretical and historical works on the theater, including *Towards a New Theatre* (1913), *Henry Irving* (1930), and *Ellen Terry and Her Secret Self* (1931). He also illustrated editions of *Hamlet* (1929; translated by GERHART HAUPTMANN) for Cranach Press and Daniel Defoe's *Robinson Crusoe*. *Scene*, a collection of articles and essays accompanied by a series of "Frozen Motion Studies," appeared in 1923. He exhibited his drawings and etchings on numerous occasions. Craig published his memoirs, *Index to the Story of My Days*, in 1957.

BIBLIOGRAPHY

Innes, C. D., *Edward Gordon Craig*, 1983; Innes, C. D., *Edward Gordon Craig: A Vision of the Theatre*, 1998; Price, Thomas, *Edward Gordon Craig and the Theatre of the Imagination*, 1986.

Cranko, John

(August 15, 1927–June 26, 1973)
Dancer, Choreographer

The South-African born choreographer John Cranko raised the Stuttgart Ballet from its status as a small German dance company to international prominence in the 1960s. In his work with the company and with the Sadler's Wells Ballet in England, Cranko contributed highly visual, dramatic choreography to both his original ballets and new versions of the classic ballets.

Cranko was born in Rustenburg, South Africa, and moved with his family to Johannesburg when he was eight. As a child he watched his sister's ballet classes in Cape Town, and his parents, both ballet enthusiasts, encouraged him to think about dance. When they separated, Cranko first lived with his mother and later with his father. At the age of 9, he enrolled in St. John's College but disliked the school so much that he ran away. He subsequently attended Highlands North, a government school. Cranko pursued several artistic interests as an adolescent, including music and elaborate orchestrations of puppet shows.

In 1944, Cranko began his career in dance, studying at the University of Cape Town Ballet. Cranko was soon dancing in productions of the Cape Town Ballet Club and the University of Cape Town Ballet. With the former, he performed in and directed his first major production, *The Soldier's Tale* (1944), to music by IGOR STRAVINSKY. The story takes place around a group of soldiers who come to a village and fall victim to the wiles of a conniving devil. Cranko performed the part of the devil and later danced many other roles, but his talent and interest lay more in choreography.

In 1946, he joined the Sadler's Wells Ballet, which later became the Royal Ballet, in England. Among his most famous productions with the Sadler's Wells were *Pineapple Poll* (1951) and *Harlequin in April* (1951). The story of *The Prince of the Pagodas* (1957), an original Cranko ballet, concerns an emperor and his two daughters, who have opposite personalities. The commanding Belle Epine is set to inherit her father's kingdom and succeeds in taking it from him before his death. Her gentler sister, Belle Rose, journeys to the land of the pagodas, and their prince, in the form of a salamander, proves to be her salvation and Belle Epine's undoing. *The Prince of the Pagodas* featured a score by Benjamin Britten.

In 1961, Cranko took the position of director of the Stuttgart Ballet and subsequently transformed it from a small German company into a major international dance company. Among the works he choreographed for the Stuttgart are *Romeo and Juliet* (1962); *Jeu de Cartes* (1966); the three-act *Onegin* (1965), taken from Alexander Pushkin's poem; *The Taming of the Shrew* (1969); and *Traces* (1973). In 1963, Cranko created the ballet *Song of My People* for the Batsheva Dance Company in Israel.

Cranko suffered a heart attack and died in 1973. Marcia Haydée, who danced many lead roles in his productions, became director of the Stuttgart Ballet in 1976.

BIBLIOGRAPHY

Percival, John, *Theatre in My Blood*, 1983.

Cugat, Xavier

(January 1, 1900–October 27, 1990)
Bandleader, Violinist

Born in Spain and raised in Cuba, Xavier Cugat later moved to the United States, where he was an influential force in the introduction of Latin American band music into American popular culture through live band performances, recordings, radio and television appearances, and film. Cugat's showy personality extended to both the stage and his private life.

Cugat was born Francisco De Asis Javier Cugat Mingall De Brue y Deulofeo in Barcelona, Spain. When he was 5 his family emigrated to Cuba, and Cugat spent the formative years of his life in Havana. Cugat's skill with the violin emerged when he was young, and after training as a classical violinist he performed with the Orchestra of the Teatro Nacional in Havana. Having earned enough money to emigrate, he eventually settled in Brooklyn.

A violin performance at a Barcelona café impressed the Spanish tenor ENRICO CARUSO, who asked the then 15-year-old Cugat to accompany him on a tour. Following the tour Cugat gave a series of unsuccessful solo concerts on the violin. Unable to make a living, he took a job as a cartoonist and caricaturist with the *Los Angeles Times* (1927).

The following year Cugat formed a dance band, The Gigolos, which created an instant sensation. The Gigolos soon became the resident band at the Waldorf-Astoria Hotel in New York.

For the next several decades Cugat continued to perform with dance bands in glitzy shows that featured brightly dressed dancers and attractive women. Maracas, bongo drums, and other Latin American instruments always featured prominently in his performances.

Cugat's music spanned the gamut of Latin American rhythm and dance—the cha-cha, the tango (which originated in Argentina), the conga, the Cuban-influenced rumba and mambo, and others—and coincided with the particular trends of the time. His many recordings for Mercury, RCA, Decca, Columbia, and Philips—such as *Cugat's Favorite Rhumbas, Tango With Cugat, Conga with Cugat, Mambo at the Waldorf, Mambo, Cha-Cha-Cha*, and *Bread, Love, and Cha-Cha-Cha*—also reflect the spectrum of his music.

As notorious for his love life as for his music, Cugat had a succession of five wives. His fourth wife, Abbe Lane, frequently performed with him in the 1950s, while his fifth wife, Charo, appeared with him regularly in the 1960s. Cugat and his band appeared in many films as well, including *You Were Never Lovelier* (1942; with Rita Hayworth), *Bathing Beauty* (1944), *Weekend at the Waldorf* (1945), *Holiday in Mexico* (1946), *On An Island With You* (1948), *A Date With Judy* (1948), *Chicago Syndicate* (1955), and *Desire Diabolique* (1959). Cugat had several radio hits, among which was "Perfidia" (1940), with Miguelito Valdes.

BIBLIOGRAPHY

Garrod, Charles, *Xavier Cugat and His Orchestra*, 1995.

Cusack, Cyril

(November 26, 1910–October 7, 1993)
Actor, Director

Known for his brooding air, quirky manner, and instinctive subtlety, the Irish actor Cyril James Cusack was particularly suited to introspective and stern roles. After acting for more than a decade at the Abbey Theatre in Dublin, he became a successful stage actor and director in Ireland, Britain, and the United States. Cusack also appeared in dozens of films.

Cusack was born in Durban, South Africa, and moved with his mother to Ireland in 1916. His mother founded a touring acting company with Brefni O'Rourke, and Cusack was performing on stage by the time he was 7. The company's touring schedule took him to many schools to study in his youth. After obtaining a law degree at University College in Dublin, he decided to pursue acting instead of law.

From 1932 to 1945 he was associated primarily with the Abbey Theatre in Dublin. The original force behind the Abbey was the Irish poet WILLIAM BUTLER YEATS, who cofounded its predecessor group in 1899. Although the Abbey was at first founded to promote the works of Irish Renaissance playwrights such as SEAN O'CASEY and J. M. SYNGE, the Abbey repertoire of Cusack's day also included non-Irish plays. During this time he also performed from time to time in Britain.

Cusack remained associated with the stage for the rest of his life. After managing the Gaiety Theater in Dublin in the early 1940s he founded Cyril Cusack Productions in 1944, and he directed and acted in many productions for his company. In 1957 he starred opposite Wendy Hiller in a Broadway production of Eugene O'Neill's *A Moon for the Misbegotten*. In 1963 he joined the Royal Shakespeare Company, and the following year he joined the National Theatre. Three years before his death, he appeared in a Gate Theater production of Russian dramatist Anton Chekhov's *The Three Sisters* with three of his four daughters who had become actresses, Sinéad, Niamh, and Sorcha Cusack.

Although Cusack appeared in films as early as 1917 (*Knocknagow*), his first real screen success came with his 1947 supporting role in CAROL REED's thriller about the Irish Republican Army (IRA), *Odd Man Out*. His other films include *Shake Hands with the Devil* (1959), Martin Ritt's *The Spy Who Came in from the Cold* (1965), FRANÇOIS TRUFFAUT's *Fahrenheit 451* (1967), *The Taming of the Shrew* (1967), *King Lear* (1971), *Les Misérables* (1978), *Tristan and Isolde* (1979), *The Kingfisher* (1982), *The Day of the Jackal* (1973), *Danny, The Champion of the World* (1989), and *My Left Foot* (1989). Cusack received many honorary doctorates. His *Timepieces* was published in 1970, and his *Between the Acts and Other Poems* appeared in 1990.

BIBLIOGRAPHY

Cusack, Cyril, *Timepieces*, 1970; Ryan, Kathleen Jo, and Share, Bernard, eds., *Irish Traditions*, 1990.

D

Dahl, Roald

(September 13, 1916–November 23, 1990)
Novelist, Short-Story Writer, Playwright, Writer of Children's Books, Screenwriter, Poet

During World War II, Roald Dahl began his career as a writer of war-inspired tales and macabre short stories. He is better known, however, for his popular children's works, and stories such as *The Gremlins*, *James and the Giant Peach*, and *Charlie and the Chocolate Factory* attained classic status in modern children's literature.

Dahl was of Norwegian ancestry, born in Llandaff, Wales. His father, the successful part-owner of a ship-brokering firm, died when he was 4. Dahl entered Llandaff Cathedral School in 1923 and St. Peter's School in Weston-Super-Mare two years later. The harsh disciplinary atmospheres of both schools alienated Dahl from formal education and took an emotional toll on him.

He continued his studies at the elite Repton Public School in Derby until 1934 but chose to end his education there. At Repton, he acquired his agnosticism as well as a love for photography. Upon his graduation, he took a job with the Shell Oil Company, working first in London and then in East Africa. With the outbreak of World War II, Dahl enlisted in the Royal Air Force and served as a fighter pilot.

Tragedy indirectly led to his decision to become a writer. When the plane he was flying ran out of fuel, Dahl was forced to crash land in the Libyan desert and was seriously wounded. Upon his recovery, he returned briefly to active service but was eventually posted at the British Embassy in Washington, D.C. In the United States, he met the author C. S. Forester, who encouraged him to write about his war experiences.

Dahl began with "A Piece of Cake," retitled as "Shot Down Over Libya" and published in the *Saturday Evening Post* in 1942. Soon his stories appeared in other major American periodicals such as *Harper's* and the *New Yorker*. The volume *Over to You* (1945) collected some of these stories, which range in style from realistic to fantastic and are largely drawn from his war experiences.

In 1953, Dahl married the actress Patricia Neal. Alfred Knopf published a second and very successful short-story collection, *Someone Like You*, the same

Roald Dahl (CFCL)

year. In this and a subsequent volume, *Kiss, Kiss* (1960), Dahl's stories began to take on darker elements. Extraordinary circumstances often force his characters to reveal sinister aspects they succeed in hiding under normal conditions. They sometimes fall tragically, victims of their own vices and weaknesses. Troubled relationships between men and women are another prominent theme in the stories.

Dahl published his first full-length book, a children's story entitled *The Gremlins*, in 1943. Originally written for Walt Disney, it later formed the basis of a popular film. Gremlins appear in the book as tiny creatures with horns sabotaging RAF planes during World War II. The pilot Gus devises a scheme to tame the mischievous creatures, who then help him return to flying after an accident. The gremlins are more obnoxious in their second incarnation in *Some Time Never: A Fable for Supermen* (1948). Their leader ends their campaign to rid the earth of humans, correctly observing that humans are predisposed to kill themselves off.

Having become the father of several children, nearly losing a son, and losing his daughter to encephalitis, Dahl devoted much of his time to children's stories in his later life. *James and the Giant Peach* (1961) originated as a story he told his own children and repeats a theme that recurs in his children's stories—an innocent child victimized by callous adults. The orphaned James is sent to live with his cruel aunts. When he spills the contents of a bag given to him by a mysterious old man, a nearby peach tree grows a giant peach. James's aunts seek to profit from the curiosity, but the peach is for the young boy a place of refuge. Inside, he befriends a group of insects. The peach becomes a vehicle, running over the nasty aunts, traveling, and eventually settling in New York, where James lives happily ever after.

Charlie and the Chocolate Factory (1964), like *James and the Giant Peach*, was a huge success. Dahl, who himself loved chocolate and taste-tested chocolates for Cadbury with his schoolmates at Repton, imagined a mysterious chocolate factory operated by the eccentric and energetic Willy Wonka. Charlie is one of five children to win a tour of the factory, along with the blabbermouth Violet Beauregarde, the obese glutton Augustus Gloop, the brat Veruca Salt, and the television-watching Mike Teavee. The other children's vices lead them into trouble inside the factory, where they encounter dwarfish workers called Oompa Loompas. Charlie is the only one to finish the tour, and he inherits the factory from Wonka.

Dahl adapted the story into a screenplay for the film *Willy Wonka and the Chocolate Factory* (1971). At the insistence of his publisher, he completed a sequel, *Charlie and the Great Glass Elevator* (1972), which earned much less critical and popular acclaim than did the original work.

Dahl did not abandon adult writing entirely in his later life. During the 1970s he wrote a number of sexually oriented stories for *Playboy*, some of which appeared in the collection *Switch Bitch* (1974). The main character of two of them, "The Visitor" and "Bitch," is the womanizing playboy Oswald Hendryks Cornelius, protagonist of Dahl's later novel *My Uncle Oswald* (1979).

For young children, Dahl wrote *The Magic Finger* (1966), *Fantastic Mr. Fox* (1970), and *The Enormous Crocodile*

(1977), the first of several books on which he collaborated with illustrator Quentin Blake. His other children's works include *Danny, the Champion of the World* (1975), *George's Marvelous Medicine* (1981), *The BFG* (1982), *The Witches* (1983), winner of the Whitbread Award, and *Matilda* (1988).

Among Dahl's other works are the autobiographical works *Boy: Tales of Childhood* (1984) and *Going Solo* (1986); screenplays for the James Bond movie *You Only Live Twice* (1967) and *Chitty Chitty Bang Bang* (1968); the verse collections *Roald Dahl's Revolting Rhymes* (1982), *Dirty Beasts* (1983), and *Rhyme Stew* (1989); and the play *The Honeys*, produced in New York in 1955.

BIBLIOGRAPHY

Treglown, Jeremy, *Roald Dahl: A Biography*, 1994; Warren, Alan, *Roald Dahl*, 1988; West, Mark I., *Roald Dahl*, 1992.

Dalí, Salvador

(May 11, 1904–January 23, 1989)
Painter, Illustrator, Costume Designer, Novelist

The Spanish artist Salvador Dalí led the Paris Surrealists in the 1930s until his expulsion from the movement in 1934. Although he is best known for Surrealist paintings, such as *The Persistence of Memory*, that juxtapose and distort everyday objects in bizarre combinations, Dalí worked with a wide variety of styles, themes, and art forms over his long career.

Dalí was born Salvador Felipe Jacinto Dalí y Domenech in Figueras, Catalonia, Spain. From the beginning of his life to the end, he was used to being the center of attention. Dalí was born nine months after the death of his elder brother, also named Salvador, and both parents doted on him. (His father was a prosperous notary.) Dalí attended a number of schools as a boy but never excelled academically. He began painting around the age of 10, and his father nurtured his interest in every way he could. Dalí also frequented the home of the artistically inclined Pichot family. His early impressionistic paintings reflect the Spanish landscape in which he spent his time, including the fishing village of Cadaques, where his family kept a summer home. Typical of this period is the impressionistic oil painting *View of Cadaques with Shadow of Mount Pani* (1917).

In the early 1920s Dalí began studying draftsmanship at the Municipal Drawing School, and in 1922 he enrolled in the San Fernando Academy of Fine Arts in Madrid. He never graduated from the latter on account of his refusal to take his final exam, but he continued to paint and met other Spanish artists such as the film maker LUIS BUÑUEL and the poet and playwright FEDERICO GARCÍA LORCA. He began experimenting with the Cubist style, evident in such works as *Femme Couchée* (1926) and the ink drawing *Cubist Study of Figures on a Beach* (1923–1925).

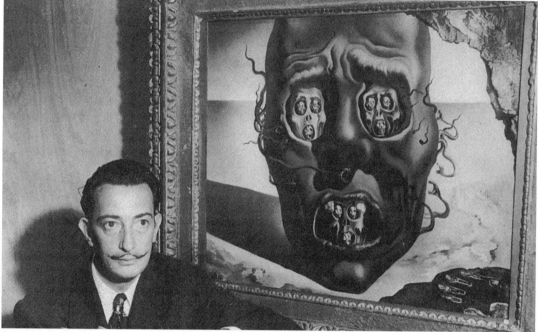

Salvador Dalí with his painting *Face of War* (AKG)

Assisted by his father, Dalí held his first show in 1925 in Barcelona. He collaborated with Buñuel in the films *An Andalusian Dog* (1928) and *The Golden Age* (1930) and designed the set for García Lorca's play *Mariano Pineda* (1927). In 1928, his photorealistic oil painting *The Basket of Bread* first brought him international attention when it was displayed in the United States. The following year he met Gala Éluard, then married to the French Surrealist poet PAUL ÉLUARD. Her marriage to Dalí in 1934 lasted until Gala's death in 1982, and she was intimately involved with Dalí's work throughout his life.

Although he was exposed to a wide variety of artistic influences, a primary influence on his career was his interest in the theories of Sigmund Freud (whom he met in London in 1938). After moving to Paris at the age of 25, Dalí also became

involved with the French Surrealist group and continued his friendship with PABLO PICASSO. Dalí and the other Surrealists consciously sought to employ subconscious elements in their paintings, often in the form of bizarre, distorted images rendered in bright color and realistic detail. To tap into his subconscious Dalí used a process he called the paranoid critical method, which involved creating hallucinations without using drugs.

Dalí's most famous paintings come from the 1930s, known as his Surrealist period. Typical of the paintings of this decade are contorted objects, such as the limp, drooping watches in one of his most famous works, *The Persistence of Memory* (1931). *The Weaning of Furniture, Nutrition* (1934), set in a Catalonian fishing village, features his childhood nurse with a rectangular hole cut in her back. A mock trial among the Surrealists ended in Dalí's ejection from the movement in 1934, but he continued to paint in a Surrealist style for several years afterward.

Around 1940 Dalí began to paint in a more traditional style, and this later period in his work is often called his "classic" period. His later paintings also reflect his growing interest in science, the molecular world, religion, and history. In the same year he and his wife fled the impending German invasion of France and, with the help of money from Picasso, moved to the United States. The Metropolitan Museum of Art held a major exhibition of his work in New York in 1941. Dalí's works on religious themes include the watercolor *The Madonna of the Birds* (1943), *Madonna of Port Lligat* (1949), *Crucifixion* (1954), and *The Sacrament of the Last Supper* (1955). Historical themes characterize works such as *The Discovery* *of America by Christopher Columbus* (1959).

In addition to painting, Dalí experimented with other art forms. He illustrated a number of books, including editions of Shakespeare's *Macbeth*, Cervantes's *Don Quixote*, the Bible, and Dante's *Divine Comedy*. Among his writings are the autobiography *The Secret Life of Salvador Dalí* (1944), *Diary of a Genius* (1965), and the novel *Hidden Faces* (1944). His other works include costume and set designs, ballet scenarios, and jewelry. Dalí died of heart failure in 1989. The Salvador Dalí museum in St. Petersburg, Florida, houses many of his paintings.

BIBLIOGRAPHY

Ades, Dawn, *Dalí and Surrealism*, 1982; Lear, Amanda, *Persistence of Memory: A Personal Biography of Salvador Dalí*, 1987; Maddox, Conroy, *Salvador Dalí: Eccentric and Genius*, 1990.

D'Annunzio, Gabriele

(March 12, 1863–March 1, 1938)
Poet, Novelist, Short-Story Writer, Playwright, Journalist

A controversial, often egocentric figure who was never a stranger to scandal, Gabriele D'Annunzio was Italy's most notorious writer of the pre–World War I era. A sensual, passionate, and lyrical writing style pervades his poetry and fiction. D'Annunzio knew no inhibitions in his critical and sometimes cruel portrayals of others. He created several successful plays for the actress Eleonora Duse, the most famous of his many well-known mistresses.

D'Annunzio was born in Pescara, Italy, where his father, a wealthy landowner, and very influential in the area, was once elected mayor. From a young age he showed a rebelliousness and independent spirit given to trouble-making. Both D'Annunzio and his father believed he was destined for greatness. Raised in a household full of superstitious aunts, nurses, and sisters, D'Annunzio began to write at a young age, sparing no criticism of his nurses or anyone else he felt like

Gabriele D'Annunzio (Ann Ronan/Image Select)

sexual pleasure, devoting a number of the poems to famous adulterers.

D'Annunzio's scandalous love affairs and tireless pursuit of women found their way into his fiction. Among his early novels are *L'innocente* (1892; *The Intruder*), his best-known novel *Il trionfo della morte* (1894; *The Triumph of Death*), and *Le vergini delle rocce* (1896; *The Maidens of the Rocks*). *The Triumph of Death* is a macabre story depicting the affair and ultimate death of the lovers Giorgio and Ippolita. D'Annunzio also wrote short stories that appeared in collections such as *Il Libro delle Vergini* (1884; *The Book of Virgins*).

D'Annunzio used flowery, passionate, and sensuous language. *Il piacere* (1898; *The Child of Pleasure*) follows the adventures of the autobiographical Nietzschean seducer Andrea Sperelli. Sperelli meets Elena Muti, Duchess of Scerni, at a dinner and falls wildly in love with her. Elena leaves him, and his successive seductions of other women lead him into a series of troubles, among which is a duel with his mistress's lover.

The three-volume work *Laudi del cielo del mare della terra e degli eroi* (1899; *In Praise of Sky, Sea, Earth, and Heroes*) is his best-known poetic effort. His love of the outdoors manifested itself particularly in the third volume, *Alcyone* (1904), a celebration of the Tuscan landscape.

In 1894 D'Annunzio began the most infamous of his love affairs—with the actress Eleonora Duse. For her he began to write plays, among which was *La gioconda* (1899), an enormous success when it was staged in Palermo. The tragic story concerns a sculptor who finds himself torn between his wife, Silvia, and his model, Gioconda. His

criticizing. During his childhood he also developed the great love of nature and the outdoors that emerges in his poetry. His family sent him to the College of Prato, a Catholic school, where he studied Latin with great success but was not the least bit respectful of religion.

Bound for the University of Rome and soon to become a journalist for the paper *Tribuna*, D'Annunzio moved to Italy's capital in 1881. Around this time his first volumes of poetry appeared—*Primo vere* (1879; *In Early Spring*) and *Canto novo* (1882; *New Song*). Both collections of lyrical verse reflect an ecstatic, youthful spirit and sold well upon their publication. *New Song* sold 10,000 copies in three years time. The decadent and sacrilegious poems of *Intermezzo di rime* (1883), originally printed on pink paper, provoked a scandal when they appeared. In these D'Annunzio celebrated vice and

Francesca da Rimini (1901), first staged in Rome, is based on the life of a thirteenth-century noblewoman murdered by her husband for having an affair with his brother. *La figlia di Iorio* (performed 1904; *The Daughter of Jorio*), taken from Abruzzi peasant life, was written after his breakup with Duse and is often considered his best theatrical work.

D'Annunzio's often cruel nature was at its worst in *Il fuoco* (1900; *The Flame of Life*), a pointed fictional account of his relationship with Duse. In a vengeful manner he revealed Duse's secrets and private details of her life. His increasingly nationalistic outlook manifests itself in the play *La Nave* (1908; *The Ship*), a historical drama.

Given to extravagant living and spending more than the considerable sum he earned, D'Annunzio fled his creditors and moved to France in 1912. There he gained the friendship of Anatole France and continued to write stories and plays, among which was the verse drama *Le martyre de Saint Sébastien* (1911; *The Martyrdom of Saint Sebastian*). D'Annunzio also collaborated with the ballet impresario Sergey Diaghilev, composer Claude Debussy, and artist Léon Bakst in a production for Diaghilev's Ballets Russes.

The outbreak of World War I was to lead to D'Annunzio's status as national hero. After working briefly as a propagandist for the French government, he actively sought action and adventure, urging Italy to enter the war and eventually obtaining a commission as a lieutenant. Serving in the navy, infantry, and air force, d'Annunzio managed to involve himself in the most dangerous missions he could.

In 1919 D'Annunzio, with 300 followers, occupied the Dalmatian Adriatic seaport of Fiume (now Rijeka, in Croatia) in a direct violation of the Treaty of Versailles. The treaty gave the port to the new Yugoslav state, but D'Annunzio believed it was Italy's, occupied it, and ruled it until his expulsion in 1920. Italy eventually was able to keep possession of the port. After the war D'Annunzio established himself as an enthusiastic supporter of Fascism and a personal friend of dictator Benito Mussolini. Mussolini promoted his works, having them printed in a national collection.

The youthful bravado and sensuality of his earlier works gave way to loneliness, despair, and a preoccupation with death in his later writings, among which is the *La Contemplazione della morte* (1912; *The Contemplation of Death*), and the memoir *Libro segreto*. Other works include the poetry collection *L'Isoteo—La Chimera* (1890); the plays *Più che l'amore* (*More than Love*) and *Le Chèvrefeuille* (1913; *The Honeysuckle*); and the novel *Forse che sì forse che no* (1910; *Perhaps So, Perhaps Not*).

Bibliography

Jullian, Philippe, *D'Annunzio*, 1972; Woodhouse, John Robert, *Gabriele D'Annunzio: Defiant Archangel*, 1998.

Day-Lewis, C.

(April 27, 1904–May 22, 1972)
Poet, Novelist, Playwright, Teacher

Cecil Day-Lewis began publishing poetry a few years before the contemporaries with whom he is usually associated—STEPHEN SPENDER, LOUIS MACNEICE, and W. H. AUDEN. Like these three, Day-Lewis rose to prominence in the 1930s with politically charged poetry, responding to the Depression and the rise of Fascism, and like them he showed a brief interest in Marxism. His mature poetry reflects a more personal outlook and lyrical style.

Day-Lewis was born in Ballintupper, Ireland. His father was a clergyman in the Church of Ireland. Two years after the family moved to London (1906), Day-Lewis's mother died. He studied at the Sherbourne School before entering the University of Oxford to study the Greek and Roman classics, from which he would draw much of the symbolism in his later poetry.

While at Oxford, Day-Lewis met Auden, Spender, and MacNeice. In 1927 he co-edited *Oxford Poetry* with Auden. Upon the completion of his studies the same year, Day-Lewis took a job teaching at the Summer Fields preparatory school in Oxford. Meanwhile, he had financed the publication of his first volume of poetry, *Beechen Vigil* (1925), which contains twenty-four poems generally regarded by critics as immature and slight. A second volume along the same lines, *Country Comets*, followed in 1928.

Day-Lewis married Constance Mary King the same year and took a job teaching at the Larchfield School in Scotland, after which he taught at the Cheltenham Public School (1930–1935). His *Transi-* *tional Poem* (1929) marked the beginning of a more mature phase in his poetry and was followed by *From Feathers to Iron* (1931).

The critical volume *A Hope for Poetry* (1934) was one of the main texts outlining the aims of the thirties poets. In it Day-Lewis argued for a socially committed poetry and rejected the notion of "pure poetry." His own leftist political outlook took full shape in the long poem *The Magnetic Mountain* (1933), one of his primary works of the period, and he joined the Communist Party. Several subsequent volumes maintained the political orientation, including *A Time to Dance* (1934) and *Overture to Death* (1938). The latter contains Day-Lewis's popular poems "Newsreel" and "Bombers" and was dedicated to the novelist E. M. FORSTER.

The advent of World War II (during which he served in the Ministry of Information) signaled another change in Day-Lewis's poetry, which became less political. *Poems in Wartime* (1940) was published during this period, and its poems reappeared in the subsequent volume *Word Over All* (1943). This period is also marked by the breakdown of his marriage, which resulted in his divorce in 1951 and his marriage to Jill Balcon the same year. In Day-Lewis's later poetry, including *Pegasus and Other Poems* (1957), *The Gate and Other Poems* (1962), *The Room and Other Poems* (1965), and *The Whispering Roots* (1970), he developed a highly personal style.

Day-Lewis maintained an intermittent academic career in the 1940s and 1950s as the Clark lecturer at the University of Cambridge (1946–1947) and as Professor of Poetry at Oxford (1951–1956). He translated the classics, notably Virgil's *Georgics* (1941), *Aeneid* (1952), and *Eclogues* (1963). His other works of criticism include a series of lectures published as *The Poetic Image* (1947) and *The Lyric Impulse* (1965).

Although most famous for his poetry, Day-Lewis wrote in other genres. His novels include *The Friendly Tree* (1936), *Starting Point* (1937), *Child of Misfortune* (1939), *The Morning After Death* (1966), and *The Private Wound* (1968). Under the pseudonym Nicholas Blake, Day-Lewis wrote the detective novels *A Question of Proof* (1934), *Minute for Murder* (1948), and *Whisper in the Gloom* (1954). Among his other works are his autobiography, *The Buried Day* (1960), the verse play *Noah and the Waters* (1936), and the poetry volumes *Italian Visit* (1953) and *Collected Poems* (1954). Queen Elizabeth II appointed him poet laureate in 1968. The Academy-award winning actor Daniel Day-Lewis is the son of Day-Lewis and Jill Balcon.

BIBLIOGRAPHY

Gelpi, Albert, *Living In Time: The Poetry of C. Day-Lewis*, 1998; Riddel, J. N., *C. Day-Lewis*, 1971.

De la Mare, Walter

(April 25, 1873–June 22, 1956)
Poet, Novelist, Short-Story Writer, Playwright, Writer of Children's Books

J. B. PRIESTLEY said of Walter de la Mare's work, "We can always recognize his hand, the work is all of a piece, but no one who has once known it can fail to appreciate that curious perfume and that most melodius twang." Known for his rhythmic, precise, and imaginative works, Walter John de la Mare wrote poetry, novels, short stories, and numerous works for children. His writing was propelled by an ever present sense of wonder, admiration of nature, an interest in spiritual matters and the imagination, and a love for children.

De la Mare was born in Charlton, Kent, England. His father was a church warden of Huguenot ancestry. De la Mare's mother's main influence was her habit of reading the Bible to him, and though he rejected organized religion he maintained a lifelong love of the Bible stories and imagery that inspired his imagination. He studied at St. Paul's Cathedral Choir School, in London, where he founded the school magazine, *The Chorister's Journal*, but did not have enough money to go on to university. From 1890 to 1908 he worked as a bookkeeper in the London office of the Standard Oil Company. De la Mare began writing while he worked for the oil company and in 1902 published *Songs of Childhood* under the pseudonym Walter Ramal.

Henry Brocken, the first of his five novels, in which the protagonist travels through old literary scenes on his mare, was published two years later, followed by *Poems* (1906), which contained many sonnets. Having received a royal grant in 1908 he quit his job at the oil company and devoted himself to writing. De la Mare quickly demonstrated his ability to evoke ethereal beauty in simplicity and the cycles of nature as well as to explore the realm of the imagination. The title piece from *The Listeners and Other Poems* (1912) may serve as an example of de la Mare's ability to create a powerful sense of mystery. An unidentified man comes back to an empty house to fulfil an unexplained promise. He speaks to no one—"'Tell them I called, and no one answered, / That I kept my word,' he said"—and a "host of phantom listeners" stand in the moonlight and listen to a "voice from the world of men."

Many of de la Mare's works are fantastic in nature, such as his acclaimed novel *Memoirs of a Midget* (1921), which treats the life of a female midget until she reaches 21, and his children's fairy play *Crossings* (1921). A man with deep interest in and admiration for children, he published many works for young readers. Among these are *Come Hither* (1923), an anthology of English poetry for children; the highly successful *Peacock Pie* (1924); *Collected Rhymes and Verses* (1944); and *Collected Stories for Children* (1947).

His children's tale "The Turnip," adapted from a Brothers Grimm tale, is a moral fable about two brothers. The elder is a wealthy merchant motivated by avarice, while his farmer-brother has little money and a lot of happiness. One day the younger brother finds a giant turnip in his fields, a gift that he presents to the king. The grateful king rewards him with a fortune, after which his elder brother determines to pursue his own reward. He sells all he owns to buy a ruby for the king, but the king understands his motivations and rewards him with only a slice of his brother's turnip. A children's fairy story, and the title story of a collection of tales, "The Lord Fish," recounts the adventures of young John Cobbler, who is out to release a fish girl from a curse.

De la Mare impressed many young poets with his kindness and willingness to help them, and many spoke highly of him. T. S. Eliot summed up de la Mare's excellence in perhaps the most striking of those tributes, "To Walter de la Mare," which ends with a reference to "the delicate invisible web you wove—/ The inexplicable mystery of sound."

De la Mare also received numerous awards for his work, including the James Tait Black Memorial Prize and the Carnegie Medal (1947). He was made Companion of Honour in 1948 and received the Order of Merit in 1953. His other books of verse include *The Burning Glass* (1945), the long poem *The Traveller* (1946), *Inward Companion* (1950), *O Lovely England* (1953), and numerous volumes of *Collected Poems*. Among his other works are the novels *The Return* (1910), about a man who undergoes a radical change in personality through possession by the spirit of a French Huguenot; and the anthology *Desert Islands* (1930).

BIBLIOGRAPHY

Hopkins, Kenneth, *Walter de la Mare*, 1957; Whistler, Theresa, *Imagination of the Heart: The Life of Walter de la Mare*, 1993.

De Sica, Vittorio

(July 7, 1901–November 13, 1974)
Director, Actor

Vittorio De Sica's best-known films belong to the post–World War II era in Italian cinema dominated by Neorealist directors such as ROBERTO ROSSELLINI and LUCHINO VISCONTI. During that time De Sica made a succession of Neorealist films, including *Shoeshine*, *The Bicycle Thief*, and *Umberto D.* De Sica's films achieved more success abroad than in his native Italy and won numerous international awards.

De Sica was born into a Neopolitan family in Sora, Italy. His family was relatively poor but not destitute. His father, a bank clerk and former journalist, admired the arts and encouraged his eldest son to participate in the theater. Reluctant at first, De Sica studied for a business career, graduating from the University School of Political and Commercial Science. At the age of 21 he did his military service.

Following his release De Sica still had a more practical career in his mind when he began to act. In 1923 he joined an acting company that performed for wounded soldiers, and he quickly gained a following for his matinee performances and singing appearances. Over the next decade De Sica appeared in many plays ranging from serious pieces to musical comedies.

De Sica's father had pushed him into a film appearance as early as 1918, but it was not until the 1930s that his screen career began to take off. His role in Mario Camerini's *Gli uomini, che mascalzoni!* (1932; *The Men, What Rascals!*), a film about an affair between a chauffeur and the daughter of a cab driver, made him a minor film star. *La compagnia dei matti* gave De Sica his first leading role in a film.

By this time De Sica had also begun to direct films, and he achieved his first directorial success with *Due dozzine di rose scarlatte* (1940; *Twenty-Four Red Roses*). During World War II he began to work with his longtime screenwriter Cesare Zavattini, completing *The Children Are Watching Us* in 1942. Filming was difficult during the war, especially during the Nazi occupation. In 1944 De Sica filmed *The Gate of Heaven* (1944), a religious work for the Catholic Film Center in Rome that depicts a pilgrimage to the Santa Casa shrine at Loreto.

Sciuscià (1946; *Shoeshine*) was the first of the Neorealist films for which De Sica is best known. A film about poverty-stricken children who shine the shoes of American soldiers in postwar Rome, the work has the key characteristics of the Neorealist style—the use of amateur actors, realistic depictions of ordinary people, scenes shot in the streets instead of the studio, and a documentary-like atmosphere.

Ladri di biciclette (1948; *The Bicycle Thief*), *Miracolo a Milano* (1951; *Miracle in Milan*), and *Umberto D.* (1952) are also in the Neorealist vein. In these films De Sica evoked the atmosphere of postwar Italy and treated the effects of social difficulties on individual people. The central figure in *Umberto D.* is a pensioner, lonely, old, and poor, who has only the company of his dog to comfort him. The dog, too, passes away.

After a succession of Neorealist films De Sica traveled to the United States and planned to work with a number of Hollywood directors. However, his traditional mode of working did not fit in with the polished studio productions and professional actors that Hollywood preferred. Many planned projects never materialized, and those that did—such as *Indiscretion of an American Wife* (1954)—proved to be commercial failures.

De Sica returned to Italy and made two more major Neorealist films: *L'Oro di Napoli* (1954; *The Gold of Naples*), based on short stories by Giuseppe Marotta, and *The Roof* (1956). After the latter he continued to act and began a series of what many critics regard as unsuccessful experiments with other film styles. Nevertheless, it was for his later films that he earned numerous awards.

La ciocara (1961; *Two Women*), based on ALBERTO MORAVIA's book, starred Sophia Loren in an Oscar-winning performance. De Sica first used color in *The Last Judgment* (1961). Other later films include *Ieri, oggi, domani* (1963; *Yesterday, Today and Tomorrow*); *Matrimonio all'italiana* (1964; *Marriage Italian Style*); *Woman Times Seven* (1967), starring Shirley MacLaine; *Il giardino dei Finzi-Contini* (1970; *The Garden of the Finzi-Continis*), which won an Academy Award for best foreign film; and *Una breve vacanza* (1974; *A Brief Vacation*). His final film *Il viaggio* (1974; *The Voyage*) starred Loren and RICHARD BURTON.

BIBLIOGRAPHY

Daretta, John, *Vittorio de Sica: A Guide to References and Resources*, 1983.

Debussy, Claude

(August 22, 1862–March 25, 1918)
Composer, Critic, Pianist

The twentieth-century composer Achille-Claude Debussy, as he was christened, developed original sounds and musical structures from the diverse artistic and cultural elements that dominated Paris during his lifetime. His work owes much of its influence to the French Symbolists and Impressionists and is often classified as "musical Impressionism."

Debussy was born into an impoverished family in Saint-Germaine-en-Laye, France, and became interested in the piano as a young boy. At age 9 he took his first piano lesson, and at age 11 he began studying composition (under Ernest Guiraud) and piano in the Romantic style (under Antoine Francois Marmontel) at the Paris Conservatory. He later met the wealthy Russian Nadezhda Filaretovna von Meck, who hired him to play for her family. In this position Debussy was able to travel around Europe, where he gained exposure to the work of composers such as Richard Wagner (1813–1883), Aleksandr Borodin (1833–1887), and Modest

Mussorgsky (1839–1881). In 1884 he won the Grand Prix de Rome for his cantata *The Prodigal Child.*

Debussy seldom performed his music for the public and preferred instead to compose. Soon after his studies at the Paris Conservatory, he began to reject the traditional Romantic techniques in which he was trained and experiment with new compositional styles. The primary influences on his work were poetry and painting, particularly the work of the Impressionists and Symbolists. *Prélude à l'après-midi d'un faune* (1894; *Prelude to the Afternoon of a Faun*), his first orchestral composition, is based on a poem by the French Symbolist Stéphane Mallarmé (1842–1898) and was later used in a widely performed ballet. Among his other early works are *La demoiselle élue* (1888; *The Blessed Damozel*), *Cinq poèmes de Baudelaire* (1889; *Five Poems of Baudelaire*), and the popular orchestral suites *Nocturnes* (1893–1899).

Pelléas et Mélisande (*Pelléas and Mélisande*), Debussy's first and only opera, was based on a play by Maurice Maeterlinck and written with his cooperation. Maeterlinck claimed to have no ability to critique music, but he was impressed, as were many others, with the smooth, lyrical quality of Debussy's finished composition. However, a quarrel erupted between them when Maeterlinck's mistress was removed from the leading role. The opera, first performed in 1902, presented a dark, dreamy score tightly integrated with Maeterlinck's libretto and proved to be both controversial and popular.

Debussy's compositions from the early twentieth century also include a number

Claude Debussy (Ann Ronan/Image Select)

of piano works. Among them are *Engravings* (1903), *Images* (1905 and 1907), two collections of Preludes in 1910 and 1913, and *Douze Études* (1915; *Twelve Études*). His most famous piano composition is *Clair de lune* (*Moonlight*) from the *Suite Bergamasque*, completed in 1905. The piano suite *Children's Corner* (1908) was written for his daughter, Claude-Emma. The three-part *La Mer* (1905; *The Sea*) stretched string color to new boundaries and is Debussy's most famous orchestral work. His other compositions include the ballet score *Games* (1912), a violin sonata, a cello sonata, and a sonata for flute, viola, and harp. His death from cancer prevented him from pursuing his longtime desire to write a piece based on Edgar Allan Poe's *The Fall of the House of Usher.*

Among Debussy's musical innovations are his use of the whole-tone scale and his experimentation with tonality and harmonic structure. Debussy's abandonment of fixed tonality, in which the music centers around multiple tones instead of a single tone, significantly influenced later twentieth-century composers and lends an ethereal quality to his music. Along with other musical impressionists, such as MAURICE RAVEL, Debussy aimed at creating mood and tonal color rather than melody.

BIBLIOGRAPHY

Dumesnil, Maurice, *Claude Debussy: Master of Dreams*, 1940; Lockspeiser, Edward, *Debussy: His Life and Mind*, 1962; Nichols, Roger, *Debussy Remembered*, 1992; Wenk, Arthur; *Claude Debussy and Twentieth Century Music*, 1983.

Deighton, Len

(February 18, 1929–)
Novelist, Journalist, Producer, Short-Story Writer, Illustrator

With JOHN LE CARRÉ and James Bond creator IAN FLEMING, Len Deighton is part of a generation of British Cold-War spy-thriller novelists. He is best known for his long series starring the British secret agent Bernard Samson, but he has also written histories of World War II, cookbooks, and other fiction.

Deighton was born in Marylebone, London. After doing his national service as a photographer for the Special Investigation Branch, he entered St. Martin's School of Art in London. Deighton studied further at the Royal College of Art. During his years of study he worked as a waiter, inaugurating his lifelong interest in cooking. Following his graduation, Deighton worked alternately as a pastry cook, writer, illustrator, and art director.

Dissatisfied with his career, or the lack of one, Deighton moved to the Dordogne and began to write. His first novel, *The Ipcress File*, appeared in 1962 and concerns the disappearance of leading biochemists in England. Having gained popular success with *The Ipcress File*, Deighton followed with several other spy novels: *Funeral in Berlin* (1964), *The Billion Dollar Brain* (1966), *Only When I Larf* (1968), and *Bomber* (1970). *Close-Up* (1972), not a spy novel, explores the intrigue of the Hollywood film industry through the film star Marshall Stone.

Since the 1980s Deighton has released several series featuring the British intelligence officer Bernard Samson. *Berlin Game* (1983), *Mexico Set* (1984), and *London Match* (1985) pit Samson against Soviet KGB agents. These three novels were later collected as *Game, Set, Match* and serialized on PBS. Deighton orchestrates in his work fast-paced narratives and webs of intrigue—defection, treason, and suspicion. A second series, consisting of *Spy Hook* (1988), *Spy Line* (1989), and *Spy Sinker* (1990), finds Samson immersed in the intrigue of his own agency as he uncovers scams and finds himself under suspicion for treason.

Between the *Spy* trilogy and his next, Deighton published *Mamista* (1991), a complex story set in a South American jungle. The Cold War enemies are pulling strings behind the scenes as Marxist revolutionaries try to wrest control of the government while the White House intends to prop up the current right-wing regime to enable the United States to exploit oil fields.

Faith (1994) began another Bernard Samson trilogy. Set in 1987, in the years before the Berlin Wall fell, the story concerns Samson's efforts to return an agent named Verdi from the East and Samson's tenuous relationship with his wife, Fiona. Fiona's return from the East is accompanied by the death of her sister, Tessa Kosinski. *Hope* (1996) finds Samson investigating the disappearance of Tessa's husband in Poland. In *Charity* (1996) Samson is still obsessed with Tessa's death; he ultimately discovers that the British Secret Service ordered the execution.

Aside from Cold War spy thrillers, Deighton has written numerous fiction and nonfiction works concerning the World War II era. *Declarations of War* (1971) consists of short stories about the experiences of soldiers and the horrors of death they face on the battlefield. His novel *Winter* (1987) concerns the brothers Peter and Pauli Winter, sons of a German banker and American mother. The Winter brothers are not at all alike but find their fates intertwined as war ravages their native land. *Blitzkreig* (1979), a nonfiction work, examines the rise of Hitler in Nazi Germany and German military strategy in World War II. In *Blood, Tears, and Folly* (1993), a history of World War II, Deighton probes the early years of the war leading up to the entry of the United States.

Deighton's fast-paced and dramatic spy thrillers have enjoyed immense commercial and critical success in the United States and England. Many of his works have been adapted for film and television. Deighton's historical works have earned citical acclaim for their clarity in style, depth of research and detail, and objective approach. Among his other writings are the novels *Yesterday's Spy* (1975), *XPD* (1981), and *Goodbye, Mickey Mouse* (1982), and several cookbooks.

BIBLIOGRAPHY

Sauerberg, Lars Ole, *Secret Agents in Fiction: Ian Fleming, John le Carré, Len Deighton*, 1984.

Delaunay, Robert

(April 12, 1885–October 25, 1941)
Painter, Designer, Costume Designer

Robert Delaunay, husband of the painter and decorator SONIA DELAUNAY, developed as a painter by studying the dominant Paris styles of his day—Fauvism, Cubism, the Nabis, and other movements. His mature paintings combine purely abstract, circular forms with vibrant color, a style the poet Guillaume Apollinaire (1880–1918) called Orphism.

Delaunay was born into a middle-class family in Paris. His father left the family when he was 4, and he was raised by his mother and an uncle. School never excited Delaunay. He began drawing when he was young and in 1902 was apprenticed to a theater designer—essentially his only training as an artist. Two years later he exhibited his first paintings at the Salon des Indépendants in Paris, and he was soon showing his work in other Paris Salons.

In the early 1900s he experimented with a number of the painting styles that emerged in Paris. Some paintings show the influence of the Nabis (see MAURICE DENIS and PIERRE BONNARD), whereas he rendered works such as *Landscape with Disk* (1905) and the *Portrait of Wilhelm Uhde* (1907) in a Neo-Impressionist style. The influence of the Fauves is apparent in the brightly colored *Saint-Séverin* (1909) series, a succession of interiors in blues, yellows, and other colors.

By 1910 Delaunay was painting in a Cubist style, generally with a brighter palette than Cubist originators PABLO PICASSO and GEORGES BRAQUE used. A *Cities* series begun around the same time combines Cubism with Pointillism, as in *Window on the City* (1910–1911). The Eiffel Tower, the central symbol in his popular *Tour Eiffel* series in 1910–1911, became a recurring symbol in his paintings and drawings throughout his life. *The City of Paris* (1910–1912), a colorful rendition of the Eiffel Tower, the river, and a Three Graces motif, was exhibited at the Salon des Indépendants and attracted a lot of attention to Delaunay's work. A 1926 painting depicts the tower in bright red, reaching into a blue sky and viewed from the bottom up.

In 1910 Delaunay married Sonia Terk (formerly married to the Wilhelm Uhde of his portrait), who was to become his intimate companion and collaborator. The following year saw the birth of their son Charles, who later became a jazz historian. Other paintings from this period include *The Cardiff Team* (1912–1913), *Disk* (1912), and *Simultaneous Contrasts: Sun and Moon* (1912–1913). The latter, with its abstract, and wavy forms in bright colors, characterizes the Orphist style Delaunay finally adopted, although he did not completely abandon representation until the early 1930s.

Delaunay's work gained recognition more quickly than did his wife's. By World War I he was exhibiting regularly in France and, through the influence of WASSILY KANDINSKY, in Germany. The Delaunays spent the war in Spain and Portugal, which provided the subject matter for the series *Portuguese Markets* and *Still Lifes*. While there, both of the Delaunays contributed scenery and costume designs to a 1918 Ballets Russes production of *Cleopâtre*. After the war ended, the Delaunays returned to France and began to associate with the Paris literary avant-garde, most closely with Dadaist founder Tristan Tzara.

Delaunay painted many portraits of his friends and acquaintances, including the *Portrait of Henri Rousseau* (1914), a charcoal portrait of Surrealist ANDRÉ BRETON (1922), *Portrait of Tristan Tzara* (1923), and the unfinished *Portrait of Jean Cocteau* (1924). He preferred to work with series, creating a group of paintings on the same theme. Among these are the *Windows*, the *Circular Forms*, a series of *Color Disks*, a *Windows* series, *Sprinters* (1924–1926), and *Rhythms* (1938).

In the 1920s Delaunay and his wife designed a number of sets for film. In the next decade he devoted himself to pure abstraction. In his work he also experimented with a variety of materials, including sprayed sand, casein, lacquered stone, and wax. Among his best-known later works are the large panel *The Woman and the Tower* (1935) and his murals for the Paris Exposition in 1937, in the Railroad Pavilion and the Pavilion of the Air. The following year, the Delaunays, with other artists, decorated the interior of the sculpture hall of the Tuileries Salon. With the unique brand of abstraction he formulated early in the development of nonobjective art, Delaunay was a pioneer in the broad movement toward abstract painting that dominated twentieth-century canvases.

BIBLIOGRAPHY

Hoog, Michel, *R. Delaunay*, 1976; Vriesen, Gustav, *Robert Delaunay: Light and Color*, 1967.

Delaunay, Sonia

(November 14, 1885–December 5, 1979)
Painter, Designer, Costume Designer

Influenced by the developments in French art at the turn of the century, Sonia Terk Delaunay and her husband, ROBERT DELAUNAY, developed very similar painting styles after their marriage in 1910. Early in her career as a painter, she settled on a purely abstract style characterized by broad, flat, areas of pure color dominated by but not limited to circular forms.

Delaunay was born Sonia Stern in Gradizhsk, Ukraine. Her father worked in a nail factory, and she did not get along well with her mother. As a young child she left both of them to live with a wealthy uncle, an attorney in St. Petersburg. In her new family Delaunay learned several languages and was taught by governesses at home until, at the age of 16, she was sent to a prestigious secondary school in St. Petersburg. More importantly, she gained exposure to Europe's art museums through her adoptive family's extensive European travels.

Delaunay received her first paints from MAX LIEBERMANN, who was an acquaintance of her uncle. At age 18 she entered the academy of fine arts in Karlsruhe and also studied in a painter's studio. Surviving works from her early years include a number of realistic charcoal portraits—of her aunt, peasants, and others. In 1905 she settled permanently in Paris, where she studied briefly at the Académie de la Palette in Montparnasse.

In Paris she frequented art exhibits, quickly adopting the bright colors and expressive lines of the Fauves and Postimpressionists, and she was particularly influenced by the work of Paul Gauguin (1842–1903). *Young Finnish Girl* (1906) depicts a vivid, multicolored head of a girl against a bright yellow background. Radiant reds dominate paintings such as *Philomène* (1907).

After a brief marriage to and amicable divorce from the Paris art dealer Wilhelm Uhde, she married Robert Delaunay in 1910. By that time her paintings had become almost entirely abstract, consisting of interplay of areas of bright color—for example, the large oil *Bal Bullier* (1913). Unlike her husband, however, she would have to wait many years for her paintings to gain international recognition.

Financial circumstances spurred her to devote her energies to the applied arts—pottery, rugs, carpets, handbags, dishes, furniture, tapestries, and other items. Her designs, particularly in fabrics, met with considerable success. Delaunay founded her own company to produce fabric designs in the 1920s, and the Amsterdam department store Metz & Co. was a principal purchaser of them for many years.

She did not, however, give up painting entirely. The Delaunays spent World War I in Spain and Portugal, where she painted *The Market at Minho* (1916), self-portraits, dancers, flamenco singers, and a series of *Disks*. In 1917 she created designs for a production of the opera *Aïda* in Madrid, and the following year both Delaunays contributed designs to a Ballets Russes production of *Cléopâtre*. After the war they returned to France and began to associate with many prominent Paris writers, including their particular friend Tristan Tzara. With him she collaborated on "poem dresses," and she contributed costume designs to his *Le coeur gaz* (1923).

In the 1920s the Delaunays designed a number of costumes and sets for film. Delaunay also painted advertisements and book designs, among which are end-papers for Blaise Cendrars's *Pâques à New York* (1912; *Easter in New York*). The following year she illustrated the poet's *La Prose du Transsibérien et de la Petite Jeanne de France* (1913; *The Prose of the Trans-Siberian and of Little Jehanne of France*), a "simultaneous book," or a foldout poem with decorated pages.

Delaunay returned to painting in the 1930s, producing for the 1937 Paris Exposition a mural featuring a large airplane propellor for the Palais de l'Air. After her husband's death in 1941, her work began to gain international recognition, particularly in the 1950s. In 1964 she became the first living female artist to have an exhibition at the Louvre. Her late paintings, which include *Rhythme couleur* (1939) and many gouache-on-paper paintings entitled *Rhythme coloré*, follow the abstract, colorful style of her work from 1910 onward. Among her more unusual works is a painted automobile, which was exhibited in the Musée Nationale d'Art Moderne in 1967.

BIBLIOGRAPHY

Baron, Stanley, *Sonia Delaunay: The Life of An Artist*, 1995; Cohen, Arthur Allen, *Sonia Delaunay*, 1975.

Delius, Frederick

(January 29, 1862–June 10, 1934)
Composer, Pianist, Violinist

In spite of his general disdain for England, Frederick Theodore Albert Delius (to give him his full name) contributed to a revival of English music at the end of the nineteenth century. Influenced by the Norwegian composer Edvard Grieg (1843–1907), Delius's style has a romantic, lyrical quality that derives from unique harmonies achieved by unusual juxtapositions of chords.

Delius was the fourth of fourteen children and was born in Bradford, Yorkshire, England.

Both of his parents immigrated to England from Germany. Although his father loved music, he wanted Delius to pursue a more practical career in his wool business. Nevertheless, Delius learned to play the violin and the piano in his youth. He studied at the Bradford Grammar School and later at the International College in London. After working briefly for his father, he decided to move to Florida and grow oranges.

Delius settled at Solano Grove, near Jacksonville, in 1884. Although his orange-growing enterprise was unsuccessful, he took with him from his time in Florida two influences significant to the development of his music. The first was the teaching of the organist Thomas F. Ward, whom Delius would later acknowledge as his most valuable instructor. He also absorbed the local African-American folk music, the influence of which is evident in early compositions such as his *Florida Suite* (1888).

After the failure of his orange-growing venture, Delius moved up the East Coast, supporting himself by singing and teaching in Danville, Virginia, and in New York. In 1886 he moved to Germany to study at the Leipzig Conservatory, where he took violin lessons and began to devote himself to composing. There he met Grieg, who had gained world fame with his incidental music for Henrik Ibsen's *Peer Gynt* (1867). Grieg's harmonic constructions and Romantic style were to greatly influence Delius's mature work.

From Grieg, Delius also acquired a love of Scandinavian culture, and he made numerous excursions to Norway throughout his life. Delius's body of work includes many Danish and Norwegian songs. Many other influences on Delius were literary—the philosopher Friedrich Nietzsche, the author Jens Peter Jacobsen, and the poet Walt Whitman (whose texts he used in *Sea Drift*, 1904). Delius's great love of nature inspired many of his works, such as *The Song of the High Hills* (1912). His work first attracted attention in Germany, where in 1897 Hans Hym conducted a performance of his tone poem *Over the Hills and Far Away*. Hym enthusiastically promoted Delius's work in Germany and the same year gave an entire concert of his music.

Also in 1897, Delius settled permanently near Paris, where he lived much of the rest of his life. There he married the painter Jelka Rosen. Hym again conducted at the premiere of *Appalachia* (1907; composed 1902), a set of variations on an African-American spiritual. Owing to the efforts of the English conductor Sir Thomas Beecham, Delius's music began to gain a following in England.

Of Delius's six operas, *A Village Romeo and Juliet* (1900–1901) is his most famous. It recounts a tragic tale of two lovers from feuding Swiss families and features the popular orchestral interlude, "The Walk to the Paradise Garden." Others include *Irmelin* (1890–1892); *The Magic Fountain* (1894–1895); *Koanga* (1895–1897), which incorporates African-American folk music; *Margot la Rouge*, a one-act opera with piano arrangement by Maurice Ravel; and *Fennimore and Gerda* (1908–1910), based on *Niels Lyhne*, an important novel by the Danish poet and novelist, Jens Peter Jacobsen (1847–1885).

In the mid-1920s Delius suffered blindness and paralysis. He continued to compose with the assistance of Eric Fenby, who moved into his home and transcribed at his dictation. Also among his works are symphonies, including the *London Symphony*, the *Paris Symphony*, and the *Pastoral Symphony*. His orchestral works include *Brigg Fair* (1907), *Caprice and Elegy* for cello and small orchestra, two *Dance Rhapsodies* (1908 and 1916), *On Hearing the First Cuckoo in Spring* (1912), *North Country Sketches* (1913–1914), *A Song Before Sunrise* (1918), and *Poem of Life and Love* (1918). Delius also composed *A Mass of Life* (1904–1905) and *Requiem* (1914–1916) on texts by Nietzsche, string quartets, piano concerti, sonatas for violin and piano, and incidental music for *Hassan*, a drama by James Elroy Flecker. He was admitted to the Order of the Companions of Honour in 1929.

BIBLIOGRAPHY

Beecham, Sir Thomas, *Frederick Delius*, 1959; Fenby, Eric, *Delius As I Knew Him*, 1981; Jefferson, Alan, *Delius*, 1972; Palmer, Christopher, *Delius: Portrait of a Cosmopolitan*, 1976; Redwood, Christopher, ed., *A Delius Companion*, 1980.

Delvaux, Paul

(September 23, 1897–July 20, 1994)
Painter, Designer, Costume Designer

Paul Delvaux's mature painting style combines unusual juxtapositions of imagery, brooding atmosphere, and recurring images that include trains, classical architecture, female nudes, and skeletons. His work formed a major contribution to the Surrealist movements of 1930s Paris. He also taught painting and designed sets and costumes for the stage.

Delvaux was the son of a barrister, born in Antheit, Liège, Belgium. In 1904 he entered the École Primaire de Saint-Gilles in Brussels, where he studied music and acquired a fascination with skeletons that eventually manifested itself in his paintings. He also enjoyed Jules Verne's *Voyage to the Centre of the Earth*, from which he later drew his depictions of the character Professor Otto Lindenbrock. From 1910 to 1916 he studied at the Athénée de Saint-Gilles in Brussels, concentrating on Greek and Latin.

Delvaux's family discouraged his ambition to paint. He studied architecture under Joseph Van Neck and painting at the Académie des Beaux-Arts in Brussels. His earliest paintings are forest landscapes in the realist manner. Railway scenes, found in many paintings over the course of his career, also began to appear in the works of the early 1920s. Then in the year 1926 he met the Surrealist painter GIORGIO DE CHIRICO, a turning point in his career.

Influenced by de Chirico, RENÉ MAGRITTE, SALVADOR DALÍ, and other Surrealists, Delvaux left his early realism behind, and began to exhibit with them during the 1930s. Paintings such as *Young Woman Dreaming* (1930) and *Women and Stones* (1934) date from this period. In accordance with the Surrealist emphasis on the unconscious and strange juxtapositions of imagery, *The Break of Day* (1937) depicts a group of creatures who are half female nude, half tree.

Delvaux's figures are realistic and academic in appearance, but imbued with an eerie quality through lighting effects and bizarre combinations of imagery. Female nudes are often found walking amidst elements of classical architecture, as in *Entry into the City* (1940). In the most famous of his *Sleeping Venus* paintings (1944), a female nude reclines on a sofa in the midst of classically styled architecture under a threatening night sky. At her head a standing nude reaches toward the dark sky, while at her feet a woman appears to be conversing with a skeleton.

Other noteworthy paintings from the 1940s and 1950s include *The Sleeping City* (1938); his *Phases of the Moon* series; *The Anxious City* (1941), painted after the German invasion of Belgium during World War II; *The Public Voice* (1948); and *The Iron Age* (1951) a blue-tinged painting with a female nude in the foreground and a threatening train emer-

ging from the background. Train scenes recur in many of his 1950s paintings, such as *Evening Trains* (1957).

In 1952 Delvaux married his longtime love Anne-Marie De Maertelaere. In the next decade he produced the erotic and controversial paintings *The Visit* (1962) and *The Sabbath* (1962), the latter of which is a dimly lit portrayal of a gathering of female nudes. To the left, a man wearing a suit stares into a full-length mirror.

Delvaux continued to paint until his eyesight failed in the 1980s. From 1950 to 1962 he also taught painting at the École Nationale Supérieure d'Art et d'Architecture in Brussels. Later paintings include *Abandon* (1964), *The Blue Sofa* (1967), *Homage to Jules Verne* (1971), and *The Choir* (1983).

Aside from painting, Delvaux designed sets for the ballet, film, and the theater. Among these is JEAN GENET's ballet *Adame miroir* (1947). He also designed sets for two plays by Claude Spaak at the Vieux Colombier Théâtre in Paris in 1950 and created costumes for ROLAND PETIT's ballet *La nuit transfigurée* (1976). Delvaux completed several public commissions, such as the murals for the Palais des Congrès in Brussels (1960) and for the Liège in Belgium (1960) and the diptych *The Legendary Voyage I* (1974) for the casino at Chaudfontaine.

The Paul Delvaux Museum opened in 1982 at Sint-Idesbald on the North Sea coast. Delvaux is most remembered for his ability to express on canvas the fears that filled the conscious and unconscious mind of humanity at mid-century.

BIBLIOGRAPHY

Scott, David, *Paul Delvaux: Surrealizing the Nude*, 1992.

Denis, Maurice

(November 25, 1870–November 13, 1943)
Painter, Illustrator

Maurice Denis was a prolific painter of murals and smaller works, but he gained more recognition during his lifetime for his writings about painting and the theories they expressed. Motivated by his staunchly Catholic outlook, he studied the history of religious art and sought to revive it in France. His murals decorate several cathedrals in France and Switzerland. Denis also accepted secular commissions and painted on nonreligious themes. He worked in other media as well, producing stained glass windows, tapestries, mosaics, and ceramics.

Denis was born into a Catholic family in Granville, France, and was to remain a devout Catholic his whole life. His mother was a milliner, and his father was a railway official. For a time Denis considered becoming a monk. By the time he was a teenager, Denis knew he wanted to devote his life to art. He took drawing lessons and excelled in his studies at the Lycée Condorcet, where he studied the Greek and Latin classics from 1882 to 1887. During this time he met ÉDOUARD VUILLARD and began his lifelong habit of writing in a diary. In 1888 he entered the Académie Julien (1888), where he met PIERRE BONNARD and studied under Jules Lefebvre. Denis subsequently studied at the École des Beaux-Arts.

It was also during this time that he frequented the Louvre and began to develop his love of Italian art.

With Vuillard, Bonnard, and others, Denis formed a group of painters, the Nabis, in 1888. The Nabis, influenced by Paul Gauguin, the German Expression-ists, and the Art Nouveau movements, rejected the work of the Impressionists. In their paintings the Nabis used broad, flat areas of bold color. Denis's religious bent influenced him to treat many biblical subjects, as in *Jacob Wrestling with the Angel* (1893), but he also worked with many secular subjects. The Nabis also contributed to a revival in the decorative arts, and Denis designed screens, lampshades, ceramics, and other items. For the Baron Denys Cochin, a Catholic statesman, Denis in 1897 created *La legende de Saint Hubert* (1897) in seven panels. His paintings were first exhibited two years later in Paris, and in 1891 he exhibited at the Salon des Indépendants.

At this time his subjects included still lifes, such as *Dish of Plums* (1889), portraits, and almost mystical landscapes. In *Forest with Anemones* (1889), ghostlike trees rise from the green forest floor into a blue sky. In his *Green Christ* (1890) and *Orange Christ* (1890), both of which depict the crucifixion scene, the figures in the crowd and Christ on the cross appear as silhouettes among flat areas of color. Several paintings demonstrate an acknowledged debt to Paul Cézanne (1839–1906), whom he visited, including *Homage à Cézanne* (1901) and *Monsieur Cézanne au motif* (1906). Working with Lugne-Poe's Symbolist Théâtre de l'Oeuvre, Denis contributed scenery design to the theater.

In 1892 he met ANDRÉ GIDE, and he illustrated Gide's *Le Voyage d'Urien* the next year. The year 1893 also saw his marriage to his first wife, Marthe Meunier, who appears in *Portrait of the Artist and His*

Wife at Dusk (1897) and other paintings. Denis first visited Italy in 1895. Broadening the scope of his love for Italian art, he absorbed the works of the fresco painters of the fourteenth and fifteenth centuries. Toward the end of the decade he embraced a neoclassical style. He subsequently decorated many churches, receiving in 1899 his first commission, *La glorification de la croix* for the chapel of the College Sainte-Croix at Vesinet. The mural *Pentecost* (1934) decorates the apses of Saint-Esprit church in Paris.

In 1919 Denis, with Georges Devallières, founded the Studios of Sacred Art. His wife died the same year, and in 1922 he married Elizabeth Graterolle. He executed many stained glass windows, including *The Life of Joan of Arc* (1916) for the home of Gabriel Thomas in Meudon.

Denis illustrated St. Francis of Assisi's *Fioretti* (1913); *Eloa*, a poem by the nineteenth-century French Romantic, Alfred de Vigny; and a number of books published by Ambroise Vollard. His theoretical writings on art include *Theories* (2 vol., 1920, 1922) and *History of Religious Art* (1939).

Among Denis's other works are *Life of Saint Paul* (1916) for St. Paul's in Geneva; *Justice and Peace* (1928) for the staircase ceiling of the Senate in Paris; the paintings *Eurydice* (1906), *The Golden Age: The Spring* (1911), and *The Raising of Lazarus* (1933); the four-panel *Screen with Doves* (1896); mosaics; and tapestries. Outside of France, Denis's work gained little recognition during his lifetime, and his work has not often been exhibited since his death. He was elected to the Académie des Beaux-Arts de l'Institut de France in 1932. Denis died at 73 when a tram ran over him on the Boulevard St. Michel.

BIBLIOGRAPHY

Cogeval, Guy, et al., *Maurice Denis, 1870–1943.*

Dennis, Nigel

(January 16, 1912–July 19, 1989)
Novelist, Playwright, Journalist, Editor

Nigel Forbes Dennis made his living for many years as a book reviewer for major publications in the United States and England. In the realm of fiction and drama, he was best known for his novel *Cards of Identity* (1955), which, like his plays, is sharply satirical and explores aspects of psychology.

Dennis was born in Bletchingley, Surrey, England. During his childhood he lived in Southern Rhodesia (now Zimbabwe). He later studied at the Odenwald School in Germany and finally settled in England. In 1930 he finished his first novel, *Boys and Girls Come Out to Play* (published 1949), a fictional investigation of the Austrian psychiatrist Alfred Adler's theories on the development of personalities, in the characters of the liberal journalist Max Divver and the wealthy Jimmy Morgan, who owns the periodical where Divver works.

Beginning in 1934 he spent a lot of time in the United States, where he worked for the National Board of Review of Motion Pictures in New York City in 1935–1936. Dennis subsequently reviewed books for *The New Republic* and *Time*, and he served as associate editor at the former. He returned to London in 1949 and worked as a book reviewer (1960–1963) and co-editor (1967–1970) for *Encounter*. He continued to write book reviews for the *Sunday Telegraph* into the 1980s.

Dennis finished his best-known novel, *Cards of Identity*, in 1955, and it was later adapted as a play. As the title suggests, the novel is about the search for identity. In a sharply satiric manner, Den-

nis depicts a group of psychologists (members of the Identity Club), who gather at an English country house to hear papers on problems of identity. *A House in Order* (1966) also concerns the question of identity. The protagonist is a prisoner and a pawn in a rivalry between military factions, and he is able to successfully preserve his identity during his confinement. Dennis's other works include *August for the People* (1961), an indictment of the media; the play *The Making of Moo* (first performed in 1957), a satire on religious zeal; *A House in Order* (1966); and *Exotics: Poems of the Mediterranean and Middle East* (1970). Among his nonfiction works is *Jonathan Swift: A Short Character* (1964).

Derain, André

(June 10, 1880–September 8, 1954)
Painter, Sculptor, Graphic Artist, Illustrator, Designer

André Derain's paintings were part of the famous Fauve exhibition at the Paris Salon d'Automne in 1905. Before his break with the movement around 1908, he was a chief proponent of its brilliant color, broken brush strokes, and free forms. After 1908 Derain experimented with Cubism and other styles before evolving the Neoclassical forms of his late work. Derain also illustrated books, designed sets for the ballet and for theater, and sculpted.

Derain was born in Chatou, France. His father was a pastry chef, and both

parents encouraged his early love of painting. At the age of 15, he went to study with a local landscape painter. When it came to finding a career, however, his parents had more practical ideas. Derain studied at the Lycée Chaptal and under his parents' influence intended to go into engineering. Bored with his studies, he spent much of his time painting and frequenting Paris museums. He later studied painting at the Académie Carrière and at the Académie Julien. At the Louvre he met Georges Florentin Linaret, who introduced him to HENRI MATISSE and other painters of the Paris avant-garde. Derain also gained the close friendship of MAURICE DE VLAMINCK.

In the early years of his career, Derain painted numerous landscapes, such as *The Road to Carrières* (1899), and city scenes. After completing his military service (1901–1904), Derain returned to Paris and met the Symbolist poet Guillaume Apollinaire. In 1905 the Paris art dealer Ambroise Vollard (who handled the work of other artists, notably GEORGES ROUAULT) purchased almost all of his work.

Derain exhibited paintings with the Fauves at the 1905 exhibition at the Salon d'Automne. At this time, like the other Fauves, he used pure pigment and brilliant color—notably rich blues and greens—in his paintings. In 1906 he went to London, where he painted a series of London scenes, among which is *Hyde Park*. The following year, PABLO PICASSO introduced him to his future wife, Alice Princet. Derain soon moved away from the Fauvist style, however, and began to develop his own. A tragic studio fire in 1908 destroyed many of his paintings up to that time. In 1909 art dealer Daniel Henry Kahnweiler began to buy his work.

Although Derain maintained his friendships with other painters, he also came to be friends with literary figures such as the poet Guillaume Apollinaire and also acquired an interest in mysticism. The painter Paul Cézanne (1839–1906) influenced the next phase of development in his art. Derain used milder color in many of his paintings, although works such as *Trees on the Banks of the Seine* (1912) retain the intense color of his Fauvist paintings. Other works from this period include *Bathers* (1908), *The Old Bridge at Cagnes* (1910), and *Last Supper* (1911).

Paintings such as *La Samedi* (1913) and *Chevalier X* (1912–1914) are dominated by long, thin figures and muted earth tones. In his later years, Derain painted in a neoclassical style, and his subjects included nudes (*Nu au chat*, 1923; *Nu à la cruche*, 1921–1923), harlequins (*Arlequin et Pierrot*, 1924), ballet dancers, portraits, and still lifes (*Still Life with Dead Game*, 1928). A number of his paintings prior to World War II were destroyed when German soldiers occupied his home in 1940.

In addition to painting, Derain contributed illustrations to editions of books by Max Jacob, ANDRÉ BRETON, Oscar Wilde, and George Gabory as well as to editions of many classical texts. In 1919 he designed sets for SERGEY DIAGHILEV's production of *La boutique fantasque*. He contributed designs to a number of other ballets, including *Le diable l'emporte* (1948), for ROLAND PETIT. In 1933 he designed the ballets *Les fastes* and *Les songes*. His work for theater includes designs for a production of Paul Claudel's *L'annonce faite à Marie* (1918). In 1927 he completed a series of lithographs entitled *Metamorphoses*, and he also executed sculptures.

He won the Carnegie Prize in 1928.

BIBLIOGRAPHY

Lee, Jane, *Derain*, 1990.

Diaghilev, Sergey

(March 31, 1872–August 19, 1929)
Impresario, Editor

The legendary Russian-born ballet impresario Sergey Pavlovich Diaghilev was perhaps the most influential figure in modern dance. Between 1909 and 1929 he ran the Ballets Russes, an international dance company that launched the careers of many of the twentieth century's best-known dancers and choreographers. Diaghilev's efforts to integrate the talents of the leading musicians and painters of his day into ballet productions that had roots in the Russian classical tradition with which he was familiar—largely through the choreographer MICHEL FOKINE—revolutionized the conception of ballet in his day.

Diaghilev was born in Perm, Russia, and raised by his father, a military man, and his stepmother. As a youth he studied music and attended the Perm Gymnasia, and in 1890 he entered the University of St. Petersburg to study law. After he graduated he intended to pursue a career writing music, but the Russian composer Nikolay Rimsky-Korsakov (1844–1908), whom he met in St. Petersburg, convinced him that his true talents did not lie in music.

Next Diaghilev began to associate with prominent painters, writers, and musicians, including LÉON BAKST. From 1899 to 1904, he edited the influential art review *Mir Iskusstva* (*The World of Art*). His entrance into the world of theater came in 1899, when the director of the Imperial Theatres gave him a post and appointed him editor of the *Annual of the Imperial Theatres*. As Diaghilev's responsibilties grew, he began to oversee productions of operas and ballets.

Diaghilev spent most of the years between 1904 and 1908 organizing art exhibitions, and in 1906 he settled in Paris, where he was based for the rest of his life. His debut as an independent theatrical impresario came in 1908, when he secured FEODOR CHALIAPIN to sing his famous title role in Modest Mussorgsky's (1839–1881) *Boris Godunov* at the Paris Opera. The following year he founded Les Ballets Russes de Diaghilev.

Drawing from a pool of talents he had known in Russia, he secured such noted dancers as TAMARA KARSAVINA, ANNA PAVLOVA, and VASLAV NIJINSKY to perform in a series of ballets (including *Les Sylphides*) largely choreographed by Michel Fokine. The season in Paris met with resounding success, and for the next two decades the Ballet Russes was the dominant force in dance on international stages.

In 1910, the company performed the first of three operas by IGOR STRAVINSKY, *The Firebird*, which showcased the talents of Karsavina and the dancer Adolph Bolm. The following year the Ballet Russes expanded its productions to international stages, performing in Rome, London, and Monte Carlo as well as in Paris. For the next two years Karsavina and Nijinsky dominated lead roles in productions such as *Petrouchka* and *Le Spectre de la Rose*, while Fokine continued to provide the bulk of the choreography.

Following Fokine's temporary departure from the Ballet Russes in 1913, Nijinsky, who had done some choreography for the company before, began to choreograph more, notably for Stravinsky's *Le Sacre du Printemps* (*The Rite*

Sergey Diaghilev, an illustration by Serov, 1903 (Ann Ronan/Image Select)

of Spring). Soon afterward, however, Nijinsky, with whom Diaghilev had maintained a long and close homosexual relationship, married a female dancer, and an enraged Diaghilev dismissed him from the company.

Fokine returned to choreograph several ballets in 1914, and the same year LÉONIDE MASSINE made his dancing debut with the Ballet Russes in *La Légende de Joseph* (*The Legend of Joseph*). The company made its American debut in 1915, and Nijinsky returned to dance with the Ballet Russes during the 1916 season. Massine's choreographic debut for the company came the same year with *Le Soleil de nuit* (*The Midnight Sun*), and until the mid-1920s he was a major contributor, with Bronislava Nijinska, to the company's choreography with such works as *La Boutique Fantasque, The Three-Cornered Hat,* and *Mercure*. In the company's final years, GEORGE BALANCHINE became Diaghilev's principal choreographer, creating such works as *La Chatte* and *Les Dieux Mendiants*.

The Ballet Russes gave its final production with a trio of ballets at Covent Garden on July 26, 1929, and Diaghilev's death less than a month later ended the existence of the company as it was. Season after season until then, his productions became huge international successes. CLAUDE DEBUSSY, PABLO PICASSO, JEAN COCTEAU, MAURICE RAVEL, HENRI MATISSE, MANUEL DE FALLA, GEORGES BRAQUE, and RICHARD STRAUSS were among many avant-garde musicians and painters who contributed costumes, set designs, and music scores to Ballet Russes productions.

BIBLIOGRAPHY

Buckle, Richard, *Diaghilev,* 1977; Drummond, John, *Speaking of Diaghilev,* 1997; Garafola, Lynn, *Diaghilev's Ballet Russes,* 1998; Garafola, Lynn, and Nancy Van Norman Baer, eds., *The Ballet Russes and Its World,* 1999; Spencer, Charles, *The World of Serge Diaghilev,* 1974.

Dietrich, Marlene

(December 27, 1901–May 6, 1992)
Actress, Singer

Propelled from the German stage to international stardom almost overnight by film director JOSEF VON STERNBERG, Marlene Dietrich commanded admiring audiences for more than fifty years as a film actress and nightclub singer. Using shadow, contrast, and innovative camera work, Sternberg created the haunting mystique associated with her in their first film, *The Blue Angel,* in which she starred as the sensuous singer Lola-Lola.

Dietrich was born Marie Magdalene Dietrich von Losch in Berlin; many details of her childhood remain unknown. Her father was an officer in the Royal Prussian Police, and in her first years her family had ample financial means. After the death of her father, and subsequently her stepfather, her family's fortunes declined markedly. She attended the Augusta Victoria School for Girls and later enrolled at the Berlin Hochschule für Musik, where she studied the violin.

Marlene Dietrich in a scene from the film *Knights without Armour* (Ann Ronan/Image Select)

However, she gave up her ambition to play professionally after injuring her arm with overpractice.

Dietrich next studied acting under the director Max Reinhardt. In 1921 she made her stage debut in the chorus line of a touring review, and a short time later she returned to Reinhardt to act in his theater company. Reinhardt aimed to steer theater away from strict literary interpretations, emphasizing decor, costumes, and choreography. While acting in his company, Dietrich also appeared as an extra in films for the Universum Film AG. In 1924 she married the director Rudolf Sieber.

Two years later she accepted a part in British director ALEXANDER KORDA's *Eine Du Barry von Heute* (*A Modern Du Barry*). It was Sternberg, however, who was responsible for making Dietrich an international star and sex symbol. After seeing her in the play *Two Bow Ties*, he insisted on casting the then unknown actress as the cabaret singer Lola-Lola in his *Der blaue Engel* (1930; *The Blue Angel*), an adaptation of Heinrich Mann's novel and the first sound film made in Germany. Sternberg's shadow and light contrasts and Dietrich's sensuous singing contributed to overnight fame, particularly in the United States.

From 1930 to 1935 Dietrich worked with von Sternberg and Paramount Pictures in Hollywood, appearing again as a cabaret singer in *Morocco* (1930), as a secret agent in *Dishonored* (1931), and as a wife who leaves her husband in *Blonde Venus* (1932). In the action-packed *Shanghai Express* (1932), she played Shanghai Lily, one of several characters aboard a Shanghai-bound train that has been taken by revolutionaries. Dietrich appeared as Catherine the Great in *The Scarlet Empress* (1934), and the following year she finished her final film with Sternberg, *The Devil Is a Woman* (1935).

Desire (1936) and *Destry Rides Again* (1939) are among Dietrich's other notable movies prior to World War II. An ardent opponent of Nazism, she renounced her German citizenship and devoted the years between 1943 and 1946 to entertaining Allied troops. After the war Dietrich continued to appear in films, including *A Foreign Affair* (1948), *The Monte Carlo Story* (1956), and *Witness for the Prosecution* (1957; adapted by Billy Wilder from AGATHA CHRISTIE's play). In Orson Welles's visually appealing *Touch of Evil* (1958), she played a madam and fortuneteller opposite Welles's alcoholic sheriff in a Mexican-American border town. In 1961 she appeared in *Judgment at Nuremberg* (1961), a film about the Nazi war trials.

In the later years of her life Dietrich became a popular nightclub and concert hall singer, appearing in her characteristic top hat and tails. She toured the United States giving concerts in 1973. *Just a Gigolo* was one of the few films in which she appeared. Her autobiography, *Ich bin, Gott sei Dank, Berlinerin* (*I Am, Thank God, a Berliner*; English translation, *Marlene*), appeared in 1987.

BIBLIOGRAPHY

Bach, Steven, *Marlene Dietrich: Life and Legend*, 1992; Dickens, Homer, *The Complete Films of Marlene Dietrich*, 1992; Dietrich, Marlene, *Marlene*, 1989; Morley, Sheridan, *Marlene Dietrich*, 1976; O'Connor, Patrick, *Dietrich: Style and Substance*, 1991; Spoto, Donald, *Blue Angel: The Life of Marlene Dietrich*, 1992; Walker, Alexander, *Dietrich*, 1984.

Dinesen, Isak

(April 17, 1885–September 7, 1962)
Novelist, Short-Story Writer

Isak Dinesen was the pseudonym of Karen Christence Dinesen, Baroness Blixen-Finecke. Best known for her memoirs *Out of Africa*, Dinesen published several collections of romantic tales beginning in the 1930s. Her work first attained popularity in the United States and inspired a number of films, including *Babette's Feast*.

Dinesen was born in Rungsted, Denmark. Her father, a military officer, acquired the family's property in Rungsted, where Dinesen spent the majority of her life. His hanging suicide during her childhood left an emotional scar on Dinesen, made more serious by the local scandal that followed. Nevertheless, her childhood had many happy moments. For example, as a child, she enjoyed dressing up and putting on pantomime shows with her siblings. She was educated privately, studied at the Academy of Fine Art in Copenhagen, and traveled widely in Europe, visiting Paris in 1910. Four years later, she married a cousin, Baron Bror Blixen-Finecke, and settled with him in Africa.

The Blixens ran a coffee plantation in Kenya, where she developed a deep love for the landscape, natives, and traditions of Africa. By 1921 their marriage had dissolved, in part due to his frequent absence and extramarital affairs. Dinesen stayed to run the plantation until 1931, when financial and other difficulties forced her to leave. During that time she fell in love with the English hunter Denys Finch Hatton, whose death in a plane crash devastated her. She recorded her experiences of these years in her memoirs *Out of Africa* (1937) (the basis for an Oscar-winning film directed by Sydney Pollack). A sequel, *Shadows on the Grass*, appeared in 1960.

Dinesen began to write seriously upon her return to Denmark. She wrote in English and translated her works into Danish. The short stories collected in *Seven Gothic Tales* (1934) marked her first success. *Winter's Tales* followed the same year. A successful American lecture tour in 1959 followed her early popularity in the United States.

During the Nazi occupation of Denmark, Dinesen embarked on her only novel, *The Angelic Avengers* (1944), published under the pseudonym Pierre Andrézel. She contradicted those who saw the story, which concerns a group who liberate themselves from an evil captor, as a wartime allegory.

Dinesen's short stories fall in the Romantic tradition. She often combined multiple narrations in her stories, which were also influenced in style by her longtime love of the theater. Dinesen was particularly fascinated with the commedia dell'arte and was often known to dress as the commedia dell'arte persona Pierrot, the clown. Themes of self-searching, the past, the meaning of art, and the mythological and supernatural characterize her work.

A 1987 film based on "Babette's Feast," directed by Gabriel Axel, popularized the story of a servant who spends all her money to prepare an elaborate feast for a group of rigid and skeptical diners. "The King's Letter" is based on the true story of a letter Dinesen brought from the King of Denmark to Africa. Orson Welles produced a film based on "The Immortal Story" in 1968. In "Deluge at Norderney," the young Calypso, living with her uncle, is the victim of his obsession with dressing her up as a boy.

Illness hampered Dinesen's writing efforts from the 1950s onward. Her *Last Tales* were published in 1957, followed by the posthumous volume *Carnival: Entertainments and Posthumous Tales* (1977). Her other works include *Daguerreotypes, and Other Essays* (1979) and *Letters from Africa, 1914–31* (1981). Her stories, and particularly *Out of Africa*, were highly regarded for their mystical atmospheres, drama, and sensitivity.

BIBLIOGRAPHY

Hannah, Donald, *'Isak Dinesen' and Karen Blixen: The Mask and the Reality*, 1971; Juhl, Marianne, *Diana's Revenge: Two Lines in Isak Dinesen's Authorship*, 1985; Lasson, Frans, *The Life and Destiny of Isak Dinesen*, 1970; Migel, Parmenia, *Titania: The Biography of Isak Dinesen*, 1967; Pelensky, Olga Anastasia, *Isak Dinesen: The Life and Imagination of a Seducer*, 1991; Thurman, Judith, *Isak Dinesen: The Life of a Storyteller*, 1982.

Dolmetsch, Arnold

(February 24, 1858–February 28, 1940)
Musician, Violinist, Pianist

The musical career of French-born Eugène Arnold Dolmetsch revolved around three focal points—restoration and construction of old instruments, research into early English music, and performing of old English music on authentic instruments—all of which sparked renewed interest in long-forgotten music. Dolmetsch's ideas, unique approach to music, uncompromising enthusiasm for his work, and often unforgiving outlook rendered him a controversial figure in an era that championed musical experimentation.

Dolmetsch was of German and French ancestry and was born in Le Mans, France. Several of his immediate ancestors had musical interests. His father, an organ and piano builder who worked for his father-in-law, was a stern and disciplined man. The skill of both men contributed to a successful business. Dolmetsch remained close to his grandfather and often accompanied him on organ-repairing journeys. His mother, too, had musical talent—she played the cello.

At the age of 4, Dolmetsch began taking piano lessons. The cruelty of his teacher, however, caused disillusionment with the piano, and many years passed before he seriously played keyboard instruments again. Dolmetsch next studied the violin, and at the age of 6 he entered the Lycée du Mans. There, as in all of his studies, he received the highest marks. At the age of 14 he quit school to help out in his father's business.

Within two years, both his beloved grandfather and his father died. Dolmetsch was left, as a teenager, to run the family business, impeded by interfering relatives. He joined the local orchestra as a violinist. Before long had eloped with the young widow Marie Morel. They had a daughter, Hélène, who would later become a talented musician, and after her birth they married in England. After a brief stay in the United States, the Dolmetsches returned to France. There he continued the family business, successfully, with his mother's new husband Alphonse Gouge.

Dolmetsch next studied at the Brussels Conservatory, at first playing the viola. Under the influence of Ferdinand Kufferath he overcame his aversion to the keyboard and took up the study of the pianoforte. He acquired an old piano and, unable to find someone to restore it for him, did the work himself. This early acquisition was one of many old instruments he purchased and restored over the years. Lutes, violas, and many other instruments he restored were prominent features of his concerts.

After leaving the Conservatory, Dolmetsch moved to England and attended the Royal College of Music, where he studied the violin under Henry Holmes and performed regularly in the school's concerts. Upon the completion of his studies, E. D. Rendell hired him as a part-time violin teacher at Dulwich College. Dolmetsch took on private students as well, and he developed a teaching style that focused on developing feeling for the music before the introduction of formal technique.

Both in the libraries at the Royal College and in the British Museum, Dolmetsch grew increasingly fascinated with early British music, particularly viol music. Around the same time he acquired a viola d'amore, an unfretted instrument with vibrating sympathetic strings underlying bowed melody strings. He poured himself into research, finding new music to perform and studying how to play it authentically. He gave his first viol concert in 1890, gave many concerts and lectures over the course of his life, and frequently appeared with the Elizabethan Stage Society. Dolmetsch often appeared with a trio consisting of himself, Kathleen Salmon, and his wife. He found an enthusiastic supporter in the playwright GEORGE BERNARD SHAW, who attended many of his performances and promoted his work.

In 1902 he embarked on a tour of the United States. From 1905 to 1909 he immersed himself in the building and restoration of lutes, harpsichords, and other instruments. From 1911 to 1914 he worked at the Gaveau factory in Paris, and following World War I he began constructing some of the first modern recorders. In addition to performing and building instruments, Dolmetsch published many editions of old music and a book, *The Interpretation of Music of the XVII and XVIII Centuries* (1915 and 1944). The Dolmetsch Foundation, founded in 1928 to advance his ideas on music, published the magazine *The Consort*. He received an honorary doctorate in music from Durham University.

BIBLIOGRAPHY

Campbell, Margaret, *Dolmetsch: The Man and His Work*, 1975.

Domingo, Plácido

(January 21, 1941–)
Singer, Actor, Conductor

An operatic tenor renowned for his warm voice and versatility, Plácido Domingo is a household name around the world. The thousands of productions in which he has appeared include standard opera roles, concerts of popular music and Spanish songs, films, traditional Spanish light operas, and modern operas.

Domingo was born into a Catholic family in Madrid. From his earliest childhood, he spent much of his time around music and the theater. His mother, a popular singer, was of Basque ancestry. Domingo's father, a talented singer and violin player, was of Catalan and Aragonese background. Both parents earned their living performing in zarzuelas, a form of Spanish light opera that dates to the seventeenth century and involves singing, dancing, and acting. Domingo appeared from time to time in these productions as a boy, for example, in Manuel Penella Moreno's *The Wildcat* (*El gato montés*).

In 1946 Domingo's parents decided to move to Mexico and form their own zarzuela troupe. Domingo and his sister joined them there three years later. In Mexico he began to study the piano, first under Manuel Barajas and then at the National Conservatory of Music. At the latter Domingo studied under Cerlo Morelli, the brother of Chilean tenor Renato Zanelli. He also observed classes by the National Opera, giving him his first real introduction to modern opera.

A marriage, child, and subsequent divorce cut short Domingo's formal music training. He took to performing in his parents' zarzuelas, singing in nightclubs, playing the piano, and appearing in musicals, often singing baritone roles. In 1959 he joined the National Opera, where he started out singing supporting roles such as Borsa in Giuseppe Verdi's (1813–1901) Rigoletto and Gaston in Verdi's *La traviata*. During this time he continued to perform outside of the opera and began to appear in music shows on television. Domingo also dabbled in acting, preparing for his roles using the Stanislavsky method (see KONSTANTIN STANISLAVSKY).

In 1961 he made his debut in a lead operatic tenor role as Alfredo in *La traviata*. The following year he married his second wife, Marta Ornelas, with whom he later formed a chamber opera group. After his debut in Mexico, Domingo joined an opera company in Dallas. Among his most successful roles there was his performance in *Lucia di Lammernour* with JOAN SUTHERLAND. From 1962 to 1965 Domingo sang with the Hebrew National Opera in Tel Aviv.

In Philadelphia in 1965 Domingo sang his first performance as the German poet E. T. A. Hoffmann in Jacques Offenbach's *Les Contes d'Hoffmann*. It became one of his best-known roles, the other outstanding one being his Chevalier des Greiux in Puccini's *Manon Lescaut*. He took a contract with the New York City Opera in 1965, debuted at the Hamburg Opera in 1967, made his first appearance at the Metropolitan Opera House in New York in 1968, and debuted at Milan's La Scala in 1969.

Domingo had by this time become an international star and sang regularly at

Plácido Domingo as Alfredo in *La traviata* (Ann Ronan/Image Select)

dard repertoire and also appearing in modern operas such as *Don Rodrigo*. Although his range is not as broad as that of his contemporary LUCIANO PAVAROTTI, he is renowned for the warmth, color, and timbre of his voice. In 1984 he was instrumental in founding the Los Angeles Music Center Opera, and the following year he sang in the world premiere of ANDREW LLOYD WEBBER's *Requiem*. He accepted the post of artistic director of the Washington Opera in 1996.

Domingo has made many recordings of opera, Spanish songs, and other music. He has also appeared in film versions of numerous operas and conducted. His video *The Songs of Mexico* features performances of popular Mexican music. *My First Forty Years*, an autobiography, was published in 1983.

BIBLIOGRAPHY

Domingo, Plácido, *My First Forty Years*, 1983; Schnauber, Cornelius, *Plácido Domingo*, 1997; Snowman, Daniel, *Plácido Domingo's Tales From the Opera*, 1995.

the major opera houses of the world, as he still does, performing all of the stan-

Douglas, Keith

(January 20, 1920–June 9, 1944)
Poet

Like the World War I poet WILFRED OWEN and other poets of that generation, Keith Castellain Douglas lost his life fighting for England at a young age. Mortally wounded in World War II at the age of 24, Douglas had already begun to publish verse that expresses the turmoil and misery of his wartime experi-

ence. His reputation as a poet was established with several posthumous collections of his verse.

Douglas was born in Royal Tunbridge Wells, Kent, England. His mother worked as an artist's secretary, and his father faced perpetual financial difficulties. A wilful, determined personality emerged early in the young Douglas. In 1926 he entered the Edgeborough School, where he was given to rebellious behavior but still earned good grades. From 1931 to 1938 Douglas studied at Christ's Hospital, a boarding school. His first published poems, "Pan" and "Ave Atque Vale," appeared in the school's literary periodical *The Outlook* in 1934.

Douglas's poetry soon began to appear regularly in *The Outlook*; it expressed a youthful optimism as yet untainted by the disappointment of relationships and the misery of war. As the years wore on, Douglas's independence and determination brought him into conflict with the Christ's Hospital authorities. His military activity began in 1935 and continued for the rest of his brief life.

Upon the completion of his studies (mainly in history) at Christ's Hospital, Douglas won a scholarship to study at Merton, Oxford. The years at Merton marked the beginning of numerous stormy love affairs, the difficulties of which found their way into his poetry. Douglas served as editor of the school's *The Cherwell* and regularly contributed verse to its pages.

With the outbreak of World War II Douglas enlisted in the military. From 1941 to 1944 he served in the Middle East, where he wrote much of the poetry for which he became famous. Douglas framed images of soldiers, battlefield miseries, and death in the Middle Eastern setting where he served, and in several poems he seems to predict his own death. Although principally concerned with his wartime experiences, Douglas's verse lacks the strong antiwar sentiment found in the World War I poetry of Owen and SIEGFRIED SASSOON, and instead carries the subtle tone and attitude of a detached observer.

Single poems such as "Dead Men," published in *Citadel* in 1943, found their way into print in various periodicals. Much of his verse was collected, with sketches, in *Alamein to Zem-Zem* (1946). After serving in the Middle East Douglas was sent back to England. He was mortally wounded during the invasion of Normandy in 1944. Following his death several editions of his poetry appeared, including *Collected Poems* (1951) and *Selected Poems* (1951). TED HUGHES compiled an edition of his poetry entitled *Selected Poems* (1964) that contributed significantly to the posthumous recognition of his work for its eloquent and ironic treatment of war themes in verse.

BIBLIOGRAPHY

Fraser, G. S., *Keith Douglas: A Poet of the Second World War*, 1957; Graham, Desmond, *Keith Douglas, 1920–1944: A Biography*, 1974; Scammell, William, *Keith Douglas: A Study*, 1988.

Douglas, Norman

(December 8, 1868–February 9, 1952)
Novelist, Essayist

Though of Scottish and German ancestry, Norman Douglas lived much of his life in the warm Mediterranean climate of southern Italy, the setting of his most famous novel, *South Wind*. Douglas wrote only two other novels, devoting most of his time as a writer to his travel books, acclaimed for their rich and colorful detail; and opinionated essays, all of which reveal his pointed sense of humor and his mastery of conversational style.

Douglas's father was Scottish, his mother Scottish-German, both of aristocratic families; Douglas was born in Thüringen, Austria. His father, an enthusiastic outdoorsman whom he deeply admired, died in a hunting accident in 1874. Four years later, Douglas's family sent him to study at Yarlet Hall, Staffordshire, England. Douglas disliked the rigid atmosphere of this and the other English schools he attended, and in 1883 he went to study at the gymnasium in Karlsruhe, Germany. During his time there, he wrote for *The Zoologists* and learned a handful of languages, including German, French, and Russian. The looser discipline better suited his outlook and temperament, and he remained at the gymnasium until 1888.

By this time, Douglas had already developed his lifelong interest in the natural sciences. His first published work was an article entitled "Variation of Plumage in the Corvidae" for the journal *Zoologist*. In 1893, without having attended a university, Douglas entered the British Foreign Office. His diplomatic work took him to St. Petersburg, Russia, where he served until 1896; he then left the service for reasons that remain unclear.

Douglas married a cousin, Elsa Fitzgibbon, in 1898. They collaborated on *Unprofessional Tales* (1901), a book of short stories, mostly conceived by his wife, published under the pseudonym "Normyx." Their marriage ended bitterly in 1903. *Unprofessional Tales* was Douglas's only major work of fiction until the publication of *South Wind* in 1917. In the meantime, he occupied himself with traveling and writing travel books.

Douglas particularly liked the Mediterranean area and lived much of his life in southern Italy, the subject of many of his travel books, which combine his impressions with philosophy and local history. Among them are *Siren Land* (1911), *Fountains in the Sand* (1912), *Old Calabria* (1928), *Alone* (1921), *Together* (1923), *One Day* (1929), *Summer Islands* (1931), and *A Footnote on Capri* (1952).

In all his works, Douglas was an outspoken and opinionated writer. He cultivated a reputation for hedonistic, bohemian living. Principal targets of his pen were Christianity in particular and organized religion in general. His lifelong atheism and antireligious sentiment is evident in *Goodbye to Western Culture* (1929; published in Europe as *How About Europe*) and other essay collections. An interest in the culture of ancient Greece and a fundamentally scientific approach to nature also influenced his writing.

From 1912 to 1916 Douglas worked as assistant editor of FORD MADOX FORD's *English Review*. The first and best-known of his three novels, *South Wind*, is a philosophical and conversational work set on the fictional island of Nepenthe, modeled on Capri, his home of many years. The rather proper and orthodox English Bishop Mr. Heard comes to Nepenthe to fetch his cousin and take her back to England. The hedonistic atmosphere of the island, where each of Douglas's assortment of characters seems to embody some form of rebellion against conventional morality, slowly transforms the bishop. By the end of the novel, he is defending his cousin's murder of her no-good ex-husband.

The setting of Douglas's second novel, *They Went* (1920), moves to an island that resembles England; it was inspired by an old Breton legend. A princess renowned for her beauty, her cruelty, and her love of architecture falls in love with the unattractive Theophilus, also a lover of architecture. Together they transform the city into a model of beauty and craftsmanship, and Theophilus softens the formerly harsh princess. In the weak and elderly King, a convert to Christianity who is not the princess's real father, Theophilus identifies an enemy. He urges the princess to dispose of the Christian missionary Kenwyn, which she does with initial but not lasting regret. Nevertheless, the couple fails to save the city from disaster in the end and flees elsewhere to start anew. Although the novel received some critical acclaim, it was less successful commercially than *South Wind.*

Douglas derived his final novel, *In the Beginning* (1927), from the legend of Ninus and Semiramis, founders of the Assyrian Empire. Among his other works are *Goodbye Western Culture* (1930), the autobiographical *Looking Back* (1933), and the essay collections *London Street Games* (1916), *Experiments* (1925), *Birds and Beasts of the Greek Anthology* (1927), *An Almanac* (1941), *Late Harvest* (1946), *Three of Them* (1930), and *Venus in the Kitchen* (1952).

BIBLIOGRAPHY

Dawkins, R. M., *Norman Douglas,* 1954; Greenless, Ian, *Norman Douglas,* 1957; Leary, Lewis Gaston, *Norman Douglas,* 1968; Lindeman, Ralph D., *Norman Douglas,* 1965.

Doyle, Arthur Conan

(May 22, 1859–July 7, 1930)
Novelist, Short-Story Writer

Sir Arthur Conan Doyle created the most popular sleuth in detective fiction, Sherlock Holmes, whose name has become synonymous with good detective work. Doyle also wrote novels in other genres, practiced medicine, lectured, and became an ardent advocate of spiritualism in his later life.

Doyle was born in Edinburgh, Scotland. His father, a civil servant of Norman ancestry, suffered from both mental and physical ailments, and he was primarily raised by his mother. The family was

The adventure of the final problem, a scene from an Arthur Conan Doyle story (Ann Ronan/Image Select)

Catholic, and Doyle first attended the Jesuit schools Hodder House and Stonyhurst College in Lancashire, where he studied classics and mathematics. After an additional year at Feldkirsch School in Austria, he studied medicine at the University of Edinburgh, where he also began to write stories. After obtaining his degree in 1881, Doyle set up a practice in Southsea, England. The most important legacy from his time at Edinburgh was his meeting the surgeon Joseph Bell, who inspired the character of Sherlock Holmes. Four years later he married Louise Hopkins; after her death from tuberculosis in 1906 he married his mistress of many years, Jean Leckie.

Magazines began to publish Doyle's short stories in the 1880s. The character of Sherlock Holmes, a brilliant sleuth who applies rational deduction to solve cases, first appeared in *A Study in Scarlet* (1887), published in *Beeton's Christmas Annual.* Over the next few years, Holmes, accompanied by his sidekick, the less brilliant but reliable and lovable Dr. Watson, solved mysteries in the pages of *Strand* and other magazines. The stories gained enormous popularity with British and American audiences, and fans besieged Doyle with letters (often addressed to Sherlock Holmes).

Typical of the Holmes stories is *The Sign of Four* (1890), in which the detective is drawn into a mystery surrounding the murder of Bartholomew Sholto, brother of Thaddeus Sholto. The latter Sholto is wrongly accused of murdering his brother, and Holmes unearths the true culprits. A collection of the stories, *The Adventures of Sherlock Holmes*, was published in 1892, and the next year Doyle decided to end the detective's life in *The Final Problem*. The resulting protest included thousands of angry letters to Doyle and the magazine, and he eventually complied with public demand and resurrected the detective.

With *The Hound of the Baskervilles* (1901), set before Holmes's death, Doyle reintroduced the detective. The popular story focuses on his investigation of a mysterious, apparently supernatural hound implicated in the deaths of Sir Charles Baskerville and his family. Not until the series of thirteen stories in *The Return of Sherlock Holmes* (1905) did Doyle resurrect Holmes from the dead. Stories about Holmes, which appeared in collections such as *His Last Bow* (1917), continued to appear until 1927.

In the meantime, Doyle's other fiction also began to draw a large audience. *Micah Clarke* (1888) is set in seventeenth-century Scotland during the time of the Monmouth Rebellion and is one of his many historical novels. The story's hero, Micah Clarke, embodies Doyle's ideal of a good individual. Clarke shuns dogmatic church doctrines—as Doyle had by this time—and is moral, courageous, and intelligent. The hero of *The White Company* (1890), Alleyne Edricson, is a similar character; he has been raised in a monastery and is at first reluctant to leave its shelter, but his father's will forces him to spend a year in the world. He opens himself up to broader experiences in a series of adventures, eventually coming to see ordinary human life as more worthwhile than "holy" seclusion.

All Doyle's historical novels, which also include *The Refugees* (1891), *Rodney Stone* (1896), and *Sir Nigel* (1906), are filled with adventure and also carry strong moral messages. He experimented with a variety of other genres, such as the scientific romance *The Lost World* (1912), the play *A Story of Waterloo* (1894), and the verses collected in *The Tragedy of the Korosko* (1897).

Doyle's dislike of the clergy and organized religion, particularly the Catholic Church, is evident in works such as *Micah Clarke* and *The White Company*, in which the clergy are often portrayed as self-serving hypocrites. A fictional series of letters to a Catholic friend, the character of J. Stark Munro in *The Stark Munro Letters* (1894), expresses Doyle's own reasons for rejecting the Catholicism of his upbringing. After the death of his son in World War I, Doyle became increasingly and publicly devoted to spiritualism. Among his writings on this subject is his two-volume *History of Spiritualism* (1926).

Around the turn of the century, Doyle was heavily involved in the Boer War in South Africa, serving as a physician at Bloemfontein Field Hospital. His *The Great Boer War* (1900) and *The War in South Africa: Its Causes and Its Conduct* (1902) address issues associated with the war. Doyle was knighted for his service in 1902.

Among Doyle's other works are his six-volume *History of the British Campaign in France and Flanders* (1916–1920), the autobiography *Memories and Adventures* (1924), and the novels *A Duet: With Occasional Chorus* (1898) and *The Firm of Girdlestone* (1890). He also lectured widely and did a bit of detective work himself, collecting evidence and launching publicity campaigns that eventually freed two men wrongly convicted of crimes.

BIBLIOGRAPHY

Cox, Don Richard, *Arthur Conan Doyle*, 1985; Jaffe, Jacqueline A., *Arthur Conan Doyle*, 1987; Pearson, Hesketh, *Conan Doyle*, 1974.

Du Maurier, Daphne

(May 13, 1907–April 19, 1989)
Novelist, Playwright, Short-Story Writer

Most famous for her novel *Rebecca* (1938), Daphne du Maurier reintroduced the genre of the gothic romance to English literature in the World War II era. Alfred Hitchcock directed several successful screen adaptations of her mystery-shrouded stories. Du Maurier's interest in British history also inspired a number of historical novels.

Du Maurier was the daughter of the actor and manager Sir Gerald du Maurier, born in London. She deeply admired her father, the primary influence in her younger life. Her grandfather, George du Maurier, was also a novelist. In 1916, she entered a day school in Oak Hill Park, and the following year she began her studies with a tutor at home. She attended finishing school at Camposena outside of Paris for six months beginning in 1923. Du Maurier read a lot of French and English literature and cited Guy de Maupassant (1850–1893) and KATHERINE MANSFIELD as authors she admired. She began writing short stories in the 1920s but grew disappointed with her early efforts.

When she finished school, du Maurier lived a somewhat adventuresome life filled with traveling and boating. In 1932 she married Leiutenant Colonel Frederick Arthur Montague Browning, whose military career forced them to move often, much to her dismay. Du Maurier's real love was the Cornwall coast, the setting of many of her novels. Her first novel, *The Loving Spirit*, was published in 1931, followed by *I'll Never Be Young Again* (1932) and *The Progress of Julius* (1933).

Jamaica Inn (1936), the film version of which Hitchcock directed in 1939, is a gothic romance inspired by her visit to a hostelry of the same name. From the outset, du Maurier creates a mysterious, brooding atmosphere. The main character, the 23-year-old Mary Yellan, is one of the numerous strong female figures that inhabit the pages of du Maurier's fiction.

Following the death of her mother, Mary goes to stay with her aunt Patience and her uncle Joss, who run the Jamaica Inn. She finds Patience weary and broken, while the larger-than-life Joss seems to be evil incarnate. It soon emerges that Joss is a "wrecker" who puts false lights on the coastline to cause shipwrecks, and then loots the wrecks. Behind this scheme is Frances Davey, a mysterious and malevolent vicar, who orders the murders of Patience and Joss. Mary emerges from the adventure that follows a much stronger woman than when she came to the inn, and she is now ready to marry Jem, her uncle's brother.

The film version of *Rebecca* (1938), which Hitchcock transformed for the screen in 1940, starred LAURENCE OLIVIER and Joan Fontaine and earned an Academy Award for Best Picture. Stage versions were also produced in London and New York. As in *Jamaica Inn*, the opening pages of *Rebecca* immediately reveal a dark and mysterious atmosphere. The action of the story takes place on the estate Manderley, where the Rebecca of the title was the first wife of the mysterious Maxim DeWinter. Rebecca's memory haunts the house, now inhabited by DeWinter, his innocent and timid second wife (who narrates the story), and the wicked housekeeper Mrs. Danvers. Like Mary Yellan, the second Mrs. DeWinter comes through the strife and emerges victorious as a stronger woman. Du Maurier published a sequel to Rebecca, *Mrs. DeWinter*, in 1971.

Du Maurier's works often explore individual psychological obsessions within a mysterious setting. Her belief in living for the present and her rejection of religious sentiment also inform her stories. Her love of history, particularly that of the British Isles, frames the narratives of several novels such as *Hungry Hill* (1943; filmed in 1947), *The King's General* (1946), and *Mary Anne* (1954), set during the madness of George III. *The King's General* tells the story of the romance between Sir Richard Grenville, a naval hero of the time of Queen Elizabeth I, and the beautiful Honor Harris. The du Maurier family history, which she

researched extensively, inspired her novel *The Glass Blowers* (1963). *Rule Brittania* (1972), set in a fictional near future when Britain has withdrawn from the Common Market and decided to form a union with the United States, reflects du Maurier's fundamental dislike of American culture.

My Cousin Rachel (1951), another of du Maurier's successful novels, was filmed in 1952, with RICHARD BURTON and Olivia de Havilland playing the leads. A tone of mystery again dominates the story, set in Cornwall and narrated by Philip Ashley. Ashley, who has grown up distrustful of women thanks to his cousin and guardian Ambrose, receives a desperate letter from him. Ambrose begs him to come before his mysterious and domineering wife, Rachel, does him in. Ashley arrives to find Ambrose dead and is given unsatisfactory explanations of his death. He seeks out Rebecca, who eventually comes to his home and seduces him. Throughout the narrative, du Maurier teases the reader with hints of Rebecca's involvement in Ambrose's murder, but Rebecca dies in an accident and leaves the mystery unsolved.

Du Maurier also wrote plays, short stories, the travel books *Vanishing Cornwall* (1967) and *Enchanted Cornwall* (1989), and the autobiography *Growing Pains* (1977). The drama *The Years Between* was staged in Manchester in 1944 and in London the following year. Her short-story collections include *The Apple Tree* (1952; published in the United States as *Kiss Me Again, Stranger*), *The Breaking Point* (1959), *Not After Midnight* (1971; American title *Don't Look Now*), and *The Rendezvous and Other Stories* (1981). *Gerald: A Portrait* (1934) and *The du Mau-*

riers (1937) are among the works she wrote on her family.

Du Maurier's other novels include *Frenchman's Creek* (1941), *The Parasites* (1949), *The Scapegoat* (1957), *The Infernal World of Branwell Bronte* (1960), *The House on the Strand* (1969), *Golden Lads* (1975), and *The Winding Stair* (1976). She became a Fellow of the Royal Society of Literature in 1952 and was made Dame Commander in the Order of the British Empire in 1969.

BIBLIOGRAPHY

Cook, Judith, *Daphne: A Portrait of Daphne Du Maurier*, 1992; Forster, Margaret, *Daphne du Maurier*, 1993; Kelly, Richard, *Daphne du Maurier*, 1987; Shallcross, Martin, *The Private World of Daphne du Maurier*, 1991.

Dubuffet, Jean

(July 31, 1901–May 12, 1985)
Painter, Sculptor, Graphic Artist, Illustrator

Jean-Philippe-Arthur Dubuffet (as he was christened) is primarily remembered for his development of *art brut*, or "raw art," a violent, brutal style into which he assimilated the art of the mentally ill, primitive cultures, and children. In the 1960s Dubuffet began creating a series of puzzle-like pictures constructed of interlocking areas. Dubuffet was among the few French artists to impact modern art after the World War II era.

Dubuffet was born in Le Havre, France. His father was a wine merchant. He studied art at the Ecole des Beaux-Arts in Le Havre beginning in 1916, and two years later went to the Académie Julien in Paris. For a short period of time, Dubuffet involved himself with the latest developments in the Paris art world, befriending such figures as RAOUL DUFY. From 1920 to 1924 he immersed himself in philosophy, literature, painting, and music, and he was also interested in the work of the Dadaists.

In 1923 Dubuffet acquired a copy of a book by Dr. Hans Prinzhorn, in which the author asserted that the art of the mentally ill deserved attention as serious art. Dubuffet became fascinated with the art of the mentally ill as well as art produced by children and primitive cultures. These three influences were to shape his body of work, but not for another two decades.

The following year Dubuffet abandoned painting altogether and took over his father's wine business. Six years later he founded his own wine business and continued in that trade until 1934. He then turned to painting again for three years, but only decided to devote himself permanently to art in 1942.

Dubuffet held his first one-man show at the Galerie René Drouin in 1944. Three years later he held a one-man show in New York, and the same year he began holding the first *art brut* exhibitions, the first of which took place at the Galerie René Drouin. The following year he founded La Compagnie de l'Art Brut, and in 1949 he wrote *L'Art Brut préféré aux arts culturels.*

Dubuffet's *art brut* assimilated the influences of the art of the insane and children's art. Primitive human figures populate his paintings, lithographs, and drawings. These include male and female nudes (such as the *Large Charcoal Nude* of 1944) as well as people in everyday situations, as in the 1943 series of gouaches entitled *Métro (Subway)*. In his paintings, Dubuffet created thick, rough surface textures formed by mixing a variety of materials, including ashes, sand, and tar.

In the 1960s he turned to creating puzzle-like compositions with interlocking striped or colored areas. Among these are *La gigue irlandaise* (1961; *Irish Jig*) and *Nunc Stans* (1965) as well as the *Hourloupe* series begun in 1962. In some of the works, the interlocking pieces cover the whole canvas, sometimes obscuring faces hidden among them. In others, barely recognizable figures themselves are formed of interlocking areas, as in the large work *Coucou Bazar (Le Bal de l'Hourloupe)* [1972–1973; *Coucou Bazaar (The Hourloupe Ball)*]. Dubuffet also applied these concepts to three-dimensional sculptures formed of epoxy and styrofoam.

Among Dubuffet's other works are a series of *praticables* for theater and a series of *costumes de théâtre* (both 1971); the *Group of Four Trees* at Chase Manhattan Plaza in New York (1972); and illustrations for books. In his later career, Dubuffet designed a series of large sculptures of black-and-white-painted fiberglass.

BIBLIOGRAPHY

David and Aldfred Smart Gallery, *Jean Dubuffet: Forty Years of His Art*, 1984; Messer, Thomas M., et al., *Jean Dubuffet: A Retrospective*, 1973.

Duchamp, Marcel

(July 28, 1887–October 2, 1968)
Painter, Sculptor, Actor, Director

A major force in nonobjective art in the twentieth century, the French-born painter and sculptor Henri-Robert-Marcel Duchamp created "readymades," or everyday objects exhibited as sculpture, a series of motorized works in glass, and his major sculpture, *The Bride Stripped Bare By Her Bachelors.* His work strongly influenced the development of conceptual art and pop art in the United States, and he is credited with introducing Dadaism and Surrealism to American audiences. Duchamp also painted, although he did little in that medium after 1913, and worked in film.

Duchamp was born in Blainville, France. His father was a notary, and his grandfather was an engraver. The youngest of three brothers (see JACQUES VILLON and RAYMOND DUCHAMP-VILLON) and a sister who all became artists, Duchamp attended the École Bossuet in Rouen and graduated in 1904. From a young age he demonstrated an ability to draw, and at 15 he painted his first known work, *Landscape at Blainville* (1902), in an impressionistic style. In 1904 he moved to Paris and entered the Académie Julien, where his two brothers also studied. The following year he began contributing comic cartoons to the magazines *Courrier Français* and *Le Rire*.

The next several years were ones of experimentation for Duchamp. The influences of Impressionism, Postimpressionism, Paul Cézanne (1839–1906), Fauvism (see HENRI MATISSE), Cubism (see PABLO PICASSO and GEORGES BRAQUE), and Italian Futurism (see F. T. MARINETTI and UMBERTO BOCCIONI) all successively appeared in his painting. His first exhibition at the Salon des Indépendants came in 1909.

Two years later he painted, in a manner that combines Cubism and Futurism, the first version of his *Nude Descending a Staircase*, based on a text by the Symbolist poet Jules Laforgue. The subsequent version of the painting, which depicts a nude female figure in successive phases of motion, earned universal disdain when it was exhibited at the Salon des Indépendants in Paris in 1912 and attracted a great deal of attention at the Armory Show in New York in 1913, the first major exhibition of modern art in the United States.

Around 1912 Duchamp, under the influence of friends who included the Symbolist poet Guillaume Apollinaire (1880–1918) and the French avant-garde artist Francis Picabia (1879–1953), abandoned representational art altogether. He ceased painting in 1913 and took a job as a library clerk at the Bibliothèque Sainte-Geneviève. He began to construct sculptures of everyday objects. *Bicycle Wheel*

(1913) was the first of these sculptures, which he called "readymades"; it consisted of a bicycle wheel mounted upside down on a wine rack. Others include *In Advance of the Broken Arm* (1917), a snow shovel; and a urinal exhibited as *Fountain* (1917).

Having moved to New York in 1915, Duchamp began work on his *The Bride Stripped Bare by Her Bachelors* (1915–1923; also known as *The Large Glass*), widely considered his masterpiece. The work consists of a large object made of various materials—lead, paint, and metal—as well as a collection of notations. The latter were published in 1934 as *Boite Verte (Green Box)*. *Tu M'*, Duchamp's final painting, was exhibited in 1918 and combined painting with everyday objects.

He returned to Paris in 1919 and the following year exhibited *L.H.O.O.Q.* (1919), a reproduction of the *Mona Lisa* on which he drew a moustache and a goatee. Over the next two decades Duchamp loosely associated himself with the Dadaists and the Surrealists. In 1920 he began, with *Rotary Glass Plate (Precision Optics)*, a series of mobile glass constructions entitled *Precision Optics*. The same year he adopted the pseudonym Rrose Sélavy.

Duchamp worked in film as well. He appeared in RENÉ CLAIR's film *Entr'acte* in 1924 and made, with Man Ray, the short film *Anemic Cinema* two years later. While working in art and film Duchamp devoted much of his time to playing chess and was one time chess champion of Haute-Normandie.

Duchamp returned to New York in 1942 and became a U.S. citizen in 1955. During the last years of his life he worked on a massive piece entitled *Étant donnés:*

1. la chute d'eau. 2. le gaz d'éclairage (*Given: 1. the waterfall. 2. the illuminating gas,* 1946–1966), now held at the Philadelphia Museum of Art, consisting of a leather female figure lying on a bed of leaves near a waterfall. Walter Arensberg, a friend of Duchamp since 1915, donated a large collection of the artist's work to the Philadelphia Museum of Art when the artist died in 1954. Duchamp's use of everyday objects in his artwork influenced the pop art movement in the 1950s and 1960s, which borrowed imagery from pop culture. Duchamp's work also significantly influenced the conceptual art movement of the 1960s, in which the concept of an artwork is more important than the actual work.

BIBLIOGRAPHY

Hopkins, David, *Marcel Duchamp and Max Ernst: The Bride Shared*, 1998; Hulton, Pontus, ed., *Marcel Duchamp: Work and Life*, 1993; Masheck, Joseph, *Marcel Duchamp in Perspective*, 1974; Schwarz, Arturo, *The Complete Works of Marcel Duchamp*, 1969; Tomkins, Calvin, *Duchamp: A Biography*, 1996.

Duchamp-Villon, Raymond

(November 5, 1876–October 7, 1918)
Sculptor

Before his premature death, Raymond Duchamp-Villon was among the earliest sculptors to work in the Cubist style. Although he had only a few years to develop his style, he influenced a succeeding generation of abstract sculptors.

Duchamp-Villon was born Raymond Duchamp in Damville, near Evreux, France. His father was a notary, and he was the half-brother of the painter JACQUES VILLON and the brother of the sculptor MARCEL DUCHAMP. After studying medicine, he decided to pursue sculpture as a career around the turn of the century. His early works were influenced by the naturalistic style of the French sculptor Auguste Rodin (1840–1917), who sought to portray the inner state of his subjects.

Works such as the terra cotta *Le torse de jeune homme* (*Torso of a Young Man*, 1910; also titled *The Athlete*), which depicts the athletic torso of a male figure, show Rodin's influence in their representational portrayals of the subject. Duchamp-Villon executed portrait sculptures in this manner as well, such as his head of the Symbolist poet *Baudelaire* (1911).

Like his brothers, Duchamp-Villon fell under the influence of Cubism as it developed under PABLO PICASSO and GEORGES BRAQUE. Pursuing a more abstract and simplified style than in his earlier work, he executed such sculptures as *Maggy* (1911) and *The Seated Woman* (1914). *Le cheval majeur* (*Large Horse*, 1914), an abstract, half-animal, half-machine creation based on geometric shapes, is widely considered his masterpiece. Duchamp-Villon's career was cut short by his death from exposure to poison gas in World War I.

BIBLIOGRAPHY

Cabanne, Pierre, *The Brothers Duchamp: Jacques Villon, Raymond Duchamp-Villon, Marcel Duchamp*, 1976.

Dufy, Raoul

(June 3, 1877–March 23, 1953)
Painter, Ceramicist, Graphic Artist, Designer

The Impressionists and Postimpressionists were the first influences on the French painter Raoul Dufy. Dufy was then influenced by the Fauves and the Cubists before he evolved his personal style, in which his typical outdoor scenes convey motion, activity, and light through simple, sensuous forms and bright color.

Dufy was born into a poor family in Le Havre, France. Like his fellow Fauve MAURICE DE VLAMINCK, he came from a family of musicians. His brother, Jean Dufy, was also a painter. With eight siblings and parents with little money, Dufy had to work at the expense of some of his schooling. He did, however, study art at the École Municipale des Beaux-Arts du Havre, where he met the future Cubist GEORGES BRAQUE and cubist painter Émile-Othon Friesz. In 1900 he went to the École des Beaux-Arts in Paris.

Dufy was not terribly attracted to the formal study of art. He developed an interest in the Impressionists and Postimpressionists, both of which influenced early works such as his *Self Portrait* (1898). The treatment of line in Japanese prints also shaped his work. Dufy began to exhibit his work in Paris, first at the Salon des Artistes Français in 1901 and then at the avant-garde Salon des Indépendants.

By 1904, Dufy was painting with the Fauves, whose bold compositions employed vibrant colors designed to make a strong visual impact. His work appeared in the famous 1905 exhibition at the Salon d'Automne with paintings by HENRI MATISSE, ANDRÉ DERAIN, Maurice de Vlaminck, and Braque. Like the rest of the Fauves, Dufy soon abandoned the style and developed his own. He spent the year 1906 in Normandy with the painter Albert Marquet, another Fauve, producing such works as *Old Houses at Hornfleur* (1906) that reveal the subject matter he was to treat for the rest of his life—scenes that reveal the dynamic movement associated with human activity. His colors, always vibrant, were nonetheless more subdued than those in the works from his Fauvist period.

In 1907, Dufy worked with Braque in Provence. Braque's evolution toward Cubism briefly affected Dufy's style, evident in the angular forms of such works as *Homage to Mozart* (1915). Dufy's forms grew increasingly simple and flowing, as his paintings placed more emphasis on

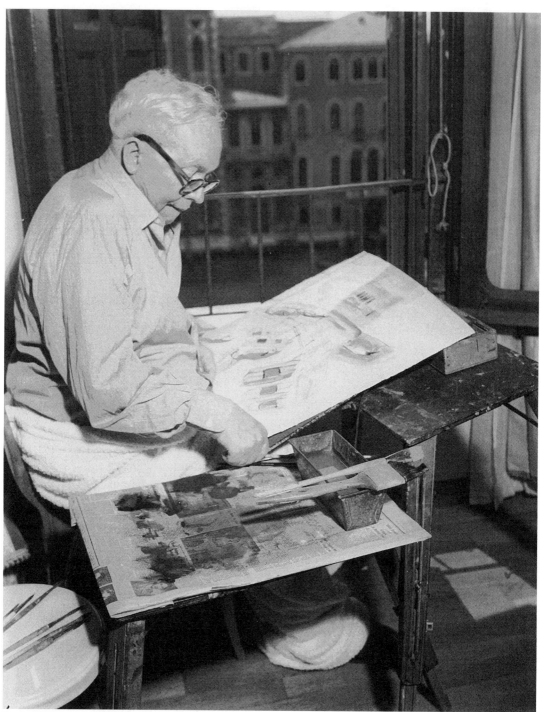

Raoul Dufy (Gamma)

the vibrant motion, color, and light of his subject matter.

Popular subjects in his work were regattas (*Henley Regatta*, 1934, and *Deauville Regatta*, 1936), circuses, city scenes from London and Paris, farming scenes (*The Threshing Machine*, 1946), and major events (*The Coronation of King George VI*, 1937). Particularly in his later years, Dufy often painted musical instruments, operas, and orchestras, for example, *Orchestra* (1942), *The Double-Bass Players* (1946), *The Pink Violin* (1948), and *Homage to Bach* (1952). His nudes include many standing nudes and reclining nudes.

Dufy did not confine himself exclusively to painting canvases. He worked on a series of murals for the Palais de Chaillot in Paris. His fabrics, used by the fashion designer Paul Poirot, were worn in fashionable Parisian society. Dufy also executed woodcuts and ceramics. An edition of Guillame Apollinaire's *Le bestiaire* with his illustrations appeared in 1911.

BIBLIOGRAPHY

Brion, Marcel, *Raoul Dufy: Paintings and Watercolours*, 1958; Lancaster, Jan, *Raoul Dufy*, 1983; Perez-Tibi, Dora, *Dufy*, 1989.

Durrell, Lawrence

(February 27, 1912–November 7, 1990)
Novelist, Poet, Playwright, Short-Story Writer

Lawrence George Durrell is best known for his fictional tetralogy set in Alexandria, Egypt, *The Alexandria Quartet*, published between 1957 and 1960. His literary output, which also includes poetry, short stories, plays, and travel books, was shaped by the many places in which he lived and, more basically, by his interest in a deeper reality, the Heraldic Reality, as he called it.

Durrell was of Irish and English ancestry, born in Jullundur, India, where he lived until he was 11. The Indian background of his early childhood played a significant role in his development, and in his adulthood he retained an interest in Eastern thought and liked to think he had a Tibetan mentality. At the age of 11, Durrell's parents sent him to school in

England. After attending a series of preparatory schools, he repeatedly failed his entrance examinations for the university and never went on with formal study.

England made a negative impression on Durrell, and he was to live there only briefly during his life. In 1936 he moved with his family and his first wife, Nancy Myers, to the Greek island of Corfu. During the time he lived there he became a friend of the Nobel-Prize-winning author GEORGE SEFERIS and taught at the British Institute in Athens.

His first novel, *Pied Piper of Lovers*, was published in 1935. The same year, he read the American writer Henry Miller's *Tropic of Cancer* and wrote a letter to the author, inaugurating a forty-five-year friendship and correspondence between the two men. With the intention of marketing the book to the public, Durrell published *Panic Spring* in 1937 under the pseudonym Charles Norden. His more serious work *The Black Book* was published in Paris the following year.

With the approach of the German army, Durrell fled Greece with his wife and daughter in 1941 and settled in Cairo. The couple separated the following year, and Durrell moved to Alexandria, where he worked as a press attaché in the British Information Office. Alexandria provided the setting for his popular tetralogy of novels, *The Alexandria Quartet*, and his second wife, Eve Cohen, whom he met in Egypt, served as the model for Justine in the first volume.

Durrell returned to Greece, settling on the island of Rhodes, in 1945 and worked as a public relations director. In 1947 and 1948, he served as director of the British Council Institute during an unpleasant stay in Cordoba, Argentina. During that year he wrote *A Key to Modern British Poetry* (1948), and his novel *White Eagles Over Serbia* appeared in 1949. From that year until 1952, he lived in Belgrade, Yugoslavia, and again worked as a press attaché.

In 1952, Durrell moved to Cyprus, taught English literature, and worked as a public relations officer. The political situation there grew unstable as tensions mounted among the British and Cypriot Greeks and Turks. The turmoil placed Durrell in danger, and in 1956 he moved to Dorset, England. His experiences in Cyprus form the substance of his travel book *Bitter Lemons* (1957). He married Claude-Marie Vincendon in 1961.

Justine, the first volume of *The Alexandria Quartet*, was published in 1957, the year Durrell settled in the south of France. There he continued work on the subsequent volumes, *Balthazar* (1958), *Mountolive* (1958), and *Clea* (1960). The best-selling tetralogy earned praise from critics and the public. The series is narrated from multiple perspectives, with the most significant voice being that of the middle-aged, Anglo-Irish schoolteacher L. G. Darley. Darley is recovering from an affair with Justine Hosnani, and he is assisted in understanding the things that have befallen him by the doctor-mystic Balthazar. *Mountolive* deviates from Darley's story and uses third person narration, but Darley returns to the narrator's spot in *Clea* and tells of his love for the painter Clea Montis.

In his fiction, Durrell presents subjective pictures of people and events, entering into the souls of his characters as they search for deeper meaning in their lives. Durrell himself saw deeper meaning as to be found in a fusion of Western physics (particularly the theories of Albert Einstein) with Eastern metaphysics. He believed in the existence of a realm of higher consciousness toward which one should strive, which he called the Heraldic Reality. Durrell investigated various mystic traditions that seemed to offer paths to that reality, including the Cabbala (the tradition of Jewish mysticism), Eastern mysticism, and the tarot.

His novels are subjective both in substance and in structure; subjectivity of structure is particularly evident in *The Avignon Quintet*, in which he purposely confuses the division between fiction and reality. The series consists of *Monsieur; or, The Prince of Darkness* (1974), *Livia; or, Buried Alive* (1978), *Constance; or, Solitary Practices* (1982), *Sebastian; or, Ruling Passions* (1983), and *Quinx; or, The Ripper's Tale* (1985). Critics were less enthusiastic about *The Avignon Quintet* than *The Alexandria Quartet*. Durrell published a third multivolume novel, *The Revolt of Aphrodite*, consisting of *Tunc* (1968) and *Nunquam* (1970).

Durrell's varied living situations provided the material for a number of critically acclaimed travel books, often considered equal to his fiction. In addition to Cyprus in *Bitter Lemons*, Durrell treated two other Greek islands in *Prospero's Cell* (1945) and *Reflections on a Marine Venus* (1953). His final book, *Caesar's Vast Ghost: Aspects of Provence* (1990), describes the landscape and culture of Provence in the south of France.

Among Durrell's other works are the volumes of poetry *A Private Country* (1943), *Cities, Plains and People* (1946), *The Tree of Idleness* (1953), *The Ikons* (1966), and *Collected Poems 1931–74* (1980); the plays *Sappho* (1961), *Acte* (1961), and *An Irish Faustus* (1964); *Antrobus Complete* (1985), a series of humorous sketches inspired by his work in the Civil Service; and paintings under the pseudonym Oscar Epfs.

BIBLIOGRAPHY

Bowker, Gordon, *Through the Dark Labyrinth: A Biography of Lawrence Durrell*, 1997; Kaczvisnky, Donald P., *Lawrence Durrell's Major Novels, or, The Kingdom of the Imagination*, 1997; Pine, Richard, *Lawrence Durrell: The Mindscape*, 1994; Weigel, John A., *Lawrence Durrell*, rev. ed., 1989.

Dürrenmatt, Friedrich

(January 5, 1921–December 14, 1990)
Playwright, Short-Story Writer, Essayist

Influenced by experimental stylists such as BERTOLT BRECHT, the German-language playwright Friedrich Dürrenmatt emerged as one of the most prominent figures in post–World War II German theater. His plays, which include *The Visit* and *The Physicist*, convey a sense of the absurdity and futility of ordinary human endeavor, yet the possibility of achieving authenticity, even in defeat. Dürrenmatt's work has been widely translated and is frequently performed around the world.

Dürrenmatt was the son of a Protestant minister, born in Konolfingen, near Bern, Switzerland. He attended a local school before his family moved to Bern, where he studied at the gymnasium. At the universities of Zurich and Bern, Dürrenmatt studied philosophy and literature, also developing an interest in painting. He married Lotti Geissler in 1947.

Dürrenmatt began his career as a writer with the publication of his first short story, "The Old Man," in Bern in 1947. Over the next several years, his stories continued to appear in Swiss and German periodicals. Among them were several detective stories, including "The Judge and His Executioner" and "The Suspicion," both published serially in the early 1950s. He contributed theater criticism to *Die Weltwoche* in Zurich in 1951–1952. A number of his stories were collected and published as *The City* (1952).

Es steht geschrieben (*It Is Written*), Dürrenmatt's first play, premiered in Zurich in 1947 and was published the same year in an edition he illustrated. The story, set during the siege of Münster in 1534–1536, a conflict that ended in the suppression of the radical Protestants by the Roman Catholic authorities, reflects Dürrenmatt's cynical attitude toward religion. The story incorporates several parodies of historical participants and in part concerns a power struggle between the literalist-religionist Knipperdollinck and the sensualist Bockelson. *Der Blinde* (*The Blind Man*) followed in 1948.

Romulus der Grosse (1949; *Romulus the Great*) proved to be Dürrenmatt's first success in the theater and typifies the tragicomic style of his mature works. The hero is Romulus, the last emperor of the crumbling Roman Empire, usually called Romulus Augustulus, or Romulus the little Augustus, so ineffectual was he believed to be. In the playwright's portrayal, Romulus has genius, although it does not emerge until well into the drama. His greatness lies in his recognition of the emptiness of the empire, the end of which he makes every effort to hasten.

In his early plays, Dürrenmatt borrowed stylistic elements from Brecht, who employed various devices to break the usual connection between the actors and the audience. Broken chronology, interruptions, chaotic atmosphere, and actors who step out of their roles to speak to the audience recur frequently in Dürrenmatt's work, making the audience remember that what they are seeing is not real, and think about its message. Human attempts to control fate or establish ideal societies, whether religious or political, are portrayed as futile.

Die Ehe des Herrn Mississippi (1952; *The Marriage of Mr. Mississippi*, produced in New York as *Fools Are Passing Through* in 1958) brought Dürrenmatt his first real success abroad. The play opens with the final scene in chronological time, three men shooting another. In the action that follows, the three men each represent an idealist of a different philosophical leaning. The devious Anastasia leads all to their downfalls. *An Angel Comes to Babylon* was produced in Munich in 1953.

In *Der Besuch der alten Dame* (1956; *The Visit*), Dürrenmatt painted a grim picture of greed, mob mentality, and the destruction of a community. The impoverished prostitute-turned-multimillionaire Claire Zachanassian returns to Güllen, a now economically depressed city from which she was driven years before. The town's citizens hope to secure a sizable donation from her with the assistance of her former lover, Alfred Ill, whose corruption had led to her earlier disgrace. Instead, Claire agrees to give a billion dollars, but only if the townspeople will kill Ill. Outraged at first, they slowly warm to the idea as the economic situation worsens, rationalizing their crime as punishment for the no-good Ill. The city's moral demise is complete when the townspeople carry out the act, but Ill himself achieves a certain redemption by the way he accepts his doom.

Along with *The Visit*, many critics consider *Die Physiker* (1962; *The Physicist*) Dürrenmatt's best play. Framed in a more conventional structure than most of his plays, it relates his skepticism over the role of rapidly advancing science and shows an individual powerless to stop impending disaster. The central character, Möbius, is faking madness to prevent the spread of a potentially destructive discovery he has made. Two other insane scientists are spies for rival powers of the East and West, who want access to Möbius's discovery. In the end, it is their unscrupulous psychiatrist who obtains the damaging secrets, leaving them confined to the sanatorium and the world destined for disaster.

Der Meteor (1966; *The Meteor*), a two-act play, caused an uproar at its Zurich premiere. The protagonist is a nihilistic Nobel Prize winner who actively seeks death and in the process ruins everyone in his path. At the end of the play, he has not been able to die. Dürrenmatt's other plays include *Frank V* (1959); *Hercules and the Augean Stables* (1962), originally written as a radio play in 1954; and *Porträt eines Planeten* (1970; *Portrait of a Planet*).

Among his other works are *Theaterprobleme* (1955; *Problems of the Theatre*) and a number of radio plays—*The Double* (1946); *The Case of the Donkey's Shadow* (1951); *Stranitzky and the National Hero* (1952); *Nocturnal Conversation With a Despised Person* (1952); *Operation Vega* (1954); and *Traps* (1956).

BIBLIOGRAPHY

Chick, Edson M., *Dances of Death: Wedekind, Brecht, Dürrenmatt, and the Satiric Tradition*, 1984; Peppard, Murray B., *Friedrich Dürrenmatt*, 1969; Tiusanen, Timo, *Dürrenmatt: A Study in Plays, Prose, Theory*, 1977; Urs, Jenny, *Dürrenmatt: A Study of His Plays*, 1981; Whitton, Kenneth S., *Dürrenmatt: Reinterpretation in Retrospect*, 1990.

Eco, Umberto

(January 5, 1932–)
Novelist, Essayist, Critic, Scholar, Teacher, Writer of Children's Books

A professor of the obscure discipline of semiotics (the study of signs and symbols), Umberto Eco was little known outside of Italy until the 1980 publication of his blockbuster novel *The Name of the Rose*. Although sometimes criticized for their obscure language and overly complex plots, his three novels to date have sold millions of copies world wide.

Eco was born in Alessandria, Italy. As a youth he was precocious; he enjoyed drawing cartoons and making parodies and games. He studied at the Liceo Plana and later at the University of Turin, where he received his Ph.D. in 1954. At Turin he studied under the aesthetics theorist Luigi Pareyson, and Eco devoted his earliest intellectual endeavors to aesthetics. Early in his career Eco saw himself as a Catholic intellectual and wrote regularly for the publication of the Gioventù Italiana di Azione, a Catholic youth organization. Eco and his colleagues sought to move away from the conservative policies of Pope Pius XII and to counteract his influence on the Church. He also worked for Italian Radio-Television.

Having written his thesis on the aesthetics of St. Thomas Aquinas, he continued to explore the subject of aesthetics in *Opera aperta* (1962; *The Open Work*).

Umberto Eco (Gamma)

Eco examined modern music, poetry, and literature, arguing that the works leave themselves open to multiple interpretations. He later imposed boundaries on this idea in *The Limits of Interpretation* (1990), in which he decries the explosion of nonsensical interpretations.

Eco made his mark as a semiotician, or student of signs and symbols, with *A Theory of Semiotics* (1976) and *Semiotics and the Philosophy of Language* (1984), both originally written in English. His real fame, however, came with the publication of his first novel *Il nome della rosa* (1980; *The Name of the Rose*). Ostensibly a murder mystery set in a medieval Italian monastery, the novel probes commonly accepted notions of truth.

The story centers on the middle-aged English monk William of Baskerville, who arrives at the monastery in 1327. Seven murders occur in seven days, leaving Baskerville to pore through manuscripts, signs, and symbols to solve the mystery. Eco's Baskerville is a modern monk who believes in the power of reason, leading him into conflict with the rest of the establishment. In spite of its difficulty and complexity, *The Name of the Rose* proved an international hit and was the basis of a successful film.

Eco took the title of his next novel, *Foucault's Pendulum* (1988), from inventor of the pendulum Leon Foucault (1819–1868). Many have pointed out possible links to the French philosopher Michel Foucault (1926–1984), although Eco has denied the connection. The bulk of the story concerns three editors in a Milan publishing house who, with their boss's approval, decide to publish the works of previously rejected authors who have ideas on the mysteries of the universe. Overwhelmed with strange theories, they begin to compile the ideas into a master plan that will explain life's mysteries conclusively. With the work Eco wove together hundreds of conspiracy theories and occult beliefs that he had researched in more than 1,000 volumes.

L'isola del giorno prima (1995; *The Island of the Day Before*), Eco's most recent novel, features the adventurer-protagonist Roberto de la Griva in a complex narrative that weaves back and forth in time. Griva has embarked on a search for the Island of Solomon, believed to be on the hundred and eightieth meridian. He is shipwrecked on the *Daphne* and never reaches the island, but he begins to write his own narrative of his past.

Eco's essays have appeared in numerous volumes. *Apocalypse Postponed* (1968) is a collection of writings on mass media and culture. *Misreadings* consists of fifteen critical and satirical essays that explore imagined scenarios, such as Dan Rather and other modern media figures covering Columbus's arrival in America and modern publishing companies refusing to publish great works such as the Bible. The five essays in *Serendipities: Language and Lunacy* (1988) concern the use and power of language. *Six Walks in the Fictional Woods*, an analysis of the creation of fiction, was published in 1994.

Eco has also written children's books, among which are *The Bomb and the General*, a story about a general who constructs an atomic bomb, only to find that his atoms prefer to live peaceably; and *The Three Astronauts*, which relates the story of three astronauts from different countries who land on Mars. Aside from his writing career, Eco has lectured and taught at numerous universities in Italy.

BIBLIOGRAPHY

Bondanella, Peter, *Umberto Eco and the Open Text*, 1997.

Eisenstein, Sergey

(January 23, 1898–February 11, 1948)
Director, Theorist, Essayist

Perhaps the most influential figure in twentieth-century cinema, the Soviet film director Sergey Mikhaylovich Eisenstein was the most important early technical innovator in film, particularly in his pioneering experiments with visual sequences he termed "the montage of film attractions." A prolific theorist as well, he established the centrality of the director to the production, a tenet that lay at the heart of later movements in film, such as Neorealism and the French New Wave. His best-known films include *The Battleship Potemkin*, *Alexander Nevsky* and the two-part *Ivan the Terrible*.

Eisenstein was born in Riga, Latvia, into a middle class family. His father was of German Jewish ancestry and a stern figure; his mother came from a middle-class Russian family. Eisenstein was a well-behaved and well-educated child—fluent in four languages at the age of 10 and an avid reader. He was exposed to film at a young age. During a trip to Paris with his family in 1907 he saw his first film, Georges Mélèis's *Les 400 farces du diable* (*400 Jokes of the Devil*). The potent visual impact of the film left an imprint on the young child's mind—particularly a scene depicting the skeleton of a horse pulling a carriage. Eisenstein's home life was unpleasant on account of the frequent violent arguments between his parents. His family moved to St. Petersburg in 1910, and soon afterward his mother abandoned the family. After following in his father's footsteps by studying at the Petrograd Institute of Civil Engineering, Eisenstein studied at the School of Fine Arts.

Eisenstein supported the Bolsheviks in the 1917 revolution and joined the Red Army. In addition to his military duties, he organized a theatrical group to entertain soldiers. In 1920 he became a designer at the Proletkult Theater in Moscow. After having studied at the State School for Stage Direction, Eisenstein eventually became the theater's co-director and began to direct many of its plays. Among his influences was Japanese Kabuki theater, which places more emphasis on costuming, music, scenery, dance, and other special effects than on drama and plot.

Eisenstein's film career was confined to the years of the Stalin regime. His first major film, *The Strike* (1924), applied his early ideas on montage, in which unrelated images that deliver a strong, often shocking, visual impact are inserted into the drama. A film, he argued, "cannot be

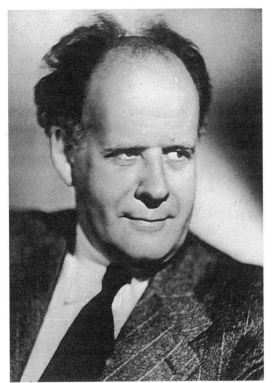

Sergey Eisenstein (AKG)

a simple presentation or demonstration of events; rather it must be a tendentious selection of, and comparison between, events, free from narrowly plot-related plans and moulding the audience in accordance with its purpose." Eisenstein also used "typage," selecting actors based on their physical appearances rather than their training or acting ability.

Caricatures and grotesque depictions of wealthy capitalists contribute to *The Strike*'s brutal portrait of the tsarist government, and a montage sequence that intersperses images of cattle being slaughtered with shots of government soldiers massacring striking workers foreshadowed Eisenstein's famous "Odessa Steps" sequence in the silent film *The Battleship Potemkin* (1925).

Created to celebrate the Revolution of 1905, *The Battleship Potemkin* was largely filmed on a ship used for mine storage in Odessa and depicts a mutiny aboard a ship following the crew's refusal to eat spoiled food and the subsequent confrontation with tsarist troops. The "Odessa Steps" sequence, which became a model for montage for many directors who followed Eisenstein, graphically portrays the massacre of citizens fleeing down a long flight of steps. Notable, too, in the otherwise black-and-white work, are the frames bearing the *Potemkin*'s red flag, which Eisenstein painted onto the film.

A number of other films followed in the late 1920s and early 1930s. *October* (1928), later renamed *Ten Days that Shook the World*, depicted the Bolshevik Revolution and Lenin's rise to power. *The General Line* (1929) renamed *Old and New*, was a propagandistic film supporting the extensive Stalinist collectivization projects imposed on the Russian countryside. In 1929 Eisenstein traveled to Paris, where he filmed *Sentimental Melody*. The following year he went to the United States to work on films based on the novels of Theodore Dreiser and Blaise Cendrars. However, Eisenstein grew dissatisfied with the projects and left to film *Que Viva Mexico!* in Mexico in 1932. He originally conceived the film as a comprehensive cinematic treatment of the varied aspects of Mexican culture, but he quarreled with the film's financial backer, the novelist Upton Sinclair, and never finished the project.

With the advent of sound in film, Eisenstein sought to apply the visual juxtapositions of images to audio. He returned to Russia in 1933 and was well into the production of *Bezhin Meadow*, which would have been his first sound film, when government criticism forced him to abandon it. Eisenstein completed his next and most popular film, *Alexander Nevsky*, in a matter of months in 1938. The Battle on the Ice scene, which depicts German soldiers chaotically plunging into the water and drowning as the ice underneath them cracks, showcased his "orchestral counterpoint" technique and recounts the story of the thirteenth-century Novgorod prince who drove the Teutonic Knights from Russia. A score written by the Russian composer SERGEY PROKOFIEV accompanied Eisenstein's epic tale.

In 1943 Eisenstein began work on the first part of *Ivan IV*, a heroic portrayal of the Russian tsar known as Ivan the Terrible. The cinematic portrayal of the sixteenth-century tsar (played by Nikolai Cherkasov) who centralized power in Russia pleased Soviet authorities who wished to inspire patriotism during World War II. By the beginning of 1946, Eisenstein had all but finished part two of *Ivan IV* when he suffered a serious heart attack. Stalin disliked the film, objecting that it evoked sympathy for the noblemen, or boyars, and it was officially banned until 1958. Eisenstein had also begun work on a third part, but the work was destroyed during the critical furor over the second. Another heart attack took his life in 1948.

Eisenstein also wrote extensive theoretical notes and essays on film, published in English as *The Film Sense* (1942), *Film Form* (1949), *Notes of a Film Director* (1959), and *Film Essays with a Lecture* (1968). He received the Order of Lenin in 1939 and the Stalin Prize (for *Ivan the Terrible*) in 1946.

BIBLIOGRAPHY

Barna, Yon, *Eisenstein*, 1966; Bergan, Ronald, *Eisenstein: A Life in Conflict*, 1997.

Elgar, Edward

(June 2, 1857–February 23, 1934)
Composer, Teacher

The composer Sir Edward William Elgar revitalized British choral music and orchestration in the late nineteenth and early twentieth centuries. Elgar composed in the late Romantic style, but he is considered the first of Britain's major modern composers.

Elgar was born into a musical family in Broadheath, Worcestershire, England. His father was an organist and violinist with his own music business. The young Elgar delighted in listening to his mother, who had wide literary tastes, read poetry to him. Although he was an intelligent and sensitive child, his family's financial situation kept him from formal study after he was 15. He took his first piano lessons at school at the age of 7. Elgar had little further musical training. He taught himself to play several instruments and studied theory from his father's books.

Edward Elgar (Ann Ronan/Image Select)

Although he wanted to pursue a career in music, Elgar went to work in a law office as a solicitor's clerk in 1872. His legal career was brief, and he soon quit to devote his time to music. In 1873 he joined the Worcester Glee Club, for which he played, conducted, and composed. During the next few years, Elgar played with several local orchestras and listened extensively to area church music. By 1877 he was able to afford a few violin lessons from Adolphe Pollitzer in London. In 1885 he replaced his father on the organ at St. George's Roman Catholic Church, a position the elder Elgar had held for thirty-seven years.

Elgar married Caroline Alice Roberts in 1889 and moved to London the same year. His failed attempts to launch a career in London prompted him to move to Malvern in 1891. By this time, he had given up his previous determination to become a professional violinist and was actively composing. With the cantatas *The Black Knight* (1893) and *The Banner of St. George* (1896) as well as the oratorio *The Light of Life* (1896) and *Variations on an Original Theme* (also known as the *Enigma Variations)* for orchestra (1898), Elgar began to gain a reputation in England as a composer.

The *Enigma Variations* proved to be one of Elgar's most popular and enduring compositions. Hans Richter conducted a performance of the work in London in 1899; it consists of a number of musical portraits of Elgar, his wife, his friends, and his dog. The title continues to generate controversy, as Elgar allegedly wrote the theme as counterpoint to a popular melody, but refused to identify the song and left the matter open for speculation. With the *Enigma Variations*, Elgar finally secured an interna-

tional reputation. The intriguing work consists of fourteen variations on a theme. Each variation reflects Elgar's perception of how one of his acquaintances or relatives might approach the theme. The "enigma" referred to in the title is the tune. Elgar based the composition on a tune he never revealed.

Elgar's most important compositions are his vocal and choral works. At the time he wrote, choral composition in England was at a low, and his work helped revitalize the medium. Although he developed a unique style, his work belongs to the tradition of the late Romantics. Elgar was the first major composer to come from Britain in two centuries, and his work sparked a musical revival that led to the development of British national music (see VAUGHAN WILLIAMS).

The Dream of Gerontius (1900), for mezzo-soprano, tenor, bass, full choir, and orchestra, is considered by many to be Elgar's masterpiece, a witty, lyrical, and dramatic oratorio. He based the composition on a poem by Cardinal John Newman, eleven years after he received the poem as a wedding present, and the work gained popularity in Germany before it did in Britain. During a 1902 visit to Düsseldorf, where *Gerontius* was enthusiastically received, Elgar met the composer RICHARD STRAUSS.

Elgar produced many other vocal works in the early 1900s. He selected the biblical texts for *The Apostles* (1903), an oratorio in two parts based on the actions of the apostles prior to the resurrection. *The Kingdom* (1906), also a two-part oratorio, picks up after the resurrection. He intended to write a third religious oratorio, but his plan never materialized. His other early vocal works include the choral cantata *Caractacus*

(1898), the song cycle *Sea Pictures* (1900), and the concert overture *Cockaigne* (1901).

From 1905 to 1908 Elgar taught music at the University of Birmingham. He completed his two symphonies before the outbreak of World War I. Symphony No. 1 in A-Flat Major (1908) consists of four movements and uses a recurring theme. The music in Symphony No. 2 in E-Flat Major (1911) is a more musically complex interweaving of themes, suffused with tragedy, conflict, and nostalgia.

With the outbreak of World War I, Elgar began writing a number of patriotic works. These include *Carillon* (1914) based on a poem by Emile Cammaerts, and the choral work *The Spirit of England* (1916), incorporating verse by the war poet Lawrence Binyon. Elgar joined the Hampstead Volunteer Reserve and donated the proceeds from some of his works to war charities. The bloodshed and suffering associated with the war, combined with the devastating emotional effect his wife's death in 1920 had on him, affected his creativity during the last years of his life.

Elgar's other works include church music, the overture *Froissart* (1890), *Coronation Ode* (1902), the symphonic study for orchestra *Falstaff* (1913), the marches *Pomp and Circumstance* (1901–1930), Introduction and Allegro for Strings (1905), Violin Concerto (1910), Cello Concerto (1919), and *Nursery Suite* (1931). Elgar was working on his third symphony when he died in 1934. He received numerous honorary degrees in music and was knighted in 1904. Elgar's mastery of orchestral and choral music and his sensitivity to drama, color, and lyricism sparked a revitalization in English music and paved the way for later composers such as BENJAMIN BRITTEN and WILLIAM WALTON.

BIBLIOGRAPHY

Anderson, Robert, *Elgar*, 1993; Moore, Jerrold Northrop, *Edward Elgar: A Creative Life*, 1984; Reed, W. H., *Elgar*, 1949.

Eliot, T. S.

(September 26, 1888–January 4, 1965)
Poet, Playwright, Critic, Editor, Scholar

Thomas Stearns Eliot, always referred to as T. S. Eliot, profoundly influenced twentieth-century verse not only by his example as a poet, but also through his many essays on literature and in his roles as an editor and patron. His poetry combines modern imagery with innovations in style and versification to convey powerfully his sense of dismay with contemporary culture and his hope for spiritual renewal, an outlook heightened by his conversion to Christianity in 1927. He received the Nobel Prize for Literature in 1948 "for his outstanding, pioneer contribution to present-day poetry."

Eliot was born in St. Louis, Missouri. His family came from a long line of distinguished New England writers and teachers, and among his ancestors was Andrew Eliot, the first member of the family to settle in America and a juror in the Salem Witch Trials. The Eliots, like many other liberal New England families, converted to Unitarianism in the nineteenth century. Eliot's father, an amateur painter and businessman, was president of the Hydraulic-Press Brick Company in St. Louis. From the beginning of his education—first at Miss Lockwood's primary school and then at Smith Academy (founded, along with Washington University, by his grandfather)—Eliot proved himself an outstanding student and was routinely at the top of his class. After studying at Milton, a well-known college-preparatory school in Massachusetts, where many of his relatives still lived, Eliot entered Harvard University.

At Harvard he edited the literary *Harvard Advocate* and fell under the influence of critic Irving Babbitt's "new humanism," which rejected the scientific and deterministic underpinnings of Naturalism and Realism and championed a restoration of individuality and moral foundation, and antiromantic outlook. Numerous other influences shaped Eliot's perspective at this early stage in his life—the philosophers T. E. Hulme (1883–1917), a founding figure in the Imagist movement, and F. H. Bradley (1846–1924), who saw reality as a product of the mind, as well as Henri Bergson, whose lectures he attended at the Sorbonne in Paris in 1911. In Paris he also met the poet ALAIN-FOURNIER.

Having earned his M.A. in philosophy at Harvard in 1910–1911, he returned to the university from 1911 to 1914 for his doctoral degree. His real interest, however, had shifted to poetry, and when he settled in London in 1915, he continued to study poetry, particularly that of the French Symbolist Jules Laforgue (1860–1887), the seventeenth-century lyric poet John Donne (1592–1631), and the great medieval epic poet Dante (1265–1321), author of the *Divine Comedy*. The same year he married Vivien Haigh-Wood, whose later decline into mental illness caused great personal despair to Eliot. In 1916 he wrote a dissertation entitled "Knowledge and Experience in the Philosophy of F. H Bradley," but the outbreak of war prevented him from taking his oral examinations at Harvard, and he never completed his doctorate.

Eliot attended the University of Oxford and in 1914 gained the friendship of his fellow American expatriate, the poet Ezra Pound, who was instrumental in arranging for the publication of Eliot's first volume of poetry, *Prufrock and Other Observations* (1917). The volume's title poem, "The Love Song of J. Alfred Prufrock," was his first major poetic work, largely unrhymed and lacking traditional form. In fact, it was so daringly unconventional that Eliot had not been able to get it published in the United States. The often quoted opening lines of the poem illustrate Eliot's wry and ironic tone as well as his use of "unpoetic" (as poetic was then defined) imagery, antiromantic imagery that reflected the realities of the modern world:

Let us go then, you and I,
When the evening is spread out against
  the sky
Like a patient etherised upon a table . . .

These lines from the ending are perhaps even more memorable as a description of modern alienation: "I have heard the mer-maids calling, each to each. / I do not think that they will sing to me."

In both "Prufrock" and "Gerontion," an interior monologue in the traditonal form of blank verse, Eliot's modern imagery again conveys powerfully a sense of the despair and alienation of contemporary urban life, a sense of the near impossibility of living an authentic life.

Eliot's indisputably modern poetic style might be a rejection of the Romanticism that had dominated poetry throughout the nineteenth and early twentieth century, but it was not a rejection of tradition. In his famous essay "Tradition and the Individual Talent," which appeared in his first volume of criticism, *The Sacred Wood* (1920), he argued that a poet should develop a comprehensive familiarity with the whole of European literature: " . . .[T]he poet must develop or procure the consciousness of the past and . . . should continue to develop this consciousness throughout his career," he wrote. And in fact he filled his poems with allusions to other works, particularly in "The Waste Land" (see below), which contains so many allusions to literary works and religious traditions that he published notes for the poem.

As examples of what effective poetry should be, where thought and feeling are one, where wit and passion work together, Eliot championed early seventeenth-century English poets like Donne; he believed that the later English poets had contributed to what he called the "dissociation of sensibility," a divorce of thought and feeling in poetry. These ideas are reflected in the famous essays "The Metaphysical Poet" and "Andrew Marvell," both of which appeared in *Selected Essays 1917–32* (1932). Other early volumes of criticism include *For Lancelot Andrewes* (1928) and *The Use of Poetry and The Use of Criticism* (1933).

"The Waste Land," published in 1922, established Eliot's reputation as a poet outside of Britain; although the poem's modernism infuriated the more conservative, the vision of Western civilization after World War I as a wasteland resonated with many readers. Written in the midst of a personal mental crisis as well as the crisis of a post–World War I civilization, the five-part work reflects the poet's alienation from the greed, vice, and other human ills of his surroundings. Broken meter underscores a sense of fragmentation and dismay. Again the opening lines have become part of our culture, and they convey Eliot's despair:

> April is the cruelest month, breeding
> Lilacs out of the dead land, mixing
> Memory and desire, stirring
> Dull roots with spring rain.

Nevertheless, a sense of the possibility of personal redemption and renewal of meaning admist the cultural debris was never absent from Eliot's work, and it can be found even in "The Waste Land."

In the 1920s Eliot's spiritual quest, particularly reflected in "The Hollow Men" (1925), culminated in his 1927 confirmation in the Church of England. (In the same year he became a naturalized citizen of Great Britain.) From that point onward, his poetry became more reflective. "Ash Wednesday," his first major poem after his conversion, is a meditative poem that opens in despair, with lines such as, "Because I cannot drink / There, where trees flower, and springs flow, for there is nothing again," but moves on to the possibility of redemption, invoking the one who "made strong the fountains and made fresh the springs / Made cool the dry rock and made firm the sand. . . . In other poems, such as "Choruses from 'The Rock'" (1934), Eliot's disillusionment with modern culture is expressed within the context of his faith.

Eliot wrote many essays on a variety of subjects in the 1930s and 1940s, which were collected in volumes such as *Thoughts After Lambeth* (1931), *The Idea of a Christian Society* (1939), and *Notes Towards the Definition of Culture* (1948). He also turned increasingly to writing plays, the first of which was *Sweeney Agonistes* (1926). First performed in 1934, it was followed by his most successful play, *Murder in the Cathedral* (1935), a tragedy about the martyrdom of the twelfth-century archbishop of Canterbury, Thomas à Becket, who refused to subordinate the church to the state. Other plays include *The Family Reunion* (1939), *The Cocktail Party* (1949), and *The Elder Statesman* (1959). Through his poetic drama, Eliot was able to reach a much wider audience with his vision of the possibility of spiritual renewal.

Aside from the considerable influence he exercised on modern poetry through actual contributions to poetry and literary criticism, Eliot was personally responsible for launching the careers of other poets. As editor of the quarterly review, *The Criterion* (1922–39) and an editor at the publishing house Faber & Faber Ltd., he published and supported young poets he admired.

The widely celebrated *Four Quartets* were published in 1943 and consisted of four separate but related poems, "Burnt Norton," (1936), "East Coker" (1940), "The Dry Salvages" (1941), and "Little Gidding" (1942). In these poems, he con-templates his own life in terms of a cohesive understanding of its fragments, its momentary glimpses of eternity, of "the still point of the turning world," given full meaning by the magnificent vision of unity regained at the end of "Little Gidding," a vision that begins with the often quoted lines,

> We shall not cease from exploration
> And the end of all our exploring
> Will be to arrive where we started
> And to know the place for the first time.

The *Quartets* were among Eliot's favorites of his own work and led to a Nobel Prize in 1948.

Eliot married Valerie Fletcher in 1947 and found in that second marriage the emotional fulfillment so absent in his first. A late poem, one of his rare completely personal poems, is "A Dedication to my Wife," "To whom I owe the leaping delight/ That quickens my senses in our wakingtime/ And the rhythm that governs the repose of our sleepingtime." He lived with her happily until his death.

In 1948 he received the Order of Merit. Among his other works is the volume of children's verse *Old Possum's Book of Practical Cats* (1939), made newly popular in the 1980s as the basis of *Cats* (1981), a musical by ANDREW LLOYD WEBBER.

BIBLIOGRAPHY

Ackroyd, Peter, *T. S. Eliot*, 1993; Bergonzi, Bernard, *T. S. Eliot*, 1978; Bush, Ronald, *T. S. Eliot: A Study in Character and Style*, 1984; Dale, Alzina Stone, *T. S. Eliot: The Philosopher-Poet*, 1988; Gordon, Lyndall, *T. S. Eliot: An Imperfect Life*, 1998; Hughes, Ted, *T. S. Eliot: A Tribute*, 1987; Pinion, F. B., *A T. S. Eliot Companion: Life and Works*, 1986; Sharpe, Tony, *T. S. Eliot: A Literary Life*, 1991.

Éluard, Paul

(December 14, 1895–November 18, 1952)
Poet

The French poet Paul Éluard helped found the Surrealist movement that developed out of Dadaism in France after World War I. Having written more than seventy volumes of verse, he ranks as one of the major lyric poets of the twentieth century.

Éluard was born Eugène Grindel in Saint-Denis, an industrial suburb of Paris. His mother was a seamstress, and his father was an accountant. He attended the Ecole Communale and the Ecole Primaire Supérieure Colbert in Paris. As a teenager, he suffered from tuberculosis and went to a sanatorium in Switzerland to recover. During his two years abroad, he read poetry and began to write his own. It was there that he met his first wife, Gala, who left him in 1930 for the Surrealist painter SALVADOR DALÍ. They had one daughter, Cécile. Éluard served in the French Army during World War I, and was gassed.

Éluard's early volumes of poetry include *Le Devoir* (1916; *The Duty*) and *Poèmes pour la Paix* (1918; *Poems for Peace*). In 1919, he began his association with a number of writers who later formed the vanguard of the Surrealist movement, including ANDRÉ BRETON, Philippe Soupault, and Louis Aragon. All of these writers, including Éluard, first associated themselves with the anarchic Dadaist movement that started in Switzerland in 1917. The Dadaists were a nihilistic group who disliked Western culture and rejected traditional art forms. By 1923, Éluard and the others had rejected Dadaism, and Breton's *Surrealist Manifesto*, which Éluard signed, in 1924 inaugurated the Surrealist movement. Later that year, spurred by the end of his marriage, he took off on a voyage around the world.

The Surrealists emphasized the importance of the subconscious in creative activity and often blurred the distinction between dream and reality in their work. Automatic writing, in which one spontaneously writes whatever comes into the mind, was an integral part of Éluard's poetry and other Surrealist literature. Some believed supernatural forces were behind automatic writing, and others saw the subconscious as the source of their words. Éluard maintained his association with the Surrealists until 1938.

Paul Éluard (AKG)

The major volumes of Éluard's Surrealist poetry include *Capitale de la douleur* (1926; *Capital of Grief*), *L'amour, la poésie* (1932; *Love Poetry*), *La rose publique* (1934; *The Public Rose*), and *Les yeux fertiles* (1936; *The Fertile Eyes*). Also among his Surrealist writings is the prose work *The Reversals of Life, or the Human Pyramid* (1926). During his Surrealist period, he collaborated with painters such as Max Ernst and Pablo Picasso in efforts to combine painting with poetry. His early poetry was largely personal, tinged with a sense of loneliness and isolation. Éluard and Breton also explored mental disorders in their joint poem *L'immaculée conception* (1930; *The Immaculate Conception*).

Éluard broke with Surrealism in 1938. He had joined the Communist Party in 1926 and rejoined it in 1942. His later poetry is more politically and socially oriented, expressing his ideal of a universal brotherhood and his identification with the underclasses. Three of his volumes of poetry, *Poésie et verité* (1942; *Poetry and Truth*), *Au rendez-vous allemand* (1944; *To the German Rendezvous*), and *Dignes de vivre* (1944; *Worthy of Living*), circulated among the fighters in the French Resistance in Nazi-occupied France. The poem "Liberty" from *Poetry and Truth* became especially popular in the Resistance underground.

Éluard married twice after his separation from Gala: Maria Benz (Nusch), in 1934, and Dominique Lemor in 1951, five years after Nusch's death. His later volumes of poetry include *Political Poems* (1948), *Tout dire* (1951; *Say Everything*), and *Le phénix* (1951; *The Phoenix*). He died of a stroke in 1952.

BIBLIOGRAPHY

Nugent, Robert, *Paul Éluard*, 1974.

Ernst, Max

(April 2, 1891–April 1, 1976)
Painter, Sculptor, Graphic Artist

Max Ernst was at the center of the avant-garde painters in Europe in the early twentieth century, participating in both the Dadaist and Surrealist movements after World War I. Beginning with his Surrealist works, Ernst's paintings are often vivid depictions of apocalyptic gloom. He is also noted for his experiments with painting and drawing techniques.

Ernst was born into a Catholic family in Brühl, Germany. His father was a teacher and administrator at a school for the deaf. From him, Ernst gained his first exposure to painting. The elder Ernst was an amateur painter thoroughly devoted to the realistic style his son later rejected. Ernst began drawing as a child and underwent several traumatic experiences that shaped his outlook, among which was the death of his sister in 1897.

Ernst attended a gymnasium and in 1909 enrolled in the University of Bonn, where he studied psychiatry and philosophy. His interests around this time encompassed the occult (with which he had his first contact in 1906), the human psyche, philosophy, and painting. Although he had little formal art training, he increasingly devoted his time to painting at the expense of his studies.

In 1910 he met the poet Auguste Macke, who was connected to the Expressionist group Der Blaue Reiter (The Blue Rider). Ernst's paintings were first exhibited in 1912, and he began to associate with many leading avant-garde painters of Germany and France. Ernst served in the German army during World War I, and the horrifying experiences he endured manifested themselves in postwar creations such as his *Collage* of 1920. In the work, he altered photoengravings and shaped a human figure as an airplane.

Following the war, Ernst joined the Dadaists and formed a Dadaist group in Cologne. Dadaism grew out of the disillusionment with Western civilization caused by World War I, and its adherents rejected all past conventions associated with art. Their nihilistic, chaotic approach to creation produced distorted figures and unconventional associations. Ernst and other Dadaists refused to restrict themselves to traditional materials and began to experiment with others, such as bits of magazines and photoengravings.

The periodical *Der Sturm*, to which Ernst contributed, promoted his work in the postwar period. With JEAN ARP, he organized a controversial exhibit in a public restroom. In 1919 he met PAUL KLEE, who with GIORGIO DE CHIRICO was one of the major influences on his subsequent work. The same year he completed a series of eight lithographs entitled *Fiat Modes*

Pereat Ars and began to publish *Der Ventilator*, quickly banned by the authorities. *Elephant of Celebes* (1921), one of his best-known Dadaist paintings, depicts a mechanical, elephant-like figure staring at a headless nude.

His work from this period is marked by his use of photoengravings, photomontage, and collage, as in *The Swan is Very Peaceful* (1920) and *Here Everything Is Still Floating* (1920). In 1922 he settled in Paris, where in 1924 he helped found Surrealism and became an early advocate of automatism. The Surrealists emphasized the role of the unconscious in artistic creation, giving rise to bizarre, distorted images and associations. Forests full of menacing trees, monstrous figures, birds, and nudes began to dominate ominous paintings like *Two Children Are Threatened by a Nightingale* (1924).

In 1925 Ernst began to incorporate his *frottage*, or pencil rubbing, techniques into his work, as he made rubbings of leaves, wood grains, and other surfaces. His *Earthquake* (1925) forms part of a major series of frottage drawings entitled *Histoire naturelle* (1926), and he also used frottage in his paintings. Always one to experiment with new techniques, Ernst next turned, in paintings such as *Two Sisters* (1926), to *grattage*, an adaptation of *frottage* for paint, in which paint is scraped from the canvas after the artist applies it. In the late 1920s he wrote the first of his autobiographical fragments, many of which later appeared in *Beyond Painting* (1948).

Although his association with the Surrealists lasted until 1938, Ernst found himself at odds with them as early as 1926. The Surrealists looked unfavorably upon his 1926 contributions, with JOAN

MIRÓ, to the design for a Ballets Russes production of *Romeo and Juliet*. In 1929, he finished the first of his collage-novels, *La Femme 100 têtes (The Hundred Headless Women)*, which still followed the surrealist vein, and began to sculpt. He also appeared in LUIS BUÑUEL's film *L'age d'or*.

In the early 1930s, Ernst began to experiment with decalcomania, which involves rubbing two surfaces together to transfer paint from one to the other. His sculptures, among which are *Oedipus II* (1934) and *Gypsy Dream Rose* (1959), evince the same experimental directions he followed in his paintings.

As a German alien, Ernst fell under the suspicion of the French government as World War II approached and was interned twice. He fled to the United States with his third wife, the collector and heiress Peggy Guggenheim, and settled in New York. Ernst's work had already been exhibited in America in 1931, and he had a son, Jimmy, also a painter, in the United States already. Paintings from this period include the oil paintings *Europe after the Rain* (1940–1942), *Napoleon in the Wilderness* (1941), and *The Eye of Silence* (1943–1944).

In the early 1940s, Ernst experimented with another technique, oscillation, in paintings such as *Vox Angelica* (1943). His method involved swinging paint from a container over a canvas. After living in Sedona, Arizona, with his fourth wife Dorothea Tanning, Ernst returned to France in 1949. His later works, less experimental than his early endeavors, include the 1956 collage series *Dada Forest, Dada Sun*. Ernst's other works include *The Couple* (1923), *Woman, Old Man and Flower* (1923), *Vision Provoked by a String Found On My Table* (1927), and *The Great Forest* (1927). The Museum of Modern Art in New York held a major exhibition of his work in 1958.

BIBLIOGRAPHY

Lieberman, William S., ed., *Max Ernst*, 1961; Russell, John, *Max Ernst: Life and Work*, 1967; Schneede, Uwe M., *Max Ernst*, 1972.

Evans, Edith

(February 8, 1888–October 14, 1976)
Actress

At the time of her death at the age of eighty-eight, Dame Edith Mary Evans was a seasoned veteran of the British stage and a world-renowned screen actress. Though known for her ability to portray varied and complex characters, especially in the plays of William Shakespeare, GEORGE BERNARD SHAW, and Oscar Wilde (1854–1900), she was particularly adept at comic roles. From the 1940s onward, Evans starred in a succession of films, often in strong supporting roles.

Evans was born in London. While working as a milliner's apprentice, she

Edith Evans (Universal Pictorial and Press Agency)

began to study acting at night. Her stage debut came in 1912, when she acted the part of Cressida in William Poel's production of Shakespeare's *Troilus and Cressida*. Evans was soon appearing on London stages in other Shakespearean roles as well as in the works of Shaw, Anton Chekhov, Wilde, NOËL COWARD, and others. She joined London's Old Vic' company in 1925, and she later attained considerable success on Broadway.

Among the major productions in which she appeared are stage versions of Fyodor Dostoeyevsky's *Crime and Punishment* (1866) and HUGH WALPOLE's *The Old Ladies*. CHRISTOPHER FRY created the part of the Countess in *The Dark Is Light Enough* (1954) specifically for her. Evans

also starred as Judith Bliss in Coward's *Hay Fever*, the Ghost of Christmas past in Charles Dickens's *A Christmas Carol*, Mrs. Millamant in William Congreve's *Way of the World*, and Gertrude in *Hamlet*. Her most famous role, however, was that of Lady Bracknell in Wilde's *The Importance of Being Earnest*.

Although she appeared in the silent films *A Welsh Singer* and *East Is East* in 1915 and 1916, she stayed away from the cinema after that until 1949. Then, hampered by fading memory in her later years, she turned increasingly to film as she aged. In 1949 she starred in the film version of Alexander Pushkin's short story "The Queen of Spades." Evans's performance in that work established her as an international film star, and she subsequently appeared with RICHARD BURTON in *The Last Days of Dolwyn* (1949) and as Lady Bracknell in Anthony Asquith's film version of *The Importance of Being Earnest* (1952).

Evans's other film credits include roles in *Look Back in Anger* (1959), *The Nun's Story* (1959), *Tom Jones* (1963), *The Chalk Garden* (1964), *Young Cassidy* (1965), *Prudence and the Pill* (1968), *The Madwoman of Chaillot* (1969), *Crooks and Coronets* (1969), and *A Doll's House* (1973). Her 1967 performance as Mrs. Ross in Bryan Forbes's *The Whisperers* won her a number of awards, including Best Actress from the New York Film Critics and the British Film Academy and a Golden Globe Award. Evans was created a Dame of the British Empire in 1946.

BIBLIOGRAPHY

Batters, Jean, *Edith Evans: A Personal Memoir*, 1977; Forbes, Bryan, *Ned's Girl: The Authorised Biography of Dame Edith Evans*, 1977.

Evans, Geraint

(February 16, 1922–September 19, 1992)
Singer

Geraint Evans sang operatic baritone at London's Covent Garden for more than thirty years. Best known for his roles in Mozart's *Don Giovanni*, Verdi's *Falstaff*, and Wagner's *Die Meistersinger von Nürnberg*, Evans also appeared in the major opera houses of the world, sang in television productions, and recorded many of his roles.

Evans was born in Cilfynydd, Glamorganshire, Wales. His father was a coal miner as well as, like so many of the Welsh, a music lover. His mother, too, was musically inclined, but she died in childbirth before his second birthday. After her death, Evans went to live with his maternal grandparents, where he remained until he was 10. His family spoke Welsh, and he learned the Welsh language before learning English. Evans's music career started early. At the age of 4, he won a gold medal in a singing competition, and two years later he won a prize for best singer-actor in the Children's Action Song Competition.

Evans attended local schools until he was 14, at which time he left to work for a window dresser. In his spare time he immersed himself in music and theater, playing the violin in the YMCA orchestra, joining a local dramatic society, and obtaining a role on the Welsh Rarebit radio program. Evans enthusiastically volunteered for the Royal Air Force in World War II, during which time he spent most of his time working and performing for the British Forces Radio Network. While in this job he eventually lived in Hamburg, where he was able to absorb the city's musical life and take singing lessons from Theo Hermann—his first real musical training.

Following his release from military obligations, Evans returned to England and entered the Guildhall School of Music. In 1948 he joined the opera company at London's Covent Garden, where he debuted as the Nightwatchman in Richard Wagner's *Die Meistersinger von Nürnberg;* The same year he sang Schaunard in Puccini's *La Bohème*, and the next season saw his debut in one of his most popular roles—the title role in Mozart's *Marriage of Figaro*. (He repeated his Figaro for his debut at Milan's La Scala in 1960.) In 1952 Evans sang his first Leporello in *Don Giovanni* at the Sadler's Wells Theatre.

In 1957 he peformed his first Falstaff, another of his popular roles, at the Glyndebourne Festival, at which he would appear on many occasions. Evans's American debut came in 1960, when he sang the title role of Paolo in Verdi's *Simon Boccanegra* in San Francisco. Two years later he sang Lemuel in *The Harvest* at the Chicago Lyric Opera. In 1965 sang the title role in *Don Pascuale* in Argentina.

Aside from his performances in the standard repertoire, Evans appeared in roles in modern works—as Herald in Ralph Vaughan Williams's *The Pilgrim's Progress* in its 1951 premiere at Covent Garden, and as Balstrode in Benjamin Britten's *Peter Grimes*. Evans performed around the world but centered his activity in London until he retired. For his final performance at Covent Garden, he sang the role of Dulcamara in Donizetti's *L'elisir d'amore*.

In the 1970s Evans appeared in a number of television performances for Harlech Television and the BBC Television—as Sesto in *Murder, the Magician* (1976), as Scrooge in Charles Dickens's *A Christmas Carol* (1978), and as Jack Vandeleur in *The Rajah's Diamond* (1979). Among his numerous recorded roles are Figaro, under Otto Klemperer conducting the New Philharmonia (1971); Ned Keene in *Peter Grimes* (1959); the title role in *Falstaff*, conducted by Sir GEORG SOLTI (1964); and Beckmesser in *Die Meistersinger* with HERBERT VON KARAJAN conducting in Dresden (1971). He was made Commander of the Order of the British Empire in 1959 and knighted a decade later. His autobiography, *A Knight at the Opera*, was published in 1984.

BIBLIOGRAPHY

Evans, Sir Geraint, *A Knight at the Opera*, 1984.

Falla, Manuel de

(November 23, 1876–November 14, 1946)
Composer

Manuel de Falla's work drew from elements of traditional Andalusian dance and song as well as the impressionistic influence of French composers such as Claude Debussy, and was associated with a revival of nationalistic music in Spain in the early twentieth century. De Falla was the most widely renowned Spanish composer of the twentieth century. By the time of his death he had increasingly withdrawn from the public eye and was composing in Castilian style, but the warm and colorful Andalusian works of his early career form the cornerstone of his reputation as a composer.

De Falla was born in Cádiz in southern Spain. As a child he took music lessons from his mother and from other teachers. He subsequently moved to Madrid and began to study under Felipe Pedrell (1841–1922), an influential composer and musicologist deeply rooted in many forms of traditional Spanish music. Pedrell became one of the primary influences on de Falla's work.

In 1905 de Falla won recognition from the Real Academia de Bellas Artes in Madrid, which honored him for his first opera, the lyrical drama *La vida breve* (*Life Is Short*). The opera, first performed in 1913, shows strong influences of Andalusian music. Its story centers around Salud, a gyspy girl who dies at the feet of the lover who deserted her. De Falla also composed *zarzuelas*, or traditional Spanish musical comedies. From 1905 to 1907, he taught piano lessons in Madrid. In 1907, he moved to Paris, where he gained the friendship of several French composers, including Claude Debussy, whose impressionistic compositions were to influence his later work. De Falla returned to Spain in 1914.

De Falla's ballet *Wedded by Witchcraft* (1915) is noted for its rhythmic variety, which the composer uses to create interesting rhythmic contrasts, and draws from Andalusian dance rhythms. In the story, Candélas, a gypsy girl, is haunted by memories of her deceased lover, a cruel and unfaithful Andalusian. When a new lover, Carmélo, appears, so does her dead lover's ghost. Carmélo is only able to win her affections when he enlists her friend, Lucía, to distract the ghost by seducing him.

One of de Falla's most famous compositions was the score for Léonide Massine's ballet, *El sombrero de tres picos* (1919; *The Three-Cornered Hat*), staged by Sergey Diaghilev's Ballets Russes with a set designed by Pablo Picasso. Among his other works is the widely performed *Nights in the Gardens of Spain* (1916) for orchestra and piano.

The music for *El retablo de Maese Pedro* (1924; *Mastro Pedro's Puppet Show*), a one-act puppet show based on an episode in the second part of Miguel de Cervantes's *Don Quixote*, was written for a small orchestra and makes extensive use of muted instruments. Concerto for Harpsichord (1926) drew from the work of the Italian composer Domenico Scarlatti (1685–1757). His other work includes the vocal pieces

Siete canciones populares españoles (1915; *Seven Popular Spanish Songs*) and guitar music.

After moving to Granada, de Falla co-organized a festival of *cante jondo*, or deep song, a traditional form of Andalusian folk music, with FEDERICO GARCÍA LORCA in 1922. In 1939 de Falla moved to Argentina. He was working on *Atlántida*, a choral work, when he died in 1946.

BIBLIOGRAPHY

Demarquez, Suzanne, *Manuel de Falla*, 1968; Pahissa, Jaime, *Manuel de Falla: His Life and Works*, 1954; Trend, J. B., *Manuel de Falla and Spanish Music*, 1929.

Fassbinder, Rainer Werner

(May 31, 1946–June 10, 1982)
Director, Actor, Playwright, Screenwriter

A leading German film director in the post–World War II era, Rainer Werner Fassbinder earned critical acclaim for his films, which indict middle-class values and probe social themes such as oppression and homosexuality. A prolific writer, actor, and director, he made more than one hundred films, plays, and television shows during his short lifetime, and was a major force in postwar German film.

Fassbinder was born in Bad Wörishofen, Germany. His father, who left the family when he was 6, was a doctor who practiced in the red-light district and often treated prostitutes, some of whom the young Fassbinder befriended. His mother suffered from tuberculosis and spent periods of time in the sanatorium. Being a student proved difficult for Fassbinder, and he transferred from school to school before he finally quit at the age of sixteen.

In 1967 he helped found the Antitheater, an avant-garde theatrical group. The actors and actresses from the Antitheater, notably the actress Hanna Schygulla, later appeared frequently in his films. Fassbinder finished the first of his forty-one full-length films, *Liebe is kälter als der Tod* (*Love Is Colder Than Death*), in 1969. The same year he finished *Katzelmacher* (1969), the first of what he called his "bourgeois films," in which he sharply satirized middle-class norms. The story concerns a working-class Greek who bursts into the lives of a group of bored German middle-class people living silly lives.

The Third Generation (1978–1979) is a satiric commentary on capitalism. In the story, an enterprising computer dealer attempts to boost his sales to the government by financing its terrorist enemies. Exploration of sexuality is another major theme is Fassbinder's films. Erwin/Elvira, the main character of *In einem Jahr mit 13 Monden* (1979; *In a Year of 13 Moons*), is a transexual in confusion and despair following a sex change. *Die Ehe der Maria Braun* (1979; *The Marriage of Maria Braun*), one of Fassbinder's best-known films, relates the story of a troubled relationship between a German soldier and his wife, ending with their destruction.

Rainer Werner Fassbinder (AKG)

in, and often wrote the screenplays for his films, which carry a strong line of commentary on social, political, economic, and sexual matters. His other films include *Die bitteren Tränen der Petra von Kant* (1972; *The Bitter Tears of Petra von Kant*); *Angst essen Seele auf* (1974; *Fear Eats the Soul*), about the relationship between an elderly cleaning lady and a Moroccan garage mechanic; *Lola* (1981); and *Veronika Voss* (1982), based on the life of the German actress Sybille Schmitz.

In addition to his films and plays, he also wrote for television and radio. His major television work is the fourteen-part adaptation (1978–1979) of Alfred Döblin's novel *Berlin Alexanderplatz*, about the efforts of the convicted criminal Franz Biberkopf to fit into society after his release from prison.

BIBLIOGRAPHY

Hayman, Ronald, *Fassbinder Film Maker*, 1984; Thomsen, Christian Braad, *Fassbinder: The Life and Work of a Provocative Genius*, 1997; Watson, Wallace Steadman, *Understanding Rainer Werner Fassbinder: Film as Private and Public Art*, 1996.

Fassbinder worked feverishly, producing an enormous output of plays and films during his short career. He directed, acted

Fellini, Federico

(January 20, 1920–October 31, 1993)
Director, Screenwriter

Working with ROBERTO ROSSELLINI, Federico Fellini was initially associated with the Neorealist movement in Italian film. With such movies as *La Dolce Vita*, *8 1/2*, *La Strada*, and *Fellini-Satyricon*, he developed his own cinematic style, which blended the worlds of imagination, dreams, and reality.

Fellini was born in Rimini, Italy, and spent much of his childhood there among a large, middle-class family. He attended a Catholic boarding school in Fano. Fellini's first aspirations were in the field

Federico Fellini instructing an actor during the making of *Fellini-Satyricon* in 1969 (AKG)

of journalism. In 1938 he moved to Florence and began to work on science-fiction and humor periodicals. The following year he moved to Rome and began selling caricatures to restaurants. In 1940, he became the editor of a weekly satire magazine, *Marc'Aurelio*. Three years later he married Giulietta Masina, who had appeared in one of his radio scripts.

His film career began around that time when he gained the friendship of the director ROBERTO ROSSELLINI, a leader in Italy's Neorealism movement in cinema. Fellini worked with him on films such as *Paisan* (1946; *Peasant*) and *L'Amore* (1948) and began to write scripts for other directors. One of them, Alberto Lattuada, asked Fellini to work with him on the production of *Variety Lights* (1950).

Fellini's films contained many autobiographical elements. *The White Sheik* (1952) was his first production on his own. His next film, *I Vitelloni* (1953), was based in part on his own experiences with his friends when he was young. The story centers around five men in their twenties who live with their families, lack the ambition to look for jobs, and are doomed to remain in their hometown. The film became Fellini's first success, and it won an award at the Venice Film Festival.

La Strada (1954), one of Fellini's most famous films, was the first to earn widespread international fame and an Academy Award. His wife, who starred in many of his movies, played a naive girl named Gelsomina who joins a traveling circus under the brutal Zampano (Anthony Quinn). Gelsomina dutifully remains with Zampano in spite of his re-peated cruelties, rejecting several opportunities to escape him. In the end, Zampano abandons her. In 1956, Fellini finished *The Nights of Cabiria*, again starring his wife, who this time played a Roman prostitute. The strong character portraits of these two films are characteristic of his early work.

Beginning with *La dolce vita* (1961; *The Sweet Life*), Fellini began to work with Angelo Rizzoli. The film is set in Rome and sharply satirizes an array of unscrupulous high society characters—intellectuals, the wealthy, journalists, paparazzi, and others. The principal character in Fellini's next film, *8 1/2*, is a film director who encounters a creative block; he is tormented by a series of dreams and flashbacks relating to his past and his relationships with women. The fantasy-like *Juliet of the Spirits* (1965) was Fellini's first film shot in color. The star, a housewife named Juliet (again Fellini's wife), is troubled by an inattentive husband and a series of supernatural visions. *Fellini-Satyricon* (1969), set in pre-Christian Rome, was loosely based on Petronius's *Satyricon*, written in the first century A.D. during Nero's rule, and like the *Satyricon*, it depicts the hedonism and decadence of ancient Rome. Fellini's next major project was an autobiographical film for television, *The Clowns* (1971).

Among Fellini's later films are *Roma* (1972), *Casanova* (1976), *Prova d'Orchestra* (1979), *The City of Women* (1980), *The Ship Sails On* (1983), *Ginger and Fred* (1986), and *Intervista* (1987).

The storylines in Fellini's films, most of which he wrote or co-wrote, are loosely constructed and the plot is sometimes left hanging. More important to his message are the elaborate and emphatic costumes, film sequences, and sets that make symbolic statements. Fellini's work earned four Academy Awards and many other international film awards. He received an Academy Award for lifetime achievement in 1993.

BIBLIOGRAPHY

Baxter, John, *Fellini: A Life*, 1993.

Ferrier, Kathleen

(April 22, 1912–October 8, 1953)
Singer

Kathleen Ferrier's warmth with her audiences and rich contralto voice made her a favorite among concertgoers in postwar Europe and America. She is best known for her contralto parts in oratorios and for her interpretations of Bach, Sir EDWARD ELGAR, and Gustav Mahler's song cycles, but she also performed folk songs and appeared in operas. Her career was cut short by cancer in 1953.

Ferrier was born in Higher Walton, Lancashire, England. Her first ambition was to play the piano professionally, and she won a number of prizes. But for many years she earned a living as a telephone switchboard operator. She sang with a local choral society and attracted the attention of Malcolm Sargent, who advised her to go to London to study—advice which Ferrier took, and won a competition at Carlise in 1937. She did not, however, make her professional singing debut until 1942. The following year she debuted in London, performing in *The Messiah* at Westminster Abbey.

Ferrier soon gained an international reputation, touring both the United States and Europe. She often performed

Kathleen Ferrier (Ann Ronan/Image Select)

at parish churches in England and in major festivals, such as the Edinburgh Festival. It was for her that BENJAMIN BRITTEN wrote his opera *The Rape of Lucretia*, which was performed at Glyndbourne in 1946, one of only two operas that she ever appeared in, the other being Gluck's *Orfeo et Euridice*.

Among the works in her extensive repertoire were her postwar performances of Mahler's song cycles, which she learned under the direction of BRUNO WALTER—notably *Das Lied von der Erde*. Ferrier recorded many works for Decca, which released a major compilation of

her music entitled *The Decca Ferrier Edition* in 1997. "Blow the Wind Southerly" is the best known of the folk songs she recorded.

After having many operations Ferrier lost her battle with breast cancer in 1953. In the middle of her final performance earlier that year, in *Orfeo* at Covent Garden, she broke her hip, but she still managed to finish the show.

BIBLIOGRAPHY

Cardus, Sir Neville, *Kathleen Ferrier: A Memoir*, 1969.

Feuchtwanger, Lion

(July 7, 1884–December 21, 1958)
Novelist, Playwright, Journalist, Critic, Translator

Most famous for his novels, Lion Feuchtwanger wrote historical fiction that addresses personal and political issues he faced during his lifetime—his Jewish identity, the rise of Hitler in Germany, the relationship of artists and intellectuals to society, and the place of political action. Feuchtwanger also wrote a number of plays.

Feuchtwanger was born into an orthodox Jewish family in Munich. His father, a wealthy industrialist, inherited a fortune gained in margarine manufacturing. When Feuchtwanger was 6, he entered the Sankt Anna Schule; four years later he enrolled in the Humanistic Wilhelms-Gymnasium. Feuchtwanger was an outstanding student but found himself in perpetual conflict with his family, who did not approve of his ambition to write.

Their strict religious observance did not suit his nature either, and Feuchtwanger left to study literature and philology at the University of Munich, where he later earned his doctorate.

In 1903, Feuchtwanger helped found the Phoebus, a literary society. He was later instrumental in the establishment of the Phoebus's paper *Der Spiegel* (*The Mirror*). From 1908 to 1911 he worked for *Die Schaubühne* (*The Stage*). Writing for *Der Spiegel* and other reviews, Feuchtwanger gained a reputation for harsh and pointed criticism. His first efforts as a writer were in the theater, and plays such as *Die Prinzessin Hilde*, the antiwar play *Die Kriegsgefangener* (*Prisoners of War*), and *König Saul* (*King Saul*) were staged in Munich. However, he later gave up the theater and devoted his time to literature. In 1912 he married Marthe Löffer. Two years later he was taken prisoner of war in Tunis.

From the outset, Feuchtwanger the novelist wrote in an even-handed style, often using historical interpretation to comment on the contemporary climate. His first historical novel, *Die Hässliche Herzogin* (*The Ugly Duchess*), appeared in 1923; it examines the character of Margaret Maultasch, Duchess of Tirol. Hampered by her unattractiveness, the duchess struggles with her beautiful rival, Agnes of Flavon. The duchess's sharp intelligence cannot save her from defeat at the hands of her competitor. Feuchtwanger, self-conscious about his short, frail, constitution, struggled with the duchess's problem himself. The book brought Feuchtwanger his largest success to that date.

Jew Süss and Power (1925) evolved from Feuchtwanger's earlier play *Jud Süss*. The central character is Joseph Süss Oppenheim, a powerful Jewish financier who works for the Duke of Württemberg. Süss refuses to convert to Christianity and is tried and executed by his enemies. Feuchtwanger's story was adapted as a film in Britain, and the Nazis later produced a distorted, propagandistic, antisemitic version.

Erfolg (1930; *Success*) attacks the German justice system; it was inspired by an actual incident in Feuchtwanger's life. While he was dining in Munich with acquaintances, the group suddenly found itself at the mercy of soldiers who stormed in and accused them of radical political activity. Feuchtwanger was later called to testify against his hostess, whom the police had arrested on trumped-up charges. In the novel an art critic is ar-rested on false charges and sentenced to five years in prison.

Feuchtwanger spent much of 1932–1933 in the U.S., and with the rise of the Nazis in 1933, he and his wife fled to France. Feuchtwanger found himself in danger on several accounts—as a Jew, a socialist, and a vocal critic of National Socialism. His struggles of this period are depicted in *The Oppermanns* (1933), about Gustav Oppermann, a pensive intellectual who leads a relatively pleasant life until the Nazis come to power. When his family suffers, Gustav resolves to take action, but he finds he is lost when it comes to knowing exactly what to do.

French authorities imprisoned Feuchtwanger several times as tensions grew between France and Germany. He was released the first time after protests from abroad but not granted an exit visa. With the help of American diplomats in Marseilles, Marta, who was interned for a time herself, engineered his final escape from Nîmes. The U.S. deputy consul smuggled him out dressed as an elderly woman. The Feuchtwangers later escaped through Spain and Portugal to the United States; Lion was himself instrumental in the escape of Heinrich Mann, brother of THOMAS MANN. Feuchtwanger's *The Devil in France* (1941) portrays these events.

During these tumultuous years, Feuchtwanger worked on *The Josephus Trilogy* (1932–1945), a fictional interpretation of the life of the first-century Jewish scholar and historian Josephus. Feuchtwanger's Josephus is a rational man who envisions a society that transcends sectarian nationalism but still retains a certain pride in his Jewish identity. In his later works, Feuchtwanger turned to other historical subjects, including the Salem witch trials (*The Devil in Boston*) and the French Revolution. Among these are *Waffen für Amerika* (1947; *The Proud Destiny*), written shortly after his arrival in the United States and originally titled *Arms for America; This is the Hour* (1951), a portrait of an artist and his relationship to society using the figure of the Spanish painter Francisco Goya (1746–1828); and *Jeffa und seine Tochter* (1957; *Jephthah and His Daughter*) on a story from the Hebrew Bible.

Feuchtwanger's other works include the novels *The Pretender* (1936); *Moscow 1937*, written after his visit to the Soviet Union and interview with Joseph Stalin; *Paris Gazette* (1939); *'Tis Folly to Be Wise;* and *Raquel*. With his close friend BERTOLT BRECHT, he translated Christopher Marlowe's *Edward II*. Feuchtwanger earned critical acclaim for his penetrating analysis of the human psyche and exploration of Jewish culture.

BIBLIOGRAPHY

Kahn, Lothar, *Insight and Action: The Life and Work of Lion Feuchtwanger,* 1975; Spalek, John M., *Lion Feuchtwanger, The Man, His Ideas, His Work: A Collection of Critical Essays,* 1972.

Ffrangcon-Davies, Gwen

(January 25, 1891–January 27, 1992)
Actress

In an acting career that spanned 80 years and a lifetime that spanned 101, Gwen Ffrangcon-Davies appeared in an array of roles on both the stage and screen. She was particularly noted for her portrayals of leading Shakespearean and Shavian women, and her best-known role was that of Juliet in *Romeo and Juliet*. Ffrangcon- Davies also appeared in modern dramas.

Ffrangcon-Davies was born in London and was the daughter of the Welsh clergyman and oratorio singer David-Thomas Ffrangcon-Davies. She made her debut as an actress with a minor part in William Shakespeare's *A Midsummer Night's Dream* (1911). Over the next several years she continued to play supporting parts, gradually working her way up to leading roles. She appeared with great success in the role of Etain in Rutland Boughton's music drama *The Immortal Hour,* and the following year she acted the part of Phoebe Thrassel in J. M. Burrie's *Quality Street* in London. She appeared regularly with the Birmingham Repertory Company, which she joined in 1921, and in 1923 played the original Eve in GEORGE BERNARD SHAW's *Back to Methusaleh* (1923).

The following year Ffrangcon-Davies played her first major Shakespearean role, appearing as Cordelia in *King Lear,* and around the same time starred in a production of *Romeo and Juliet* opposite Sir JOHN GIELGUD. She continued to play Shakespeare heroines, including Ophelia

Gwen Ffrangcon-Davies with Anthony Quayle (Ann Ronan/Image Select)

in *Hamlet*, Portia, Lady Macbeth, Cleopatra, and Queen Katharine.

Aside from her Shakespearean roles, Ffrangcon-Davies appeared in contemporary roles. In 1927 she appeared as Eliza Dolittle in Shaw's *Pygmalion* and Anne Witefield in Shaw's *Man and Superman*. Among others, she played Elizabeth Barrett in *The Barretts of Wimpole Street* (1930), Mrs. Manningham in Patrick Hamilton's *Gas Light*, Gwendolen in Sir JOHN GIELGUD's production of Oscar Wilde's *The Importance of Being Earnest* (1939; with EDITH EVANS and Gielgud), Madame Ranevskaya in Anton Chekhov's *The Cherry Orchard*, and Amanda Wingfield in Tennessee Williams's *The Glass Menagerie* (1965). In 1958 she appeared as Mary Tyrone in a production of Eugene O'Neill's *A Long Day's Journey Into Night*, and three years later she appeared in the London premiere of JEAN GIRAUDOUX's *Ondine* with the Royal Shakespeare Company.

After appearing as Madame Voynitsky in Chekhov's *Uncle Vanya* at the Royal Court Theatre in 1970, Ffrangcon-Davies retired from the stage. She continued to appear in films, on the radio, and on television. Among her films are Terence

Fisher's *Devil Rides Out* and *The Master Blackmailer* (1992). She was made Dame Commander of the Order of the British Empire in 1991.

BIBLIOGRAPHY

Hartnoll, Phyllis, *The Oxford Companion to the Theatre*, 4th ed. "Ffrangcon-Davies, Gwen," 1983.

Fields, Gracie

(January 9, 1898–September 27, 1979)
Actress, Singer

Known to millions as "Our Gracie," the English-born comedienne Gracie Fields entertained British and American audiences with music hall ballads and light comedy in films, live performances, radio and television appearances, and recordings. Fields was a popular wartime entertainer during the World War II era, and her career spanned more than seventy years.

Fields was born Grace Stansfield in Rochdale, Lancashire, England. From a young age she was exposed to the music hall scene, and she first made a name for herself playing Sally Perkins with the touring review Mr. Tower of London, with which she appeared between 1918 and 1925. Her fame already established in England, she appeared regularly in the United States from 1930 onward.

During World War II Fields was a popular entertainer, often giving benefit performances for British war relief efforts. Fields made many recordings of songs (such as "Singing In The Bathtub," "You've Got To Be Smart To Be In The Army," "Smile When You Say Goodbye," "My Blue Heaven," "The Biggest Aspidistra in the World," and the ballad "Sally") as well as sketches that reflect the culture of her native Lancashire.

Fields appeared regularly on the radio and scored her biggest film success with *Sing as We Go* (1934). Among the films she appeared in are *Sally in Our Alley* (1931), *Looking on the Bright Side* (1931), *Love, Life and Laughter* (1933), *Look up and Laugh* (1935), *Queen of Hearts* (1936), *This Week of Grace* (1938), *We're Going to Be Rich* (1938), *The Show Goes On* (1938), *Holy Matrimony* (1943), *Stage Door Canteen* (1943), *Paris Underground* (1945), and *Molly and Me* (1945).

Sing As We Go, Fields's autobiography, was published in 1960. She was made Dame Commander of the Order of the British Empire in 1938.

BIBLIOGRAPHY

Bret, David, *Gracie Fields: The Authorized Biography*, 1996; Fields, Dame Gracie, *Sing As We Go*, 1960; Moules, Joan, *Our Gracie: The Life of Dame Gracie Fields*, 1983.

Gracie Fields (Ann Ronan/Image Select)

Firbank, Ronald

(January 17, 1886–May 21, 1926)
Novelist, Short-Story Writer, Playwright

Arthur Annesley Ronald Firbank's eccentric novels never achieved success during his lifetime, but they gained recognition after his death for their comic burlesques, unique structure and language, and rich characterizations.

Firbank was born in London into a family that had risen from rags to riches. His grandfather escaped straitened circumstances as a coal miner's son and became a wealthy railroad contractor. Firbank's mother tutored him at home until he was 14; he later studied at the Mortimer Vicarage School in Eton, Buckinghamshire, and then at Uppingham as well as with private tutors.

In 1898, Firbank wrote *Lady Appledore's Mesalliance*, a story about the wealthy Wildred Forrester, who loses all of his money and takes a pleasant job as a gardener on Lady Appledore's estate. His identity is only revealed to Lady Appledore when his aunt comes to visit her. In 1901 he traveled to France to continue his studies. His first work to appear in print, "The Artificial Princess," was published in *Les Esais* after he moved to Paris in 1904.

In 1905 Firbank began to publish fiction at his own expense. His first volume contained the stories *Odette D'Antrevernes* and *A Study in Temperament*. The former is about a young orphan girl who passes her youth in a convent and envies St. Bernadette. More than anything, Odette wants to see a vision of the Blessed Virgin. When she goes to receive the vision, she is surprised to find instead a painted lady who teases her. Upon understanding Odette's earnestness, the woman is repentant. Firbank revised and republished *Odette* in 1916. From 1906 to 1909, he studied at Trinity Hall, Cambridge, where he was a contemporary of RUPERT BROOKE, and published short pieces in *The Granta*.

Firbank was an eccentric both in person and on paper, given to heavy drinking and extreme shyness. The innocent Odette stands in sharp contrast to the many grotesque burlesques and exaggerations of socialites, clergy, artists, writers, and other figures that appear in his works, for example, in the novel *Vainglory* (1915). His plots generally take second place to his multitude of characterizations, and his writing style is marked by odd usages of words.

Like *Vainglory* and almost all of Firbank's work, *Caprice* (1917) was published at his own expense and illustrated by AUGUSTUS JOHN. Its main character, Sarah Sinquier, is the daughter of staunchly Victorian parents. Sarah dreams of escaping her family and playing Juliet on the West End. Her parents disapprove of her aspirations, so she pawns some of their silverware and uses the money to escape. Sarah finally realizes her dream of playing Juliet and dies the following day.

Valmouth (1919) takes place in the west of England at a resort where the wealthy go to recover their health. The action takes place around a central event: the marriage of Dick Thoroughfare to the mysterious Niri-Esther. *Santal* (1921), written while Firbank was in Tunisia, takes place in the North African setting and temporarily departs from the character burlesques. The central character is Cherif, a young Arab boy who embarks on an unsuccessful spiritual journey to find a holy prophet.

The Flower beneath the Foot (1923) is an unheroic portrait of St. Laura de Nazianzi. *Sorrow in Sunlight* (1924) is the only novel Firbank did not pay to publish. The story takes place in the exotic and decadent setting of Tacarigua and its capital, Cuna-Cuna, which is struck by an earthquake. *Concerning the Eccentricities of Cardinal Pirelli* (1926) again returns to satirizing the clergy.

Firbank died in Rome in 1926. Among his other works are *The Princess Zoubaroff* (1920), about two couples va-cationing in Florence, Adrian and Nadine Sheil-Meyer and Eric and Enid Tresilian, who break up when the wives enter a convent under the influence of Princess Zoubaroff; *The New Rhythm*, a novel set in New York, which he began in Rome and never finished; and *Inclinations* (1916).

BIBLIOGRAPHY

Benkovitz, Miriam J., *Ronald Firbank: A Biography*, 1969; Kiechler, John Anthony, *The Butterfly's Freckled Wings: A Study of Style in the Novels of Ronald Firbank*, 1962; Merritt, James Douglas, *Ronald Firbank*, 1969.

Fleming, Ian

(May 28, 1908–August 12, 1964)
Novelist, Short-Story Writer, Writer of Children's Books

The British novelist Ian Lancaster Fleming invented James Bond, the flashy British Secret Service agent 007. His dozen novels have sold more than 18 million copies, and Bond's taste for high living and fast-paced, high-drama adventures has made him a popular motion picture hero since the 1960s. Since Fleming's death, a number of other authors have continued to write James Bond stories.

Fleming was born in London and studied at Eton, where he was an excellent athlete. In the early 1930s, he worked for Reuters as a journalist; his most notable assignment sent him to Moscow to cover the trial of British citizens accused of spying. During World War II, Fleming held a high rank in British Naval Intelli-gence and helped orchestrate a number of secret missions.

After the war ended, Fleming moved to Jamaica, living in a house called "Goldeneye." There Fleming indulged his taste for fast living, his love of alcohol and tobacco, and interests that ranged from black magic to biology. He continued as a journalist, working as foreign manager for the London *Sunday Times* until 1959.

It was in Jamaica that he wrote his first book, *Casino Royale* (1953), a Cold War thriller set in France. The novel introduces the strong and cold-hearted James Bond, who differs dramatically from the suave playboy depicted on the movie screen. Bond is a British Secret Service agent licensed to kill; in *Casino Royale* he battles the villainous Le

Chiffre. He loves fine cuisine, women, danger, and fine cigarettes. The origin of his name is thought to be the James Bond who wrote *The Birds of the West Indies*. The fictional Bond's code name 007 probably came from a short story by RUDYARD KIPLING, in which a train was numbered "007."

In 1957, Fleming wrote a non-Bond work, *The Diamond Smugglers*, about diamond smuggling in Africa. A series of the immensely popular James Bond stories continued until Fleming's early death in 1964. *From Russia, with Love* (1957) pits Bond against Soviet SMERSH agents. *Dr. No* (1958), set on a tropical island, was the first of many of Fleming's Bond stories to appear on screen. *Goldfinger* (1959) introduces the evil character Auric Goldfinger, with whom Bond crosses paths as he tries to solve the murder of a woman. *The Spy Who Loved Me* (1962) is narrated by Vivienne Michel, whom Bond saved from the villains Slugsy and Horror. Other Bond novels include *Diamonds Are Forever* (1956), *Thunderball* (1961), *Moonraker* (1955), *You Only Live Twice* (1964), and *The Man with the Golden Gun*, published posthumously in 1965.

Fleming also wrote a number of short stories featuring Bond. "The Living Daylights," originally titled "Berlin Escapes," finds Bond trying to protect another agent from a KGB assassin. The story appeared with two others, "The Property of Lady" and "Octopussy," in a collection entitled *Octopussy*. The volume *For Your Eyes Only* (1960) consists of five stories, including "From a View to Kill," the basis for the film *A View to a Kill* (1985).

Fleming's death did not put an end to the James Bond series. Several other well-known writers have written novels featuring 007, including John Gardner, Raymond Benson, and KINGSLEY AMIS (under the pseudonym Robert Markham). On screen, several actors have portrayed the popular spy-hero—Sean Connery, Roger Moore, and most recently Pierce Brosnan.

Among Fleming's other works are the children's story *Chitty Chitty Bang Bang* (1964); the travel book *Thrilling Cities* (1964); and *On Her Majesty's Secret Service* (1963). Fleming died of heart failure at the age of 56.

BIBLIOGRAPHY

Bryce, Ivar, *You Only Live Once: Memories of Ian Fleming*, 1975; Lycett, Andrew, *Ian Fleming*, 1995; McCormick, Donald, *17F: The Life of Ian Fleming*, 1993; Rosenberg, Bruce A., *Ian Fleming*, 1989.

Fo, Dario

(March 24, 1926–)
Playwright, Actor, Director

Since World War II Dario Fo has entertained audiences in his native Italy and around the world with his semi-improvisational productions that combine mime, acting, and social commentary. His bawdy, outrageous, and often sacrilegious plays have made him a highly controversial figure and resulted in numerous conflicts with the authorities. He received the Nobel Prize for Literature in 1997 for "strength in the creation of texts that simultaneously amuse, engage, and provide perspectives." The committee also described him as one "who emulates the jesters of the Middle Ages in scourging authority and upholding the dignity of the downtrodden."

Fo was the son of a railway worker born in Leggiuno-Sangiamo, Italy. The chief sources of diversion in his rural native region were the puppeteers, actors, and traveling storytellers who entertained peasants with, among other things, tales that mocked their wealthy landlords. Both the tradition of the traveling entertainer and the element of social protest were to be strong influences on Fo's work.

Originally, Fo studied architecture at the Brera Gallery's art school in Milan, but he soon abandoned it and pursued his interest in the theater. He took jobs working as a comic mime in satirical reviews and was soon appearing regularly on the radio as Poer Nano (Poor Dwarf). The satirical *Il dito nell'occhio* (1953; *Finger in the Eye*) was Fo's first major independent production and mocked the prevailing versions of history put out by the authorities. From this production Fo took away two significant influences: the "black mime" style of pantomime advanced by Jacques Lecoq, and his acquaintance with his future wife and collaborator Franca Rame.

Rame and Fo married in 1954 and continued to stage their work. Their often outlandish productions combined satire, farce, comedy, social protest, and mime, drawing from the traditions of the commedia dell'arte, the traditional Italian improvisational theater, and the *guillare*, a sort of medieval jester. Fo's performances of the same work differed from night to night (as they still do) and sometimes involved audience participation and discussion. His merciless criticism of the then-ruling Christian Democratic regime, the pope, the Church, and the Vatican earned him many enemies and brought frequent trouble with the authorities.

Both Fo and Rame had strong ties to the Communist Party, and their work grew increasingly political. *I sani da legare* (*Fit to Be Tied*, 1954) poked fun at the Red Scare and other efforts to silence dissent. In 1959 they founded the Campagnia Dario Fo–Franca Rame, opening the same year for a season at Milan's Odeon Theatre. Fo acted the lead in the production, *Gli arcangeli non giocano a flipper* (*Archangels Don't Play Pinball*). Both also appeared in satirical roles on the television show *Canzonissima*. Plays such as *Isabella, tre caravelle e un cacciaballe* (1963; *Isabella, Three Ships, and a Con Man*) mocked the traditional story of Columbus's discovery of America and poked fun at the Spanish monarchs Ferdinand and Isabella. His final production for conventional theater, *La signora non è da buttare* (1967; *The Lady's Not for Discarding*), attacked the United States and resulted in another brush with the authorities.

Dissatisfied with the conventional theater, Fo and Rame formed the short-lived Nuova Scena in 1968. The group was closely tied to the Communist Party and toured not in theaters but in unions, factories, and parks. Both internal dissension and disagreement with the Party led to the group's breakup in 1970. That year Fo and Rame formed Colletivo Teatrale la Comune and continued to tour public places. They now considered themselves members of the "unofficial left." The most successful of Fo's productions from this period was *Mistero Buffo* (1974; *Comic Mystery*), a one-man show that irreverently mocks the life of Christ and borrows from the medieval mystery plays known as *misteri buffi*.

Morte accidentale di un anarchico (1974; *Accidental Death of an Anarchist*), another of Fo's popular successes, was inspired by the death of the anarchist Giuseppe Pinelli. Pinelli fell out of a window while under interrogation. Fo's tale concerns the death of such an agitator and a harsh satire of the official attempts to cover it up. He treated the theme of civil disobedience in *Non si paga, non si paga!* (1974; *We Can't Pay? We Won't Pay!*).

Also among Fo's later works are *Storia di una tigre* (1980; *Story of a Tiger*), an allegorical monologue based on a Chinese folk tale; *L'uomo nudo e l'uomo in frak* (1985; *One Was Nude and One Wore Tails*); and *Coppia aperta* (1983; *The Open Couple—Wide Open Even*). *Il papa e la strega* (1989; *The Pope and the Witch*), with the everpresent anticlerical bent in his work, examines the problem of drug addiction and potential solutions. *Johan Padan a la desoverta de le Americhe* (1992; *Johan Padan and the Discovery of America*) returns to the Columbus theme. In the story a *guillare* stows away on Columbus's ship. When they arrive in America, he instigates a rebellion of the Native Americans against the Conquistadors.

Rame has been perhaps even more politically active than her husband. In 1973 she was kidnaped by Fascists and badly beaten. She tours with Fo and has written her own shows, including *Tutta casa letto e chiesa* (1977; *She's All Church, Home, and Bed*) and *Female Parts* (1981). Together they have written more than sixty plays. Among Fo's other works is *Manvale minimo dell'attore* (*The Tricks of the Trade*), in which he relates his extensive research on the history of jesters and political clowns.

BIBLIOGRAPHY

Hirst, David L., *Dario Fo and Franca Rame*, 1989; Hood, Stuart, Introduction to *The Pope and the Witch*, 1992; Mitchell, Tony, *File on Fo*, 1989.

Fokine, Michel

(April 26, 1880–August 22, 1942)
Choreographer, Dancer

The most influential choreographer in the early twentieth century, Michel Fokine reformed the classical Russian ballet style in which he was trained. After creating *The Dying Swan* for ANNA PAVLOVA, Fokine joined SERGEY DIAGHILEV's Ballets Russes as its chief choreographer in 1909. In both his ballets for Diaghilev's company and his later works, he sought to integrate all elements of the production into a cohesive whole.

Fokine was born Mikhail Mikhaylovich Fokine into a middle-class family in St. Petersburg, Russia. The youngest of five children, he enjoyed playing ballet with his siblings. Fokine's father, a prosperous businessman, objected to his ambition to dance. His mother, however, prevailed upon him to send Fokine to the Imperial Ballet School at the Mariinsky Theatre. The school accepted him in 1889. Fokine took his first classes from Platon Karsavin, father of the renowned ballerina TAMARA KARSAVINA.

Fokine's varied talents—painting, dancing, and mime—soon emerged at the school. He performed from time to time as part of the corps de ballet and in 1898 passed his final exam. His debut with the Imperial Russian Ballet came on his eighteenth birthday. Pavlova first partnered with Fokine in such productions as *Harlequinade* at the Mariynsky. At this time Fokine was dancing, teaching classes, and beginning his work in choreography.

In 1905 he achieved his earliest choreographic success with *The Dying Swan*, a solo dance he created for Pavlova. He had already begun choreographing for his students—*Acis et Galatée*, *A Mid-summer Night's Dream* (in which VASLAV NIJINSKY danced), and *The Animated Gobelins*—and was soon orchestrating works for the Maryinsky. The year 1908 saw the production of three major Fokine ballets: *Le pavillon d'Armide*; *Une nuit d'Égypte* (*Cléopâtre*), in which he danced the role of Amoun and Pavlova danced Berenice; and *Chopiniana* (*Les Sylphides*), a classical ballet with music by Frédéric Chopin (1810–1849).

Diaghilev enlisted Fokine's talent for his Ballets Russes, and in 1909 the company performed revised versions of all three ballets in Paris. Fokine remained with the Ballets Russes as principal choreographer until 1914, creating such works as *L'oiseau de feu* (1910; *The Firebird*) and *Petrushka* (1911), both with music by IGOR STRAVINSKY; *Daphnis et Chloé* (1912), to which MAURICE RAVEL contributed the score; *Schéhérazade* (1910), with music by Nikolai Rimsky-Korsakov; *Le spectre de la rose* (1911); *Le carnaval* (1911); *Le légende de Joseph* (1913); and *Le coq d'or* (*The Golden Cockerel*, 1914). The Ballets Russes performed Fokine's creations all over the world.

Fokine was trained in the conservative classical style, as taught by Marius Petipa (1818–1910), the longtime head of the St. Petersburg Ballet. Petipa emphasized dance steps above all else in his ballets, subordinating costumes, sets, and music to movement. Fokine, in contrast, sought to equalize and integrate these elements. He tried to render movement more expressive and interpretive of the action of the ballet. "For such interpretive dancing," he said, "the music must be equally inspired. In place of the old-time waltzes, polkas, pizzicati, and galops, it is necessary to create a form of music which expresses the same emotion as that which inspires the movement of the dancer."

To achieve the unified effect he envisioned, Fokine employed leading composers and artists of his day for the music and set design. His interest in ancient legend led him to draw from old myths and stories for his plots. He was meticulous in the creation of his ballets, often showing up at early rehearsals with complete, detailed pictures of what he envisioned for the ballet. Dancers sometimes found him demanding and difficult to work with.

Fokine left the Ballets Russes in 1914, after which other choreographers such as LÉONIDE MASSINE extended his work. He left Russia after the Bolshevik Revolution in 1917 and spent much of 1919–1920 in Sweden and Denmark. In 1921 he and his wife, the ballerina Vera Fokina, moved to the United States. They danced the leading roles in his *The Thunder Bird*, which premiered in New York the same year.

From then on Fokine worked mainly in the United States, both dancing and choreographing, although he also continued to work with companies in Europe. He and his wife formed the Fokine Ballet. His other works include *Adventures of Harlequin* (1922); *Frolicking Gods* (1923); *The Return from the Carnaval* (1923); *Medusa* (1924), with music by Tchaikovsky; *The Immortal Pierrot* (1925); *L'Épreuve d'amour* (1936); and *Don Juan* (1936). Vera Fokina appeared in many of her husband's productions, and he choreographed many dances specifically for her.

Upon his death in 1942 Fokine was working on his final ballet, *Helen of Troy*, which later premiered in Mexico City. In revised form, many of his ballets have become part of the standard repertory.

BIBLIOGRAPHY

Beaumont, Cyril W., *Michel Fokine and His Ballets*, 1981; Horwitz, Dawn Lille, *Michel Fokine*, 1985.

Fonteyn, Margot

(May 18, 1919–February 21, 1991)
Dancer

Known for her technical precision as a dancer and her fifteen-year partnership with RUDOLF NUREYEV, Dame Margot Fonteyn rose to stardom on the British stage in the 1930s. Stepping comfortably into leading classical roles left vacant by ALICIA MARKOVA's departure from the Vic Wells Ballet, she also appeared in numerous ballets choreographed by FREDERICK ASHTON.

Fonteyn was born Margaret Hookham in Reigate, Surrey, England. Her father was a businessman and engineer for a British cigarette company. From her

Margot Fonteyn (Rex Features Ltd.)

mother, who was part-Irish and part-Brazilian, Fonteyn took her name, an anglicized form of her mother's name, Fontes. At the age of 4 Fonteyn was taken by her mother to Miss Grace Bosustow's dance school to learn tap dancing. Eventually, Fonteyn studied in both China and England under such well-known teachers as Serafima Astafieva and Ninette de Valois. Through Valois Fonteyn was apprenticed to the Vic Wells Ballet in London.

Fonteyn went on to make her professional debut with the Vic Wells. When Markova left in 1934, Fonteyn soon stepped into her spot, dancing the lead in *Giselle* and other parts. Fonteyn's biggest success up to that time, however, came in 1939 when she danced Aurora with ROBERT HELPMANN in *The Sleeping Beauty*. Impressed with Fonteyn, Frederick Ashton recruited her for many of his productions. Among these are *Le baiser de la fée (The Kiss of the Fairy)*, *Horoscope*, *Symphonic Variations*, *Daphnis and Chloë*, and *Ondine*. Fonteyn continued to dance classical roles as well, including *Coppélia* and *Les Sylphides*.

In 1955 Fonteyn married Roberto Emilio Arias, who was the son of a former Panamanian president and became Panama's ambassador to England shortly after their marriage. They had met and fallen in love nearly twenty years earlier when Arias was studying in England. After having returned to Panama and married, he saw Fonteyn perform with the Royal Ballet in New York in 1953 and rekindled their romance. In 1964 Arias was shot in an assassination attempt and paralyzed from the neck down. Fonteyn nursed him through the initial trauma and remained devoted to him for the rest of his life.

Her celebrated partnership with Nureyev began in 1962, the year after he defected from the Soviet Union. Because she was nearly twenty years his senior, she harbored serious doubts about their ability to work together. However, her technical perfection proved to be the perfect match for Nureyev's energetic flamboyance, and their partnership won international popularity that lasted for fifteen years. They danced together in productions of *Swan Lake* (in which she appeared as the Swan Queen), *Raymonda*, *Le Corsaire pas de deux*, and *Mar-*

guerite and Armand. Kenneth MacMillan's Romeo and Juliet (1965) proved to be one of their biggest hits. At its performance in London's Covent Garden she and Nureyev took forty-three curtain calls.

After having danced a farewell performance at the Royal Opera House in London, Fonteyn retired from the ballet at the age of 60. She had already become president of the Royal Academy of Dancing in 1954 and been created Dame of the Order of the British Empire in 1956. The Royal Ballet awarded her the title of prima ballerina assoluta in 1979. Fonteyn wrote several books, among which are Margot Fonteyn: Autobiogra-phy (1975), A Dancer's World (1979), and The Magic of Dance (1979).

Among the other ballets in which she appeared are Apparitions (with Helpmann); MICHEL FOKINE's The Firebird and Petrushka; and JOHN CRANKO's Poème de l'extase (1970; Poem of Ecstasy). Fonteyn appeared in numerous films, including The Royal Ballet (1959), two versions of Romeo and Juliet in 1966 and 1982, Swan Lake (1967), and I Am a Dancer (1973).

BIBLIOGRAPHY

Bland, Alexander, Fonteyn and Nureyev: The Story of a Partnership, 1979; Fonteyn, Dame Margot, Margot Fonteyn: Autobiography, 1976.

Ford, Ford Madox

(December 17, 1873–June 26,1939)
Novelist, Poet, Critic, Essayist, Editor

The English writer Ford Madox Ford published eighty-one books during his lifetime. His novels, poetry, and essays touch on history, the European cultural climate of the World War I generation, literature, and other subjects. In addition to his own writing, he was well known for promoting the work of young authors in the two major literary reviews he edited, the English Review and the Transatlantic Review.

Ford was born Ford Madox Hueffer, the eldest of three children, in Merton, Surrey, England. An artistic and intellectual atmosphere prevailed in his home. His mother, Catherine Brown, was the daughter of the painter Ford Madox Brown, and his father was a German musicologist, librettist, and music critic for the Times. Ford's younger brother, Oliver, also became a successful author. Beginning in 1881 Ford attended the Praetorius School at Folkestone, Kent, and he later attended University College School in London. Thanks to his home life as well as his schooling, Ford acquired a broad education.

The year 1891 saw the publication of Ford's first major work, the fairy story The Brown Owl. A second fairy story, The Feather, appeared in 1892, as did his first novel, The Shifting of the Fire. The same year he joined the Roman Catholic Church, and he remained a less-than-devout Catholic for the rest of his life. In 1893 he published the poetry collection

The Questions at the Well and a third fairy story, *The Queen Who Flew*. He married Elsie Martindale in 1894.

Ford met the Polish-born writer JOSEPH CONRAD in 1898, around the time the latter retired from sea life and was just beginning his literary career. The two writers eventually collaborated on three works, *The Inheritors* (1901), *Romance* (1903), and *The Nature of A Crime* (1909). After Conrad's death in 1924, Ford published *Joseph Conrad: A Personal Remembrance* (1924).

With Arthur Marwood, Ford founded the *English Review*, an influential literary journal he edited in 1908 and 1909. The *Review* published the works of both young and established writers; among them were Thomas Hardy, D. H. LAWRENCE, E. M. FORSTER, and H. G. WELLS. In this position and in his later editorship of the *Transatlantic Review* (1924–1925), Ford helped bring to public notice the work of many writers who later became famous.

Ford joined the army in 1915, the same year his novel *The Good Soldier* was published. Critics, who sometimes fault Ford for hasty, mediocre writing, often consider this novel, which examines the flaws in human relationships, his best piece of work. His poetry and writing, modern for his time, is generally characterized by careful attention to technique, at times at the expense of content. Among his other most noteworthy novels are a trilogy set in the time of Henry VIII,

which begins with *The Fifth Queen* (1906), and the wartime tetralogy *Parade's End* (1924–1928). The latter series reflects Ford's pessimistic perceptions of Western civilization during and after World War I.

Ford had actually taken part in the war himself; in 1916 he suffered gassing and shell-shock at the Battle of the Somme. Three years later, Ford, then still using the name Hueffer, changed his name to Ford Madox Ford. In 1922 he moved to France with his mistress, the Australian painter Stella Bowen, and their daughter, Julie. Ford spent his last years living in France (where he founded the *Transatlantic Review*) and the United States. In 1938 he received an honorary professorship in Michigan.

His other works include a biography of his grandfather, *Ford Madox Brown* (1895); the novel *The Rash Act* (1933), about an individual who assumes the identity of a wealthy man who commits suicide, and its sequel, *Henry for Hugh* (1934); the critical works *The Critical Attitude* (1911), *Henry James* (1914), and *The March of Literature from Confucious' Day to Our Own* (1938); the long poems *Antwerp* (1915), *A House* (1921), and *Mister Bosphorous and the Muses* (1923); and his *Collected Poems* (1936). Ford died in France in 1939.

Bibliography

Judd, Alan, *Ford Madox Ford*, 1990.

Forster, E. M.

(January 1, 1879–June 7, 1970)
Novelist, Essayist, Critic, Journalist, Editor, Librettist

The English writer Edward Morgan Forster is most famous for two of his novels, *Howard's End* and *A Passage to India*, which explore the intricacies of human relationships, especially when people of different classes or cultures meet. Forster was also a noted critic and essayist.

Forster was born in London and lost his father before he was 2. His upbringing fell to three women in particular: his mother; his great-aunt, Marianne Thornton, who came from a family of wealthy bankers and about whom Forster wrote a biography in 1956; and his grandmother, whose cleverness and vivacity he particularly liked. He attended a preparatory school in Eastbourne, followed by Tonbridge School in Kent. At King's College, Cambridge, he later studied classics and history.

Forster's years at Cambridge were crucial to his development as a writer. He rejected the evangelical Protestant influences of his background and adopted the agnostic and secular outlook that underlies his work. At Cambridge Forster also acquired a dislike of the educational system to which he had been exposed, a dislike that is evident in his novel *The Longest Journey* (1907). His first published pieces appeared in college periodicals.

After his graduation, Forster traveled extensively in Europe. In England, he associated himself with the unconventional Bloomsbury Group, an informal social and intellectual group whose other writers, artists, critics, and theorists included VIRGINIA WOOLF and the economist John Maynard Keynes. His first novel, *Where Angels Fear to Tread* (1905), introduces the theme of social and cultural clash common throughout his work. An upper-middle-class English family, the Herritons, strongly oppose Lilia Herriton's marriage to an Italian, Gino. This theme continues in *A Room with a View* (1908), a light and humorous story about a woman torn between the man she loves and the man convention would have her marry.

The complexities of human relationships are the dominant theme of Forster's fiction. Class, ethnicity, gender, and conflicting values complicate the connections between his characters. In his smooth and concise writing style, he frequently contrasted materialism with the ideals of rich imagination and appreciation of nature. Some characters remain hopelessly trapped in their faults, but the life-changing experiences of others move them in the direction of these ideals.

Forster fully developed these motifs in the first novel to bring him success, *Howard's End* (1910). A sharp divide exists between the cultured, imaginative sisters Margaret and Helen Schlegel and the materialistic Wilcoxes. The exception to the rule in the Wilcox family is Ruth Wilcox, the owner of the beautiful country house, Howard's End, who becomes particularly attached to Margaret and leaves the house to her. The surviving Wilcoxes refuse to honor her request, but Margaret acquires the house anyway after she marries Henry Wilcox. By that time, Henry's lifestyle has beaten him down, and he symbolically and physically connects to the beauty and continuity that Margaret and the house symbolize. The novel's message, stated in an epigraph, is "only connect." The house in Howard's End is modeled on Forster's childhood home, Rooksnest. Director James Ivory's excellent film version of the novel was released in 1992.

During World War I, Forster spent three years in Alexandria working for the Red Cross. His experiences there are reflected in the travel book *Alexandria: A History and a Guide* (1922). After the war, he became increasingly active in leftist thought and activity. He edited the Labour Party newspaper the *Daily Herald*, was a member of the Humanist Society, and served twice as the President of the National Council for Civil Liberties.

Before he wrote *A Passage to India* (1924), Forster had traveled to India twice, and he was to return again in 1945. In the story, Adela Quested is a young English visitor to India, then part of the British Empire. Her personal conflict with a respected Indian, Dr. Aziz, whom she accuses of attacking her, represents and causes larger cultural conflicts between the British and Indians, a conflict that Forster handled adeptly and delicately. *A Passage to India* wan the James Tait Black Memorial Prize in 1925.

Part of what put Forster at odds with conventional British society was his homosexuality. Forster wrote several works that address homosexual themes but left them unpublished when he died. *Maurice*, written just before World War I, was not published until 1971. The novel concerns two college-age men who fall in love in a society that does not tolerate homosexuality. *The Life to Come*, a volume of short stories published in 1972, also treats homosexual themes.

During World War II Forster vocally opposed the Nazis. In 1946 he received an honorary fellowship from King's College that enabled him to live in financial comfort. His other works include the short-story collections *The Celestial Omnibus* (1914) and *The Eternal Moment* (1928); the travel book *The Hill of Devi* (1953), based on his experiences in India; *Abinger Harvest* (1932), a collection of previously published articles and reviews; and *Two Cheers for Democracy* (1951). In 1927 he gave the Clark Lectures at King's College, resulting in the critical work *Aspects of the Novel* (1927). He also wrote *Billy Budd* (1951), a libretto based on the classic work by Herman Melville (cowritten with Eric Crozier for an opera by BENJAMIN BRITTEN). Many of Forster's novels were adapted for theater and radio during his lifetime and made into films in the 1980s and 1990s.

BIBLIOGRAPHY
Ackerley, J. R., *E. M. Forster: A Portrait*, 1970; Colmer, John, *E. M. Forster: The Personal Voice*, 1975.

Fowles, John

(March 31, 1926–)
Novelist, Essayist, Poet

John Robert Fowles is best known for two of his novels, *The Magus* and the award-winning *The French Lieutenant's Woman*, which combine engaging storylines with psychological portraits. Fowles's works have proved particularly popular in the United States, and several have been adapted for the screen. In addition to novels, Fowles has written text for photographic books, poems, and a number of essays.

Fowles was born into a middle-class family in Leigh upon Sea, Essex, England. His father was a tobacco importer, who held orthodox religious beliefs against which Fowles rebelled. Fowles studied at Bedford School from 1939 to 1944, concentrating on French and German. During World War II, he served as a lieutenant in the Royal Marines and studied at the University of Edinburgh.

After the war, Fowles entered New College, Oxford, where he earned his B.A. in 1949. French writers ranging from Gustave Flaubert to the existentialist AL-BERT CAMUS were Fowles's main interests at the university. From 1950 to 1963, Fowles taught in England and on the Greek island of Spetsai (1951–1952). He married Elizabeth Whitton in 1954.

Although he had begun to write *The Magus* and other novels much earlier, his first published novel, *The Collector*, appeared in 1963. A typical Fowles plot is tightly constructed with unexpected twists and focuses on the psychological and sexual aspects of his characters. Fowles's love of nature and a Zen-influenced humanistic philosophy underlies his works. He moved to the country set-ting of Underhill Farm, near Lyme Regis, Dorset, in 1966 and has been active in environmental and ecological causes.

The Collector (1963), adapted for film in 1965, explores the psychosexual obsessions of a young, lower-class antihero, Clegg. The novel immediately established Fowles's reputation as a writer, and it received favorable reviews from the *Times Literary Supplement* and other publications. Aside from his entomological hobbies, Clegg develops an obsession for the middle-class Miranda Grey. When Clegg wins a large sum of money in a football pool, he quits his job and eventually buys an isolated country house. After having fitted its old chapel as a prison, he kidnaps Miranda and keeps her there, where she becomes an object for Clegg's sexual obsessions. Miranda dies, and the story ends with a new seed of obsession germinating in Clegg's head. Fowles accomplishes a multifaceted view of Miranda's ordeal by interrupting Clegg's first-person narrative with her own perspective on her life and her imprisonment.

The main action of *The Magus* (1965), also adapted for film (1968), takes place on a Greek island. The semiautobiographical protagonist Nicholas Urfe has just finished his studies at Oxford and gone to Greece. The enigmatic millionaire Maurice Conchis draws him into a mysterious and far-reaching game involving many players, leading Urfe to rediscover himself and forcing him to define his relationship with his girlfriend Alison.

The French Lieutenant's Woman (1969), filmed in 1981, is Fowles's best-known work, was a bestseller in the

United States, and won the W. H. Smith literary award in 1970. The mysterious Sarah Woodruff, a farmer's daughter who has nevertheless acquired an education, is the woman of the title. Woodruff, the former lover of a married French lieutenant, has an affair with the engaged and wealthy paleontologist Charles Smithson. Critics praised Fowles's novel not only for its engaging story, but for its depiction of the Victorian England atmosphere in which it is set.

Daniel Martin (1977), one of the most straightforward of Fowles's works, stands out among his later novels. The central character is the middle-aged Daniel Martin, whom Fowles traces through his complicated relationships and self-analysis. Other later novels include *A Maggot* (1985), a story set during the eighteenth century.

Fowles has also written poems, essays, novellas, and text for books of photographs. Among his other works are the book of nonfiction sketches *The Aristos* (1964); *Poems* (1973); *Shipwreck* (1975), a pictorial record of shipwrecks off Britain's coasts; *Islands* (1978), a study of the island metaphor in literature; *The Tree* (1979); *The Ebony Tower* (1974), a volume of novellas; the novel *Mantissa* (1982), and *Wormholes* (1998), a collection of essays. Fowles has also translated Charles Perrault's *Cinderella* (1974) and Claire de Durfort's *Ourika* (1977).

BIBLIOGRAPHY

Barnum, Carol M., *The Fiction of John Fowles: A Myth for Our Time*, 1988; Foster, Tom C., *Understanding John Fowles*, 1994; Huffaker, Robert, *John Fowles*, 1980; Tarbox, Katherine, *The Art of John Fowles*, 1988.

France, Anatole

(April 16, 1844–October 12, 1924)
Novelist, Poet, Critic

Cynicism, irony, and pointed satire mark the novels of Anatole France, who began his writing career with a skeptical, humanistic outlook and ended it as an impassioned social critic and political activist. France also wrote poetry and criticism; he received the Nobel Prize for Literature in 1921, "in recognition of his brilliant literary achievements, characterized as they are by a nobility of style, a profound human sympathy, grace, and a true Gallic temperament."

France was born Jacques-Anatole-François Thibault. His father was a Paris bookseller, and his father's book shop, which specialized in works on the French Revolution, introduced him to literature at a young age. From 1855 to 1862, France studied at the Collège Stanislas, where he received a classical education. His first book, *Alfred de Vigny* (1868), was a biography of the nineteenth-century French Romantic poet and author.

Anatole France (Ann Ronan/Image Select)

In the 1870s, France published poetry largely influenced by the Parnassians, advocates of classical verse and a strict, disciplined approach to poetic style. Two of his poems appeared in *Le Parnasse contemporain* in 1869, and his own collection, *Les Poèmes dorés (Gilded Poems)* was published in 1873. France's verse incorporates myth and legend, as in "La Fille de Caïn" ("The Daughter of Cain") as well as contemplation of nature, God, the universe, and death. A second volume of poetry, *Les noces corinthiennes (The Corinthian Wedding)*, was published in 1876.

The two novelettes published as *Jocaste et le chat maigre* (1879; *Jocasta and the Thin Cat*) were his first major works of fiction. Of his early fiction, *Le crime de Sylvestre Bonnard* (1881) proved to be one of the most successful and won a prize from the Académie Française the same year. The story, told in the form of diaries written by the scholar and antiquarian Sylvestre Bonnard, recounts the path that leads him away from the academic achievement toward which he aims.

The first part of the book finds Bonnard in furious pursuit of a fourteenth-century manuscript of great value to his work. When he loses all hope of obtaining the manuscript, it shows up as a gift from a formerly impoverished woman to whom he had shown kindness years before. It is the events of the second part that lead Bonnard to abandon his scholarly work. He takes an interest in Jeanne-Alexandre, the orphaned granddaughter of his former lover. After a series of mishaps and an illness, he becomes her legal guardian. Bonnard sells his library (the "crime" of the title being his secret removal of some of the books before the sale) to finance Jeanne-Alexandre's dowry and gives up his life as a scholar.

In 1886, France began to write for *Le Temps*. *La Rôtisserie de la Reine Pédauque* (1893; *At the Sign of the Reine Pédauque*), one of his most acclaimed novels, is set in eighteenth-century France. In the character of the fraudulent M. d'Astarac, France derides occult beliefs and practices. The protagonist of the story is the Abbé Jérôme Coignard, an unlucky and unorthodox Catholic. With his pupil, Jacques, who narrates the story, Coignard becomes involved with the unscrupulous occultist M. d'Astarac, leading both of them into intrigues that end in his death. Coignard is again the central character in *Les opinions de Jérôme Coignard* (1893); other novels of this period are *Thaïs* (1890), set in Egypt; *Le Lys rouge* (1894; *The Red Lily*), a love story set in Florence; and *Le Jardin d'Epicure* (1894; *The Garden of Epicurus*).

With his major series *L'Histoire contemporaine* (1897–1901), which presents the government, church, and other contemporary institutions in an unfavorable light, France began to turn his attention to contemporary political and social matters. The series begins with *L'orme du mail* (1897; *The Elm-Tree on the Mall*), and focuses on the first of two major plot threads, the political rivalry between the Abbé Lantaigne and the more conniving Abbé Guitrel over the post of Bishop of Tourcoing. The second thread concerns M. Bergeret, a scholar turned socialist activist. The second volume, *Le mannequin d'osier* (1897; *The Wicker Work Woman*), involves Bergeret's unhappy relationship with his dressmaker wife, who comes from a higher social background, and their ultimate parting.

The narrative of the third volume, *L'anneau d'améthyste* (1899; *The Amethyst Ring*), returns to the fight for the bishop's post. Bergeret emerges as a political advocate in *Monsieur Bergeret à Paris* (1901; *Monsieur Bergeret in Paris*), in which, like his creator, he becomes a vocal defender of Alfred Dreyfus. (Dreyfus was a Jewish-French army officer wrongly convicted of divulging military secrets to the Germans in 1894. A victim of the anti-Semitism so prevalent at the time, in fact convicted on the basis of documents forged by anti-Semites, he was defended by some of the most important writers in France and only vindicated twelve years later, after a struggle that almost brought down the French Republic.) From the period of the Dreyfus Affair onward, France developed increasingly radical political beliefs, which eventually lead him to join France's Communist Party.

The novel *Le livre de mon ami* (1885; *My Friend's Book*) began another of France's series, followed by *Pierre Nozière* (1899), *Le Petit Pierre* (1918; *Little Pierre*), and *La Vie en fleur* (1922; *The Bloom of Life*). Among his other works are the comedy *Crainquebille* (1903); *La Vie de Jeanne d'Arc* (1908), a life of Joan of Arc; *L'Île des Pingouins* (1908; *Penguin Island*), a satire on French history; *Les Dieux ont soif* (1912; *The Gods are*

Athirst), a tragic story set during the French Revolution; and *Le Révolte des Anges* (1914). France was elected to the French Academy in 1896 and to the Royal Society of Literature in London in 1908.

BIBLIOGRAPHY

Jefferson, Alfred Carter, *Anatole France: The Politics of Skepticism*, 1965; Tylden-Wright, David, *Anatole France*, 1967; Virtanen, Reino, *Anatole France*, 1968.

Friel, Brian

(January 9, 1929–)
Playwright, Short-Story Writer, Teacher

Known for his masterful treatment of everything Irish in plays and short stories, Brian Friel places his characters against the backdrop of his native Irish landscape, sketching character portraits and examining the cultural, historical, and political climate of Ireland. Among his best known plays are *Philadelphia, Here I Come!*, *The Loves of Cass McGuire*, and *Translations.*

Friel was born to a schoolteacher near Omagh, County Tyrone, Northern Ireland. He studied at Long Tower School and Saint Columb's College before entering Ireland's national seminary, St. Patrick's College, Maynooth. His unpleasant years at the seminary ended with a degree in 1948, after which he attended St. Joseph's Teacher Training College in Belfast. Upon the completion of his studies in 1950, he taught in Londonderry for the next decade. Friel married Anne Morrison in 1954.

While still teaching, Friel began to write short stories and plays. His first play, a radio play called *A Sort of Freedom*, was broadcast on the BBC in 1958. *The Francophile (A Doubtful Paradise)* was Friel's first effort for the stage, and

following an unsuccessful production at the Group Theatre in Belfast in 1958, it was adapted for radio and broadcast on the BBC in 1962.

The Blind Mice, another early work for the stage, premiered at the Eblana Theatre in Dublin in 1963. *The Enemy Within* marked Friel's first success as a playwright. A three-act play that premiered at the Abbey Theatre in Dublin in 1962, the drama is Friel's character study of the sixth-century Irish missionary St. Columba, who founded a monastery on the Scottish island of Iona. Friel portrays a flawed Columba, torn between his spiritual work and the worldly distractions his family imposes on him, although ultimately able to choose the former.

In 1963, Friel traveled to the United States, where he spent several months studying with the British director TYRONE GUTHRIE at the Tyrone Guthrie Theater in Minneapolis. His American travels provided the inspiration for two of his popular works, *Philadelphia, Here I Come!* (1963) and *The Loves of Cass McGuire* (1966).

Philadelphia, Here I Come! (1963), Friel's most commercially successful play, was first produced by the Dublin Theatre Festival in 1964. The play later moved to Broadway in New York and to the West End in London. The protagonist of the story is the young Irishman Gar O'Donnell, of whom the audience learns through a series of flashbacks, conversations, and glimpses into the future. Gar, bound for Philadelphia, is about to flee the emotional vacuum of his home, a vacuum created by his strained relationship with his pragmatic father and his failed relationship with Kate Doogan.

The aged female protagonist of *The Loves of Cass McGuire* (1966), also produced on Broadway, returns to Ireland after having lived most of her adult life as a waitress in New York City. Her reunion with her inhospitable family is anything but happy, and she soon finds herself in a home for the elderly, Eden House. After listening to two of the other inmates, Trilbe Costello and Mr. Ingram, deliver idealized versions of their lives, Cass, too, is reduced to believing an illusory version of her own past.

Friel's dramas unfold in Ireland and Northern Ireland, particularly in Donegal, where he made his home. Many of his early plays amount to individual character studies, whereas later plays turn to political and other themes. Several of his plays employ unusual dramatic devices, as in *Philadelphia, Here I Come!*, where two different actors portray Gar's public and private aspects. The story of *Faith Healer* (1979), about the life and death of faith healer Frank Hardy, unfolds in a series of monologues delivered by three different characters.

Friel's political plays include *The Freedom of the City* (1973), inspired by Bloody Sunday in Ireland in 1972, and *The Mundy Scheme* (1969). The un-

scrupulous cast of characters in the latter form the substance of Friel's satire on Ireland's political climate. The intrigue and power plays of the story center around a scheme to alleviate a troublesome financial situation by converting barren Irish land into an international burial ground, a plan advanced by Michael Maloney, Minister of Foreign Affairs.

Translations (1980), winner of the Ewart-Biggs Memorial Award, was the first play performed by the Field Day Theatre Company, which Friel founded with Stephen Rea. The play takes place at an Irish hedge school and attempts to show the impact of English culture on Ireland. *Molly Sweeney* (1994) relates the story of a woman blind from birth who gains her sight through the efforts of an alcoholic surgeon.

Friel, better known for his plays, began to publish short stories around the same time he wrote his first dramatic works. His first story, "The Skelper," appeared in *The New Yorker* in 1959. Among his volumes of short fiction are *A Saucer of Larks* (1962), the title story of which depicts two Germans who come to Donegal to find the burial site of a World War II casualty. A second collection, *The Gold and the Sea*, was published in 1966.

Friel was elected to the Irish Academy of Letters in 1972, received an honorary doctorate from the National University of Ireland in 1983, and was nominated for a seat in the Irish Senate in 1986. His other plays include *Lovers: Winners and Losers* (1967), *Crystal and Fox* (1968), *The Gentle Island* (1970), *Volunteers* (1975), *Living Quarters* (1977), *Aristocrats* (1979), *The Communication Chord* (1982), *Making History* (1988), and *Dancing at Lughnasa* (1990).

BIBLIOGRAPHY

Andrews, Elmer, *The Art of Brian Friel: Neither Reality Nor Dreams*, 1994; Dantanus, Ulf, *Brian Friel: A Study*, 1988; Duncan, Dawn, *Studies in the Plays of Brian Friel*, 1994; O'Brien, George, *Brian Friel*, 1990; Pine, Richard, *Brian Friel and Ireland's Drama*, 1990.

Fry, Christopher

(December 18, 1907–)
Playwright, Actor, Director, Screenwriter, Translator

At the height of his career in the late 1940s and early 1950s, Christopher Fry produced a series of successful verse dramas on London's West End that attracted top British actors of the era. His West End plays and others often carried religious themes and used historical settings. After 1961, Fry devoted himself primarily to writing adaptations, screenplays, and television plays.

Fry was born Christopher Harris in Bristol, Gloucestershire, England. His father, a builder and a minister, died when he was 3. Following his father's death, Fry's mother moved the family to Bedford, where Fry attended the Froebel Kindergarten. As a student his main interests were music and Greek, and for a time he contemplated going into the ministry. In 1918, Fry entered the Bedford Modern School. He adopted the name of his maternal grandmother. At the age of 18, he went to work as a teacher.

Over the next several years, Fry held a number of odd jobs around the theater. He began to write plays in the early 1920s and also acted and directed. In 1934 he accepted a position as director of the Tunbridge Wells Repertory Players. The same year, his own play *Youth and the Peregrins* was billed with the British premiere of GEORGE BERNARD SHAW's *A Village Wooing*. His other early plays include *Open Door* (1935) and the musical comedy *She Shall Have Music* (1935). Fry married Phyllis Hart in 1936.

Fry's *The Boy with a Cart* was first performed in Chichester in 1939. The play tells the story of St. Cuthman, who, as a boy, travels with his widowed mother, pulling her in a homemade cart. Cuthman's complete trust in the guidance and wisdom of God enables him to overcome his adversities. The play conveys a recurring theme in Fry's work, presenting a vision of an ordered universe in which God's hand guides all for the best, even in tragedy. In this respect Fry's outlook directly conflicted with the dominant view of contemporary European absurdist playwrights (see EUGÈNE IONESCO, ALBERT CAMUS, and JEAN-PAUL SARTRE), who took an atheistic perspective and viewed the world as chaotic and meaningless, or only to be given meaning by the individual who insists on living an authentic life. *The Boy with a Cart*, though not initially successful, was performed at the Lyric Theatre in 1950, with RICHARD BURTON in the leading role.

In style, too, Fry's plays differed from those of his absurdist contemporaries. Whereas absurdist dialogue often consists of idle or incoherent chatter whose only purpose seems to be to make a point about the absurdity of ordinary human life, Fry wrote his plays in polished verse. He became director of the Oxford Playhouse in 1939 and continued to write plays, among which was *The Tower* (1939). The following year he was drafted into the army as a noncombatant; he received a medical discharge in 1944. The Mercury Theatre staged his play *A Phoenix Too Frequent* in 1946.

Fry's first real success as a playwright came with the comedy *The Lady's Not For Burning* (1948), with a story set in the year 1400. The young and attractive Jennet Jourdemayne, accused of turning a man into a dog, finds herself the victim of a witch-hunt. During her attempt to escape, Jourdemayne meets and falls in love with Thomas Mendip, who, disgusted with a corrupt world and wanting to escape it by death, has confessed to murdering two men he did not kill. Jourdemayne's love for Mendip and her own resolve to live cure Mendip of his desire to die. The play was produced at the Globe Theatre in 1949 with JOHN GIELGUD as Mendip. The play, popular on the American stage as well as on the West End, won the Shaw Prize (1951) and the New York Drama Critics' Circle Best Play Award.

Thor, with Angels (1948), along with several of Fry's other plays, was written for a religious festival. The story unfolds amidst the competing forces of paganism and Christianity in sixth-century England. St. Augustine has arrived to reconvert the island to Christianity. The tragic hero Hoel finds himself caught in the middle—he is a Briton and a Christian convert captured by a family of pagan Jutes. The Jute captors are amazed to find themselves acting against their own wills in their treatment of Hoel and eventually convert to Christianity. The conversion, however, comes too late for Hoel, who is murdered. *The Firstborn* (1948), another of Fry's plays for a festival, is an adaptation of the biblical story of the exodus of the Israelites from Egypt.

A series of other plays in the 1950s marked the peak of Fry's career as a dramatist. *Venus Observed* (1950) was produced at the St. James Theatre with LAURENCE OLIVIER and was followed by *A Sleep of Prisoners* (1951). *The Dark Is Light Enough* (1954), staged at the Aldwych Theatre with EDITH EVANS, unfolds around the characters of the Countess Rosmarin, her acquaintances Jakob, Belmann, and Dr. Kassel, and Gettner, an author-turned-drunk and army deserter. Fry finished the historical play *Curtmantle* in 1961.

Aside from his own creations, Fry adapted and translated the work of others. Among them are JEAN ANOUILH's *L'invitation du château*, as *Ring Round the Moon* (1950); Anouilh's *The Lark* in 1955; several plays by JEAN GIRAUDOUX, including *Duel Angels* (1963) from *Pour Lucrèce* and *Tiger at the Gates* (1955) from *La Guerre de Troie n'aura pas lieu (The Trojan War Will Not Take Place)*; Henrik Ibsen's *Peer Gynt* (1970); and Edmond Rostand's *Cyrano de Bergerac* (1975).

Fry finished a number of screenplays and plays for radio and television. He wrote screenplays for *The Beggar's Opera* (1953), *Ben Hur* (1959), *Barabbas* (1962), and *The Bible: In The Beginning*

(1966). His television adaptation of Anne Brontë's *The Tenant of Wildfell Hall* aired in 1968, and he completed a series of four television plays entitled *The Brontës of Haworth* (1973). Fry's other works include the play *A Yard of Sun* (1970); *Can You Find Me: A Family History* (1978) and the children's book *The Boat That Mooed* (1965).

BIBLIOGRAPHY

Leeming, Glenda, *Christopher Fry*, 1990; Leeming, Glenda, *Poetic Drama*, 1988.

Fuentes, Carlos

(November 11, 1928–)
Novelist, Short-Story Writer, Playwright, Critic, Diplomat

The chief theme in the work of Mexican writer Carlos Fuentes, best known for novels that reach into the past to analyze the present, is the history and culture of Mexico. His use of innovative combinations of literary techniques, such as flashback, stream of consciousness or interior monologue, and blurred chronology, to create his narratives made him one of the most popular Latin American writers of the twentieth century and won him international audiences as well. His writings are among the most popular and influential in Latin America.

Fuentes was born to a middle-class diplomat and his wife in Mexico City. His father's career took the family all over the Americas and Europe when he was young. Fuentes attended schools in many North and South American capitals as a boy, earned a law degree at the University of Mexico, and pursued further study in law in Geneva, Switzerland. Early in his career he rejected his upbringing and became an avowed Marxist. He worked chiefly in political posts in the years immediately following his graduation and represented Mexico in a number of international delegations. His most important post, as ambassador to France, lasted from 1975 to 1977. In addition, Fuentes edited several literary journals.

Fuentes's first collection of stories, *The Masked Days*, appeared in 1954. The first of his novels, *Where the Air is Clear* (1958), is a harshly critical portrait of twentieth-century Mexico City; it secured his fame in his native country. *The Good Conscience* followed in 1959. *The Death of Artemio Cruz* (1962) was widely translated and made Fuentes an international success. The novel's unheroic protagonist, Artemio Cruz, is a wealthy and powerful veteran of the Mexican Revolution who has betrayed its ideals. As he lies dying, Cruz recalls the major events of his life and is tormented by his ruthless actions.

Fuentes used doubles in several subsequent works. *Aura* (1962) is a fantastic, dreamlike love story steeped with elements of witchcraft and sorcery. The four central characters are in reality two sets of doubles who represent different aspects of the same individual. The doubles in the psychological novel *Zona Sagrada* (1967), which explores the sexual obsessions of a young man, and *Birthdays* (1969) are even more complex.

In *A Change of Skin* (1967) and *Terra Nostra* (1975), Fuentes returned to Mexican culture and history. *The Old Gringo* (1985) was inspired by the mysterious disappearance of the American writer Ambrose Bierce in Mexico in 1914. *Christopher Unborn* (1987) takes place in dismal, polluted, and overpopulated Mexico City. A man who had the honor of being the first child born on the five-hundredth anniversary of Columbus's arrival in the West narrates the story. *The Campaign* (1991) is set in the revolutionary climate of nineteenth-century Latin America. In the autobiographical *Diana, The Goddess Who Hunts Alone* (1995), Fuentes treats his brief affair with the American actress Jean Seberg. Fuentes's latest work, *The Crystal Frontier: A Novel in Nine Stories* (1997), focuses on the relationship between the United States and Mexico. The unifying character in all nine stories is Leonardo Barroso, a powerful boss with extensive connections on both sides of the border.

In addition to his novels and short stories, Fuentes has also written several plays. Among them is *Orchids in the Moonlight* (1982), set in Los Angeles, about two failed Mexican actresses who move to Hollywood and deceive themselves about their success. His other books include the critical work *The New Hispano-American Novel* (1969), *House With Two Doors* (1970), *Mexican Time* (1971), his essay *Buried Mirror* (1992), a detective novel called *The Hydra Head* (1978), the novel *Distant Relations* (1980), *The Orange Tree* (1994), and *A New Time for Mexico* (1996).

BIBLIOGRAPHY

Brody, Robert, and Rossman, Charles, eds., *Carlos Fuentes: A Critical View*, 1982; Faris, Wendy B., *Carlos Fuentes*, 1983; González, Alfonso, *Carlos Fuentes: Life, Work, and Criticism*, 1987; Williams, Raymond L., *The Writings of Carlos Fuentes*, 1996.

Fugard, Athol

(June 11, 1932–)
Playwright, Actor, Director

The South African playwright Harold Athol Lannigan Fugard has produced a steady stream of anti-apartheid plays since the early 1960s. His dramas examine the social consequences of South Africa's apartheid laws and use representative characters to probe particular segments of society.

Although constrained by poverty and prejudice, Fugard's characters do not live in a hopeless world. His latest play, *Valley Song*, looks toward the future of postapartheid society in South Africa.

Fugard was born in Middleburg, Great Karroo, Cape Province, South Africa and grew up in the industrial town of Port

Elizabeth. His father, a former jazz pianist of British descent, was handicapped and could not work. In order to support the family his mother, of Afrikaaner ancestry, managed a boarding house and later ran a tearoom. The racism he observed in his mother's tearoom had a profound impact on shaping his attitude toward apartheid. Fugard studied at a Catholic elementary school, studied motor mechanics at the Port Elizabeth Technical College, and eventually enrolled at the University of Cape Town. There he majored in philosophy and social anthropology.

Before he finished, however, Fugard went north to Port Sudan and joined the crew of a British merchant vessel, the SS *Graigaur.* As the only white crew member, he made friends with a number of his African shipmates and came to thoroughly oppose apartheid. From 1955 to 1957 he worked as a journalist for the *Evening Post,* and from 1958 to 1960 he worked as a clerk in the Native Commissioner's Court in Johannesburg. His observance of the poor treatment of blacks in that position further strengthened his resolve against apartheid, and he determined to combat the apartheid system with his dramas.

Fugard's initial success came in 1961 with *The Blood Knot* (1961), the first in a trio of plays entitled *The Family Trilogy.* The story demonstrates South Africa's racial divide in the characters of two brothers. In *The Blood Knot,* Morris, intelligent, practical, and very literate, is so light-skinned that he passes for white. His brother Zach, a dejected and illiterate figure, is so dark he is considered black. The two begin a pen-pal correspondence with a white girl named Ethel—using Morris's words and Zach's name—which

inevitably causes problems. In a second episode, Morris and Zach act out a series of roles that parody the expected behaviors of blacks and whites.

The Blood Knot immediately won international attention and was produced for television in 1967. *Hello and Goodbye* (1965) and *Boesman and Lena* (1969) completed the trilogy, later published as *Three Port Elizabeth Plays* (1974). *Boesman and Lena,* which premiered in South Africa in 1969, is set during a night in the life of the title characters, just after their shanty town has been destroyed.

The strong antiapartheid statements of Fugard's plays, coupled with his use of black and white actors together, inevitably led to conflict with the authorities. The government confiscated his passport from 1967 to 1971. Other early plays include *No-Good Friday* and *Nongogo,* which appeared as *Two Early Plays* (1977).

Fugard usually acts in and directs his plays. The characters in his dramas are symbolic of strains, trends, or laws in society and are not developed as individuals. There is little action in his dramas— more important is the confrontation of the symbolic forces embodied in the characters. Set among the lower and working classes, the plays employ sparse scenery that reflects the circumstances in which the characters live. A dead tree, for example, stands as the dominant visual symbol of the characters' desolation in *Boesman and Lena.*

In *Sizwe Bansi Is Dead* (1972) and *The Island* (1973), Fugard collaborated with the black actors John Kani and Winston Ntshona. Kani and Ntshona supplied dialogue for Fugard's scenarios. In the former, Sizwe Bansi is an illiterate man from Port Elizabeth looking for work. He gets a chance to better his lot when he finds the pass book of a deceased man. The man had more legal privileges than he has, and Siswe takes on the new identity. Kani and Ntshona won a Tony in 1975 for their performances in these two plays. Together with *Statements after an Arrest under the Immorality Act*, they were published as *Three Plays* in 1974.

"*Master Harold*" . . . *and the Boys* (1982) enjoyed success in both London and New York. Based on Fugard's own childhood mistreatment of a Basuto waiter at his mother's tea shop, which he felt terrible about, the play concerns the relationship between the 17-year-old Hally (the Master Harold of the title), who is white, and his family's two black servants, Sam and Willie ("the Boys").

With his latest play, *Valley Song* (1995), Fugard examines life in post-apartheid society. The story takes place in a valley town in the Karoo region, and each of the three characters represents a strain in the new society. Abraam Jonkers is an older black farmer whose family has worked a small piece of land for generations. Abraam, a representative of the older generation, is dedicated to the land. His daughter Veronica, however, is a member of the younger generation and aspires to bigger things—she wants to become a singer. The Author is a white playwright who represents a third sector of the new society. In the original production Fugard acted the parts of both Abraam and The Author, and he instructs that the same actor is to play both in his stage directions.

Among Fugard's other plays are *Dimetos* (1977); *Orestes* (1978); *A Lesson from Aloes* (1978); *The Road to Mecca* (1985); *My Children, My Africa!* (1988), inspired by a real-life story and about a black teacher who dies at the hand of a mob; *Playland* (1992); and *The Captain's Tiger* (1999). Fugard has appeared in several films, including *The Killing Fields* (1984) and *Gandhi*.

Fugard's other writings include the novel *Tsotsi* (1980) and his *Notebooks, 1960–1977* (1983). He received an honorary doctorate of literature from the University of Port Elizabeth, and the city also gave him the Freedom of the City.

BIBLIOGRAPHY

Benson, Mary, *Athol Fugard and Barney Simon: Bare Stage, A Few Props, Great Theatre*, 1997; Gray, Stephen, ed., *Athol Fugard*, 1982; Vandenbroucke, Russell, *Truths the Hand Can Touch: The Theatre of Athol Fugard*, 1985; Walder, Dennis, *Athol Fugard*, 1984.

Fuller, Roy

(February 11, 1912–September 27, 1991)
Poet, Novelist, Teacher, Essayist, Journalist

Roy Broadbent Fuller emerged as a poet in England during World War II, part of the generation between the Thirties poets and the Movement poets of the 1950s. The war and political issues inspired his early verse, and he later wrote more personal and contemplative poetry. Although he was better known for his poetry, he also wrote a number of novels.

Fuller was born in Failsworth, Lancashire, England. Although he was an avid reader with intellectual interests, his lower-middle-class origin deprived him of the luxury of attending fine schools. Fuller's father worked for a rubber-proofing firm; he died when Fuller was 8. His mother moved the family to Blackpool after his death, and there Fuller enrolled in the Blackpool High School. Anxious to leave the area, he decided to pursue a career in law. At the same time, he nursed an interest in poetry, and his first published poem appeared in the *Sunday Referee* in 1928.

In 1935, Fuller went to work in Kent, and he married Kathleen Smith the following year. In 1938, he became assistant solicitor for the Woolwich Equitable Building Society, a position he held for twenty years, becoming solicitor in 1958 and holding that post until 1969. In his early years as a poet and lawyer, Fuller was active with Socialist political groups. He admired the Thirties poets with similar political leanings, such as STEPHEN SPENDER and W. H. AUDEN, both of whom influenced his early verse.

With the outbreak of World War II, Fuller served in the Royal Navy, providing him with the experiences for his early volumes of poetry. The first, *Poems*, was published in 1939 and attracted little attention. It was followed by the more successful *The Middle of a War* (1942), a book of war-inspired verse that evokes the bombing of London, giving a semiautobiographical view of his early experiences during the war.

Fuller wrote the verse for a third volume, *A Lost Season* (1944), while he was stationed in Africa. The African landscape of the poems contrasts with the English atmosphere of those in the previous volume and adds a new dimension to his war poetry. Fuller's African experience also inspired his children's work *Savage Gold* (1946).

With *Epitaphs and Occasions* (1949), Fuller began to move away from the political orientation of his earlier verse. *Counterparts* (1954), although it still contains some political poems such as "Socialist's Song," marked a turn to more introspective and philosophical verse. The nature of art, poetry, and the poet's place in society emerge as themes. Fuller addressed poems to cultural figures he admired, such as ANDRÉ GIDE. *Brutus's Orchard* (1957), often considered his finest work, completed Fuller's introspective turn.

At this point, Fuller often framed his verse in sonnet form. *Buff* (1965), which contains a series of Shakespearean sonnets entitled "The Historian," followed the publication of his *Collected Poems 1936–61* (1962). His later volumes of poetry include *New Poems* (1968), *Tiny Tears* (1973), *From the Joke Shop* (1975), written in iambic stanzas, and *New and Collected Poems, 1934–84* (1985).

Although better known for his poetry, Fuller completed a number of novels. Thrillers such as *The Second Curtain* (1953) and *Fantasy and Fugue* (1954) appeared in the early 1950s. *Image of Society* (1956), informed by his work in the legal profession, in part concerns a power struggle between two men, one a pragmatic, unfeeling soul and the other a careless egotist. Among his other novels are *The Ruined Boys* (1959), *The Fa-*

ther's Comedy (1961), The Perfect Fool (1963), and The Carnal Island (1970).

My Child, My Sister (1965) was Fuller's favorite of his own works. Narrated by the protagonist Albert Shore, it concerns a novelist's attempt to sort through the emotional wreckage of his life. Shore is a successful and aging novelist living in the difficult milieu left from family strife. His son, Fabian, marries Frances Leaf, the stepdaughter of Fabian's mother and Shore's ex-wife. Opposed to the union at first, he later finds the marriage a source of healing and comfort. Shore's own relationship with the much younger art student Flip, the Leafs' daughter, proves tragic when Flip loses her sanity and is confined.

Fuller taught poetry at the University of Oxford from 1968 to 1973. His lectures from those years are collected in the volumes Owls and Artificers (1971) and Professors and Gods (1973). Throughout his career, he contributed reviews, articles, and essays to numerous periodicals. His four volumes of memoirs were published between 1980 and 1991. Fuller was made Commander of the Order of the British Empire in 1970.

BIBLIOGRAPHY

Austin, Allan E., Roy Fuller, 1979; Powell, Neil, Roy Fuller: Writer and Society, 1995; Tolley, A. T., ed., Roy Fuller: A Tribute, 1993.

Furtwängler, Wilhelm

(January 25, 1886–November 30, 1954)
Conductor, Composer

One of the foremost conductors of the first half of the twentieth century, Gustav Heinrich Ernst Martin Wilhelm Furtwängler, to give him his full name, was best known for his exuberant interpretations of the Romantic composers and for his long association with the Berlin Philharmonic Orchestra. Widely criticized in the United States for remaining in Germany during World War II, he was more successful with European audiences than with American ones. Furtwängler also composed his own music.

Furtwängler was born the son of a distinguished archaeologist in Berlin. He was educated privately and studied for a time under the German theorist Heinrich Schenker. As a teenager his first ambition was to become a composer, and a large symphony was an early effort in the body of work he composed over his career. His Symphonic Largo was featured in his conducting debut with the Kaim Orchestra in 1906.

From 1907 to 1909 Furtwängler assisted the conductor Felix Mottl. He worked in Lübeck between 1911 and 1915 before taking a directorship at the Mannheim Opera (1915–1918). In 1920 he replaced RICHARD STRAUSS as conductor of the Berlin Opera concerts. The year 1922 brought appointments as conductor of the Gewandhaus Concerts in Leipzig and, more importantly, as Chief Conductor for Life of the Berlin Philharmonic Orchestra.

Furtwängler's years at the Berlin Philharmonic are usually considered his greatest as a conductor. Under his direction the orchestra developed a lush string sound and excelled in the works of the Romantics. The works of Anton Bruckner, Johannes Brahms (particularly the First Symphony), Richard Wagner, Ludwig von Beethoven, and Wolfgang Amadeus Mozart were central in Furtwängler's repertoire.

In 1930 Furtwängler began conducting the Vienna Philharmonic Orchestra, and in 1933 he took a conducting post at the Berlin State Opera. He was also associated with the Bayreuth Festival (1931–1932) and the Salzburg Festival (after World War II). His decision to remain in Germany under the Nazi regime haunted him for the rest of his life. Furtwängler never joined the National Socialist Party, and he used his influence to help several Jewish associates escape from Germany. He was cleared of involvement with the Nazis in denazification hearings after the war, but his residence in Germany under Hitler cost him conducting posts at the New York Philharmonic and the Chicago Symphony Orchestra. Furtwängler's denazification hearings were the subject of Ronald Harwood's 1994 play *Taking Sides*.

Furtwängler made many recordings of his work, particularly of his live performances. He died of bronchitis at the age of sixty-eight. *Wilhelm Furtwängler: Notebooks, 1924–54* was published in 1989.

BIBLIOGRAPHY

Ardoin, John, *The Furtwängler Record*, 1994; Furtwängler, Elisabeth, *About Wilhelm Furtwängler*, 1993; Furtwängler, Wilhelm, *Wilhelm Furtwängler: Notebooks, 1924–54*, 1989; Shirikawa, Sam H., *The Devil's Music Master: The Controversial Life and Career of Wilhelm Furtwängler*, 1992.

G

Jean Gabin (AKG)

Gabin, Jean

(May 17, 1904–November 15, 1976)
Actor

Jean Gabin emerged as one of the most popular actors on the French screen in the mid-1930s. From that time until his death in 1976, he appeared in more than ninety films. His strong, tough image led to many roles as social outcasts, criminals, and gangsters.

Gabin was born Jean-Alexis Moncorgé into a family with intimate ties to the theater in Paris. His father was a music-hall comedian who also used the stage name Jean Gabin. By 1923 Gabin had decided to pursue a career in the theater, and he appeared regularly at the Folies-Bergère in Paris as well as in cabarets and vaudeville shows.

In 1928 he appeared in his first film, *Ohé! Les Valises* (1928). By the time he made *Chacun sa chance* (1930), he had decided to give up the theater for film. His first success on screen came in 1934, when he appeared in *Maria Chapdelaine*. In Julien Duvivier's *Pépé le Moko* (1937), set in French Algiers, Gabin again scored a success as the Casbah-based gangster Pépé. In JEAN RENOIR's classic antiwar film *Grande Illusion* (*Grand Illusion*, 1937), he was among a group of prisoners in a World War I German prison camp.

Gabin appeared in various popular roles over the next several years—entangled in a love triangle in *La Bête Humaine* (1938), as an army deserter in Marcel Carné's *Quai des brumes* (American title *Port of Shadows*, 1938), and as a loner-murderer in Carné's *Le Jour se lève* (*Daybreak*, 1939). He served in World War II, took part in the invasion of Normandy, and was awarded the Croix de Guerre.

Gabin's later films include *La Marie du port* (1950); *Le plaisir* (1951); *Touchez pas au Grisbi* (1953); *Des gens sans importance* (1956); *Les Misérables* (1957); *Speaking of Murder* (1959); *Money, Money, Money* (1962); *The Upper Hand* (1967); *The Sicilian Clan* (1969); and *L'année sainte* (*Pilgrimage to Rome*, 1976). *Inspector Maigret* (1958) inaugurated a series of films in which he starred as Inspector Maigret. Awards for Best Actor at the Venice and Berlin Festivals are among the honors Gabin received.

BIBLIOGRAPHY

Barbier, Philippe, and Moreau, Jacques, *Jean Gabin: Album Photos*, 1983; Thomas, Nicholas, ed., *International Dictionary of Films and Filmmakers*, 1992.

Galsworthy, John

(August 14, 1867–January 31, 1933)
Novelist, Playwright, Poet, Short-Story Writer, Essayist

Best known for his two trilogies of novels about the propertied Forsyte family, John Galsworthy scrutinized upper-middle-class British society and treated other socioeconomic themes in his fiction and dramas. He was awarded the Nobel Prize for Literature in 1932 "for his distinguished art of narration, which takes its highest form in *The Forsyte Saga.*"

Galsworthy was born in Kingston Hill, Surrey, England. His father was a solicitor whose family acquired a considerable fortune. Galsworthy was tutored at home until he was 9, when he enrolled in the Saugeen Preparatory School at Bournemouth. As at the schools at which he later studied, he was an above average student with interests in acting and athletics. Galsworthy later attended Harrow and New College, Oxford, where he studied law and obtained a degree in 1889.

Law was his father's choice for Galsworthy's career, but the legal profession did not suit the younger Galsworthy. He was called to the bar in 1890 and, with the idea of pursuing marine law, decided to travel around the world. While aboard the *S. S. Torrens*, Galsworthy met the author JOSEPH CONRAD, then serving as the ship's first mate. Conrad's career at sea was drawing to a close, and he was subsequently to become a dedicated friend to Galsworthy.

Galsworthy gave up law and devoted his time to writing. A volume of short stories, *From the Four Winds*, appeared in 1897. Using the pseudonym John Sinjohn, he published his first novel, *Jocelyn*, in 1898, followed by *Villa Rubein* in 1900. *Island Pharisees* (1904) appeared under his own name and addressed themes that recur throughout his work—the complacency of upper-class English society and failures of romantic relationships. The protagonist, Shelton, is an upper-middle-class Englishman engaged to be married and increasingly disillusioned with the class divisions of society and with his own family.

In 1905, Galsworthy married Ada Pearson, his cousin's former wife, with whom he had been having an affair for ten years. The following year saw the publication of the first in a long series of novels about the Forsyte family. The first series, a trilogy with two shorter interludes, is collectively known as *The Forsyte Saga. The Man of Property* (1906), its first novel, introduces the strong-willed, narrow-minded patriarch Soames Forsyte, a solicitor and the owner of a considerable amount of property. Soames's wife, Irene, has an affair with the architect Philip Bosinney, who incurs Soames's wrath and later dies in an accident.

After serving with the Red Cross during World War I in 1916 and refusing a knighthood in 1917, Galsworthy continued the story in the interlude "Indian Summer of a Forsyte" (1918), the novel *In Chancery* (1920), the interlude "Awakening" (1920), and the novel *To Let* (1921). The first interlude takes place in 1892, when Irene separates from Soames and grows close to Jolyon Forsyte. Irene and Soames divorce in *In Chancery*, which also recounts another significant event in *The Forsyte Saga*—the birth of

Soames's daughter Fleur. Jon Forsyte, Irene's son, is a central character in "Awakening," and *To Let* recounts the troubled romance between Jon and Fleur and Fleur's marriage to Michael Mont, the son of a baronet and a man she does not truly love.

The first Forsyte trilogy is primarily concerned with relationships and attitudes in the Forsyte circle. In the second trilogy, *A Modern Comedy*, Galsworthy expanded the sphere to the realm of political and social issues. *The White Monkey* (1924) begins the series, focusing on the relationship between Fleur and Michael. Again, Galsworthy separated the novels with interludes. "A Silent Wooing" finds Jon Forsyte growing peaches in South Carolina, where he meets and marries Anne Wilmot, daughter of a prominent southern family.

Her brother, Francis, travels to England in *The Silver Spoon* (1926), the second novel in the trilogy. But the main story revolves around Michael, who has abandoned his publishing career and decided to go into politics. He wins a seat in Parliament but grows disillusioned with his inability to effect change. As a politician Michael espouses "Foggartism," which some critics have seen as a satire on Fabian socialism (see GEORGE BERNARD SHAW). Also central to *The Silver Spoon* is the libel case that rages between Soames and Fleur on one side, and the aristocrat Marjorie Ferrar and her fiancé on the other. Although Fleur wins a legal and moral victory, a society Galsworthy viewed as corrupt awards the victory to Marjorie.

"Passers By," a second interlude, brings the major Forsyte characters together in a Washington, D.C., hotel, where Fleur, Soames, Jon, Anne, and Irene happen to be staying at the same time. The interlude was followed by *Swan Song* (1928), the last of Galsworthy's Forsyte novels. Michael, who often reflects Galsworthy's own philosophy, defends striking underpaid miners during the General Strike of 1926, while the romance between Jon and Fleur rekindles. *Swan Song* also recounts the death of the aged patriarch Soames.

Galsworthy's Forsyte novels became very popular in both Britain and the United States, and the *Forsyte Saga* was the basis of the British Broadcasting Corporation's major production of the same title in 1967. His other novels include *The Country House* (1907); *The Patrician* (1911); *The Freelands* (1915); *Beyond* (1917), about a woman's troubled marriage to a Swedish violinist; and the trilogy *End of the Chapter* (1934).

Aside from novels, Galsworthy also wrote many plays. *Justice* (1910) was one of his most influential social commentaries, inspired by his own visits to Britain's prisons. In the story, a young clerk, Falder, falsifies a check to obtain money to move to South America with a woman whose husband beats her and her children. After his arrest and conviction, he is sentenced to a prison term. The brutal environment in which he finds himself leaves permanent psychological scars, and he is unable to function normally when he is released. Falder commits suicide when he faces a second arrest for failing to report to his parole officer. Galsworthy particularly objected to the practice of solitary confinement, and he corresponded with British prison officials about reforms.

The Skin Game (1920)—about a property conflict between the wealthy, established Hillcrists and the newly rich Hornblowers, who want to build a factory that will ruin the view from the Hillcrist home—premiered at St. Martin's Theatre and was one of Galsworthy's most successful plays. His other plays include *The Silver Box* (1906), a critical commentary on the English justice system; *Strife* (1909); *The Pigeon* (1912); *The Mob* (1914); *Loyalties* (1922); and *The Roof* (1929). Galsworthy's other works include the volumes of poetry *Moods, Songs, and Doggerels* (1912), and *The Bells of Peace* (1921); the short-story collections *A Man of Devon* (1901), *Five Tales* (1918), and *Captures* (1923); and the essay collections *The Inn of Tranquility* (1912), *A Sheaf* (1916), and *Castles of Spain* (1927).

In 1921 Galsworthy became the first president of the writers' club PEN. He received honorary degrees from Dublin University, Cambridge, Princeton, Oxford, and other universities, and in 1929 he was made a member of the Order of Merit.

BIBLIOGRAPHY

Gindin, James, *John Galsworthy's Life and Art*, 1987

Gance, Abel

(October 25, 1889–November 10, 1981)
Director, Screenwriter

Abel Gance was the most experimental of the post–World War I generation of film makers in France and a significant technical innovator in the development of film. Although he continued working well into the eras of sound and color, his masterpieces, such as *I Accuse!* and *Napoleon*, belong to the era of silent film.

Gance was born in Paris and attended the Collège de Chantilly and the Collège Chaptal. His father tried to steer him into a career in the legal profession, but Gance quickly rejected law and turned to the theater. By 1907 he had decided to pursue acting, and in 1909 he acted in his first film, *Molière*. The major work of his theater period was the lengthy play *Victoire de Samothrace*. Gance began writing screenplays and, after recuperating from tuberculosis, founded the company Le Film Français in 1911. His codirected first film, *The Dike* (1911) with Pierre Renoir, brother of the film maker JEAN RENOIR and son of the major Impressionist painter Pierre-Auguste Renoir.

The comic farce *La Folie du Docteur Tube* (1916; *The Folly of Dr. Tube*) marked the beginning of Gance's long period of technical innovation. The story, about a scientist who discovers a means of altering people's shapes, spurred Gance to experiment with mirrors to achieve the required distortions.

Another early film, *Barberousse* (1916), first used the horizontal wipe, while in *Mater Dolorosa* (1917; *Sorrowful Mother*) Gance experimented with contrasts. Typical of Gance's early subject matter is the drama *La Dixième Symphonie* (1918; *Tenth Symphony*), which concerns a composer who marries a woman with a secret that ultimately jeopardizes their relationship.

In his film-making style, Gance was particularly influenced by the American director D. W. Griffith, whom he met in New York in 1921. *J'Accuse* (1919; *I Accuse!*), an antiwar statement inspired by World War I, was Gance's most technically innovative film to date, incorporating montages (see also SERGEY EISENSTEIN), tinting, superimposed images, and other techniques. The public and critics responded favorably to the film, and it was Gance's first international success. (Gance was to produce another antiwar work in his first major sound film, *La Fin du monde* (1931; *The End of the World*).

La Roué (1923; *The Wheel*) turned to another issue in the early twentieth century—the increasing mechanization of society. The story itself centers around three characters, Sisif, a railway mechanic; his son, Elie; and his adopted daughter, Norma. The rhythm of Gance's carefully orchestrated montages mimics the repetitive turning of the wheel of fate, which leads to disaster in the film. In this work, he removed cameras from their tripods and placed them on moving trains.

Gance's epic *Napoléon vu par Abel Gance* (1927; *Napoleon as Seen by Abel Gance*) was shown in Polyvision, a technique Gance designed (and had patented the year before) in which three projectors showed three images on an enlarged screen. Polyvision never became popular due to its high cost and the advent of sound, but it anticipated Cinerama in the 1950s and 1960s, in which films were shown from three projectors on a curved screen. *Napoleon* earned as much praise for its portrayal of Napoleon Bonaparte as it did for its technical aspects. Gance researched his life extensively and presented a heroic portrait of Bonaparte in his early life, although some critics fault him for sacrificing historical accuracy. *Un Grand Amour de Beethoven* (1936; *The Life and Loves of Beethoven*), a sound film about the composer, was Gance's other major biographical work; he never finished his long-planned film on Christopher Columbus.

The advent of sound ended Gance's greatest period of creativity and popularity, although he continued to produce films. He made sound versions of earlier films such as *Sorrowful Mother*, *I Accuse*, and *Napoleon*, but these never gained the popularity or critical acclaim of their silent predecessors. His later films include *La Tour de Nesle* (1954; *The Tower of Nesle*); *Austerlitz* (1960; *The Battle of Austerlitz*), his first major film in color; and *Cyrano et d'Artagnan* (1963; *Cyrano and d'Artagnan*).

BIBLIOGRAPHY

King, Norman, *Abel Gance: A Politics of Spectacle*, 1984; Welsh, James M., and Kramer, Stephen P., *Abel Gance*, 1978.

García Lorca, Federico

(June 5, 1898–August 19/20, 1936)
Poet, Playwright

In spite of his early death in 1936, Federico García Lorca remains one of the most popular literary figures in Hispanic culture. His popular trilogy of plays, *Blood Wedding*, *Yerma*, and *The House of Bernarda Alba*, are still widely performed. As a member of the Spanish poets dubbed the Generation of 1927, he wrote poetry and plays inspired by the Andalusian peasant culture that surrounded him in his youth, and was instrumental in reviving *cante jondo*, a traditional form of Spanish song.

García Lorca was born into a Catholic family in Fuente Vaqueros, near Granada, in the province of Andalusia in southern Spain. His mother was a teacher and his father a prosperous farmer. García Lorca was an introverted child and liked to write poems and play music. His mother taught him how to play the piano. After the family moved to nearby Granada in 1909, he attended a Jesuit school, and he later continued his studies in law at the University of Granada. In 1918, he paid to publish *Impresiones y Viajes* (*Impressions and Landscapes*), a collection of prose inspired by his travels in Castile.

The Residence of Students at the University of Madrid, where he transferred in 1919, provided García Lorca with the creative platform he needed to launch his literary career. He met other Spanish artists and writers, such as SALVADOR DALÍ and Rafael Alberti, and frequented cafés where the Spanish literary vanguard held discussions. García Lorca became well known among his circle of friends for his poetry readings but did not publish any poetry until his *Libro de Poemas* (1921; *Book of Poems*). Its seventy-nine poems, most of them written in 1918–1919, intimately addressed themes connected with Andalusian peasant life—the passing of time, women, death, fate, and melancholy.

It was the culture of the Andalusian peasantry that inspired most of García Lorca's work. With the Spanish composer MANUEL DE FALLA in 1922, he organized a festival of Andalusian gypsy songs known as *cante jondo*, or deep song. The publication of his *Romancero gitano* (1928; *Gypsy Ballads*), and *Poema del cante jondo* (1931; *Poem of the Cante Jondo*), poems based on the *cante jondo*, brought him his first international acclaim. The former used the traditional Spanish ballad form to convey Andalusian gypsy themes.

In addition to his poetry readings, García Lorca began writing and performing plays. His first, the two-act *El maleficio de la mariposa* (*Butterfly's Evil Spell*), debuted in 1920 in Madrid and flopped on its first night. Far more successful was his verse drama *Mariana Pineda* (1927), performed in Barcelona and Madrid with a set designed by Dalí. In the story, Mariana Pineda, a widow, refuses to denounce a group of rebels led by the man she loves, who has fled, and pays with her life. Dalí also helped García Lorca organize an exhibition of the latter's drawings the same year.

García Lorca spent 1929–1930 in New York and in Cuba, where he wrote a series of pessimistic poems, critical of the mechanization of modern civilization, that were not published until after his death, *Poeta en Nueva York* (1940; *Poet in New York and Other Poems*). His experiences in America left a negative impression on him, and in 1931 he returned to Madrid and began working with a government-sponsored theater group commissioned to bring excellent theater to the provinces. The group, known as La Barraca and composed of students, performed the classic works of Spanish dramatists such as Lope de Vega, Tirso de Molina, Miguel de Cervantes, and Pedro Calderón de la Barca.

In addition to his work for La Barraca, García Lorca continued to write and stage his own plays. A true story inspired *Bodas de Sangre* (performed in 1933; *Blood Wedding*), celebrated by many critics for its masterful blend of tragedy, verse, music, and surrealism and widely considered García Lorca's dramatic masterpiece. In the play, a farm girl leaves her groom for her lover, a member of a family involved in a longstanding feud with her own, on her wedding day. The two men end up killing each other. The same year, García Lorca traveled to Buenos Aires and watched another company perform the play there. *Yerma* (1934) is a tragedy in verse about a woman who kills a husband who refuses to give her a child. In *Doña Rosita the Spinster* (1935), a girl naively waits for more than twenty-five years for her cousin to return from South America to marry her, only to find out in the end he had married someone else.

Meanwhile, 1935 had seen the publication of *Llanto por Ignacio Sánchez Mejías* (*Lament for Ignacio Sánchez Mejías*), a poem widely considered one of the best in Hispanic literature. A touching elegy for a bullfighter who García Lorca had known, its drumlike refrain, "at five in the afternoon," repeats itself like clockwork throughout the poem, driving home the time of the bullfighter's death.

García Lorca did not live to see the performance of his final play, *La Casa de Bernarda Alba* (1936; *The House of Bernarda Alba*), in which five rebellious sisters are ordered to mourn their deceased father for eight years by their cruel and spiteful mother, Bernarda Alba. Spanish nationalists arrested and executed García Lorca sometime on the morning of August 19–20, 1936, during the fury of the Spanish Civil War. His other works include the comedy *La Zapatera prodigiosa* (*The Shoemaker's Prodigious Wife*), first performed in 1930; *Amor de don Perlimplín con Belisa en su jardín* (*Love of Don Perlimplín*), first performed in 1933; the poetry collection *Diván del Tamarit* (1936; *Divan of Tamarit*); and two puppet plays, *Los títeres de cachipurra* (*The Billy Club Puppets*), and *Retabillo de Don Cristóbal* (*The Puppet Play of Don Cristóbal*).

BIBLIOGRAPHY

Adams, Mildred, *García Lorca: Playwright and Poet*, 1977; Cobb, Carl, *Federico García Lorca*, 1967; Gibson, Ian, *Federico García Lorca: A Life*, 1989; Morris, C. Brian, *Son of Andalusia: The Lyrical Landscapes of Federico García Lorca*, 1997.

García Márquez, Gabriel

(March 6, 1928–)
Novelist, Short-Story Writer, Screenwriter, Journalist

One of the most influential literary figures in the Spanish-speaking world, the Colombian writer Gabriel José García Márquez developed a literary style known as "magical realism" that combines elements of realism and fantasy. He was awarded the Nobel Prize for Literature in 1982 "for his novels and short stories, in which the fantastic and the realistic are combined in a richly composed world of imagination, reflecting a continent's life and conflicts."

García Márquez was the first child of an impoverished telegraph operator. He was born in Aracataca, a small banana town in northern Colombia. Aracataca, where his maternal grandparents lived, was his home for the first seven years of his life. As a child he was generally shy and enjoyed listening to his grandparents tell stories. His grandfather was a war veteran, and his grandmother was a superstitious woman who, with his aunts, frequently told stories about ghosts and spirits. The matter-of-fact style in which his grandmother delivered her fantastic stories was to significantly shape García Márquez's later writing style. The violence and economic hardship that followed the end of the banana boom in 1928 was also to have a strong impact on his stories.

After his grandfather's death, García Márquez returned to his parents and enrolled in a boarding school. At age 12, he began attending a Jesuit school north of Bogotá. He later studied law and journalism at the National University of Colombia and the University of Cartagena but never graduated from either. Instead, he spent most of his time away from his studies writing and talking with other budding artists and writers.

García Márquez identifies one of the formative experiences of his career as his reading of Franz Kafka's "The Metamorphosis," which freed his mind from the notion that literature has to follow certain forms. He began to write professionally in Bogotá and contributed the first of many stories, "The Third Resignation," to *El Espectador* in 1946. After moving to Cartagena he wrote newspaper articles for *El Universal*. In 1950, García Márquez moved to Barranquilla, began to associate with a small literary circle, and read the works of authors such as William Faulkner, James Joyce, and Virginia Woolf. He was particularly influenced by Faulkner's style. He also continued working as a

Gabriel García Márquez (Ann Ronan/Image Select)

journalist for *El Heraldo*, writing under the pseudonym "Septimus." García Márquez spent the next few years primarily as a journalist in Europe, the United States, Colombia, Venezuela, and Cuba. In 1958 he married Mercedes Barcha Pardo, to whom he is still married.

In addition to his journalistic articles he began to publish short stories. In *La hojarasca* (1955; *Leaf Storm*), a novella, a colonel carries out a promise to bury a disgraced doctor in spite of a hostile town's wishes to the contrary. The imaginary town of Macondo, used frequently in García Márquez's works, first appears in *Leaf Storm*. *No One Writes to the Colonel* (1961) recounts the unhappy plight of an impoverished Colombian war veteran waiting for his promised pension check. In *In Evil Hour* (1962), again set in Macondo, the town suffers a new wave of political oppression after they have lived through a period of relative peace.

In the early 1960s García Márquez moved to Mexico, where he continued working as a journalist and began to take an interest in screen writing. He also wrote what is perhaps his most famous work, the novel *One Hundred Years of Solitude* (1968). It was García Márquez's first novel to win international acclaim and his first novel to employ magical realism. The story revolves around the Buendía family and is again set in the fictional town of Macondo. A young member of the Buendía family founds Macondo with his wife, who is also his cousin. The people of Macondo suffer from the same hardships that in fact plagued Latin Americans under colonial rule.

García Márquez became increasingly active in leftist political causes all over Latin America after the publication of *One Hundred Years of Solitude*. He founded HABEAS, an organization dedicated to assisting political prisoners. Political activism did not, however, keep him from his writing. He moved to Barcelona in 1973 and subsequently moved back to Mexico. Several collections of his stories appeared in the 1970s, including *Innocent Eréndira and Other Stories* (1972) and *Eyes of a Blue Dog* (1972).

Using a more developed style of magical realism, García Márquez wrote his novel *The Autumn of the Patriarch* (1975), a harsh portrayal of the corruption, intrigues, and paranoia of a stereotypical Latin American dictator. The novella *Chronicle of a Death Foretold* (1981) takes place in a small Colombian town. Two brothers plot to kill the alleged lover of their sister, a bride who is rejected by her new husband when he discovers she is not a virgin. By the time the murder takes place, everyone but the victim has heard about the plot, but nobody takes the brothers' intention seriously until it is too late. *Love in the Time of Cholera* (1985) recounts the lives of two lovers, Florentino Ariza and Fermina Daza. After a teenage romance, the two marry other spouses. Not until the death of Fermina's husband many years later do they end up together. *The General in His Labyrinth* (1989) is a historical novel about the last months of Simón Bolívar's life. Bolívar succeeded in throwing off Spanish rule in Colombia in 1820 and became the country's first president.

In 1981 García Márquez settled in Mexico City, where he still lives. The following year he was awarded the Nobel Prize for Literature. García Márquez's other works include the screenplay *Viva*

Sandino (1982), based on the Sandinistas in Nicaragua. His most recent writings are *Strange Pilgrims* (1992) and *Love and Other Demons* (1994).

BIBLIOGRAPHY

Bell, Michael, *Gabriel García Márquez: Solitude and Solidarity;* Bell-Villada, Gene H., *García Márquez: The Man and His Work,* 1990.

Garnett, David

(March 9, 1892–February 17, 1981)
Novelist, Editor

David Garnett, one of many English Garnetts who achieved literary recognition, was associated with the Bloomsbury Group in the early twentieth century. He enjoyed popularity with his fantastic stories *Lady into Fox* and *A Man in the Zoo* in the 1920s and went on to write more than twenty novels. Garnett also edited the letters of T. E. Lawrence and fellow Bloomsbury member Dora Carrington.

Garnett was the son of Edward and Constance Garnett, born in Brighton, East Sussex, England. The Garnetts had a long and distinguished literary history. Constance was the noted translator of nineteenth-century Russian literature, and Edward established himself as a famous literary critic. When he was young, Garnett was introduced to many prominent literary figures through his parents' acquaintances. He grew up with FORD MADOX FORD and met older writers such as JOSEPH CONRAD and JOHN GALSWORTHY. Garnett attended schools sporadically, first in Limpfield and then in France, where his mother went to recover her health. He later studied at University College, London.

Garnett attended the Royal College of Science and studied botany. Having learned Russian and French from his mother, he earned money translating. During the World War I era, Garnett associated himself with the Bloomsbury Group, whose members included the economist John Maynard Keynes, VIRGINIA WOOLF and her husband Leonard, Lytton Strachey, DUNCAN GRANT, and Clive and Vanessa Bell. He later married the Bells' daughter, Angelica, but his first wife was Ray Marshall, whom he married in 1921. He began to write, sometimes just to make money, as with the story *Dope Fiend* under the pseudonym Leda Burke.

Illustrated with his wife's woodcuts, Garnett's fantastic novel *Lady into Fox* (1922) was his first success and remains one of his most popular works. The story's protagonist is a man whose wife turns into a fox. *A Man in the Zoo* (1924), about a man placed on exhibition as homo sapiens in the London Zoo, was also successful. *The Sailor's Return* followed in 1925. Garnett achieved less success with his later novels, which include *No Love* (1929), *The Grasshoppers Come* (1931), *Beany-Eye* (1935), *Two By Two: A Story of Survival* (1963), *Ulterior Motives* (1966), and *A Clean Slate* (1971). *Aspects of Love* (1955) unfolds in Italy and France and treats the relationships among four people.

The Golden Echo, the first of Garnett's three-volume autobiography, was published in 1953. Completed by *The Flowers of the Forest* (1955) and *The Familiar Faces* (1962), the work outlines the impressions of his youth, his parents, his relationships with the other Bloomsbury members, and his first successes in writing. *Great Friends: Portraits of Seventeen Writers* (1979) contains Garnett's sketches of other writers of his acquaintance. He edited the correspondence of both T. E. Lawrence and Dora Carrington, *The Letters of T. E. Lawrence* (1938) and *Carrington: Letters and Extracts from Her Diaries* (1978). His other works include *A Rabbit in the Air*, a journal he kept while he was learning to fly. Garnett helped found the Nonesuch Press and served as literary editor of the *New Statesman*.

BIBLIOGRAPHY

Garnett, David, *The Familiar Faces*, 1962; Garnett, David, *The Flowers of the Forest*, 1955; Garnett, David, *The Golden Echo*, 1953.

Genet, Jean

(December 19, 1910–April 15, 1986)
Novelist, Playwright, Poet

Jean Genet stands apart from most authors in that he completed much of his work as a prisoner. His shocking, anarchistic, and often obscene subject matter depicts the life he lived as a tramp, thief, and homosexual prostitute in the streets and prisons of Europe, and the criminal acts his characters commit are often elevated to religious acts.

Genet was born in Paris to a prostitute, Gabrielle Genet, who abandoned him in his infancy. He did not discover his identity until he was 21. His supervision fell to the National Foundling Society, and he was raised by a peasant family in the Morvan region of France. Genet's long career as a criminal began at the age of 10, when he was caught stealing. When his behavior grew too unbearable for his adoptive family, they sent him to the strict Mettray Reform School. Having escaped from the school in 1929, he enlisted in the French Foreign Legion in order to get the enlistment bonus, but quickly deserted to return to the streets of Europe.

During the 1930s, Genet traveled in Europe and engaged himself in criminal activity. Until 1948, Genet spent much of his time in and out of prison for theft and prostitution. For Genet crime evolved into much more than a means of survival. Thefts and forbidden sexual experiences became religious acts of self-assertion against society, as they so often are for the characters in his works. While serving time in Fresnes prison, he wrote his first poem, "Le Condemné a Mort" ("The Man Condemned to Death"). There he also wrote his first novel, *Notre Dame des Fleurs* (1943; *Our Lady of the Flowers*), on the paper used to make brown bags. The narrator of the story admires the toughest, most fearless criminals,

Jean Genet (Fragment Publishing)

In 1948, Genet was convicted a tenth time for theft, which in France carried a sentence of life in prison. However, his novels had by then impressed a number of leading French artists and writers, including JEAN-PAUL SARTRE, ANDRE GIDE, and JEAN COCTEAU. Sartre, Cocteau, and others successfully petitioned France's president for Genet's pardon.

After his release, Genet turned to writing absurdist plays. The characters in his early dramas resemble those of his novels. *Les Bonnes* (1947; *The Maids*) was inspired by two servant girls who murdered their master and mistress. Genet transformed the real-life story into a psychological and spiritual treatment of two sisters, Claire and Solange, who enjoy acting the part of their mistress and her maid and plan to murder the mistress. When she refuses to drink the poisoned tea they have prepared for her, they ritually and religiously prepare for Solange to murder Claire with the tea while the latter plays the mistress. In *Haute Surveillance* (staged in 1949; *Deathwatch*), set in a prison cell, Lefranc and Maurice vie for the love of Green Eyes, whom they idolize because he killed a prostitute in a fit of rage. Different motives have led each character to crime. The motivations of Snowball, who has murdered out of calculation and greed, are presented as superior to the motives of other characters who have comitted crimes out of rage and other reasons.

such as Our Lady of the Flowers. Our Lady of the Flowers is a young murderer who boldly faces his fate, execution.

Genet's next novel, *Miracle de la rose* (1945–1946; *Miracle of the Rose*) describes his experience at the reform school in Mettray and was written in a Paris penitentiary. *Pumpes funèbres* (1947; *Funeral Rites*) is set during the Paris Liberation and unfolds over two days after the death of the narrator's lover. The main character in *Querelle de Brest* (1947; *Quarrel of Brest*) is George Quarrel (a character based on Genet's lover Jean Descamin), a heroic murderer and drug smuggler, and the story examines the dynamics of homosexual relations. *The Thief's Journal* (1949), Genet's last novel, recounts his own sordid existence as a prostitute and thief. In these novels, Genet's narrative is fragmented, utilizing flashbacks, stream of consciousness, confused time elements, and street jargon.

Genet's later plays, *Le Balcon* (1956; *The Balcony*), *Les Negrès* (1958; *The Blacks*), and *Les paravents* (1961; *The Screens*), are more structurally complex. *The Blacks* creates an atmosphere of uncertainty and unreality, using techniques designed to shock, offend, and confuse the audience. Genet designed the play as a clown show, cast all black actors, and intended the play for a white audience, stipulating that at least one white person be present in a crowd wherever it was performed.

In his later life, Genet traveled widely, lending support to the Palestinians in the Middle East and the Black Panthers in the United States. He died of throat cancer in 1986.

BIBLIOGRAPHY

Knapp, Bettina L., *Jean Genet*, 1989; White, Edmund, *Genet*, 1993.

Giacometti, Alberto

(October 10, 1901–January 11, 1966)
Sculptor, Painter

The Swiss-born sculptor Alberto Giacometti established himself among Paris's avant-garde in the 1920s and 1930s, producing a series of Surrealist-inspired sculptures between 1930 and 1935. After parting ways with the Surrealists, he began to sculpt male and female figures characterized by their excessive height, extreme thinness, and appearance of frailty.

Giacometti was born to parents of Italian ancestry in Borgonovo, Switzerland. He was deeply attached to his mother and gained early exposure to the world of art from his father, a Postimpressionist painter. Giacometti grew up in the Swiss village of Stampa, where he passed a very happy childhood. He began to draw at a young age and eagerly devoured the art books in his father's library. Among the numerous works he copied was Albrecht Dürer's *Knight, Death, and the Devil*. In 1914 he made his first sculpture—of his brother Diego, who was later to serve as his assistant. As a child he studied at the Evangelical Secondary School in Schiers, excelling in all his studies but focusing especially on art.

In 1919 Giacometti went to Geneva to study art. He again traveled to Italy with his father in 1920 and 1921 and during that time developed an interest in Egyptian art. By this time he was sculpting busts on a regular basis. Giacometti did his military service in 1922 and the same year landed in Paris. Paris was to become the primary center of his work as he absorbed the city's diverse artistic influences. From 1922 to 1925 he attended the Académie de la Grande-Chaumière, and among his teachers there was ÉMILE-ANTOINE BOURDELLE.

Giacometti frequented the Louvre and investigated African, Egyptian, Cycladic, and Oceanic Art. These influences are evident in one of his best-known early works, the abstract spoon-shaped figure entitled *The Spoon-Woman* (1926). He was sensitive to many different artistic trends in Paris. The Cubist experiments begun by GEORGES BRAQUE and PABLO PICASSO manifested themselves in his *Torse and Composition Cubiste (Deux Tetes)* (1925; *Cubist Composition [Two Heads]*), *Cubist Composition* (1926), and other works. The works of CONSTANTIN

Alberto Giacometti modeling a sculpture, a portrait of his brother Diego (AKG)

BRANCUSI, Henri Laurens, and the Dadaists also shaped Giacometti's style.

In the late 1920s Giacometti sculpted abstract, often flat compositions in wood and metal. The exaggerated vertical dimensions of his later works had not yet appeared. Around 1930 he fell under the influence of the Surrealists (see SALVADOR DALÍ) and began to produce pieces that more obviously reflected emotional and psychological states. In *The Suspended Ball* (1930), a ball missing a wedge-shaped piece from the bottom dangles from the top of a cage over a larger wedge resting on a platform.

The Suspended Ball was one of several "caged" works Giacometti finished during his Surrealist period. *The Cage* (1931) consists of a wooden cage housing an array of suspended objects. *The Palace* at 4 A.M. (1932–1933) is a caged work in wire, wood, and string. In another Surrealist work, *The Displaced Table* (1933), the head of a woman rests on a table with a displaced hand and other objects. *Woman with Her Throat Cut* (1932) is one of Giacometti's most violent works.

Dissatisfied with what he considered inadequate representation of the human figure, Giacometti broke with the Surrealists in 1935 and sought a new method working from nature. Over the next decade he produced very little sculpture, instead devoting himself to paintings and drawings. Among his notable paintings of the era are his *Apple on a Sideboard* (1937) and *Portrait of the Artist's Mother* (1937). His new conception of the human figure was partly shaped by his stay as a patient in a hospital in Geneva, where he observed the movements of injured patients.

In the mid-1940s Giacometti returned to sculpture. Some works, such as *Head of a Man on a Rod* (1947), resemble the abstract sculptures from the late 1920s. *The Nose* (1947) features a suspended figure with a long, thin nose. At this time Giacometti also began creating the tall, thin, vertical figures for which he is best known. Stationary female figures and walking male figures (such as *Walking Man I* in 1960) recur throughout the sculptures of the 1950s and 1960s. His other works include *The Chariot* (1950), *Women of Venice* (1956), and many *Tall Figures*. In 1959 the Chase Manhattan Bank in New York commissioned him to sculpt three large figures. After several changes in plan Giacometti planned to proceed with a standing woman more than twenty-five feet tall, but he never finished the commission. He also designed the set for SAMUEL BECKETT's *Waiting for Godot* in 1963.

Although his work was known among the Paris avant-garde during the 1930s, Giacometti was not known to international audiences until the 1940s. Two New York exhibitions in 1948 and 1950 brought his work to a wider audience. Many of his works are now housed in the Art Gallery (Kunsthaus) in Zürich and the Beyeler Gallery in Basel, Switzerland.

BIBLIOGRAPHY

Lord, James, *Giacometti: A Biography*, 1983; Sylvester, David, *Looking at Giacometti*, 1995.

Gide, André

(November 22, 1869–February 19, 1951)
Novelist, Playwright, Critic, Short-Story Writer, Editor, Translator, Essayist

André-Paul-Guillaume Gide helped found the French literary review *La nouvelle revue française*, which was instrumental in popularizing the work of many French avant-garde writers. Through the *revue* and through his own writing, Gide was one of the most influential writers in France in the pre–World War II generation. He received the Nobel Prize for Literature in 1947 "for his comprehensive and artistically significant writings, in which human problems

André Gide (Ann Ronan/Image Select)

and conditions have been presented with a fearless love of truth and keen psychological insight."

Gide was an only child born in Paris. His father, who died when he was a child, was of Huguenot, that is, French Protestant, ancestry. His mother came from an established Catholic family but was raised as a Protestant, and her religious devotion dominated Gide's environment as a child. His upbringing in the Protestant moral atmosphere had a marked effect on his life and career. Many of Gide's works deal with the conflict between human desire and moral strictures as well as his own search for spiritual fulfillment. He enrolled in the École Alsacienne in Paris when he was 8, and a tutor supplemented his education during his frequent illnesses.

After Gide finished his studies, he decided to pursue a career in writing. The protagonist of his first book, the autobiographical *Les cahiers d'André Walter* (1891; *The Notebooks of André Walter*), is a troubled and isolated young man who loses his sanity and dies. The work also introduced Gide's often-used journal form. That same year, Gide fell under the influence of the Symbolists, who used fluid literary forms, rather than the strict forms of the classical French tradition, and emphasized the role of the imagination in creativity. Gide's early works influenced by the Symbolists include *Traité du Narcisse* (1891; *Narcissus*) and *The Lovers' Attempt* (1893).

In 1893, Gide traveled to Tunisia, where he experienced a feeling of liberation from his moralist upbringing. He returned for a second visit in 1894, when he met the Irish writer Oscar Wilde and Lord Alfred Douglas. They encouraged Gide to open himself up to his homosexuality, a theme that appears in his writings. *Corydon* (1924), a defense of homosexuality, caused an uproar when it was published. Nevertheless, he married his cousin, Madeleine Rondeaux, upon his return to France in 1895.

The lyrical prose work *Les Nourritures terrestres* (1897; *Fruits of the Earth*) captures the sense of liberation Gide felt after his travels to North Africa. It consists of eight chapters pulsing with energy, and in it Gide advocated freedom to satisfy human desires. At this point in his life and career, Gide was primarily concerned with individual moral and spiritual questions.

Gide wrote many tales he called *récits*, characterized by narration in the first person and a central character grappling with moral dilemmas. Among these are

L'immoraliste (1902; *The Immoralist*), *La Porte Étroite* (1909; *Strait is the Gate*), and *La Symphonie pastoral* (1919; *The Pastoral Symphony*). The latter examines questions of religion, morality, and love. The main character is a married clergyman who falls in love with a blind girl, Gertrude, whom he has sheltered and taught. His obsession with Gertrude violates his religious mores and disturbs his family. Like his *récits*, Gide's plays, including *Philotète* (1897; *Philoctectes*), the verse drama *Le Roi Candaule* (1901; *The King Candaule*), and *Saul* (1903), are marked by their engaging character portraits.

Les Caves du Vatican (1914; *The Caves of the Vatican*) is a work of unconventional structure consisting of a number of parallel episodes. While the characters lead their own lives unaware of each other, their lives and fates are intertwined without their knowledge. After its publication, *Les Caves du Vatican* was widely attacked for anticlericalism. The complex story of the only work Gide called a novel, *Les Faux-Monnageurs* (1926; *The Counterfeiters*), explores human hypocrisy and false images.

Gide also established himself as a literary critic and translator. In 1909 he helped found the *Nouvelle revue française*, which, until World War II, published many prominent progressive and avant-garde French writers. His studies of other literary figures include *Dos-toïevsky, articles et causeries* (1923; *Dostoevsky*). Among his translations are Shakespeare's *Antony and Cleopatra* and *Hamlet;* portions of Walt Whitman's poetry; and William Blake's *The Marriage of Heaven and Hell.*

After a 1925–1926 journey to French Equatorial Africa, Gide returned to France and published *Voyage au Congo* (1927) and *Le Retour du Chad* (1927), both of which appeared in English as *Travels in the Congo* (1929), and criticized the French presence in Africa. Gide's brief optimistic espousal of Communism dimmed when he visited the Soviet Union in 1936. His travels to and thoughts on the Soviet Union are reflected in *Retour de l'U.R.S.S.* (1936; *Return from the U.S.S.R*) and *Afterthoughts on the U.S.S.R.* (1937).

While the Germans occupied France during World War II, Gide lived in North Africa, where he completed *Theseus* (1946). Gide's four volumes of journals, which he began keeping in 1889, were published in 1950. His other works include *Prometheus Misbound* (1899); *Isabelle* (1911); *Marshlands* (1894); and the autobiography *Si le grain ne meurt* (1926; *If It Die*).

BIBLIOGRAPHY

Brée, Germaine, *André Gide*, 1963; Painter, George Duncan, *André Gide: A Critical Biography*, 1968.

Gielgud, John

(April 14, 1904–May 21, 2000)
Actor, Director, Producer

Most famous on the stage for his portrayals of Hamlet and other leading Shakespeare roles, Arthur John Gielgud rose to prominence on London stages in the late 1920s. His reputation as both an actor and a director subsequently grew worldwide. Gielgud has also acted in numerous films and television shows.

Gielgud was born into a family with a history in theater in London. His father, a stockbroker of Lithuanian ancestry, was a less formative influence on his life than was his mother, a relative of the actress Ellen Terry (1847–1928). Gielgud and his three siblings built a play theater and staged their own productions as children. He attended the Hillside preparatory school, where he acted his first role as the Mock Turtle in *Alice and Wonderland.* After studying at the Westminster School, he enrolled at Lady Benson's dramatic school. Gielgud finished his education at the Royal Academy of Dramatic Art in London.

With the reluctant support of his parents, who in spite of the theatrical successes in the family preferred more stable methods of earning a living, Gielgud devoted himself to the theater. His professional acting debut came in 1921, when he played the Herald in Shakespeare's *Henry V* at the Old Vic Theatre in London. For Gielgud, the debut marked both the first of many professional roles in Shakespeare productions and the first of many roles at the Old Vic.

In 1924–1925, Gielgud appeared in more than a dozen productions with the Oxford Playhouse, mostly plays by modern dramatists such as GEORGE BERNARD SHAW. The year 1924 also saw him in his earliest performances as Romeo (opposite GWEN FFRANGCON-DAVIES's Juliet). Some critics charged that his calculated stage manner limited his portrayal of the passionate Romeo. More successful were his many portrayals of Hamlet, especially his performance in the Broadway production of 1936. Other noteworthy successes in the 1920s were his roles as Trofimov in Anton Chekhov's *The Cherry Orchard* (1925); as an understudy to NOËL COWARD in the latter's *The Vortex* (1925); and as Lewis Dodd in a West End production of *The Constant Nymph* (1926), adapted from a Margaret Kennedy novel.

In his early career, Gielgud worked to overcome difficulties with diction and movement, eventually earning acclaim for the precision and clarity of his speech on stage. His Broadway debut came in 1924, when he played Alexander in a disappointing production of Alfred Neumann's *The Patriot* in 1927. Although he acted in a number of modern plays, Gielgud strongly preferred the classics. He acted with the Old Vic company from 1929–1931, playing many leading Shakespearean and Shavian roles. Particularly successful were his Richard II and, as was mentioned before, Hamlet.

Gielgud's first directing effort came in 1932 with the Oxford University Dramatic Society—*Romeo and Juliet.* He later directed many shows on the West End, at the Old Vic, and elsewhere in

John Gielgud in *Prospero's Books* (Ann Ronan/Image Select)

both Britain and North America. In 1937–1938 he directed the season at the Queen's Theatre in London, and in 1944–1945 he directed the season at the Haymarket Theatre. With TYRONE GUTHRIE, Gielgud directed Shakespeare productions at the Old Vic in 1940. He also worked with HARLEY GRANVILLE-BARKER and directed the first major English version of Hector Berlioz's opera *The Trojans.*

By the 1940s, Gielgud was touring the world as both an actor and director. His other noteworthy roles include Nicholas in *Dear Octopus* in 1938–1939; Leontes in *The Winter's Tale* (1951); Gaev in *The Cherry Orchard* (1961); Joseph Surface in Richard Sheridan's *The School for Scandal* (1962); the Headmaster in ARNOLD BENNETT's *Forty Years On* (1968); and Spooner in HAROLD PINTER's *No Man's Land* (1975). Gielgud first performed his one-man Shakespeare show *Ages of Man* at the Edinburgh Festival in 1957. Over the next several years, the show took him around the world, winning significant popularity on Broadway.

Gielgud's career in film and television began with silent films, and in 1936 he appeared in Alfred Hitchcock's *The Secret Agent.* During the 1950s he played Cassius in *Julius Caesar* (1952) and the Duke of Clarence in *Richard II* (1955). Other roles came in *Murder on the Orient Express* (1974), *Chariots of Fire* (1980), *Arthur* (1981, for which he earned an Academy Award for best supporting actor), and *Prospero's Books* (1991). Gielgud's writings include his autobiography *Early Stages* (1938), *Stage Directions* (1963), *Distinguished Company* (1972), and *Shakespeare: Hit or Miss* (1991; also published as *Acting Shakespeare*). He was knighted in 1953.

BIBLIOGRAPHY

Bandredth, Gyles Daubeney, *John Gielgud: A Celebration,* 1984; Tanitch, Robert, *Gielgud,* 1988.

Gill, Eric

(February 22, 1882–November 17, 1940)
Sculptor, Typographic Designer, Graphic Artist, Essayist, Illustrator

As the designer of the Stations of the Cross at Westminster Cathedral in London, Arthur Eric Rowton Gill was an accomplished sculptor of figures and bas-reliefs. Gill also illustrated books for his own presses and for others with wood engravings and created lettering for them. His work in lettering produced a number of modern typefaces, including Perpetua and Gill Sans Serif.

Gill was born into a large family in Brighton, Sussex, England. His father, at the time of Gill's birth a Congregationalist minister, enjoyed painting and encouraged his son's artistic ambitions. Formal study interested Gill very little. Along with his siblings, he attended a local school before moving on to the Arnold House School, Hove. As a child he began to draw and developed an interest in lettering, evident in his carefully lettered drawings of locomotives. His father joined the Church of England in 1897 and moved the family to Chichester.

In Chichester, Gill studied at the Chichester Technical and Art School. In 1900, he was apprenticed to William Caröe, architect to the Ecclesiastical Commissioners. Bored with both architecture and the Church, he studied stonemasonry and inscription cutting at the Westminster Technical Institute. He also studied lettering at the Central School of Arts and Crafts, where the most important influence on him was his instructor Edward Johnston. With Johnston Gill came to share a dislike of modern type, which they believed removed the beauty of natural writing from the letters.

By 1902, Gill was carving letters and tombstones as well as dabbling in book design.

During this period Gill attended meetings of the Fabian Society (see GEORGE BERNARD SHAW), read H. G. WELLS, and for a time embraced a Socialist philosophy. In 1904, he married Ethel Mary Moore. He began sculpting figures around 1909 and achieved his first major success with *Mother and Child* in 1912. He rejected an offer to study with ARISTIDE MAILLOL, who, unlike Gill, worked from clay models.

The major influence on Gill's subsequent work was his conversion to Roman Catholicism in 1913. Although he disliked the cathedral's architecture, he designed and carved the Stations of the Cross, a series of bas-reliefs, for the Westminster Cathedral in London (1914–1918). Gill created his relief *Christ Driving the Money-Changers Out of the Temple* (1922–1923), in which he presented politicians, financiers, and other figures in contemporary clothing, as a war memorial at the University of Leeds.

Gill completed his famous torso *Mankind* (1928) in Hoptonwood stone, a medium he used for many other sculptures. In 1929 he carved three "winds" at St. James Park Underground Station. Two years later he finished his relief *Prospero and Ariel* (1931), drawn from two characters in Shakespeare's *Tempest*, over the main entrance of Broadcasting House, London. Gill was also commissioned to create bas-relief panels for a hotel at Morecambe (1933) portraying the story of Nausicaa and Ulysses as well as a series of carved panels for the Palestine Archaeological Museum in Jerusalem (1933). Later works include *The Creation of Adam* (1935–1938), a series of three bas-reliefs at the Palace of Nations in Geneva.

Gill also continued his work in printing. With Douglas Pepler, he founded St. Dominic's Press in 1915. To the press's books Gill contributed many wood engravings—elegant but not complex—including twenty-two for Frances Cornford's book of poems *Autumn Midnight* (1923). His association with Golden Cockerel Press also produced many woodcuts and examples of elegant lettering. Among the works he illustrated for them are *Sonnets and Verses* (1925), a book of poetry written by his sister, Enid Clay; an edition of the biblical Song of Songs (1925) with eighteen wood engravings; an edition of Geoffrey Chaucer's *Canterbury Tales* (1927); and an edition of the Four Gospels (1931). The Golden Cockerel printed Gill's own essay *Art and Love* (1928). With his son-in-law René Hague, Gill founded a private press in 1931.

Gill designed nearly a dozen typefaces, among which are Perpetua (1925), Gill Sans Serif (1927), and Joanna (1930). His own essay *Art Nonsense* (1929) was printed in Perpetua type. Throughout his adult life he also wrote articles and essays on many different subjects, such as art, religion, clothes, architecture, typography, pacifism, and the industrialization and mechanization of society. Gill was a passionate and opinionated writer who generated controversy with his ideas and his manner. He contributed to a number of periodicals, including *The Game, Order,* and *The Listener.*

His longer writings include *Christianity and Art* (1927); *Money and Morals* (1934); *The Necessity of Belief* (1936); *Work and Property* (1937); and his *Autobiography* (1937).

Among Gill's other works are erotic drawings and sculptures; nudes, some of which appeared in *Twenty-Five Nudes* (1938); a memorial tablet to Lady Ottoline Morrell; and illustrations for G. K. CHESTERTON's poem *Gloria in Profundis* (1927). He was made associate of the Royal Academy in 1937. Gill died of lung cancer in 1944, having designed his own gravestone.

BIBLIOGRAPHY

MacCarthy, Fiona, *Eric Gill,* 1989; Speaight, Robert, *The Life of Eric Gill,* 1966; Yorke, Malcolm, *Eric Gill: Man of Flesh and Spirit,* 1981.

Giraudoux, Jean

(October 29, 1882–January 31, 1944)
Playwright, Novelist, Short-Story Writer, Screenwriter, Critic, Essayist, Diplomat

Hyppolyte-Jean Giraudoux, as he was christened, introduced his impressionistic plays to a French theater then under the influence of Realism. Drawn largely from Greek and Roman myth and biblical sources, they derive their originality from his carefully constructed dialogue, irony, and exploration of universal contrasts. Giraudoux also wrote novels, essays, and literary criticism.

Giraudoux was born in Bellac, France. His father, a civil servant, moved the family around as his job required. Giraudoux attended a local school in Bellac and in 1893 entered the lycée of Châteauroux. After completing his studies at the École Normale Supériéure at Lakanal, he went to the University of Munich on a scholarship. During this time he developed a particular interest in German culture and literature. A year at Harvard University in 1907–1908 finished his academic career, after which he entered the diplomatic service. Giraudoux fought in World War I and suffered slight wounds.

Giraudoux established himself as a writer of fiction before he embarked on his more famous work in the theater. His early works include *L'école des indifférents*, consisting of novellas, and *Suzanne et le Pacifique* (1921). *Siegfried et le limousin* (1922; *My Friend from Limousin*), an allegorical story about the relationship between France and Germany, is one of his best-known works of fiction and is the basis for his first successful play, *Siegfried* (1928). Giraudoux also published short stories in French literary reviews.

A desire for freedom from the constraints of everyday routine permeates Giraudoux's other novels. In *Aventures de Jérome Bardini* (1930), the prosperous protagonist grows tired of his monotonous life and leaves his family. Among the characters he meets on his sojourns is Kid, a symbol of complete independence. Maléna, the main character of *Combat avec l'ange* (1927; *Combat with the Angel*), is wealthy and attractive but fundamentally dissatisfied with her life. She develops an obsession for Jacques of which she is finally cured, and then settles in to accept her life. A desire for freedom recurs in subsequent generations in *Choix des Elues* (1939). Edmée, the protagonist, leaves her husband Pierre and their two children, Jacques and Claudie. When she returns to the family many years later, she finds the grown Claudie pining for freedom as she had.

Giraudoux entered the theater with the modestly successful *Siegfried* in 1928. Many of his subsequent plays draw from Greek and Roman mythology as well as biblical and apocryphal sources. *Amphitryon 38* (1929) draws from the myth of Jupiter and Alcmene, and the tragedy *La Guerre de Troie n'aura pas lieu (The Trojan War Will Not Take Place)* uses the story of the Greek embassy to Troy that tried in vain to prevent the Trojan War by persuading the Trojans to return Helen, whom the Trojan prince Paris had stolen from her Greek husband. The English playwright CHRISTOPHER FRY translated this work as *Tiger at the Gates* in 1955. *Électre* (1937) is based on the story of Electra, daughter of Agamemnon, the leader of the Greek forces in the Trojan War who was killed by his unfaithful wife on his return home. Electra helps her brother to avenge her father by killing their mother.

In his plays, laden with humor and sometimes described as impressionistic, Giraudoux crafted the dialogue and structure to explore ideas and orchestrate confrontations of opposites, not necessarily aiming to present a realistic drama. The structure of his 1937 play *L'Impromptu de Paris* provided him with a platform to express ideas on the theater. In the story, the employees at a theater answer questions from a government official who has come to ask about the theater's work.

Giraudoux's biblical and apocryphal plays include *Judith* (1931), *Sodom and Gomorrha* (1943), and *Cantique des cantiques* (1938; *Song of Songs*). *Judith* tells the story of the apocryphal Israelite heroine who kills Holofernes, general of the enemy Assyrian army. In *Sodom and Gomorrha* (1943), Giraudoux dramatized incompatibility between men and women in the characters of Lia and Jean. The lovers of the biblical Song of Songs, King Solomon and the Shulamite, are modernized characters in Giraudoux's play, the former as Monsieur le Président and the latter as a modern woman.

Giraudoux's most famous play, *La Folle de Chaillot* (1946; *The Madwoman of Chaillot*), reflects his distaste for the exploits of the wealthy and powerful. Several such characters plot to destroy the area of Chaillot in order to search for oil they believe awaits them under the surface. The "madwoman" Aurélie and her cohorts will have none of it, and they lure the prospectors into her home and slam a trap door over them. Their symbolic action heralds a new era of peace and happiness.

Among Giraudoux's other plays are *Intermezzo* (1933) and *Ondine* (1939). His other works include the film scripts *La duchesse de Langeais* (1942) and *Les anges du péché* (1944; *The Angels of Sin*); essays on political and other subjects; and literary criticism.

BIBLIOGRAPHY

LeSage, Laurent, *Jean Giraudoux: His Life and Works*, 1959; Mankin, Paul A., *Precious Irony: The Theatre of Jean Giraudoux*, 1971; Reilly, John H., *Jean Giraudoux*, 1978.

Godard, Jean-Luc

(December 3, 1930–)
Director, Critic

The filmmaker Jean-Luc Godard has been a prominent figure in the French cinema since the early 1960s. His first feature film, *À bout de souffle* (1959; *Breathless*), established him as the leader of the New Wave, the movement that revitalized the French cinema in the late 1950s and 1960s.

Godard was born into an upper-middle-class family in Paris and spent much of his childhood in Switzerland. He studied ethnology at the University of Paris, but spent much of his time in discussion at cafés and in cinema clubs. Godard taught himself to make films using a small camera he owned and contributed film criticism to the New Wave journal *Cahiers du Cinéma (Notes on the Cinema)*.

Godard's job working on a dam inspired his first short film, *Opération Béton* (1954). His first feature film, *À bout de souffle*, was produced by FRANÇOIS TRUFFAUT. Its main character, Michel Poiccard, shoots a police officer and moves in with his American girlfriend, Patricia. He wants to go to Rome, but Patricia turns him in to the authorities, who shoot him.

The actor Jean-Paul Belmondo, who appeared in many of Godard's films, plays Michel.

Truffaut, Godard, and other New Wave directors shot their films in an informal style, often improvising scenes and dialogue. Jump cuts, long tracking shots, and sparse, unpolished production were important elements of New Wave cinema. New Wave directors involved themselves in all aspects of a film's production. Until 1968, Godard employed an experimental narrative style in his films. Critics sometimes fault him for producing indecipherable plots, but his efforts as a director established him as a leading innovator in modernist cinema. Godard's films are generally pessimistic and critical of people and society.

In *Un femme est une femme* (1961; *A Woman Is a Woman*), the actress Anna Karina plays a stripper, Angela, who would like to marry her boyfriend and start a family. Karina, to whom Godard was married for a period of time, starred in leading female roles in many of his movies. When Angela's husband refuses,

Jean-Luc Godard (Gamma)

she turns to another man to help her conceive a baby. The Austrian director Fritz Lang plays himself in *Contempt* (1963), based on a story by the Italian writer ALBERTO MORAVIA.

Alphaville (1965) is framed in a futuristic scenario that takes place in a town run by a computer, Alpha–60. Lemmy Caution is dispatched to kill Alpha–60's administrator, Dr. von Braun. Caution destroys Alpha–60, throwing the town into chaos. After killing von Braun, he escapes with his daughter. The main characters in *Pierrot le fou* (1965; *Pierrot the Fool*), Ferdinand and Marianne, flee from the lives they have been living in Paris and move to the south of France. Marianne has been involved with gangsters, and her Paris life soon catches up with her. The ensuing turmoil eventually leads to her death, after which Ferdinand resolves to kill himself. He changes his mind too late—the explosives he has strapped to himself ignite.

Godard made many other films during the 1960s. Among them are *Le petit soldat* (1960; *The Little Soldier*), which deals with the subject of torture in political groups; *My Life to Live* (1962), concerning a Paris prostitute played by Karina; *Une femme mariée* (1965; *The Married Woman*); *Made in U.S.A.* (1966), a sordid tale of murder and intrigue set in Atlantic City, New Jersey; *Two or Three Things I Know About Her* (1966); *La Chinoise* (1967), about young Maoists in Paris; *Weekend* (1967), a bizarre story of greed, death, murder, and cannibalism meant as a commentary on French society; and *One Plus One* (1968), featuring THE ROLLING STONES.

In the late 1960s and early 1970s, Godard abandoned his earlier narrative style and began making didactic and propagandistic films that reflected his increasing devotion to Marxism. Most famous among these is *The Joy of Knowledge* (1968), consisting of discussion between two people in a dimly lit room.

Godard returned to feature films in the late 1970s. His later films include *Sauve qui peut la vie* (1979; *Every Man for Himself*); *Je vous salve Marie* (1984; *Hail Mary*), a revised and modernized account of the biblical Mary and Joseph; *King Lear* (1986); *Nouvelle vague* (1990; *New Wave*); *Helas pour moi* (1993; *Woe is Me*); *JLG by JLG* (1994); and *Forever Mozart* (1996).

BIBLIOGRAPHY

Cameron, Ian, ed., *The Films of Jean-Luc Godard*, 1969; Collet, Jean, *Jean-Luc Godard*, 1970; Kreidel, John Francis, *Jean-Luc Godard*, 1980.

Golding, William

(September 19, 1911–June 19, 1993)
Novelist, Short-Story Writer, Critic, Essayist, Teacher, Actor

Sir William Gerald Golding, to give him the title he eventually won as well as his full name, achieved popular success with his novel *The Lord of the Flies*, a story about a group of boys who become savages after being stranded on an island. This and Golding's subsequent novels give vivid and memorable pictures of fallen societies in which evil seems to triumph over good. Golding was awarded the Nobel Prize for Literature in 1983 "for his novels, which, with the perspicuity of realistic narrative art and the diversity and universality of myth, illuminate the human condition in the world of today."

Golding was born in St. Columb Minor, near Newquay, Cornwall, England. His mother actively campaigned for women's suffrage, and his father was a multitalented teacher with interests that ranged from the sciences to music. Golding studied at the Marlborough Grammar School, where his father taught, and then at Brasenose College, Oxford. At the latter he abandoned the science course his father wanted for him and studied literature. His first work, *Poems*, was published in 1934.

Upon his graduation, Golding spent several years acting with small theater groups. In 1939, he married Ann Brookfield and began teaching English and philosophy at Bishop Wordsworth's School in Salisbury. He enlisted in the Royal Navy in 1940 and served in World War II. After the war, Golding returned to his teaching post and began to read Greek literature.

The Lord of the Flies (1954) was Golding's first published novel and proved to be one of his most popular. The title derives from Beelzebub, lord of the flies, a devil figure in ancient religious traditions. The story concerns a group of young boys who have not yet reached their teenage years. During a nuclear war, they find themselves stranded on an island with no adults. The boys polarize into factions, one led by the savage and evil hunter Jack Merridew and the other by the more noble Ralph, who advocates a sort of democratic organization. Jack's hunters triumph, and their cruelty culminates in the murder of Simon, an intelligent boy who wears glasses and is utterly helpless in the face of savagery.

The Inheritors (1955), inspired by Golding's reading of H. G. WELLS's *Outline of History*, paints another picture of an amoral, evil human race. Golding had less faith in humanity than Wells, who believed education might steer humanity in a progressive direction. The focus of the novel is the end of the gentle Neanderthal man, according to evolutionary theory the immediate predecessor of homo sapiens, and the dawn of the era of the violent homo sapiens. Wells saw evolution as taking the world in a positive direction and presented the Neanderthals as morally inferior, but Golding, using one of the Neanderthals as his narrator, suggests otherwise.

Pincher Martin (1956) switches its focus to a single individual. Told in the form of flashbacks, the story is about Christopher Hadley Martin, the only survivor of a torpedoed British war ship who at the beginning of the novel is drowning. The novel alternates between the story of his desperate and ultimately unsuccessful attempts to survive and flashbacks to his former life. Flashback is also important in the presentation of *Free Fall* (1959), about Sammy Mountjoy's quest to find out what in his troubled past caused him to lose his freedom and become trapped in greed.

Golding received his M.A. in 1961 and retired from teaching to devote himself to writing. He reviewed books for the *Spectator* from 1960 to 1962. His next novel, *The Spire* (1964) adapts its form from a Greek tragedy. Its protagonist, Jocelin, is obsessed with building a spire on the Cathedral of the Virgin Mary. His unwise pursuit of the project leads to tragedy.

Darkness Visible (1979) is a violent, allegorical novel. Its two main characters are the tragic figure Matthew Septimus, reader of the Bible and victim of trouble in the world, and the less sympathetic Sophy Stanhope. Sophy, who leads a careless life and believes in nothing, involves herself in a failed plot to kidnap the son of an oil sheik. The aftermath of the scheme leaves Matthew dead. *The Paper Man* (1984) is Golding's attack on the academic world. The overambitious professor Rick L. Tucker relentlessly goes after the story's protagonist, novelist Wilfred Barclay.

Golding's other works include *The Pyramid* (1967); *The Scorpion God* (1971), consisting of three stories set in ancient civilizations; *Rites of Passage* (1980); *A Moving Target* (1982); *An Egyptian Journal* (1985); *Close Quarters* (1987); and *Fire Down Below* (1989). His play *The Brass Butterfly* (1958) was adapted from "Envoy Extraordinary," one of the stories in *The Scorpion God*. Golding was elected fellow of the Royal Society of Literature in 1955, received an honorary doctorate of letters from Sussex University in 1970, and was knighted in 1988. He has been most admired for his willingness to be completely honest about his vision of the dark side of human nature and the utter absence of any sign of God, an honesty that was particularly striking in the 1950s, when many thinkers in England and the United States were expressing a more positive view. Those who saw their efforts as based on denial were among Golding's greatest admirers.

BIBLIOGRAPHY

Boyd, S. J., *The Novels of William Golding*, 1990; Dick, Bernard F., *William Golding*, rev. ed., 1987; Gindin, James Jack, *William Golding*, 1988; McCarron, Kevin, *William Golding*, 1994; Subbarao, V. V., *William Golding: A Study*, 1987.

Gordimer, Nadine

(November 20, 1923–)
Novelist, Short-Story Writer, Essayist

In a narrative style often characterized as humorless, unsentimental, complex, and challenging, the South African novelist Nadine Gordimer sets a variety of characters against the backdrop of South Africa's political and social climate and shows in intimate and often startling detail the impact of the policies of apartheid on individual lives. Her works examine many facets of racial relations and the consequences of racial segregation policies. Her aim is not to suggest solutions but to deepen our understanding of the problem as it affects human beings like ourselves. Gordimer received the Nobel Prize for Literature in 1991; the committee described her as one "who through her magnificent epic writing has—in the words of Alfred Nobel— been of very great benefit to humanity."

Gordimer was born in the mining town of Springs, Transvaal, South Africa. Her mother was English, and her father was a Jewish-Lithuanian immigrant and a jeweler. Gordimer liked to read and write as a child, and her first story appeared in print when she was 15. She studied English literature at the University of Witwatersrand. By this time, she had already developed her opposition to the policies of apartheid in South Africa, and the impact of the country's racial segregation laws on the lives of its citizens is the major theme in her writing.

Gordimer's first book of short stories, *The Soft Voice of the Serpent*, was published in 1952, followed by *Six Feet of the Country* (1956). Her first novel, *The Lying Days*, appeared in 1953. The protagonist of *A World of Strangers* (1958) is typical of her many naive and liberal-minded characters. Toby Hood, a London publisher who has come to South Africa to visit an extension of his firm, becomes involved in South Africa's dilemmas and decides to remain there permanently.

Occasion for Loving (1963), which earned Gordimer more critical acclaim than anything she had yet written, examines the lives of two couples. Ann Davis, who is married to Boaz Davis, researcher of African musical instruments, has a brief affair with the black artist Gideon Shibalo. The other couple consists of a professor who studies the history of southern Africa and his wife, Jessie.

Nadine Gordimer (AKG)

The Late Bourgeois World (1966), banned in South Africa, was the first of Gordimer's novels to win international acclaim. The narrative unfolds during a pivotal day in Liz Van De Sant's life and is set against the backdrop of the failure of liberalism in South Africa. Liz's ex-husband, Max, was a member of an outlawed political group in South Africa. Liz learns that Max has drowned himself and taken with him some incriminating papers. When surviving members of his group approach her for financial help, she ultimately chooses to assist them.

Burger's Daughter (1970), noteworthy for its experimental syntax in which Gordimer leaves out quotation marks, examines the life and self-discovery of Rosa Burger, the daughter of parents who were political activists. Her father was imprisoned for his activities and died behind bars. Rosa, too, grows up and finds herself jailed for political activity.

Gordimer's 1973 novel *A Guest of Honour* won the James Tait Black Memorial Prize. The action takes place in a Central African setting but examines the same racial divisions present in her South African novels. Evelyn Bray is a former British administrative officer who had been active in working for the country's independence. Bray returns to the newly liberated country as a guest of honor, takes a minor post in the new government, and finds himself in opposition to the Neocolonialists. In the end, Bray strays from his ideals and dies in the tumultuous political atmosphere.

In *July's People* (1981), Gordimer orchestrates a racial role reversal. When political tensions rise in South Africa, Bam and Maureen Smales, who have always treated their longtime black servant, July, very kindly, find themselves under July's protection. Again, Gordimer omits quotation marks in the text, substituting dashes instead. *My Son's Story* (1990) relates the emotional and psychological struggle of Will, a black youth who finds his father with a white woman who, like his father, is an antiapartheid activist.

With *None to Accompany Me* (1994), Gordimer begins to write about the postapartheid era in South Africa, taking as her protagonist Vera Stark, an aging white attorney with the Legal Activist Foundation who is working for the restoration of land taken during government relocation programs. Vera's personal life is as chaotic as the social climate. Her son in London is getting divorced, she is unhappy with her husband, and her daughter begins a relationship with a woman. Her black friends, Didymus and Sibongile Maqoma, have been exiled members of "the Movement" and have their own problems to overcome within the group and outside of it.

Gordimer's latest novel, *The House Gun* (1998), also takes place in postapartheid South Africa. In her story, Harald and Claudia Lindgard have been living in an illusion. Liberal-minded but complacent, they have distanced themselves from South Africa's political turmoil. The shocking arrest of their son, Duncan, an architect, turns their lives upside down. Duncan, accused (and guilty) of murdering an ex-lover, forces his parents to confront their historically violent surroundings.

Among Gordimer's other works are the novels *Friday's Footprint* (1960), *Not for Publication* (1965), *The Conservationist*

(1974; winner of the Booker McConnell Prize), and *A Sport of Nature* (1987); the short-story collection *A Soldier's Embrace* (1980); *The Black Interpreters* (1973), a study of African literature; and *Writing and Being* (1995), a collection of essays. She has lectured widely in the United States.

BIBLIOGRAPHY

Clingman, Stephen, *The Novels of Nadine Gordimer: History From the Inside*, 2d ed., 1992; Cooke, John, *The Novels of Nadine Gordimer: Private Lives/Public Landscapes*, 1985; Head, Dominic, *Nadine Gordimer*, 1994; Heywood, Christopher, *Nadine Gordimer*, 1983; Newman, Judie, *Nadine Gordimer*, 1988.

Gorky, Maxim

(March 28, 1868–June 14, 1936)
Novelist, Playwright, Essayist

The Soviet writer and revolutionary Maxim Gorky was instrumental in founding the literary school of Socialist Realism, the Soviet Union's only officially sanctioned literary style for more than fifty years. His work exerted a profound influence on later Soviet writers.

Gorky was born Aleksei Maksimovich Peshkov in Nizhny Novgorod, Russia. His father, an upholsterer, died when he was 5 years old, and he spent the remainder of his childhood with his maternal grandparents, both of whom had a profound influence on him. Gorky's grandfather, a former Volga boatman and a dyer, taught him to read, and his grandmother's love of telling stories helped shape his sensibility. He received less than two years of schooling and was sent to work at odd jobs before his tenth birthday. At the young age of 12, Gorky left home and took a job washing dishes on a Volga steamer. His boss, a cook named Smury, sparked his interest in literature. Gorky moved to Kazan in 1884 and continued working in menial jobs while he tried to educate himself by reading on his own. After surviving a suicide attempt in 1887, he left Kazan and became interested in the revolutionary ideas gaining popularity in Russia. He first associated with a Populist revolutionary, Mikhail Romas.

Gorky adopted his pseudonym (meaning "bitter") in 1892, the year his first story, "Makar Chudra," was published in *The Caucasus*. In 1896, he married Ekaterina Pavlovna Volzhina. The publication of *Sketches and Stories* two years later brought him widespread fame in Russia. Romantic portrayals of the Russian lower classes, outcasts, criminals, and the poor, among whom Gorky had spent much of his time, characterized his early stories. One of his most famous, "Twenty-Six Men and a Girl" (1899), depicts harsh working conditions in a Russian bakery modeled on a bakery in which Gorky worked in the 1880s.

In *Foma Gordeyev* (1899), Gorky's first novel, the confused son (Foma) of a wealthy merchant (Ignat Gordeyev) rebels against his father's lifestyle and values, preferring instead to seek out meaning in life. *Mother* (1906), the most revolutionary of his early novels, glorifies the revolutionary spirit then growing in Russia and portrays socialism as a necessary step for the people of the country.

Among Gorky's many plays, the most famous is *The Lower Depths* (1902), a title that stemmed from his observations of what he called "the lower depths" of society he observed during his post–suicide attempt wanderings around Russia. By the time of its production, Gorky was a familiar figure to tsarist censors, who had all but banned his play *Smug Citizens*. The censors permitted *The Lower Depths*, however, and it became an international success. The characters in the play lead miserable lives working for the tyrranical Mikhail Kostylev. A roaming philosopher, Luka, appears on the scene full of comforting words and advice for the sufferers. The character of Satin scoffs at Luka's passive acceptance of oppressive circumstances and reflects Gorky's own advocacy of revolutionary action.

In the early 1900s Gorky became interested in Marxism and joined the Social Democratic Party; when the party split into two factions, he sided with the more revolutionary Bolsheviks. Tsarist police arrested him for his participation in the 1905 revolution, and his release followed a storm of international protest. In St. Petersburg he founded the Bolshevik paper *Novaya Zhizn* (*New Life*), and in 1906 he traveled to the United States with his mistress, Maria Andreeva. The incident sparked an uproar and resulted in expulsion from their hotel. He subsequently settled in Capri, Italy, where he founded a sort of Bolshevik training school. He returned to Russia in 1914.

Maxim Gorky (Ann Ronan/Image Select)

Gorky's autobiographical trilogy (1914–1923) covers the early years of his life. *My Childhood* (1914) concerns his difficult early years from age 3 to age 11, a time span that included the deaths of both of his parents and the family's plunge into poverty. The second volume, *In the World* (1916) covers his adolescence. *My Universities* (1923), the third, details Gorky's years living in Kazan, his suicide attempt, and the beginning of his devotion to revolutionary action. In these works, he made more of an attempt to bring out the personalities of individual characters than he had done in previous novels.

The Artomonov Business (1925) depicts the rise of a large family enterprise—a linen factory—after the freeing of the serfs in 1861 and its subsequent demise after the Bolshevik Revolution. From 1925 to 1936 Gorky worked on *The Life of Klim Samgin*, a comprehensive view of the Russian intelligentsia in the years leading up to the 1917 revolution. The central character, Klim Samgin, is a liberal intellectual whom Gorky portrays as a weak-minded, selfish, and hypocritical opponent of real change through revolution.

Due to poor health, Gorky spent several years in Sorrento, Italy, in the 1920s. He returned to Russia in 1928, was instrumental in the formation of the Soviet Writers Union, and became its first chairman in 1934. He was a major contributor to the development of Socialist Realism, the literary style Soviet leaders would demand of the country's writers until the 1980s. Gorky's other works include *Three of Them* (1900), *The Life of Matvey Kozhemyakin* (1910), essays, and biographical works on Leo Tolstoy, Anton Chekhov, and Leonid Andreyev.

BIBLIOGRAPHY

Borras, F. M., *Maxim Gorky: The Writer*, 1967; Levin, Dan, *Stormy Petrel: The Life and Work of Maxim Gorky*, 1986; Scherr, Barry P., *Maxim Gorky*, 1988.

Grahame, Kenneth

(March 8, 1859–July 6, 1932)
Writer of Children's Books, Short-Story Writer

Remembered chiefly for his classic children's tale *The Wind in the Willows*, Kenneth Grahame published relatively little in his lifetime. The work was preceded by his two major volumes of short stories, *The Golden Age* and *Dream Days*, mostly tales of the happy lives of a family of children in turn-of-the-century England.

Grahame was born in Edinburgh, Scotland. After his mother's death from scarlet fever in 1864, his father, a barrister who paid little attention to his children, sent them to live with their grandmother in England. Grahame was tutored privately in his early childhood and later attended St. Edward's School, Oxford. Caving into family pressure, he decided to pursue a career at the Bank of England, where he worked from 1879 to 1908 and eventually obtained the position of secretary of the bank.

From the time he started to work at the bank, he pursued writing on the side. In 1880 he became honorary secretary of the Shakespeare Society. His first known published essay, "By a Northern Furrow," appeared in the *St. James Gazette* in 1888. Two years later, he began to publish in the *Scots Observer*, edited by the conservative-minded man of letters William Ernest Henley. Henley's *Observer* was later called the *National Observer* and published many of Grahame's pieces, collected in *Pagan Papers* in 1893.

Two collections of short stories preceded *The Wind in the Willows* (1908)—*The Golden Age* (1895) and *Dream Days* (1898)—and feature five English children in rural, late-nineteenth-century England.

The children's story "The Reluctant Dragon" first appeared in the latter. In the narrative, a shepherd tells his son, called Boy, about a large creature he has found resting by a cave. Boy understands this creature to be a dragon and resolves to go and talk to it. He befriends the benevolent beast but encounters trouble with the arrival of St. George. St. George is won over, and to combat superstitions about dragons, they stage a successful mock battle; in the eyes of the villagers, the dragon is defeated and "reformed," and they are able to accept him.

The Headwoman (1898), first published in the *Yellow Book* four years earlier, is an adult story set in the sixteenth century in the fictional French town of St. Radegonde. The attractive and competent Jeanne inherits her job as executioner, a post she accepts over many protests. She meets the seigneur of the village and is attracted to him, but when he is mistakenly brought for execution the following day, she resolves to do her duty. He is rescued from death in the nick of time, and his attraction to Jeanne only increases. They marry, and Jeanne eventually quits her job, leaving it to a cousin.

Grahame married Elspeth Thomson in 1899. Their marriage was a troubled one complicated by the emotional problems of their son, Alastair, who died at the age of 20. As a child, Alastair was the first to hear the stories of the animal characters who appear in *The Wind in the Willows* (1908), Grahame's most popular work. Despite initial difficulties in finding a publisher, the story has become a children's classic in the English-speaking world.

In the story, the industrious Mole is enticed to give up his spring cleaning and leave behind his dark hole by the smell of spring in the air. As he wanders enchanted beside a river, he meets the Water Rat, who likes to write poetry. Ratty invites the Mole to stay in the larger world as his friend and housemate. Nearby lives the rich and adventurous Toad, owner of Toad Hall, who has just taken up as his latest craze journeying on the country roads in a horse-drawn caravan. He persuades the pair to set out on the road with him, but is soon distracted by the car that tips their caravan and abandons Mole and Rat, who return home while Toad disastrously pursues his infatuation with cars.

Later, Mole and Rat end up at the home of Badger during a snowstorm, and together the three animals unsuccessfully try to mend Toad's ways by holding him captive. Toad escapes, wrecks a car, is imprisoned, escapes, and again ends up with Mole, Rat, and Badger. The animals successfully recapture Toad Hall, which, in the newly reformed Toad's absence, has fallen into the hands of weasels, and all settle down again to the idyllic country life Grahame describes with such charm. A. A. Milne dramatized the story as *Toad of Toad Hall* (1930), and Walt Disney made it into a movie in the 1950s.

Grahame's later life was marked by ill health and family difficulty, and he produced little writing. In 1916 he edited *The Cambridge Book of Poetry for Children*. But he had already done enough to win himself lasting fame and great influence on later children's literature. Moreover, the skill with which Grahame evokes the beauty of his benevolently ordered world and brings alive his characters won him admirers among adults as well as children even before the publication of *The Wind in the Willows*. Theodore Roosevelt, then president of the United

States, wrote to him after *The Wind in the Willows* appeared to say that he had been unhappy to hear that the new book was not about the same family of children as the earlier books, but that in fact he had found it even more delightful.

BIBLIOGRAPHY

Green, Peter, *Beyond the Wild Wood: The World of Kenneth Grahame, Author of* The Wind and the Willows, 1983; Kuznets, Lois R., *Kenneth Grahame*, 1987; Prince, Alison, *Kenneth Grahame: An Innocent in the Wild Wood*, 1994.

Grant, Duncan

(January 21, 1885–May 10, 1978)
Painter, Designer, Costume Designer

Exhibiting in a Postimpressionist show in England two years after the label was first applied to the works of the Dutch painter Vincent van Gogh and the French artists Paul Cézanne and Paul Gauguin, the British painter Duncan James Corrowr Grant (to give him his full name) helped inaugurate Postimpressionism in England. His paintings share with the French Postimpressionists an emphasis on free, expressive forms and the use of color to create atmosphere and evoke subjective experience.

Grant, an only child, was born in Rothiemurchus, Inverness, Scotland. His father was a well-read military officer and talented musician, and his mother, to whom he was closer, was frequently complimented for her beauty. A governess tutored Grant during the part of his early childhood he spent in India. In 1894, he went to England and lived with his grandmother while he attended the Hillbrow Preparatory School, Rugby, where his classmates included the future poet RUPERT BROOKE. From 1899 to 1901, he studied at St. Paul's School, London, and lived with the family of Sir Richard and Lady Strachey, his aunt and uncle.

From his childhood, Grant showed an inclination toward art. In the Strachey home, creativity was encouraged at every turn, and it was his aunt who suggested he go to art school. Grant was also encouraged to pursue his artistic inclinations by his cousin Lytton, the biographer and the most famous of the Strachey children, to whom he became attached during this time. From 1902 to 1905, he studied at the Westminster School of Art. In 1906, he studied briefly under Jacques-Émile Blanche in France. His decorative style, however, was influenced less by his academic studies than by paintings—such as *Massacius*—that he saw and copied during a trip to Italy in 1902–1903 and by the French Postimpressionists. After finishing his studies, Grant opened his own studio.

Through Lytton Strachey, Grant was immersed in both the creative climate and the tangled web of relationships and affairs in the Bloomsbury Group. The group's members included Clive and Vanessa Bell, Leonard and VIRGINIA WOOLF, DAVID GARNETT, the economist John Maynard Keynes, and the art critic Roger Fry. Fry organized a controversial and widely publicized exhibition of Postimpressionist art in 1910, and Grant's paintings, among which was a portrait of Fry's daughter, appeared in a second Postimpressionist exhibit in 1912.

Grant was now exhibiting with increasing frequency, and his reputation as an artist began to grow. In 1911 he joined the Camden Town group, which was influenced by the French Impressionists and Postimpressionists and included AUGUSTUS JOHN. The same year, Grant completed two murals, *Bathing* and *Football*, for the dining room of the Borough Polytechnic. By 1913, Roger Fry had organized his Omega Workshop, to which Grant, Vanessa Bell, and others contributed designs for pottery, fabrics, and other decorative art. Grant was to continue working in the decorative arts for the rest of his life, and among his more successful designs was his *Apollo and Daphne* (1932–1933), winner of an award at the Paris International Exhibition in 1937.

Grant's works vary considerably in style and medium. A number of early paintings are rendered in abstract style, including *Abstract Kinetic Collage Painting With Sound* (1914) and *In Memoriam: Rupert Brooke* (1915), the latter a tribute to his classmate, who had died of blood poisoning during World War I. His later Postimpressionistic work applies expressive form, contour, and color to nudes and erotica, particularly studies of the male form; bathing scenes; still lifes; and landscapes such as *The French Window, Charleston* (1953). Grant was also well known for his ability to convey a strong sense of the inner reality of his subjects in his portraits, as in, for example, *John Maynard Keynes* (1909), *David Garnett* (1918), and many portraits of Vanessa Bell.

With Vanessa Bell, Grant maintained a close relationship that lasted until the end of her life. Beginning in the 1920s, they worked together on numerous interior design commissions. With Bell or working on his own, Grant designed interiors in restaurants, churches, Keynes's rooms at Cambridge, and the homes of Adrian and Karin Stephen and Lady Dorothy Wellesley (1931).

Grant's work extended to the theater and to ballet. He designed costumes and scenery for a Jacques Coupeau production of *Twelfth Night* (1914) as well as costumes for the Russian ballerina Lydia Lopokova. A somber Lopokova, who married Keynes, was also the subject of a Grant portrait (1923). When SERGEY DIAGHILEV's Ballets Russes came to London in the years before World War I, Grant met the dancer VASLAV NIJINSKY, whom he commemorated in his *Still Life with Nijinsky* (1972).

BIBLIOGRAPHY

Shone, Richard, *Bloomsbury Portraits: Vanessa Bell, Duncan Grant and Their Circle*, 1993; Spalding, Frances, *Duncan Grant*, 1997; Turnbaugh, Douglas Blair, *Duncan Grant and the Bloomsbury Group*, 1987; Watney, Simon, *The Art of Duncan Grant*, 1990.

Granville-Barker, Harley

(November 25, 1877–August 31, 1946)
Director, Playwright, Actor, Theorist, Producer, Critic

Harley Granville-Barker revolutionized English theater in the first two decades of the twentieth century, stripping his productions of elements designed to entertain in an effort to capture the heart of a play and present audiences with a genuine work of art. Many of GEORGE BERNARD SHAW's plays premiered under Barker's direction or with his help. Barker was also a playwright himself and wrote a number of dramas with a strong vein of social commentary.

Barker was born in Kensington, Middlesex, England. His mother was an entertainer, and his father was an architect. Many details of Barker's early life are mysterious. At the age of 13 he joined an acting troupe, and the following year enrolled in a theatrical school at the Theatre Royal, Margate. He first entered the theater as an actor and delivered his first London performance at the Comedy Theatre in a production of Charles Brookfield's *The Poet and the Puppets* in 1892.

Throughout the 1890s, Barker acted with several theater companies in London, including Florence Farr's company at the Avenue Theatre and Mrs. Patrick Campbell's Company. Lillah McCarthy, Barker's future wife, played lead female roles in Ben Greet's Company, with which he toured in 1895. Among his early acting roles were Gordon Jayne in *The Second Mrs. Tanqueray* and Richard II in Shakespeare's *Richard II*.

In 1900, Barker joined the progressive Stage Society, which opposed mainstream theaters and sought to establish a forum for the production of plays with artistic merit. As Marshbanks in *Candida*

the same year, Barker played the first of many roles in productions of Shaw's dramas. Shaw became Barker's patron and lifelong friend, and many of Shaw's plays were originally performed in conjunction with Barker. Among Barker's other Shaw roles were Captain Kearney in *Captain Brassbound's Conversion* in 1900; Napoleon in *The Man of Destiny* (1901); and Frank in *Mrs. Warren's Profession* (1902).

In 1904, Barker became manager (with J. E. Vedrenne) of the Court Theatre in London, a position he held until 1907. Several of Shaw's plays premiered at the Court Theatre under his own direction, with Barker acting in them and sets designed by GORDON CRAIG. Barker also directed plays by Henrik Ibsen, the Belgian dramatist MAURICE MAETERLINCK, and many others. He acted his 1905 role of Jack Tanner in Shaw's *Man and Superman* opposite McCarthy, whom he married the following year.

Aside from the works of other playwrights, Barker wrote and staged many of his own. He cowrote his earliest dramas with Herbert Thomas, including *A Comedy of Fools*, *The Family of the Oldroyds*, *The Weather-Hen; or Invertebrata* (1897), and *Our Visitor to 'Work-a-Day'*. Of these, only *The Weather-Hen; or Invertebrata* was produced.

The tone of social commentary in Barker's plays is much like that found in Shaw's. Barker shared many of Shaw's philosophical beliefs and in 1901 joined the socialist Fabian Society (cofounded by Shaw). Barker's first major play to see production (for the stage society) was

The Marrying of Ann Leete (1901), a commentary on turn-of-the-century English society. The story revolves around Ann Leete, the daughter of a Whig-turned-Tory politician, Carnaby Leete. Carnaby secretly seeks to further his new political connection by marrying Ann to the son of a Tory politician. Ann backs out of the marriage at the last minute and decides to marry the gardener. The dialogue in the play is sparse and artificial, in accordance with the shallow natures of the characters.

Barker wrote several other plays before World War I, including *The Voysey Inheritance* (1905), *Prunella* (1906), *Waste* (1907), and the comedy *The Madras House* (1910). He continued to direct at various theaters around London—the Duke of York's Theatre, the Court Theatre (to which he returned in 1911 to direct Shaw's *Androcles and the Lion*), the St. James's Theatre, and the Kingsway Theatre.

Barker kept the exaggerated theatricality that had been so common on the English stage out of his productions, aimed to create a unified atmosphere with the players and action on the stage, and used relatively little scenery. He applied these principles to his famous Shakespeare productions at the Savoy Theatre between 1912–1914, *Twelfth Night*, *The Winter's Tale*, and *A Midsummer Night's Dream.*

After World War I, Barker never resumed the same level of activity in the theater. He divorced McCarthy in 1918 and married Helen Huntington, a rich American, with whom he moved to Paris. Barker was elected president of the British Drama League in 1919, became director of the British Institute at the University of Paris in 1937, and lectured in the United States and Canada. His most significant works from the postwar period are his six volumes of *Prefaces to Shakespeare*, written from the perspective of a stage director.

BIBLIOGRAPHY

Kennedy, Dennis, *Granville Barker and the Dream of Theatre*, 1985; McDonald, Jan, *The New Drama, 1900–1914: Harley Granville Barker, John Galsworthy, St. John Hankin, John Masefield*, 1986; Salmon, Eric, *Granville Barker: A Secret Life*, 1983.

Grass, Günter

(October 16, 1927–)
Novelist, Poet, Playwright, Essayist, Graphic Artist

Günter Wilhelm Grass, winner of the Nobel Prize for Literature in 1999, is Germany's most prominent novelist from the World War II generation, "whose frolicsome black fables," in the words of the Swedish Academy, "portray the forgotten face of history." A follower of no particular literary style, Grass combines realism with elements of fantasy and the grotesque in experimental narrative structure to, in general, explore the German political

Günter Grass (Gamma)

Grass enrolled in the Academy of Art in Düsseldorf in 1949 and later studied at the Academy of Fine Arts in Berlin. In 1954 he married Anna Schwarz, a ballet student. Die Gruppe 47 (Group 47), a writers' association, gave Grass the assistance he needed to launch his literary career. In 1956 he went to Paris, where he published a volume of poetry and several plays. In 1959 he finished his first novel *Die Blechtrommel* (*The Tin Drum*), which, with his next two volumes, unified by their Danzig settings, formed the *Danzig Trilogy*. *The Tin Drum* won a prize from Die Gruppe 47 and was made into a film in 1979.

"When Günter Grass published *The Tin Drum* in 1959," the Swedish Academy stated upon announcing Grass as the Nobel Prize winner, "it was as if German literature had been granted a new beginning after decades of linguistic and moral destruction." Entertainingly and vividly written, the story is at once an account of individual protest and the impact of the encroachment of Nazism on the German-Polish culture of Danzig. The main character in *The Tin Drum* is the dwarf Oskar Matzerath, who narrates from a mental hospital, and Grass interweaves Oskar's past with his observations on his present circumstances in postwar German society. The tin drum, which Oskar bangs incessantly, is his symbol and weapon of protest.

Katz und Maus (1961; *Cat and Mouse*) and *Hundejahre* (1963; *Dog Years*) completed the *Danzig Trilogy*. A portrait of adolescence in wartime Germany, *Cat and Mouse* uses the incident of a cat landing on a young boy's oversized Adam's apple to trigger a chain of events that ultimately lead to his status as a hero. The epic novel *Dog Years* ex-

and social climate from the World War II era on. Grass has also authored plays and poetry.

Grass was born in Danzig, Germany, now Gdánsk, Poland. His father was a grocer. He was 5 when Adolf Hitler rose to power and 11 when the National Socialists took control of Danzig, and he went through the Hitler Youth Program as an adolescent. At the age of 16, he volunteered for the German Air Force, was wounded, and was taken to an American prisoner of war camp. The war experience brought Grass a profound sense of disillusionment, and he subsequently worked in a series of odd jobs, including apprenticing to a stonemason and drumming in a jazz band.

amines the German mentality through the rise and fall of National Socialism.

Aus dem Tegebuch einer Schnecke (1972; *From the Diary of a Snail*) probes a number of themes connected with Germany, from the Holocaust to Grass's own involvement with the politics of the Social Democratic Party in the 1960s. *Das Treften in Telgte* (1979; *The Meeting at Telgte*) takes place in 1647, in the middle of the Thirty Years' War, among German writers and musicians, and it presents an unkind portrait of intellectuals engaged in rivalries and quarrels.

Grass's other novels include *Örtlich Betäubt* (1969; *Local Anaesthetic*), which blends fantasy and reality in a story told through the eyes of a patient sitting in a dentist's chair; *Der Butt* (1977; *The Flounder)*, a tale about relationships between men and women in both the past and present; *Kopfgeburten, oder die Deutschen sterben aus* (1980; *Headbirths, or, the Germans Are Dying Out*); and *Die Rätten* (1987; *The Rat*).

Two of Grass's latest works, *Unkenrufe* (1992; *The Call of the Toad*) and *Ein weites Feld* (1995; *A Broad Field*), examine contemporary political issues in Germany. The former paints a portrait of greed in Danzig in the flawed efforts of the German man Alexander Reschke and the Polish woman Alexandra Piatkowska to establish a memorial cemetery for both Polish and German Danzigers. *A Broad Field* probes the German reunification process, about which Grass was openly critical. In 1999 Grass published *Mein Jarhundert* (*My Century*), a collection of 100 different stories, each of them told by a different person from each year of the twentieth century. Grass's plays include *Hochwasser* (1956; *Flood*), and *Die bösen Köche* (1961; *The Wicked Cooks*), both of which appeared in *Four Plays* (1967). Among his collections of poetry, which he illustrated himself, are the volumes *Die Vorzüge der Windhühner* (1956; *The Advantages of Windfowl*); *Gleisdreieck* (1960; *Railroad-Track Triangle*); *Questioned* (1967), a book of political poems; *Inmarypraise* (1973); and *Tested By Love* (1974).

Grass had close ties with the Social Democratic Party in West Berlin and was a personal friend of Willy Brandt, chancellor of West Germany from 1969 to 1974. His outspokenness on political issues has long made him a controversial figure in Germany. In the 1960s he opposed the introduction of nuclear missles in his country, and he was critical of the German reunification process. His essays and political writings appear in *Speak Out: Speeches, Open Letters, Commentaries* (1968); and *Writing and Politics* (1985).

BIBLIOGRAPHY

Hayman, Ronald, *Günter Grass*, 1985; Keele, Alan Frank, *Understanding Günter Grass*, 1988; Lawson, Richard H., *Günter Grass*, 1985.

Graves, Robert

(July 24/26, 1895–December 7, 1985)
Poet, Novelist, Scholar, Short-Story Writer

Primarily known for his love poetry and his novels *I, Claudius* and *Claudius the God*, Robert von Ranke Graves was born in London and grew up in the strict religious atmosphere his mother created. He shared his father's love of poetry and literature, particularly of the Celtic tradition. After attending numerous primary schools, he enrolled in the Charterhouse School in London at the age of 14. At the latter he began to write poems, experimenting with different styles. Graves enlisted in the Royal Welch Fusiliers and served as a British officer during World War I. During this time he met the young antiwar poet SIEGFRIED SASSOON, who for a time was one of his closest friends. An exploding shell nearly ended his life at the Battle of Somme in 1916, an experience recounted in poems such as *Escape* (1916), which begins: "But I was dead an hour or more / I woke when I'd already passed the door."

The same year saw the publication of his first volume of poetry, *Over the Brazier*, which, along with *Fairies and Fusiliers* (1917) was based on his war experiences. After his recuperation, Graves studied at Oxford, where he earned his doctorate. His subsequent marriage to Nancy Nicholson produced four children but was unhappy and fraught with troubles. Graves's autobiography *Good-Bye to All That* (1929) recounts his early life with particular emphasis on his traumatic experience in trench warfare during World War I. The work's success enabled Graves to move to Mallorca with the American writer Laura Riding, with whom he maintained a difficult relationship for the next ten years.

Of Graves's fifteen novels, the historical novel *I, Claudius* (1934) is his most well known and became the basis for a popular television series. The story takes place in the corrupt political atmosphere of Rome during the rules of the Roman autocrats Augustus (63 B.C.–14 A.D.), Tiberius (42 B.C.–37 A.D.), and Caligula (12 A.D.–41 A.D.), as seen through the eyes of the ineffectual Claudius. Its sequel, *Claudius the God* (1934), continues into Claudius's own reign. *The Story of Marie Powell: Wife to Mr. Milton* (1942) is an unsympathetic portrait of the poet John Milton, told from the point of view of his first wife, Marie Powell. Among Graves's other novels are *Count Belisarius* (1938), a fictional biography of the Byzantine military leader; and *Hercules, My Shipmate* (1944), originally published in Britain as *The Golden Fleece*; and *Homer's Daughter* (1955).

Crucial to the understanding of Graves's later poetry and novels is his work *The White Goddess: A Historical Grammar of Poetic Myth* (1948). The White Goddess, Graves argued, is a feminine force that has existed from ancient to modern times. In his philosophy, the goddess is the source of truth and the poetic muse found in pagan traditions. Christianity and Greek philosophy, Graves argued, had destroyed the muse—or at least done their best to destroy her.

In the novel *King Jesus* (1946), Graves portrays Jesus's crucifixion as a consequence of his defiance of the White Goddess. *King Jesus* was also colored by Graves's friendship with Joshua Podro, a Polish Hebrew scholar with extensive knowledge of rabbinical tradition. With Podro he also coauthored the nonfiction work *The Nazarene Gospels Restored* (1945).

In form Graves's poetry followed English tradition, with careful attention to form and meter, and he is most remembered for his melancholy love verses. His collections of poetry number more than fifty and include *Whipperginny* (1923) and *Poems About Love* (1969) as well as his earlier war poetry and several volumes of collected poems. Graves outlined his ideas on poetry in works such as *On English Poetry* (1922) and taught poetry at Oxford from 1961 to 1966.

During the 1960s, Graves developed an interest in several new areas. He had long been interested in hallucinogenic mushrooms used in religious rites and began experimenting with mind-altering drugs himself. Graves shared a belief with other intellecutals such as ALDOUS HUXLEY that hallucinogenic drugs led one to deeper spiritual insight, an idea that became popular among a generation of youth in the 1960s.

In addition to psychedelic drugs, Graves turned to a series of young female "muses," whom he believed embodied the White Goddess, for inspiration in his poetry. His most controversial work of this period, a new translation of *The Rubáiyát of Omar Khayyàm* (1967), quite different from the one done in the nineteenth century by Edward Fitzgerald, stemmed from his growing interest in Sufism, the mystical tradition of Islam. Fitzgerald had taken Omar's praise of love and wine completely literally, but Graves claimed superior knowledge; the Sufi poet Omar Ali-Shah, who claimed to be a direct descendant of Mohammed, had given Graves copies of the *Rubáiyát*'s verses, and communicated the tradition that Omar, like other Sufi poets, was really singing of the love of the Divine and the intoxication of direct contact with it. Shah's refusal to produce the original manuscript he claimed was in his family's possession led to widespread critical objection to Graves's translation.

Graves's other works include a biography of T. E. Lawrence, *Lawrence and the Arabs* (1927); *Greek Myths and Legends* (1968); and short stories.

BIBLIOGRAPHY

Canary, Robert H., *Robert Graves*, 1980; Graves, Richard Perceval, *Robert Graves*, 1986; Graves, Richard Perceval, *Robert Graves and the White Goddess*, 1995; Seymour, Miranda, *Robert Graves: Life on the Edge*, 1995.

Greene, Graham

(October 2, 1904–April 3, 1991)
Novelist, Short-Story Writer, Playwright, Poet

Henry Graham Greene achieved success as a writer with the 1932 publication of his "entertainment" *Stamboul Train*. The engaging narratives of his novels and stories are shaped by his Catholicism; they focus on

Graham Greene (Ann Ronan/Image Select)

England and was followed by *The Name of Action* (1930) and *The Rumour at Nightfall* (1931). Meanwhile, Greene had also converted to Roman Catholicism (1926), married Vivien Dayrell-Browning (1927), and begun a career in journalism. He worked for the London *Times* from 1926 to 1930 and subsequently wrote literary and film criticism for the *Spectator* and *Night and Day*.

Not until the publication of *Orient Express* (1932; British title *Stamboul Train*) did Greene achieve popular success. The story unfolds around passengers on a train to Istanbul, among whom are the currant merchant Carleton Myatt and the chorus girl Coral Musker. Greene called this and his next three novels "entertainments." The novels—*A Gun for Sale* (1936), *The Confidential Agent* (1939), and *The Ministry of Fear* (1943)—are mainly fast-paced thrillers. *A Gun for Sale* pits James Raven against the detective Mather, who is engaged to Anne Crowder. Raven is hired to kill the minister of a European nation and is betrayed by all who know him.

Greene's characters throughout his fiction are flawed, morally fallen, and struggling with spiritual dilemmas. The political and social orders in which they live are equally flawed. With *Brighton Rock* (1938), he began to examine questions of heaven and hell, faith and faithlessness, and good and evil. Its protagonist, the teenage gangster Pinkie Brown, was raised as a Catholic and consciously chooses hell. A trip to Mexico inspired Greene's *The Power and the Glory* (1940), about the downfall and execution of a soul-searching, alcoholic priest who tries to perform his clerical duties under the threat of death at the hands of Communists.

characters grappling with moral and spiritual dilemmas. Greene's essentially pessimistic outlook is reflected in the decay and chaos which form the backdrops of his work.

Greene was the fourth child of six, born in Berkhamsted, Hertfordshire, England. He attended the Berkhamsted School, where his father taught and where Greene was miserable. Greene was a rebellious child, in trouble at school and at home, and toyed with suicide on several occasions in his adolescence. At the age of 17, Greene entered Balliol College, Oxford and became active in the University's literary scene.

The poetry collection *Babbling April*, Greene's first published work, appeared in 1925. His first novel, *The Man Within* (1929), gained a measure of popularity in

Greene worked in the Foreign Office during World War II and was stationed in West Africa, the locale that provided the setting for *The Heart of the Matter* (1948). The protagonist, Henry Scobie, deputy commissioner of police, is a sympathetic character forced to choose between his wife, Louise, and Helen, with whom he has an affair. His feelings of guilt over this dilemma and other matters lead him to choose damnation and commit suicide.

Greene presents *The End of the Affair* (1951), which explores the question of sainthood, through alternate perspectives. The formerly agnostic Bendrix tells the story of an affair he had with Sarah, who is married to Henry Miles. Sarah dies with a faith strong enough to elevate her to sainthood, and through his affair with her, Bendrix comes to accept belief in God. Query, the protagonist of *A Burnt-Out Case* (1961), undergoes a spiritual awakening when he goes to a leprosarioum in the Belgian Congo.

Many of Greene's later novels are set in scenes of impending revolution. These include *The Quiet American* (1956), set in Vietnam; *Our Man in Havana* (1958), which takes place in pre-Communist Cuba; and *The Comedians* (1966), set in Haiti during the rule of François "Papa Doc" Duvalier. Among his other novels are the entertainment *Travels With My Aunt* (1969); *The Honorary Consul* (1973); *The Human Factor* (1978); *Doctor Fischer of Geneva or The Bomb Party* (1980); *Monsignor Quixote* (1982); and *The Tenth Man* (1985).

Aside from novels, Greene wrote short stories and plays that continue the themes he addressed in his novels. His short-story collections include *Nineteen Stories* (1947) and *May We Borrow Your Husband? and Other Comedies of the Sexual Life* (1967). Among his plays are *The Living Room* (1952), which centers around a love triangle in which Michael Dennis struggles between his love for Rose Pemberton and his pity for his wife; *The Potting Shed* (1957); *Carving a Statue* (1964); and *The Return of A. J. Raffles* (1975). His memoirs, *A Sort of Life* and *Ways of Escape*, were published in 1971 and 1980.

BIBLIOGRAPHY

DeVitis, A. A., *Graham Greene*, rev. ed., 1986; McEwan, Neil, *Graham Greene*, 1988; Watts, Cedrick Thomas, *A Preface to Greene*, 1997.

Grierson, John

(April 26, 1898–February 19, 1972)
Producer, Director, Teacher

The originator of the term "documentary," John Grierson introduced documentary filmmaking to Great Britain and founded the documentary film movement in that country. He directed his first film in 1928 and thereafter spent most of his time finding talent and resources for the production of other films. Over the course of his career, he worked for the governments of Britain and Canada as well as the United Nations Educational, Scientific and Cultural Organization (UNESCO).

Grierson was born in Deanston, Stirlingshire, Scotland. His father, a teacher, was headmaster at the school he entered in 1903. Grierson's mother, also a teacher, was a feminist and an early advocate of suffrage for women. A good student with a strong personality, Grierson attended the High School in Stirling beginning in 1908. During World War I, he did munitions work before joining the crew of a minesweeper as a telegraphist.

With the end of the war, Grierson entered the University of Glasgow and studied philosophy. He joined the university's chapter of the Fabian Society, which sought to promote socialism in Britain through nonviolent means (see GEORGE BERNARD SHAW). When the chapter dissolved, Grierson became involved with the New University Labour Club, which backed H. G. WELLS as a candidate for Lord Rector in university elections. Wells lost the election, but Grierson developed a reputation for his boisterous speeches and vocal and physical taunting of the opposing candidates.

In 1923, the Rockefeller Foundation awarded Grierson a research fellowship that enabled him to study in the United States. Over the next five years, Grierson traveled extensively in America, studying in Chicago, Wisconsin, and New York (at Columbia University). His area of concentration was sociology, and in particular the effect of mass communication on society. In 1925, he met Walter Lippmann in New York and developed an interest in the potential use of film in influencing the public.

While in the United States, Grierson began to contribute articles and film reviews to a number of periodicals. It was in a review of the film *Moana* (1926) for the New York *Sun* that he first used the term "documentary" in describing a film. He returned to England in 1928 and went to work for the Empire Marketing Board (E.M.B.), putting together its film unit.

Grierson directed his first documentary, *Drifters*, in 1928. The film, about the lives of herring fishermen in the North Sea, was shown at the Film Society before SERGEY EISENSTEIN's *Battleship Potemkin* (1925). Eisenstein, with whose work Grierson had become familiar in the United States, attended the showing. *Drifters* earned praise from film critics and inspired a number of young directors to begin working in the same vein. In 1930 Grierson married Margaret Taylor, who had helped him edit *Drifters*.

Grierson believed documentaries should both entertain and educate. During his lifetime he was involved with productions of propaganda films, public interest pieces, documentaries of the lives of ordinary people, and many other projects, though seldom directing the films himself. He supervised the work of many other filmmakers and worked with other noteworthy figures in film, including JORIS IVENS and the Brazilian director Alberto Cavalcanti. Those who worked under him knew him as demanding, passionate, and sometimes difficult.

When the E.M.B. dissolved in 1933, the film unit fell under the General Post Office. Grierson headed the G.P.O.'s film office and produced many films for the British government. He solicited financing for films and sought out new directors to undertake projects. In 1935, he founded the Film Centre in London, which coordinated and financed other documentary film units. Grierson also founded and published *World Film News*, wrote film criticism, and lectured to other groups.

Grierson's efforts in film shifted to Canada in the late 1930s. In 1939 he helped draft the National Film Act in Canada and was responsible for its main ideas. The same year, he helped found the National Film Board of Canada and served as its head. During World War II, he produced and supervised a number of government propaganda films. From 1946 to 1948, Grierson worked for UNESCO. He returned to the British government in 1948, working as film controller at the Central Office of Information until 1950.

With John Baxter the following year, Grierson headed Group 3 of the National Film Finance Corporation and was involved in promoting the work of young filmmakers and actors, among whom was the actor Peter Sellers. In 1957, Grierson began his program *This Wonderful World*. He taught at McGill University in Canada from 1968 to 1971 and died of cancer in 1972.

BIBLIOGRAPHY

Evans, Gary, *John Grierson and the National Film Board: The Politics of Wartime Propaganda*, 1984; Forman, Sir Denis, *John Grierson: The Man and the Memory*, 1978; Hardy, Forsyth, *John Grierson: A Documentary Biography*, 1979; Sussex, Elizabeth, ed., *The Rise and Fall of British Documentary: The Story of the Film Movement Founded by John Grierson*, 1975; Winston, Brian, *Claiming the Real: The Griersonian Documentary and Its Legitimations*, 1995.

Gris, Juan

(March 23, 1887–May 11, 1927)
Painter, Graphic Artist, Illustrator

J uan Gris was a lesser-known figure in the group of painters who worked in the Cubist style developed by PABLO PICASSO and GEORGES BRAQUE, but his Synthetic Cubist still lifes, which combine harsh, angular forms with bold, vibrant colors, formed an important contribution to the body of Cubist art in the World War I era.

Gris was of Castilian and Andalusian ancestry, born José Victoriano González in Madrid. From 1902 to 1904 he studied engineering at the Madrid School of Arts and Sciences. During this time he began to contribute drawings to such publications as *Blanco y Negro* and *Madrid Comico*. José Maria Carbonero, under whom he studied painting from 1904 to 1906, gave Gris his only formal art training. He moved to Paris in 1906, settling in Montmartre in Le Bateau Lavoir, where his countryman Picasso also lived.

At this time, Gris had not yet begun to paint in earnest. His drawings, with which he primarily concerned himself, derived from the Art Nouveau style then popular in Germany. The Cubist experiments of Picasso and Braque, however, were soon to transform Gris into a Cubist painter, and he began painting seriously in 1910. Through Picasso he also met such avant-garde figures as Guillaume Apollinaire and Max Jacob. In 1908 he met Daniel Henry Kahnweiler, his most important early patron, who in 1912 purchased all his works. The American expatriate Gertrude Stein also admired Gris's work and enthusiastically promoted it.

Gris essentially followed Picasso and Braque through Analytical and Synthetic Cubism. The curvilinear forms of his earlier drawings gave way to severe, angular creations in his paintings. Early Cubist works such as *Still Life with Bottle* (1910) and *Portrait of Picasso* (1912), the latter of which employs a blue, monochromatic color scheme, are rendered in the Analytical Cubist style. Even at this point, however, Gris used more striking colors than the grays and muted earth tones Picasso and Braque preferred.

When Picasso and Braque began to employ brighter colors in their Synthetic Cubist works, Gris used even bolder colors. *Violin and Guitar* (1913), an oil on canvas, mixes brilliant reds, blues, greens, and purples reminiscent of the color palettes of the Fauves. In his mature style, Gris also distinguished himself from Picasso and Braque by his use of more severe and angular forms.

In 1912 Gris spent a summer with Picasso and Braque in Céret, France. There they began to experiment with *papier collé*—shapes cut from paper. The three of them were soon affixing shapes cut from wood, glass, and paper to their works, and the resulting "collages" dominate Gris's work in 1914. He combined paper, wood, and glass, intermingling them with watercolor, charcoal, pencil, or crayon. He affixed a piece of mirror to *The Marble Console* (1914).

Because he was a Spanish citizen, Gris was not required to fight in World War I. He passed the war in Paris, living in near-poverty. While the works of Picasso and Braque brought large sums of money, Gris remained virtually unknown outside of Paris art circles. He did not have his first one-man show until 1919, after which he exhibited frequently.

Although still lifes undoubtedly dominated Gris's subject matter, he also painted landscapes and café scenes, such as his *The Man in the Café* (1912) and *Landscape* (1917). After 1920 Gris's severe geometric compositions gave way to looser, curvilinear forms, as in *Pierrot with Guitar* (1922) and *Seated Harlequin* (1923). Between 1922 and 1924 he designed two sets for SERGEY DIAGHILEV's Ballets Russes, *Les tentations de la bergère* (*The Temptations of the Shepherdess*) and *La colombe* (*The Dove*).

Among Gris's other works are book illustrations; lithographs; and a single Cubist sculpture, *Harlequin* (1917). Gris died of blood poisoning in 1927.

BIBLIOGRAPHY

Green, Christopher, *Juan Gris*, 1992; Soby, James Thrall, *Juan Gris*, 1958.

Gropius, Walter

(May 18, 1883–July 15, 1969)
Architect, Theorist, Teacher, City Planner

As the founder and director (1919–1928) of the Bauhaus, the most influential school in modern architecture, Walter Adolph Gropius exerted a profound influence on the development of twentieth-century public buildings. The International Style, to which he was a major contributor, was the dominant force in architecture between the two world wars; it is marked by its rejection of the then-prevalent decorative approach in favor of a strong emphasis on functionality. His major works include the school building and faculty housing at the Bauhaus in Dessau (1925–1926), the Graduate Center at Harvard University, the United States Embassy in Athens, Greece (1960), and the University of Baghdad (1960).

Gropius was the son of an architect, born in Berlin. He studied architecture at the Universities of Munich (1903–1904) and Berlin-Charlottenburg (1905–1907). He worked in an architect's office in Berlin in 1904 and soon afterward did his military service. He began to design buildings before he graduated, notably the farm laborers' cottages in Pomerania in 1906. In 1907 he joined PETER BEHRENS's office in Berlin and worked as his chief assistant until 1910.

That year he opened his own office, and in 1911 he joined the German Labor League (Deutscher Werkbund). The Labor League's goal fit in with the purpose Gropius held to throughout his career as an architect: to bridge the gap between designers and the requirements of the modern machine age.

Gropius's mature style emerged early in his career, in the Fagus Works at Alfeld-an-der-Leine (1911) and the model office and factory buildings in Cologne (1914), both collaborative efforts with Adolph Meyer. The Fagus Works, a rectangular structure, is noteworthy for its massive use of glass and its horizontal bands of windows divided by steel supports. The Cologne buildings are less functional but also use a large amount of glass. The office building features a large, circular, glass-enclosed staircase.

In World War I Gropius served as a cavalry officer on the Western Front; during his period of service he was injured by a bomb explosion and received the Iron Cross for bravery. In 1915 he married Alma Schindler Mahler, the widow of composer Gustav Mahler (1860–1911). Their short marriage ended in 1919 following her affair with FRANZ WERFEL, and the only child of their marriage, Alma Manon, died tragically in 1935. Gropius married Ise Frank in 1923.

In 1918 he founded the Staatliches Bauhaus in Weimar by uniting two schools, the Grand Ducal Saxon School of Applied Arts and the Grand Ducal Academy of Arts, of which he was director. For the next fifteen years, the Bauhaus would train hundreds of architects and craftsmen and exert a profound influence on modern architecture. Gropius was responsible for the Bauhaus curriculum, which sought to train students to create architecture for the modern machine age. First and foremost, every student underwent training in the crafts at the Bauhaus's numerous craft shops. An architect, Gropius believed, was first a craftsman.

Gropius engaged for the Bauhaus faculty the most prominent figures of progressive art in his day, including PAUL KLEE, WASSILY KANDINSKY, and LÁSZLÓ MOHOLY-NAGY (who later established the New Bauhaus in Chicago). His aim of designing buildings for the machine age was born of his belief in creating structures for the requirements of the social environment rather than from any fixed preference for mechanization. The complexity and large-scale demands of modern buildings, Gropius believed, required collaboration with other architects, and he rarely worked alone. A centerpiece of the Bauhaus curriculum was a design course formulated by the Swiss painter and sculptor Johannes Itten, who encouraged exploration of rhythm, color, contrast, and form.

Gropius, arguably better known for his teaching and ideas on architecture than for his actual designs, continued to design buildings in the 1920s. Among these designs are the Chicago Tribune Tower in 1922 and the Siemensstadt Housing in Berlin (1929). He also designed furniture and smaller items such as silverware and door handles, many for commercial production. Among his more unusual projects were a self-propelled diesel railroad car (1913), a sleeping car for the Germany Railway (1914), and a car, the Adler Cabriolet (1930). Although he did some work on private dwellings, his major focus was public buildings and city planning.

When the Bauhaus relocated to Dessau in 1925, Gropius designed what was to become his best-known work, the school building and faculty housing (1925–1926). The asymmetrical, flat-roofed, white buildings are based on rectangular shapes, and, like many of his designs, feature horizontal bands of windows. These characteristics are hallmarks of the International Style (also sometimes referred to as the Bauhaus Style or the Functional Style), which emerged as the dominant force in architecture between World War I and World War II.

When the Nazis rose to power in the early 1930s, the Bauhaus was quickly closed, and its style was labeled "art Bolshevism." Gropius's functional style was looked upon unfavorably by people in other quarters as well—charges of inhumanity, overmechanization, and coldness were not uncommon in critical descriptions of his work. Gropius fled with his wife to Italy and ultimately settled in England in 1934. There he worked in association with Maxwell Fry on the design for the Village College at Impington, Cambridgeshire (1936).

Gropius moved to the United States in 1937, settling in Cambridge, Massachusetts, and accepting a professorship of architecture at Harvard University. In 1938 he became chairman of the department. In accordance with his belief that buildings should serve the needs of the current social climate, he rejected all historical reference in architecture and attempted, unsuccessfully, to purge the class on architectural history from the curriculum. Although he was able to teach the philosophical tenets of the Bauhaus at Harvard, he remained unable to establish the training in crafts he espoused.

Gropius became an American citizen in 1944. His later buildings were all collaborative efforts. From 1937 to 1940 he worked with Marcel Breuer, a former Bauhaus student and fellow teacher.

Together they designed Gropius's home in Lincoln, Massachusetts as well as Black Mountain College, Lake Eden, North Carolina. In the decade between 1942 and 1952 he served as vice president of the General Panel Corporation, a company that manufactured prefabricated housing.

The center of his work, however, was The Architects Collaborative (TAC), which he founded in 1946 with six former Harvard students and remained involved with until his death. TAC designed the Harvard University Graduate Center (1949–1950) as well as the U.S. Embassy in Athens (1960) and the University of Baghdad (1960).

Gropius received innumerable awards for his work throughout his life. Among these are honorary doctorates from the Hannover Institute of Technology (1929), Western Reserve University in Cleveland (1951), Harvard University (1953), and the University of Sydney in Australia (1954). From 1929 to 1957 he was vice president of the International Congresses of Modern Architecture (CIAM) in Zurich.

BIBLIOGRAPHY

Fitch, James Marston, *Walter Gropius*, 1960; Giedion, Siegfried, *Walter Gropius: Work and Teamwork*, 1954; Sharp, Dennis, *Bauhaus, Dessau: Walter Gropius*, 1993.

Grosz, George

(July 26, 1893–July 6, 1959)
Painter, Graphic Artist, Illustrator

Influenced by the German Expressionists, the Dadaists, and his own vision of the corruption and decadence of German society, the artist and painter George Grosz framed his violent social and political criticism in expressive line drawings and paintings with jagged, angular forms and grotesque caricatures. Intermingled with these works, particularly in his later years, were landscapes, portraits, and other less violent works.

Grosz was born Georg Ehrenfried Gross in Berlin. After the death of his father in 1900, he moved with his mother to Stolp in Pomerania in 1902. He attended a local grammar school and took drawing lessons. A talent for satire and caricature emerged in Grosz early on and first manifested itself in cartoons. He sold his first to *Ulk* in 1910 and continued selling them to other magazines.

Grosz enrolled in the Royal Academy in Dresden, but more influential in his development was his time of study at the Kunstgewerbemuseum in Berlin, beginning in 1912. In Berlin he began to sketch objects and barren cityscapes as well as sympathetic portraits of down-and-outs, such as *Unemployed Men* (1912). Circus drawings, nudes, sex scenes (*Orgy*, 1913), and violent murder sketches (*Murder*, 1912–1913) also began to appear in his work. In 1913, Grosz went to Paris, where he was further influenced by his studies at the Atélier Colarossi and his acquaintance with the draftsman Jules Pascin.

By this time, Grosz had already become a harsh and vehement social critic. His graphic sketches portrayed chaos and decay, a vision that his disastrous years of military service would only make more negative. Grosz enlisted during World War I, was released on a medical discharge, and was recalled in 1917 before being permanently discharged. The horrors of war began to dominate his drawings, such as *Landscape with Dead Bodies* (1915) and *The Shell* (1915). War veterans, prostitutes, profiteers, and complacent, ignorant middle-class figures appeared in grotesque form in his work.

Beginning with two volumes of lithographs published in Berlin in 1917, he began to publish his drawings. Subsequent collections include *Republican Automatons* (1920), *The Face of the Ruling Class* (1921), and *Ecce Homo* (1923; *Behold the Man*). The Expressionists had influenced Grosz earlier (see ERNST LUDWIG KIRCHNER), but two later movements influenced his work during the 1920s. In 1918, he joined both the Communist Party and the Dadaists, the latter an anarchistic artistic movement sharply critical of all facets of postwar society. He married Eva Peter in 1920.

Burlesques by Grosz of religious establishments, the bourgeois, militarists, and capitalists, such as the paintings *Diamond Racketeer* (1920) and *Pillars of Society* (1926), appeared frequently. At this time, Grosz turned more of his attention to drawings than he did to painting. Through his political drawings, such as *The Bourgeois Stirs up Trouble and The Proletarian Must Shed His Blood* (1923), his name became well known, and he

was arrested and tried for his outspoken criticism more than once.

Toward the end of the 1920s, however, Grosz lost his enthusiasm for Communism and began to create less highly charged subjects along with his controversial material. Among his "less offensive" works of the 1920s are a series of portraits and self-portraits, a painting of the boxer Max Schmeling (1926), and the costumes for George Bernard Shaw's *Androcles and the Lion* in 1924.

The emergence of Adolf Hitler provided Grosz with a new enemy, and critical sketches of the future dictator, such as *Hitler the Savior* (1930), appeared in his work several years before Hitler's rise to power in 1933. Having thought of emigrating to the United States for several years, Grosz finally made the move in 1933, the same year the Nazis deprived him of his German citizenship. His works were exhibited widely in Germany up until this time; in 1937 the Nazis included them in an exhibit of "degenerate art," and many were subsequently destroyed.

Although he continued to produce politically charged works, Grosz toned down his social criticism in the United States. Photographs of New York, paintings of New York scenes and people (*New York Types*, 1934), and landscapes all began to emerge in his work. He painted more than he had in Germany but also continued to sketch. This new and less controversial mode provided him with little popular success, and he turned to teaching to earn money. In 1953 he opened an art school on Long Island.

Even after he moved to the United States, however, Grosz still set his pen and paintbrush to work against the Nazis, as in *Letter to an Anti-Semite* (1935). *He Was a Writer* (1934) was inspired by the death of his friend Erich Mühsam in a concentration camp. The Spanish Civil War formed the subject matter of another series of works, such as *The Radio General* (1937), a savage caricature of General Francisco Franco. Toward the end of Grosz's life, attacks on American commercialism appeared in his work.

Grosz's autobiography *A Little Yes and a Big No* was published in 1946, and he was elected to the National Institute of Arts and Letters in 1954. Among his other works are the illustrations for Bertolt Brecht's children's book *The Three Soldiers* (1930) and Heinrich Mann's *Kobes* (1925).

BIBLIOGRAPHY

Flavell, Kay, *George Grosz: A Biography*, 1988; Lewis, Beth Irwin, *George Grosz:, Art and Politics in the Weimar Republic*, 1971; Schneede, Uwe M., *George Grosz: His Life and Work*, 1979.

Guilbert, Yvette

(January 20, 1865–February 4, 1944)
Singer, Actress, Novelist

The French artist Henri de Toulouse-Lautrec memorialized Yvette Guilbert in his poster of the singer in her characteristic black gloves and yellow dress. Guilbert gained fame in late nineteenth-century Paris as a cabaret singer performing innuendo-filled songs. In her later career she appeared on screen, recorded her songs, and wrote novels and autobiographical works.

Guilbert was born Emma Laure Esther Guilbert in Paris. Her father was of peasant background and worked in several unsuccessful business ventures. From him Guilbert received her first exposure to music as she sang to his instrumental accompaniment. When she was 12, however, her father abandoned the family, leaving her with her mother, a seamstress. Guilbert attended the Pension Couard as a day student and worked with her mother in the shop.

At the age of 16 Guilbert took a modeling job, and she later went to work as a sales-girl. After watching a performance by Sarah Bernhard, she began to think about singing professionally. M. Landrol, a member of the company at the Gymnase, took her on as a student, and in 1887 she made her professional debut as Madame de Nevers in *La Reine Margot* at the Bouffes-du-Nord.

The French author Guy de Maupassant suggested she use the stage name Yvette, and from her debut onward she was known as Yvette Guilbert. In 1891–1892 she gave a series of successful performances at the Horloge. Guilbert soon became a popular cabaret singer, appearing at the Moulin Rouge, the Folies-Bergère, the Ambassadeurs, and elsewhere. From the mid-1890s on she appeared on international stages as well.

Later in her career Guilbert made popular recordings of her songs (many written by Léon Xanrof and Aristide Bruant), made international appearances, and appeared in such films as *Les Misérables* (1934) and *Pêcheurs d'Islande* (1934). Her writings include *Struggles and Victories* (1910; with Harold Simpson), *L'art de chanter une chanson* (*How to Sing a Song*, 1918), the autobiography *La chanson de ma vie* (*Song of My Life: My Memories*, 1929), and the novels *La vedette* and *Les demi-vieilles*.

BIBLIOGRAPHY

Guilbert, Yvette, *Song of My Life: My Memories*, 1929; Knapp, Bettina, and Chipman, Myra, *That Was Yvette: The Biography of Yvette Guilbert, the Great Diseuse*, 1964.

Guillén, Jorge

(January 18, 1893–February 6, 1984)
Poet, Teacher, Critic, Scholar

The Spanish poet Jorge Guillén released most of his poetry in three major collections, *Canticles*, *Clamor*, and *Homages*. His lyrical, exuberant verse is rich in metaphor and extols his natural surroundings, celebrates the joys of love, and considers the passing of time. Guillén also lectured at major universities all over the world.

Guillén was born the son of a newspaper publisher in Valladolid, Castile, Spain. At the age of 10, he enrolled in the Institute of Valladolid, and from 1909 to 1911, he studied with the french Fathers of the Oratory in Friebourg, Switzerland. Returning to Spain in 1911, Guillén lived at the Residencia de Estudiantes and studied at the University of Madrid. In 1913, he earned a licentiate in letters from the University of Granada, and in 1923 he returned to the University of Madrid to earn his doctorate (1924).

Guillén's first collection of poetry, *Cántico* (*Canticle*), was published in 1928. The first edition contained seventy-five poems, and after undergoing three expansions over period of more than twenty years, the final edition appeared in 1950 with 334 poems. The *Canticle* poems are musical, rhythmic, contemplative celebrations of life. The cycles of nature form an important part of them, as in "April of the Ash," describing the spring leaves emerging on the ash tree. "Beyond" finds the poet enraptured with his surroundings as the day dawns.

Many poems, such as "I Close My Eyes," are introspective and evoke dreams, whereas others, such as "A Springtime of Salvation" and "Love Fulfilled," are sensual. The passage of time ("Along the Illustrious Shores") and his own mortality ("Death in the Distance") are also frequent themes in *Canticles*. In poetic style Guillén was influenced in part by the Spanish poet JUAN RAMÓN JIMÉNEZ, whose painstaking attention to craftsmanship lent his poetry a lyrical, sonorous quality. Guillén's poetry, too, was carefully tailored to bring out musical qualities that complemented his subjects. He turned to a more negative tone in *Qué van a dar en la mar* (1960; *That Flow into the Sea*) and *A la altura de las circunstancias* (1963; *The Rise to the Occasions*).

Like many other Spanish writers and intellectuals, Guillén found himself an exile during the Spanish Civil War (1936–1939). He was arrested in Pamplona in 1936 and two years later moved to the United States; he did not return permanently to Spain until 1978.

From 1957 to 1963, Guillén published his second major series of poetry, the three-volume *Clamor: Time of History.* As a whole, the poems of the three volumes of *Clamor* are more pessimistic than those of *Canticles*. In the first volume, Guillén offered his first social criticism. In a series of "Clover Leaves," or short, often humorous poems, Guillén attacks the excesses of modern civilization. The prose poem "The Holdup Men" questions the American dream. In "The Power of Perez" and "Police Chorus," Guillén criticizes Spain's Fascist police state. His poetic commentary led Spanish authorities to ban *Pandemonium.*

The two volumes that complete the *Clamor* trilogy back away from social themes and return to the more personal subjects considered in the *Canticles.* The former contains a section entitled "In Remembrance," dedicated to the memory of Guillén's first wife, Germaine Cahen, who died in 1947. Many poems in *To Rise to the Occasion* again evince the optimistic, exuberant spirit of the *Canticles*, as do the poems in Guillén's last major collection, *Homenaje* (1967; *Homage: A Gathering of Lives*), which pays poetic homage to writers and also has love lyrics written to his second wife.

Guillén's lifelong academic career started in 1917, when he began lecturing at the Sorbonne in Paris. He lectured at universities all over the world: from 1926 to 1929, he taught Spanish language and literature at the University of Murcia; from 1929 to 1931 he taught at Oxford; from 1931 to 1938 he was professor of Spanish literature in Seville. Guillén was a professor at Wellesley from 1940 to 1957; he also lectured in Romania, Colombia, Mexico, and Puerto Rico as well as many other universities in the United States.

Guillén's other works include *Aire nuestro* (1968; *Our Air*), a massive volume that includes *Canticles, Clamor,* and *Homages; The Poetry and the Poet* (1979), a selection of his poetry; *And Other Poems* (1973); and the critical works *Language of Poetry: Some Poets of Spain* (1961) and *The Theme of the Work* (1961). Guillén received the Miguel de Cervantes Prize from the Spanish Royal Academy in 1976.

BIBLIOGRAPHY

MacCurdy, G. Grant, *Jorge Guillén,* 1982; Matthews, Elizabeth, *The Structured World of Jorge Guillén: A Study of Cántico and Clamor,* 1985.

Guinness, Alec

(April 2, 1914–)
Actor, Producer, Director

The English actor Alec Guinness was a private personality with a talent for portraying pensive, introverted characters. He lacked the flashiness and dramatic flair of LAURENCE OLIVIER and other British actors of his generation, but was recognized for his versatility and was also a popular personality in *The Lavender Hill Mob* and *Kind Hearts and Coronets*. Like many of the English actors of his generation, he established himself on the British stage before earning international fame as a film star, particularly in the films of DAVID LEAN and in the *Star Wars* trilogy.

Guinness was born in Marylebone, England. He was the illegitimate child of a mother named Agnes and a father he rarely saw but who provided for him—a Scottish bank director. He spent his childhood moving with his mother from one boarding house to another in England. At the age of 6, he was sent to the boarding school Pembroke Lodge at Southbourne. Soon afterward he fell ill with colitis. During his illness he began constructing model theaters, dreaming up dramatic plots, and acting them out himself. After his recovery, he returned to school and entertained his fellow students with his dramatic performances.

At the age of 12 Guinness entered Roborough, near Eastbourne, where he became involved with the school's dramatic society. He did well in school but was not at the top of his class, and he abandoned formal study when he was 17. While working as a copywriter for the advertising agency Arks Publicity, he attended theater performances whenever he could, particularly at London's Old Vic Theatre.

Guinness soon began to consider a career in theater seriously. He called JOHN GIELGUD to ask him for his advice, and from then on, Gielgud helped him. He was eventually invited to join Gielgud's company at the New Theatre in 1934. With that company he appeared in a variety of Shakespearean and non-Shakespearean roles, beginning first as a versatile character actor. Guinness joined the Old Vic company in 1936 and appeared in a number of plays directed by TYRONE GUTHRIE and Michel Saint-Denis. He was especially successful as Sir Andrew Aguecheek (opposite Olivier's Sir Toby Belch) in *Twelfth Night* in 1937.

With Gielgud's company, he appeared in such plays as *Richard II* (1937), *The School for Scandal* (1937), *The Three Sisters* (1937), and *The Merchant of Venice* (1938). He took his first leading role as Louis Dubedat in GEORGE BERNARD SHAW's *The Doctor's Dilemma* in 1938. The same year he starred in the title role in a popular modern-dress version of *Hamlet* at the Old Vic. Guinness's first major West End role was in Clemence Dane's *Cousin Muriel* at the Globe Theatre in 1940.

Guinness served in the Royal Navy during World War II and while on leave made his stage debut in New York in TERENCE RATTIGAN's *Flare Path* (1942–1943). PETER BROOK directed Guinness's own stage adaptation of Fyodor Dostoeyvsky's *The Brothers Karamazov* at the Lyric Theatre, in which he starred as

Alec Guinness (second from left) in a still from the film *The Bridge on the River Kwai* (Ann Ronan/Image Select)

Mitya in 1946. In 1948 he produced *Twelfth Night*, his first directorial effort, for the Old Vic. Later stage roles include the poet DYLAN THOMAS in *Dylan* (1964).

In his first major film role (1946), Guinness appeared as Pip's friend Herbert Pocket in a screen version of Charles Dickens's *Great Expectations*. (Guiness later adapted the story for the stage.) In *Oliver Twist* (1948), he co-starred as Fagan. *Kind Hearts and Coronets* (1949) was one of several Ealing studio comedies to bring him international recogni-

tion. Guinness would appear in a number of films directed by Lean, including *Dr. Zhivago* (1963), in which he portrayed General Yegraf Zhivago.

Other films in which he appeared include *The Bridge on the River Kwai* (1957), for which he won an Academy Award for best actor; Lean's epic *Lawrence of Arabia* (1962), as Prince Feisal; FRANCO ZEFFIRELLI's *Brother Sun, Sister Moon* (1973), as the pope; Lean's *A Passage to India* (1984), as Professor Godbole; and *Little Dorrit* (1987), in which he acted the part of William Dorrit. Guinness also played Obi-Wan Kenobi in the trilogy *Star Wars* (1977), *The Empire Strikes Back* (1980), and *Return of the Jedi* (1983). He was knighted in 1960. His autobiography, *Blessings in Disguise*, was published in 1986.

BIBLIOGRAPHY

Guinness, Alec, *Blessings in Disguise*, reissue, 1996; O'Connor, Garry, *Alec Guinness: Master of Disguise*, 1994; Tanitch, Robert, *Guinness*, 1989; Taylor, John Russell, *Alec Guinness: A Celebration*, 1984; Von Gunden, Kenneth, *Alec Guinness: The Films*, 1987.

Guthrie, Tyrone

(July 2, 1900–May 15, 1971)
Director, Producer, Actor

Most famous for his Shakespeare productions, William Tyrone Guthrie established himself as a major director at the Sadler's Wells and Old Vic theatres in London. In his later life, he brought his Shakespearean productions to Canada and the United States and helped reestablish repertory theater in both countries. Guthrie also produced operas and other works by modern playwrights.

Guthrie was born in Tunbridge Wells, Kent, England. His mother, the daughter of a general, came from a theater-going family and introduced him to the theater at a young age. One excursion in particular excited his interest in the theater—a production of Gilbert and Sullivan's *Yeomen of the Guard* when he was 8. Guthrie was a successful student and attended a local school before studying at the preparatory schools of Hurstleigh and Templegrove, Eastbourne. With the outbreak of World War I, the 14-year-old Guthrie entered the military college of Wellington.

When the war ended, Guthrie entered the University of Oxford, where he studied history, joined the Oxford University Dramatic Society, and began to act. In 1924 he took a job with the British Broadcasting Corporation (BBC) and over the next two years put together a number of radio productions, including Euripides's *Iphigenia in Tauris* and his own *A Night in a Mid-Victorian Drawing-Room.*

In 1926, Guthrie began a season of directing with the Scottish National Players. Among his many productions there was *The Glen is Mine*, by the Scottish playwright John Brandane. He continued to write material for the BBC, among which is his "microphone play" *Squirrel's Cage*, about a man who dreams of traveling to Africa but submits to an average daily work routine under the influence of his father. His *The Flowers Are Not For You To Pick* (1929) depicts a young minister's final minutes before he drowns.

Guthrie began to develop his mature directing style when in 1929 he took the position of artistic director of the Anmer Hall Company, which performed at the Festival Theatre in Cambridge, and later at the Westminster Theatre in London. He preferred to work with actors who worked together over a period of time and got to know one another, and he did not like to use extras. Whereas later directors such as BERTOLT BRECHT purposely tried to establish distance between the performers and the audience, Guthrie tried to cultivate a relationship between the two. To foster this relationship, he preferred the thrust stage, designed to create a sense of intimacy between performers and spectators.

Among Guthrie's successful productions with the Anmer Hall Company was his first major independent production, James Bridie's *The Anatomist* (1931). His production of Luigi Pirandello's *Six Characters in Search of an Author* (1932) also proved a success. *Follow Me* (1931), Guthrie's own play about a Scottish working-class man, fared less well. During this time Guthrie married the actress and playwright Judith Bretherton, who was from then on intimately involved in her husband's work.

Throughout the 1930s and 1940s, Guthrie directed many plays at the Old Vic and Sadler's Wells theatres in London. Under the management of Lilian Baylis, the Old Vic staged mainly Shakespeare's plays and English language operas. Its management later passed to the French director Michel Saint-Denis. Productions of Shakespeare's plays were always in Guthrie's repertory during these years, but he also produced many works by Anton Chekhov as well as plays written by modern figures such as W. H. AUDEN, JOYCE CARY (*Sweet Aloes*, 1934), and GEORGE BERNARD SHAW.

By this time Guthrie had emerged as a major director and attracted prominent actors to his productions. LAURENCE OLIVIER starred as Hamlet at an Old Vic production in 1937. From time to time Guthrie directed his own plays, which never proved very successful. Among these was *Top of the Ladder*, staged at the St. James Theatre in London in 1950, about an executive ruined by the influences of his parents.

Along with plays, Guthrie produced many operas, the most successful of which were Giuseppe Verdi's *La Traviata;* BENJAMIN BRITTEN'S *Peter Grimes* (1946), the first show at the Sadler's Wells after World War II; Edmond Rostand's *Cyrano de Bergerac* (1946), with a set designed by his longtime collaborator Tanya Moisiewitsch; and an English version of Bizet's *Carmen*, staged at the Sadler's Wells in 1949, the Metropolitan Opera House in New York in 1952, and The Opera House in Düsseldorf in 1968.

Throughout his career, Guthrie sought to bring both theater and opera to the general English-speaking public. In the last fifteen years of his life, he increasingly devoted his energies to establishing repertory theater in North America. For several seasons, beginning in 1953, he served as artistic director at the Shakespeare Festival Theatre in Stratford, Ontario, dividing his time between Canada, Britain, and the United States. The Tyrone Guthrie Theater in Minneapolis opened in 1963, with Guthrie as artistic director of the Minnesota Repertory Theatre Company.

Among Guthrie's writings are *Theatre Prospect* (1932), *A Life in the Theatre* (1959), and *Tyrone Guthrie on Acting*

Harrison, Rex

(March 5, 1908–June 2, 1990)
Actor, Director

Known for his seemingly effortless performances and comic-aristo-cratic air, Rex Harrison established himself as an actor on London's West End before he became an international film star. He is best known for his roles of Professor Henry Higgins in the Broadway and film productions of *My Fair Lady*.

Harrison was born Reginald Carey Harrison in Huyton, Lancashire, England. His father was a practical sort, a businessman and engineer, who nevertheless allowed him to pursue his interest in acting. When Harrison was a child, he decided he did not like the name "Reggie" and asked his mother to call him Rex. He was often ill, and his parents sent him to school at the nearby Liverpool College. Although not a great student, he began acting in the school plays. Upon his graduation and with his father's help, he obtained an interview with the director of the Liverpool Repertory Theatre and was subsequently accepted.

Harrison appeared in many of the company's productions for the next several years, including J. M. BARRIE's *A Kiss for Cinderella* and JOHN GALSWORTHY's *Old English* (as a footman). After moving to London in 1927, he secured a role in Brandon Thomas's *Charley's Aunt*, a comedy about two boys at Oxford trying to sneak their girlfriends into their room against the rules. Until 1930 he toured, appearing in Ben Travers's *A Cup of Kindness* and other productions.

A 1930 production of Shakespeare's *Richard III* at the New Theatre marked

Rex Harrison (Ann Ronan/Image Select)

Harrison's debut on the London stage. Over the next several years, he continued to tour and to act on West End stages. Among his successful roles of the 1930s were Tubbs Barrow in a New York production of JOYCE CARY's *Sweet Aloes* (1936) and Alan Howard in TERENCE RATTIGAN's comedy *French Without Tears* (1936). The latter, a comedy marked by the characters' use of bad French, ran for more than 1,000 performances in London and was Harrison's most successful role to date.

With *The Great Game* (1931), Harrison embarked on his long career in film. He appeared in a series of productions for London Films during the 1930s—as

Thomas Newbiggin Stapleton in *Men Are Not Gods* (1936); and acting in *Storm in a Teacup* (1937), based on a James Bridie play, with Vivien Leigh. Harrison also appeared in *The Citadel* (1938), *Ten Days in Paris* (1940; American title *Missing Ten Days*), and a film version of George Bernard Shaw's *Major Barbara* in 1941.

Although he and other popular entertainers were exempt from military service during World War II, Harrison enlisted in the Royal Air Force. After the war, he returned to both film and the stage. He starred in the film version of Noel Coward's *Blithe Spirit*, directed by David Lean as well as *The Rake's Progress* (1945; American title *The Notorious Gentleman*). During this period of time, he appeared in several film and stage productions with his second wife, actress Lilli Palmer.

Harrison's role as King Mongkut in *Anna and the King of Siam* (1946), based on a novel by Margaret Landon, marked his debut in American film. *The Ghost and Mrs. Muir* (1947) was the first of several Harrison films directed by Joseph Manckiewicz, including *Escape* (1948); *Cleopatra* (1963), as Julius Caesar, with Richard Burton as Mark Antony and Elizabeth Taylor as Cleopatra; and *The Honey Pot* (1967).

The most popular of Harrison's roles came with the 1956 production of the Broadway musical *My Fair Lady*, an adaptation of Shaw's *Pygmalion*. He took voice lessons for his "sing-speak" performance of Professor Henry Higgins,

opposite Julie Andrews as Eliza Dolittle, and for his role earned a Tony Award. Similarly, he won an Oscar for his performance in the film version (1964) opposite Audrey Hepburn.

Among Harrison's other films are *Anne of the Thousand Days* (1948); *Unfaithfully Yours* (1948), directed by Preston Sturges; *King Richard and the Crusaders* (1954*); The Reluctant Debutante* (1958); *Midnight Lace* (1960), with Doris Day; two films directed by Carol Reed, *Night Train to Munich* (1940, as Dickie Randall; American title *Night Train*) and *The Agony and the Ectasy* (1965); *Doctor Dolittle* (1967); and numerous films for British and American television.

In spite of the success of his career in film, Harrison never left the stage. Until his death, he appeared in plays such as Jean Anouilh's *The Fighting Cock* (1959); *Platonov* (1960); *In Praise of Love* (1973); Luigi Pirandello's *Henry IV* (1974); Shaw's *Heartbreak House* (1983, as Captain Shotover); and Barrie's *The Admirable Crichton* (1988). Peter Ustinov's play *The Love of Four Colonels* (1953), staged in Canada and the United States, was Harrison's first effort as a director. Harrison authored two autobiographies, *Rex* (1974) and *A Damned Serious Business: My Life in Comedy* (1991) and was knighted in 1989.

Bibliography

Harrison, Rex, *A Damned Serious Business*, 1991; Moseley, Roy, *Rex Harrison: The First Biography*, 1987.

Hauptmann, Gerhart

(November 15, 1862–June 6, 1946)
Playwright, Novelist, Poet

Gerhart Johann Robert Hauptmann established himself as a leader of naturalist drama in Germany at the end of the nineteenth century with a series of plays that addressed issues affecting the peasant classes. His later plays moved away from the strict realism of the naturalist style, employing symbolism, fantasy, and mythology. Hauptmann also wrote novels and poems; he received the Nobel Prize for Literature in 1912, "primarily in recognition of his fruitful, varied, and outstanding production in the realm of dramatic art." Hauptmann was born in Obersalzbrunn, Silesia, Prussia (now Szczawno-Zdrój, Poland), where his modestly successful father owned a hotel. His early childhood was pleasant, but the year 1874 marked the beginning of four miserable years of school in Breslau. At the end of that period, Hauptmann's father lost his money and sent him to live with an uncle in the country. In 1880 he enrolled in the Breslau Academy of Art to study sculpture, and two years later he entered the University of Jena to study philosophy and natural science.

Hauptmann worked in Rome with the intention of making a living as a sculptor, and in 1884 he studied graphic art in Dresden. He married Marie Thienemann in 1885. The couple settled outside of Berlin, and her money enabled him to begin intense periods of personal study as well as to associate with progressive scientists and intellectuals. The Norwegian playwright Henrik Ibsen particularly influenced Hauptmann's early dramas, which introduced naturalism into the German theater, previously marked by its stylized productions. Naturalists sought to depict subjects in a realistic and scientific manner without moral judgment.

Vor Sonnenaufgang (1889; *Before Dawn*), Hauptmann's first play, depicts the demise of a working-class family's morals after the discovery of coal on their property makes them rich. The play, produced by the Free Stage Society, was an instant popular success. *Hanneles Himmelfahrt* (1894; *The Assumption of Hannele*) relates the dreams of an abused child before she dies and combines naturalism with fantasy.

Die Weber (1892; *The Weavers*), based on the Silesian weavers' revolt in 1844, is one of Hauptmann's most enduring and tragic works. The play revolves around a group of weavers who live in squalid conditions, showing them moving toward revolt. When police try to suppress the rebellion, a man who has not taken part in it becomes the first casualty. *Die Biberpelz* (1893; *The Beaver Coat*) is a humorous satire on corrupt Prussian justice. Its protagonist, the washerwoman Mrs. Wolff, succeeds in pulling off thefts and confounds Prussian justice officials.

Environmental circumstances shape individual and social morality in Hauptmann's earlier dramas. In *Rose Bernd* (1903), a woman enters into marriage with a man she does not love. She then falls in love with a bailiff, whose own wife is bedridden. The woman's disintegration ultimately leads her to murder her infant child.

The difficulties of love and family relationships form the central theme of many

Hauptmann plays. In *The Coming of Peace* (1890), an initially peaceful family-Christmas gathering disintegrates toward tragedy. The naturalist tragedy *Fuhrmann Henschel* (1898; *Drayman Henschel*) depicts the ruin of a man's life after his wife dies and he remarries in defiance of his deceased wife's wishes. *Karls Geisel* (1908; *Charlemagne's Hostage*), written in blank verse, presents Charlemagne as an aging man of 60 who is infatuated with the young hostage Gersuind but suppresses his desire and resists her advances.

The theme recurs in *Gabriel Schillings Flucht* (1912; *Gabriel Schilling's Flight;* staged in Lauchstedt with scenery painted by MAX LIEBERMANN) but adds the dimension of an artist's relationship with women. The verse-fantasy play *Die versunkene Glocke* (1896; *The Sunken Bell*), a parable in verse, marked a turn toward romanticism in Hauptmann's work and portrays an artist's relationship with society and with a wife who does not understand him. This conflict was close to Hauptmann's heart, as he divorced his own wife in 1904 and married the actress and violinist Margarete Marschalk. Hauptmann, however, continued to write naturalist dramas such as *Michael Kramer* (1900) and *Rose Bernd*. He showed a capacity for fantasy in plays such as *Und Pippa tanzt* (1906); comedy in works such as *Die Jungfern vom ßis chofsberg* (1907); and an interpretation of the classic myths in *Der Bogen des Odysseus* (1914), a play in blank verse.

Hauptmann's later plays moved away from naturalism and mixed elements of fantasy with symbolic language. Most notable among them is *The Tetralogy of the Atrids* (1941–1945), drawn from the Greek myth of the House of Atreus. His other plays include *The Lonely Lives* (1891), *The Rats* (1911), *Dorothea Angermann* (1926), and *Hamlet in Wittenberg* (1935).

Aside from plays, Hauptmann wrote several works of fiction, including *The Heretic of Soana* (1918) and *The Fool in Christ, Emanuel Quint* (1910). The latter's protagonist is an impoverished peasant who feels a calling to preach the gospel in his youth. The calling develops into fanaticism, until he finally believes Christ has entered his body. Hauptmann's other works include the epic poems *Till Eulenspiegel* (1928) and *The Great Dream* (1942); the autobiographical works *Adventure of My Youth* (1937 and 1949); and *Book of Passion* (1930). Although not known for philosophical depth, Hauptmann's prolific output and mastery of many dramatic and literary forms made him a major figure in twentieth-century drama.

BIBLIOGRAPHY

Behl, C. F. W., *Gerhart Hauptmann: His Life and Work*, 1956; Marshall, Alan, *The German Naturalists and Gerhart Hauptmann: Reception and Influence*, 1982.

Havel, Václav

(October 5, 1936–)
Playwright, Essayist, Statesman

Václav Havel, president of the Czech Republic since 1993, gained international recognition as a dissident playwright in Communist-ruled Czechoslovakia in the 1960s. Drawing from the style of the Theater of the Absurd playwrights, he targeted the Communist bureaucracy in his dramas. From a young age he was a vocal political activist, and his dissident activities resulted in numerous arrests and several years in prison.

Havel was born in Prague, Czechoslovakia, now the Czech Republic. His father was a prosperous restauranteur and businessman before the Communist government confiscated much of the family property in 1948. Because he was the son of "bourgeois" parents, Havel was prohibited from attending school during the day. When he was old enough he drove a taxi to support himself and went to night school. As a teenager Havel developed an interest in poetry, read eagerly, and formed his own intellectual circle, the Thirty-sixers. He later studied at the Czechoslovak University of Technology.

Among the members of the Thirty-sixers was future film director Miloš Forman, who studied film at the Academy of Performing Arts. Forman and Havel co-wrote a film script for one of his classes. In 1959 Havel took a job as a stagehand in Prague and began acting on a regular basis. He also began to write his own plays, which were staged at the Theatre of the Balustrade Company. There he met his future wife Olga Äplichalová, whom he married in 1964.

In writing his own plays Havel was influenced by the Czech-born FRANZ KAFKA and by Theater of the Absurd playwrights such as EUGÈNE IONESCO and SAMUEL BECKETT. Many of his plays evoke the absurd atmosphere of the Communist bureaucracy under which he lived. *An Evening with the Family* was the first of his absurdist efforts. *Zahradní slavnost* (1963; *The Garden Party*), the satire of which targets de-Stalinization, was inspired by a story Havel heard about a man who lost his identity and went looking for himself at his own apartment. The play marked Havel's first success as a playwright, and it was translated into many languages.

Vyrozumení (1965; *The Memorandum*) satirized the Communist bureaucracy and proved particularly objection-

Václav Havel (Fragment Publishing)

able to the authorities. The characters in the play embrace a new language, Ptydepe, which transforms communication. The same year Havel joined the editorial board of the Writers' Union literary monthly *Tvář*. Havel finished *Ztížená moznost soustredení* (*The Increased Difficulty of Concentration*) in 1968, the year of the Prague Spring (the reform movement that attempted to establish in Czechoslovakia a more humane form of Communism) and its brutal suppression by the Soviet Union. In spite of the suppression of his plays in Czechoslovakia, he began to earn enough money from the publication of his works abroad to drive a Mercedes to his job at a brewery.

Havel had long since established himself as a vocal opponent of the Communist system and increasingly found himself under the watchful eyes of the police. In 1956 he stood up at a writers' conference and demanded recognition for the suppressed work of dissident poets. He took an active role in the reforms of the Prague Spring. After the Soviet suppression authorities banned his works, revoked his passport, and kept him under constant surveillance. Havel helped found Charter 77 in 1977, which expressed opposition to human rights violations.

Havel continued to write in the 1970s, including *The Beggar's Opera* (1972),

based on the eighteenth-century ballad opera by the English poet and playwright John Gay; and the one-act plays *Audience* (1975), *Private View* (1975), and *Protest* (1978). The year 1977 brought an arrest and a short term in jail. After his release he was rearrested and spent the years from 1979 to 1983 in prison.

During the 1980s Havel established himself as a leading dissident voice in Czechoslovakia. Demanding democratic reforms, he participated in the Civic Forum and the Velvet Revolution of 1989, the year the Communist government fell. From 1989 to 1993 he served as president of Czechoslovakia. When the nation split in 1993 he became president of the Czech Republic, a position he still holds.

Havel has been nominated repeatedly for the Nobel Peace Prize. His later plays include *Largo Desolato* (1985), which takes its title from a movement in an ALBAN BERG work; *Slum Clearance* (1987); and *Temptation* (1988), a play on the Faust theme. Among his other works are the nonfiction collection *Summer Meditations* (1992) and *Letters to Olga* (1988), a volume of his prison correspondence to his wife.

BIBLIOGRAPHY

Kriseová, Eda, *Václav Havel: The Authorized Biography*, 1993.

Head, Bessie

(July 6, 1937–April 17, 1986)
Novelist, Short-Story Writer

The novels and short stories of the South African–born writer Bessie Amelia Emery Head primarily address racism, sexuality, and cultural conflict in southern Africa in straightforward prose. Head spent her early life in South African cities but moved to rural Botswana in 1964, and the latter setting furnished the basis for most of her fiction.

Head was born in Pietermaritzburg, South Africa, to a white mother and a black father. She grew up without both of them. Authorities placed her mother in a mental hospital, and she died in 1943. Her father inexplicably vanished. After spending her youth in foster care and orphanages, Head trained as a teacher and taught primary school until 1959. She subsequently worked as a journalist for the *Golden City Post* and *Drum* magazine. In 1962 she married Harold Head, a journalist.

In 1964 Head's marriage broke up, and she moved to Botswana with her son, Howard. She took a teaching job in Serowe, a large village and the center of the Bangwoto ethnic group. Life in Serowe was difficult for Head. She lived as an exile and did not obtain citizenship in Botswana until 1979, just a few years before her death. From 1967 to 1970 she suffered from mental illness, which culminated in a breakdown in 1969. Nevertheless, Head adopted Serowe as her new home, and almost all of her writing is set in rural Botswana.

Her first novel, *When Rain Clouds Gather*, was published in 1969. Its protagonist, Makhaya, is an exile who has escaped the shackles of apartheid and regains his sense of humanity in an adopted village. A different form of racism dominates Head's second novel, *Maru* (1971). Its central event is a controversial marriage that crosses the racial boundaries between the dominant Botswana and the weaker Basarwa people. Both novels mirror Head's own experience under apartheid in South Africa as a light-skinned woman among a predominantly dark-skinned people in Botswana.

A Question of Power (1973), her third novel, is also rife with autobiographical elements and recounts a woman's struggle with insanity and sexuality. Sexuality is the other major theme in Head's writings, which contain many sympathetic portraits of women who are physically and psychologically abused by men.

The sexual element is particularly evident in *The Collector of Treasures* (1977), a volume of short stories. Most of the sketches it contains were published earlier in periodicals. Many reflect women's struggles in Botswana in both historical and modern settings. The title story concerns a woman, Dikeledi, who is imprisoned for murdering her abusive husband.

Head also wrote two historical works, *Serowe: Village of the Rain Wind* (1981) and *A Bewitched Crossroad* (1984). Despite their heavy social content, Head's writings are not directly political and, with the exception of the historical works, are derived largely from her personal experience. Her criticism of apartheid and European colonialism did not condemn all Europeans, nor did her efforts to reach back into history result in complete respect for African traditions, particularly with regard to customs that belittled women. Before her early death from hepatitis in 1986, her work attained moderate success both in Africa and elsewhere in the world.

BIBLIOGRAPHY

Eilerson, Gillian Stead, *Bessie Head, Thunder Behind Her Ears: Her Life and Writing*, 1995; Ibrahim, Huma, *Bessie Head: Subversive Identities in Exile*, 1996; Mackenzie, Craig, ed., *A Woman Alone: Autobiographical Writings*, 1990; Ola, Virginia Uzoma, *The Life and Works of Bessie Head*, 1994.

Heaney, Seamus

(April 13, 1939–)
Poet, Teacher, Essayist, Translator, Critic, Short-Story Writer

Seamus Justin Heaney's work springs from both the stormy cultural-political climate in Northern Ireland and his background as one brought up on the land. His poetry is reflective in nature, combining elements of Irish culture, history, and politics with his own experiences. Heaney was awarded the Nobel Prize for Literature in 1995 (the fourth Irish writer to win that honor), "for works of lyrical beauty and ethical depth, which exalt everyday miracles and the living past." In his speech of acceptance, he defined what "the necessary poetry always does, which is to touch the base of our sympathetic nature while taking in at the same time the unsympathetic reality of the world to which that nature is constantly exposed." His own poetry seems to many necessary poetry.

Heaney was born at his family's farm, Mossbawm, in County Derry, Northern Ireland. He attended the Anahorish School and St. Columb's College. Childhood memories of the farm life at Mossbawm furnished the material for many of Heaney's early poems. In 1953, the family moved to another farm, The Wood. Heaney studied English literature and language at Queens College in Belfast, where he received his degree in 1961. The following year, he attended St. Joseph's College of Education.

After teaching at St. Thomas's Intermediate School, Heaney returned to St. Joseph's as a lecturer and embarked on his career as a poet. His first published poem, "Tractors," appeared in the *Belfast Telegraph* in 1962. An important influence on his work at this time was his association with Philip Hobsbaum's "Group," in which he and such poets as James Simons and Michael Longley met to discuss their work. Heaney subsequently lectured at Queens College and married Marie Devlin in 1965.

Death of a Naturalist (1966), Heaney's first collection of poetry, won several awards after its publication, immediately winning praise from both the critics and the reading public. Along with its successor, *Door in the Dark* (1969), its poetry is deeply rooted in his youth on the farm.

The natural landscape, customs, rituals, and memories of specific incidents form the subject matter of many of the poems, such as *Death of a Naturalist*'s title poem, the story of the day he saw the frogs, "the great slime kings . . . gathered there for vengeance," and gave up gathering their spawn, and "Churning Day," with its vivid re-creation of every detail of the ritual of churning day:

Arms ached.
Hands blistered. Cheeks and clothes were
    spattered
with flabby milk.
Where finally gold flecks
began to dance,

and finally the butter itself emerges, "heavy and rich, coagulated sunlight." Sometimes also Heaney takes the reader into his sense of what it means to be a poet, as in "Personal Helicon": "As a child, they could not keep me from wells," where buckets drop into darkness, and now that such exploration can no longer be a literal prying "into roots," "I rhyme / To see myself, to set the darkness echoing."

Heaney's poetry, both early and later, is crafted and honed, following traditional forms and utilizing a variety of poetic devices. The poems are rhythmic, generally short, and often characterized by abruptness. The publication of *The Bog People* (1969), by P. V. Glob, steered Heaney into a new thematic direction. Glob's presentation of archaeological finds in Jutland (Denmark) included accounts of remains of victims of sacrifice and execution preserved in the bogs. Heaney's discovery of Glob's book coincided with renewed violence in Northern Ireland, and poems such as "The Tollund Man" in *Wintering Out* (1972) compare the ancient victims with modern ones, as Heaney brings to life both the ancient suffering and the modern. Bog imagery figures prominently in much of his later work.

North (1975) contains many poems that address the Protestant-Catholic conflict in Northern Ireland. Heaney, a Catholic, mourns violence on both sides, refusing to make any direct political statement, but working for peace in a way that is appropriate for poetry. And in fact the Nobel Foundation praised him for his subtle and profound approach to the violence in his country. *Field Work* (1979) returned to themes of his early writings, but it also includes a series of elegies for friends that make their own kind of plea for peace. One of them, "Casualty," memorializes the death of Louis O'Neill, who died when an Irish Republican Army bomb exploded in a Protestant bar, and brings O'Neill alive so completely, in such homely detail, that the full horror of using that kind of violence has to be felt. Heaney's "Glanmore Sonnets," written at his 1970s home in County Wicklow, Ireland, and celebrating poetry, the countryside, and his marriage, also form part of *Field Work*.

Many poems in *Station Island* (1984), *The Haw Lantern* (1987), and *Seeing Things* (1991) are personal and reflective. "Clearances," a sequence of elegies in sonnet form about his mother's death, belongs to *The Haw Lantern*, and a series of elegies for his father forms part of *Seeing Things* (1991). Heaney's latest work, *The Spirit Level* (1996), reflects his search for balance in various aspects of life. The title refers to a carpenter's level (called a spirit level in Ireland), a symbol of evenness.

Beginning in 1982, Heaney taught at Harvard University for the spring semester every year, a part of the Irish world in Boston, always approachable by ordinary people, active in encouraging young poets, and a conscientious and stimulating teacher. The celebration in Boston when he won the Nobel was almost as enthusiastic as the one in Dublin. He also lectured at the University of Oxford from 1989 to 1994. Aside from his poetry, Heaney has contributed essays and articles to numerous publications in the English-speaking world.

His other works include *Preoccupations: Selected Prose, 1968–1978* (1980); *The Rattle Bog* (1982), a collection of poetry for children he edited with TED HUGHES; *Sweeney Astray* (1983), a translation of the medieval Irish poem *Buile Suibhne; Government of Tongue* (1988); *Selected Poems, 1966–1987* (1991); *The Cure at Troy* (1991), a version of Sophocles's *Philoctectes; The Midnight Verdict* (1993); *The Redress of Poetry* (1995), a collection of his lectures at Oxford; and *Opened Ground: Selected Poems, 1966–1996* (1998), which gives a more complete picture of his poetic accomplishment than is usual in a *Selected Poems*, and ends with the text of his Nobel acceptance address, "Crediting Poetry." Some critics saw the book, which came out in paperback in 1999, as confirming Heaney's status as the best poet writing in English today. His critically acclaimed translation of *Beowulf* (2000) contributed further to that reputation.

BIBLIOGRAPHY

Corcoran, Neil, *Seamus Heaney*, 1986; Curtis, Tony, ed., *The Art of Seamus Heaney*, 3d ed., 1994; Foster, Thomas C., *Seamus Heaney*, 1987; Murphy, Andrew, *Seamus Heaney*, 1996.

Hélion, Jean

(April 21, 1904–October 27, 1987)
Painter

First attracting attention in the world of abstract art in Paris, Jean Hélion painted, during the span of his career, in styles that range from pure abstraction to strikingly realistic detail. Characterized by their use of cool colors, symbols, shapes, and flat planes, his paintings were exhibited widely around the world during his lifetime.

Hélion was born in Couterne, Orne, France. Before determining on a career as a painter, he studied engineering and architecture in Lille. After moving to Paris as an architect's apprentice, he turned to painting. Assisted by the Uruguayan artist Joaquen Torres-Garcea, he met the avant-garde painters of Paris and began to experiment with the various influences flourishing in the city's artistic climate.

Strongest of these influences in the late 1920s was Cubism, which appears in the angular planes of such works as *Tête de femme* (1925), depicting the side profile of a woman's face. Toward the end of the decade Hélion moved toward pure abstraction, creating series of paintings composed of interplays of flat areas of color and bearing such titles as *Abstraction* (1929) or *Composition* (1930). With the Dutch painter Theo van Doesburg, he helped found the Association Abstraction-Création. Several works entitled *Composition orthogonale* (1929–1930) consist of flat areas of color bounded by thick, black lines, reminiscent of PIET MONDRIAN's paintings of the 1920s. *Tensions circulaires* (1931–1932) depicts an interplay of circular and straight lines against a white background. He also began to include three-dimensional shapes in his abstract depictions, as in *Figure tombée* (1937; *Fallen Figure*).

Hélion moved to the United States in the late 1930s but returned to France to fight in World War II. He was taken prisoner by German soldiers and interned on the Polish border until he escaped. His war experiences are reflected in the autobiographical book, *They Shall Not Have Me* (1943). In 1945 he married Pegeen Guggenheim, daughter of the influential patron of modern art Peggy Guggenheim.

During and after World War II Hélion reintroduced representation into his work. In the late 1930s he painted a number of male heads and full-length bodies, such as *Eduoard* (1939) or *Charles* (1939). These figures have angular, flat-featured faces and bodies in simplified form, sometimes in blue-dominated canvases. In the 1940s he painted still lifes and many nude females characterized by their simplified, rounded forms and expressive poses.

Embarking on another dramatic change in his style, Hélion in the 1950s painted realistic still lifes. *Le goûter* (1953; *The Lunch*), for example, depicts a table strewn with coffee cups, garments, food, silverware, papers, and other items, while on the floor sit plants and a bottle of wine. *L'atelier* (1953) shows the inside of a studio with Hélion's own paintings sitting about. The artist is seated in his chair as a woman stands pensively on the stairs in the background.

Two major developments occurred in Hélion's work in the 1960s. The first was his switch from oil to acrylic paints due to his allergic reactions to oil solvents, and the second was the beginning of a series of large-scale triptychs. His first triptych, a scene from the rue du Dragon, was begun in 1967. The twenty-seven-foot *Last Judgment of Things* (1979), one of his last major works, depicts a flea market scene.

Hélion's eyesight began to fail in the 1970s and by 1983 he was completely blind. His work gained international attention in the 1930s and has been exhibited widely since then. The popularity of his paintings benefitted from his proficiency in English and his numerous trips to the United States and England. Portions of his notebooks were published as *Journal d'un peintre (Journal of a Painter)* in 1992.

BIBLIOGRAPHY

Gallery of Modern Art, *Paintings by Jean Hélion*, 1964.

Helpmann, Robert

(April 9, 1909–September 28, 1986)
Choreographer, Dancer, Actor, Director

A commanding presence as a both a dancer and an actor, Sir Robert Murray Helpmann was a regular in lead roles in British theater and ballets in the mid-twentieth century. As a choreographer he brought highly dramatic and theatrical ballets to both British and Australian stages. Helpmann also directed for the theater and appeared in a number of films.

Helpmann was born in Mount Gambier in southern Australia. He made his first stage appearance in a musical comedy in 1923. His first big break as a dancer came when he joined and began touring with ANNA PAVLOVA's company three years later, and he subsequently toured in Australia with J. C. Williamson's company. In 1933 Helpmann moved to London and joined what was then the Vic –Wells Ballet (later the Sadler's Wells), performing in such roles as Satan in Ninette de Valois's *Job* (1933).

The following year he was promoted to premier danseur, a position he held until 1950. He began to appear in leading roles opposite such ballerinas as ALICIA MARKOVA and MARGOT FONTEYN, and his partnerships with Fonteyn proved especially popular. His other dance roles include the Prince in *Sleeping Beauty*, the lead role in *Miracle in the Gorbals* (1944), the lead role in *Adam Zero* (1946), and Mr. O'Reilly in de Valois's *The Prospect Before Us*. He appeared often in works choreographed by both de Valois and Sir FREDERICK ASHTON.

As a choreographer Helpmann produced his first major work (in which he also danced the lead role), *Hamlet*, in 1944. A loose interpretation of Shake-

speare's play, the ballet begins with the hero's death and focuses on his psychological state in the time leading up to the fateful event. He went on to choreograph a number of successful works for the Australian Ballet, of which he served as artistic director from 1965 to 1973. Helpmann made his final stage appearance in Australia in 1986, when he appeared as the Red King in *Checkmate*.

Running parallel to his ballet career was his career on stage. In 1937 he played his first major role at the Old Vic—Oberon in Shakespeare's *A Midsummer Night's Dream*. He often played Shakespearean roles, including Shylock in *The Merchant of Venice* and the title role in *Hamlet*. In 1948 he performed at the Shakespeare Memorial Theatre at Stratford with Sir Barry Jackson's company. Helpmann directed plays as well, including *Murder in the Cathedral* (1953), *Antony and Cleopatra*, *Romeo and Juliet*, *As You Like It* (1955), and *Duel of Angels* (1960).

Films in which Helpmann appeared include *One of Our Aircraft Is Missing* (1942); *Henry V* (1944); *The Red Shoes* (1948), which he also choreographed; *Tales of Hoffman* (1950); *Big Money* (1956); *Don Quixote* (1973), which he codirected with dancer RUDOLF NUREYEV; *The Mango Tree* (1977); and *Patrick* (1978). Helpmann was knighted in 1968.

BIBLIOGRAPHY

Anthony, Gordon, *Robert Helpmann*, 1946; Brahms, Caryl, *Robert Helpmann, Choreographer*, 1943; Salter, Elizabeth, *Helpmann: The Authorised Biography of Sir Robert Helpmann*, 1978.

Henze, Hans Werner

(July 1, 1926–)
Composer, Essayist

Best known for his operas, the German composer Hans Werner Henze has also produced a vast output of symphonies, chamber works, song cycles, ballet scores, and other music. After working with ARNOLD SCHOENBERG's twelve-tone system in his early career, Henze turned to more traditional tonality in his later works but did not entirely abandon his roots. During the 1960s he became an ardent political activist and has since infused his music with a political spirit.

Henze was the eldest of six children, born in Gütersloh, Germany. His father was wounded in World War I and afterward became a teacher. It was with his mother's encouragement that Henze, who at a young age developed an interest in music, began to compose. Henze's father, who supported the Nazis, forced him to join the Hitler Youth against his will. At school he spent less time on his nonmusical studies than on music.

Henze was drafted in 1944; during the last years of the war he listened to foreign broadcasts as often as he could. He later studied music under Wolfgang Fortner and René Leibowitz, the latter of whom had studied with Schoenberg. For the first years of his composing career, Schoenberg's twelve-tone system and other directions in serialism (see PIERRE BOULEZ and KARLHEINZ STOCKHAUSEN) dominated Henze's work, such as the Violin Concerto (1947). However, Henze never carried serialism to the extremes that Boulez and Stockhausen did.

To date Henze has composed nine symphonies, the first of which he completed in 1947. The four-movement First Symphony premiered under Fortner in 1948, and he later (1964) reworked the music as a three-movement chamber symphony. Henze completed the Second Symphony in 1949. The Third Symphony (1940–1950), for large orchestra, followed his new interest in ballet music. The New York Philharmonic commissioned his Fifth Symphony, which premiered under Leonard Bernstein in 1962. It was followed by his Sixth Symphony (1969), composed after a much publicized visit to Communist Cuba, and full of the spirit of revolution. Henze's most recent symphony, the Ninth (1996),

Hans Werner Henze (AKG)

is a choral symphony inspired by his war experiences.

After watching the Sadler's Wells ballet company in 1948, Henze began to compose ballet music. In 1949–1950 he completed three ballet works in rapid succession, *Ballet Variations*, *Jack Pudding*, and *Rosa Silber*. From 1950 to 1953 he was ballet adviser at the Wiesbaden State Theatre. Working with the Italian film director Luchino Visconti, he wrote *Maratona di danza* (1956; *Dance Marathon*), a jazz-infused ballet about a boy who dies in postwar Rome amidst the dance marathon frenzy. More successful was his jazz-infused ballet *Undine*, which premiered at Covent Garden in 1958 with choreography by Sir Frederick Ashton and Margot Fonteyn dancing in the lead role. *Orpheus*, one of many collaborations with the left-wing British playwright Edward Bond, was completed in 1979.

Henze's best-known works, however, are his operas. With *König Hirsch* (1956; *The Stag King*), he moved away from Schoenberg's twelve-tone system and the serialists, marking one of many turning points in his career. The opera was first performed in an abbreviated version at the Berlin Festival in 1956 under Hermann Scherchen. Henze was unappreciative of Scherchen's cuts, and the performance sparked strong reactions—both negative and positive—from the audience. The opera was not performed as Henze intended it until 1985.

Having settled permanently in Italy in the early 1950s, Henze gained the friendship of the poet W. H. Auden and the British composer William Walton. Walton eagerly embraced his work, while Auden became one of his chief collaborators. The opera *Elegy for Young Lovers* (1959–1961) was a joint effort with Auden, as was *The Bassarids* (1964–1965). Henze again collaborated with Bond in *We Come to the River* (1974) and the satiric opera *The English Cat* (1978). His other operas include *Das Wundertheater* (1948; *The Wonder Theatre*), the popular success *Der Prinz von Homburg* (1958; *The Prince of Homburg*), the comic opera *Die Junge Lord* (1965; *The Young Lord*), *Das verratene Meer* (1986–1989; *The Betrayed Sea*), and *Venus and Adonis* (1993–1995).

In the mid-1960s, Henze's music underwent another radical change. Inspired by the social protests and antiwar demonstrations of that decade, he embraced socialism and added to his works a political dimension. Henze subsequently became a strong advocate for the politicization of music. *Das Floss der "Medusa"* (1968; *The Raft of the "Medusa"*), a requiem for the executed revolutionary leader Che Guevara, provoked a storm of protest when it premiered. *Voices* (1973), a politically charged song cycle, employs revolutionary texts.

Among Henze's other works are *Kammermusik* (1958; *Chamber Music*), a song cycle for tenor, guitar, and eight performers dedicated to Benjamin Britten; many settings of poetry, by Arthur Rimbaud, Walt Whitman, the Italian Renaissance poet Torquato Tasso, Auden, and others; *Fünf neapolitanische Lieder* (1958; *Five Neopolitan Songs*); the choral works *Novae de infinito laudes* (1962; *New Praises of the Infinite*) and *Cantata della fiaba estrema* (1963; *Song of the Final Fairytale*); *Tristan* (1972), a piano concerto; and *Requiem*

(1989–1993). His books include *Essays* (1964) and *Music and Politics: Collected Writings 1953–81* (1982).

Bibliography

Richards, Guy, *Hindemith, Hartmann and Henze*, 1995.

Hepworth, Barbara

(January 10, 1903–May 20, 1975)
Sculptor

With her mature style, which developed in the 1930s, Jocelyn Barbara Hepworth was a pioneer in English abstract sculpture. Her work is marked by rounded surfaces, pierced forms with color or string in the interiors, and the use of a wide variety of woods, stones, and metals. In her later life, she created a number of abstract sculptures on a large scale.

Hepworth was the eldest child in her family, born in Wakefield, Yorkshire, England. Her parents supported her artistic ambitions, which emerged at a young age. As a child, Hepworth enjoyed drawing and painting. She developed an interest in sculpting and on occasion cast her sisters' heads. At the Wakefield Girls' High School, Hepworth earned high marks and numerous awards. The headmistress of the school took a particular interest in her and encouraged her to develop her artistic abilities. From her numerous talents, among which was playing the piano, Hepworth chose to pursue sculpting.

In 1920 she studied drawing at the Leeds School of Art, where she met the abstract sculptor Henry Moore, her lifelong friend and one of the major influences on her work. She (together with Moore) next entered the Royal College

of Art in London, where she studied until 1924. The first public exhibition of her work, a bronze head, accompanied the works of other Royal College students at the Red Fern Gallery. Upon her graduation Hepworth received a scholarship that enabled her to travel to Flo-

Barbara Hepworth (Universal Pictorial & Press Agency)

rence. In 1925, she married the sculptor John Skeaping.

Skeaping and Hepworth exhibited jointly and received some critical acclaim during their short marriage. At this time, Hepworth's figures, such as *Mother and Child* (1927) and *Musician* (1929), were still somewhat representational and show African, Chinese, and Egyptian influence. The birth of her son Paul in 1929 inspired her *Infant*, a primitive, black figure rendered in Burmese wood. During this period, Hepworth sculpted masks, faces, and figures, including her woman's *Head* (1930).

In the early 1930s, Hepworth increasingly concerned herself with the interplay of mass, volume, and space within her sculptures. With the abstract painter BEN NICHOLSON, whom she married in 1936, she traveled to Paris and became acquainted with the work of PABLO PICASSO, JEAN ARP, CONSTANTIN BRANCUSI, and others. She and Nicholson also joined the Association Abstraction-Création. Her own work, such as the *Mother and Child* of 1934 (the year she gave birth to triplets) and *Two Forms* in ironstones from the same year, grew more abstract.

Hepworth worked with a variety of woods, metals, and stones. Her mature sculptures are often characterized by their finished, rounded surfaces and organic forms. *Two Forms* (1935) and other works that used angular forms and straight edges were exceptions. Her *Pierced Form* (1931) inaugurated her lifelong interest in rendering pierced forms. In later works, such as the *Pierced Form* (1957) in mahogany and string and *Merryn* (1962), she covered concaves and cavities with string or color.

In the 1940s, Hepworth often painted the interiors of her sculptures and in general began to use more color, as in *Sculpture with Colour Deep Blue and Red* (1940). *Two Figures* (1943) depicts a male and a female figure. Other noteworthy examples of her work with interiors are *Wave* (1943–1944) and *Oval Sculpture* (1943) in wood. She created her *Cosdon Head* (1949) in blue marble. By this time, Hepworth exhibited widely and had earned respect, but not widespread renown. During World War II, the Museum of Modern Art in New York purchased some of her sculptures. In 1959, she was awarded the Grand Prix for plastic art at the Bienial of Modern Art in Brazil.

From a gift of several tons of scented guarea, a Nigerian wood, Hepworth rendered a number of sculptures in the 1950s. During that decade she also completed her series *Groups*, consisting of vaguely human forms sculpted in thin marble. Hepworth first completed a large sculpture with her *Monumental Stela* of 1936, and her later years were marked by many more works on a larger scale.

Her *Contrapuntal Forms* in blue limestone (1950), commissioned by the Institute of Contemporary Arts for the Festival of Britain, measured ten feet in height and later rested at Harlow New Town. Her *Single Form (Memorial)* (1961–1962) was placed in Battersea Park. Following the death of the United Nations Secretary-General Dag Hammarskjöld in a plane crash in 1961, Hepworth was commissioned by the U.N. to create a memorial. Other large sculptures include *Two Forms (Divided Circle)* 1969, consisting of two pierced semicircles, and the series *The Family of Man* (1970), massive sculptures in piled stone.

Hepworth's later life was marked by tragedy and illness. Her son Paul died in an accident in 1953. Hepworth herself developed cancer and was plagued by alcoholism. She died in a fire that broke out at her home in 1975. In 1958, she was made Commander of the Order of the British Empire, and in 1965 she was made a Dame.

BIBLIOGRAPHY

Curtis, Penelope, *Barbara Hepworth: A Retrospective*, 1994; Festing, Sally, *Barbara Hepworth: A Life of Forms*, 1995; Hammacher, Abraham Marie, *Barbara Hepworth*, 1987.

Hesse, Hermann

(July 2, 1877–August 9, 1962)
Novelist, Short-Story Writer, Poet, Essayist, Critic, Editor

The work of the German novelist Hermann Hesse, author of such novels as *Steppenwolf* and *Magister Ludi*, was shaped significantly by his interest in Eastern mysticism and the psychoanalytic theories of Carl Jung. Hesse's novels primarily address the psychological and spiritual dilemmas of intellectuals and artists. He received the Nobel Prize for Literature in 1946, "for his comprehensive and artistically significant writings, in which human problems and conditions have been presented with a fearless love of truth and keen psychological insight."

Hesse was born in Calw, Württemberg, Germany, to former missionaries, and a devout Protestant family, who had lived in India. Both parents pursued extensive intellectual interests. Although Hesse was an intelligent student and earned good grades, his lifelong dislike of formal education and institutions showed itself in the form of rebellion at an early age. After attending a series of schools in Germany and Switzerland as a boy, he enrolled in the Maulbronn seminary. Again, the environment proved disagreeable, and he began to develop nervous ailments and suicidal tendencies. Hesse subsequently worked as an apprentice in a tower clock factory and a bookstore. His first published work was the poem "Madonna" (1896).

Outside of work Hesse read voraciously and particularly admired the work of the German Romantic authors, who influenced the melancholy poetry collected in *Romantische Lieder* (1899; *Romantic Songs*). His first prose works were collected in *Eine Stunde hinter Mitternacht* (1899; *An Hour Behind Midnight*). The prose sketches *Hinterlassene Schritten und Gedichte von Hermann Lauscher* followed in 1901. In 1904 Hesse married Maria Bernoulli, who came from a prosperous family; she eventually succumbed to insanity. They had three sons, Bruno, Heiner, and Martin. His first novel, *Peter Camenzind*, was published the same year and became successful enough to enable him to quit his job in the bookstore.

Hesse moved to Switzerland just before World War I and remained there for the rest of his life. During the war he worked for the Prisoners of War Welfare Organization, which provided books and relief to German prisoners of war. He underwent a series of personal trials—including the war and the failure of his marriage—that led to a partial mental breakdown. During these years Hesse underwent psychoanalysis with J. B. Lang (a student of Carl Jung), developed a deep interest in Eastern mysticism, and explored Jung's theories. The profound influence of these factors on Hesse's outlook appears in novels such as *Demian* (1919), about the development of the young boy Emil Sinclair under the guidance of his mentor Demian, the first of his books to make him famous. It was published under the pseudonym Emil Sinclair. *Siddhartha* (1922) is another obvious example; it is set in India and recounts the spiritual quest of the title character.

Hesse married his second wife, Ruth Wenger, in 1924; they divorced in 1927. The same year saw the publication of *Der Steppenwulf* (*Steppenwolf*), set in post–World War I Germany. The protagonist, Harry Haller, a depressed middle-class and middle-aged intellectual struggling to reconcile divergent elements of his life, has determined to kill himself when he turns 50. Instead of this grim end, Haller begins a journey toward self-realization that includes immersion in sensual experience and a series of symbolic hallucinations that reach into the depths of his psyche. Another notable aspect of the novel is its section of psychoanalysis,

originally numbered separately. *Narcissus und Goldmund* (1930; *Narcissus and Goldmund*), set in a medieval monastery, involves the differences between and ultimate integration of two world views, a dominant motif in Hesse's writing. Narcisssus is a young and brilliant intellectual ascetic, while Goldmund is a sensualist fascinated with Narcissus. Hesse married his third wife, Ninon Dolbin-Ausländer, in 1931.

Magister Ludi (1943), also published as *Der Glasperlenspiel* (*The Glass Bead Game*), is Hesse's last major work and has proved to be one of his most popular. Set around 2400 A.D., the novel represents Hesse's vision of highly developed human knowledge, embodied in the central character, Joseph Knecht. In the utopian Castalia, an elite group of intellectuals play the glass bead game, presided over by the Magister Ludi, the Master of the Game. The purpose of the bead game, though its intricacies are never precisely explained, is to demonstrate connections among different areas of human knowledge—science, the arts, and so forth—and thus construct a universal language. In contrast to their situation in the twentieth century, these intellectuals have achieved long-sought freedom and respect in society, but their tendency toward isolation threatens to undermine their influence. Knecht becomes the Magister Ludi and moves away from the elitist intellectuals who play the game simply because they worship knowledge; he wants the game to be played for the sake of knowledge to put into action. Knecht's symbolic death at the end makes way for the improvements in the game he has envisioned.

In addition to his novels and short stories, Hesse was a prolific contributor to literary journals such as *Simplicissimus* during his lifetime. From 1907 to 1912 he coedited *März*, and from 1919 to 1922 he coedited *Vivos voco*. His other novels include *Unterm Rad* (1906; *Beneath the Wheel*), which criticized the educational system Hesse went through; *Gertrud* (1909); *Rosshalde* (1914); and *Die Morgenlandfahrt* (1932; *Journey to the East*). *Aus Indien*, a collection of notes and poems from his travels in India, was published in 1914. He published poetry as well, and his collected poems were published in 1942. In 1947 the University of Bern awarded him an honorary doctorate in philosophy. Hesse's novels acquired enormous popularity among the beat and counterculture movements in the United States in the 1950s and 1960s, and novels such as *Steppenwolf* and *Magister Ludi* are still widely read today He won the Gottfried Keller Prize in 1936 and Frankfurt's Goethe Prize in 1946. He died at the age of 85.

BIBLIOGRAPHY

Casebeer, Edwin F., *Hermann Hesse*, 1972; Freedman, Ralph, *Hermann Hesse, Pilgrim of Crisis: A Biography*, 1978; Mileck, Joseph, *Hermann Hesse: Life and Art*, 1978.

Hindemith, Paul

(November 16, 1895–December 28, 1963)
Composer, Violist, Teacher, Theorist

Germany's most renowned composer in the first half of the twentieth century, Paul Hindemith ultimately rejected the modern work in atonality begun by ARNOLD SCHOENBERG. As an influential theorist, teacher, and composer, he promoted traditional tonality and believed a composer's music should serve a purpose rather than exist simply as artistic expression.

Hindemith was born into a working-class family in Hanau, near Frankfurt am Main. There were both Catholic and Protestant influences in his family, but Hindemith himself remained distant from organized religion. He started violin lessons at the age of 8, and when he was 13 he entered the Hoch Conservatory in Frankfurt. Soon thereafter, he was performing at Conservatory concerts and saw his own works performed at the school. When he was young he accepted a variety of musical jobs to earn money, from playing the violin in cafés to performing with dance bands.

At the age of 20, Hindemith became *Konzertmeister* (concertmaster) at the Frankfurt Opera Orchestra, where he remained for a number of years. He later married music director Ludwig Rottenberg's daughter Gertrud (1924). He was composing regularly by this time, and his String Quartet in C Major won the Mendelssohn Prize in 1915. Hindemith served in World War I, during which time he composed the Sonata for Violin and Piano (1918), Op. 11, No. 1, and a number of other works. The first public perform-

Paul Hindemith (Ann Ronan/Image Select)

ance of his music came in 1919, and international festivals were soon featuring his compositions regularly. The pianist Emma Lübbucke-Job frequently performed his early piano works.

Hindemith would eventually reject atonality, but to a certain extent he worked with the direction taken by Schoenberg and others in his early, more experimental works. The opera *Mörder, Hoffnung der Frauen* (1919; *Murder, Hope of Women*) is an expressionistic work with a text by the painter OSKAR KOKOSCHKA. *Sancta Susanna* (1921), another opera, also dates from this period.

In 1921 he helped organize the successful Amar-Hindemith Quartet, with himself playing the viola and his brother Rudolf on the cello. Hindemith composed a number of chamber works for the quartet. Other notable early works include the song cycles *Die junge Magd* (1922; *The Young Maid*), settings of poems by the Austrian poet Georg Trakl; and *Das Marienleben* (1924, rev. 1948; *The Life of Mary*), settings of fifteen poems by RAINER MARIA RILKE.

In the late 1920s and early 1930s, Hindemith's music was influenced in part by the baroque composers. He composed a number of solo concertos that were influenced by Johann Sebastian Bach's *Brandenberg Concertos*. The larger Concerto for Orchestra was finished in 1925. The following year, he created the opera *Cardillac* (1926), based on E. T. A. Hoffmann's *Das Fräulein von Scuderi* (*The Girl from Scuderi*).

Unique among his works is the brief opera *Hin und zurück* (*Roundtrip*, 1927), in which the music and the story of a marital dispute that ends in murder proceed forward and then unwind like a film running backwards. By the late 1920s Hindemith had established himself as Germany's leading composer.

Hindemith believed in composing music that served a purpose. To this end he wrote for children's games, radio plays, bands, and other groups and occasions. His numerous film scores include music for *Felix the Cat at the Circus* (1927). In the late 1920s he collaborated with KURT WEILL and the radical playwright BERTOLT BRECHT in the latter's radio play *Der Lindberghflug* (1928; *The Lindbergh Flight*). He again worked with Brecht on *Lehrstück* (1929). The late 1920s also saw the beginnings of his teaching career. He accepted a position as professor of composition at the Berlin Hochschule für Musik.

The opera *Mathis der Maler* (*Mathis the Painter*, 1933), along with the symphony Hindemith derived from it, is often considered his masterpiece. The story treats the life of the Renaissance painter Mathias Grünewald and was particularly inspired by a series of paintings for an altar at the monastery at Isenheim. WILHELM FURTWÄNGLER conducted the orchestral version at the Berlin Harmonic in 1934, after which the newly established Nazi regime began its attacks on Hindemith. Labeled by Joseph Goebbels a "cultural Bolshevist" and "spiritual non-Aryan," he eventually left Germany and accepted a teaching post at the conservatory in Ankara, Turkey.

After he left Germany, Hindemith's music was purely tonal, and he developed extensive theories on counterpoint and tonality. The ballet *Ludus Tonalis* (1943), a set of twelve fugues for all keys, specifically reflects Hindemith's ideas. Having visited the United States in 1937, he settled there and taught at a number of American universities, including Yale University (1940–1953).

Hindemith continued to compose regularly while in the United States, producing such varied works as the Violin Concerto (1939); the Concerto for Cello and Orchestra (1940); the *Symphonic Metamorphoses on Themes by Carl Maria von Weber* (1943); the opera *Die Harmonie der Welt* (*The Harmony of the World*, 1956–1957), inspired by the work of the astronomer Johannes Kepler (1571–1630); and the *Sinfonia Serena* (1946).

During the last years of his life, Hindemith lived in Zurich, where he taught at the university and wrote comparatively little. His final work was a Mass, finished in 1963. Among his other compositions are his *Kammermusik* (*Chamber Music*) pieces, composed for a variety of unconventional instruments.

Hindemith also wrote a number of books as teaching tools and to relate his theories. These include *Unterweisung im Tonsatz* (1937–1939), translated as *The Craft of Musical Composition* (1941–1942); *A Concentrated Course in Traditional Harmony* (1943); *Elementary Training for Musicians* (1946); *Exercises for Advanced Students* (1948); and *A Composer's World* (1952).

BIBLIOGRAPHY

Kemp, Ian, *Hindemith*, 1970; Noss, Luther, *Paul Hindemith in the United States*, 1998; Rickhards, Guy, *Hindemith, Hartmann and Henze*, 1995; Skelton, Geoffrey, *Paul Hindemith, The Man Behind the Music: A Biography*, 1975.

Hockney, David

(July 9, 1937–)
Painter, Graphic Artist, Photographer

Influenced by American Pop art, David Hockney developed a painting style characterized by the use of radiant light and broad, flat areas of bright color. His best-known works include his paintings of Los Angeles pool scenes and his series of double portraits in the 1960s and 1970s. Hockney has also illustrated books, created photocollages, and designed scenery for the ballet and opera.

Hockney was born in Bradford, Yorkshire, England. From 1953 to 1957 he studied at the Bradford College of Art. His paintings from that time, such as *Portrait of My Father* (1955), reflect the school's traditional and academic course of instruction, which emphasized drawing from life. When the time came for his military service, Hockney declared himself a conscientious objector and spent two years working in hospitals. Following the completion of his service, he entered the Royal College of Art in London, where he studied from 1959 to 1962.

Hockney's years at the Royal College were a period of experimentation in his artistic style. To hone his skills he executed drawings of a skeleton. After having been exposed to modern art—particularly Pop art and the works of American abstract artists such as Jackson Pollock—Hockney changed his style radically, producing a number of abstract paintings, such as *Growing Discontent* (1959–1960). His period of painting in pure abstraction was brief, and he finally settled on a style that employs bright color and flat forms that are neither representational nor abstract.

With *Tyger* (1960), a work alluding to William Blake's poem of the same title, he began to introduce graffiti-like titles and phrases in his paintings. Upon the completion of his studies at the Royal College, Hockney won a gold medal in a graduate competition. Before his graduation, he had already begun to make a name for himself. Exhibitions at the Young Contemporaries Exhibition (1961–1962) and the Paris Biennale (1963) earned him international acclaim almost overnight.

Aside from refining his style during his student years, Hockney also grew more open with his subject matter. Paintings such as *Queer* (1960) openly address his homosexual orientation, a subject that he treats repeatedly in both sexual and nonsexual contexts. In the early 1960s he executed several series of paintings, including a *Love* series, a *Marriage* series, and a *Domestic Scene* series. In the latter, he depicts men in domestic situations at home, sometimes in ways that remind the viewer of the erotic aspects of the relationship.

The American poet Walt Whitman, himself a homosexual, was another early influence on Hockney, and he borrowed from Whitman in works such as *We Two Boys Together Clinging* (1961) and *Myself and My Heroes* (1961), a series of etchings with quotes from the poet's work. At the same time, Hockney also worked on another major series of graphic prints, *A Rake's Progress*

(1961–1963), inspired by the series by the same name done by the eighteenth-century English artist William Hogarth (1697–1764) and by Hockney's visit to New York in 1961.

From 1964 to 1967 Hockney taught at American universities in Iowa, Colorado, and California and began to spend time in Los Angeles. The bright California sunlight illuminates his paintings from this period. Using bright blues, pinks, and greens, Hockney painted pool scenes, palm trees, and human figures who often look like cardboard cutouts, as in *Beverly Hills Housewife* (1966). *Sunbather* (1966) is one of many paintings to portray male figures sunbathing or swimming. *A Bigger Splash* (1967), one of his most famous paintings, depicts a large splash presumably made by an unseen figure jumping from a diving board. Instead of traditional flower vases or bowls of fruit, modern objects such as a television and a dictionary appear in Hockney's still lifes, such as *A Table* (1967) and *Still-Life with TV* (1969).

Hockney often works from photographs when he paints, and in 1967 he bought his first quality camera. The following year he began to paint double portraits, one of the first of which was *Christopher Isherwood and Don Bachardy* (1968). His subjects are indoors, seated in chairs, or, as in *American Collectors (Fred and Marcia Weisman)* (1968), outdoors in radiant sunlight. In the 1970s Hockney painted other series, such as *The Weather* series and a number of portraits of his friend Celia Birtwell. *The Weather: Sun* (1973) depicts bright sunlight filtering in through a window to a plant. Hockney lived for a short period of time in Paris, and some of his paintings have Paris settings.

In the 1980s Hockney began to devote more time to photography, creating photocollages such as *Pearblossom Hwy., 11–18th April* (1986). Among the other works he has illustrated are Constantine Cavafy's *Fourteen Poems* (1966), *Six Fairy Tales of the Brothers Grimm* (1970), and *The Blue Guitar* (1976–1977). Hockney has also contributed scenery to a number of productions, including Alfred Jarry's *Ubu Roi* (1966), Roland Petit's ballet *Septentrion* (1975) Mozart's *Magic Flute* (1977–1978; for the Glyndebourne Opera in England); and Erik Satie's *Parade*, for the Metropolitan Opera in New York in 1980. His books include *Hockney by Hockney* (1976), *Travels With Pen, Pencil, and Ink* (1978), *Paper Pools* (1980), *David Hockney Photographs* (1982), *China Diary* (1983), and *Hockney Paints the Stage* (1983).

BIBLIOGRAPHY

Adam, Peter, *David Hockney and His Friends*, 1997; Clothier, Peter, *David Hockney*, 1995; Livingstone, Marco, *David Hockney*, rev. ed., 1987; Webb, Peter, *Portrait of David Hockney*, 1988.

Hoffmann, Josef

(December 15, 1870–May 7, 1956)
Architect

The functionality, simplicity, and geometric abstraction characteristic of Josef Franz Maria Hoffmann's early architectural design anticipated the International Style of the mid-twentieth century (see Walter Gropius). Hoffmann's later works combine the functionality of the modernists with the decorative influence of the late-nineteenth-century Arts and Crafts Movement in England.

Hoffmann was born into a wealthy family in Pirnitz, Moravia, now in the Czech Republic. His father was a landowner, cotton manufacturer, and mayor of Pirnitz. As a child Hoffmann learned to play the violin and participated in his family's frequent musical activities. His parents sent him to a private German school. At the age of 9, he was sent to the gymnasium at Iglau. Among his fellow students was the future architect Adolf Loos. Loos, however, rejected the decorative element found in Hoffmann's designs, and the two never saw eye-to-eye professionally.

By all accounts, Hoffmann's years at the gymnasium were disastrous. He boarded with an excessively strict landlady and failed two years in a row. His scholastic fortunes improved, however, when he entered the State Technical School at Brünn. In 1891 Hoffmann went to Würzburg, Germany, where he helped build brick barracks. The following year he entered the Academy of Fine Arts in Vienna, where he studied under Carl von Hasenaur and the Viennese architect Otto Wagner.

Wagner's functional, rationalistic approach to architectural design was the primary influence on Hoffmann's early work. Having won the Rome prize upon his graduation from the Academy, he traveled to Italy in 1895, absorbed the country's architecture, and made numerous sketches. He returned to Vienna the following year, went to work for Wagner, and began to enter his designs in competitions. Among these was his design for a facade for Vienna's exhibition pavilion for the Jubilee Exhibition of 1898.

Somewhat uncomfortable with his close association with Wagner, Hoffmann joined the Vienna Secession in 1899. The Secessionists, and Hoffmann too at this point in his career, embraced the ideals of the Art Nouveau movement. But Hoffmann's work soon moved closer to modern strains in architectural design, developing into a style that has been called "geometric formalism," marked by its use of simplified decoration. Hoffmann quickly threw himself into the Secession's activities, designing rooms for its periodical *Ver Sacrum* and contributing to the publication as well. The same year, he took a position at the School of Applied Arts in Vienna, where he taught until 1936.

Among his earliest commissions was the interior of the Apollo soap and candle factory (1899), marked by its red-stained walnut arches. Window seats and arches appeared frequently in his early interiors, which included many private homes. Among his other early designs are the Vienna School of Arts and Crafts at the Paris Universal Exposition of 1900 and a residence for personnel of the Wittgenstein Forestry Department.

In 1901 Hoffmann designed four villas on the Hohe Warte notable for their black and white contrasts and interplay of cubic spaces. From 1901 to 1905 Hoffmann's designs stress functionality and the interplay of rectangles and squares.

Two buildings in particular exemplify his style of this period. The flat-roofed Westend Sanatorium at Purkersdorf (near Vienna), Austria (1903), was a functional design intended for patients with nervous disorders and solidified his reputation as an architect.

The opulent Palais Stoclet (1905–1911) in Brussels, perhaps Hoffmann's most famous work, was commissioned by the Beligan coal magnate Adolphe Stoclet. In the design, he combined rectangular and square patterns to form an elegant, white exterior complemented by a copper roof. Lavish marble walls lined the interior, and its vertical staircase window was imitated by many other architects. Mosaics by GUSTAV KLIMT hung on the Paonazzo marble walls. Pillars of Paonazzo and Belgian marble stood in the great hall. Hoffmann also designed a music room, with walls of Protovenere marble and red carpets, furniture, and curtains.

Hoffmann's lifelong interest in crafts began to manifest itself in more decorative designs after 1905. He helped found the Vienna Workshop, a center for arts and crafts, in 1903, and served as its director for three decades. Furniture, dresses, and jewelry are among the numerous arts and crafts he created during his lifetime. His work for the Austrian pavilion at the International Exhibition of Decorative Arts in Paris (1925) featured a gallery room with black, gridlike woodwork with decorative painting.

Hoffmann also designed numerous villas, halls, and pavilions, including the Ast House (1909–1911) and the Skywa-Primavesi House (1924–1925). The Kaasgraben Colony (1913) consisted of four one-family villas. In 1920 he was appointed city architect of Vienna, after which he designed numerous housing projects for the city, with notable series of lower-class housing taking shape in 1924–1925 and after World War II. He designed the Austrian pavilions for the 1914 Deutscher Werkbund Exhibition in Cologne and for the 1934 Venice Biennale. Many younger artists—among them OSKAR KOKOSCHKA and EGON SCHIELE—owed something to Hoffmann, who was known for going out of his way to assist those he saw as budding talents.

BIBLIOGRAPHY

Sekler, Eduard F., *Josef Hoffmann: The Architectural Work*, 1985.

Hofmann, Hans

(March 21, 1880–February 17, 1966)
Painter, Teacher

Born in Germany, Hans Hofmann contributed to the development of Abstract Expressionism in American painting. His abstract paintings of the late 1930s onward employ bright colors and improvisational techniques, such as paint splattering. Hofmann was also a noted art teacher in both Munich and the United States.

Hofmann was born in Weissenberg, Bavaria, Germany. His father was a government official in Munich. As a child he attended public schools and the gymnasium, where he showed early talent in science and math. The young Hofmann also learned to play the violin, organ, and piano. After finishing his schooling, he took a position as an assistant to the director of Public Works in Bavaria. Hofmann showed early promise as a scientist and invented an electromagnetic comptometer. To further his son's success, his father gave him a sum of money to encourage his scientific endeavors. Hofmann, however, used the money to go to art school, which he entered in Munich in 1898. Two years later he met his future wife, Maria (Miz) Wolfegg, whom he married in 1923.

Through one of his instructors, Willi Schwarz, Hofmann met the nephew of the art collector Phillip Freudenberg. Freudenberg became his earliest patron and supported him until 1914. In 1904 Hofmann settled in Paris, taking art classes and absorbing the influences of the Cubists and the Fauves. From the latter he got his preference for the use of brilliant color. His work slowly gained recognition, and he held his first one-man show in 1910 at Paul Cassirer's in Berlin. During this time he painted many expressionistic still lifes and landscapes, but he is better known for his later abstract creations.

When Freudenberg's support ended, Hofmann decided to teach and opened a painting school in Munich in 1915. He was exempted from military service in World War I for medical reasons. In 1930 Hofmann moved to the United States, teaching in both New York City and Berkeley before he founded the Hans Hofmann School of Fine Art.

From the late 1930s onward, Hofmann's paintings were entirely abstract. He used bold colors and experimental techniques in applying paint. *Spring* (1940), an oil on wood, was one of the first of his works to employ the paint dripping technique (later used by American artists such as Jackson Pollock). Works such as *Image of Fear* (1960), *Tormented Bull* (1961), and *The Phantom* (1961) also use splattered paint. Several of Hofmann's works combine large rectangular areas of color, as in *Cathedral* (1959); *Pre-Dawn* (1960), composed of rectangles of blue, red, and yellow; *Lumen Naturale* (1962; *Natural Light*); and *Ignotum Per Ignotius* (1963).

In 1958 Hofmann dissolved his school and devoted his efforts entirely to art. His work as both a teacher and a painter significantly influenced the development of Abstract Expressionism in the United States. His other paintings include *Fantasia in Blue* (1954), *The Garden* (1956), *Lava* (1960), and *Summer Night's Bliss* (1961). Hofmann also published *Form and Color: A Textbook for Instruction in Art.*

BIBLIOGRAPHY

Goodman, Cynthia, *Hans Hofmann*, 1990; Seitz, William C., *Hans Hofmann*, 1963.

Holst, Gustav

(September 21, 1874–May 25, 1934)
Composer, Teacher

The rise of Gustav Theodore Holst's career as a composer coincided with the emergence of Neoromanticism in English music in the early twentieth century. While his music has affinities with the Neoromantics, Holst was more accepting of modern developments of music than were his contemporaries such as RALPH VAUGHAN WILLIAMS.

Holst was born Gustavus Theodore von Holst in Cheltenham, Gloucestershire, England to an English mother and a Swedish father. His father, who came from a family of musicians, was a professional pianist who devoted much of his time and energy to his work. Holst's mother died when he was 8, after which he was raised in part by an aunt. He attended the Cheltenham Grammar School and played the organ, piano, and trombone. Holst began to compose in his youth, finishing his first composition, a setting of the poem *Horatius*, in 1887. Although proficient as a piano player, Holst suffered from neuritis in his right hand and could not play professionally.

Beginning in 1893, Holst studied composition under Sir Charles Villiers Stanford at the Royal College of Music in London, where he met Vaughan Williams. Vaughan Williams became a lifelong friend and kindled his interest in English folk music. Holst also developed a love for English madrigals, a significant influence on his early work. Holst's socialist sympathies led him to join the Hammersmith Socialist Club. He attended GEORGE BERNARD SHAW's lectures and also conducted the Hammersmith Socialist Choir (1896–1898). After finishing his studies in 1898, he earned his living playing the trombone for the Carl Rosa Opera Company and for the Scottish Orchestra.

In 1901 he married the soprano Isobel Harrison. In 1905 Holst took a teaching post at St. Paul's Girls' School, and two years later he became music director at Morley College. He remained in both positions until he died and composed a significant amount of music for his students. He composed *St. Paul's Suite* for strings (1913) in gratitude to the school after it built him a studio.

Another influence on Holst's work was early English music, and in particular its vocal aspects. He particularly admired Henry Purcell (1659–1695) and contributed to a revival of his music in the early 1900s. While he was at Morley (1911), the school staged a production of Purcell's *The Fairy Queen* (1692).

Among Holst's early compositions is *Lansdown Castle* (1893), an operetta produced at the Cheltenham Corn Exchange in 1893. The overture *Walt Whitman* (1899) and *The Mystic Trumpeter* (1904) for soprano solo and orchestra, a setting of Whitman's verse, are among several Holst compositions to use the work of the American poet he admired. The *Cotswolds Symphony* (1900) expresses his love of the Cotswold hills.

Holst's deep interest in Hindu literature led him to learn Sanskrit and translate texts himself. By 1903 he had already composed a symphonic poem called *Indra*, depicting the god Indra's battle against drought. Holst also set Sanskrit hymns from the Rig Veda, oldest and most sacred of the Hindu scriptures. Two operas also derive from Holst's Sanskrit studies, the three-act *Sita* (1899–1906) and the one-act *Savitri* (1908), based on a story from the ancient Indian epic, the *Mahabharata*.

As his career progressed, Holst opened himself to modern influences in his music, particularly the music of IGOR STRAVINSKY. Stravinsky's influence is particularly evident in Holst's most popular work, *The Planets* (1913). The work, an orchestral suite, consists of seven movements, each based on a planet (missing are Earth and the not-yet-discovered Pluto). Each movement reflects the spirit of the planet—Mars, bringer of war, is dominated by low bass sounds, while Saturn, associated with contemplation and old age, is characterized by a peaceful tone.

Among Holst's other works are *The Hymn of Jesus*, for chorus and orchestra (1917), an apocryphal hymn he undertook to translate himself; many songs for female voice; settings of Greek tragedies; the *Ode to Death*, for chorus and orchestra (1919), based on a Whitman text and written in the World War I climate; *Fugal Concerto* (1923) for flute, oboe, and string orchestra; *Choral Symphony* (1923–24); *Egdon Heath* for orchestra (1927), inspired in part by Thomas Hardy's *Return of the Native;* Double Concerto for Two Violins and Orchestra (1929); *Hammersmith*, for orchestra (1930); and *Choral Fantasia* (1930). Holst composed several operas, including *The Perfect Fool*, a chamber opera (1923) produced by the British National Opera; *At the Boar's Head* (1925); and the chamber opera *The Tale of The Wandering Scholar* from the book by medievalist Helen Waddell.

Holst also lectured often in the United States. He never, however, attained the popularity enjoyed by Vaughan Williams and his other contemporaries. His work combines traditional English strains with modern developments in music and has influenced later composers. His weak physical constitution, unkind critics, and a public that was sometimes unreceptive to his work contributed to bouts of depression. His work has gained more acceptance since his death, an end to which his daughter, Imogen Holst, has contributed significantly.

BIBLIOGRAPHY

Holst, Imogen, *Gustav Holst: A Biography*, 2d ed., 1988; Holst, Imogen, *The Music of Gustav Holst*, 1985; Short, Michael, *Gustav Holst: The Man and His Music*, 1990.

Horta, Victor

(January 6, 1861–September 8, 1947)
Architect

Through his designs of dozens of private homes and buildings in the early 1900s, Victor Horta popularized the Art Nouveau style in Belgium in the early twentieth century. First trained in neoclassical architecture, Horta returned to a more simplified neoclassical style in his later works. He is particularly known for his work in iron.

Horta was the son of a shoemaker, born in Ghent. He initially wanted to become a musician and in 1873 enrolled in the Ghent Conservatory. After being expelled, he went to the Académie des Beaux-Arts in Ghent, followed by the Académie des Beaux-Arts in Brussels from 1876 to 1881. After the end of his time there, he studied under the neoclassical architect Alphonse Balat, who was then architect to King Leopold II.

Horta's early buildings reflect his neoclassical training. In 1884 he won the Prix Godecharle for a project design for the parliament building, enabling him to travel. In 1892 he took a position as a lecturer in design at the Université Libre de Brussels. His first major building, the four-story Hôtel Tassel in Brussels (1892–1893), was among the earliest examples of Art Nouveau architecture in Belgium. The curvilinear facade, the mosaic floor, elaborate stained-glass window designs, and ornate wall murals marked a distinct change from the neoclassicism of his earlier work.

For the next decade, Horta worked almost nonstop, producing more than forty buildings that consisted for the most part of private dwellings in the Art Nouveau style. He sought a wholeness in his buildings that integrated all elements of the interior and was tailored to the people for whom he designed them. Known for his resourcefulness as a designer, he sometimes fashioned his designs to fit particular materials. Most prominent of these materials during his Art Nouveau period was iron. His thin, sinuous ironwork was dubbed the "noodle style." Among his major buildings from this period are the Hôtel Winssingers (1895–1896), Hôtel Solvay

(1895–1900), his own house on the rue Américaine (1898), and the House for the secretary for the Belgian Congo, Edmond van Eetvelde (1895–1897).

Perhaps Horta's best known work is the Maison du Peuple in Brussels (1896–1899), which for many years served as the headquarters of the Belgian Socialist Party (with which Horta had connections). His major public building in the Art Nouveau manner, it featured a large façade of glass and iron. Following a heated public debate, the building was destroyed in 1965.

After 1900, beginning especially with the Hôtel Max Hallet (1902–1905), Horta abandoned the ornate elegance of his previous buildings for a simplified style. His efforts, too, turned to the public arena, although he continued to design private homes. His major late projects include the Museum of Fine Arts in Tournai (1905–1928), the Palais des Beaux-Arts (1922–1928), and the railway station in Brussels begun in the late 1930s. The Brugmann Hospital (1906–1923), for which he designed several buildings and planned the site, was one of his most complex projects.

BIBLIOGRAPHY

Bernie, David, and Carew-Cox, Alastair, *Victor Horta*, 1995; Borsi, Franco, *Victor Horta*, 1991.

Housman, A. E.

(March 26, 1859–April 30, 1936)
Poet, Scholar, Teacher, Critic

Alfred Edward Housman is chiefly remembered for the two volumes of romantic, subtly pessimistic verse he published during his lifetime, *A Shropshire Lad* and *Last Poems*. One of the most highly regarded classical scholars of his day, he worked with the texts of Latin writers such as Manilius and Juvenal. In 1930 he completed his comprehensive edition of Manilius's works.

Housman was born in Fockbury, Worcestershire, England, and grew up in nearby Bromsgrove. Both parents came from clerical families and maintained an atmosphere of strict religious observance in the house. In 1870 Housman won a scholarship to study at King Edward's School. The death of his mother when he was 12 was a devastating experience for him. His father was given to heavy drinking and financial trouble, and to make family matters worse he married a stern and overbearing cousin.

As a youth Housman began to write verse. In 1877 he won a scholarship to St. John's College, Oxford, where he studied classics. Against his mother's dying wish that he keep his faith, Housman was an avowed atheist at the age of 21. Although he excelled in his studies he failed the final exams, much to the surprise of his family, his classmates, and his instructors. Many reasons have been suggested for his failure, among which are his personal despair over his homosexual desires for a fellow student and his family difficulties.

For the decade of 1882–1892 Housman worked as a civil servant, taking in 1882 a clerkship at the Patent Office in London. In his off hours Housman studied Latin texts and contributed scholarly articles to journals. His proficiency in the Latin texts led to his appointment as Professor of Latin at University College, London, in 1892.

Housman financed the publication of his first volume of verse, *A Shropshire Lad* (1896), a collection of sixty-three poems published by Kegan Paul. In form his poems derive from traditional ballads, sonnets, and classical odes. When he wrote the poems Housman had little experience with or knowledge of his Shropshire setting, and there are few autobiographical elements in his verse. He had originally intended to title the collection *The Poems of Terence Hearsay.* The fictional Terence appears in poems such as "Terence, This is Stupid Stuff" and may be seen as a voice in many of them.

What emerges most forcefully in Housman's subtle, ironic lyrics is his preoccupation with death. Whether reached prematurely through war or inevitably with the passing of time, death remains in his poetry the senseless end of a meaningless existence. His antiwar sentiment is evident in poems such as "The Day of Battle" and "1887." In the latter he attacks blind patriotism, ridiculing those who chant "God save the Queen" while their loved ones die on the battlefield. The 1901 death of Housman's brother in the Boer War reinforced his antiwar outlook. Housman often interweaves his subjects with natural imagery, particularly the seasonal cycles of nature. The widely reprinted "When I Was One and

A. E. Housman (Ann Ronan/Image Select)

Twenty" addresses the passing of youthful innocence, another recurring theme in Housman's poetry.

The initial sales of *A Shropshire Lad* were disappointing, but over the years they began to gain popularity, particularly during the First World War. The verse in *Last Poems* (1922) continues in the manner and theme of the previous volume and proved popular when it first appeared.

In spite of the success of his poetry Housman cared little for literary circles and paid little attention to criticism. He was reclusive by nature and did not openly express his views. Although popularly remembered for his poetry, he devoted most of his efforts to classical scholarship. In 1911 he became Professor of Latin at Cambridge, where he taught for the remainder of his life. The culmination of his long scholarly career was an annotated edition of Manilius (1903–1930) that took nearly thirty years to complete.

Housman's other works include the lectures *The Confines of Criticism*, originally delivered in 1911; *The Name and Nature of Poetry* (1933); the posthumous volumes of poetry *More Poems* (1936) and *Collected Poems* (1940); and his letters, published in 1971.

BIBLIOGRAPHY

Bayley, John, *Housman's Poems*, 1992; Graves, Richard Perceval, *A. E. Housman: The Scholar-Poet*, 1979; Hoagwood, Terence Allan, *A. E. Housman Revisited*, 1995; Jebb, Keith, *A. E. Housman*, 1992.

Hughes, Ted

(August 16, 1930–October 28, 1998)
Poet, Short-Story Writer, Teacher, Writer of Children's Books, Critic, Essayist, Translator

Ted Hughes's raw verses draw from his West Riding upbringing and frequently employ animals as symbols and metaphors, reflecting his vision of nature as embodying above all the basic animal need for survival, which he is apt to see also in human beings. Hughes was married to the major American poet Sylvia Plath from 1956 until her suicide in 1963, and he has been blamed for contributing to the state of mind that led to that suicide. The 1998 (posthumous) publication of his poems addressed to her, *Birthday Letters*, has renewed the controversy, yet also helped to establish Hughes as a poet of the first rank.

Hughes was born Edward James Hughes in Mytholmroyd, Yorkshire, England and was the youngest of three children. His father, a carpenter and World War I veteran, moved the family to Mexborough, a somewhat larger town in Yorkshire, when he was 7. There, Hughes attended the Mexborough Grammar School. The west Yorkshire dialect that he grew up with shaped the musical rhythms of his verse. Hughes's lifelong fascination with animals began in his childhood with collections of real and toy specimens.

After serving with the Royal Air Force for two years, Hughes entered Pembroke College, Cambridge. After graduating in 1954, Hughes continued to write poetry while he worked as a gardener and a zoo attendant, and later as a script reader in Arthur Rank's film studios.

Hughes's first published poem, "The Little Boys and the Seasons," appeared in Cambridge's *Granta* in 1954, and other poems soon followed in Cambridge publications. At Cambridge Hughes also developed a strong interest in ROBERT GRAVES's *The White Goddess*, which would shape his future poetry. After graduating, Hughes worked in a series of odd jobs until 1956. That year, he helped found the *St. Botolph's Review*, which only lasted for one issue, but that issue contained a number of his poems. In connection with the review he met the American poet Sylvia Plath, whom he married the same year.

Aside from her own successes as a poet, Plath was responsible for launching Hughes's career. In 1957 she entered the poems that eventually became *The Hawk in the Rain* in a contest in New York. The judges, among whom was STEPHEN SPENDER, chose Hughes's poems for the prize: publication. The themes that continue in most of Hughes's poetry emerged in this first volume—death, man, beast, freedom, and earth. "Griefs for Dead Soldiers" treats the theme of war. Hughes's poetry is contemplative but harsh, sometimes violent, and has been seen as gaining some of its power from the mannerisms and speech patterns of his native West Riding.

In 1957, Hughes moved to Boston with Plath. There he taught creative writing at the University of Massachusetts and wrote many of the poems that appeared in his next major volume, *Lupercal* (1960), which won the Hawthornden Prize. The couple returned to England in 1959, and Plath began her descent into the depression that led her to suicide in 1963. *Selected Poems*, with Thom Gunn, appeared in 1962. Hughes took a position as editor of *Modern Poetry in Translation* in London in 1965. In 1969 Hughes suffered another loss when his companion killed herself and their daughter. *Crow: From the Life and Songs of the Crow* (1973), consists of a series of poems built around the image of the crow and was partially inspired by the American sculptor Leonard Baskin.

The myth of Prometheus figured prominently in Hughes's play *Orghast* (1971) as well as his twenty-one-poem collection *Prometheus and His Crag*. Later volumes include *Wodwo* (1967), *Season Songs* (1976), *Moortown* (1979), *Moon Whales: And Other Moon Poems* (1988), and *Wolfwatching* (1992). The publication of *Birthday Letters* (1998), a collection of poetry that addresses his relationship with Plath, generated a storm of critical controversy. Some critics praised Hughes for honesty and forthrightness, while others charged him with insensitivity to his former wife and faulted him for remaining silent about her suicide for so many years.

Hughes has also written short stories and children's books. *Tales of the Early World* (1991) consists of ten short stories illustrated by David Frampton. In the work Hughes presents God as a benevolent force who nevertheless lacks full control over his creation. The short-story collection *Difficulties of a Bridegroom* was published in 1996. Hughes's children's works include *Remains of Elmet* (1979) and *What is the Truth?* (1984).

Hughes's literary criticism appears in *Winter Pollen: Occasional Prose* (1995). His translations include Seneca's play *Oedipus* and *Tales from Ovid* (1997), a highly praised translation of tales from Ovid's *Metamorphoses*, and a translation/adaptation of FEDERICO GARCÍA LORCA'S *Blood Wedding* (1997). He also gave poetry readings for children and was appointed Britain's poet laureate in 1984.

BIBLIOGRAPHY

Bishop, Nick, *Re-making Poetry: Ted Hughes and a New Critical Psychology*, 1993; Sagar, Keith, *The Art of Ted Hughes*, 1975; Scigaj, Leonard M., *Ted Hughes*, 1991.

Huxley, Aldous

(July 26, 1894–November 22, 1963)
Novelist, Poet, Critic, Essayist, Journalist

The English novelist Aldous Leonard Huxley is best known for his nightmarish satire of the contemporary world in the form of a novel about a scientific and technological "utopia," *Brave New World*. His body of work includes hundreds of novels, poems, and essays.

Huxley was born into a family of intellectuals. His grandfather, Thomas Huxley, was a well-known evolutionist and zoologist; his father, Leonard Huxley, a biographer; his brother, Julian Huxley, a biologist who helped found the United Nations Educational, Scientific, and Cultural Organization (UNESCO); and his mother, Judith Arnold, a relative of the important English poet and critic Matthew Arnold. Aldous attended Hillside School as a boy and excelled in his studies. In 1908 he enrolled at Eton, where he endured two difficult trials: the death of his mother and the erosion of his eyesight due to keratitis. While he studied English literature at Balliol College in Oxford, he met Lady Ottoline Morrell, at whose house an informal literary circle sometimes gathered. Through her Huxley met such literary figures as D. H. LAWRENCE, who later became his close friend. *The Burning Wheel*, a collection of poetry and his first book, was published in 1916, the year he graduated.

In 1919, Huxley married Maria Nys and began to work as a journalist and reviewer for the *London Athenaeum*, often writing under the pseudonym "Autolycus." *Crome Yellow*, his first novel, was published two years later. Along with its successor, *Antic Hay* (1923), *Crome Yellow* satirized the prevailing intellectual climate in England. In *Antic Hay*, a teacher, Theodore Gumbril, grows disgusted with his school's hollow curriculum. He abandons teaching and moves to London, where he encounters a cast of scientists, artists, scholars, and others devoting their time to pursuits he considers futile and even sinister. Yet Gumbril is himself no hero—he is fond of seducing women and teams up with a manipulative marketing strategist to sell the pants he has invented.

Huxley and his wife left England in 1923 and lived in Italy and France. His next novel, *Those Barren Leaves*, appeared in 1925. *Jesting Pilate* (1926), inspired by his world travels, offers a critical look at Western civilization as a whole. In *Point Counter Point* (1928), Huxley contrasts several forms of artists, intellectuals, and lovers who seem to be living in false worlds, deluding themselves, and lying to others. More honest and perceptive souls in the narrative respond to humanity's flaws in their own ways. Rampion, an artist modeled on D. H. Lawrence, is an optimistic visionary who never gives up hope for the improvement of mankind. The nihilistic Spandrell, filled with hate toward his fellow human beings, lashes out at others in destructive ways and thus destroys his own life. The pensive writer Phillip Quarles becomes depressed and deadened by everything he sees.

Brave New World (1932), a dark satire of authoritarian political and technological structures and utopian ideas, proved to be Huxley's most popular novel. Unlike the communist nightmare of GEORGE

Aldous Huxley (Ann Ronan/Image Select)

Orwell's *1984*, however, there is no "Big Brother" inflicting its agenda on a terror-stricken population. Instead, the comforts of technology have coaxed a blissful people into relinquishing their individuality and leading lives of conformity. People are scientifically conceived in test tubes and mentally conditioned after they are "hatched." A widely used drug, soma, helps them remain at ease with the system as it is structured. Humans with lower intelligence are created to perform menial tasks, and a few people of higher intelligence are formulated to run the world. The disgruntled Bernard Marx and the "savage" John threaten the new utopian society. Marx is troubled with love for a single woman (Lenina Crowne) in a society that encourages free sex and discourages emotional attachment, while the rebellious John enjoys reading portrayals of genuine human beings in such antiquated authors as Shakespeare.

After *Brave New World*, Huxley began to seriously explore solutions to the problems he had satirized in his earlier novels. *Eyeless in Gaza* (1936) is a fictional compilation of journal entries concerning, directly or indirectly, Anthony Beavis. The jumble of experiences that have influenced Anthony make up who he is in the present. A distressing conflict between who he is and who he wants to be leads him to Miller, an anthropologist working in Mexico. Miller helps Anthony to piece together an understanding of who he is and to take steps to improve himself.

In 1937 Huxley moved to California and pursued his growing interest in mysticism. He became involved with the Vedanta Society of Southern California and with Swami Prabhavananda and Krishnamurti. Such works as the essays of *Ends and Means* (1937) and the annotated texts of *The Perennial Philosophy* (1945), in which he suggested that heightened spiritual experience could help humanity transcend its problems, outlined his developing philosophy. Huxley sought to expand his consciousness with hypnotism, religion, and hallucinogenic drugs, and he recounted his experiments with mescaline in *The Doors of Perception* (1954) and *Heaven and Hell* (1956).

Huxley's other works include *After Many a Summer Dies the Swan* (1939); *Grey Eminence* (1941); *Ape and Essence* (1949); *The Devils of Loudun* (1952), an account of a true story about French nuns who were accused of demon possession in the 1600s; *The Genius and the Goddess* (1955); *Island* (1962); and screenplays, including Jane Austen's *Pride and Prejudice* (1941). After the death of his first wife in 1955, he married Laura Archera. A fire completely destroyed his home and papers in 1961. Nevertheless, he continued to write, and to enjoy the respect his writings had won him, until his death from cancer in 1963.

Bibliography

Bedford, Sybille, *Aldous Huxley: A Biography*, 1973–1974; May, Keith M., *Aldous Huxley*, 1972; Watts, Harold, *Aldous Huxley*, 1969.

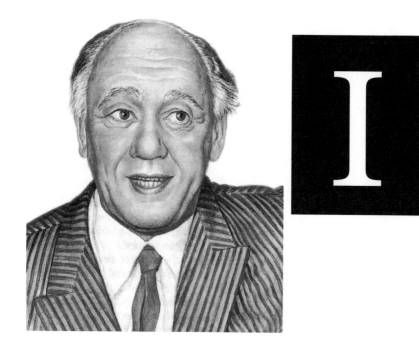

I

Ionesco, Eugène

(November 26, 1912–March 28, 1994)
Playwright, Novelist

Eugène Ionesco, with other playwrights such as SAMUEL BECKETT and Arthur Adamov, is considered a founder of the Theater of the Absurd, a post–World War II movement in English and French theater that used dramatic content and staging techniques to create a lively sense of the absurd and of the absence of meaningful patterns in life.

Ionesco was born in Slatina, Romania, to a French mother and a Romanian father. He had anemia as a young child and lived with a farming family outside of Paris. He moved back to Romania at age 13. After marrying, and graduating from the University of Bucharest, he taught French until 1938, when he moved to Paris to work on his doctoral thesis. Ionesco criticized all forms of authoritarianism and became an ardent anticommunist when his native Romania fell under Soviet control after World War II.

In Ionesco's dramatic farces, which he called "anti-plays," typical bourgeois life is portrayed as absurd. His characters are boring, mediocre, and virtually unable to communicate with one another. In *La Cantatrice chauve* (1948; *The Bald Soprano*), his first major play, the characters converse using utterly and obviously meaningless clichés inspired by Ionesco's own perusal of an English theater primer. The play takes place in a drawing room, where a Mr. and Mrs. Smith are chattering about a family of friends, all of whom are named Bobby Watson. A husband and wife enter the scene and know so little about each other that it takes a while for them to deduce they are married. Ionesco drew the inspiration for the dialog in this play from the phrasebook he used to teach himself English, and it is considered to be one of the earliest plays in the Theatre of the Absurd movement. French audiences initially scorned Ionesco's work, but it soon began to attract interest.

Short sketches and one-act plays comprise most of Ionesco's early work. They are purposely constructed in an illogical manner, and many use confused babble as dialog and other seemingly absurd elements to emphasize the senselessness of typical human life. In many of Ionesco's plays, an absurd situation disintegrates and finally ends in physical and symbolic death. Among his most fa-

Eugène Ionesco (Fragment Publishing)

mous are *La Lecon* (1951; *The Lesson*), *Les Chaises* (1952; *The Chairs*), *How to Get Rid of It* (1953), and *The New Tenant* (1955). In *The Lesson*, an egotistical teacher kills a student after overpowering her with words. The elderly man of *The Chairs* wants to deliver a speech conveying his wisdom to a crowd of acquaintances before they die. The guests are invisible, and the number of empty chairs begins to multiply. The couple kill themselves, leaving it to a hired orator to convey their message to the non-crowd. As it turns out, the orator cannot speak coherently and writes gibberish on the blackboard.

Ionesco's first full-length play was *Amédée ou comment s'en débarrasser* (*Amédée, or How to Get Rid of It*), in which a corpse, symbolic of a couple's dead marriage, grows inside their living room until Amédée floats up toward the sky on it. The character of Bérenger, introduced as an average, typical man, appears in several of Ionesco's plays, including *Rhinocéros* (1959; *Rhinoceros*). The work, an attack on conformity and totalitarianism, is Ionesco's most famous full-length play. Bérenger resists conforming to the ways of his fellow citizens, who all turn into beastly rhinoceroses.

Ionesco's other plays include *Tueur sans gages* (1957; *The Killer*), *Le Soif et la faim* (1964; *Hunger and Thirst*), *Le Piéton de l'air* (1967; *A Stroll in the Air*), *Killing Game* (1970), *A Hell of a Mess* (1973), and *The Man With Bags* (1977). His other works include his 1972 adaptation of *Macbeth*, the novel *The Hermit* (1974), and his memoirs *Présent passé passé present* (1968; *Present Past, Past Present*). He was elected to the French Academy in 1970. Ionesco also acted, and in 1951 he played in Fyodor Dostoevsky's *The Possessed*.

BIBLIOGRAPHY

Coe, Richard N., *Eugene Ionesco*, 1970; Lewis, Allan, *Ionesco*, 1972.

Ivens, Joris

(November 18, 1898–June 28, 1989)
Director

During his long career as a filmmaker, the Dutch director Joris Ivens made dozens of documentaries bearing strong social and left-wing political messages. A collaborative effort with the American novelist Ernest Hemingway in the mid-1930s established his international reputation, and Ivens subsequently made films in the United States, Indonesia, and Europe.

Ivens was born Georg Henri Anton Ivens in Nijmegen, the Netherlands. His father was a photographic supplier. He made his first short film in 1911 and the same year entered the municipal Dutch High School. Ivens studied at the Rotterdam School of Economics from 1916 to 1917 and again in 1920 and 1921. Between his two periods of study he served in World War I as a field artillery lieutenant. After further study in photography in Germany, he moved to Amsterdam to work for his father's business. He later made films for the University of Leyden.

In 1927 he helped found FILM LIGA, and he finished his first major film, *De Brug* (*The Bridge*, 1928), the following year. Along with *Regen* (*Rain*, 1929), a detailed cinematic study of raindrops, *De Brug* attracted international attention. His early films show the influence of the montage sequences of the Soviet director SERGEY EISENSTEIN. After these two films Ivens turned to overt, left-wing political themes. He traveled to the Soviet Union in 1930 and filmed *Komsomol* (*Song of Heroes*, 1932), a documentary about young Communists building the steel center Magnitogorsk. The German composer Hans Eisler, a student of ARNOLD SCHOENBERG, contributed the music score to *Komsomol* and several other Ivens films.

The following year Ivens made *Misère au Borinage* (*Borinage*, 1933), a documentary on a miner's strike in Belgium. Hemingway narrated *The Spanish Earth* (1937), an anti-Fascist documentary on the Spanish Civil War that brought Ivens international fame and is still worth watching. *The Four Hundred Million*, made in China in 1938, documented the Sino-Japanese War.

Ivens next worked in the United States, where in 1940 the U.S. government hired him to make *The Power of the Land*, a film about a New Deal electrification program. During World War II he lectured at UCLA and worked for the U.S. and Canadian governments. He made *Our Russian Front* the following year. From 1944 to 1946, when he resigned in opposition to Dutch colonialism (specifically Holland's refusal to recognize Indonesia's independence), Ivens was film commissioner in the Dutch East Indies. The immediate result of his resignation was *Indonesia Calling* (1946), a film that championed the cause of Indonesian independence and resulted in the revocation of his passport.

Ivens spent much of the 1950s in Eastern Europe. *Stromenlied* (*Song of the Rivers*, 1952) won an international peace prize, and he won a World Peace Prize in 1955 and a Lenin Prize in 1967. In 1956 he worked with Cavalcanti on *Die Vind Rose*. He codirected, with Gérard Philipe, *Les Aventures de Till l'Espiègle*. During the Vietnam War he was an outspoken foe of the American military effort and made a number of films on that subject. Ivens received an honorary doctorate from London's Royal College of Art in 1978 and Cuba's Che Guevara Prize in 1987.

BIBLIOGRAPHY

Böker, Carlos, *Joris Ivens, Film-Maker: Facing Reality*, 1981; Delmar, Rosalind, *Joris Ivens: Fifty Years of Film-Making*, 1979.

J

Jacobsen, Arne

(February 11, 1902–March 24, 1971)
Architect, Designer

Arne Jacobsen was one of Denmark's leading proponents of modern architecture in the mid-twentieth century and forged his own version of the International Style. Jacobsen's designs include many public and private buildings in Denmark notable for both their functionalist style and integration with the surrounding landscape.

Jacobsen was the son of a wholesaler, born in Copenhagen, Denmark. As a child he developed an interest in drawing and painting, but his father sought a more practical career for him and steered him toward architecture. Jacobsen left school at 15 and later attended the Copenhagen Technical College. There he met the brothers Flemming and Mogens Lassen, who were to become two of Denmark's most prominent modern architects. Jacobsen studied under Kay Fisker, Kay Gottlob, and Ivar Bentsen and with the school's assistance traveled to Italy and France. Upon the completion of his studies, he entered the Copenhagen Academy of Arts, from which he graduated in 1927.

While at the Academy, Jacobsen had already done some architectural work and had begun to exhibit furnishings, some of which won a Silver Medal at the Paris World Exhibition in 1925. After receiving his diploma, he went to work for city architect Poul Holsøe at the Copenhagen Town Hall. There he took charge of the design for a new music pavilion and other structures. Jacobsen also began to enter his designs in competitions and to receive commissions, mostly for private homes and residential districts. Among these was the yellow brick villa for Professor Sigurd Wandel, a residential district at Ordrup Mose, and a home for the lawyer Max Rothenborg.

Jacobsen designed the first section of a seaside district, the Bellavista Housing Estate, at Klampenborg in 1933. The terraced buildings of the three-wing complex allow each occupant a good view of the sea. Over the next two years, Jacobsen added the Bellevue Theatre and a restaurant to the district. The theater is notable for its sliding roof, which opens to the sky when the weather permits.

In the early 1930s, the functionalist International Style advanced by WALTER GROPIUS's Bauhaus School in Germany began to influence Danish architects, including Jacobsen. In his early works, Jacobsen used the traditional building materials of Denmark, notably brick. The new style employed modern materials such as concrete, glass, and steel, and Jacobsen, though he never abandoned brick, increasingly used them in his designs.

In 1934–1935 he designed the Novo Therapeutical Laboratory, his first factory, which used as its primary material reinforced concrete. Another notable design from this period is his gas station at Skovshoved Harbor, which has a prominent white circular roof. Before World War II he designed town halls at Århus (1937) and Søllerød (1940)—two of the numerous town halls he designed during his lifetime—as well as his own summer home (1937) and the yellow brick Ibstrupparken Housing Estate (1940).

In 1941–1942 Jacobsen designed a stadium for the City of Gentofte. Another major war-era work was his herring smoking plant at Odden Havn (1943), to which he added a round house for the manager's residence in 1957. The war forced him to live in Sweden from 1943 until its end. While there he continued to do architectural work but also began to design textile and wallpaper patterns with his wife. Their designs achieved some success in Sweden, and the National Museum of Stockholm purchased a number of them.

After the war, Jacobsen returned to Denmark and immersed himself in the postwar rebuilding. In 1947 he designed, using three-story, yellow brick structures, a housing estate in Gentofte for young married couples. He finished the Søholm Housing Estate near Bellevue three years later. Also among his works from this period is the Munkegårds School (1952–1956), a school for young children. The design consists of twenty-four paired classrooms in which each pair opens to a patio. As in all of his works, Jacobsen carefully planned the landscape. In one patio he placed a pool with aquatic plants, and another featured shrubs trimmed in animal shapes.

The Rødovre Town Hall (1955), to which he also contributed the furniture for the Council Chamber, is a long, rectangular building with horizontal ribbons of windows. With the Scandinavian Airlines System (SAS) Building (1959), Jacobsen designed both the interior and exterior and gave Copenhagen its first skyscraper. The Novo Industri A/S Factory (1961), built in reinforced concrete, is noteworthy for an emergency exit that consists of an external spiral staircase enclosed in a cylindrical glass structure.

Jacobsen worked for the most part in Denmark, but he received several notable international commissions. Among these is the Parliament Building at Islamabad, Pakistan (1962), which consists of a low-level, rectangular block with a taller, cylindrical building for the Parliament Chamber. He also designed the buildings of and some furniture for St. Catherine's College, Oxford University (1964).

Jacobsen's other architectural designs include the Jesperson Building (1955) in Copenhagen, the National Bank building at Copenhagen (1961), the Headquarters Building for the Hamburg Electricity Supply Company (1962), and numerous sports halls. He also received recognition for his silverware, dishes, and furniture, particularly his swan and egg armchairs.

BIBLIOGRAPHY

Faber, Tobias, *Arne Jacobsen*, 1964.

Jacobson, Dan

(March 7, 1929–)
Novelist, Short-Story Writer

In his novels and short stories, the South African–born writer Dan Jacobson has created a series of characters motivated by greed or prejudice that often stems from the divided cultures in which they live. In his early works, such characters spring from the climate of racial segregation perpetuated by apartheid policies in South Africa. Jacobson's later novels consider religious divisions and other factors that contribute to conflicts among humanity.

Jacobson was born in Johannesburg, South Africa, to Jewish immigrants from Eastern Europe. The family moved to Kimberley in 1933, and Jacobson attended the Kimberley Boys' High School. He studied at the University of Witwatersrand and graduated in 1948. The same year, he moved to the newly established country of Israel and worked on a kibbutz. In 1950, Jacobson moved to London and taught at a private Jewish school.

After returning to South Africa and working briefly for a press digest and for his family's feed milling business, Jacobson moved permanently to England in 1954. He had begun writing short stories in 1953, and his first novel, *The Trap*, was published in 1955. In *The Trap* and other early novels, he frames his narratives in a realistic and even naturalistic writing style.

His next novel, *A Dance in the Sun* (1956), is an indictment of the apartheid system and the whites whose mentality support it. The mysterious Mr. and Mrs. Fletcher, inhabitants of the village of Mirredal, are two such whites, who host two students that have gotten off track from their intended vacation. The students find the atmosphere of the home stifling, and everything about the Fletchers suggests an isolated and backward existence. The students learn that the Fletchers have sent away her brother, Nasie, after he fathered an illegitimate child by a black woman, Mary. Mr. Fletcher also paid Mary to leave with the child, and Mary's brother, Joseph, wants to know where they are. Nasie's return disrupts the family and he is eventually persuaded to leave again, but his appearance stimulates a change in the students' thinking, and even in the outlook of Mrs. Fletcher.

Greed is the driving factor in *The Price of Diamonds* (1957). An illegal diamond dealer accidentally gives a box of uncut diamonds to Manfried Gottlieb, when they were intended for his associate, Fink. Gottlieb gets caught up in the excitement brought on by the mistake and unsuccessfully attempts to sell them, eluding Fink's inquiries. When Fink is severely beaten, he determines to turn himself in, but complications with the police prevent his arrest.

The Evidence of Love (1960) returns to the subject of racial prejudice, examining its effect both on a light-skinned black man and a white woman. The wealthy and white Lucille Bentwisch sends Kenneth Makeer to study law in England. There he meets the South African white woman Isabel Last, who does not known he is "colored." Makeer is too ashamed to tell her, and when she finds out by other means, she leaves him and returns to South Africa. Her departure leaves Makeer devastated and confused, and Isabel's mentality begins to change following a visit from Makeer's brother. She returns to England and marries Makeer, and the pair return to South Africa, where their arrest follows.

Jacobson's short-story collections include *A Long Way From London* (1958), *Zulu and the Zeide* (1959), and *Beggar My Neighbour* (1964). The title story of *Zulu and the Zeide* concerns the relationship between an elderly Jewish Lithuanian immigrant and his son as well as the old man's friendship with a Zulu, Paulus. The son, Harry Grossman, does not get along with his senile father, who prefers the companionship of Paulus and eventually loses his life when a bicycle hits him.

The novel *The Beginners* (1966), a family chronicle about Benjamin Glickman, his wife Sarah, and their three children, marked a turning point in Jacobson's style and focus. His narratives became more complex and his writing style more experimental. *The Rape of Tamar* (1970), narrated by Yonadab, is based on the biblical story of the rape of David's daughter by her brother, Amnon. In this and other later works, Jacobson did not confine himself to South Africa for subject matter.

The Confessions of Josef Baisz (1977), told in the form of a diary narrated by the ruthless Josef Baisz, takes placed in totalitarian Sarmeda, a country "like" South Africa. Baisz is the son of a civil servant who was arrested on charges of embezzlement and committed suicide. Baisz pursues a brutal course of life, abusing, manipulating, and falsely accusing others to get ahead. His crimes even extend to murder. In the end, he, like his father, will kill himself.

In *The God-Fearer* (1992), Jacobson attempts to reverse the roles of Christians and Jews in European history. The main character, Kobus, is a bookbinder who lives in Ashkenaz, ruled by the God-Fearers, descendants of the Yehudim. The majority Yehudim blame the minority Christer for the world's ills, and the latter are treated unfairly by the legal system and the populace. Kobus sees a series of visions of two Christer children who force him to confront the mistakes of his past.

Among Jacobson's other works are the novel *The Wonder-Worker* (1973); *The Story of the Stories: The Chosen People and Its God* (1982); and *Time and Time Again: Autobiographies* (1985). He has traveled and lectured widely in the United States, England, and Israel.

BIBLIOGRAPHY

Jacobson, Dan, *Time and Time Again: Autobiographies*, 1985; Roberts, Sheila, *Dan Jacobson*, 1984.

Jennings, Elizabeth

(July 18, 1926–)
Poet

Elizabeth Joan Jennings achieved her first poetic successes in the 1950s, when she was considered part of a group of poets from that era who included JOHN WAIN, KINGSLEY AMIS, and PHILIP LARKIN. Her poetry is intimate and direct, rendered in traditional style.

Jennings was born in Boston, Lincolnshire, England. Her father was a doctor. The family moved to Oxford when Jennings was young, and she has never left other than to travel. She attended school in Oxford and then studied at St. Anne's College, Oxford from 1945 to 1949. Her first published poems appeared in *Oxford Poetry* in 1948.

During her time at Oxford, Jennings met fellow poets Wain, Amis, and Larkin. Critics dubbed the work of these poets, including Jennings's, "The Movement." They shared certain characteristics, such as the avoidance of politics as subject matter, the use of traditional forms, the use of simple language, and study at Oxford. However, the members of The Movement had no common agenda and worked independently. Jennings makes no secret of her dislike of the label.

Jennings's first volume of poetry, *Poems*, was published in 1953 and won an Arts Council prize. Poets who influenced her included T. S. ELIOT and Gerard Manley Hopkins. In *Poems*, she introduced themes that recur throughout her work, themes such as the varied aspects of love and childhood memories. Her next volume of poetry, *A Way of Looking* (1955), won a Somerset Maugham Award that allowed her to visit Italy. Jennings's love for the country and its literary tradi-

tion had a strong influence on her poetry. *A Sense of the World* followed in 1958. With *Song for a Birth or Death* (1961), Jennings achieved a new intimacy in her writing.

The poems collected in *The Mind Has Mountains* (1966) were written during a period of mental illness that culminated in a breakdown, and many movingly reflect her experiences with other patients and with the staff at a hospital where she received treatment. Most of Jennings's poetry follows traditional meter and rhyme, but in volumes such as *Growing Points* (1975), she experimented with other styles.

Many of the poems in *Consequently I Rejoice* (1977), *Moments of Grace* (1979), *Celebrations and Elegies* (1982), and other later volumes incorporate religious themes shaped by Jennings's Roman Catholic faith. Inspirational figures and art, the passage of time, and death all form prominent themes and images in Jennings's poetry, and she addresses them in straightforward terms without the extensive use of metaphor.

Her other volumes include *Recoveries* (1964), *The Animals' Arrival* (1969), *Lucidities* (1970), *Relationships* (1972), *Winter Wind* (1979), *Extending the Territory* (1985), *Tributes* (1989), and *Times and Seasons* (1992). Her latest works are *Familiar Spirits* (1994), and *In the Meantime* (1997). She has also published children's poetry, including *The Batsford Book of Children's Verse* (1958) and *The Secret Brother* (1966). Her translation of *The Sonnets of Michelangelo* was published in 1969. The prose work *Let's Have Some Po-*

etry (1960) chronicles her emergence as a poet. She has published several volumes of her collected poetry: *Collected Poems 1967* (1967), *Selected Poems* (1980), and *Collected Poems 1953–1985* (1986).

BIBLIOGRAPHY

Gramang, Gerlinde, *Elizabeth Jennings: An Appraisal of Her Life as a Poet, Her Approach to Her Work and a Selection of the Major Themes of Her Poetry*, 1994.

Jiménez, Juan Ramón

(December 23, 1881–May 29, 1958)
Poet, Translator

The Spanish poet Juan Ramón Jiménez began his career under the influence of the Modernists and evolved his own poetic style suffused with melancholy and nostalgia. He won the Nobel Prize for Literature in 1956.

Jiménez was the youngest of four children, born in Moguer, a small town in the Andalusian region of southern Spain. His father operated a successful and prosperous vineyard, and both parents treated their temperamental child well. After completing several years of schooling, he entered a Jesuit school at age 11. He subsequently studied painting and law in Seville, the latter in accordance with his father's wishes. Jiménez disliked law and quit his studies, eventually deciding to devote himself to poetry.

The year 1900 was eventful for Jiménez. During a two-month visit to Madrid, he met several noteworthy literary figures, including the Nicaraguan modernismo poet Ruben Darío and RAMÓN DEL VALLE INCLÁN. His father's death from a heart attack the same year caused a severe nervous illness from which he spent the next year recovering. His first poetry collection, *Violet Souls* (1900), consisted of eighteen poems originally printed in purple ink. Like much of his poetry, the verse in *Violet Souls* is nostalgic, brooding, and melancholy. *Water Lilies* (1900) was printed in green ink.

Early in his career as a poet, Jiménez was influenced by the nineteenth-century Spanish poets Gustavo Adolfo Bécquer and Rosalia de Castro as well as Darío and the French Symbolists. In his work Jiménez also drew from the Catholic faith he maintained throughout his life, although his views grew less orthodox with age. Much of Jiménez's early poetry is marked by careful attention to form and technique. The poems of *Sad Airs* (1903), *Distant Gardens* (1904), and *Pastorals* (1905) are generally written in four-verse stanzas with unrhymed odd lines. *Spiritual Sonnets* (1917), a book of sonnets written in traditional rhyme and eleven-syllable verse, is particularly noteworthy for its technical refinement.

In 1912 Jiménez returned to Madrid after having lived in Moguer for seven years. He worked as an editor in the Residencia de Estudiantes, where he met other writers such as ANTONIO MACHADO and MIGUEL DE UNAMUNO. The prose sketches of *Platero and I* (1914) are among Jiménez's most popular works. Jiménez set his series of sketches about a poet and his donkey, Platero, in his native town of Moguer. Many of the stories concern humankind's relationship with animals, from the poet's warm relationship with Platero to the callous cruelty people inflict on a dog, a canary, and other animals.

Diary of Newly Married Poet (1917) followed his marriage to Zenobia Camprubí Aymar, translator of the Indian poet RABINDRANATH TAGORE. The *Diary* marked a turning point in Jiménez's poetic style. Jiménez embraced what he called "naked poetry," or a pure poetry stripped of formality. Most of the volume's poems are written in free verse, and some are prose poems. They fall into six sections containing his reflections on love, his first visit to the United States, and the ocean voyages that took him across the Atlantic and back.

Upon the outbreak of the Spanish Civil War in 1936, Jiménez and his wife moved to the United States. Representing the Spanish Republic, he served as an official cultural emissary. Until his death in 1958, he lived in the United States and Puerto Rico, lecturing at major universities and continuing to write poetry. He received the Nobel Prize for Literature in 1956, the same year his wife died from cancer. Among his later collections of poetry is *Coral Gables Ballads* (1948), written during his residence in southern Florida.

Jiménez's other volumes of poetry include *Pure Elegies* (1908), *Ballads of Spring* (1910), *Rock and Sky* (1919), *Poetry, in Verse* (1923), *Poetry in Prose and Verse* (1932), *Voices of My Song* (1945), and *Animal at Bottom* (1947).

BIBLIOGRAPHY

Fogelquist, Donald F., *Juan Ramón Jiménez*, 1976.

John, Augustus

(January 4, 1878–October 31, 1961)
Painter

Like his sister, GWEN JOHN, Augustus Edwin John established his reputation as an artist with his portraiture. John used large, bold areas of color to depict gypsies, peasants, and later many prominent European artists and intellectuals.

John was born in Tenby, Pembrokeshire, Wales, and attended school there. His mother died in 1884. A decade later he entered the Slade School of Fine Art, where he studied until 1898. Although he was younger than Gwen, she began studying at the same school only a year later. John soon distinguished himself as one of the school's most talented draughtsman.

Influenced in style by the Postimpressionists and Impressionists as well as the older European masters, John chose for his early subjects the Welsh peasantry and gypsies he lived and worked among. *Lily in North Wales, Rustic Idyll* (1903), and *Encampment on Dartmoor* (1906) as well as many drawings, spring from his experiences among the peasantry.

John became friends with the painter James Dickson Innes, whose preference was for painting landscapes in mountainous regions. Although primarily known as a portraitist, John too created a number of landscapes. Some, such as *Chateau Neuf, Provence*, treat only the landscape, while others like *Woodlanders* show his ability to integrate his human figures with surrounding landscape.

In contrast with the earthy colors and subdued tones of Gwen's paintings, John used bolder colors and less subtle emotion. Shaped by his talent in draughtsmanship, his forms are clearly defined. In his later portraits, he continued to paint lesser known figures, such as his 1918 *Canadian Soldier* (1918) (among other portraits of soldiers), *Cornish Sailor Boy* (1937), and *Spanish Gypsy*. His most famous works, however, are the portraits of prominent literary, artistic, and political figures.

Among John's portraits are *Dorelia; W. B. Yeats; Smiling Woman* (1908); two *George Bernard Shaw* (1914) portraits, one in which the playwright has closed his eyes; *Arthur Symons* (1917); the cellist *Madame Suggia* (1923); *Thomas Hardy* (1923); *Lady Ottoline Morrell* (1926); *James Joyce* (1930); *Tallulah Bankhead* (1933); *Mrs. Augustus John* (1937); and *Dylan Thomas* (1938). John also painted and drew multiple-figure works, such as *Suffer the Little Children to Come Unto Me* and the cartoon *Galway*.

John attained the status as the finest portraitist in England at the height of his career and exhibited widely until 1910. Although his sister rarely exhibited, he was a prime force in the promotion of her work.

BIBLIOGRAPHY

Easton, Malcolm, *Augustus John*, 1975; Holroyd, Michael, *Augustus John*, 1996; Rothenstein, John, *Augustus John*, 1946.

John, Gwen

(June 22, 1876–September 18, 1939)
Painter

Gwendolyn Mary John's intimate, impressionistic portraits of women convey subtle emotion and evince a marked melancholy. A very private person, she did little to promote her work and exhibited few paintings during her lifetime. Her work is often overshadowed by that of her more famous brother, AUGUSTUS JOHN.

John was born in Haverfordwest, Wales, where her father was a solicitor. Her mother died in 1884, after which the family moved to Tenby. John attended school there before entering the Slade School of Fine Art in London, where she studied from 1895 to 1898. The professors Philip Wilson Steer and Fred Brown were among her numerous teachers; her brother Augustus attended the Slade School during roughly the same period. Upon her departure, she earned a first prize for figure composition.

In 1898 John went to Paris to study under James McNeill Whistler (1834–1903), the well-known American painter, at the Académie Carmen. The following year she moved to London, where she lived until 1903. In 1904 John settled permanently in France. She earned her living modeling for the French sculptor Auguste Rodin (1840–1917) and other artists and became Rodin's mistress the same year. Rodin used her as the model for his *Muse*, created as a memorial for Whistler.

Not many of John's early paintings survive. After she graduated from school, she depicted women in muted, earthy colors. Her female subjects—which include nudes and plainly dressed women—have long sad faces. Some of her models remain unknown, but many of them were close friends. Among her portraits are self portraits, *Dorelia in a Black Dress* (1903), *The Student* (1903–1904), *Chloë Boughton-Leigh* (1908; 1910), *Fenella Lovell* (1909), *Girl Praying* (1930), and several works with unknown dates—*Girl in Profile*, *Girl with Cat*, and *The Convalescent*.

John absorbed few of the modern artistic influences that dominated Paris in the early twentieth century, fashioning her style instead from the works of the old masters. In 1906 she met the poet RAINER MARIA RILKE, who served as Rodin's secretary for several years. Until 1910

John found little success as a painter. A limited number of her works appeared in scattered exhibitions, particularly those sponsored by the New English Art Club in London. The American collector John Quinn began purchasing her work in 1910 and continued to support her until his death in 1924.

In 1911 John moved to Meudon. Shortly thereafter she converted to Catholicism, after which she painted many portraits of Catholic figures. Noteworthy among these are her depictions of the seventeenth-century abbess Mère Poussepin and her small paintings of Saint Teresa of Lisieux (in the 1930s). Aside from her portraits of women, John also painted interiors—such as *A Corner of the Artist's Room in Paris* (1907–1909) and *The Teapot* (1915–1916)—and cats.

John lived a private and somewhat reclusive life, associating mainly with a handful of close friends. Augustus was among her most enthusiastic supporters and promoters. The New Cheril Galleries in London held a retrospective of her work in 1926 that included forty-four paintings and numerous drawings.

BIBLIOGRAPHY

Chitty, Lady Susan, *Gwen John, 1876–1939*, 1981; Langdale, Cecily, *Gwen John: An Interior Life*, 1985; Taubman, Mary, *Gwen John: The Artist and Her Work*, 1985; Thomas, Alison, *Portraits of Women: Gwen John and Her Forgotten Contemporaries*, 1994.

Jooss, Kurt

(January 12, 1901–May 22, 1979)
Choreographer, Dancer

An influential figure in the development of modern dance, Kurt Jooss fashioned a choreographic style that combined classic ballet steps with expressionistic movement. For more than twenty-five years he toured with his own ballet company, introducing his work to world audiences. Through his efforts as a teacher, he influenced many young dancers. Jooss's best-known work is his antiwar ballet *The Green Table.*

Jooss was born in Wasseralfingen, Germany. He studied music in his youth and later turned to ballet. The most important influence on his development was his association with the Hungarian theorist and choreographer Rudolf Laban, who devised a widely used system of dance notation. (MARY WIGMAN and Sigurd Leeder were also pupils of Laban.) Jooss studied under Laban between 1920 and 1924, also working as his assistant. After further study in Berlin and Paris, he worked as a choreographer for Neue Tanzbühne (New Dance Stage).

In 1927 he founded the Folkwang School, and the following year he established a ballet company, the Folkwang Tanzbühne (which later became the Ballets Jooss). In 1930 he took the position of ballet master at the Essen Opera House. Two years later Jooss danced in the Paris premiere of his most famous work, *The Green Table*, a satirical, antiwar ballet that featured music composed by Fritz Cohen and won first prize from a competition sponsored by the International Archives of Dance.

On tour with his company when Hitler rose to power, Jooss refused to remain in Germany and settled instead in England, eventually gaining his British citizenship. With Sigurd Leeder, he established his company at Dartington Hall, Devon, where he remained until his 1949 return to Essen. Jooss's company continued to perform until 1953, and he ran the dance school until 1968.

The subject matter of Jooss's ballets was generally modern, and he sought to express psychological and emotional themes with movement. He contributed to the development of Laban's eukinetics, a method of dance that allows for expressiveness in multiple contexts and takes into account the effect of gravity on dancers. Although he rejected what he considered excessive pirouetting and other elements of classical dance, Jooss retained its basic steps and disciplined approach. Jooss's other ballets include *The Big City* (1932), *The Seven Heroes* (1933), *Juventud* (1948), and *Colombinade* (1951).

BIBLIOGRAPHY

Coton, A. V., *The New Ballet: Kurt Jooss and His Work*, 1946.

Joyce, James

(February 2, 1882–January 13, 1941)
Novelist, Poet, Playwright

The Irish writer James Augustine Aloysius Joyce (as he was christened) is considered one of the most complex novelists of the twentieth century. He is best known for his controversial novel *Ulysses* and his extensive use of stream of consciousness, or interior monologue, in which the thoughts and impressions of a characters are fully expressed in a way that reflects the natural disorder of the mind.

Joyce was born to a large family in Dublin in 1882. His father, a civil servant, squandered the family's money on alcohol, leaving them virtually impoverished. His mother was a talented pianist. Joyce attended Jesuit boarding and grammar schools in his youth and later enrolled at the Jesuit-run University College in Dublin. He studied languages, read extensively, and worked to improve his writing. During his college years he made a final break with the Roman Catholic tradition he had earlier begun to question.

In 1904 Joyce left Dublin with the woman he eventually married, Nora Barnacle. They moved around Europe—to Austria-Hungary, Trieste, Zürich, and Paris—and never returned permanently to Ireland. The year 1904 also brought an attack of iritis, the first sign of lifelong eye troubles that required a long series of operations and left him nearly blind. Their two children, George and Lucia, were both born in Trieste. To support

James Joyce with grandson (Ann Ronan/Image Select)

himself and his growing family, Joyce at various times gave language lessons and worked at a bank.

Joyce's first book, *Chamber Music* (1907), was a collection of thirty-six poems. These were followed by *Dubliners* (1914), a collection of short stories he had begun to write for an Irish magazine. The stories included "The Dead," "Eveline," "Clay," and "After the Race," and explored with a new delicacy and exactness various ways of rebelling against and being trapped in the sterile conformity of working- and lower-middle-class life in Dublin, portraying characters at every stage of life up to maturity. Many of the stories culminate in what Joyce was the first to call epiphanies, moments of profound revelation, when, as Joyce put it in *Stephen Hero*, the "soul" of some thing or some situation "leaps to us from the vestment of its appearance." One of the main purposes of art, for Joyce, was to capture such epiphanies, and the stories of *Dubliners* are still read as magnificent examples of successfully captured epiphanies. Joyce originally wrote some of them for the magazine under the pseudonym "Stephen Dedalus," the name of the protagonist in his autobiographical first novel, *A Portrait of the Artist as a Young Man*, published in 1916.

He employed the stream-of-consciousness or interior monologue technique for which he is famous in A *Portrait of the Artist*, detailing in sequence Stephen Dedalus's emotions, thoughts, and perceptions during his youth as he questions the Catholic church, interacts with his family, decides to become a writer, and resolves to leave Dublin. Again, many crucial moments in Stephen's growth are captured in epiphanies.

With the outbreak of World War I Joyce moved his family to Zürich and began work on his most famous novel, *Ulysses*. His one play, *Exiles*, was published in 1918. Gifts from sympathetic patrons such as Harriet Shaw Weaver and Edith Rockefeller McCormick helped ease his family's poverty while he wrote the novel. Weaver, the editor of *The Egoist*, published *A Portrait of the Artist as a Young Man* as a serial in the pages of her magazine.

In 1920 Joyce joined the American poet Ezra Pound (1885–1972) in Paris, where *Ulysses* was first published. The novel was loosely (very loosely) based on Homer's *Odyssey* (the story of the wanderings and homecoming of Odysseus, called Ulysses by the Romans); it featured three main characters: Stephen Dedalus, a mature version of the protagonist of *A Portrait of the Artist*; Leopold Bloom, an Irish Jew; and Molly Bloom, his unfaithful wife. *Ulysses* broke new literary ground in many ways. Using a carefully calculated mixture of literary techniques, Joyce re-created with unparalleled vividness and completeness the characters' psychological lives as they pass through a series of events that take place on one day—June 16, 1904—and eventually cross paths. The final chapter utilizes stream of consciousness to portray Molly Bloom's inner state as she drifts off to sleep at the end of the day; the long sentences lack any punctuation, and they capture Molly perfectly. The passage, with its final words, "yes I said yes I will Yes," has become a classic.

With the publication of *Ulysses* in 1922, Joyce became an internationally recognized writer. The book was banned in the United States on account of its sexually explicit passages. A New York District Court lifted the ban in 1933, in a historic decision that helped to establish the principle that works of artistic integrity could not be censored in the United States, no matter what their content.

In Joyce's final novel, *Finnegan's Wake*, he sought to portray history as a series of events that repeat themselves, and he used one family to represent all families. The initials of the main character, Humphrey Chimpden Earwicker, also stand for "Here Comes Everybody" and other phrases in the book. To emphasize the circular nature of history, the novel begins with the second part of a sentence: "riverrun, past Eve and Adam's, from swerve of shore to bend of bay, brings us by a commodius vicus of recirculation back to Howth Castle and Environs." It ends with the beginning of the sentence: "A way a lone a last a loved along the." Joyce combined words from different languages with English and incorporated figures, traditions, and other elements from different historical and modern cultures.

Ulysses is challenging, but *Finnegan's Wake* is so much more challenging that it has never drawn a wide audience—although Joseph Campbell, American popularizer of myth, has fascinated audiences with his reading and discussion of the many layers of meaning of the work. An excellent film version of the novel (1965) has also reached a somewhat wider audience. (The film version of *Ulysses* done in 1967 was much less successful.)

Joyce died in Zürich in 1941. *Stephen Hero*, his early version of *A Portrait of the Artist as a Young Man*, was published posthumously in 1944. And if you go to Dublin on June 16, you can join in the celebration of Bloomsday, and retrace Leopold Bloom's wanderings.

BIBLIOGRAPHY

Anderson, Chester G., *James Joyce and His World*, 1963; Ellmann, Richard, *James Joyce*, 1982; Grose, Kenneth H., *James Joyce*, 1975; Gross, John J., *James Joyce*, 1970.

Kafka, Franz

(July 3, 1883–June 3, 1924)
Novelist, Short-Story Writer

The German-language writer Franz Kafka never gained fame in his lifetime, but his dark depictions of individuals alienated from twentieth-century culture became classics soon after his death. The strange, ominous, dreamlike quality of Kafka's stories gave rise to the term "Kafkaesque" used to describe such conditions in general.

Kafka was born to Jewish parents in what is now the Czech Republic. His father, Hermann Kafka, a merchant, was an overbearing and demanding figure whose shadow obscured the sun and whose expectations tormented Kafka all his life. In school Kafka was an exceptional student. He graduated from the University of Prague, studied law, and worked in insurance by day and as a writer by night—a pattern that distressed him, yet continued almost until his death. Although Kafka excelled in school and at work, he found himself philosophically at odds with both and constantly questioned the relevance of what he did.

In 1902 Kafka met his friend, editor, and biographer Max Brod, who encouraged him to write. Although his stories unfold in bizarre, fantastic ways, his writing style is clear and straightforward. Kafka's work circulated among a small number of literary enthusiasts, but with the exception of a few short stories, his writings were not published until after his death.

Two of Kafka's semiautobiographical novels, *The Trial* (1925) and *The Castle* (1926), are similar in their portrayals of an individual caught in a nightmarish world in which he cannot find the justice he craves, in which nothing turns out as he expects it to. In *The Trial*, a harmless bureaucrat, Joseph K., "without having done anything wrong," finds himself "arrested one fine morning." He is never told what his offense is. After a long series of appeals, appearances in court, and strange episodes at the bank where he works, he submits to his fate, execution. The K. of *The Castle* is a stronger, more rebellious figure but nevertheless finds himself caught in a similar web of accusations and senseless oc-

Franz Kafka (Fragment Publishing)

currences. He is sent to a village as a land surveyor, is dismayed to find that nobody believes he is supposed to be there, and is repeatedly denied admission to the castle in the village. Kafka never finished the final chapter of *The Castle*, but he allegedly told Brod that K. was to die of exhaustion. In both of these works, the character at odds with the horrors of his surroundings lacks the strength to overcome them, paralleling Kafka's own dilemma.

A second prominent theme in Kafka's work is a son's conflict with a dominant father, an obvious reflection of his own experience. This theme appears in short stories such as "The Judgment" (1912), in which a son obeys his father's order to commit suicide. Kafka's other short stories include "The Metamorphosis" (1915), "In the Penal Colony" (1919), and "A Hunger Artist" (1924).

In "The Metamorphosis," the main character, Gregor Samsa, who has sacrificed everything to take care of his family, wakes up one morning and finds he has turned into a giant insect. At first he feels a certain joy in being freed from the meaningless drudgery of a job he hates, but his family finds him disgusting and he cannot get the nourishment he craves. They continue to feed him, but he stops eating and eventually starves to death, much to his family's relief. The parallels with Kafka's own situation are obvious, but Kafka tells the story with humor, and with such clarity that it seems to shed light on a universal dilemma.

Kafka was diagnosed with tuberculosis in 1917 and was ill for much of the rest of his life. He was involved in several failed love affairs but never married. His early death in 1924, at age 41, perhaps spared him the ultimate fate of his three sisters, who died in Nazi concentration camps. Brod defied Kafka's request to burn his manuscripts and had them published instead. In addition to *The Trial* and *The Castle*, he published a third novel, *Amerika* (1927) as well as a number of unpublished short stories. Kafka's novels were first translated into English by Willa and Edwin Muir in the 1930s.

BIBLIOGRAPHY

Brod, Max, *Franz Kafka: A Biography*, 1947; David, Claude, *Franz Kafka*, 1989; Fickert, Kurt J., *Franz Kafka, Life, Work, and Criticism*, 1984; Osborne, Charles, *Kafka*, 1968.

Kahlo, Frida

(July 6, 1907–July 13, 1954)
Painter

The wife of the Mexican painter and muralist DIEGO RIVERA, Frida Kahlo de Rivera is best known for her psychologically revealing self-portraits. Influenced in her early career by Rivera and later, to some extent, by the Surrealists, she combined folk art, fantasy, and realism in her work.

Kahlo was born Magdalena Carmen Frida Kahlo y Calderón in Coyoacán, Mexico. Her father, Wilhelm Kahlo, was of Hungarian-Jewish ancestry and changed his name to Guillermo when he immigrated from Germany. His second wife, Matilde Calderón, was Frida's mother and a devout Catholic. As a child, Kahlo witnessed the Mexican Revolution (1914–1916), which reduced the fortunes of her relatively prosperous family. She was stricken with polio at the age of 6, leaving her with a permanently deformed leg.

Kahlo's father, a successful photographer and amateur painter with an interest in Mexico's archaeology, encouraged her creativity. Her mother was less influential in her life—Kahlo absorbed none of her piety and religiosity. In 1922, she entered the National Preparatory School in Mexico City. At school, Kahlo was something of a tomboy, read voraciously, and earned a reputation for her rebellious attitude toward her instructors. Rivera was then working on his mural at the school, and it was there that Kahlo first met him.

In 1925, Kahlo suffered a major physical setback when a trolley collided with the bus on which she was riding. She was pierced through her abdomen with a handrail, suffered a broken spinal column, and sustained several other injuries. After more than thirty operations throughout her life, she never fully recovered from her wounds. As she convalesced, she taught herself to paint.

Most of Kahlo's paintings are self-portraits that reflect her emotional and physical pain. Of her own features, she usually exaggerated her eyebrows. She painted in a simple, primitive style, using expanses of color and interjecting objects to emphasize her emotional state. Elements of Mexican folk art and tradition recur in the paintings, and Kahlo herself preferred to wear traditional Indian dress. Many paintings, such as her portrait of the horticulturalist and hybridist *Luther Burbank* (1931), employ fantastic elements. In this work, Kahlo depicted Burbank as part man and part plant.

While Rivera traveled in the United States working on his mural commissions, Kahlo accompanied him and continued to paint herself. Her inability to bear children was a constant source of distress for her and the subject of several works. *Henry Ford Hospital* (1932), a portrayal of a miscarriage, is one of her many graphic and bloody depictions of her struggles. *A Few Small Nips* (1933), a depiction of the murder of a young girl, is one of her most violent paintings. In *My Grandparents, My Parents and I* (1936), she depicts her family tree. As a small child, she stands in front of the imposing portraits of her parents, with the faces of her grandparents in the background. A baby is shown in her mother's womb, painted on top of a form that otherwise reveals only external features—a common element in Kahlo's work.

The stormy relationship between Rivera and Kahlo inspired many self-portraits and portraits of her with her husband. A series of affairs on both sides—which in Kahlo's case also included homosexual affairs—complicated their relationship. One of her most noteworthy extramarital relationships—with the exiled Bolshevik Leon Trotsky—came when Trotsky and his wife took refuge in Mexico in the 1930s. She and Rivera divorced in 1939 and remarried in 1941.

In 1938, Kahlo met the Surrealist ANDRÉ BRETON when he came with his wife to Mexico. With Breton's assistance, she exhibited New York City in 1938 and in Paris the following year.

Critics began to label her work "Surrealistic," and paintings such as *The Broken Column* (1944) and *Moses* (1945) employ many fantastic elements. *The Love Embrace of the Universe, the Earth (Mexico), Diego, Me and Señor Xolotl* (1949) depicts Kahlo in a red dress in the arms of an earth goddess, and a nude, infant-sized Diego in her arms. Like her husband, Kahlo was a dedicated Communist throughout her adult life and created a number of political paintings, including *Marxism Will Give Health to the Sick* (1954). After the couple's break with Trotsky, both were briefly implicated as conspirators in his 1940 assassination.

Her work grew increasingly popular during the 1940s, as her physical and emotional pain grew stronger. In 1943, she became a professor of painting at La Esmerelda, the Education Ministry's School of Fine Arts. *The Wounded Deer* (1946), a reflection of her suffering, depicts her own head on the body of a deer wounded by arrows. Kahlo painted *Tree of Hope* (1946), showing her partially nude body with surgical gashes and another figure of herself in a red dress, after one of her spinal operations.

Kahlo's first and only solo exhibition in Mexico City came in 1953, just before she died. The ailing artist, with a long-established reputation for outrageous behavior, surprised her guests when she had herself carried in on a stretcher and spent the evening on a bed in the midst of the exhibition. After the amputation of part of a gangrenous leg, Kahlo never recovered her emotional health. Her death in 1954 was attributed to an illness, but some speculate she committed suicide. Kahlo's diaries and letters were published in 1995.

BIBLIOGRAPHY

Herrera, Hayden, *Frida: A Biography of Frida Kahlo*, 1983; Herrera, Hayden, *Frida Kahlo: The Paintings*, 1991.

Kandinsky, Wassily

(December 16, 1866–December 13, 1944)
Painter, Teacher, Theorist

The Russian-born painter Wassily Kandinsky founded the Munich group Der Blaue Reiter (The Blue Rider) in 1911. His theories and paintings, which evolved toward pure abstraction beginning in 1909, contributed heavily to the later development of Abstract Expressionism.

Kandinsky was born Vasily Vasilyevich Kandinsky into a wealthy family in Moscow. His mother was descended from a Mongolian princess. As a child he traveled widely in Europe with his family. The family moved to Odessa in 1871, and Kandinsky attended school and studied music. In his youth he was a keen observer of colors, and he also began painting. In 1886 he enrolled in the University of Moscow, where he earned a doctorate in economics and law. Kandinsky also studied in the areas of ethnology and anthropology, and the Russian folk art he discovered impressed him, as did the architecture and colors of Moscow. Among painters, he was first impressed by Rembrandt.

Kandinsky taught at the university and later took a position at a Moscow printing company. In 1896, he gave up his career to become a painter and moved to Munich. For several years he attended art school, first under Anton Azbé and then at the Munich Academy under Franz von Stuck. Kandinsky associated himself and exhibited with avant-garde groups. In 1901 he helped found the Phalanx, a Munich group that sought to exhibit the work of young, unknown artists. The group exhibited until 1904, and Kandinsky's work gained a measure of critical acclaim as a result of the exhibitions.

Although his later work became highly abstract, Kandinsky used recognizable forms in his early paintings. Color was his main preoccupation in creating art during all phases of his career. He explored the relationships between color and sound and used rich color in his paintings. His early art draws from many styles, including Fauvism, Impressionism, Pointillism, and Jugendstil (or Art Nouveau). Among his early paintings are *Ancient Town* (1902) and the impressionistic *The Sluice* (1902).

In 1902 he met the painter Gabriele Münter, who was a student at Kandinsky's newly founded Phalanx School. The two traveled extensively in Europe and in Tunisia over the next few years, and in 1909 they settled in a house in Murnau. The same year, he founded the New Artists' Association with the painter Alexey Von Jawlensky. At this time, Kandinsky's ever-evolving painting style began to move toward pure abstraction. Works such as *Improvisation No. 3* (1909) and *Trojka* (1911) show his drift toward nonobjective art.

Paintings such as *The Black Arc* (1912) and *Composition 1914* announced his arrival at pure Abstract Expressionism. The latter, in addition, shows the beginning of his interest in geometric forms, a direction he would take in his art over the next several years in Russia and again in Germany. With abstraction, Kandisnky sought to portray inner spiritual perception rather than exterior objective reality.

In 1914 he returned to Russia, where he married Nina Andreevskaya in 1917. During his seven-year stay, he served in several posts in the new Soviet Union. He held professorships at the Moscow Academy of Fine Arts and the University of Moscow, became a member of the People's Commissariat for Public Instruction, and helped found the Institute of Artistic Culture, the Russian Academy of Artistic Sciences, and several museums.

By 1921, the Soviet government's increasing insistence on art created in the style of Socialist Realism spurred Kandinsky to return to Germany. He took a teaching post at the Bauhaus School of Architecture and Applied Art, where the Swiss painter PAUL KLEE also taught. He continued his study of geometric shapes and abstraction, as evident in paintings such as *Small Worlds II* (1922) and *Yellow-Red-Blue* (1925). When the Nazis closed the Bauhaus in 1933 and denounced his art as "degenerate," Kandinsky moved to Neuilly-sur-Seine, a suburb of Paris, where he spent the remainder of his life.

Kandinsky's later paintings include *Dominant Curve* (1936), *Various Actions* (1941), and *White Balancing Act* (1944).

Other works include woodcuts and his theoretical treatises on abstraction, *Concerning the Spiritual in Art* (1912) and *Point and Line to Plane* (1926).

BIBLIOGRAPHY

Grohmann, Will, *Wassily Kandinsky: Life and Work*, 1958; Selz, Peter, *German Expressionist Painting*, 1957.

Karajan, Herbert von

(April 5, 1908–July 16, 1989)
Conductor

Herbert von Karajan built his career conducting both opera and orchestra in Nazi Germany. After World War II, he emerged as one of the world's leading conductors of the standard repertoire and conducted prominent international orchestras and at the major opera houses. Unlike his contemporaries, Karajan worked primarily in Europe and relatively little in the United States.

Karajan was born in Salzburg, Austria. The original family surname—Karajanis—is of Greek origin. After moving from Greece, Karajan family members received two baronetcies. Karajan's father, however, was a doctor and played the clarinet. At a young age, Karajan showed considerable talent on the piano, and he was performing in public by the time he was 10. His parents sent him to study at the Mozarteum in Salzburg. The Mozarteum's director, Bernhard Paumgartner, took a special interest in Karajan and introduced him to Italian art. He next studied at the University of Vienna, followed by the Academy of Music. At the latter, he took his first conducting class under Alexander Wunderer.

Although he was well established as a pianist in Salzburg, he did not chance upon an opportunity to conduct an orchestra until he was 20. For his debut he conducted Gioacchino Rossini's *William Tell* overture. The following year he made his professional debut conducting Richard Strauss's tone poem *Don Juan*, Peter Ilych Tchaikovsky's *Fifth Symphony*, and other works.

The latter performance generated an offer to conduct opera in Ulm, Germany, in spite of the fact that he had no experience conducting opera. Karajan remained at Ulm until 1934, working with the limited resources of a small orchestra and a small theater. He staged six operas a year, including many works by Strauss and Richard Wagner (1813–1883). During this time he also attended many performances conducted by ARTURO TOSCANINI. After being fired from Ulm (by a superior who thought he should move on to a better position), he took a job at the Aachen Theatre. The following year he became Germany's youngest Kapellmeister (musical director) at Aachen. There he had a larger orchestra and theater to work with.

His appointment coincided with the rise of the National Socialists in Germany. While many of his Jewish and dissenting non-Jewish musical colleagues were fired and forced from the country, Karajan's ca-

Herbert von Karajan (Deutsche Gramaphone)

reer began to take off. In a decision that would later cost his reputation dearly, he joined the Nazi party in 1935 in order to keep his position. With the absence of competition (except for his rival WILHELM FÜRTWANGLER), Karajan's career blossomed in World War II Germany.

In 1937 Karajan debuted at the Vienna State Opera conducting Wagner's *Tristan und Isolde*. The following year he married Elmy Holgerloef, from whom he separated three years later. In 1938 he made his conducting debut with the Berlin Philharmonic, conducting selections from Mozart, Brahms, and MAURICE RAVEL. Karajan stayed at Aachen until 1941, when he moved full time to the Berlin State Opera.

In 1944 Karajan fled Germany. After the war ended, he was prohibited from con-

ducting until Allied authorities cleared his name, which they quickly did. In 1947 he made a series of recordings for EMI with the Vienna Philharmonic, including works by Brahms and Beethoven. With ELISABETH SCHWARZKOPF and Hans Hotter, he recorded Brahms's *German Requiem*. Karajan made many other recordings throughout his career, including *Il Trovatore* and *Madame Butterfly* with the American soprano Maria Callas. In the postwar years, his recordings contributed to his rising international reputation.

Karajan was instrumental in founding the London Philharmonia in 1948. He was chief conductor at Milan's La Scala from 1949 to 1956. In 1953 he conducted the world premiere of CARL ORFF's *Trionfo d'Afrodite*, which starred Schwarzkopf. The following year at La Scala, he conducted a highly successful production of Gaetano Donizetti's *Lucia di Lammermoor* with Callas in the lead role. In 1955 he became music director of the Berlin Philharmonic, was appointed conductor for life, and made his debut in the United States. His past membership in the Nazi party provoked a storm of protest in the United States, and Karajan made few trips across the Atlantic during his career.

From 1956 to 1964 Karajan served as principal conductor at the Vienna State Opera. Over much protest, he abolished the long established *stagione* system, in which a core group of singers perform all of the lead roles in a given season. Karajan instead believed the world's opera houses should trade productions. Among his successes in Vienna were CLAUDE DE-BUSSY's *Pélleas and Mélisande*, Wagner's *Parsifal;* and Giuseppe Verdi's *Otello.*

In his later career, Karajan was also heavily involved in the annual Salzburg Festival and in 1967 founded the Salzburg Easter Festival. He conducted many other orchestras around the world—the New York Philharmonic, the Orchestre de Paris (1969–1970), and others. Although his later years with the Berlin Philharmonic were troubled, he stayed there until just a few months before his death in 1989.

As a conductor, Karajan was known for his objective and precise approach to music. He conducted from memory and required long, rigorous rehearsals before he gave performances. Karajan was at home with both German and Italian opera as well as orchestras. He preferred the standard repertoire to modern music and conducted relatively little of the latter.

BIBLIOGRAPHY

Lang, Klaus, *The Karajan Dossier,* 1992; Robinson, Paul, *Karajan,* 1975; Vaughan, Roger, *Herbert von Karajan: A Biographical Portrait,* 1985.

Karsavina, Tamara

(March 9/10, 1885–May 26, 1978)
Dancer, Teacher

Tamara Platonovna Karsavina was a lead ballerina in SERGEY DIAGHILEV's Ballets Russes from 1909 to 1922. Originally trained in the classical Russian techniques, she later helped popularize MICHEL FOKINE's modern choreographic style. During her early years with the Ballets Russes she frequently danced lead roles with VASLAV NIJINSKY, and in the later part of her career she worked with many other prominent dancers and choreographers.

Karsavina was born in St. Petersburg, Russia. Her father, the dancer Platon Karsavin, charmed her with his stories of the theater when she was young. It was not he, however, who initially steered her into dancing. Her mother secretly took her to the retired dancer Vera Zhukova for lessons and to see ballets. When her ambi-

Tamara Karsavina (Rex Features Ltd.)

tion to dance and her talent became obvious, her father agreed to give her lessons.

As a child, Karsavina entered the Imperial Ballet School in St. Petersburg. At that time, the French-born choreographer Marius Petipa (1818–1910) was the major influence on the style of the Imperial Ballet. Petipa, a classical stylist, stressed choreography above the other elements of a production. Karsavina studied under Pavel Gerdt and the aged Swedish dancer Christian Johannson, eventually becoming one of the star pupils at the Imperial Ballet School. She danced in productions of *Paquita*, *La fille mal gardée*, and others and was chosen to dance at the coronation of Nicholas II in 1896. Among her fellow students was ANNA PAVLOVA.

At the Chinese Theatre of Tsarskoe Selo, Karsavina danced with Fokine and Julie Sedova in *Lac des Cygnes (Swan Lake)*. She appeared again with Fokine in *Le pêcheur et la perle (The Fisher and the Pearl)*. Upon her graduation from the Imperial Ballet School, Karsavina joined the company at the Mariinsky Theatre (renamed the Kirov Theatre in 1935), dancing her debut in *Javotte* in 1902.

Karsavina danced her first leading role in *The Awakening of Flora*, a one-act ballet with Fokine as Apollo. Other productions in which she appeared include *Fairy Doll* (1904), for which LEON BAKST designed the scenery; *Giselle*; *A Life for the Tsar*, *The Trial of Damis*; the one-act ballet *Graziella*; *Humpbacked Horse* (1906), in which she danced the Tsar Maiden; and *Corsair*, in which she danced Medora. In 1904 she studied briefly in Italy, practicing the Italian methods, which, in contrast with her previous training, stressed precision in movement over grace and fluidity.

In a part of *Roxana*, Karsavina first appeared with Nijinsky in 1907. Both Nijinsky and Karsavina were to join Diaghilev's Ballets Russes, Karsavina in 1909. Both danced in the 1910 Paris premiere of *Carnaval*, a Fokine-Bakst collaboration. Nijinsky and Karsavina danced the lead roles in *Daphnis et Chloé*, choreographed by Fokine with music by Maurice Ravel, in Paris in 1912.

Dancing in many other lead roles in Fokine's works, Karsavina helped popularize his modern style of choreography. Fokine rejected the division of movement from the music, scenery, and costumes Petipa and other classical choreographers sought, seeking instead to integrate all of these elements with expressive movement. With Diaghilev's help, he collaborated with many famous artists and composers for the scenery and music of the ballets. Karsavina danced lead parts in such Fokine ballets as *Les Sylphides*, *Le Spectre de la Rose* (with Nijinsky), *Firebird*, *Petrushka*, *Pavillon d'Armide*, and *Schéhérezade*.

Karsavina also worked with other prominent figures, including LÉONIDE MASSINE (in his *The Three-Cornered Hat* and *Pulcinella*) and FEODOR CHALIAPIN. She married the British diplomat Henry James Bruce and in 1918 settled with him in England. After leaving the Ballets Russes in 1922, Karsavina danced with the Ballet Rambert and for FREDERICK ASHTON.

She helped found the Royal Academy of Dancing in 1920, and among the students she taught was MARGOT FONTEYN. Karsavina's writings include articles on dance; her autobiography, *Theatre Street* (1930); and *Classical Ballet: The Flow of Movement* (1962).

BIBLIOGRAPHY

Karsavina, Tamara, *Theatre Street: The Reminiscences of Tamara Karsavina*, 1931.

Kiefer, Anselm

(March 8, 1945–)
Painter, Sculptor, Photographer

A leading Neo-Expressionist artist of the late twentieth century, Anselm Kiefer explores in his paintings symbolic mythological and religious themes. His early paintings derive from both the Germanic and Christian traditions and investigate issues of contemporary German history, notably the Nazi era. Many of Kiefer's later paintings are inspired by Hebrew themes. Kiefer's paintings are marked by their chaotic and pessimistic tones and unusual textures. With heavy brush strokes, he applies bold color in a manner that evokes a chaotic, disturbing atmosphere. Although Kiefer uses traditional themes, his way of painting them suggests a profound unease with what the modern world has made of those traditions.

Kiefer was born in Donaueschingen, Germany. Before determining to devote his life to art, he studied law and French literature at the University of Freiburg, beginning in 1966. Without completing his curriculum, he left to study art, enrolling in the State Academy of Fine Arts in Karlsruhe in 1969. Kiefer next studied in Düsseldorf under the avant-garde artist and political activist Joseph Beuys.

Kiefer's early works include many wood interiors that incorporate Christian and Germanic mythological themes. In *Father, Son, Holy Ghost* (1973), the three figures of the Trinity are represented as flames burning in three chairs untouched by the fire, which sit in a wood interior. Kiefer again depicts the Trinity as three flaming spirits in *Quaternity* (1973), and this time he adds the figure of the serpent. He created a series entitled *The Parsifal Room* (1973), inspired by the operas of Richard Wagner (1813–1883), for an exhibition in Amsterdam.

Germany's Spiritual Heroes (1973) portrays flaming spirits in a wood interior. Among his other wood interiors are *Notung* (1973), the title of which is taken from the mythological Wotan's sword; and *Resurrexit* (1973). Kiefer has also painted many bleak, pessimistic landscapes such as *March Heath* (1974) and *Painting of the Scorched Earth* (1974).

Earlier paintings allude to contemporary German history, particularly the National Socialist era, and in works such as *Operation Sea Lion* (1975) he began to address the past more directly. One of several "Operation" paintings, it takes its

Anselm Kiefer (AKG)

title from Adolf Hitler's planned but never realized invasion of England. These grim portrayals, dominated by blacks and dark blues, evoke the desolation and destruction of war.

The 1980s marked a major turning point in Kiefer's work, both in its popularity and its style. The Venice Biennale of 1980 popularized his work and established him as an international artist. Previously not well known, he now began to exhibit in major cities around the world. During that decade he also turned toward Old Testament themes in works such as *Shulamite* (1983), *Cherubim and Seraphim* (1983), and *Exodus of Egypt* (1982–1983), a bent further strengthened by his

visit to Israel in 1984. Other later paintings include *Osiris and Isis* (1985–1987) and *Zimzum* (1990).

Among Kiefer's other works are *Interiors* (1981), two works entitled *Tomb of the Unknown Painter* (1974 and 1983), *Ways of the Worldly Wisdom: Arminius's Battle* (1978–1980), *Waterloo, Waterloo, the Earth Still Shakes* (1982), sculptures, photographs, and hand-made books.

BIBLIOGRAPHY

Anselm Kiefer, 1984; Gilmour, John, *Fire on the Earth: Anselm Kiefer and the Postmodern World*, 1990; Rosenthal, Mark, *Anselm Kiefer*, 1987.

Kipling, Rudyard

(December 30, 1865–January 18, 1936)
Short-Story Writer, Novelist, Poet

The author of the well-known children's tales *The Jungle Books* and *Just So Stories*, Joseph Rudyard Kipling also wrote novels, short stories, and poetry, all immensely popular around the turn of the century. He was awarded the Nobel Prize for Literature in 1907, "in consideration of the power of observation, originality of imagination, virility of ideas, and remarkable talent for narration which characterize the creations of this world-famous author." On account of his controversial support for British colonialism, however, his literary reputation has suffered among critics since World War I.

Kipling was born in Bombay, India, to upper-middle-class British parents and learned to speak Hindi before he spoke English. His father was professor of Architectural Sculpture at the Bombay School of Art and curator of the Lahore museum. The family was well connected through his mother, Alice Macdonald. One of her sisters was the mother of the future prime minister Stanley Baldwin, and two were married to the painters Sir Edward Poynter and Sir Edward Burne-Jones.

When Kipling was 6, his parents took him with his sister to England, as was usual at that time because the climate of India was felt to be unhealthy for children, and left them with the Holloway family in Southsea. Life with Mrs. Holloway, a cruel and vindictive woman,

Kipling's *Departmental Ditties* (1886), a volume of satirical verse, was published while he wrote for the *Gazette* and targeted the prejudices of Englishmen unfamiliar with India and corruption in the British service. During his time in India he also published several volumes of short stories in a similar vein, including *Soldiers Three, The Phantom Rickshaw, Wee Willie Winkie,* and *Plain Tales from the Hills,* all of which were published in 1888.

In 1889, Kipling returned to England. He met W. E. Henly, editor of the *Scots Observer,* which published many of the verses that later became his *Barrack-Room Ballads* (1892). The volume's poems include "Mandalay" and "Gunga Din," the latter narrated by a British private praising an Indian water boy shot during battle, and ending with the famous lines,

Though I've belted you an' flayed you,
By the livin' Gawd that made you,
You're a better man than I am, Gunga Din.

Another volume of verse, *The Five Nations,* was published in 1903 and contains "Recessional," a poetic prayer urging Britain not to grow "drunk with sight of power." Much of Kipling's poetry skillfully incorporates common colloquialisms in rhymed and strongly rhythmical verse. T. S. ELIOT admired his work, praising the best of it as great verse, if not real poetry.

Kipling published his novel *The Light That Failed,* a story about the war correspondent and artist Dick Heldar, in 1890. Heldar's suffering as a child reflects Kipling's, and like Kipling, Heldar suffers from poor eyesight. He returns to England after his eyes are injured in the war

Rudyard Kipling, cartoon by Will Owen (Ann Ronan/Image Select)

proved a traumatic experience for Kipling, one that is reflected in his fiction. He left the family after five years and attended a boarding school, the United Services College at Westward Ho, Devon. There he edited the *United Services College Chronicle* and particularly liked to read the English classics.

With the assistance of his mother, he published his first book, *School Boy Lyrics,* in 1881. *Echoes,* another volume, which also contained his sister's poetry, followed in 1884. Meanwhile, Kipling had returned to India (1882) and taken a job with the *Civil and Military Gazette.* Using a number of pseudonyms, he reported for the *Gazette* and contributed short stories and verse to the paper.

and works to finish painting his masterpiece while his sight allows. The novel appeared serially before its publication in book form, and Kipling provided two different endings, the first happy and the second tragic.

In 1892 Kipling married Caroline Balestier, sister of the American publisher and writer Wolcott Balestier, with whom he coauthored the romance *The Naulahka, a Story of West and East* (1892), set in both India and Colorado. Kipling lived briefly with his wife in her hometown of Brattleboro, Vermont. They returned to England after a bitter land dispute with her brother.

The novel *Captains Courageous, A Story of the Grand Banks* (1897) is a moral tale. When the spoiled and wealthy Harvey Cheyne is swept into the water from his ocean liner, the crew of the fishing schooner *We're Here* picks him up. The captain of the schooner forces him to work with the crew and treats him with the same mixture of toughness and love he shows his own son, transforming him into a decent and hardworking individual. *Stalky & Co.* (1899), about three boys at a British school and the many ingenious ways they give their teachers a hard time, reflects Kipling's own experiences at the United Services College.

Of all Kipling's books, *Kim* (1901) reflects most strongly Kipling's intimate knowledge and love of India, and many critics see it as his best long book, and still an excellent introduction to India. Kim is the son of an Irish soldier, long dead, and an Indian mother, who has grown up utterly at home in the bazaars and on the roads of India. He is found and educated by his father's regiment, and much of the book is an engrossing account of his adventures on the roads in the company of a Tibetan lama, first during vacations from school and then as an agent for the British secret service.

In 1902, Kipling purchased a home in Sussex, where he lived for the rest of his life. From 1900 to 1908, he spent some of his time in South Africa in a house given to him by the diamond magnate Cecil Rhodes. Rhodes solidified Kipling's imperialistic outlook, born of a belief that Britain was destined to civilize other lands.

Kipling is also remembered for his classic children's tales. *The Jungle Books* (1894–1895) is a series of adventure stories connected by verses. The protagonist of the stories, Mowgli, wanders into the jungle when he is so young he can barely walk, is raised by a family of wolves, and becomes a leader among the wolves. *The Jungle Books* also include other stories that focus on animals, one a protest against the slaughter of the seals, another the famous "Rikki Tikki Tavi," about an Indian mongoose who battle the menacing cobras Nag and Nagina to protect his adoptive human family. *Just So Stories for Little Children* (1902) includes "The Elephant's Child," which tells why elephants have trunks, "How the Camel Got His Hump," and other funny and fantastic "How" tales, first told to his own children, as were the vivid stories of old England, especially the Sussex countryside he loved, in *Puck of Pook's Hill* (1906) and *Rewards and Fairies* (1910).

Kipling's other works include the short-story collections *Life's Handicap* (1891), *Many Inventions* (1893), *Actions and Reactions* (1909), and *Limits and Renewals* (1932); the travel sketches in *From Sea to Sea* (1899); *Something of Myself* (1941), an unfinished autobiographical piece; and *The Irish Guards in the Great War,* a military history of the Irish Guards, with which his only son was fighting when he was killed in World War I.

Kipling lost favor with many in the reading public after World War I, and many now dismiss his writing for adults as imperialist propaganda. Nevertheless, many of his works have an energy and a sense of life that still wins him enthusiastic readers, and his later stories, more complex and challenging, have won praise from modern critics, who see them as his best work.

BIBLIOGRAPHY

Fido, Martin, *Rudyard Kipling,* 1974; Seymour-Smith, Martin, *Rudyard Kipling,* 1989; Shahane, Vasant A., *Rudyard Kipling: Activist and Artist,* 1973; Tompkins, J. M. S., *The Art of Rudyard Kipling* (1965).

Kirchner, Ernst Ludwig

(May 6, 1880–June 15, 1938)
Painter, Graphic Artist, Illustrator

The painter Ernst Ludwig Kirchner helped found and was widely considered the leader of Die Brücke (The Bridge), the first group of German Expressionist painters. Die Brücke flourished in the first decade of the twentieth century, leading to other Expressionist movements in Germany and elsewhere in the world. After the group's dissolution in 1913, Kirchner continued to paint in expressionistic styles and produced a large body of highly acclaimed expressionistic woodcuts.

Kirchner was born in Aschaffenberg, Bavaria. His family moved to Saxony when he was 9, and he attended the Chemnitz Realgymnasium. Kirchner's interest in painting developed when he was a child. Although his father, a teacher, was also interested in painting, he discouraged Kirchner from pursuing a profession that promised little reward. Accordingly, from 1901 to 1905 Kirchner studied architecture at the Technical College in Dresden, with a year in 1903–1904 to study painting in Munich.

The earliest influences on Kirchner were the German Gothic artists, especially Albrecht Dürer (1471–1528). He was also heavily influenced by the Norwegian Expressionist painter EDVARD MUNCH, the French Postimpressionist Vincent van Gogh, and African and Oceanic art. His first paintings, such as *Self Portrait* (1904), *Deciduous Forest* (1904), and many landscapes, were influenced by Neo-Impressionism.

With fellow architecture students KARL SCHMIDT-ROTTLUFF, Fritz Bleyl, and Erich Heckel (some of whom are depicted in Kirchner's 1925 painting *The Painters of the Brücke*), Kirchner founded Die Brücke in 1905. EMIL NOLDE joined the group later. Die Brücke members opposed the stiff old order embodied in Kaiser Wilhelm II and in academic art. As stated in their 1906 manifesto, they wanted to serve as a "bridge" between the old order and a new more open German society that would encourage free expression and emotion. The members of Die Brücke worked together in Dresden, exhibited together, and frequently traveled to local lakes. Although they did not call themselves "Expressionists," the term was later applied to them, and seems to describe them accurately.

The Expressionists sought to portray the subjective and emotional aspects of their subjects with the use of loose, distorted forms and intense colors. In general, they held a pessimistic and critical view of society. Die Brücke exhibited with another Expressionist group, Der Blaue Reiter (The Blue Rider), whose members included painters PAUL KLEE, WASSILY KANDINSKY, and Gabriele Münter. The beginnings of German Expressionism, influenced by Neo-Impressionism, coincided roughly with a similar movement, Fauvism, in France. In 1911, Die Brücke relocated to Berlin.

Kirchner's painting style evolved continuously throughout his life. The smooth, rounded lines characteristic of paintings such as *Girl under Japanese Parasol* (1909) and *Nude with Hat* (1911) gave way to more violent, elongated, and jagged forms around 1912 and 1913. Aggressive, almost threatening women appear as frequent subjects in his work, as do nudes and city scenes. As with all of the Expressionists, his use of color was generally bold and intended to generate a strong emotional impact. Characteristic paintings from these years are *Street Scene* (1912), *Five Women on the Street* (1913), and *Lady with Green Hat* (1913). The year 1913 also saw the breakup of Die Brücke, largely spurred by its members' disapproval of Kirchner's history of the group, *Chronik der Brücke* (1913).

Aside from painting, Kirchner produced more than 2,000 woodcuts, prints, and lithographs. After Die Brücke's move to Berlin in 1911, he contributed a number of woodcuts to the avant-garde periodical *Der Sturm*. He also completed illustrations for the novel *Peter Schlemihl's Wonderful Story* (1915), by Adelbert von Chamisso (1781–1838).

Kirchner joined the German army in 1915, an experience that proved too traumatic for his fragile psyche. Several paintings on war themes, including *Soldiers in the Shower Room* (1915) and *Self-Portrait as Soldier* (1915), reveal his inner turmoil. The former shows a group of elongated, nude men crammed into a shower room, while the latter shows the artist in bold color with his hands cut off. Symbolically, the war had almost cut off the hands Kirchner used to paint. In 1917 he suffered a severe mental and physical breakdown. During his recovery, he painted frescoes on the sanitarium walls.

Following his recuperation, Kirchner moved permanently to Switzerland, leaving behind the tormented paintings of his life in Berlin. Into the 1920s he painted natural, serene Swiss landscapes and scenery, including *Frankfurt Cathedral* (1925). The boldness of his colors diminished somewhat in his later work, which also grew more abstract. The rise of the Nazis in Germany troubled Kirchner emotionally, and Nazi officials, who disliked the avant-garde and denounced his work, confiscated some of it. In 1938, depressed and in poor health, Kirchner committed suicide.

BIBLIOGRAPHY

Gordon, Donald E., *Ernst Ludwig Kirchner*, 1968; Selz, Peter, *German Expressionist Painting*, 1957.

Klee, Paul

(December 18, 1879–June 29, 1940)
Painter, Graphic Artist, Teacher, Theorist

Although he associated himself with German Expressionist artists in the early twentieth century, the Swiss painter Paul Klee developed an abstract artistic style that did not belong to any particular school. His drawings, paintings, watercolors, and other compositions influenced the Surrealists, who rose to prominence in the mid-1920s, and the later development of Abstract Expressionism.

Klee was born in Münchenbuchsee, near Bern, Switzerland. His father was a music teacher who came from a line of distinguished organists, and his mother was also a musician. He attended the local gymnasium and later a literary school in Bern, but his real education took place outside these institutions. As a child he wrote poetry and plays and played the violin. His grandmother introduced him to painting, and he began to paint around the age of 10.

In 1899 Klee moved to Munich, where he studied art first under Heinrich Knirr and then under Franz von Stuck at the Munich Academy. Under the latter he learned drawing, which he mastered before he began to paint seriously. Prior to his return to Bern, Klee traveled to Italy, where the rich artistic heritage of Rome impressed him. His early work was also influenced by his extensive reading of literature.

In 1905 Klee traveled to Paris, where he discovered the Impressionists, Post-impressionists, and the Belgian painter James Ensor (1860–1949), famous for his violently-colored canvases and grotesque forms. He moved to Munich permanently in 1906 and married the pianist Lily Stumpf the same year. They had one son, Felix. He earned a living as an illustrator, art teacher, and reviewer for the Swiss review *Die Alpen*, while his wife taught piano lessons. Klee's first major works were drawings and etchings, including the series *Inventions* (1903–1905). Many of the drawings and etchings, such as *Two Men Meet, Each Believing the Other to Be of Higher Rank* (1903) and *Crown Mania* (1904), are characterized by satire and caricatures of conventional life. He also completed a series of illustrations for an edition of Voltaire's classic satire, *Candide* in 1911–1912.

Klee discovered the avant-garde in Munich. In 1911 he joined Der Blaue Reiter (The Blue Rider), a group of artists founded by the painters WASSILY KANDINSKY and FRANZ MARC, both of whom became his personal friends. He had already developed an interest in Cubism when he visited Paris the following year and particularly admired the work of the French artist ROBERT DELAUNAY, who at the time was just beginning to paint his Orphic Cubist works.

Much of Klee's early work was done in black and white, but a 1914 trip to Tunisia with the painter August Macke led to his discovery of color. He painted a series of watercolors in Tunisia, such as the abstract landscapes *Red and White Domes* (1914) and *The Heart of St. Germain (Tunis)* (1914). After being drafted for and dismissed from the Germany army, Klee continued to paint landscapes during World War I.

Klee's paintings are generally abstract, use flat forms, and blend elements of fantasy and reality. In 1920 he accepted a

Boats under Moonlight by Paul Klee (Ann Ronan/Image Select)

teaching position at the Bauhaus, where Kandinsky also later taught. As Kandinsky had done several years earlier, Klee began to study geometric forms and to incorporate them into his work. Horizontal line patterns dominate watercolors such as *Parting at Evening Time* (1922) and *Architecture of Planes* (1923).

In 1930 Klee left the Bauhaus and took a position at the Düsseldorf Academy. In paintings rendered in the early 1930s, such as *Semicircle against Angle* (1932) and *Ad Parnassum* (1932), Klee used color technique derived from the Pointillists. With the rise of Hitler in Germany, Klee and his wife removed to Switzerland in 1933. He was among many artists whose work the Nazis labeled "degenerate," and some of his paintings were confiscated. In 1935 he fell ill with scleroderma, a disease affecting the connective tissues.

Klee completed many paintings in the years leading up to his death in 1940. These include *Angel, Still Feminine* (1939), *The Lovely (Female) Gardener* (1939), and the gloomy *Death and Fire* (1940). His theoretical work *Pedagogical Sketchbook* was published in 1925.

BIBLIOGRAPHY

Geelhaar, Christian, *Paul Klee: Life and Work*, 1982; Selz, Peter, *German Expressionist Painting*, 1957.

Klimt, Gustav

(July 14, 1862–February 6, 1918)
Painter, Designer

As the founder of the Vienna Secession in 1897, Gustav Klimt rejected the naturalistic, academic style that characterized Viennese painting around the turn of the century. He combined symbolic and allegorical elements with decorative design in his many murals and portraits. Klimt's work had a strong influence on a generation of younger German painters that included EGON SCHIELE and OSKAR KOKOSCHKA.

Klimt was born in Baumgarten, Austria, a suburb of Vienna. His mother was musically inclined but was never really able to pursue her talent outside the home. Klimt's father, a gold engraver, earned little money, and the family lived in relative poverty. Two of his siblings, especially his brother Ernst, would also demonstrate talent in the arts. Klimt's parents could not afford to send him to the gymnasium, so he attended the local bürgerschule. Having demonstrated talent in drawing at the bürgerschule, he entered the School of Arts and Crafts at the age of 14.

Klimt was trained in the prevailing academic style, the dominant influence on his work until the mid-1890s. In his early years he painted many large-scale, naturalistic murals under public commission. The Austrian emperor financed his murals for the Vienna Burgtheater, completed in 1888, and he also executed a mural for the staircase of the Kunsthistorisches Museum. During this time Klimt frequently worked in collaboration with his brother and with Franz Matsch.

The works *Idyll* (1884), a composition of male, female, and child seminudes, and *Love* (1895), depicting two lovers about to kiss, still demonstrate the naturalistic influence in his work. In 1897, however, Klimt pursued a new direction in his art when he founded the Vienna Secession. The Secessionists were influenced by both the British Arts and Crafts and the Art Nouveau movements. They sought to elevate craftsmanship to the status of art, rejecting the academic style of painting and incorporating decorative elements into their work.

Klimt's *Nuda Veritas* (1899), *Water Snakes* (1904–1907), and many subsequent works treat allegorical, often mythological themes. The former depicts a nude woman holding the mirror of truth with a snake—symbolic of deception—at her feet. His allegorical murals for the University of Vienna auditorium ceiling, *Philosophy*, *Medicine*, and *Jurisprudence* (1900–1902), are controversial, erotic works. *Medicine* combines sensuous female nudes, a skeleton symbolic of death, and an elaborately dressed Hygeia, the Greek goddess of health. The depiction generated complaints of pornography and was also controversial because it emphasizes the failures of medicine rather than its accomplishments.

Decorative elements are prominent in Klimt's well-known *Beethoven Frieze* (1902), but he attained the height of his decorative phase with his work for the Stoclet House (1909–1911). The house, designed by the Secessionist architect JOSEF HOFFMANN, was commissioned by the Belgian coal magnate Adolphe Stoclet. Stoclet gave his home's designers virtually unlimited finances to work with, and Klimt formed his resulting mosaics of precious stones, gold leaf, glass, enamel, coral, and other expensive materials.

Klimt's mosaic designs are flat, two-dimensional designs marked by their emphasis on decorative elements. Among his best-known works is *The Kiss* (1908), an erotic, mosaic-style picture of a man and woman in embrace. He contributed a number of designs to Hoffmann's interiors and also collaborated with Emilie Flöge in the creation of clothing and fabric. (Flöge, whose portrait he painted in 1902, was one of the numerous mistresses for whom he earned a reputation.)

Also among Klimt's works are numerous portraits of Viennese women, including *Frau Fritza Riedler* (1906), *Frau Adele Bloch-Bauer* (1907), and *Friederike-Maria Beer* (1916). Again, the figures are two-dimensional, with emphasis on the skin and the clothing. He painted numerous landscapes, such as *Unterach on the Attersee* (1915), inspired by the mountainous region of western Austria. Also among his works are many drawings, particularly of female nudes.

BIBLIOGRAPHY

Hofmann, Werner, *Gustav Klimt*, 1972; Whitford, Frank, *Gustav Klimt*, 1995.

Kokoschka, Oskar

(March 1, 1886–February 22, 1980)
Painter, Playwright, Poet, Short-Story Writer

The psychological portraits and landscapes of the Austrian painter Oskar Kokoschka are part of the German Expressionist movement in the early twentieth century. Aside from painting, for which he is most famous, Kokoschka wrote several plays that helped inaugurate Expressionism in the theater.

Kokoschka was born in Pöchlarn, Austria. His father, a talented goldsmith, could not support the family in an economy in which commercial production increasingly replaced the small craftsman. When Kokoschka was 3, his father moved the family to Vienna and made his living as a salesman. The family's unhappy financial circumstances were further aggravated by the death of Kokoschka's brother when Kokoschka was 5. Despite their poverty, Kokoschka acquired both his father's love of literature and his mother's love of nature. During his childhood and adolescence, he attended school in Vienna.

Kokoschka's first exposure to visual art came from his visits to museums and from the art that adorned the church his family attended. At the museums he developed an interest in masks, Japanese woodcuts, and Austrian baroque painters. At age 18, Kokoschka won a scholarship to study at the School of Arts and Crafts in Vienna, where he also taught.

In 1908, Kokoschka met the Viennese architect ADOLF LOOS. Loos was very interested in his work and introduced Kokoschka to other artists and intellectuals, some of whom he subsequently painted. Throughout his painting career, Kokoschka was primarily concerned with the human form. Before World War I, he painted many works he called "black portraits," in which he depicted people showing fear, discomfort, sadness, and insecurity. In his early work in general, he tailored color and form to express the psychological aspects of his subjects. Among the subjects of these portraits are the art historians *Hans Tietze and Erica Tietze-Conrat* (1909), the actor depicted in *The Trance Player* (1907–1908), and the poet *Peter Altenberg* (1909).

In 1909, Kokoschka traveled to Switzerland, where he continued painting portraits and began painting landscapes. Among the former is his portrait of the scholar *Auguste Forel* (1910), and among the latter is *Winter Landscape, Dent du Midi* (1909). In 1910, Kokoschka went to Berlin with Herwath Walden, to whose periodical *Der Sturm* (*The Storm*) he contributed a number of sketches. The following year he began a three-year affair with Alma Mahler, the widow of the Austrian composer Gustav Mahler (1860–1911). She appears in several of his works, which began to show heavier outline and more fluid forms than his earlier portraits. They include *Double Portrait (Oskar Kokoschka and Alma Mahler)* (1912) and *The Tempest* (1914).

Kokoschka enlisted in the Austrian army in 1914, fought in World War I, and was severely wounded on the Russian front in 1916. He had written Expressionist plays prior to the war, including *Murderer the Women's Hope* (1907) and *Sphinx and Strohmann*. Both were performed in Vienna and generated a scandal that cost him his teaching position at the School of Arts and Crafts. During his recovery from his wounds in Dresden, he wrote three plays, including *Orpheus and Eurydice* (1918).

From 1919 to 1924, Kokoschka taught at the Dresden Academy. His most noteworthy paintings between the two world wars are his numerous landscapes reflecting his extensive travels in Europe and the Middle East, including *Harbor of Marseilles* (1925), *Tower Bridge* (1925–1936), *London: Large Thames View* (1926), and *Jerusalem* (1929–1930). Like his portraits, Kokoschka's landscapes capture the human emotions associated with the subject, and they are characterized by his combination of light colors with heavy, broken brush strokes. In 1931 he again returned to Vienna, and in 1934 he moved to Prague, where he met his future wife Olda Palkovska.

Kokoschka's political paintings, many of which he completed during World War II, reflect his objection to the forms of totalitarianism that threatened Europe after World War I. The Nazis denounced Kokoschka's art as "degenerate," and he and his wife fled to London in 1938. There he painted a series of political works, including *The Red Egg* (1940–1941), *Anschluss-Alice in Wonderland* (1942), and *What We Are Fighting For* (1943).

Kokoschka's work was widely exhibited in Europe and the United States after World War II. In 1953 he settled in Switzerland. Among his later paintings are two three-part series on mythological themes, *Prometheus Saga* (1950) and *Thermopylae* (1954); *View of Hamburg Harbor* (1951); *Delphi* (1956); and

Herodotus (1960–1963). Kokoschka's other works include the short stories collected in *A Sea Ringed with Visions* (1956) and his autobiography, *My Life* (1964).

BIBLIOGRAPHY

Hodin, J. P., *Oskar Kokoschka, the Artist and His Time: A Biographical Study*, 1966; Kokoschka, Oskar, *My Life*, 1964; Whitford, Frank, *Oskar Kokoschka, A Life*, 1986.

Kollwitz, Käthe

(July 8, 1867–April 22, 1945)
Graphic Artist, Sculptor

Käthe Schmidt Kollwitz began her career in the atmosphere of the Expressionist movement in Germany in the early twentieth century. After 1893, she abandoned the painting of her formative years and devoted herself to lithographs, woodcuts, drawings, and sculpting. The personal devastation of war and the plight of the urban poor form the major themes in her work.

Kollwitz was born Käthe Schmidt into a middle-class family in Königsberg, East Prussia (now Kaliningrad, Russia). Both of her parents were associated with the Latitudinarian Community, a movement that formed as a reaction against Calvinism. After studying briefly with the painter Gustav Naujok, Kollwitz studied drawing and painting at the Women's Art College in Berlin, where she later taught, in 1885–1886. She began painting professionally in 1887, and in 1888–1889 she studied at the Women's Art College in Munich.

Her marriage to Dr. Karl Kollwitz in 1891 proved to be a significant influence on her life's work. Dr. Kollwitz, a physician, practiced and lived with his family in a working-class district in Berlin. The poor conditions around her and the sufferings of the people of the district moved his wife, and they began to figure prominently in her drawings. In 1893, Kollwitz attracted the attention of critics when she exhibited at the Free Berlin Art Exhibition.

Shortly thereafter, she stopped painting and concentrated on graphic art, characterized by the use of bold, dark, and expressive lines. She completed her first major series, a collection of etchings entitled *Weavers' Revolt* (1894–1898), for the playwright GERHART HAUPTMANN. The drawings of *Weavers' Revolt* were shown successfully at the Great Berlin Art Exhibition in 1898. The same year, she joined the Berlin Secession.

Another of Kollwitz's series, *Peasants' War* (1902–1908), earned the Villa Romana Prize, enabling her to travel to Florence. She traveled elsewhere in Europe and visited the sculptor Auguste Rodin in France. In her lithographs and drawings, Kollwitz depicted the plight and conditions of the poor in expressive forms that carry intense emotion in series such as *Pictures of Misery* (1909). In addition to drawing, she began sculpting around 1910.

The death of her son, Peter, in World War I was the strongest influence on her work for the remainder of her life. Series such as *Seven Woodcuts on War* (1924) and *Parting and Death* (1924) depict distraught mothers with dead children, as in "Mother and Dead Son," and mothers trying to protect their children. Social themes also continued to appear in her work, including the series *The Proletariat* (1925), consisting of three woodcuts.

Kollwitz, who had long had socialist leanings, visited the Soviet Union in 1927 but grew disillusioned with Soviet-style communism. She was the first woman elected to the Prussian Academy of Arts, where she served as head of the Master Studio for Graphic Arts from 1928 until her resignation from the Academy in 1933. That year saw the rise of Adolf Hitler in Germany, and, along with the work of many other artists, her work was declared "decadent" by the Nazis. She subsequently lost much of it when her home was bombed during the war. Her last major series of prints, *Death*, a collection of lithographs, was completed between 1934 and 1936.

Peter Kollwitz's death inspired her best-known sculptures, *The Parents*, rendered in granite and placed as a memorial in the Soldiers' Cemetery Roggevelde in Flanders in 1932. Compounding the grief caused by the loss of her son during World War I was the loss of her grandson during World War II. Among her other works are many self-portraits and posters, which she began to publish in 1906. Her extensive diaries were published as *The Diary and Letters of Kœthe Kollwitz* in 1988.

BIBLIOGRAPHY

Henz, Renate, ed., *Käthe Kollwitz: Graphics, Posters, Drawings*, 1981; Klein, Mina C., *Käthe Kollwitz: Life in Art*, 1972; Meckel, Christoph, et al., *Käthe Kollwitz*, 1967; Noun, Louise R., *Three Berlin Artists of the Weimar Era: Hannah Höch, Käthe Kollwitz, Jeanne Mammen*, 1994.

Korda, Alexander

(September 16, 1893–January 23, 1956)
Director, Producer

A major founding figure in Hungarian cinema, Alexander Korda later worked in the film industries of Vienna, Berlin, and Hollywood before founding London Film Studios in England. His work was a major force in British cinema in the mid twentieth century. Known for his insistence on technical expertise and taste for lavish costume and set designs, he produced and/or directed nearly 150 films during his lifetime. Korda's films helped launch the careers of many actors and actresses, including Vivien Leigh, Charles Laughton, and his second wife, Merle Oberon.

Korda was born Sándor Laszlo Kellner in Pusztatúrpásztó, Hungary. His father was a former soldier and oversaw the family estate. Korda was a good student, entering a local Jewish school at the age of 5. (His two brothers, Zoltan and Vincent, later directed and contributed sets to his films.) Four years later he won a scholarship to secondary school. Several years after his father died in 1906, Korda moved to Budapest and got a job as a journalist, writing mostly reviews and crime stories. He adopted part of his pseudonym from the Catholic *sursum corda*, or "lift up your hearts."

After traveling to Paris in 1911, he got his first film job writing captions in 1912. Two years later he founded the film periodical *Pesti Mozi* (*Budapest Cinema*), which published in-depth film reviews. He codirected his first film, *A becsapott újságíró* (*The Duped Journalist*), in 1914. Korda was soon directing a succession of films for the large studio Corvin, eventually rising to the position of co-owner. He remained there until 1919, when he went to Vienna and made four films between 1920 and 1922. He spent the next three years making films in Berlin.

The Berlin films generated attention in Hollywood, and from 1927 to 1930 Korda lived in California and made several films, including *The Private Life of Helen of Troy* (1927). He was to find his true calling, however, in England, where he founded London Film Productions in 1931. Dissatisfied with the state of British filmmaking, he brought in technical experts and modern equipment and enlisted writers such as GRAHAM GREENE and H. G. WELLS for his film scripts.

The Private Life of Henry VIII (1933) marked the beginning of a series of lavish films Korda produced and/or directed, followed by *Catherine the Great* (1934), *The Scarlet Pimpernel* (1935), *Rembrandt* (1936), *The Ghost Goes West* (1936), *The Man Who Could Work Miracles* (1937), *Elephant Boy* (1937), and *The Four Feathers* (1938). Korda's taste for extravagance in his films led him into financial trouble more than once, and in 1939 he lost his Denham Studios, where many of these films were produced. In 1940 he made *The Thief of Baghdad* (1940), a fantasy film in Technicolor based on *The Arabian Nights* that also featured set designs by his brother Vincent.

In 1941 Korda made *That Hamilton Woman* in Hollywood, a story about a woman who rises from poverty to become the mistress of Horatio Nelson, revered admiral of the British fleet in the early nineteenth century. *Jungle Book* (1942; based on the children's classic by RUDYARD KIPLING) was again directed by Zoltan Korda and featured designs by Vincent Korda. He returned to England in 1942 and was awarded the first knighthood given to anyone in film.

In London Korda resurrected London Film Productions, which produced such works as *Anna Karenina* (1948), CAROL REED's *The Third Man* (1949) and *Outcast of the Islands* (1952), *Seven Days to Noon* (1950), *The Sound Barrier* (1952), and LAURENCE OLIVIER's *Richard III* (1955).

BIBLIOGRAPHY

Kulik, Karol, *Alexander Korda: The Man Who Could Work Miracles*, 1975; Stockham, Martin, *Korda Collection: Alexander Korda's Film Classics*, 1992; Tabori, Paul, *Alexander Korda*, 1966.

Koussevitzky, Serge

(July 26, 1874–June 4, 1951)
Conductor

Trained as a double-bass player, the Russian-born conductor Serge Alexandrovich Koussevitzky was known for the beauty of his orchestral tone and his ebullient and unconventional interpretations of modern as well as classical works. His long tenure at the Boston Symphony Orchestra, during which he conducted more than one hundred world premieres, was his most important conducting post. His efforts to promote the works of young French, Russian, and American composers helped launch many careers.

Koussevitzky was born Sergey Aleksandrovich Kusevitsky into a poor family in Vyshny, Volochyok, Russia. His family was a musical one, and in his youth he learned to play the piano, the trumpet, and other instruments. As a teenager he entered the Moscow Conservatory, where, because there was a scholarship associated with the instrument, he mastered the double bass under Josef Rambusek.

In 1894 Koussevitzky joined the Bolshoi Theatre Orchestra as a double-bass player, and from 1901 to 1905 he was solo double-bass player in the orchestra. The year 1905 also marked the beginning of a series of solo performances that took him to a number of European cities. His own double-bass concerto (1905) was one of many pieces he composed and played himself. That year, too, he married Natalie Ušhkkov, daughter of a wealthy tea merchant who financed his ambition to conduct. In the realm of conducting Koussevitzky was largely self-taught—he learned the technical aspects by observing Artur Nikisch and other conductors.

With his father-in-law's financial assistance, he hired the Berlin Philharmonic Orchestra in 1907 and with it made his conducting debut. After the well-received performance, he returned to Moscow (1909) and founded the Koussevitzky Orchestra. Over the next several years he toured Russia with the orchestra. In an effort to take orchestral music to provincial towns, he, on several occasions, hired a steamboat to take his orchestra up the Volga River.

Promoting the works of young contemporary composers was the primary focus of Koussevitzky's efforts as a conductor—then and for the remainder of his career. To that end he founded the Russian Music Publishing house (1915), which published the works of SERGEY RACHMANINOFF, SERGEY PROKOFIEV, IGOR STRAVINSKY, Aleksandr Scriabin (1872–1915), and others.

After the 1917 revolution Koussevitzky briefly directed the State Symphony Orchestra in Petrograd (now St. Petersburg). Unhappy with the new Soviet regime, he moved to Paris in 1920. There he conducted a series of concerts featuring new compositions by French composers and continued to promote the work of young Russian composers.

In 1924 Koussevitzky began his long incumbency as conductor at the Boston Symphony orchestra. There he began to perform the works of American composers such as Aaron Copland, Roy Harris, William Schuman, David Diamond, Leonard Bernstein, and Walter Piston, many of whose careers he launched. In that post Koussevitzky also commissioned what later became major works from other composers. For the orchestra's fiftieth anniversary in 1930, he commissioned Stravinsky's *Symphony of Psalms*, Arthur Honegger's Symphony No. 1, Prokofiev's Symphony No. 4, and PAUL HINDEMITH's *Konzertmusik* op. 50.

Koussevitzky was instrumental in founding the Berkshire Music Festival in 1936 as well as its outgrowth, the Berkshire Music Center (1940), which he directed for the remainder of his life. With the intent of assisting promising young composers and musicians, he engaged top musical talents as instructors—including his own former student Bernstein, who taught there between 1948 and 1955. In memory of his wife, who died in 1942, he founded the Koussevitzky Foundation (1943) to commission and promote new works, one of which was British composer BENJAMIN BRITTEN's opera *Peter Grimes*.

BIBLIOGRAPHY

Smith, Moses, *Koussevitzky*, 1947.

Kraus, Karl

(April 28, 1874–June 12, 1936)
Playwright, Poet, Journalist, Critic, Essayist, Editor

Known for his boldly expressed opinions, gift of satire, and exact use of language, the Viennese writer Karl Kraus attacked major figures and institutions of his day through essays, plays, and his periodical *Die Fackel* in an effort to restore what he saw as lost precision in language in both journalism and literature. His other works include poetry and books of aphorisms.

Kraus, of Jewish ancestry, was born in Gitschin, Bohemia, now Jićin, Czech Republic. His father, a wealthy paper manufacturer, moved the family to Vienna, where Kraus was to spend the remainder of his life, in 1877. From 1884 to 1892 Kraus attended the Franz-Josephs-Gymnasium. There and at the University of Vienna, where he studied law, philosophy, and literature, he was an average student and never took much interest in formal education.

By 1892, Kraus was contributing satire and criticism to a number of periodicals in Vienna and elsewhere. He tried acting in 1893 but met with little success. Kraus directed his first major piece of characteristic satire, *Die demolirte Literatur* (1896; *A Literature Demolished*), toward the literary and intellectual elite of his day. Written as an obituary for the recently burned Café Griensteidl, it attacks the intellectual circles that met at the café.

His real success as a writer, however, came with *Die Fackel (The Torch)*, a periodical he founded with his father's assistance in 1899. *Die Fackel* was Kraus's vehicle for attacking journalists, politicians, intellectuals, the middle class, and other figures of his day. He sought to expose corruption, dispose of sloppy and cliché-ridden writing in the press, return precise language to literature, and preserve European cultural tradition. After 1910, Kraus was the journal's only writer, and he continued to publish *Die Fackel* almost until his death in 1936. *Weltgericht* (1919; *Last Judgment*) collected some of his articles.

In politics, Kraus was an ardent pacifist and a proponent of women's rights. His essay *Eine Kron für Zion* (1898; *A Crown for Zion*) attacked the aims of Zionism and one of its main proponents, Theodor Herzl. The Austrian justice system was the target of his *Sittlichkeit und Kriminalität* (1908; *Morality and Criminality*). World War I inspired a torrent of antiwar pieces from Kraus's pen, including an address given in Berlin, *In dieser grossen Zeiten* (1914; *In These Great Times*). In 1932 he attended an international pacifist meeting in Amsterdam. Kraus did not maintain consistent religious loyalties—he renounced Judaism in 1899, was received into the Catholic Church in 1911, and angrily left the Church in 1923.

Kraus waged literary war against specific enemies, past and present, including the poet Heinrich Heine (1797–1856), the press baron Imre Békessy, Alfred Kerr, Felix Salten (author of the story *Bambi*, which formed the basis of Disney's classic children's film), the police chief Johannes Schober, and the periodical *Neue Freie Press*. The pamphlet *Heine und die Folgen* (1910; *Heine and the Consequences*) identified Kraus's central objection to Heine, whom he accused of fathering feuilletonistic writing.

The feuilleton, which Kraus despised, was a portion of the paper that vendors could sell separately. It was devoted to gossip and informal discussion of political, artistic, and other events.

When it came to language, Kraus was an extreme perfectionist, devoting hours to informing himself of details and fine-tuning his writing. The 1922 *Untergang der Welt durch schwarze Magie* (*End of the World By Black Magic*) also targeted the press.

In the realm of literature, Kraus published aphorisms, poetry, and plays. His books of aphorisms include *Sprüche und Widersprüche* (1909; *Dicta and Contradictions*) and *Nachts* (1919; *At Night*). His poetry, collected in the nine-volume *Worte in Versen, 1916–30*, is more introspective and contemplative than his other writings.

Like his essays, his plays are often satirical and critical. *Die letzten Tage der Menschheit* (published 1922; *The Last Days of Mankind*) is an antiwar play often considered his masterpiece. He directed his operetta *Literatur oder Man wird doch da sehn* (*Literature Or We Shall See About That*) against literary Expressionism. His other plays include the one-act verse drama *Traumstück* (*Dream Play*); *Wolkenkuckucksheim* (1923; *Cloudcuckooland*), a verse play inspired by Aristophanes's *The Birds*; and *Die Unüberwindlichen* (1928; *The Unconquerable*), a drama about Schober. Kraus also staged plays by the Austrian dramatist Johann Nestroy, whose work he helped revive with his *Nestroy und die Nachwelt* (1912; *Nestroy and Posterity*), and translated the works of William Shakespeare.

If Kraus made enemies through his writing, he had many friends. He never married, but the main love of his life was the Baroness Sidonie Nádherny, whom he met in 1913 and remained close to for the rest of his life. Also among his friends was the architect ADOLF LOOS, whose funeral oration he gave in 1933. He admired and helped promote the work of the ailing poet Peter Altenberg. His other works include *Literatur und Lüge* (1929; *Literature and Lies*) and *Die Sprache* (1937; *Language*).

BIBLIOGRAPHY

Timms, Edward, *Karl Kraus, Apocalyptic Satirist: Culture and Catastrophe in Habsburg Vienna*, 1986; Zohn, Harry, *Karl Kraus*, 1971; Zohn, Harry, *Karl Kraus and the Critics*, 1997.

Kundera, Milan

(April 1, 1929–)
Novelist, Short-Story Writer, Poet, Playwright, Teacher, Essayist

The Czech-born writer Milan Kundera, author of the novels *The Joke* and *The Unbearable Lightness of Being*, began his writing career in Communist-run Czechoslovakia. After his expulsion from the Communist Party and the banning of his works in his native country, he emigrated to France and continued to write novels, gaining increasing international acclaim.

Kundera was born in Brno, Czechoslovakia, now the Czech Republic. From his father, the concert pianist Ludvik Kundera, he acquired an interest in music. Kundera studied musicology at Charles University in Prague and took classes from the Film Faculty of the Prague Academy of Art. Having studied the twelve-tone system of composition developed by the Austrian composer ARNOLD SCHOENBERG, he composed a number of works before he decided on writing.

At this time, Kundera's other main interest was the Communist Party, which he joined in 1947 and from which he was expelled in 1950. He was reinstated in 1956 and expelled again in 1970, in part for his participation in the Fourth Czech Writers' Congress in 1967. *Clovek Zahrada Sira* (*Man: A Broad Garden*), published in 1953, was the first of his volumes of poetry published during the 1950s, followed by *Posledni Maj* (1955; *The Last May*) and *Monology* (1957; *Monologues*). From 1958 to 1969 he taught film at the Academy of Music and Dramatic Arts. His *The Art of the Novel*, a study of the Czech novelist Vladislav Vancura not to be confused with a later volume bearing the same title, was published in 1960.

From the outset of his writing career, Kundera embraced modernist and avantgarde trends in literature. Flashbacks, interior monologues, and the use of multiple narrators are common devices in his work. Particularly in his early novels, several of his characters embark on personal quests against a backdrop of chaotic political events. Kundera's musical training, which included not only his studies of the twelve-tone system but an interest in jazz, is often cited as an influence on the structure of his writing. He wrote his early novels in the Czech language, later began to write in French, and has often been involved in the translations of his works.

In 1963, Kundera became a member of the editorial board for the literary journal *Literarni noviny*. During that decade he began to write fiction in earnest. *Směšné lásky* (1963–1968; *Laughable Loves*), a collection of short stories, appeared in 1963. Its "The Hitchhiking Game" is one of many of his erotic stories. The two main characters, a couple, engage in a game that triggers a sexual awakening in the woman, who has previously been shy. The game leaves both unsure of the division between fiction and reality. Two additional volumes of *Laughable Loves* followed in 1965 and 1968.

Kundera's first novel, *Zert* (1967; *The Joke*), won the Czechoslovak Writers Union Prize and established him as an international writer. The reader learns the story of the protagonist, Ludvik Jahn, through the eyes of several narrators. Jahn is expelled from the Communist Party after sending a postcard to his girlfriend containing parodies of Marxist slogans and a statement of support for the exiled and murdered Leon Trotsky. Thorough humiliation follows—Jahn is expelled from the university, labeled a "Trotskyite," and called to the military for back-breaking work. He seeks redemption from the absurdity of these events through his relationships with women. *The Joke* was followed by *Zivot je jinde* (1974; *Life Is Elsewhere*).

Kundera himself was ejected from the Communist Party in 1970, fired from his teaching position, and forbidden to publish his work. After living off of his wife's earnings teaching English for several years, they emigrated to France. There, Kundera taught comparative literature at the University of Rennes from 1975 to 1978 and later taught at the École des Hautes Études in Paris. The Czech authorities deprived him of his citizenship in 1978, and he became a French citizen in 1981. His novels of the 1970s include *Valcík na rozloucenou* (1976; translated in English as *The Farewell Party*) and *Kniha smíchu a zapomnení* (1979; *The Book of Laughter and Forgetting*).

Nes nesitelná lehkost byti (1984; *The Unbearable Lightness of Being*) was the basis for a successful film in 1988. The story unfolds in the climate of the Soviet invasion of Czechoslovakia in 1968, and its protagonist is a young physician drawn into a series of erotic escapades.

With *Nesmrtelnost* (1990; *Immortality*), Kundera creates a series of characters preoccupied with immortality and interweaves his fictional characters with historical figures, including Beethoven and Goethe. In *La Lenteur* (1995; *Slowness*), he contrasts the slow, contemplative spirit of the eighteenth century with the modern spirit of "forgetfulness" and "speed." The principal characters in *Identity* (1998), the middle-aged Chantal and her younger lover Jean-Marc, both suffer from uncertainty about who the other really is.

Among Kundera's other works are the second *The Art of the Novel* (1986), winner of the Académie française prize; *Testaments Betrayed: An Essay in Nine Parts* (1995), also relating his ideas on artists and the creation of art; and the plays *Majitelé Klícu* (1962; *The Keepers of the Keys*), *Ptakovina (A Farce)* (1969), and *Jacques and His Master: An Homage to Diderot in Three Acts* (1971). He received an honorary doctorate from the University of Michigan in 1983, became a member of the American Academy of Art in 1986, and has won numerous awards, including the Nelly Sachs Prize in 1987.

BIBLIOGRAPHY

Banerjee, Maria Nemcová, *Terminal Paradox: The Novels of Milan Kundera*, 1990; Misurella, Fred, *Understanding Milan Kundera*, 1993.

Kurosawa, Akira

(March 23, 1910–September 6, 1998)
Director

The Japanese motion picture director Akira Kurosawa, noted for strong character portrayals, epic samurai films, and his blend of Japanese and western cinema styles, was the most internationally renowned Japanese director and was responsible for introducing Japanese productions to world cinema.

Kurosawa was born in Tokyo, the youngest of seven children. His father was a stern teacher and former military man, and he was well known for shaping young athletes. Kurosawa was never inclined to athletics as a youth, however. He enrolled in the Doshusha School of Western Painting and planned to pursue a career in painting, but his poor economic circumstances hampered his ambition. His elder brother Heigo was a film commentator and, before his suicide, a significant influence on Kurosawa.

In 1936 Kurosawa began his career in cinema. He became an assistant director at the P.C.L. Cinema studio and worked under the Japanese director Yamamoto Kajiro, noted for his films about World War II. Kurosawa's natural talent for writing scenarios quickly became evident to Yamamoto and others. In 1943 he attained the position of director and completed his first film, *Sanshiro Sugata*, about the growth and development of a Japanese judo student. A sequel followed in 1945.

The following year saw the release of his second film, *The Most Beautiful*, a documentary-like story of Japanese girls who work in an optics factory during wartime. Kurosawa married the lead actress in the movie, Yaguchi Yoko, by whom he had a son and a daughter. His third film, *They Who Step on the Tiger's Tail*, was shot in 1945; it borrowed its story and style from Kabuki and No theater, traditional forms of Japanese drama. In *No Regrets for Our Youth* (1946), an accused spy is arrested and eventually executed for espionage during the war. After the execution, his lover abandons her life in Tokyo, takes his remains to his family in the country, and stays on to work in the rice fields.

Drunken Angel (1948) was the first film to bring Kurosawa international fame. Set in the ruins and corruption of a postwar Japanese city, the story portrays the stormy relationship between a gangster who goes to an alcoholic doctor (Takashi Shimura) to have a bullet removed from his hand. The doctor diagnoses him with tuberculosis, and their quarrels eventually end in the gangster's

Akira Kurosawa (Gamma)

knows will soon end. At first he is unsuccessful in his resolve; he experiences alienation from his son and drowns himself in unfulfilling sensual pleasures. Finally, he finds fulfillment after immersing himself in building a playground in a slum.

Seven Samurai (1954), an entertaining period film, proved to be Kurosawa's most popular production; it effectively combines elements of the classic American western with the Japanese tradition of tales of the samurai, the professional warriors of Japan's feudal age. The fast paced action takes place in a small village bracing itself for an annual invasion of bandits. The villagers engage seven samurai to help them defend their people and farms. After losing four of their own, the samurai bring about the final defeat of the bandits. In *Record of a Living Being* (1955), a dentist and volunteer in family court, Harada, is called in to help preside over a dispute between a man who wants to move to South America and his family members who refuse to go. The man's desire to leave stems from his intense fear that Japan will soon experience an atomic holocaust, and he initially fails to convince either his family or the court to decide in his favor. After the official decision against him, his family begins to warm to the idea in response to his pleading, and the court officials who handed down the judgment harbor some feelings of guilt. However, the man eventually ends up in a mental institution, yet is portrayed as perhaps more sane than those who refused to listen to him. Kurosawa also adapted European literature into films, including *The Idiot* (1951), based on Fyodor Dostoevsky's book of the same title; *The Throne of Blood* (1957), based on Shakespeare's *Macbeth*,

death. *Drunken Angel* was the first film to star Toshiro Mifune (as the gangster), the powerful actor who appeared in almost all of Kurosawa's subsequent productions.

Rashomon (1950) won the Grand Prix at the Venice Film Festival in 1951, the first time a Japanese director had received the prize. The film is adapted from two stories by Ryū Nosuke Akutagawa, *Rashomon* and *In a Grove*, and relates completely different versions of the rape of a woman and the murder of her husband through the eyes of four different people—a man, his wife, a bandit, and a woodcutter. *Ikiru* (1952) portrays a terminally ill bureaucrat who searches for meaning in a life that he and *The Lower Depths* (1957) based on MAXIM GORKY'S play of the same title.

The Hidden Fortress (1958), set during the civil wars of the sixteenth century, depicts a Japanese princess trying to cross enemy territory into safety. In 1960 Kurosawa began to produce films for his own company, Kurosawa Productions. Its first film was *The Bad Sleep Well* (1960), a cinematic portrayal of rampant corruption in the ranks of a government housing corporation. Kurosawa's other films of the 1960s include *Yojimbo* (1961), *Sanjuro* (1962), *High and Low* (1963), and *Red Beard* (1965).

In the 1960s and early 1970s, Kurosawa experienced difficulties financing his films and worked on several failed projects with Hollywood producers. *Dodes'-ka-den* (1970), a humorous look at urban poverty, was his first color film. Following its commercial failure, Kurosawa attempted suicide. He subsequently filmed *Dersu Uzala* (1975) in Siberia at the invitation of the Soviet Union. The story depicts the relationship between a Siberian hermit and a Russian surveyor. The samurai epic *Ran* (1985), based on Shakespeare's *King Lear*, became a commercial success.

Akira Kurosawa's Dreams (1990) is a visually striking compilation of eight distinct episodes. The same year Kurosawa received an Academy Award for Lifetime Achievement. His films after 1990 include *Rhapsody in August* (1991) and *No, Not Yet* (1993); and his other productions include *The Quiet Duel* (1949), *Stray Dog* (1949), *Scandal* (1950), *One Wonderful Sunday* (1947), and *Kagemusha* (1980).

BIBLIOGRAPHY

Kurosawa, Akira, *Something Like an Autobiography*, 1982; Richie, Donald, *The Films of Akira Kurosawa*, 1965.